CATHAY
AND THE WAY THITHER

Bas-relief of Odoric from the shrine at Udine

CATHAY
AND THE WAY THITHER

BEING A COLLECTION OF
MEDIEVAL NOTICES OF CHINA

TRANSLATED AND EDITED

BY

COLONEL SIR HENRY YULE, R.E., C.B., K.C.S.I.

CORR. INST. FRANCE

WITH A
PRELIMINARY ESSAY

ON THE INTERCOURSE BETWEEN CHINA AND THE WESTERN NATIONS PREVIOUS TO THE DISCOVERY OF THE CAPE ROUTE

NEW EDITION, REVISED THROUGHOUT IN THE LIGHT OF RECENT DISCOVERIES

BY

HENRI CORDIER, D. LITT., HON. M.R.A.S.,
HON. COR. M.R.G.S., HON. F.R.S.L.

MEMBER OF THE INSTITUT DE FRANCE
PROFESSOR AT THE ECOLE DES LANGUES ORIENTALES VIVANTES, PARIS

VOL. II

MISSIONARY FRIARS—RASHIDUDDIN—PEGOLOTTI—
MARIGNOLLI

GYAN

Published by

Gyan Publishing House
5, Ansari Road
Daryaganj, New Delhi-110002
Phone: 011-47034999, 9811692060
E-mail: books@gyanbooks.com

Distribution Network
gyanbooks.com
India, USA, Canada, UK, Australia, France

ISBN : 978-81-212-3198-5 (Set)
ISBN : 978-81-212-4818-1 (HB)
First Published, London, 1913

2nd Impression 2020

Printed at: Gyan Press, Delhi.

Cathay and the Way Thither Vol. II
Author: Colonel Sir Henry Yule

CATHAY
AND THE WAY THITHER

BEING A COLLECTION OF
MEDIEVAL NOTICES OF CHINA

TRANSLATED AND EDITED

BY

COLONEL SIR HENRY YULE, R.E., C.B., K.C.S.I.
CORR. INST. FRANCE

WITH A

PRELIMINARY ESSAY
ON THE INTERCOURSE BETWEEN CHINA AND THE WESTERN
NATIONS PREVIOUS TO THE DISCOVERY OF THE CAPE ROUTE

NEW EDITION, REVISED THROUGHOUT IN THE LIGHT
OF RECENT DISCOVERIES

BY

HENRI CORDIER, D.LITT., HON. M.R.A.S.,
HON. COR. M.R.G.S., HON. F.R.S.L.
MEMBER OF THE INSTITUT DE FRANCE
PROFESSOR AT THE ÉCOLE DES LANGUES ORIENTALES VIVANTES, PARIS

VOL. II

ODORIC OF PORDENONE

LONDON:
PRINTED FOR THE HAKLUYT SOCIETY
MDCCCCXIII

TABLE OF CONTENTS

CATHAY AND THE WAY THITHER

I. THE TRAVELS OF FRIAR ODORIC OF PORDENONE (1316–1330)

ILLUSTRATIONS

CATHAY AND THE WAY THITHER,

edited by Sir Henry YULE, was issued by the HAKLUYT SOCIETY, in 1866, and has been out of print for many years past; copies occasionally offered for sale have commanded a very high price. The preparation of a new edition was entrusted to me after I had brought out the third edition of the *Book of Ser Marco Polo.* Recognizing that a thorough revision of the work was necessary, I have, whilst keeping almost all the notes of Sir Henry Yule, supplemented them by new information which has greatly increased the bulk of the book. The new edition of *Cathay* will therefore form four volumes instead of two: Vol. I, with the *Preliminary Essay on the Intercourse between China and the Western Nations previous to the Discovery of the Cape Route*, will be issued last; Vol. II, the present volume, contains *Odoric of Pordenone*; Vol. III will include *Reports of Missionary Friars, Rashiduddin, Pegolotti* and *Marignolli*; Vol. IV will include *Ibn Batuta, Benedict of Goës* and the *Index*.

H. C.

October 1913.

I

ODORIC OF PORDENONE

View of Pordenone from near the Railway Station

ODORIC OF PORDENONE

BIOGRAPHICAL AND HISTORICAL NOTICES

THE first place in this collection has been given to the narrative of Odoric of Pordenone, a Beatus or semi-saint of the Roman Church, not as the first in time, nor perhaps in value, but as on the whole the most curious and as that which was the original nucleus of the volume.

Odoric was a native of Friuli, a country which was perhaps better known to travellers before there was a railway through it. Few now, in passing from Trieste to Venice, or from Venice to Vienna, think it worth while to break their journey for the sake of seeing such places as Pordenone, Udine, or Cividale; and thus those interesting cities, though on or near a great thoroughfare, still keep a rare old-world flavour and simplicity.

This border land had in old times closer relations to Germany than to Italy. It has again close relations of a certain kind to Germany, but in no region of Italy, it is believed, is the Italian feeling stronger.

The Patria del Friuli borrowed its name from Forum Julii, a city represented by modern Cividale, and became the seat of a dukedom [568] under the nephew of Alboin when the Lombards first burst into Italy.

Charlemagne extinguished the Lombard dukes, and from Friuli for a time was governed the Eastern March of the Frankish empire. In the end of the ninth century or thereabouts, the administration of the province fell into the hands of the Patriarchs of Aquileia, whose seat had been at Cividale since 737; and in 1029 the Emperor Conrad II formally conferred on the Patriarch Wolfgang Poppo the Duchy of Friuli and the Marquisate of Istria.

This ecclesiastical principality continued to exist; with territory of fluctuating extent, until 1420, when the Patriarch [Lud. II di Teck], engaging in war with Venice, lost his temporal dominion, and Friuli became subject to the Republic. It was remarkable as perhaps the only Italian state, excluding Sicily, which possessed a genuine Parliament. This consisted of three Estates, assembling in one house.

Friuli divides naturally into three zones. The first and widest is a great level, subsiding near the Adriatic into swamp, elsewhere well cultivated and fairly productive, but without irrigation, and far behind the wealth of the Lombard plain, excepting towards the west, where water lies nearer the surface, the streams have a more perennial character, and there is seen an almost tropical luxuriance of vegetation.

The second zone consists of undulating hills, dotted with white villages, and covered with fine grass carefully reserved for the scythe. The brilliant verdure of these undulating meadows, as seen under a July sun, was alike surprising and delightful. The third zone is that of the mountain country.

The dialect of the Friuli country is a Romance one, said to be very distinct from the Venetian, and to come very near to Provençal. Many of the local names are alleged to be quite French in character, and I remember one, *Martignac*, which struck me particularly. It may be only a fancy that this quasi-French idiom may sometimes be traced through the thin veil of Odoric's Latin.

The native district of Odoric was Pordenone, in that richer part of the Friulian plain which lies towards the river Livenza. Pordenone itself, called in Latin, I know not of what antiquity, Portus Naonis, [in German, Portenau] is a quaint but thriving little city of some seven thousand inhabitants, standing on the banks of the Noncello, a tributary of the Livenza, and by which boats ascend from the sea to the town. The beautiful gardens which environ it, and the very fine campanile which rises beside the cathedral, group into a singularly pleasing picture, even as seen by a railway traveller.

Odoric is said to have sprung from one of the garrison established in this district by Ottokar, King of Bohemia, to whom the territory had passed from his cousin Udalric, Duke of Carinthia and Lord of Pordenone[1]. A curious confirmation of this tradition is found in the manuscript from which we print the Latin text of his travels, for in it he is designated "*Frater Odericus* Boemus[2]." The name

[1] "*De reliquiis seminis eorum quos olim Rex Otakerus apud Portum Naonis ad custodiam deputavit.*" This is quoted from an anonymous chronicler of Laybach, in *Monumenta Ecclesiæ Aquilejensis*, etc., Argentinæ, 1740, p. 866. Ottokar succeeded to the throne of Bohemia in 1254; Rudolf of Hapsburgh was chosen King of the Romans in 1272; their wars about the Austrian provinces held by Ottokar, including part of Friuli, terminated in 1279 in the rout and death of Ottokar. See also *Venni*, p. 3.

[2] [Sig. V. Savi has taken a good deal of trouble in an article of the *Nuovo Archivio Veneto* (Anno VI, 1896, T. XI, Pt. II, pp. 301–325: *Della patria e della nazionalità del Beato Odorico da Pordenone*) to prove that Yule, J. von Zahn (*Revue historique*, XXI, II, mars—avril 1883, pp. 386–390) and myself (French ed. of Odoric) are wrong in saying that Odoric was of Bohemian origin. I do not think it

of his family is alleged to have been Mattiussi[1], and the place of his birth was Villa Nova, a hamlet of cottages dispersed among vineyards and mulberry trees, about a mile and a half from the town.

A substantial two-storied cottage is still shown at Villa Nova as the house in which Odoric was born; and in the half-open arcade which forms a part of the lower story, a rude old fresco, representing the friar holding forth the crucifix, much defaced by the contact of firewood and farming gear, is evidence at least of the antiquity of the

necessary to discuss the whole paper; only one point shall I refer to: the Latin MS. No. 2584 of the National Library of Paris beginning: *Descripcio Orientalium Partium Fratris Odorici Boemi de Foro Iulii* has been examined by M. Tille who found that the three passages, f. 118 *a*, f. 126 *b* (not *a*) twice wherein Odoric is called *boemus* had been erased and rewritten; M. Tille is apparently a Tcheque gentleman and though this nationality has nothing to do with the examination of a *Latin* MS., Sig. V. Savi exults and writes: "Di fronte all' adulterazione del MS. proprio nel punto sostanziale per la controversia, egli è chiaro che la testimonianza del Codice parigino non può essere più accolta perchè sospetta," p. 313. The MS. is not "suspect" in the least: the three erasures of the titles or passages in red ink have been made by a scribe contemporary of the MS., and probably by the same hand who wrote the running-title of the MS.; there is no argument to be drawn from this fact against the genuineness of the MS.: it is probable that the scribe had misread the text he was writing from and subsequently corrected his error. What could be the interest of a XIVth century scribe or of his employer to make Odoric of Bohemian origin: Italian patriotism was not yet awake; Odoric was not "tedesco" but "boemo," not German but Slav.

Savi winds up: "Finchè quindi lo Zahn ed il Cordier non porteranno innanzi più valevoli argomenti, sarà permesso e logico affermare che quelli da loro addotti non bastano per impugnare la nazionalità italiana di Odorico da Pordenone. Di lui noi italiani, e particolarmente noi veneti potremo dire, applicando al caso un' augusta espressione: *Odoricus noster est.*"

I wonder what patriotism has to do in this case: there was no Italian unity in the XIVth century, and it matters little that Odoric was of Bohemian origin, since he was a Friulan by birth, and Friuli being now part of the kingdom of Italy, well may he be claimed as an Italian. No one objects to this.—H. C.]

[1] This name does not seem to appear in print before the work of Gabelli in 1639. Zeno quotes as authority for it a MS. work on the Patriarchs of Aquileia by Jac. Valvasone (*Dissertaz. Vossiane*, 1751, ii, 297). It is also given by Asquini in his *Life of Odoric*, on the authority of a MS. of Lugrezio Treo, author of *Sacra Monumenta Prov. Forojulii*, 1724.

tradition. Even the room is pointed out in which the traveller and saint was born! and the bed, a vast and ponderous expanse of timber, looked as if it also might have officiated at the auspicious event. The parish priest asserted that the house had passed through only a second transfer since it quitted the family of Mattiussi.

The name Odorico is the same that occurs north of the Alps as Ulric, and it is found in various shapes besides, such as Udalric, Vodaric, etc. It would seem to have been

Traditional Birthplace of Odoric

common in this region of the world, for it turns up frequently in old Friulan lists, and was borne by Aquileian patriarchs and Carinthian dukes. And it is said to be still common about Pordenone, both as surname and Christian name. Our friar, therefore, might come by it in many ways, but perhaps he got it actually from the patron saint of his parish church, for that is saint Udalric. One of the old Franciscan writers calls our traveller *Ludovicus* Odoricus[1], but it seems likely that this was a mistake.

[1] Bartholomew Albizzi of Pisa, in the work cited below, *ed. Mediolan.* 1510, f. cxxiiii.

The date of his birth is assigned to 1286, whilst the Patriarch Raymond della Torre was reigning in Friuli. In naming this date later writers appear to have followed Gabelli, who published a life of Odoric in 1639. Asquini, another biographer in the last century, quotes as authority for it "*Osuald. Ravenn.*[1]," a reference respecting the age or value of which I have no knowledge. Judging, however, from the effigies of Odoric on his tomb at Udine, I should have guessed the date of his birth to stand a dozen years earlier than that mentioned.

The authorities for the circumstances of Odoric's life, exclusive of such as can be gathered from the story of his travels, are the annalists or hagiologists of his order. Whether the man whom they describe after the regular saint-model of the middle ages answers in any degree to the author of the travels, as he indicates his own likeness however faintly, appears to me most questionable. The contemporary notices of him, except the local records of the miracles which were said to have followed his death, are very .brief.

It is alleged that Odoric is treated of in a catalogue of Franciscan saints, written only five years after his death[2]; but I find no quotation from this work, and the earliest notice of him that I can discover (apart from the exceptions just specified) is in the chronicle of his German contemporary, John of Winterthur, who seems to have written about 1348–50, and whose reference shows that he was already acquainted with the Itinerary[3]. His travels,

[1] *Vita e Viaggi del B. Odorico*, etc., Udine, 1737.

[2] *Sbaralea, Supp. et Castigatio ad* Scriptores Trium Ordinum S. Francisci, etc. Romæ, 1806, p. 443.

[3] After giving a notice of the martyrdom at Tana, and some other circumstances related by our author, the chronicler adds: *Hæc testatur Sanctus Odoricus de Padua oriundus, qui peragratis cunctis regionibus orientalibus et incolumis ad terram nativam reversus, hæc et alia mira et stupenda illic visa et audita ab eo, rogatus et compulsus a suis confratribus minoribus in scripturam redegit; opusculum valde*

alleged missionary work, and miracles are also briefly spoken of by Bartholomew Albizzi, of Pisa, in his treatise concerning the *Conformity of the Life of St Francis to the Life of Our Lord Jesus Christ*, from which the passages are quoted in the *Acta Sanctorum*[1]. This work was written, according to Professor Kunstmann, about 1380, fifty years after Odoric's death, but the author was fully entitled to be termed a contemporary, for one of his works, cited by Wadding, was dated as early as 1347, and at his death in 1401 he is said to have been over a century old[2].

According to the ecclesiastical biographers, however, having in early years taken on him the vows of the Franciscans, and joined their convent in Udine, he speedily became eminent for ascetic sanctity, living on bread and water, going barefoot, scourging himself severely, and wearing ever next his skin hair-cloth or iron mail. His humility refused promotion, and with the leave of his superior he retired for a long time into the wilds to pass a solitary life. A local reputation for sanctity and miracles is ascribed to him before his wanderings began[3].

On these he started sometime between 1316 and 1318 (inclusive), and from them he returned shortly before the spring of 1330. That he was in Western India soon after 1321, that he spent three of the years between 1322 and 1328 in Northern China, and that he died in January 1331, are all the chronological facts that we know, or can positively deduce, from his narrative, and contemporary evidence[4].

solatiosum et delectabile, de hujusmodi raris et a seculo quasi inauditis, relinquens." (*Joan. Vitodurani Chron.* in *Eccard Corp. Historicum*, i, 1894.)

[1] *De Conformitate*, etc., bk. i, pa. 2, conf. 8.

[2] *Cave*, *Script. Eccles.*, App., p. 48; *Wadding*, vol. vii.

[3] *Acta Sanctorum*, January 14th; *Wadding*, vol. vi, under 1331; *Liruti*, *Notizie delle Vite ed opere scritte da' Letterati di Friuli.* Venez., 1760, i, 274 *et seq.*

[4] D'Avezac, in the very valuable dissertation prefixed to Carpini's account of the Tartars, says that Odoric reached Trebizond in 1317, and Tana in 1322; but I do not trace the authority for such precision.

I shall not here give any detailed view of his travels; the particulars of these, with the fullest explanations that I can provide, will be found in the ensuing text and notes. Suffice it to say that his route lay by Constantinople to Trebizond; thence to Erzerum, Tabriz, and Soltania; and that in all probability he spent a considerable part of the time previous to 1322 in the Houses of his Order in those cities. From Soltania he passed to Kashan and Yezd, and thence turning by Persepolis he followed a somewhat devious route, probably by Shiraz, and perhaps a part of Kurdistan, to Baghdad. From Baghdad he wandered to the Persian Gulf, and at Hormuz embarked for Tana in Salsette. Here, or from Surat, where Jordanus had deposited them, he gathered the bones of the four brethren who had suffered there in 1321, and carried them with him on his voyage eastward. He went on to Malabar, touching at Pandarani, Cranganor, and Kulam, and proceeded thence to Ceylon and the shrine of St Thomas at Mailapúr, the modern Madras. From this he sailed tediously to Sumatra, visiting various parts of the coast of that island, Java, probably Southern or Eastern Borneo, Champa, and Canton. Hence he travelled to the great ports of Fu-kien, and from Fu-chau across the mountains to Hang-chau and Nan-king. Embarking on the Great Canal at Yang-chau, he proceeded by it to Cambalec or Peking, and there remained for three years, attached, it may be presumed, to one of the churches founded by Archbishop John of Montecorvino, now in extreme old age. Turning westward at length through Tenduc (the Ordo country of our maps), and Shen-si, to Tibet and its capital Lhása, we there lose all indication of his further route, and can only conjecture on very slight hints, added to general probabilities, that his homeward journey led him by Kabul, Khorasan, and the south of the Caspian, to Tabriz, and thence to Venice by the way he had followed thirteen or fourteen years before, when outward bound.

The companion of Odoric on a part, at least, of these long journeys was Friar James, an Irishman, as appears from a record in the public books of Udine, showing that on the 5th April after Odoric's death a present of two marks was paid to the Irish friar "*Socio Beati Fratris Odorici, amore Dei et Odorici*[1]."

The assertion of Wadding and the other biographers that Odoric had sowed everywhere the seed of the Gospel, and had baptised more than 20,000 Saracens, would appear to rest on a basis of pure imagination only. No hint of such a thing appears in his travels, nor indeed any indication of his having acted as a Missionary at all; though probably in the years he spent at Cambalec, and perhaps also in Armenia, he may have taken part in the missionary duties of his brethren. In his contemporary Jordanus the spirit of the missionary breaks out strongly and clearly, showing his heart in the work. Odoric's narrative again gives one decidedly the impression of a man of little refinement, with a very strong taste for roving and seeing strange countries, but not much for preaching and asceticism. *Qui peregrinantur raro sanctificantur*, says Thomas à Kempis. And one wonders what odd chance picked out Odoric as the wanderer to be accredited with such exceptional sanctity. "*Molto diverso il guiderdon dall' opre!*" Had the simple and hardly bestead Jordanus of Séverac, or that zealous patriarch John of Montecorvino striving for the faith at the world's end to the age of fourscore years, been made a saint of, one could have understood it better.

Miracles also, and miraculous experiences, are assigned to the friar by his biographers, of which no trace will be found in his own story. Thus we are told that as he was on his way back from Tartary, commissioned by the Great Khan to call more brethren to the work of preaching to that monarch's subjects (a commission which seems again

[1] *Venni*, p. 27.

to be purely imaginary) he was met by the Great Enemy[1], who reviled him, and taunted him with the bootlessness of his errand, seeing that he was fated never to return. The assailant was repelled by the sign of the cross, but his words proved true.

So bowed and changed was Odoric by the hardships and starvation that he had endured in his years of wandering, say the biographers, that his nearest of kin could scarcely be brought to recognise him[2].

It was after visiting them no doubt that he betook himself to the House of his Order attached to St Anthony's at Padua, and there in the month of May, 1330, he related his story, which was taken down and done into homely Latin by William of Solagna, a brother of the Order; Friar Marchesinus of Bassano also afterwards lending a hand in the redaction, and adding at least one interesting anecdote from his recollection of Odoric's stories. Whether the traveller had not already written or dictated a brief sketch of his journeys will be spoken of below.

From Padua he is said to have proceeded to Pisa in order to take ship for the Papal Court at Avignon, that he might make his report of the affairs of the church in the far East, and ask recruits for the missions in Cathay. At Pisa he was sorely troubled by what he heard of the mischief wrought in the fraternity by the schisms of Cesana and Corbara[3], and became all the more anxious to prosecute his voyage. But he fell into serious illness,

[1] *Wadding*, l. c. "Sub formâ mulieris gravidæ!" says Mark of Lisbon, quoted in the *Acta Sanctorum*.

[2] *Wadding; Petrus Rodulphius, Hist. Seraphicæ Religionis*, Ven., 1586, p. 125.

[3] Petrus Rainalduccius de Vico Corbario [Rainalluci, born at Corbara] was a Minorite venerated for his age, learning, and piety, who to the great scandal of his Order let himself be set up at Rome as Antipope by the Emperor Lewis of Bavaria. In 1330 he asked pardon of Pope John with a halter on his neck. Michael Cesana was the general of the order [elected 1316], who absconded from Avignon to take part with the emperor (*Wadding*).

and being warned in a dream by St Francis to "return to his nest," he caused himself to be transported back to his own province.

There at Udine, he took to his bed, to rise no more. Having confessed, on the priest's pronouncing the absolution, Odoric is related to have said: "Do thine office, reverend Father, for I desire like a humble child to submit to the keys of the church; but know that the Lord hath signified to me that he hath pardoned all my sins." And so he died on the 14th January, 1331[1].

The friars of the convent were about to bury him the same day privately, contrary to the custom of the country. But when this became known in the city, Conrad Bernardiggi, the Gastald or chief magistrate of Udine, who had a great regard for Odoric, interfered to prevent such a hurried interment, and appointed a solemn funeral for the next day. This was attended by all the dignitaries, and created a public excitement. The people began to push forward to kiss the hands and feet of the dead friar, or to snatch a morsel of his clothing. Rumours of miracles rose and spread like wildfire. A noble dame, the Patriarch's sister, who had long suffered from a shrunken arm, declared aloud that she had received instant relief on touching the body. The whole town then rushed to the convent church. Lucky were those who could put but a finger on the friar's gown, whilst those who had such a happy chance grasped at his hair and beard; just as I have seen the Bengalis snatch at the whiskers of a dead tiger, and from like motives. One

[1] This is the date given by the postscripts to Odoric's narrative, and all the subsequent accounts. Wadding adds, "On a *Monday*, about the ninth hour." The 14th January 1331 might mean in modern style 14th January 1332, especially as the postscript to the narrative in the extracts published by the Bollandists specifies "*Anno Dominicæ Incarnationis*," which I believe indicates properly the year commencing on Lady Day. But it seems not to be so. For the date assigned fell on a Monday in 1331, and, moreover, the order by the Patriarch for an inquiry into the miracles is dated May 1331, which is not open to ambiguity.

virago made a desperate attempt to snip off the saint's ear with her scissars, but miraculously the scissars would not close! The public voice urged that such wonder-working matter should be kept longer available, and the interment was deferred for two days. The third day the body was buried in the church, but only to be taken up again on the day following. For the excitement had now spread far beyond the walls of Udine. The country gentlemen from the castles of the district with their wives and families began to throng in. Then came the nobles and burgesses of the neighbouring cities; the nuns of Cividale and Aquileia followed, walking two and two in procession; and, at last, the stream arrived from the remoter parts of Friuli, and from Carniola, and crowds continued to flock in, day and night, scourging themselves, and chaunting the praises of God and his servant Odoric. The great lady of the country, Beatrice of Bavaria, Countess Dowager and Regent of Goritz, came with a vast cortège; the Patriarch himself, Pagano della Torre, was present, and superintended the transfer of the body to another and more splendid coffin. The sanctity of the friar was now fully recognised, and the notion was at last taken up by his own community, who employed an eminent preacher to declaim to the people the history and pious deeds of this brother, whom it is most likely they had till now regarded only as an eccentric, much addicted to drawing the longbow about the Grand Cham and the Cannibal Islands[1].

The Patriarch, or the Municipality (for they supplied the funds), then gave orders for the construction of a noble shrine[2]; whilst three discreet persons, the Canon Melioranzi,

[1] *Wadding; Documenti per la Storia del Friuli, raccolti dall' Abbate G. Bianchi*, Udine, 1844–5, ii, 471.

[2] Records extant in the last century showed that the cost of the shrine, and of the formalities attending the miracle-commission, was defrayed by the city. (See *Tiraboschi*, *Storia della Letteratura Italiana*, 1789, vol. ii, pp. 124–129.)

Maffeo Cassini, and the notary Guecelli or Guccelli, were commissioned to investigate and compile the miracles ascribed to the deceased.

Seventy such miracles are alleged to have been authenticated[1]; and indeed so says the heading of the notary's report of the commission (which is extant), though (like the cotton reels of Manchester which profess to contain two hundred yards of thread), as a matter of fact it only enumerates twenty-seven. The miracles are all much alike, and substantially in this strain: "A. B. was very ill, and vowed a lump of wax to Odoric, and began immediately to mend, and is firmly convinced that it was all owing to Odoric."

Two alleged miracles which unfortunately have not found a place in this authenticated report, but only in recorded tradition, stand out from the rest as singular or startling.

In one case, Friar Michael, a preacher and doctor of theology at Venice, having suffered for seven years from a fistula in the throat, betook himself to Friar James, the Irish comrade of Odoric's travels, and from him got a letter of introduction to his defunct and sainted friend, begging him to do what was needful for the divine. This proved immediately effectual[2].

In the other case, it is asserted that a friar six days in

[1] There is a MS. copy, which I saw, in the Library at San Daniele in Friuli, a curious and valuable collection bequeathed by Archbishop Fontanini to the place of his birth; a place where the books enjoy almost undisturbed repose in a delicious atmosphere. The Report, however, is printed in the Roman *blue book* noticed further on. The heading runs: "*Hic inferius sunt scripta et annotata amplius quam septuaginta miracula quæ Deus operatus est per B. Odoricum*," etc. It would appear that the notary got tired of recording such matter, and perhaps trusted that no one would count them! Indeed he says in a document which is printed in Hakluyt as a postscript to Odoric's narrative: "*Scripsi sicut potui bona fide et fratribus minoribus exemplum dedi;* sed non de omnibus *quia sunt* innumerabilia, et mihi difficilia ad scribendum";—in fact "what no fellow could do."

[2] *Asquini, Vita e Viaggi*, p. 206.

his grave was raised to life by the power of the saint, in answer to the prayers of a sister[1].

The official detail of the miracles was sent to Guido Candidus (Bianchi?) Bishop of Udine, then at the Papal court, in order that the name of Odoric might be enrolled among the saints; but nothing was effected at that time, owing it is said to the death of the prelate[2]. Nor, perhaps, had Pope John any great zeal towards the exaltation of members of an Order which had bred such thorns in his side as Corbara, Cesana, and Occam.

In the very year of Odoric's death, we find recorded the bequest by a certain woman of Vercelli of a legacy to the altar of the Beatus at Udine; whilst a long chain of incidental notices of bequests, of repairs to his chapel, of celebrations of his festival, etc., show that his memory has been continuously preserved as sacred in Udine since his death[3].

But for four centuries his claim to the honours of beatification rested only on popular acclamation sanctioned by the Aquileian patriarch. It was not till 1755 that the question was formally discussed by the Roman court, whether the cult rendered to Odoric from time immemorial should be solemnly sanctioned by the Pontiff.

I have inspected the record of the process which then took place, a very curious ecclesiastical *Blue-book* of more than one hundred and twenty folio pages. The discussion is entitled "*Positio super dubio an sententia lata per Eminentissimum et Reverendissimum Ordinarium Utinensem super cultu ab immemorabili tempore prædicto Beato præstito, sive casu excepto a decretis sanc. mem. Urbani Papæ VIII*

[1] "Quem vidit suscitatum F. Henricus Generalis Minister, ut mihi Magistro Bartholomæo dixit ipse ore tenus" (*Barth. Pisanus* in *op. sup. citat.*; from the *Acta Sanctorum*). This legend was commemorated in an inscription which stood in the convent church at Pordenone, but dating only from 1591. (MS. copy of Gabelli's Panegyric on Odoric at S. Daniele.)

[2] *Asquini*, p. 199.

[3] Roman documents cited below.

sit confirmanda in casu, etc. The first part is entitled *Informatio super dubio*, etc. This alleges the grounds and maintains the validity of the Bishop's judgment, traces the worship of the Friar from the time of his death, and gives a long list of those who have borne testimony to his virtues. This is followed by a *Summarium super dubio*, etc., which is a sort of collection of *pièces justificatives* in which every creditable mention of Odoric is cited at length, with the whole detail of his alleged posthumous miracles, and the official report of a visitation of his shrine by Daniel [Delfin] Patriarch of Aquileia in 1749. The next document in the series consists of *Animadversiones R. P. D. Promotoris Fidei super dubio*, etc., being, in fact, the counterpleading of the official vulgarly termed the Devil's Advocate. He raises objections to the beatification, hints that Odoric and his sanctity were scarcely other than mythical, and almost sneers at the marvels of the Itinerary. In fact, this R. P. D. is worse than a profane Lutheran in the way he treats the Beatus. There is then a *Responsio super dubio*, etc., which disposes of these gibes; and though the book in question does not contain the Pope's decision, we know that it was issued by Benedict XIV, July 2nd, 1755, fully sanctioning the beatification of Odoric[1].

In May 1332, the monument, which had been commissioned by the authorities of Udine from Philip de' Santi at Venice, was completed, and a solemn transfer of the body was celebrated by the Patriarch, Pagano della Torre. The shrine consisted of a handsome sarcophagus of oriental

[1] The copy of the process in question which I examined was kindly shown me by Count Pietro Montereale of Pordenone. The Pope's decision is given by Venni, p. 32 [and by us at the end of these notices]. Authorities do not seem precisely to agree as to what constitutes beatification; an article in the *English Cyclopædia*, however, may be referred to for an explanation in what respects it falls short of canonisation. The word *canonisation* is indeed used in the Papal decision of 1755, but in terms it only sanctions the worship rendered to Odoric from time immemorial.

alabaster, adorned with small reliefs and statuettes, and elevated on dwarf columns of white marble[1].

In 1735, when the church of the Franciscans in Udine was "repaired and beautified," a new chapel was erected for Odoric, and a second solemn translation accomplished on the 27th February, 1735[2]. But he was not yet to lie quiet. In 1771 the Franciscans were compelled to remove to a house which had belonged to a suppressed Society of

The Sarcophagus as it stood in the last century

Carmelites near the Aquileian gate, their own buildings being given up for a public hospital. In their removal they carried with them all their reliques, including the body of Odoric, which was accompanied in solemn procession by all the civil and ecclesiastical authorities, headed by the lieutenant of the Venetian Republic, to its new

[1] According to the process just quoted this elevation of the body above the ground was one of the honours paid to a beatified or canonised person.

[2] *Venni*, p. 29.

Altar containing Odoric's remains

resting place in the church of the "Beato Vergine del Carmelo[1]." The Franciscan Convent was also suppressed in the days of the first Napoleon, and the church was then made over to parochial use. Odoric still lies there, but shorn of his sepulchral glories. Whether to facilitate the removal, or by accident during that operation, the sarcophagus was broken up, and never again put together as such. Portions have, however, been built into an altar dedicated to Odoric, and within this his coffin is deposited[2].

I could hear nothing of the other reliques, such as fragments of an iron girdle, portraits, etc., which existed in the last century, before the removal of the convent. But the body is there still, and is still exposed, on every fourth recurrence of his festival, to the eyes of the congregation. Had I but known this when at Udine, perhaps my Protestant eyes also might have been permitted (for a consideration) to behold the very *corpus beatum* whose hands had presented the Grand Cham with a trencher full of apples, and whose stout heart carried him chaunting the *Credo* through the Valley Perilous! It is perfect, they say, except one leg, which was frittered away in reliques; Pordenone obtaining a tibia, and Villa Nova an ankle-bone.

[1] It is now called both the "Carmine" and "San Pietro." [Chiesa del Carmine e San Pietro, 49 Via Aquilea.]

[2] The information as to the past in this paragraph has been kindly supplied by Dr Vincenzo Joppi of Udine.

The altar of Odoric is the second on the left as you enter the church. [I have given in the French edition full particulars of the various transfers of Odoric's body to its last resting place in the Carmelite Church where I saw it in 1881; I think it unnecessary to reproduce these details here; they are accompanied by a number of illustrations.] It bears the following inscription, whatever may be the meaning thereof:

† "Altare hoc Omnipotenti Deo
In honorem B. Odorici Con: erectum
privilegio quotidiano perpetuo ac libero
pro omnibus defunctis ad quoscumq: sacerdotes
vigore Brevis Benedicti Papae xiv.
die iv. Octobris MDCCLII insignitum
atque a Ministro Generali Ordinis
die x. mensis Maij MDCCLIII designatum." †

The virtues of the Odorician reliques were still in high esteem in the last century, if they be not now. Venni assures us that in his day *Polvere del B. Odorico* was (like the James's powders of our youth) potent in fevers, and in demand as far as Florence.

Odoric seems to have been the subject of a good deal of bad verse in the sixteenth and seventeenth centuries, the chief perpetrators being, in the latter age, John Baptist Gabelli, priest of Villa Nova, and in the former Girolamo Monteniani or Montignac, a zealous devotee, and syndic of the convent in Udine. This gentleman had the convent copy of the Friar's travels, with the documents about his miracles, etc., re-transcribed at his own expense in 1542. His hymns to Odoric are chiefly composed of prayers for his own unbounded comfort and prosperity.

> "Da nunc Alme tuis, da mihi jugiter
> Pacem, Divitias, Sæcula Nestoris!"

is but a sample of the demands he makes upon his local *divus*[1].

As there seems to be no doubt of the date of the sculptures which originally formed part of the sarcophagus, we have in them representations of our traveller erected in the year following that of his death, and executed by no incompetent hand. There are, or were, no less than three effigies of him upon the sarcophagus, and at least two of these remain upon the altar where his body now lies[2]. One of these represents him preaching to a crowd of Indians; in the other, he is being lowered into the tomb by the hands of the Patriarch, the Gastald, and the Brethren of the Order. In these two the heads are fairly

[1] Some of these verses, including that here quoted, are given in the *Vita e Viaggi* of Asquini.

[2] Possibly the third, but if so it escaped my notice. Unluckily my visit to Udine was on a local festival, when a constant succession of masses was going on in the church, and I had barely time to make the sketch given further on between two of them.

like each other; both presenting a bluff, benevolent, Socratic countenance, but they are certainly suggestive of sixty years rather than forty-six.

Another statuette stands in the church of his native parish of Villa Nova. It is of higher style than the sculptures at Udine, but of so much later date that it can have no authority as a likeness. The work was ascribed by the parish priest to an artist called Pilacorte, who carved the doorway of the Duomo at Pordenone[1]. It stands above the altar, paired with a corresponding statuette of St Udalric, Bishop of Augsburg, patron of the church. There are some splendid fresco heads of prophets and apostles overhead, remains of the work of John Antony Sacchiense, called Pordenone, which once covered the choir.

In the early part of the last century, there were extant other old effigies of Friar Odoric. One, in an altar piece which stood in the sacristy of the convent church, was said to have been painted only twenty-four years after his death[2]. And Venni says there was a portrait of him in the Loggia of the Parliament of Friuli[3].

Engravings of him, of course, can have no value except as they approach the old sculptures. There is one good vigorous woodcut in the old Italian style, purporting to be the *Vera B. Odorici Effigies*, in the *Historia Seraphicæ Religionis* of Petrus Rodulphius[4]. And Gabelli is said to have published a print of the "very old image of the Beatus preaching to the Indians and other barbarians, which is found in the church of S. Udalric at Villanova[5]." This would seem to be different from the work of Pilacorte. Gabelli's works will be noted below; but I have not

[1] John Antony Pilacorte was a native of Spilimbergo in Friuli. Many of his works exist in the churches of Pordenone; and the font as well as the doorway of the Cathedral are his work. The latter bears the date 1511. There is no Friulan sculptor known by name of earlier date than 1428. (*Maniago*, *Storia delle belle Arti Friulane*, Udine, 1823, pp. 158-9, 201.)

[2] *Asquini*, p. 214.

[3] *Venni*, p. 29.

[4] Venice, 1586, p. 125.

[5] *Acta Sanctorum*, l. c.

succeeded in finding any of them, nor do I know which has this engraving.

Some of the Franciscan authors assert that Odoric, besides his itinerary, left behind him various sermons and epistles[1], but if so, no one seems to know anything about them. Wadding, in the *Annales Minorum*, also repeatedly quotes as the work of Odoric a chronicle extending from the beginning of the world to the death of Pope John XXII[2]; forgetting, it would seem, that the pope survived the saint three years. Indeed, the notion that the work was written by Odoric seems to have been altogether unfounded. This chronicle is the manuscript cited in the account of Jordanus[3] as *Liber de Ætatibus*, formerly at Rome, but now in the Bibl. Nationale at Paris. From it Wadding derived the interesting letters of Montecorvino, Jordanus, and Andrew Bishop of Zaitùn, which are given in the present collection; Sbaralea considers that the real author of the book was probably another Minorite, John of Udine, otherwise of Mortiliano, who died in Friuli in 1363, and who wrote a work called *Pantheon*, supposed to be lost[4].

Very recently another work has been published in Germany as Odoric's[5], on the authority of the closing paragraph of the manuscript from which it is printed: "*Istud scripsit frater Odoricus de Foro Iulii, cum remeasset de partibus infidelium ad suam provinciam, anno Domini* M°CCC°XXX° *temporibus domini Iohannis pape XXII.*" This is a manuscript of the fifteenth century in the Berlin library, entitled *De Terrâ Sanctâ*, consisting of short chapters, containing a detailed itinerary in Palestine with

[1] *Acta Sanctorum*, l. c.

[2] See *Annales Minorum*, tom. vi and vii, *passim*.

[3] See Preface to English Jordanus, p. v.

[4] In the work cited above (at p. 8), p. 443.

[5] See *Peregrinatores Medii Ævi Quatuor*, Lipsiæ, J. C. Hinrichs, 1864; edited by J. C. M. Laurent, and containing Itineraries in the Holy Land by Burchardus de Mte. Sion, Ricold of Monte Croce, this Pseudo-Odoric, and Wilbrand of Oldenburg.

the distances, etc., and is of very little interest. It ends with a chapter on "Machomet" of a short denunciatory kind. I do not believe the book to be Odoric's[1]. It is, of course, *possible* that he returned from the East through Palestine, as we are ignorant of his route from Tibet westward. But there is no hint whatever of his having visited that country, either in his own narrative, or in the biographies. And there is not the slightest likeness in the manner of the two books.

The numbers of manuscripts of Odoric's narrative that have come down to us from the fourteenth century show how speedily his work was spread abroad, and how popular it must have been. In the next century it is easy to trace the use made of his narrative in the great map of Fra Mauro at Venice.

Liruti speaks of Odoric's "love of letters and science," whilst Meinert calls him "one of the most learned of his Order[2]"—the Order that had produced, in one little country only, such men as Occam, Duns Scotus, and Roger Bacon! These statements are even more preposterous than the very opposite view expressed by the editors of that meritorious collection called *Astley's Voyages*, when they say of Odoric's narrative in the unpleasant tone of the last century, "This is a most superficial relation, and full of lies....In short, it seems plain from the names of places and other circumstances that he never was in those countries (China and Tartary), but imposed on the public the few informations he had from others, mixed with the many fictions of his own." Whilst in the Index to the work he fares as ill, his name being thus entered: "Oderic, Friar, Travels of, IV, 620 a. *A great Liar. Ibid.*"

[1] There is a MS. of "*Oderici de F. Julii Descriptio Terræ Sanctæ*," also in the Basel Public Library (*Haenel*, *Catalogi Libr. MSS.*, etc., p. 545). [See further on, p. 58, No. 49. It is a MS. of the genuine narrative of Odoric.]

[2] In his Essay on Marignolli; see Introduction to that Traveller's notices in this collection.

It is evident, however, from the formal affidavit which Odoric was called on to append to his narrative, as well as from the tenor of the apologies of his ecclesiastical biographers, that many of his tales were considered to try the faith of readers, even of his own time, and of his own cloth since. Thus Henry of Glatz in the note appended to his transcript of Odoric, declares that if he had not heard such great things of Odoric's perfections and sanctity, he could scarcely have credited some of his stories[1]. Wadding, with scepticism scarcely disguised, says that much in the book will seem incredible, unless the holy character of the narrator find belief or force it[2]. And Asquini is reduced to plead that so saintly a man would never have told what was untrue, much less have taken his oath to it as Odoric has done[3]!

It is true indeed that our friar is not merely undiscriminating in the acceptance of what he has heard, but also sometimes looser in his statements of what he relates, or professes to relate, from actual experience, than other travellers of his day such as Jordanus and Marignolli. But this seems to come rather from the fact that Odoric is a man of inferior refinement, both morally and intellectually, than that he introduces wilful figments; whilst the notes attached to his narrative will prove I trust how certainly they are the footsteps of a genuine traveller that we are following. And in judging him we must not forget the disadvantages under which his story labours in coming to us by dictation, or mainly so, and that a dictation accomplished in illness[4], and taken down by a friar of probably still less literature than his own[5].

[1] In *Acta Sanctorum*.

[2] "*Nisi fidem exstruat vel extorqueat sanctitas auctoris.*"

[3] *Vita e Viaggi*, p. 13.

[4] "*Dum jaceret infirmus,*" says Wadding after some older writer.

[5] It is singular that the narratives of Marco Polo, Odoric, Nicolo Conti, and Ibn Batuta, the four most remarkable Asiatic itineraries

I must, however, after the examination of a considerable number of versions and MSS., entirely reject the notion put forward so positively by Tiraboschi[1], and accepted by later writers, that Odoric's narrative has been largely interpolated with lying wonders by medieval editors and copyists. Though there are great differences of expression in the various MSS., and some unaccountable ones of fact, the *substance* of all the chief MSS. is the same, and especially in regard to the principal difficulties; whilst some of the stories that Tiraboschi brands as interpolations and fictions, are indeed the very seals of truth[2].

It may be well here to point out a few of those passages which stamp Odoric as a genuine and original traveller. He is then the first European who distinctly and undoubtedly mentions the name of Sumatra. He also (though on this the variety of readings may cast a shade of doubt) mentions the Rejang of the same island, a people not known to Europe otherwise for centuries after his time. The cannibalism and community of wives which he

of the middle ages, should all have come down to us under the disadvantages of dictation.

[1] See *Storia della Letteratura Italiana*, Modena, 1789, v, pp. 124–129.

[2] I am excluding here those few Italian MSS. which are classified below as the fourth type of versions of Odoric. Some remarks will be made on them separately.

One of the examples of interpolation adduced by Tiraboschi is Odoric's account of the Tulsi trees before the doors of the Hindus, a passage, apparently, a little obscured by the misapprehension of the scribe. Another is the statement about the king of Champa's having fourteen thousand elephants, the printed version in Ramusio giving only fourteen. But here it is certain that it is the Ramusian version which has dropt the M, and not the others which have interpolated it. The region in question is the very metropolis of elephants, and for Odoric to have said that the king kept *fourteen* elephants would have been a ludicrous bathos.

On the other hand the real difficulties of Odoric's story are the accounts of the Islands of Nicoverra and Dondin, and the Passage through the Terrible Valley, with, perhaps, one or two more. The former of these are found in *all* the versions of Odoric, and the latter in all but the truncated narrative which we call here the *Minor Ramusian*.

attributes to certain races in that island do certainly belong to it, or to islands closely adjoining. And it is to be remembered that Odoric travelled with neither the scepticism of a man of science nor the experience of a man of the world. His good faith is indicated if his stories are those really current about the places which he visited. His description of sago in the Archipelago is not free from errors, but they are the errors of an eyewitness. His mention of the annoyance from leeches in the forests of Ceylon, and of a two-headed bird in that island, are shown to be the notes of a real visitor; so is his whole account of southern China. His notices of the custom of fishing with cormorants, of the habits of letting the finger-nails grow long, and of compressing the women's feet, as well as of the division of the Khan's empire into twelve provinces, with four chief Vizirs, are peculiar to him, I believe, among all the European travellers of the age. Polo mentions none of them. The names which he assigns to the Chinese post-stations, and to the provincial Boards of Administration; the technical Turki term which he uses for a sack of rice, &c., &c., are all tokens of the reality of his experience.

No two versions or MSS. that I have compared are exactly alike, and in all there are considerable differences of expression, difficult to account for unless we suppose that the practice in multiplying copies of such works was not to attempt verbal transcription, but merely to read over a clause, and then write down its gist in such language as came uppermost. Yet why should a practice have applied to the transcription of these narratives different from that which applied to the multiplication of the classics?

But apart from the slighter differences of expression and the accidental omissions which may be supposed thus to arise, the various versions of Odoric's story appear to divide themselves into *four* distinct types.

The first type is probably that which comes nearest to Odoric's actual dictation, or would do so if we had really good MSS. of it. It is represented by the Latin MS. in St Mark's library (No. 45 of the list below), and by the copious extracts which are given in the *Acta Sanctorum* from another MS. transcribed at Avignon the year after Odoric's death, by Henry of Glatz, a Silesian Franciscan. These copies make no mention of William of Solagna, but have two postscripts appended. The first, written by Friar Marchesino of Bassano, adds as a supplementary story, from his own recollection of Odoric's conversation, an anecdote[1] which the other versions introduce as part of the dictated narrative. The second postscript relates briefly the circumstances of the traveller's death.

The second type is that from which Venni published, and is that of the best existing MSS. both Latin and Italian, so far as I have seen them. It differs from the first in the points just noticed, and ends with a postscript, in which William of Solagna declares himself to have been the amanuensis of the traveller, whilst he, or some other, also records Odoric's death.

The third type is that of the MSS. in the British Museum (Nos. 5 and 7 below), of which one was published and translated by Hakluyt. These MSS. also contain the postscript of W. of Solagna, but they differ a great deal from those of the two preceding types in expression, often substituting passages of more diffuse phraseology, which are in fact glosses on the narrative, but are often quite erroneous in the turn they give to the meaning.

The fourth type is that which appears in what is

[1] There is a freshness and simple picturesqueness about this little story which suggests the notion that perhaps Odoric was a higher style of man than we see him through the penmanship of William de Solagna; and that the tone of the latter scribe may have deteriorated the rest of the narrative.

quoted hereafter as the *Minor Ramusian* version. For Ramusio, or the editor who took up his work after his death[1], without preface or explanation gives two versions of Odoric's narrative, the second being much shorter than the first, and exhibiting some remarkable differences from it, whilst at the same time it contains some additional touches which carry with them a strong stamp of genuineness. I know of only two copies partaking of this type besides that printed in Ramusio, the original of which seems not to have been traced. These two are both at Florence, one a truncated copy in the Riccardian library, and the other in the Palatine; both in Italian. This last has some remarkable differences from the version of Ramusio, and is much fuller in the latter part, as if completed from a version of the first type.

The extracts given below from Latin copies of the first three types, and from a most careful Italian MS. at Venice, will illustrate what has been said of their variations in expression, though it is difficult to select one passage which shall well show the peculiarities of each.

From the version of Henry de Glatz in the ACTA SANCTORUM.

"Deinde magnas duas sportas accepit plenas, quæ mensæ superfuerant fragmentorum, et apertâ portâ nos in quoddam viridarium introduxit. Erat autem in eo monticulus quidam plenus arboribus amœnis: acceptoque vno tintinnabulo cœpit pulsare. Ad cujus sonitum

From Venni's published Text in ELOGIO STORICO DEL B. ODORICO.

"Tunc ergo duos magnos mastellos accepit plenos hiis que superfuerant menssa; et aperiens cuiusdam viridarii portam in ipsum intravimus. In hoc viridario est monticulus quidam plenus arboribus amenis. Accepit ergo timpanum quemdam quem pulsare cepit; ad cuius

[1] Ramusio himself died in 1557, after having published only the first (1550) and third (1556) volumes of his *Navigationi*. The second volume came out under the editorship of the printer, Thomas Giunti, in 1559, but Odoric did not appear therein till the publication of the second edition in 1574. (*D'Avezac* in *Rec. de Voyages*, iv.)

mox animalia multa et diuersa de illo monticulo descenderunt, sicut essent simiæ, cati,...et plura alia, et quædam quæ faciem hominis videbantur habere. Et cùm videremus de bestiis vsque ad tria millia circa ipsum ordinatè conuenisse, ille paropsides posuit, et illis sportis secundùm naturæ suæ...distribuit illis cibum. Et cùm comedissent, iterum cymbalum pulsans, animalia ad loca propria remeabant. Ego autem multùm ridens illi seni dixi: Edissere mihi, quid ista significent," etc. [P. 990.]

sonum multa animalia varia et diversa de hoc monticulo descenderunt, sicut sunt symie gati maymones, et multa alia animalia que faciem habebant humanam, que erant circa tria millia. Que circa se aptaverunt ad se invicem ordinata. Dum autem sic circa ipsum ordinata manerent, parassides possuit ante illa et sicut competebat eis comedere dabat. Que dum comedissent cimbalum pulsare cepit; et sic ad loca sua cuncta reversa sunt. Tunc multum ridere cepi, dicens: Dicas quid hoc indicare vellit?" etc. [P. 69.]

From Manuscript in British Museum (*No.* 7 *below*).

"Tunc accepit ille religiosus duo magna vasa fragmentis quæ superaverant de mensâ repleta, et duxit me ad unam cujusdam viridarii parvam portam. Quam cum clave aperiens viridarium intravimus illo simul. In illo autem viridario erat unus monticulus amœnis herbis et arboribus plenus. Sub quo dum ad invicem staremus, ipse unum cimbalum accepit et illum incepit percutere et pulsare. Ad cujus sonitum multa animalia varia et diversa, aliqua ut simiæ, aliqua ut cati et maymones, et aliqua faciem hominis habentia, de illo monticulo descenderunt. Et dum sic

From Italian MS. in St Mark's Library (*No.* 63 *below*).

"Et allotta tolse duo grandi bigonci di quello che gl' era avanzato da desinare, et aperse la porta d' uno giardino per la quale noi entramo in quello giardino. Et in quello era un monticello pieno d' alberi dilettevoli. Et stando cosi et egli tolse uno cembalo e cominciollo a sonare. Al suono del quale molti e diversi animali di quello monticello discesono, fatti a modo di simie ghatti maimoni e molti altri animali et quali avenno faccia d' uomo. Et essendo venuti cosi questi animali ch' erano apresso di iii^{m}, et ordinatamente s' acconciorono intorno a costui, et essendo cosi

staremus animalia illa bene cciii millia se circa ipsum aptaverunt ad invicem ordinata. Quibus sic circum ipsum ordinatis et positis ipse paropsides ante ea posuit et ut competebat comedere eis dabat. Et cum comedissent cymbalum suum iterum percussit et omnia ad loca propria redierunt. Tunc admiratus quæ essent animalia ista, quasi ridendo multum inquisivi," etc.

intorno costui egli mise le scodelle dinanzi di loro, e davagli mangiare come si conveni. Et quando ebbono mangiati egli cominciò a sonare il cembalo, et tutti ritornavano agli lor luoghi. Et io vedendo cosi queste cose cominciai a ridere dicendo: Dimmi che vuole dimostrare questo?" etc.

The differences exhibited by the Italian copies of the *fourth* type are much more perplexing. Many of these differences either show marked character which looks genuine, or contain true information not contained in the other versions, so that I am strongly inclined to believe that the basis of this type of narrative has been a genuine document, and very possibly one written by Odoric himself, prior to the dictation of his longer story at Padua. But it bears also traces of having passed through ignorant hands which have misrendered the narrative put into them. In a note below I give examples of what is meant under each of the characteristics that have been named[1].

The greatest difficulty in the whole of Odoric's narrative lies in his account of the Islands of Nicoverra and Dondin,

[1] I. *Statements and peculiarities in the* MINOR RAMUSIAN *Version of Odoric that have a look of genuine character, whether true or not.* 1. The assertion that Odoric commenced his travels in 1318. 2. The repeated oaths (*per lo vero Iddio*) to the truth of the statements. 3. The story of a convent of loose women at Erzrum. 4. The Description of the Sandy Sea. 5. Description of a Marriage at Baghdad, and of another at Tana in India. 6. Comparison of the crowds in China to those in Venice on Ascension Day, etc.

II. *Statements of true or probable circumstances, not found in the Latin copies.* 1. Says nothing of going abroad for love of souls, but merely that he went with leave of his superiors. 2. Mentions mines of copper [and silver] near Trebizond. 3. Mentions that snow covers two-thirds of Ararat and renders it inaccessible. 4. Mentions Minorite

and the manner in which these are introduced in the longer versions of his story.

In the minor version of Ramusio no mention is made of Malabar or Maabar, though many particulars regarding the continent of India, which in the longer versions are connected with those two countries, are in the shorter embraced in the account of Tana.

Moreover the Minor Ramusian mentions intermediately between India and China only the islands of Nicoverra and Dondin, whereas the longer versions speak in detail of Sumatra, Java, Thalamasin (certainly a part of the Archipelago), and Champa. After Champa China should naturally follow; but here come in quite anomalously Nicoverra and Dondin, and between them *Ceylon*, which does not appear at all in the Minor Ramusian.

The only probable suggestion I can offer in explanation of this state of things is that the original incomplete sketch which forms the substance of the Minor Ramusian, whether written or dictated by Odoric, was handed over to the amanuenses to aid them in the redaction of the longer narrative, and that they interpolated this part about Nicoverra, &c., where they thought most convenient.

This notion is somewhat strengthened by the following circumstance. Under Malabar, in the longer narrative, the practice of Suttee is thus mentioned: "If the dead man had a wife, they burn her alive with him, saying that she

convent at Tauris. 5. [Mentions crossing Fiume Rosso (Araxes) before reaching Tauris.] 6. Locates the Wise Men of the East at Sabba instead of at Kashan, as the other copies do. 7. [The Sumpit or Blow-pipe in the Eastern Archipelago], etc.

III. *Instances of ignorant alteration or interpolation.* 1. Emperor of *Constantinople* substituted for Emperor of Trebizond, near the beginning. 2. Raisins of Yezd called very *big*, instead of very *little*, as in the other copies. 3. Houses in China said to be eight or ten stories high. 4. Assertion that he *saw* the plant called the Tartar Lamb, etc.

The references in brackets are to the copy in the Palatine Library at Florence.

should abide with her husband in the other world." And again the same version, in concluding the account of Champa, says: "When a married man dies in this country his body is burnt, and his wife is burnt alive along with him; for they say that she should go with her husband, to keep him company in another world." And this is immediately followed by the account of Nicoverra.

Now a reference to the translation will show that the passage about Suttee in Champa comes in inappropriately, after the author had apparently done with that country. And I do not think we have any reason to believe that Suttee was practised in Champa or Cambodia, countries whose Indian religion seems to have been Buddhism and not Brahmanism[1]. The last extract, therefore, I conceive, may have been merely a portion of the shorter narrative relating to India Proper, which was accidentally interpolated into the longer narrative along with the account of Nicoverra and Dondin. And its appearance confirms in some degree my suggestion as to the fact of this interpolation. Other and minor difficulties or exaggerations are, I dare say, to be accounted for by accidents of dictation, and must not be judged too hardly. For instance, the narrative says that Odoric saw at Champa a tortoise as big as the dome of St Anthony's at Padua. The Friar, be it remembered, was in the convent of St Anthony, when he dictated the story; perhaps lying ill, as some of his biographers assert. He tells William de Solagna that he saw *a very big tortoise*. 'How big?' quoth Gulielmo all agape; 'Was it as big as the dome yonder?' 'Well, yes,' says the sick traveller, perhaps without turning to look, and certainly without making a very accurate comparison, 'I dare say it might be.' And down it goes in regular

[1] I find, however, since writing the above, that the *Sommario de' Regni* in Ramusio ascribes the practice of suttee to the people of Cambodia. (*Ramusio*, i, 336.) [Cremation was practised in Champa; see note to Chapter XXIII.]

narration : " *Vidi ibi testudinem majorem revolutione trulli eglesiae Sancti Antonii de Padua.*"

Odoric's credit was not benefited by the liberties which Sir John Mandeville took with his narrative. Because ignorance formerly accused Herodotus and Marco Polo of multiplying falsehoods, the fashion of "rehabilitation" would extend itself too widely, and try to cover also such writers as Ferdinand Mendez Pinto and Mandeville. No one, of course, could regard Mandeville as throughout writing *bonâ fide*; but he has been treated by respectable authorities as if he had really travelled in the far East.

Domes of St Anthony's at Padua

Now the fact is that the substance of his travels to the Indies and Cathay is entirely stolen from Odoric, [and other writers][1], though largely amplified with fables from Pliny and other ancients, as well as from his own imagination, and garnished with his own wonderfully clear astronomical notions.

These *coincidences* were so obvious to former ages that Mandeville is, I think, said to have been termed on his tomb, *Odorici Comes*[2], whilst the MS. of Odoric in the

[1] [See French edition of Odoric, pp. xlix–lii ; and our note in the third edition of *Marco Polo*, II, pp. 598–605.]

[2] This phrase is from the book *De Orbis situ ac descriptione*, quoted § 114 of the *Preliminary Essay*.

library of Mentz Cathedral entitles the latter, "*Socius Militis Mendavill.*" Sir Thomas Herbert, too, calls Odoric "travelling companion of our Sir John."

I subjoin in a note details which will give an idea of the extent of these wholesale robberies[1]. Naturally Mandeville has often misunderstood what he appropriates, and that in a way which shows that he never travelled in the countries spoken of; of this many instances might be given if it were worth while. He is crafty enough now and then to suggest the probability of his having travelled in company with Odoric, and having thus shared his experiences. For instance he says, in describing the Perilous Valley (which loses nothing in his telling), that there were with him "two worthy men, Friars of Lombardy, who said that if any man would enter they would go in with us." (p. 269.)

Indeed his borrowings are so large, and date from a

[1] The following passages of Odoric are appropriated bodily by Mandeville. 1. The notice of Trebizond, and that of the body of Athanasius there. (*Mand.*, p. 202.) 2. The account of Erzrum (p. 203). 3. About Ararat, and including the difficult name of Sobissacalo (*ib.*). 4. Notices of Cassan and the Three Kings; of the Sandy Sea; of Comum or Cornaa and its ruins; and the land of Job (p. 205). 5. Of the Tower of Babel, and the dress of the men and women of Chaldæa (p. 206). 6. Of Ships without nails (with the addition of the legend of the loadstone rocks) (p. 211). 7. Notice of Thana (called Chana) *ib.* 8. All about Malabar, and the pepper, &c., with fictions added (pp. 213–14). 9. The odd passage of Odoric, about the women drinking and shaving, is repeated (p. 215). 10. Notice of Mabar; but giving the city of St Thomas the name of Calamy (the Calamina of ecclesiastical tradition) which is not used by Odoric (*ib.*). 11. Voyage to Lamori, &c.; Notices of Sumatra, Java, Sago-making, &c. (pp. 218–223). 12. Notice of Champa, with Odoric's stories of shoals of fish, of 14,000 elephants, &c., and fictions of his own added (pp. 224–5). 13. The accounts of Nicoverra, Ceylon, and Dondin, and *all out of place* just as in Odoric (pp. 226–8). 14. The whole account of Manzi and Cathay, &c., &c. It might be worth while if I had time and space to try to trace all the originals which Mandeville stole from. I suspect the knight would come out of the process almost in his buff. A large part is taken from Haiton, and something from Plano Carpini [and from Vincent de Beauvais, Jacques de Vitry, Boldensel]. It *might* even prove on examination that his minute account of the Holy Land, the best part of his book, is stolen likewise. (The preceding references are to Bohn's edition of Mandeville.) [See Warner's edition, Westminster, 1889, and my note in *Marco Polo*, II, p. 602.]

time so nearly contemporary with Odoric, that his *readings* of the proper names have some positive value for collation, and have occasionally suggested amendments of the text, which in some instances have afterwards been confirmed by superior MSS. of Odoric, and in others still need that corroboration[1].

DECRETUM

Utinen. canonizationis

BEATI ODORICI MATTHIUSSI

Sacerdotis Professi Ordinis Minorum S. Francisci.

Admissa ad relationem Eminentissimi et Reverendissimi Domini Cardinalis Prosperi Columnae de Sciarra Ponentis à Sacrorum Rituum Congregatione Ordinaria, ex dispensatione Apostolica absque interventu Consultorum, habita die 14. Aprilis 1753. Commissione Introductionis Causae Canonizationis praedicti Beati Odorici Matthiussi Sacerdotis Professi Ordinis Minorum Sancti Francisci, illaque subinde die 25. ejusdem Mensis, et Anni a Sanctissimo Domino Nostro *BENEDICTO PAPA XIV.* manu propria signata cum in ejus executionem instante Patre Fratre Laurentio Ganganelli ejusdem Ordinis Minorum Sancti Francisci Conventualium Postulatore, propositum fuerit ab eodem Eminentissimo Ponente in Sacrorum Rituum Congregatione Ordinaria, atque discussum Dubium : *An Sententia lata per Eminentissimum, et Reverendissimum Ordinarium Utinensem super Cultu ab immemorabili tempore praedicto Beato praestito, sive casu*

[1] Thus I first got the true name of the city *Chilenfu* (see § 34 of Odoric) instead of Chileso, Chilerapha, &c., from Mandeville, though I have since found it in MSS. of Odoric. And the Cornaa which Mandeville has instead of Comum (see § 3) has suggested another reading and identification.

Old Purchas's judgment of the relative claims of the two travellers is most unjust. Mandeville he calls next to Polo, "if next...the greatest Asian traveller that ever the World had"; whilst he has nought but ill to say of "Odericus, a Friar and Traveller, in whom perhaps some Friar hath travelled with him at least in this author [*i.e.*, Mandeville], whose age was before him, and therefore could not cite anything out of him" [the reverse of the truth]. *Purchas's Pilgrims*, iii, 65, 127.

excepto a Decretis san. mem. Urbani Papae VIII. sit confirmanda in casu, et ad effectum, de quo agitur. Sacra eadem Congregatio praevio maturo examine Processus informativi super praefato casu excepto in Civitate Utinen. ab Eminentissimo et Reverendissimo Ordinario ejusdem Civitatis constructo, ac audito R. P. D. Benedicto Veterani Fidei Promotore, qui suam sententiam scripto exposuit, rescribendum censuit: *Affirmativè*, si Sanctissimo Domino Nostro placuerit. Die 14. Junii 1755.

Et factâ deinde per me infrascriptum Secretarium de praedictis eidem Sanctissimo Domino Nostro relatione, Sanctitas Sua benignè annuit. Die 2. Julii ejusdem Anni 1755.

D. F. Card. TAMBURINUS *Praefectus*.
Loco ✠ Sigilli.

M. Marefuscus Sac. Rit. Cong. Secretarius[1].

FUNERALS OF BEATO ODORICO.

We give an account of the funeral expenses of our traveller from Dr V. JOPPI, of Udine; it was printed by Domenichelli, pp. 397–9, and reprinted with the corrections of Dr Joppi in the Introduction of the French edition of Odoric, pp. LX–LXIII.

Ex Quadernis Camerariorum Comunis terrae Utini, tom. X; in copia presso la Biblioteca Civica di Udine, Collez. Fabrizio.

MCCCXXXI. Expense Sepulture Beati Fratris Odorici.

Die XV mensis januarij, dedit de mandato dñi Gastaldionis et Consilij pro solutione Casse in qua fuit primo Beatus Frater Odoricus repositus. . . . denarios xvj.

Item, Pro Clavis positis in spangata facta in dicta Ecclesia occasione predicta. . . . . . dñr. xvj.

Item, Dedit illis qui vigilaverunt Beatum Fratrem Odoricum, et fecerunt sepulturam ejus. . . . . dñr. xij.

Item, Magistro Nicolao Marangono, pro lignamine, agutis et vino expenditis per ipsum cum sociis suis, de mandato Andreottis et Federici notarii olim dñi Galvagni, deputatorum de mandato Consilii, fort. tres, et dñr. ij Aquilegenses.

[1] *Venni*, pp. 32–33.

Item, Pro seratura posita ad spaltum Sepulture Fratris Odorici. dñr. xij.

Item, Pro duobus doplerijs et candellis emptis per predictos Andreottum et Federichum ad dictum opus faciendum. dñr. xxiiij.

Item, Magistro Nicolao Marangono pro se et sociis suis et aliis qui laboraverunt ad dictum opus, pro labore suo. dñr. Lviiij.

Item, Pro solutione secunde Casse in qua repositus fuit Frater Odorichus, et pro assidibus emptis que posite fuerunt super Sepultura corporis Beati Fratris Odorici. . dñr. xxviij.

Item, Dedit pro conducturis assidum et lignorum positorum in spalto ante dicto. . . . . dñr. iiij.

Item, Pro lastra sive lapide empto a presbitero Martino, qui repositus fuit super sepulturam corporis Fratris Odorici, mediam marcham deñar.

Item, Pro uno doplerio empto pro opera supradicta. dñr. xviij.

Item, Marcho qui laboravit circa spaltatam predictam. dñr. iij.

Item, Pro vino dato laboratoribus qui laboraverunt ad spaltatam. dñr. ij.

Item, Zinando Marangono, qui fecit spaltatam ante altare majus et iuxta altare apud ejus sepulcrum. . . dñr. xvj.

Item, Marcho qui iuvit dictum Magistrum laborari ad dictam spaltatam. . . . . dñr. iij.

Item, Filio Comassij, qui conduxit calcem et sabolonum pro dicta sepultura. . . . . dñr. sex.

Item, Menaccio Fabro genero Ortasij pro agutis positis in dicta opera. . . . . dñr. x.

Item, Magistro Jacobo Fornesario pro duobus ceuris calcine, et pro uno curru saboloni positis ad sepulturam predictam. dñr. xij.

Item, Magistro Rizardo staderario pro tribus seraturis et ferris positis ad Arcam Fratris Odorici. . . dñr. xxxvj.

Item, Magistro Petro Fabro pro agutis positis ad spangatam factam in dicta Ecclesia, et pro laqueis Arche Fratris Odorici. . . . . dñr. XLiij.

Item, Magistro Burlo muratori, qui laboravit per unum diem circa dictum Monimentum Fratris Odorici. . . dñr. sex.

Item, Dedit pro dimidio miliare de modonibus, et tribus ceuris de calce emptis a magistro Jacobo Fornesario. dñr. xxxv.

I give now the cost of the monument erected in 1332, from Domenichelli, pp. 399–400, corrected by my friend Dr V. Joppi, of Udine.

1332

Ex quadernis Camerariorum Comunis terrae Utini, etc.

Die tertio januarij Benevenuto notario qui exemplavit Miracula Beati Fratris Odorici ad petitionem dñi Gastaldionis de mandato Consilij, marcham unam.

Die X januarij dedit de mandato dñi Gastaldionis et Consilij Wecilo notario ex provisione sibi facta per Consilium pro testimonijs miraculorum que ivit scribendo per provinciam. marchas iij.

Item, Manfeo dñe Bertoline eadem de causa. . marchas ij.

Item, Dño Meliorantie simili de causa. . . marchas ij.

Mense Aprili. Ratio incastri Beati Fratris Odorici.

Dedit dictus Camerarius magistro Mene Marangono qui laboravit iiij diebus in faciendo incastrum ad Archam Beati Fratris Odorici. . . . . denarios xxxvj.

Item, Danieli Marangono de Grazano, qui duobus diebus laboravit ad dictum opus. . . . . . . dñr. xij.

Item, Duobus Manualibus, qui eos iuverant in tribus diebus. dñr. xviij.

Item, Romano manuali pro iiij diebus . . dñr. xvj.

Item, Pro uno curru qui duobus diebus laboravit conducendo lignamina et alia. . . . . . . dñr. xvj.

Item, Pro vino predictis. . . . . dñr. v.

Item, Pro laqueis ferri qui fuerant librarum viij onziarum iij ad dictum opus. . . . . dñr. xiij.

Item, Pro faciendo spizari clavos ad dictum opus. dñr. v.

Die X maij Fratribus Minoribus pro provisione eis facta per dñum Gastaldionem et Consilium. . . . marchas xij.

Item, Dedit Iuratis et Notario Comunis quando elegerunt homines debentes custodire apud ecclesiam Sancti Francisci in festo translationis beati Fratris Odorici, et apud dñum Gastaldionem pro potu. . . . . dñr xvj.

Item, Quibusdam pueris qui iverunt dando scripta per terram electorum predictorum. . . . . . dñr. xij.

Item, Dedit magistro Philippo de Venetiis qui fecit Archam Beati Fratris Odorici de mandato dñi Gastaldionis et Consilij. soldos x grossorum.

Die XV maij dedit Magistro Rizzardo staderario, qui fecit retem ferream circa Archam Beati Fratris Odorici. marchas ij.

The MSS. of Odoric's Travels scattered over Europe are numerous, as has already been mentioned. Here is a list of those which I have seen personally or found notice of.

BIBLIOGRAPHY

A.—LIST OF MSS. OF ODORIC'S NARRATIVE SO FAR AS THEY ARE KNOWN

See the numeration of the MSS. on p. 75.

I.—LATIN MSS.

A.—Great Britain.

1-1-1-**Cambridge**, *Corpus Christi College*, CCLXXV.

Vellum, sm. fol., 2 col., 42 lines, xvth cent.—Contains 21 pieces, of which (13) *Itinerarium fratris* Odorici *ordinis fratrum minorum de mirabilibus orientalium Tartarorum*, fol. 149. Cf. pp. 316–17, *Cat. lib. ms. quos Collegio Corporis Christi et B. Mariae Virginis in Acad. Cantab. legavit Rev. in Christo Pater M. Parker, archiep. Cantuariensis*, ed. J. Nasmith...Cantab., 1777, 4to.—English handwriting; the works are written without any interruption of text.—This MS. was marked 1280, 4 (11) of *Lib. Ms. Collegii S. Benedicti* in the *Catalogi*, Oxon., 1697, fol.—The late Henry Bradshaw wrote to me that this MS. is No. 21 of the collection of books left to *Corpus Christi College* by Thomas Markaunt, of Cambridge, in 1439; a catalogue of the whole library will be found in the 4to collection of publications of the Cambridge Antiquaries.

Odoric begins f. 149: *Incipit Itinerarium....Licet multa et varia de ritibus et condicionibus huius seculi enarrentur a multis. Ego tamen frater Odoricus de Foro-Iulii de P'tu Vahonis volens ad partes infidelium transfretare...* and ends f. 162: *...qui pulsant* *citharas vt homines alliciant intrare et interficiant, Hec de visis certitudinaliter Ego frater Odoricus hic inscripsi et multa mirabilia omisi ponere quia homines non credidissent nisi vidissent. Explicit Itinerarium fratris Odorici*, etc.

This MS. does not include the supplementary pieces of the other Corpus Christi MS.—The present MS. is probably one to which Yule refers, p. 30, No. 4, in these words: "Asquini in his life of Odoric says that the old MS. of his narrative, which formerly existed in the Convent at Udine, was sold in his own day to an English gentleman passing through Friuli, by the heirs of a priest to whom it had been lent, and he understood that it was preserved in St Benet's College, Cambridge. The MS. in question, however, only dated from 1448 (see *Venni*, p. 38)."

2-2-2-**Cambridge**, *Corpus Christi College*, CCCCVII.

[Yule, No. 4.]—Vellum, 8vo, end of xivth cent.—Contains six pieces: 1. *Itinerarium fratrum Symonis Semeonis et Hugonis illuminatoris, ordinis fratrum minorum professorum ad terram sanctam* A.D. 1322.—2. *Itinerarium fratris Willelmi de Rubruk de ordine fratrum minorum anno gratiae MCCLIII ad partes orientales* (incomplete at the end).—3. *Itinerarium fratris Odorici ordinis fratrum minorum de mirabilibus orientalium Tartarorum.*—4. *Liber de terrae partibus et diversis provinciis.*—5. *Liber secreti secretorum* sive *de regimine principum et dominorum ad instantiam Alexandri magni ab Aristotele editus.*—6. *Aliud documentum de complexione humana.* Cf. Nasmith's *Cat.*, pp. 384-5.

English Handwriting.—Odoric, which is the third of the collection, is from W. of Solagna's version; two small 4to quires, 6 ff., narrow, on a single column, 30 lines a page. Begins, f. 1 recto: *Incipit Itinerarius*... ends f. 21 verso: *...nisi vidissent*; then *De honore et reverencia factis dño Kano.* Vnum tamen referam de magno Kane quod vidi. Consuetudo est in partibus illis... then comes *De morte fratris Odorici* and ends f. 23 recto *...difficilia ad scribendum*; ff. 23 v. and 24 are blank.

This is one of the MSS. used by Francisque Michel and Thomas Wright for their edition of W. of Rubruck. (*Rec. Soc. Géog.* IV. p. 209); they gave a fac-simile.—See pp. xviii-xxiv, *The Texts and Versions of John de Plano Carpini and William de Rubruquis...edited by* C. Raymond Beazley, Lond., Hakluyt Soc., MDCCCCIII, 8vo; Beazley says it is of the earliest xvth century.

3–3–3–**Cambridge,** *Gonville and Caius College.*

[Yule, No. 5.]—Contains seven pieces: 1. *De ortu, processu, et actibus Machometis;* 2. *Wilhelmus Tripolitanus de statu Saracenorum, et de Machomete;* 3. *Paulus Venetus de conditionibus et consuetudinibus Orientalium regionum;* 4. ODORICUS *de ritibus Orientalium;* 5. *Petrus Archiepiscopus, de Russia, et de ortu Tartarorum;* 6. *Itinerarium Hierosolymitanorum. Ad finem tractatus habetur dimensio sepulchri Dominici;* 7. *Historia Hierosolymitana, et Orient. regionum.*—Cf. No. 1100. 46 of *Lib. MS. Colleg. Caio-Gonvilensis* in *Cat. lib. ms. Angliae et Hiberniae in unum collecti*, Oxoniae, 1697, fol.—No. 162, pp. 80–1 of *A Cat. of MS. in the Lib. of Gonville and Caius College*, Cambridge, by the Rev. J. J. Smith, Cambridge, 1849, 8vo.—*Marco Polo*, II, p. 533, No. 12.

4–4–4–**Middlehill** (Worcestershire).—Library of Sir Thomas Phillips, Bart.

[Yule, No. 8.]—Described in 1827 by Haenel, col. 859: "1789. 650. *Palladii Rutilii Tauri Æmiliani opus agriculturae; fr. Oderici de Foro-Iulii, ordinis Minorum, itinerarium in partibus infidelium a. 1331 compositum;* saec. XIV. membr. (Ex libris *Ioannis Iulii.*)"

5–5–5–**London,** *British Museum, Royal Collection,* 14. C. XIII.

[Yule, No. 1.]—Handsome fol. vol., vellum.—*Incipit itinerariū fris Odrici ordinis frm mion de mirabi^ba Orienta^u Tartaro^m.*—Contains: *Cronica Ranulphi monachi Cestrensis, siue Policronicon.*—*Praefationes historiographorum.*—*Historia vaticinalis Gyraldi Cambrensis de conquestu Hyberniae.*—*Libellus de mirabilibus scãe terrae.*—*Itinerarium fratris Odrici de mirabilibus orient.*—*Itinerarium fratris Willmi Rubrik de gestis Tartarum Orient.*—*Libellus Marcij Pauli de mirabilibus Orient.*—*Versus Magistri Michaelis Cornubiensis.*—*Expositio Triuet poemata et histor. tact. in libro Ciuitate Dei.*—Odoric's Itinerary begins on f. 216 and ends f. 224 verso (9 ff.); it seems to be the MS. reproduced by Richard Hakluyt: *The second volume of the Principal Navigations*, Lond., 1599, pp. 39–53: *Incipit itinerarium fratris Odorici fratrum minorum de mirabilibus Orientalium Tartarorum.*—*Marco Polo*, II, p. 530, No. 3.—Beazley, p. xviii, I.

6–6–6–**London**, *British Museum, Cottonian, Otho*, D. I.

[Yule, No. 3.]—One of the MSS. damaged by the fire at Ashburnham House, Westminster, on the 23d October 1731; leaves mounted on sheets of strong paper; large folio, of course in a very bad state of preservation.—Contains among other pieces: *Tractatus Bedae* and *Rog. Bacon.*, *Ranulphi Cestrensis Polychronicon*, etc.

7–7–7–**London**, *British Museum, Arundel*, No. 13, fol. 38 verso.

[Yule, No. 2.]—Small 4to, vellum, pale ink and much discoloured; 51 ff.; xivth cent. Yule says: "In the earlier part the agreement with the MS. Royal Coll., XIV, C. XIII, Brit. Mus., is pretty close; afterwards the variations are greater. The two MSS. have, however, a great general conformity and marked peculiarities common to both. 'These two MSS. are pronounced on good authority to be of the earlier half of the xivth century, and most probably a short time after the death of the author.' (*Major's* Preface to *Herberstein.*) However that may be, they afford a version which has been in some manner and degree tampered with. I have examined this MS. and had a transcript before me."

This is the text of Hakluyt with variants.—In the French edition I gave an heliogravure of the beginning.—Marked in our notes ARUND., and B. M.: Odoric (Latin) takes f. 38—f. 51 verso.

8–8–8–**London**, *British Museum, Harleian*, No. 562, f. 22 verso.

Not mentioned by Yule.—Incomplete Latin MS.—Includes with slight modifications the text of Hakluyt from the beginning until the passage in which Odoric relates that he collected the bones of the four Tana Martyrs (*Navigations*, II, pp. 39–43). The MS. then reproduces the paragraph relating to Tana (p. 41 of Hakluyt) until *dummodo adhibeatur sibi aqua*, when the copy stops at the top of a blank page.

Vellum, 4to; 30 ff.; the beginning includes *Topographia Urbis Romae*; Odoric begins f. 22 verso.

9–9–9–**Oxford**, *Bodleian Library.*

[Yule, No. 6.] Vellum, 8vo, xivth cent.—*Codices Digbeiani*, No. 11, Piece No. 3, f. 44.—This collection includes 31 pieces, 8vo, vellum; Odoric's relation is followed f. 59^b by Carpini's.

Incipit Itinerarium fratris Odorici de ordine Minorum, approbatum sub manu notarii publici, de mirabilibus Indie.

Incip. prol.: *Noverint universi quorum interest quod quidam frater ordinis Minorum, Odoricus nomine.* Incip. liber: *Licet multa et varia de condicionibus hujus seculi enarrantur a multis.* Expl. lib. :—*In quibus vivere et mori me dispono, si placuerit Deo meo altissimo.* Expl. append. :—*Sed non de omnibus, quia sunt innumerabilia, et mihi difficilia ad scribendum.*

Cf. *Catalogi Cod. MSS. Bib. Bodleianae Pars nona, Codices a viro clarissimo Kenelm Digby, Eq. Aur., anno 1634 donatos, complectens.* Confecit G. D. Macray, Oxon., 1883, 4to, p. 7.

10–10–10–**Oxford**, *Bodleian Library.*

[Yule, No. 7.] *Codices Digbeiani* (cf. *Cat. ut supra*, p. 166), No. 166, Piece No. 10, f. 36.—Includes 55 pieces folio, vellum, and of the xiith and xivth cent.; Odoric's relation is followed f. 46 by *Epistola Sathane ad universalem ecclesiam.*

Narratio Odorici, fratris Ordinis Minorum, provinciae Paduanae, de mirabilibus quae vidit in partibus Orientis.

Hic desinit ad finem narrationis martyrii quatuor fratrum Minorum.

11–11–11–**Glasgow**, *Library of the Hunterian Museum.*

Vellum, $10\frac{3}{4} \times 7\frac{1}{4}$, ff. 340, originally ff. 352, well written in single cols. of 36 lines.—xvth cent.—No. 84.—See *A Catalogue of the Manuscripts in the Library of the Hunterian Museum... planned by*...John Young...*continued*...*by* P. Henderson Aitken.—Glasgow, 1908, 4to, pp. 89–90.—Includes six pieces: 1. Guido de Colonna's *Destruction of Troy*; 2. Julius Valerius' (?) *History of Alexander the Great's Exploits*; 3. Archbishop's Turpin's *Itinerary* (*Exploits of Charlemagne*); 4. Marco Polo's *Travels, &c. in the East*; 5. Friar Odoric; 6. Sir John de Mandeville's *Travels*.

84–5. Frater Odoricus Forojuliensis (Imperfect).

Begins (33, 4 [f. 254 (260)] r°. lines 1–3): *L* [illuminated initial] *Icet multa et varia de ritubus et condicionibus | huius mundi a multis enarrentur. sciendum est | tamen quod ego frater Odoricus de foro Julij.*

Ends (35, 8 [f. 268 (280)] v°. lines 12, 13): *bat sic iste scribebat ad hoc vt omnes facilius intellegerent que dicerentur. Deo gracias Amen.*

12–12–12–**Glasgow,** *Library of the Hunterian Museum.*

Vellum, 8½ × 5¾, ff. 134, well written in French hand, in single cols. of 27 lines.—xivth cent. No. 458.—See *Cat....of the Hunterian Museum*, as above, pp. 378–379.—Includes two pieces: *Marco Polo* and *Odoric.*

458–2. Friar Odoric of Pordenone's Travels in Tartary and the East:

Begins (15, 1 r°. lines 1–6): *Incipit liber fratris ordorici de foro Julio de | ordine minorum de mirabilibus tartarorum | et orientalium Regionum*...[rubric] *Q* [gilt historiated initial with gestures] *Vamuis alia multa et ua | na de conditionibus et ritibus | huius mundi a multis enar.*

Ends (18, 3 v°. lines 20–24): *intelligerentur que dicuntur. Amen* | [one line vacant] | *Explicit liber de mirabilibus tartarorum compositus | a fratre Odorico de foro iulij ordinis fratrum | minorum...* | [one line vacant] | *V* [ornamental initial with grotesque head and wine cup] *Inum scribenti : debetis de meliori.*

B.—Germany.

13–13–1–**Berlin,** *Royal Library*, Latin MS., theol. 4to, No. 131.

[Yule, No. 15.]—Paper MS., pp. 440; title on the back: *Vitae Sanctorum et alia*; xvth cent., says Laurent (*Peregrinationes medii aevi quatuor*); more probably xivth cent.—Ff. 1–17 contain a description of the Holy Land supposed to be written by Odoric; it has been published by Laurent, *l.c.*; but it includes also from f. 49 the text of Odoric's Itinerary published by Hakluyt; it begins: *Licet multa*, etc.; the death of Odoric appears on pp. 94–95; it is the version of Henry of Glatz; in the French edition we have given facsimiles of ff. 93, 94 and 95; mentioned by Pertz, *Archiv*, VIII, 1843, p. 846; marked in our notes Berlin.

14–14–2–**Bremen,** *Stadtbibliothek*, MS. b. 2.

[Yule, No. 22.]—xivth cent., parchment, 4to, bound in vellum; pale yellow ink. Contains: I. *Hist. SS. trium regum.* —II. *Nobili viro domino suo carissimo domno Engelberto comiti de Marka Leuoldus de Northof*... —III. Fol. 111: *Ista infrascripta sunt mirabilia que vidit frater* Odoricus *de foro Iulii ordinis fratrum Minorum ultra mare et que idem frater ad pre-*

ceptum sui provincialis...scribi fecit per...fratrem Guillelmum de Solagna, ejusdem ordinis sub anno, mense et die infrascriptis.—Licet multa et magna de ritibus.... —Fol. 135: *Exprimebat. Anno domini Millesimo Trecentesimo tregesimo, de mense Madii padue In loco sancti Antonii confessoris. Nec curavit de latino difficili et ornato set sicut ille enarrabat sic iste scribebat. Ad hoc ut ipsum omnes legentes facilius intelligerent. que dicuntur supra dictus frater Odoricus transiuit de hoc mundo ad deum in conuentu Utini. Anno domini 1330 die 4. Ianuarii qui postmodum coruscat miraculis. Amen.*

Mentioned by Pertz, *Archiv*, VII, 1839, p. 700.—26 ff., long lines.

15–15–3–**Breslau,** *University Library.*

Not mentioned by Yule.—*Fratris Oderici de Foroiulii itinerarium.*—Pertz, *Archiv*, XI, 1858, p. 700.

16–16–4–**Mentz,** Library of the Chapter of the Cathedral, No. 52.

— *Incipit Itinerarius fidelis Fratris* ODERICI, *socii Militis* MENDAVIL, *per Indiam; licet hic prius, et alter posterius peregrinationem suam descripsit.*

"*Licet multa et magna de ritibus et condicionibus huius mundi enarrentur*; tamen sciendum est, *quod ego Frater Odericus* de *Foro Iulii*, volens transfretare, et ad partes infidelium dirigere gressus meos, ut fructus aliquos lucrifacerem animarum; multa, magna, et mirabilia vidi et audivi, que veraciter possum enarrare. Nam primo, cum transirem mare maius, me transtuli ad terram Trapesundam, que Pontus olim vocabatur. Hec terra valde bene situata est...(*quae superflua sunt*). In hac eciam terra vidi unum, quod valde placuit michi; nam vidi hominem secum perducentem plus quam quatuor milia perdicum. Iste homo per terram veniebat, perdices vero per aera volabant, iuxta quoddam castrum quod vocatur *Zanega*, distans a Trapesunda tribus dietis: He perdices erant huius condicionis et proprietatis: Nam cum ille homo vellet quiescere vel dormire, omnes perdices se ponebant iuxta eum more pullorum gallinarum; et sic isto modo ducebat eas Trapesundam, usque ad pallacium Imperatoris. Que cum essent ante eum, de eis tot accipiebat quot ipse volebat; alias autem ad locum a quo ipse prius illas acceperat, perducebat.

"In hac civitate positum est corpus B. *Anastasii*, qui fecit

Symbolum *Quicunque vult salvus esse.* Inde redii in Armeniam maiorem ad quandam civitatem, que vocatur *Arciron*, etc., etc."

In fine huius operis: "Ego Frater *Odericus* de *Foro Iulii*, de quadam terra que dicitur sive vocatur *Portus Naonis*, de Ordine Fratrum Minorum, testificor, & testimonium prebeo Reverendo Fratri et Domino meo Fri *Gvvidoco*, Provinciali S. Anthonii in Marcha Travisana, cum per eum fuerim requisitus per obedienciam, quod omnia que superius scripta sunt, propriis oculis vidi, et quedam audivi a fide dignis, ut predixi. Communis eciam locucio illarum contentarum est, ut illa que non vidi, non testarer esse vera apud homines, nisi illa propriis oculis conspexissem. Ego autem de die in diem me preparo ad illas contratas ire, in quibus dispono me mori et vivere, ut illi placuerit, a quo bona cuncta procedunt.

"Predicta autem fideliter Fr. *Guilhelmus* de *Solagna* in scriptis redegit, sicut predictus *Odericus* ore proprio exprimebat. anno Domini MCCCXXX die mensis Maii, *Padue*, in loco S. Antonii Confessoris, nec curavit de Latino difficili et ornato; sed, sicut ille sibi narravit, sic ipse scripsit; ad hoc, ut omnes hec legentes facilius intelligerent que dicuntur. Qui Fr. *Odericus* transivit de hoc mundo ad Deum in Conventu *Utini*, anno Dni MCCCXXX, die XIIII Ianuarii, qui postmodum choruscat miraculis multis.

"Explicit Itinerarius *Oderici*[1]."

This MS. is the second of fol. LII including: (*a*) *Marco Polo*; (*b*) *Odoric*; (*c*) *Ricold*; (*d*) William of Boldensel.

With regard to the text of this voyage, V. F. de G. remarks:

"Nota; iste Fr. *Odericus* non scripsit libellum hunc de mirabilibus Asie; sed ad preceptum superioris sui referente, aliqui Fratres Minores ex ore eius scripserunt. Et inde venit, quod libelli huiusmodi frequenter in aliquibus verbis et clausulis sint differentes; quia plures scribentes non potuerunt eundem ordinem verborum, pronuntiando, in mente servare, sine aliqua variacione."

I have vainly looked for this MS. at Mentz; it may have been destroyed in the bombardment of 18th June 1793.—Yule, No. 21.—*Marco Polo*, II, p. 549, No. 81.

[1] *Sylloge I variorvm Diplomatariorvm monvmentorvmqve vetervm ineditorvm adhvc, et res germanicas in primis vero Mogvntinas illvstrantivm*...Decrevit Val. Ferd. de Gvdenvs immed. ordinis eqvestris imperii Circ. Rhen. svper. Francofvrti ad Moenvm, Anno MDCCXXVIII, 8vo, Voir p. 381/3.

17–17–5–Wolfenbüttel, *Ducal Library*, No. 40, *Weissemburg.*

[Yule, No. 24.] Latin MS.; paper; xvth cent.; fol., long lines; from the abbey of Weissemburg, in Alsace; seals of the Wolfenbüttel and Paris Libraries; the foot of the pages is damaged by water. Contains:

(1) ff. 1–57 verso. *Marchi Pauli de Venetiis de conditionibus et consuetudinibus orientalium regionum* (Pipino's version).

(2) ff. 57 verso–73 verso. *Itinerarius fratris Oderici per Indiam.*

Begins: *Incipit itinerarius fidelis fratris Oderici socii militis Mandauil per Indiam. Licet hic prius et alter posterius peregrinacionem suam descripsit. Licet multa et magna de tribus et conditionibus huius mundi enarrentur, etc.*

Ends: *Qui frater Odoricus transivit de hoc mundo ad deum in conventu Utum anno domini millesimo tricentesimo tricesimo, die decima quarta Januarii, qui postmodum choruscat miraculis multis. Explicit itinerarius Oderici.*

(3) ff. 73 verso–95. *Itinerarius Richoldi ordinis fratrum predicatorum.*

(4) ff. 95–110. *Itinerarius nobilis viri Wilhelmi de Beldensele compillatus anno millesimo tricentesimo tricesimo sexto.*

Laurent, *Peregrinatores.*—*Marco Polo*, II, p. 548, No. 74.—In the French ed. of Odoric, a facsimile has been given of the page relating to the Great Khan.—Marked in our notes WOLF. 40.

18–18–6–Wolfenbüttel, *Ducal Library*, No. 41, *Weissemburg.*

Not mentioned by Yule; Latin MS., paper, xvth cent., fol., long lines, at times, text on 2 col.; same origin as No. 40. Contains:

(1) ff. 1–50. *Ciceronis orationes in Verrem.*

(2) ff. 51–88 verso. *Chronicon Flandriae.*

(3) ff. 91–120 verso. *Rogerus Bacon, de regionibus ad papam Clementem.*

(4) ff. 122–160 verso. *Marcus Paulus, itinerarium de regionibus et partibus majoris Asiae.*

(5) ff. 160 verso–179. *Ricoldi frat. ord. min. itinerarium.*

(6) ff. 179 verso–224. *Jacobus de Vitriaco, descriptio terrae sanctae.*

(7) ff. 224–235 verso. *Itinerarius Odorici.*

Begins: *Licet multa et varia de ritibus et condicionibus huius mundi narrentur...*

Ends: *Predictus frater Odericus transivit de hoc mundo ad deum in conventu vinci anno domini M°CCC°XXXI, die* XIIII *Januari. Qui postmodum multis et magnis miraculis choruscavit. Deo gratias. Explicit itinerarius fratris Oderici de partibus transmarinis et remocioribus.* (Added with a different hand and a small writing: *Qui Odericus fuit frater ordinis minorum.*)

(8) ff. 236–253 verso. *Johannes de Plano Carpino libellus Mongolorum, qui Tartari appellantur, vel de moribus Tartarorum.*

The MSS. 40 and 41 Weiss. are bound in calf.—The name of William of Solagna appears in the declaration at the end of both MSS.—A facsimile of the last page of Odoric is given in the French edition.—Marked in our notes WOLF. 41.—*Marco Polo*, II, p. 549, No. 75.

C.—ALSACE.

19–19–1–**Strasburg,** *University Library.*

Oderici ord. minorum itinerarium a. 1340 (A. VI. 7).

Pertz[1], *Archiv*, VIII, 1843, p. 461.—Yule, No. 11.

20–20–2–**Strasburg,** *University Library.*

Incipit peregrinacio fratris Odorici de ordine minorum: "In nomine patris, etc." Paper, s. XV, in-fol.

Pertz, *Archiv*, VIII, 1843, p. 466.—Yule, No. 12.

21–21–3–**Strasburg,** *Public Library.*

MS. 4to: *Vita Romoaldi; Relatio Oderici de terris ignotis; hist. de Alexandro M.; vita Nic. de Tolentino; Fr. Petrarca de insigni obedientia et fide uxoria Ioan. Boccaccii; Lotharii Abactoris lib. de miseria conditionis humanae.* (Haenel[2], 1828, col. 462. —Yule, No. 13.)

It is probable that these three MSS. are to-day destroyed.

[1] *Archiv der Gesellschaft für ältere deutsche Geschichtskunde zur Beförderung einer Gesammtausgabe der Quellenschriften deutscher Geschichten des Mittelalters* herausgegeben von G. H. Pertz... Hannover...8vo.

[2] *Catalogi lib. manuscriptorum, qui in bibliothecis Galliae, Helvetiae, Belgii, Britanniae M., Hispaniae, Lusitaniae asservantur,* nunc primum editi a D. Gustavo Haenel. Lipsiae, I. C. Hinrichs, 1830, 4to.

D.—AUSTRIA.

22–22–1–**Admont**, Styria, *Archiv der Abtei.*

No. 583, 4to, vellum; xvth cent.; fol. 49^b–76^a: *Odorici de Foro Julii Historia orientalis.*—Begins: *Cum multa et varia narrantur...*

Pertz, *Archiv*, x, 1851, p. 641.

23–23–2–**Admont.**

No. 639, 4to, vellum; xivth cent.; fol. 80^a–94^a; title *ut supra*; begins: *Licet multa et varia de ritibus hominum et condicionibus huius mundi a pluribus enarrentur...*

24–24–3–**Melk.**

H. 17. ch. f.; xivth cent.—*Fr. Odorici descriptio partium Orientis.* Licet multa et varia. Kr. p. 35.—Saec. xv. *Burckardi de Monte Syon Descr. Terrae Sanctae*, ib. p. 52. *Descriptio Terrae S.* in 158 chap. Terra sancta promissionis Deo amabilis, ib., p. 58.

Pertz, *Archiv*, x, p. 603.

25–25–4–**Prague**, *Doms Capitel.*

[Yule, No. 18.]—Paper MS., xivth cent., sm. fol., text on 2 col.—Odoric's Itinerary takes 6 ff.; differs greatly from Hakluyt's version.—*Marco Polo*, II, p. 550, No. 82.

Yule and Domenichelli, after Pertz, have mentioned *two* MSS. of Odoric in the Library of the Chapter of Prague; but when I visited this library, the keeper told me that there was but one MS. —Pertz, *Archiv*, IX, 1847, writes, p. 474: *Odorici de Foro Iulii descriptio Tartarorum*; and p. 476: *Fr. Odoricus de moribus hominum.*

26–26–5–**Prague**, *Böhmisches Museum* (Am Graben).

[Yule, No. 20.] Vellum MS. mentioned by Pertz, *Archiv*, IX, 1847, p. 478: *Oderici fratris itinerarium in Orientem.*

27–27–6–**Vienna**, *Palatine Library*, No. 545.

Latin MS., vellum, 4to, xivth cent., includes several pieces: 1. *Chronica Hungarorum* (without beginning); 2. *Gesta Alexandri Magni*; 3. *Notata de Germaniae ducibus*; 4. *Odoricus...*followed by several treaties of no interest to us and among them a *Tractatus de Urina.*—Odoric takes ff. 80 recto–103 verso; differs greatly from Hakluyt's version.—Version of W. of Solagna; does not contain M. of Bassano.—Includes interesting variants, those of the Farsetti made use of by Yule, pp. 43–4: *Wherefore I purpose to relate...fourteen years*, etc.; *the galleys from Venice*, etc.

28–28–7–**Vienna,** *Palatine Library*, No. 3559.

Latin MS., fol., paper (exc. 1st f. vellum); 2 col.; xvth cent.; contains seven pieces, the last of which, Odoric, takes ff. 165 recto–179 verso.—Complete until the death of Odoric (there are 2 ff. numbered 165).—Begins: *Incipit frater Odericus de terra magni chani. Licet multa...*

29–29–8–**Vienna,** *Palatine Library*, No. 4459.

Latin MS., fol., paper; xvth cent., contains a great number of pieces of all kinds, a Latin *Mandeville* among others.—Odoric is the 23rd and last piece of this collection and takes ff. 190 recto–200 verso. Begins: *Infra scripta sunt mirabilia q. vidit frater Odoricus de Foro julii...Licet multa et magna*...This is the MS. marked No. 14, by Yule, p. 31, who knows but two of the Palatine MSS.

30–30–9–**Vienna,** *Palatine Library*, No. 4761.

Latin MS., 4to, paper; xvth cent.—Includes a number of pieces of various nature such as a *Tractatus medicus de Gonorrhoea*, a *Descriptio Urbis Romae*, a *Soliloquium de arrha animae* by St Bernard, etc. Odoric is the seventh piece, ff. 160 recto–172 verso.—Same text with different abbreviations as MS. 3559.

E.—Bavaria.

31–31–1–**Eichstaett,** *Bischoeflichen Seminar zu Eichstaett.*

Odorici itinerarium de mirab. mundi.—Pertz, *Archiv*, IX, 1847, p. 559.—Yule, No. 23.—See French ed. of Odoric, pp. lxxx–lxxxi.

32–32–2–**Munich,** *Royal Library*, Cod. lat. 903.

Latin MS., 4to, paper, of 1422; brought from Ireland to Bavaria in 1529.—Contains 24 works; Odoric, ff. 153–173.—Text of Henry of Glatz.—Published by Marcellino da Civezza, *Storia univ. delle Missioni Francescane*, III, pp. 739–781; reproduced by Domenichelli, pp. 153–200.—Marked in our notes Civ. et M. da Civ.—Yule, No. 16.

33–33–3–**Munich**, *Royal Library*, No. 21,259.

Latin MS.; vellum; xivth cent.; 2 col. fol.; 296 ff.—Odoric, ff. 13–28; the other pieces are of a quite different nature.

Odoric begins f. 13: *In noie pris & filij & sps sti. Amen. Multa et varia scribunt a diversis maxime qui terras ignotas perambulaverunt maria navigaverut. prop. q. et ego frater Odoricus de ordine minorum volo et ego ea que vidi in scriptis redigere ad pluriu solacione.*

After Odoric's declaration, *Ego frater Odoric*, comes the anecdote of the Great Khan, and then the note, f. 24: *Predicta frater qda dicete fre Odorico redegit i scpto Anno dni M°CCC°XXX° in mse Maij Padove in loco Sa Anthonij. Infradictus aute frat. Odoricus post Anno Dni M°CCC°XXXI° Januarij die xiij migravit ad dnm i Coventu fratru Minorum Vtini. In foro Iulii*...Then a description of the seventh wonder of the world.

Some allusions to Essling, Worms, Mentz, show that the scribe was a German, probably from Swabia.—Marked in our notes MUN.—Yule, No. 17.—See t. II, Ps. III of *Cat. Cod. latin. Bibl. regiae Monac.*, 1878, 8vo, p. 303, 21,259 (Ulm. 59).

34–34–4–**Nürnberg**, *City Library*.

Latin MS., bad handwriting; contains: Marco Polo, St Brandan, Mandeville, Odoric, Schildtberger.

F.—FRANCE.

35–35–1–**Paris**, *Bibliothèque nationale*, lat. 2584 (olim Colbertinus).

Latin MS., vellum, fol., 2 col., 196 ff.; xivth cent. Contains 25 pieces, of which Odoric is the fourteenth, letters or treaties of various Saints. Cf. *Cat. Cod. MSS. Bibl. Reg. Pars tertia*, t. III, Paris, 1744, p. 300. It is a handsome vol.; in a good state of preservation in full red morocco, with ornamented letters.

Odoric begins f. 118 recto: *Descripcio* Orientalium Partium Fratris Odorici *Boemi* de Foro Julii, and it ends f. 126 verso: *Ego frater Odoricus Boemus de Foro Julii.*

This version is very important, showing Odoric's nationality. Yule printed it in *Cathay*, App. I, pp. i–xlii; we also reproduce it in the App.—Marked in our notes B.N. and B.N. lat. 2584.—Yule, No. 9.

36–36–2–**Paris,** *Bibliothèque nationale*, lat. 3195 (olim *Mazarinaeus*).

Latin MS., vellum, small fol., 2 col., 64 ff., xvth cent.—Contains four pieces, of which Odoric is the second; the first is *Petri Amphusi clericalis disciplina*; the third *Marco Polo*; the fourth *Bernardi cujusdam ad Raymundum Castri Ambrosii epistola de modo rei familiaris utilius gubernandae*. Cf. *Cat. Cod. MSS. Bibl. Reg. Pars tertia*, t. III, Paris, 1744, p. 385. This MS. is dirty and some ff. are damaged, *i.e.* ff. 56 and 57.

Odoric begins f. 19 recto with the table of 37 chapters and *Licet multa et varia de ritibus*, etc., and ends f. 26 recto (verso is blank). The end is so damaged as to be hardly legible.—Marked in our notes B.N. lat. 3195.—Yule, No. 10: "I believe it is one of what I have called the *first type*, after Henry of Glatz."—*Marco Polo*, II, p. 538, No. 24; this is the old Latin version published by the Société de Géographie.

37–37–3–**Paris,** *Bibliothèque nationale*, *Dupuy Collection*, No. 686.

Latin MS., paper, fol., long lines, 76 ff.; xviith cent. F. 1 recto: "*Itineraria in Tartariam: Fr. Ioannis de Plano Carpini Ordinis Minor.*, p. 1; *Fr. Simonis de S. Quintino ordin. Praedicator.*, p. 19; *Fr. Gulielmi de Rubruquijs ordinis Minorũ.*, p. 38; *Fr. Odorici de Foro julij ord. minor.*, p. 60; CIϽIϽCXLVII. P. Dupuy, 686."

This MS. is mentioned: Vol. 686, *Itineraria Variorum in Tartariam*, p. 1286 of the MS. Vol. *Catalogue des Manuscrits de M. Dupuy*. [Bib. nat., *Catalogues*, 217, A], and under the title of: 686. *Voyages en Tartarie*, p. 548, of the *Cabinet historique*, sér. nouv., I, 1882, Inventaire abrégé de la collection Dupuy (by M. Léopold Delisle).

Odoric begins f. 60 verso: "Incipit Itinerarium Fratris Odorici fratrum Minorum de mirabilibus Orientalium Tartarorum.—Licet multa et varia de ritibus et conditionibus huius mundi ennarrentur a multis ego tamen frater Odoricus de Foro Julij de Portu Nahonis volens ad partes infidelium transfretare, magna et mira vidi et audiui, quae possum veraciter enarrare. Primo transiens mare Maius me de Pera iuxta Constantinopolim transtuli Trapesundam..."

Ends: "DE MORTE FRATRIS ODORICI. Anno igitur Domini 1331, disponente se praedicto Fratre Odorico ad perficiendum iter suae peregrinationis prout mente conceperat, et etiam ut via et labor esset sibi magis ad meritum decrevit primo praesentiam adire Domini et patris omnium Summi Pontificis Domini Joannis Papae 22. cuius benedictione, obedientiaque recepta cum societate fratrum secum ire volentium ad partes infidelium se transferret. Cumque sic eundo versus Summum Pontificem, non multum distaret a civitate Pisana...

"Anno Domini 1331 decima quarta die mensis Januarij, obijt in Christo Beatus Odoricus ordinis fratrum Minorum, cuius precibus omnipotens Deus, multa et varia miracula demonstravit, quae ego Guecelus notarius communis Utini, filius Domini Damiani de Portu Gruario de mandato et voluntate nobilis viri Domini Conradi de Buardigio (*read* Bernardigio) Castaldionis, et Consilij Utini, scripsi, sicut potui bona fide, et fratribus Minorum exemplum dedi; sed non de omnibus, quia sunt innumerabilia, et mihi difficilia ad scribendum."

Not mentioned by Yule.

38–38–4–**Paris**, Cat. Saulcy[1], No. 308.

Peregrinatio fratris Udalrici trans mare magnum.—Visio sancti Brandonis.

MS., paper, fol., beginning of the xvth century.—Sold francs 20.

39–39–5–**Saint Omer**, *Library*, No. 737.

MS., paper, fol., xvth cent.—*Incipit Itinerarium fratris Oderici, ordinis fratrum Minorum, de Mirabilibus orientalium Tartarorum.* "Licet multa et varia de ritibus et conditionibus," etc. Finit: *Innumerabilia et mihi difficilia ad scribendum.*

Abbaye de Saint-Bertin.—Quire of 18 ff. in a bad state, damaged by water, written in gothic, with summary and red initial letters. At the end: "Et ego Michael de Lira scriptor nil plus inveni in exemplari, et explicit hic iste liber, quem scripsi Mechlinie in domo habitationis mee, anno Domini millesimo quadringentesimo quadragesimo octavo, xxi° die mensis februarii, secundum stilum et modum scribendi curie Cameracensis diocesis." This itinerary of Odoric has been published by the Bollandists. V. *Acta Sanctorum*, Januar., t. 1, p. 986, col. 2. (*Cat. des Ms.*

[1] *Catalogue de livres anciens et modernes sur la Terre Sainte et les Indes orientales* formant la riche collection de M. F. de Saulcy, membre de l'Institut, dont la vente se fera le mercredi 27 novembre 1872 et les trois jours suivants...Paris, Tross. 1872, 8vo.

de la Bib. de Saint-Omer, pp. 328/329 of vol. III of *Cat. des Ms. des Bib. des Dép.*, Paris, 1861, 4to.)

Not mentioned by Yule.

G.—ITALY.

40-40-1–**Assisi**, *Biblioteca comunale*, No. 343, late No. 20.

Latin MS., fol., parchment, xivth cent. Begins f. 1 recto: *Incipiunt hic multae et diversae hystoriae Beati Odorici Fratris Minoris, de ritibus et conditionibus huius mundi et de martyrio IIII fratrum minorum.*—Then, *Licet multa et varia de ritibus et conditionibus hujus mundi a multis enarrentur tamen est sciendum quod ego fr. Hodoricus de Foroiulii volens transfretare et ad partes infidelium volens ire, ecc.*—F. 3 recto: *hic superius incipit hystoria martyrii IIII fr. minorum;*—F. 8 recto: *hic explicit martyrium istorum quatuor fratrum minorum.*—Ends f. 23 v°.: *et obtulimus eis de predictis pomis, qui cum maximo gaudio ipsa recipientis, ita videbantur letari ac si eis prebuissemus familiariter magnum manus.*—Then follows: *Ego fr. Odoricus de Foroiulii de ordine fratrum minorum testificor et testimonium perhibeo reverendo patri fratri Guideto* [sic] *ministro provincie S. Anthonii, cum ab eo fuerim per obedientiam requisitus, quod hoc omnia que superius scripta sunt aut propriis oculis ego vidi aut ab hominibus fide dignis audivi...... autem illarum...illa quae non vidi testantur esse vero. Multa etiam alia dimisi que scribi, non feci, cum ipsa quasi incredibilia apud aliquos viderentur nisi illa propriis oculis perspexissent*—(the ...show the words which are not legible). *Predicta autem ego fr. Guilgelmus de Solagna in scriptis redegi sicut fr. Odoricus ore proprio exprimebat an: dom. MCCCXXX de mense maii Padue in loco S. Anthonii; nec curavi de latino difficili et ornato, sed sicut ille narrabat sic ego scribebam ad hoc ut omnes facilius intelligerent que scribuntur vel dicuntur. Supradictus autem fr. Odoricus postea ex hoc seculo, transivit ad dominum in conventu Utini an. dom. MCCCXXXI die* XIII (sic) *ianuarii* (cf. Venni, p. 82).—It has been added f. 24 r°: *antiphona et oratio de b. Odorico confessore ord. min.*—F. 25 r°.: *hic inferius sunt scripta amplius quam septuaginta miracula que deus operatus est per beatum Odoricum fratrem minorem hic in Utino sepultum apud fratres minores.*—Begins: *Miraculum Fantusii de Murruciis apud Tercium.*—Ends f. 57 r°: *postquam mater sua duxit eam Utinum ad corpus b. Odorici sanato est.*—Then in another hand: *Hic sunt septuaginta duo miracula scripta que deus operatus est per b. Odoricum, et alia multa fecit que non sunt hic scripta.*—Finally, in a more modern writing, f. 57 v°: *In isto libro sunt multae hystoriae b. Oderici de ordine fratrum minorum de Foroiulii qui est sepultus in conventum Utini; et est etiam hic possio et martyrium quatuor fratrum minorum, et plus quam septuaginta miracula que operatus est deus per b. Odericum; et etiam est hic cingulus ferreus inter reliquios quem portavit ad carnem, et capellus de capite suo et etiam alie res sue.*

Dominichelli writes that this MS. was in the convent of Udine, and that Venni's MS. *Udinese* seems to be a copy of it, as except the title, the two MSS. are similar.

41–41–2–**Milan**, *Ambrosian Library*, H. 188, P. Inf.

Paper, sm. fol., xvth cent.; 109 ff. c.—Contains seven pieces, one of which is *Mandeville* in Italian and the table of Mandeville's Travels. Odoric in Latin is the fifth piece; it takes ff. 80 recto–91 verso. The initial letters have not been written, so the paragraphs begin with the second letter of the first word, i.e. *icet* [for *licet*] *multa*, etc. Belonged formerly to the Convent of St Ambrose, Milan.—Yule, No. 25.—*Begins:* "Licet multa et varia de moribus hominum et mirabilibus mundi a diversis et solempnibus sive diversimode facta, ad majorem tamen fidem faciendam posteris ego frater Odoricus de Foro Iulii ordinis fratrum minorum de quamplurimis mirabilibus, quae oculis clarius vidi in diversis mundi partibus ultramarinis. Ego quidem predictus frater Odoricus volens me ad partes infidelium transfretare, ut fructus ibidem facerem animarum, multa magna et mirabilia audivi et vidi, quae veraciter possum cum attestatione narrare." (Antonio Ceruti, *Appunti di Bibliografia storica veneta contenuta nei mss. dell' Ambrosiana*, in *Archivio Veneto*, XI, 1876, Venezia, p. 195.)

42–42–3–**Milan**, Library of Count Girolamo d'Adda.

Latin MS., beginning of the xvth cent.—Varies greatly with Ramusio's text.—Mentioned by Dominichelli.

43–43–4–**Roma**, *Biblioteca apostolica Vaticana*, Fondo Vaticano, No. 5256.

Latin version following an Italian version.—See Italian versions, No. 61–11–9, p. 63.

Montfaucon, *Bibliotheca Bibliothecarum Manuscriptorum nova*, I, Paris, 1739, p. 17, mentions: No. 171, *Odericus de Ordine Minorum, descriptio de partibus Infidelium.*

44–44–5–**Roma,** *Biblioteca Casanatense*, Cod. B, IV, late 13; now No. 276.

Latin MS. small 4to, parchment, xivth cent. F. 1 recto (in red): *Incipit liber Fratris Odorici de foro Julii provintie sancti Antonij de quadam terra que dicitur Pontus* (sic) *Naonis.* Then follows the table of chapters ff. 1^a, 2^b; the text of the itinerary begins in the second column of f. 2^b with the first chapter entitled *De pernicibus que per aerem ducebantur* which includes also the short prologue; and ends with chapter xxxviij *De reverentia quam Magnus Canis fecit sanctissimo signo crucis* followed by the passage containing the author's attestation.

This MS. includes five different MSS. of which Odoric is the last, 28 ff.

45–45–6–**Udine,** *Biblioteca de l'Archivio Capitolare della Città.*

In vol. XXII of *Miscellanea*, with sundry other opuscula; 4to MS. of 26 ff., the last lines of which are lost; begins: *Istoria beati Odorici. Licet varia et multa de ritibus*...great similarity with the text given by Venni.—This Latin text follows an Italian text of the itinerary, apparently of the xvith cent.—Yule, No. 28.

46–46–7–**Udine,** Library of the heirs of Count Jacopo de Concina, at San Daniele del Friuli.

MS. 8vo, paper, first half of the xvth cent.; binding of the time in red leather; contains 38 ff.; the text is carefully written; begins: *Incipit opusculum Peregrinationis Fratris Odorici Ordinis Fratrum Minorum*, etc....Ends: *Magnis corruscavit miraculis.* Then follow an *Antiphona* and an *Oremus* reproduced by Domenichelli, p. 403. The MS. ends:

Qui scripsit scribat semper cum Domino vivat
Vivat in celis semper cum Domino felix.

47–47–8–**Venice,** *Biblioteca Marciana*, Clas. XIV.—Cod. XLIII.

Latin MS., xivth cent. (xvth wrote Sig. Veludo to me); paper; 4to, 171 ff., h. 0^m 27; wide 0^m 21. Contains a number of pieces having nothing to do with Odoric whose itinerary takes ff. 73 recto–96 verso. A note at foot of f. 96 says that copies of this MS. have been taken by Prof. F. Kunstmann of Munich (in May 1857), and by Col. Yule (August 1864). Yule writes (*Cathay*, I, p. 33, No. 26): "I have had a transcript of it in preparing this translation, but it has not proved so useful as I expected."—Described (No. LXXII) in *Biblioteca manoscritta di Tommaso Giuseppe Farsetti*, Venezia, 1771, 8vo, I, p. 116.—It passed to the Marciana Library from the Farsetti Family. Title: *Opera Fris Odorici Ord. minor.*

Begins: "Quamvis multa et varia de ritibus et conditionibus hujus mundi enarrentur a multis, tum sciendum est quod ego frater Odoricus ordinis minorum de natione forojulii (*volens*) transfectare et ad partes infidelium transmigrare, ut fructus aliquos lucrifacerem animarum, multa magna et mirabilia audivi et vidi quae possum veraciter enarrare. praesens itaque opuschulum in capitula dividens de multis gestis quae vidi et audivi in oriente, septentrione et meridie, etc."

Ends: "Nam ipse beatus frater Odoricus, cum de ultra marinis partibus ad suam provinciam remeasset, marchiam scilicet tarvisanam presentiarum (*sic*) summi pontificis adire volebat ut ab eo hoc etiam peteret, quod L fratres de quacumque provincia essent dummodo ire vellet secum ducere posset, recessit de foro Julii unde ipse natus est. dum esset pisis gravi infirmitate correptus quamobrem compulsus est ad propria remeare, qua propter in utino de foro Julii civitate anno ab incarnacione domini M.CCC.XXXI. pridie idus ianuarii de hoc mundo triumphans pervenit ad insulam beatorum, ubi virtutibus et miraculis quamplurimis corruscat. nam per eum ceci claudi muti surdi sunt permittente domino restituti. deo gratias. amen."

48–48–9–Venice, *Museo Civico e Raccolta Correr.*

MS. formerly 2389, now 2408; paper; large 4to.—This MS. belonged to Gian-Giuseppe Liruti, a Friulan scholar, and to E. A. Cicogna. It is covered with parchment and contains two works; the first is an abstract of the Voyages of *Marco Polo* from p. 1 to p. 36. See *Marco Polo*, II, p. 541, No. 35.—From page 37 to page 43, it contains *Novitates quas notavit frater Odoricus in peregrinatione sua.* It was written in 1401, as may be read twice, on p. 36 and p. 46 verso.

This MS. was used for the edition of Odoric printed at Venice in 1766, by the care of Giuseppe Venni, M.C. See preface,

p. 39 and p. 45.—In the same MS. are verses having nothing to do with the Voyages.

Odoric's Itinerary begins: *Licet multa et varia de ritibus* and ends: *corruscat miraculis*; then follows a note (*explicit*) of the scribe, who after the praises to the Lord signed: *Ego Philippus* natus Ser Petri de Faganea [Fagagna, in Friul] publicus ac imperiali auctoritate notarius scripsi istos libros...et ipsos complevi die martis 16 [Venni, 15] mensis februarii die carnis privii hora tercia dum morabar Padue pro afirmatore Antoni fili quondam nobilis viri Raymundi Sulumani in contrata heremitarum tempore quo studebam in rethoricali scientia legente magistro Marino de Rachanato. Currentibus annis Domini 1401 (*sic*) indictione secunda? [Venni, *nona*, which is exact] die ut supra.—Cf. Venni, pp. 82–3.—See Yule, No. 27.

H.—Switzerland.

49–49–1–**Basel**, University Library, D. iv. 8.

Latin MS. 4to; xivth cent., vellum; wood binding covered with leather; 60 ff.; described by Haenel, p. 545, and by Pertz, *Archiv*, vii, 1839, p. 174, under No. E. iii. 20.

1° *Epla Dni Gwilhelmi de Boldensèle preclarissimi viri r griosi militis ad dum petru abbatem aule regie De descripcone terre sancte*, ff. 1–26 recto; 2° *Epystola ad dnm petrum abbatem aule regie*, ff. 26 recto–26 verso; 3° *Descpco qruda miracl'orum peractoru in Waltsassen*, ff. 26 verso–34 recto; ff. 34 verso–36 blank; 4° *Des'cpc'o terrae sanctae fris Odi'ci de foro julij*, ff. 37–60 recto.
Begins: *Licet multa et varia de ritibus*, etc.

50–50–2–**Bern.**

—Liber Sancti Odorici fratris minoris de vicino ordinis fratrum minorum de exitibus diversarum gentium. *Licet multa et varia de exitibus et condicionibus mundi a multis enarrentur tamen sciendum est—in illa ualle dicebant esse homines cum demonibus dampnatos. Explicit liber Sancti Odorici fratris minoris.*

MS. No. 141 (327), f. 1^a–f. 11^a—xvth cent.—parchment.—With *Excerpta ex fabulis Æsopi quas Romulus de Graeco in Latinum transtulit*, f. 11^b–f. 12^b.

Catalogus Codicum Bernensium (Bibliotheca Bongarsiana).—Edidit et Praef. est H. Hagen, 1875, p. 203.

II.—ITALIAN MSS.

A.—Great Britain.

51–1–1–**Cheltenham**, Library of Sir Thomas Phillips, Bart., Middlehill (Worcestershire).

MS. xivth or xvth cent.; thick paper; 7 ff. ½. Begins, f. 1: *Anno MCCCXVIII, jo frate Oderigo de Frioli, dell' ordine de Frati Minori, della provincia di Padova, partivi della dicta provincia e veni Ingonstantinopoli* (sic)... This MS. catalogued at Cheltenham, under No. 8268, was marked in Heber's Catalogue (1836, Pt. xi, MS.), No. 1165; it belonged formerly to Lord Guilford. Ff. 8–13 last, have nothing to do with Odoric and offer no interest whatever.

B.—France.

52–2–1–**Paris.**

"Inchominccia la storia di frati odorico. Ani domini Mcccxviij, Jo frate odoricho da friolli delordine de frati minori de la provincia di padova partimi dela deta prouincia zuani ī Chostantinopoli, etc." 25 ff.—"Inchominccia la storia di tra monacci chandaro nel paradiso terestro (Holy Land), etc." 8 ff. 4to.

Fine MS., xivth cent.; thick paper; bound in velvet.

Catal. Saulcy, No. 307, Paris, 1872.

C.—Italy.

53–3–1–**Florence,** *Biblioteca Riccardiana*, No. 683.

MS. paper, small 4to; xvth century, with the title: *Oderigo de Frigoli, Viaggio da Padova a Costantinopoli e alla terra del Ponto.* The MS. is incomplete. Yule writes, No. 3, p. 33: "This is one of the peculiar type which I have classed with Ramusio's Minor Version. It seemed to me, as far as I went through it, to be the same as the next on the list (Pal., Florence, E. 5, 9, 6, 7), but it is truncated, going no further than the sons and daughters of the King of Champa."—Brunet, *Man. du Libraire*, iv, col. 160, writes: "Oderico en écrivit d'abord une ébauche en italien (vers l'année 1318), dont le ms. est conservé dans la Bibliothèque Riccardienne à Florence." Fancy the date 1318!

Lami in his *Cat. Cod. MSS. qui in Biblioth. Riccardiana Florentiae adservantur*...Liburni, 1756, fol., gives, p. 203, the following description of this MS.:

"FRIGOLI, o Friuli. F. Oderigo de. Descrizione del suo Viaggio in Costantinopoli e Trabisonda, e altrove. M. IV. *Codex chartac.* in-4, n. XXXIII.

"*Initium exhibimus:*

"Anno MCCCXVIII. io Frate Oderigo de' Frigoli dell' ordine de' Frate Minori della provincia di Padova volendo fare memoria de' paesi e provincie, le quali trovai partendomi di Padova, e venni in Costantinopoli, e di quindi passai il mare maggiore, e venni in Trebisonda nella contrada detta Metropoli di Ponto, nella qual terra giace il corpo di S. Atanasio, che fece il Simbolo. E in questa terra viddi una mirabil cosa, che un uomo menava più di due mila pernice, le quali il seguitavano per mirabile modo, perchè andavano e volavano e stavano con lui per più diete, e ubbidivallo, e parea quasi che parlassero con lui nella lingua sua; e quando andava allo Imperadore, lo 'mperadore prendea delle pernici quante ne voleva, e l' altre se ne venivano con lui quasi per quattro diete a Trebisonda insino al castello chiamato Zavecca. Da Trebisonda andai a Zavecca, ch' è castello dello Imperadore e quasi inespugnabile, e quivi si cava l' ariento, ed eziando il cristallo, secondo che dicono alquanti. Quindi andai in Ermenia maggiore, e pervenni ad Arzelone, dove presso a una dieta è il fiume del Paradiso detto Eufrates. In questa terra sentì che una grande donna lasciò per suo testamento, che de' beni suoi si facesse un munistero di meritrici, che sempre fossero apparecchiate a servire a gli uomini in ogni carnalitade, e questo fece per l' anima sua maladetta. Di quindi venni al monte dove è l' Arca Noè, e volentieri sarei salito alla cima del monte, avvegnachè mai non si trovò chi vi potesse salire, ma perchè non volli aspettare la carovana, non me ne volli provare. Quello monte è altissimo e bellissimo, e sempre ve l' aveva insino alla terza parte del mondo ec."

See LUCCA, infra, No. 58–8–6, p. 61.

54–4–2–**Florence,** *Biblioteca Nazionale, sezione Palatina,* E. 5, 9, 6, 7.

xivth cent.; 8vo. "Containing only Odoric and a short narrative about three monks who visited the Terrestrial Paradise.

According to the Ms. Catalogue by G. Molini it is of the 14th century. It is written somewhat carelessly, and in a most barbarous style, but has remarkable peculiarities. The earlier part coincides with the Minor Ramusian (not minutely), and traces of the same basis appear throughout, but also many things that are in no other copy that I know of. For this reason it has been thought desirable to print it." Yule, *Cathay*, I, p. 34, No. 4.

Printed by Yule, *Cathay*, App. II, pp. XLIII–LXIII, and reprinted in our Appendix.—Partly reproduced by De Gubernatis, *Storia dei Viaggiatori italiani*, pp. 138–141.—Marked PAL. in our notes.

55–5–3–**Florence,** *Biblioteca Nazionale,* Cod. Magliabech., ch. XIII, No. 68.

Quoted by Domenichelli: "È la versione italiana pubblicata da noi, pigliandola dal Codice di Venezia, Biblioteca Marciana, Cl. VI, nº 102, ed ha il titolo: *Viaggio in Tartaria di Odorico da Udine.*"

At the end: "Compiuto di scrivere lunedi sera a dì ventisette d' Ottobre 1377." (DOM., p. 255.)—Marked MAGL. in our notes.

56–6–4–**Florence,** *Biblioteca Nazionale,* Cl. XXII, cod. 20.

Itinerarium Fratris Odorici de Foro Iulii, quoted by Domenichelli.

57–7–5–**Genoa.**

MS. paper, XVth cent.—*Viaggi del Beato Oderico da Pordenone.*

Quoted by Amat di S. Filippo, from the *Atti della Società ligure di Storia patria.*

58–8–6–**Lucca,** *Biblioteca governativa,* Col. Lucchesini.

Paper, XVth cent.; 4to; ff. 75.—Yule, p. 34, No. 5.—Contains: *Marco Polo* and *Odoric* in the Venetian dialect.—See Lazari, *Marco Polo*, p. 452.—*Marco Polo*, II, p. 544, No. 49.—This MS. had No. 26 in the Giacomo Lucchesini collection, and it has now No. 296 at Lucca. Its title is *Viaggi di frate Oderigo del Friuli e di Marco Polo.* The vol. begins with the table of contents, then comes: "Libro delle meravigliose cosse vedute per frate Odericho dell' ordine de' frati Menori della patria di

Friuli con i suo' compagni dicesse aver trovato oltra mare in le terre de le tre Indie, et in molte altre region e paesi ne li quali el feze dimora anni xiiij: el qual frate Odoricho al suo fine fu Sancto canonizato con miracoli in Udene ne li anni del nostro Signor Misser Jesu Cristo MCCCXXXI a di xiiij di Zenaro et in Udine jace el suo corpo.—Conzo sia che per molti sia narrato e scrito diverse nuove e stranie cosse." Ends somewhat like the MS. of the Riccardiana described by Lami in his *Catalogus codicum manuscriptorum qui in Bibliotheca Riccardiana Florentiae adversantur*, Liburni, Santinij, 1756, p. 203, and is marked by Zambrini, *Opere volgari*, p. 715, see *infra*.

"Io frate Odericho di Friul di una terra chiamata Porto Neone appresso Udene e la provincia della Marca Trivisana, e de la diocesi di Aquilezia de l' ordene de frati menori testifico e con verita rispondo al mio ministro per vera obedientia che tute le cosse che sono scrite in questo libro parte le vidi con li ochi mei e parte le audi dire ad homini degni di fede come di sopra le ho notate, e quale che non vidi pareno che sia vere. Molte e molte chosse io ho lassiate, ch' io non o' fatto scrivere perchè sono quasi incredibile a chi con proprii ochi non le vedesse. E de in di in di io me aparechio d' andare a quele contrade, ne le quali mi dispono di vivere a morir secondo la volonta di Dio. Amen, Amen, amen."

The text varies somewhat from the texts of Ramusio and of the Riccardiana. Marco Polo's text is practically Ramusio's, Baldelli-Boni's and Bartoli's but differs as to the language and is shorter. At the end: "*Complito el libro de le cosse mirabile vedute per lo nobile homo Messer Marcho Polo gientelomo de Venesia a di 12 de Marzo 1465 per mi Daniele da Verona in sul Ponte de' Berettari al onore e laude dell' Omnipotente.*"

Sig. Amat di S. Filippo mentions two Italian MSS. in the Public Library at Lucca, but the Librarian, Sig. Boselli, speaks of one only.

59-9-7-**Pisa**, Private Archives of Count Alfred-Augustine Della Seta.

Small fol., xvth cent.—Contains: "Il libro delle nuove strane e maravigliose cose che Frate...Hodoricho di Friuli dell' Ordine Minori disse che avea trovate ultra mare nelle tre Indie e in molte altre regioni e paesi nelle qualli elli fue personalmente quattordici anni." Mentioned by Domenichelli from a description of Sig. Cesare Guasti; he adds: "Nelle carte precedenti è copiato il *Libro lapidario* che il Re d' Etiopia inviò a quello di Armenia, tradotto già dell' Indiano al latino da Fra Tommaso de' Minori di Pisa, e che parla delle pietre preziose che si trovano nell' India."

60–10–8–**Roma**, *Biblioteca apostolica Vaticana*, Fondo Vaticano-Urbinate, No. 1013.

Paper; small fol., xvth cent.

Begins: "Cominceno i capitoli de lo libro de le nove strane e meravĩose cose che frat. Odorigo de Friul de lo ordine di fra minori...." There are fifty chapters, with a good many illustrations.

Ends: "E anchora io me apparecchio d' andare i quelle contrade ĩ le qual mi despono de viver e de morir alla voluntade de Dio, Am̃. Am̃."

Then follow some other works.

61–11–9–**Roma**, *Biblioteca apostolica Vaticana*, Fondo Vaticano, No. 5256.

Paper; 4to; xivth cent.—*Begins:* "Libro de le cose meravigliosse chosse le qual vide frate Oderigo de Friul."

Ends: "me apparecchio de andare in quelle contrade ne le q̃le me dispongo de vivere e morire secondo la volontade de Dio. Amen."

After this is to be found the Latin version of William of Solagna: "*Incipiunt diversae historiae* B[ti]. Odorici de Utino ordinis Minorum: Supradic̃us aut fr. Odoricus postea ex hoc seculo migravit ad Dñ in conventu Utini Anno MCCCXXXI die xiiij Jan. qui postmodum multis et magnis coruscavit miraculis."—At the end: "*praedicta autem ego fr.* Guilielmus de Solagna in scriptis redegi sicut praedictus fr. Odoricus ore proprio exprimebat, anno Dñi mill. trecent. vicesimo, de mense Maji. Paduae in loco S[ti]. Antonii."

62–12–10–**Roma**, *Biblioteca Casanatense*, Cod. E, V, formerly 1; now No. 1548.

Paper; xvth cent.; Odoric, pp. 174–211.

Begins f. 174[a]: "Questo libro trata de Frate Odorico, de diverse bele e stranie cosse lui ha visto per molti strani luogi del mondo." *The text begins* f. 175^a: "Avegnadio che molte e diverse instorie dele cosse e dele condizion de questo mondo da molti sien raxonade..." *Ends* f. 211^a: "Molto si me honoravano digandome che io scia cristiano batizato e queli li quali sono in quela vala morti lor dixerano che queli omeni sono demoni infernali."

The first leaves of the MS. contain an Italian translation in *ottava rima* of the *Pharsalia* of Lucan ascribed to a "L. di Montichilto cardinalem dignissimum."

63–13–11–**Udine**, Archiepiscopal Seminary.

Paper; 8vo; 182 ff., of which 54 contain the *Vita del Beato Odorico della Patria del Friuli de' Minori...per il Padre Maestro Cornelio di Navarra, Ferrarese, Vicario generale del Santo Ufficio*, 1671.—See Domenichelli, p. 145 and p. 366.

64–14–12–**Udine**, Library of the *Archivio Capitolare della Città*.

See *supra*, Latin text 45–45–6.—I presume it is the text marked by Domenichelli, p. 366, No. 46: "Biblioteca del Capitolo.—MS. cartaceo, contenente una versione italiana dei Viaggi del Beato Odorico preceduta da un testo latino."

65–15–13–**Venice**, *Marciana*, It. Cl. VI. Cod. CII.

Paper; 8vo; XIVth cent.; 31 pages numbered, 26 to 28 lines; $0^m 20 \times 0^m 14$.—Belonged formerly to the family Nani; it has been described by J. Morelli in *I Codici manoscritti volgari della Libreria Naniana riferiti da Don Jacopo Morelli*...Venezia, Ant^o Zatta, 1776, 4to, XCV, pp. 90–1.—Yule says, p. 33, No. 1: "It is the most careful and intelligently executed copy of Odoric that I have seen. I have examined the MS. and used a transcript of it in preparing this work."—Printed by Domenichelli, pp. 201–255.

Begins: "Aveggia che molte et varie cose de costumi et de le conditioni di questo mōdo da molte altre p'sone siano state ditte et narate percio e da saper, etc."

Ends: "et presentamogli di quelle pome et eglino, con grāde alegreza, recevendole cosi si pareano alegrare, come, se noy glavessimo fatto un gran dono, etc....Et io frate Odorigo di friuli duna tēra che chiamata porto di naone, ec. Molte altre cose io o lasciate, le quali, io no feci scrivere, p'chelle parebbono incredibile apresso alchuna p'sona, che nolle vedesse con li ochi.

Et io de di in di maparechio dandare in quelle contrade nele quale io oe diliberato, di vivere et dimorare si come piacera a cō lui dal quale tutti e beni p'cedono."

66–16–14–**Venice**, *Marciana*, It. Cl. IV. Cod. CCVIII.

Paper; 4to; xvith cent.; ff. 260, 30 to 36 lines; $0^m 22 \times 0^m 16$; the title of the MS. is *Viaggiatori antichi* (*i.e.* Miscellanea di viaggi) *ed altre cose ascetiche in fine.*

After the index, come pp. 1–18: "Incomenza el tractato over el viazo lo qual fece el beato Udorico da Utine frate de l' ordine de sancto francesco d'le cose che lui vide e parte udite da p'sone digne d' fede quādo lui fo nele p'te d' oriēte. E queste cose sono vere, e fu nel 1322."

Begins: "Benche varie e molte cose di costumi e cōdictione de questo mōdo multi habiano nārato, niēte di meno, ec. ec."

Ends: "e donassemo a loro d' q'lli pomi e loro li ricevetono cū tāta alegreza. como fosse stato qualche grā presente.—Questo he q'to io frē Udorico d' la patria del friul ho veduto e parte udito da p'sone digne d' fede. E d' q'sto vēdo dio p' testimonio avāti al prē frē guidoto, mist° d' la p'vicia d' s'cto Ant° q'ste cose esser vere, cum sit ch esso mīstro me comando p' obīa che de questo dovesse dir la vita, senza fallo alcuno. Et fratre *Udorico* (this name written by another hand) da Salogna ho scripte le presente cose, secondo chel sudicto fratre Udorico me le dicea cum la propria bocha nel año del segnor 1324 del mese de mazo nel loco de s̄cto Ant° de Padua. Da poi el sopradicto fratre Udorico passò di questa vita nel 1331 a 14 de zenaro nel convento de Udene, el qual in vita e da puo la morte resplende de molti miracoli. A laude del segnor."

After the martyrdom and the miracles of the friars.—This MS. belonged to J. Morelli. Yule, p. 33, writes: "The volume contains other matter, including Polo, Alonzo Cadamosto, Voyages of Vasco da Gama and Columbus. It is noticed in Marsden's Polo, p. lxii. I have examined it, but made no use of it." See *Marco Polo*, II, p. 540, No. 34.

Domenichelli, p. 367, writes: "Il Cicogna nel Catalogo dei suoi libri rammenta un codice italiano dei viaggi del Beato Odorico, esistente nella Marciana, e segnato classe VI, No. 109, marca 103, 1." Sig. Veludo, the late chief of the Marciana to whom I owe the description of the MSS. entrusted to him, wrote to me that he may assure me that the cod. 109, cl. VI (marca 103, 1) contains only: *Giovanni Michele Vanslebio. Relazione dello stato presente dell' Egitto scritta nel 1668 a Ferdinando II. Gran Duca di Toscano*; and that only four MSS. of Odoric, three Italian and one Latin, are kept in the Marciana.

67–17–15–**Venice,** *Marciana* (R. Biblioteca Nazionale di S. Marco), It. Cl. XI. Cod. XXXII.

Paper; fol.; xvth–xvith cent.; ff. 466; $0^m\ 32 \times 0^m\ 24$; miscellanies with the title *Estratti d' opere varie ec.* Odoric (xvith cent.) takes ff. 231–242 verso: "Chominziamo lolibro dele nuove et stranie et maraviglosse chosse che fratte Odoricho di friuli delordene de minori disse ch' aveva trovate oltra mare nelle tre indie et in molte altre regioni et paesi neli quali elli fue santo ch'o molti miracholli, in udine di friulli. ne l' anno domini MCCCXXXI adi XIIII di genaro et quine (*i.e.* QUI) giaze lo suo chorppo."

Begins: "Chonciosia chossa che p' molti sia narrato et deto diversse et nuove et stranie chosse delusāze et chondicioni et riti del mondo darovi adintendere et asapere io frate Odorigo di friulli del ordene de minori, che io trapassai lo grande mare et andai in trapezonda che antichamente hera chiamata ponto; la quale trapesonda, etc."

Ends: "et p' questa chagione tuti issarazinii maveano in grāde reverencia dicendo che io era battizzato et sancto. E quelli che erano morti in quela vale erano stati hõi del diavolo dello inferno.

"Io frate Odoricho ec. ec."

The preface differs from that of Cod. CII, but the text is the same.—Belonged to Amadeo Svaier, a wealthy Venetian merchant during the xviiith century.

68–18–16–**Venice,** *Museo Civico e Raccolta Correr.*

MS. new 2613.—Described, p. 354 of *Saggio del Catalogo dei Codici* di Emmanuale A. Cicogna (*Archivio Veneto*, t. IV, Venezia, 1872); formerly No. 2611; 4to; $0^m\ 29 \times 0^m\ 22$; paper; xvth cent.; contains a *Cronaca Veneta* from the origin to the year 1405, with some additions till 1425; at the end is Odoric. *Ends:* "Io frate Odorigo de Friul de l' ordene de' frati menori rendo testemonianza al reverendo padre frate Guidoto ministro de la provenzia de santto Antonio siando da quela p. obidienzia requirido che tutto quelo che io ne la presedentte opera o ditto io veramente e lo visto con li miei ochj propri e veramente loldido dire da persone degne di fede de queli paixi moltte altre chosse o viste et aldide le qual a schriverle pareriano chose inchredibile et pero non le o voiude schrivere. Laus Y^u X^o dno. nro. amen. Finitto."

This MS. belonged to Count G.-D. Tiepolo; it was purchased in 1837 by Cicogna.

III.—FRENCH MSS.

A.—GREAT BRITAIN.

69–1–1–**London,** *British Museum, Royal Coll.*, 19. D. 1.

MS. large fol., 267 ff., text on 2 col.; xvth cent.—Mentioned by M. Paul Meyer[1]; unknown to Yule.—Contains eight works: *Le livre d'Alexandre;* Jehan le Venelais, *la Vengeance d'Alexandre;* Marc Pol; Odoric; Ascelin, *Mission chez les Tartares; le Directoire;* Primat, *Chronique des règnes de Louis IX et de Philippe III; Extraits de la Bible.*

Odoric *begins* f. 136: "Ci commencent les merveilles de la terre d'Ou // tremer..." (*See* p. 2 of French ed.).—*Ends* f. 148 c: "Frere Guil // laume Sollengin de l'ordre des meneurs mist // loiaument en escript toutes les devant dites // choses si comme le dit frere Odoric li devisa de sa // propre bouche en l'an de Nostre Seigneur mil CCC. // et XXX. el mois de mai en la cité d'Espade [read *de Pade*] el // lieu Saint Anthoine ne li chaloit de par // ler latin fors curieus et ordené et tout aussi // comme frere Odoric le racontoit, frere Guilleme escri // voit en tel maniere que touz entendissent // legierement les choses dites. Et le dit frere O//doric trespassa de cest siècle en nostre Seigneur // assez tost apres c'est assavoir l'an de nostre Seigneur // mil CCC.XXXII[2]. et. XIIII iour de ienvier el convent // de Venise[3]. et est ennobli el dit convent par moult // de grans miracles."

It is a very handsome MS.—The translation of Jean de Vignay is a poor one.—Cf. French ed. of Odoric, p. CVI.

[1] *Documents manuscrits de l'ancienne littérature de la France conservés dans les bibliothèques de la Grande-Bretagne.* Rapports à M. le Ministre de l'Instruction publique par M. Paul Meyer. Première partie. Paris, Imp. nat., 1871, 8vo, pp. 69–80.

[2] Read 1331. [3] Read *Udine.*

70–2–2–**London**, *British Museum*, 18 *Cotton.*, *Otho*, D. II.

French MS.; small fol.; 2 col.; miniatures.—Contains Voyages to the Holy Land, etc.; and an Itinerary of Odoric, unfortunately too damaged by fire to be of great use.

B.—France.

71–3–1–**Paris**, *Bibliothèque nationale*, *Français* 1380 (late 7500 C.).

Small fol.; vellum; xvth cent., 2 col.; from Bigot's collection, 165; f. 1 recto, coloured drawing; the place of the other drawings, blank. The Table in the three first preliminary leaves:

1° *Begins* recto f. 1: "Ci commence vn traittie de l'estat et des condicions de xiiij. royaumes de ayse et des empereurs qui puis lincarnacion de ñre seigneur ont regne en y ceulx et regnent encore et du passage doultre mer a la terre sainte. Et de la poissance du soubdam de egipte que nous appellons le soudam de babiloine. Et fut ce traittie fait premierement en latin par tres hault et tres noble home monseigneur Aycon Seigneur de courcy cheualier et nepueu du roy darmenie la grant..."

2° *Begins* verso f. 53: "Ci cõmence la itinerance de la peregrinacion et du voiage que fist vn bon preudome des freres prescheurs qui ot nom frere Bicult..."

3° *Begins* recto f. 95: "Ci cõmence le chemin de la peregrinacion et du voiaige que fist vns bons homs de lordre des freres mineurs qui ot nom frere Odric de Foro julii ne dune terre que on appelle port de Venise..."

Ends recto f. 117. See French edition, pp. 491/2.

4° *Begins* recto f. 119: "Cy commence vn traictie de lestat de la terre sainte et aussy en partie de la terre de Egipte & fut fait a la requeste de tres Reuerent seigñr mons. Talairât de pierregort..."

5° *Begins* verso f. 138: "Cest la copie des lettres qui li empereres souverains des tartres le grant caan de cathay envoia au pape Benoit xij^{e} de ce nom..."

6° *Begins* recto f. 142: "Cy commence de lestat et de la gouu'ance du grant caan de cathay..."

The MS. ends f. 146 verso; these translations by Jehan Le Long are reproduced in *l'Hystore merueilleuse...du grant Empereur de Tartarie*, 1529, see later on.

72–4–2–**Paris,** *Bibliothèque nationale, Français* 2810 (late 8392).

MS. fol., bound arms of France, La Vallière morocco, contains the following works: *Marco Polo, Odoric, Taleran de Pierregort, L'Estat du grant Kaan, Lettres du Pape, Mandeville, Hethum and Ricold.*

This magnificent MS. written in gothic letters on vellum was executed by order of the Duke of Burgundy and given by this prince to his uncle the Duke of Berry at the beginning of the xvth century. One of the miniatures at the beginning of Hethum's story, f. 226, shows the Duke of Burgundy receiving the book; the shield of Jean Sans Peur is drawn in the miniature above the doorway: *Écartelé, au 1. et 4. semé de France, à la bordure componnée d'azur et de gueules, qui est* BOURGOGNE MODERNE; *Au 2. et 3. bandé d'or et d'azur de six pièces à la bordure de gueules qui est* BOURGOGNE ANCIEN. *Et sur le tout, d'or au lion de sable armé, et lampassé de gueules qui est* FLANDRE. It bears the title

"Ce Liure est des // Merueilles du Monde. Cest assavoir de la Terre // Saincte. Du Grant Kaan Empereur des tartars. // Et du pays Dynde. Le Quel // Liure Jehan Duc de Bourgoingne donna // a son oncle Jehan fils de Roy dc // France Duc de Berry et Dauviergne, Conte // de Poitou, Detampes. de Bouloigne. et Dauvergne. // Et contient le dit Liure six // Livres. Cest assavoir. Marc Pol. Frere Odric de lordre des // Freres meneurs. Le Liure fait à la requeste du Cardinal Taleran de // Pierregort. L'Estat du Grant Kaan. Le Liure de Messire Guillaume // de Mandeville. Le Liure de Frere Jehan Hayton de lordre de premonstre. // Le Liure de Frere Bicul de lordre des Freres Prescheurs // — Et sont en ce dit Liure Deux cens soixante six // hystoires."

Signed by: N. FLAMEL.

Then follow:

1° *Marco Polo:* "Cy apres commence le liure de Marc Paule des merveilles daise la grant et dinde la maiour et mineur Et des diuerses regions du monde."—*Begins:* "Pour sauoir la pure verite de diuerses regions du monde. Si prenez ce liure cy et le faictes lire. Si y trouuerez les grandismes merueilles qui y sont escriptes..."

Ends (fol. 96 verso): "Et a tant fine messire marc pol son liure dc la diuision du monde et des merueilles dicelluy."

2° *Odoric:* Folio 97: "Cy cōmence le liure Frere audric de lordre des Freres meneurs. Cy commence le chemin de la peregrinacion et du voyaige que fist vn bon homme de lordre des freres meneurs. nomme frere Odric de fore iulii. ne de vne terre que on appelle port de Venisse qui par le comāt du pappe ala oultre mer pour preschier aux mescreans la foy de Dieu. Et sont en ce liure contenu les merueilles que li dis freres vit presentement. et aussy de pluseurs autres lesquelles il oy compter en ces parties sus dittes de gens disgnes de foy. Mais celles quil oy racompter et quil ne vit point. ne racompte il point pour verite fors pour oir dire. et le sōne en son langaige quant a ce vient. Et fut ce liure fait en latin par ce frere deuant nomme en lan de grace mil. CCC. XXX. p'fais le xiij iour de ianuier Et fu cilz liures translatez de latin en francois por frere Iean le lonc. dit et ne dyppre moisne de saint bertin en saint Aumer, en lan de grace M. CCC. lj."

Ends (fol. 115 r. and v.): "Explicet le yteneraire Odric de Foro Julij de lordre des freres meneurs qui fist cest liure en lan de grace mil trois cens et trente. Et puis la mort dieux a fait par lui maint miracle. Et fu cilz liures translatez par frere iehan le lonc ne dyppre et moisne de saint bertin en saint aumer. En lan de grace mil. iijc. lj. acomplis."

The MS. of Odoric begins f. 97 verso and ends f. 215 v. See p. 492, note *d* of French edition; it is illustrated with 17 (85–101) miniatures: *1. Departure, f. 97 verso (two friars); 2. Chaldaea, f. 98 verso; 3. Reception of the Reliques, f. 102 recto (two friars); 4. Gold Idol, f. 103 recto; 5. Natives of Lamory, f. 104 recto (two friars); *6. Bread Trees, f. 105 recto; 7. Champa Fishes, f. 105 verso; *8. Dog-headed men, f. 106 recto; 9. Ceylon, fishing precious stones, f. 106 verso; 10. Dondin Anthropophagi, f. 107 recto; 11. Zaïtun, f. 108 recto; *12. Fishing by hand, f. 108 verso; *13. Man-headed animals, f. 109 verso; *14. Caravan, f. 110 verso; 15. The friars travelling, f. 113 recto; 16. The rich Man of Manzi, f. 114 recto; *17. The terrible Valley, f. 115 recto. Seven of these miniatures marked *, plus three from the Book of Marco Polo in the same MS., in all 10 miniatures have been reproduced in black in the French edition of Odoric. Some of the miniatures have also been reproduced by Count de Bastard, *Librairie du duc de Berri* (1834), pl. 6–14; Silvestre, *Paléographie universelle* (1841), pl. 148; Madden, *Universal Palaeography*

(1849), pl. CXCII; Charton, *Voyageurs anciens et modernes* (1855), t. II, pp. 258 seq.; Yule-Cordier's *Marco Polo*. The whole of the 266 miniatures of the MS. have since been reproduced in facsimile in black by Berthaud frères, Paris, in two vols., with an introduction by M. H. Omont.

3° Folio 116: "Cy commence Le Liure de Taleren de Pierreguort..."

Ends (folio 132 verso):

"Par Guillaume de Boldesele."

4° Folio 133: "Cest la coppie des lettres que ly empereres souuerains des tartars le grant kaan de katay enuoya au pappe benoit le .xij^e. de ce nom en lan de grace mil trois cens. XXXVIII. enuiron la pentecouste et furent par le commandemēt dudit pappe translatees en latin, et furent translatees du latin en francois par frere iehan le lonc dit et ne de yppre moisne de saint bertin en saint aumer. en lan de grace. M. iij^c. lj."

Ends: "Escript en Cambalec en lan du s. rat. le sisiesme mois. le tiers iour de la lunison."

Followed by a commentary.

5° Folio 134: "Cest la teneur des lettres et de la responce que ly pape renuoya a ces principaux amis demourans en Cambanlech dessoubz lempereur desus dit."

Ends fol. 136: "Donne en avignon. le xiij. iour de Juing. le. v^e annee de n're regnacion de n're pappa. Explicit, etc."

6° *Estat du grant Caan:* Folio 136 verso: "Cy commence le Liure de lestat du grant Caan. Cy commence de lestat et de la gouuernance du grant kaan de cathay souuerain empereur des tartres. et de la disposicion de son empire. et de ses autres princes. Interpreté par vn arceuesque que on dist larceuesque Saltensis. au commant du pappe iehan. xxij^e de ce nom. Translate de latin en francois p' frere iehā le lōc dyppre moisne de s'. b'tī en s'. aumer."

Ends folio 140 verso: "Explicit de la gouuernance et de lestat du grant kaan souuerain empereur des Tartars."

7° *Mandeville:* Folio 141; "Cy commence le liure mesire guillaume de mandeuille—Comme il soit ainsi que la terre doultre mer cest assauoir la sainte terre de promission. entrestoutes les autres terres cest la plus excellente. et la plus digne et dame souueraine de toutes autres terres. Et benoite et saintefie et consacree du precieux corps et du precieux sang ñre seigneur Jesu Crist."

Ends verso folio 225.

8° *Hethum:* Folio 226: "Cy commence le liure frere Iehan hayton de lordre de premonstre cousin germain du roy darmenie qui parle des merueilles des .xiiij royaulmes daise. Le royaume de cathay est tenu pour le plus noble royaume et le plus riche qui soit ou monde et est sur le riuage de la mer occeane."

Ends folio 267: "Cy fine le liure des hystoires des parties dorient compile par religieux hōme frere hayton frere de lordre de premonstre iadis seigneur de core. cousin germain du roy darmenie sur le passaige de la terre sainte. p'. le commandement du souuerain pere ñre seigneur lapostole clement quint en la cite de poytiers. Le quel liure ie nicole Falcon escrips premierement en frācois. si comme le dit frere hayton le ditoit da sa bouche. sans note ne exemplaire. et de romans le translatay en latin. En lan ñre seigneur. M. CCC. sept ou mois daoust. Deo gracias."

9° "Cy cōmence Le Liure de Frere Bicul: de lordre des Freres prescheurs."

Begins folio 268: "Ci cōmence le itineraire de la peregrinacion et du voiage que fist ung bon preudōme des freres precheurs qui ot nom frere bicul. qui par le cōmant du saint pere ala oult' mer por prechier aux mescreans la foy de dieu."

Ends verso of folio 299: "Explicit le ytineraire de la peregrinacōn frere riculd de lorde des freres precheurs et sont en ce liure contenu par sobriesce les royaumes et les gens lez prouinces lez loys lez sectes lez heresies, lez monstres et les merueilles que lidis freres trouua és p'ties dorient. et fu cilz liures t'rslates de latin en françoys par frere i'han de yppre moisne de saint bertin en saint omer. En lan mil. ccc. li. acomplis."

The letters Nos. 4 and 5 have been published by E. Jacquet in the *Nouv. Journ. Asiat.*, VII, 1831, pp. 417 seq. under the title: *Notice sur quelques relations diplomatiques des Mongols de la Chine avec les Papes d'Avignon.*—Pauthier made use of this MS. for his edition of Marco Polo; marked *B.*—Since M. Louis de Backer has published Odoric, Hetum, the Letters of the Pope and the *État du Grand Khan* under the following title: Louis de Backer. *L'Extrême-Orient au moyen âge* d'après les manuscrits d'un Flamand de Belgique, moine de Saint-Bertin à Saint-Omer, et d'un prince d'Arménie, moine de Prémontré à Poitiers. Paris, Ernest Lerour, 1877, 8vo, pp. 502.—Yule (*The Athenaeum*, No. 2598, 11th August 1877) and myself (*Revue critique*, 19th May 1877) have been very severe on this bad book.

This MS. 2810 is marked No. 116 in the Catalogue of the Library of John, Duke of Berry, at the castle of Mehun-sur-Yèvre, 1416, and No. 196 of the Library of the same, p. 186 of *Le Cabinet des Manuscrits de la Bibl. nationale*, par L. Delisle, III.

Domenichelli writes, p. 365, No. 33: "Manoscritto *latino* No. 8392, Supp. français"!

73–5–3–**Paris**, *Bibliothèque nationale*, *Français* 12202 (late Supp. fr. 1103).

Paper MS.; xivth cent.; fol. long lines; 184 ff.; contains in the version of John le Long: Hetum, Ricold, etc. Odoric begins f. 108 verso, and ends f. 134 verso: *tous diables en enfer. Explicit.* See p. 492 of French ed., slight variants. Domenichelli has: "Manoscritto *latino* No. 1103, Supp. *français*."

C.—Switzerland.

74–6–1–**Bern**, *City Library*, No. 125.

Parchment; xivth cent.; fol., 286 ff.—Belonged to J. Bongars of Orleans; contains: 1. Itineraire de Marco Polo; 2. Jehan de Mandeville, de l'estat de la Terre saincte et des merveilles que il y a vues; 3. Itinéraire de Ordric; 4. Traittie de la Terre saincte de Guillaume de Bouldeselle; 5. Coppie des lettres que l'empereur des Tartres le grand Kaan de Catay envoia au pape Benoist le XII en l'an 1338; 6. L'estat du gouvernement du grand Kaan de Cathay et de la disposition de son empire, etc.; 7. Livre des hystoires des parties dorient compilé par Jehan Hayton, etc.; 8. Livre de peregrinacion de litineraire et du voiage que fist ung bon preudomme frère Ricul.

This MS. seems to be incomplete, as fol. 180 begins with these words: "seroient longues à recompter Cy nous dit de Somdoma la cite autres lapelent Sottoma. De ceste cite de thoris men party et vins lespace de dix journees en une cite qui a nom Somdoma."

Ends f. 196^b: "Mais touz ceulz qui estoient la demourez estoient touz deables d'enfer.

"Explicit le yteneraire Odric de foro Julii de lordre des freres meneurs qui fist ce livre en lan de grace mil cccxxx. Et puis sa mort dieu a fait par luy maints miracles. Et fut ce livre translate par frere Jehan le long ne dypre et moynne de Saint Bertin en saint aumer En lan de grace mil ccc cinquante et ung."

This collection is similar to the *Livre de Merveilles*, No. 70; it is mentioned, p. 458, by V. Lazari, *I Viaggi di Marco Polo*, Venezia, 1847.

IV.—GERMAN MSS.

A.—Austria.

75–1–1–**Nikolsburg** (*Moravia*), Library of Prince Mensdorf-Pouilly.

German translation of Odoric's voyage, made in 1359, by a priest called Corrado Steckel.—Mentioned by Domenichelli.

B.—Bavaria.

76–2–1–**Nürnberg**, Library?

Paper; xvth cent.; 19 ff. numbered 168–186; titles of chapters in red; the first letter of *Ich* has not been written.—Begins: "Ich Brüder Ulrich von Friaul geporen, etc."—I have been unable to find in my notes in what library this MS. is kept.

General Distribution of MSS. of Odoric

	Latin	Italian	French	German	Total
Great Britain					15
Cambridge	3				
Cheltenham ...	1	1			
London	4		2		
Oxford	2				
Glasgow	2				
Germany					6
Berlin	1				
Bremen	1				
Breslau	1				
Mentz	1				
Wolfenbüttel ...	2				
Alsace					3
Strasburg	3				
Austria					10
Admont	2				
Melk	1				
Nikolsburg				1	
Prag	2				
Vienna	4				
Bavaria					5
Eichstätt	1				
Munich	2				
Nürnberg	1			1	
France					9
Paris	4	1	3		
St Omer	1				
Italy					25
Assisi	1				
Florence		4			
Genoa		1			
Lucca		1			
Pisa		1			
Milan	2				
Rome	2	3			
Udine	2	2			
Venice	2	4			
Switzerland					3
Basel	1				
Bern	1		1		
	50	18	6	2	76

B.—BIBLIOGRAPHY OF PRINTED EDITIONS

1.—Odorichus de rebus incognitis. Pesaro [per Girolamo Soncino], 1513, 4to.

**Odorichus de rebus
incognitis.**

Small 4to; 23 ff. or 46 pages; on f. 1, title *ut supra*; then a preface of 4 pages with the title: *Ponticus Virunius Paulo Danielo Mantuano bene agere*; the first of these pages is reproduced in the French ed. of Odoric and in my *Bibliotheca Sinica*, col. 2006; this preface ends by *Ex Isauro idibus. feb. MDXIII.* Then the relation in Italian of Odoric's voyage begins: *In questo breuissimo curriculo de miserabel tempo del. M.CCC.XVIII....*This page and the last reproduced also in the French Odoric and in the *Bib. Sinica.* After the voyages comes a Latin note showing that this text was printed from the copy of Francisco Olivieri, of Jesi; the whole ends: *Impressus Esauri. M.D.XIII. idibus Martii. Laus Deo: & Curiae coelesti semper.*

There are but two copies known of this edition: one in the "Reale Biblioteca Palatina" of Parma described here; one belonging (Cat. 1900, No. 431) to the bookseller Joseph Baer, of Frankfort a. M.

On this book, written in a language *inculta* and *rozza* says Apostolo Zeno, see long note in French edition of Odoric.

2.—LHystore merueilleuse || Plaisante et Recreatiue du grād Empereur de Tar || tarie seigneur des Tartres nōme le grād Can. Cōte⸗ || nāt six liures ou parties : Dont le ¶ Premier traicte || des singularitez ꝛ conditions des .XIIII. Royaulmes de || Asye subiectz audict grand Chan. ¶ Le second parle des empereurs qui || depuis Lincarnation nostre seigñr ont regne et encore a p̄sent regnent en || Asie. Et aussi dont premier proceda le nom du grād Chan Et la seigneu || rie des Tartres | Et cōment. ¶ Le tiers descript q̄lle chose on doibt faire || auāt que commencer la guerre. ¶ Le quart parle du voyaige q̄fist vng || Religieux des freres p̄scheurs allant ꝑ le commādement du pape oultre || mer prescher les mescreās. Et sont en ceste ꝑtie cōtenuz les royaulmes | || Les gens | Les prouinces | Les loix | Les sectes | Les heresies | Et les nou= || uelles que le dit frere trouua es parties dorīēt. ¶ Le cinq̄esme cotiēt com= || mēt vng aultre religieux des freres mineurs alla oultre mer pour pres= || scher les infidelles || Et fust iusques en la terre prebstre Jan ou il vit plu= || sieurs aultres choses fort admirables Et dignes de grand memoire | cō= || me il racōpte cy dedans. ¶ Le sixiesme ꝑle du pays de surye | et des vil= || les sur mer | degipte | du desert du mōt de Synay | darabe | Et des sainctz || lieux q̄ sont entre le fleuue Jourdain ⁊ Hierusalē | Et signāment des cho || ses mōstrueuses q̄l a veues selon la diuersite des pays | cōtrees | et regiōs || Et plusieurs aultres choses cōme on pourra veoir par la table cy apres. || [Vignette.] ¶ Auec Preuilege. || ¶ On les vēd a paris en la rue neufue n̄r̃e dame a leseigne. S. Nicolas || et au pallays en la gallerie cōe on va a la chācellerie pour Jehā. S. denys.

Small folio of 80 ff. numbered and 4 prelim. ff. for the title, the permission and the table; the permit is dated "15 février 1528"; the work was printed in 1529, on the 15th of April. This volume reproduces the relations contained in the French MS. 1380 (late 7500) of the Bibliothèque nationale, Paris; see *supra*, p. 68, No. 71. The frontispiece and one page have been reproduced in the French edition of Odoric and in the *Bibliotheca Sinica*, to which I refer the reader.

3.—Viaggio del Beato Odorico da Vdine, dell' ordine de' frati Minori, Delle usanze, costumi, & nature, di diuerse nationi, & genti del mondo, & del martirio di quattro frati dell' ordine predetto, qual patirono tra gl' Infedeli. (Ramusio, *Navigationi et Viaggi*, II, Venetia, 1583, f. 245 verso–f. 253 recto.)

Version of W. of Solagna.

"The first [this one] and longest of these is almost certainly a translation from the MS. used by Venni in his edition as *Udinese*. The coincidence of peculiarities in proper names and other particulars shows this." (Yule, *Cathay*, I, p. 35.)

Though I have found a perfect similarity in most of the proper names, I am not so positive as Sir H. Yule. Venni informs us (p. 46) that *in Ms. Utinensi ante historiam habetur:*

"*Beati odorici Devotus Hieronymus Montenianus. N. D. Utin. Patr. huius, et sacri Cœnoby Conventual. Franciscanorum syndicus Itiner., et Mirac. eiusdem Beati.*

Librum hunc Omni ornatu Nudatum, et vetustate Corruptum

In hanc pristinam formam Cum omni Cultu sua Impensa restituit Anno Domini M.D.XXXXII. die XV *Mens. VIIbris.*"

It is likely that Ramusio would have reproduced this announcement.

4.—Viaggio del Beato Frate Odorico di Porto Maggiore del Frivli fatto nell' Anno MCCCXVIII. (Ramusio, *Navigationi et Viaggi*, II, Venetia, 1583, f. 253 verso–256 verso.)

See p. 8 and p. 426, note *f*, of French Edition.

5.—Incipit Itinerarium fratris Odorici fratrum minorum de mirabilibus Orientalium Tartarorum. (Pp. 39–53 of *The Second Volvme of the Principal Navigations, Voyages, Traffiques and Discoueries of the English Nation*...By Richard Hacklvyt Preacher ...Imprinted at London by George Bishop, Ralph Newberry, and Robert Barker, Anno 1599, folio.)

Begins: "Licet multa & varia de ritibus & conditionibus huius mundi enarrentur a multis, ego tamen frater Odoricus de foro Iulij de portu Vahonis..."

Based probably on the text of British Museum, Roy. Col. XIV, c. 13.—See p. 41, No. 5 *supra*.

6.—Here beginneth the iournall of Frier Odoricus, one of the order of the Minorites, concerning strange things which hee sawe among the Tartars of the East. (Pp. 53–67 of vol. II of R. Hackluyt, *ut supra*.)

Translation of the Latin text of Hackluyt less the chap. *De martyrio fratrum* and *De miraculis quatuor fratrum occisorum*.

Reprint, pp. 326 et seq. of A. W. Pollard's *Mandeville*, 1900.

7.—Elogio storico || alle gesta || del || Beato Odorico || dell' Ordine de' Minori Conventuali || con la storia || da lui dettata de' suoi Viaggj Asiatici || illustrata || da un religioso dell' Ordine stesso || e presentata || agli Amatori delle Antichita. || In Venezia || MDCCLXI. || Presso Antonio Zatta. || Con licenza de' Superiori. || Large 4to, pp. VIII–152.

All' Eminentissimo e Reverendissimo Signor Cardinale Fra Lorenzo Ganganelli, F. Giuseppe Venni M.C., p. III.—Approbations, pp. VII–VIII.—Elogio Storico, pp. 1–31.—*Decretum Utinen. Canonizationis Beati Odorici Matthiussi Sacerdotis Professi Ordinis Minorum S. Francisci*, pp. 32–33.—Indice de' Paragrafi, pp. 34–35.—Arca del B. Odorico, p. 36.—Prefazione alla Storia de' Viaggi del B. Odorico, pp. 37–45.—Historia B. Odorici, pp. 46–83.—Illustrazioni a i Viaggi del B. Odorico nell' Indie Orientali, pp. 84–149.—Indice delle illustrazioni, p. 150.—Permit to print, p. 151.—Errata, p. 152.

At the beginning a large plate, engraved and signed Philippus Pilaja, engraver, and Dominicus Scaramuccia, painter, showing Odoric baptizing the Unfaithful; below:

"B. Odoricus Matthiussi Ord. Minorum S. Francisci Conventualium Sacris Missionibus cum ingenti Animarum lucro inter Infideles peractis.

Obiit Utini Die XIV. Januarii MCCCXXXI.

Cultum, quem Concivi suo Utinenses, finitimaeque Gentes perenniter adoleverant.

Sacra Rituum Congregatio sub die XIV. Junii MDCCLV. Decreto suo probavit.

Ac sub die 2. Julii ejusdem Anni Benedictus XIV. P. O. M. confirmavit."

At the end a poor map of Asia.—P. 36: a plate showing the front and the back of Odoric's tomb in the xviiith cent.; his cilice.—P. 2, Genealogical Table of the descent of King Ottokar of Bohemia.

The Latin text given by Venni, author of this work, belonged to Giuseppe Liruti. "Altra copia scritta settant' anni dopo la morte di Odorico, e presa dall' originale da Filippo Notajo, e scolaro in Padova, figliuolo di Pietro di Fagagna l' anno MCCCCI. è in mano dell' eruditissimo Gentiluomo, e benemeritissimo delle Friulane antichità Giuseppe Liruti de' Signori di Villafredda ricco a dovizia di preziosi apografi; da lui giudicata migliore e per l' antichità, e per le diverse lezioni dalla copia Montaniana" [p. 39]. This last copy made at the expense of Girolamo Montaniani [G. del Negro says, p. 46, the count Girolamo di Montegnacco], sindaco of the Udine Convent, in Sept. 1542 from another copy of the 7th Sept. 1448 by brother Albert of Udine, was used by Venni to give variants to the Liruti text. "Posti a confronto con replicata diligenza i due Mss. Lirutiano, e Udinese, con permissione benigna del Possessore portatissimo a giovare al Pubblico abbiamo preferito il primo al secondo, come copia più antica, et tratta immediatamente, come supponesi, dall' esemplare, che custodivasi in Padova, ove dettò il Beato la sua storia. L' Udinese poi, sendo copia passata per più mani, ci fa temere della sua identità. Ciò non ostante concordi sono nella sostanza, e soltanto varianti di lezioni, delle quali le più rimarchevoli ponghiamo in veduta, sicchè l' erudito Lettore con il piacere abbia il comodo ancora di rimirare d' ambedue la varietà, e d' ambedue riscontrarne il diligente confronto" [p. 45].

This edition of Venni is one of the best of Odoric's text.

Osservazioni fatte da me Frate Francesco Antonio Maria Righini sotto la scorta del fu mio maestro Padre Maestro Giovanni Giacinto Maria Sbaraglia sopra l' Elogio storico alle gesta del Beato Odorico d' Udine dell' Ordine dei Frati Minori e le illustrazioni fatte alla di lui storia, etc.

MS. kept in the Communal Library of Rimini.

8.—B. Orderici Peregrinatio ab ipsomet descripta. (*Acta Sanctorum*, XIV Januarii, pp. 986–992.)

Begins: "Licet multa & varia de ritibus hominum, & conditionibus huius mundi, à pluribus enarrentur..."

Ends: see p. 515 of the French edition.

At the beginning a short introduction and a biography after Wadding.—Abstracts from Henry of Glatz.

9.—B. Fratris Oderici de Foro Julii, Ordinis Minorum, iter ad partes infidelium a Fratre Henrico de Glars ejusdem Ordinis descriptum, nunc vero primo in lucem editum ad fidem Mss. codicis Bibliothecae Regiae Monacensis (Cod. Lat. 903) cura Patris Marcellini a Civetia. (*Storia universale delle Missioni Francescane*, III, Roma, 1859, pp. 739–781.)

"Questa pubblicazione fu da me fatta in fine del III volume della mia *Storia universale delle Missioni Francescane*, con brevi note a piè di pagina, che dichiarano i principali luoghi percorsi dal grande Apostolo nella prodigiosa sua missione in Tartaria, in Cina, e in quasi tutto l' Arcipelago Indiano; dei quali schiarimenti mi giovai anche nel racconto che feci della sua vita e del suo apostolato nel capitolo XII dello stesso libro, dove in corrispondenza del testo latino diedi una parte del racconto in italiano. L' esemplare di questo Codice da me pubblicato l' ebbi in dono dalla gentilezza del chiaro illustratore dei viaggi di Marco Polo Vincenzio *Lazari* per gentile intramessa del mio amico Cesare *Guasti*. Il Lazari giudicò che fosse completo, e che venisse portato d' Irlanda a Ratisbona il 1539; e che fosse affastellamento di Frate Marchesino da Badaion, originalmente transcritto da Frate Enrico da Glars nel 1440. In quanto all' essere venuto in Ratisbona d' Irlanda il Lazari pensava facilmente spiegarsi con osservare, che il compagno di peregrinazione del Beato Odorico fu un tal Frate Giacomo Irlandese...

"In quanto alla vera traduzione italiana del Viaggio del Beato, com' il lettore vede, non è stata ancora pubblicata; e crediamo che sia nella Biblioteca Marciana di Venezia; ma non saprei dire se fosse quella del Codice della classe VI, numero 208, cartaceo in-4, che contiene i Viaggi del beato Odorico da Udine, di Marco Polo, di Alvise Cadamosto, di Pietro Sinzia, di Vasco di Gama, di Emmanuele Re di Portogallo, di Cristoforo Colombo, ec..., o l' altro della classe XI, numero 32, cartaceo in foglio, ove il Viaggio del beato Odorico è preceduto dall' altro *Viaggio da Venezia a San Giacomo di Galizia.*" (M. da Civezza, *Saggio di Bib. Sanfrancescana*, No. 465.)

10.—Louis de Backer.—L'Extrême Orient au Moyen Age d'après les manuscrits d'un Flamand de Belgique Moine de Saint-Bertin à Saint-Omer et d'un Prince d'Arménie Moine de Prémontré à Poitiers. Paris, Ernest Leroux, 1877, 8vo, pp. 502.

See what we say on this poor edition, *supra*, p. 72, No. 72, and in the French edition of Odoric.

11.—Cathay and the Way thither; being a Collection of Medieval Notices of China, translated and edited by Colonel Henry Yule, C.B., late of the Royal Engineers (Bengal). With a preliminary Essay on the intercourse between China and the Western Nations previous to the discovery of the Cape Route. London: Printed for the Hakluyt Society. M.DCCC.LXVI. 2 vols. 8vo, pp. ccliii, 1–250, 253–596, xcviii, 1 front., 3 maps.

The first and excellent edition of this work; see:—Odoric of Pordenone: Biographical and Historical Notices.—The Eastern Parts of the World described, by Friar Odoric the Bohemian, of Friuli, in the Province of Saint Anthony. (Yule, *Cathay and the Way thither*, I, pp. 1–162.)

12.—Storia dei Viaggiatori Italiani nelle Indie orientali compilata da Angelo de Gubernatis con estratti d' alcune relazioni di viaggio a stampa ed alcuni documenti inediti.—Pubblicata in occasione del Congresso Geografico di Parigi. In Livorno, Franc. Vigo. 1875, small 8vo, pp. VIII–400.

Chap. II of this work contains some notes and pp. 138–141 part of the Palatine Text of Florence given in full in our edition.

13.—Sopra la vita e i viaggi del beato Odorico da Pordenone dell' ordine de' minori Studi con documenti rari ed inediti del chierico francescano Fr. Teofilo Domenichelli sotto la direzione del P. Marcellino da Civezza M. O.—In Prato per Ranieri Guasti editore-libraio.—1881, 8vo, pp. 410, 1 map.

"Al Lettore (Fr. Marcellino da Civezza M. O.).—Viaggiatori Francescani.—Storia del Beato e dei suoi Viaggi.—Bibliografia di quanto finora fu scritto sul Beato Odorico.—Illustrazioni edite ed inedite.—Testo dei Viaggi del Beato Odorico in latino e in italiano.—Descriptio Fratris Oderici de ordine minorum de partibus infidelium.—Viaggio del Beato Odorico del Friuli.—Illustrazioni edite ed inedite al Viaggio del Beato Odorico.—Elenco dei Codici editi ed inediti del Viaggio del Beato Odorico.—Delle lingue indiane.—Altri Documenti e Memorie risguardanti il Beato Odorico."

Gives the Latin text of Munich, already edited by Marcellino da Civezza, see *supra*, No. 32, p. 50, and an Italian text of the Marciana Library, Cl. VI. 102, see *supra*, No. 65, p. 64. This work has no geographical value, the authority given by Domenichelli in his preface being Louis de Backer. Part of the documents supplied by Dr V. Joppi of Udine have some interest.

Notices: *Tagliamento*, 17 Sept. 1881, No. 27.—*Patria del Friuli*, 19 Sept., No. 223; 16 Sept. 1881, No. 221 (V. Joppi).—*Archivio veneto*, N.S., XXV, 1883, pp. 176–178 (C. Franzi).—*Revue historique*, XXI, 2, pp. 386–390 (J. von Zahn).

14.—Italie. Publications relatives au Frioul. Par J. von Zahn. (*Revue historique*, XXI, Paris, 1883, pp. 383–399.)

Notice on Domenichelli, pp. 386–390.

The article of v. Zahn has been translated by la *Patria del Friuli*, 27, 28 April; 1, 3, 5, 11, 14, 15 May 1883; Nos. 100, 101, 103, 105, 107, 112, 114, 115 (*Bib. Stor. Friul.* No. 711).

15.—Les Voyages en Asie au XIVe siècle du bienheureux frère ODORIC DE PORDENONE Religieux de Saint-François publiés avec une introduction et des notes par HENRI CORDIER, Professeur à l'École des Langues Orientales vivantes & à l'École des Sciences politiques.—Ouvrage orné de fac-similés, de gravures et d'une carte.—Paris, Ernest Leroux, M.D.CCC.XCI, gr. in-8, pp. XIV–CLVIII–602.

Contains: Dédicace à Sir Henry Yule.—Table des matières.—

Table des illustrations.—Introduction.—Bibliographie.—Texte.—Index.—Carte.

Vol. x du *Recueil de Voyages et de Documents pour servir à l'Histoire de la Géographie depuis le XIIIe jusqu'à la fin du XVIe siècle publié sous la direction de MM.* Ch. Schefer, *membre de l'Institut, et* Henri Cordier.—Of this collection are printed 250 copies, of which 25 are on Dutch Hand-made paper.—98 copies of the Introduction, of which 5 are on Dutch paper and 5 on simili-Japan, have been printed separately.

Notices: *Bibliografia Friulana*, in *Pagine Friulane*, Anno IV, 14 Giugno 1891, No. 4, by Vincenzo Joppi.—*La Scintilla*, 28 Giugno 1891, by the same.—*Bibliothèque de l'École des Chartes*, by Léopold Delisle, LII, 1891, pp. 452–3.—*T'oung Pao*, No. 3, sept. 1891, pp. 260–8, by G. Schlegel.—*Archivio Storico Italiano*, Serie V, T. VIII, 1891, by Eugène Müntz.—*Revue historique*, LI, Janv.–fév. 1893, pp. 210–211, by Gabriel Monod.—*Revue Critique*, No. 11, 13 mars 1893, pp. 197–202, by A. Barth.—*La Scintilla*, Venezia, 12, 19, 20 nov., 3, 15 dec. 1893, by V. Savi.—*Revue des Questions scientifiques*, Brussels, Jan. 1894, pp. 266–8, by J. van den Gheyn.—*La Géographie*, VIe année, No. 251, 21 sept. 1893, by Henry Monet.—*Revue de Géographie*, Sept. 1891, pp. 238–9, by Gabriel Marcel.

C.—SUNDRY BOOKS AND PAPERS WHICH TREAT OF ODORIC AND HIS TRAVELS

1.—Historiarum Seraphicae Religionis libri tres, seriem temporum continentes, quibus brevi explicantur fundamenta universi Ordinis, amplificatio, gradus et instituta, nec non viri scientia, virtutibus et fama praeclari, a Fratre Petro Rodulpho Tossinianensi Minorita Conventuali. Venetiis, apud Franciscum de Franciscis Senensem. 1586, fol.

(Contains a Life of Odoric.)

2.—De Origine // Seraphicae Religionis Frãciscanae // eiusq; progressibus, de Regularis // Obseruãciae institutione, forma ad // ministrationis ac legibus, admirabiliq. // eius propagatione. // F. Francisci Gonzagae // eiusdem Religionis Ministri Gñalis. // ad // S. D. N. Sixtvm V. // opus in quatuor partes diuisarum. //

Earum quid unaquaeque // contineat. // sequens pagina indicabit. // Romae. // Cū licētia Superiorū // 1587, fol.

P. 97: "B. Odoricus Forliciensis (*sic*) vir sanctus, atq; deuotus, qui Asiam, & Indiam zelo fidei euangelizando peragrauit, in conuentu Vtinensi foeliciter obdormiuit in Domino: quique in Patriarchatu Aquileiensi inter sanctos relatus est, & sanctorum quatuor martyrum corpora, de ciuitate Heroues ad superiorem Indiam in ciuitatem Carram, non sine ingenti miraculo per mare transtulit."

3.—Delle // Croniche // de' frati minori // *parte seconda*, // divisa in dieci libri, // Nella quale si contiene quello, che occorse nella Religione del Padre // San Francesco, nel tempo di ventiquattro Ministri Generali, // per lo spatio d' anni centocinquanta. // Composta dal Padre Fra Marco da Lisbona, in Lingua Portughese, // Poi ridotta nella Castigliana dal Padre Fra Filippo da Sosa. // Et tradotta nella nostra Italiana dal Sig. Horatio Diola. // Con Tauole copiosissime, & in questa quarta edittione // corretta, & migliorata. // Con privilegi. // In Venetia, appresso i Gioliti. // M.DCVI. 4to.

Odoric, lib. VIII, cap. XVIII, XIX, XX and XXI, pp. 461–465.

4.—Panegyris de Beato Odorico de Portu Naonis, Ordinis Fratrum Minorum Sancti Francisci, auctore Joanne Baptista Gabello, cum esset in Ecclesia Sancti Uldarici de Villa Nova in Dioecesi Concordiensi servus. Utini, apud Lorium, 1627, 4to.

Valentinelli.

5.—Vita del Beato Odorico da Pordenone, scritta da d. Marco da Lisbona. Udine, Schiratti, 1634.

Valentinelli.

6.—Giambattista Gabello.—Vita del Beato Odorico Mattiuzzi. Udine, Schiratti, 1639, 8vo.

Valentinelli, II ed.

7.—Vita Beati Odorici Foro-Iuliensis, Ordinis Minorum, excerpta ex praeclaris et lucidissimis annalibus Minorum, auctore Reverendo Patre Frate Luca Waddingo Hiberna eiusdem Ordinis, tom. terti. Frater Bernardinus Treus Utinensis Ordinis Minorum Conventualium, Artium et Sacrae Theologiae Doctor et in sua Provincia Divi Antonii de Patavio Diffinitor perpetuus, ex sua peculiari devotione in Beatum Odoricum, anno 1654, existente

Guardiano Admod. Reverendo Patre Fratre Francisco Barbana. Utini, Typis Nicolai Schiratti, 1654, 8vo.

Domenichelli.

8.—Historie // della // provincia del Frivli // dell' abbate // Gio : Francesco Palladio // de gli Olivi, // givreconsvlto, e patritio vdinese, // nell' academia de gli sventati detto il Ferace. // Divise in dve parti. // Dedicate all' Illustrissimo, & Eccellentissimo Sig. // Co. Giacomo Cabriel // Per la Sereniss. Republica di Venetia, &c. // Luogotenente Generale della stessa Prouincia. // In Vdine, Appresso Nicolò Schiratti. MDCLX. // Con licenza de' svperiori. 2 vols. fol.

Odoric, I, pp. 324–5.

9.—Vitae Paparvm Avenionensivm...Stephanus Balvzivs edidit...Parisiis, Muguet, 1693, 2 vols. 4to.

Odoric, I, col. 702–3, 1411, 1417.

10.—Annales Minorum seu trium ordinum a S. Francisco Institutorum auctore a R. P. Luca Waddingo Hiberno...Editio secunda, locupletior, & accuratior opera et studio R^mi^ P. Josephi Mariae Fonseca ab Ebora.—Romae, 1731–1747, 22 vols. fol.

See *Odoric*, vol. VII, Romae, 1733, pp. 123–6.—In vol. VI, under date 1321, p. 358, is related the transfer to Zaitûn of the bones carried to Supera by Friar Jordanus and disinterred by Odoric: "secum tulit in Indiam superiorem, ad Fratrum Cœnobium urbis Zaiton, Rodulphus Carram appelat."

11.—Vita, e viaggi || del || B. Odorico || da Udine || descritti || da don Basilio Asquini || bernabita, || e dedicati alli MM.RR.PP. || Guardiano, e religiosi tutti || Del Ven. Convento di San Francesco || della stessa Città. || In Udine, MDCCXXXVII. || Nella Stamperia di Giambattista Murero. || Con licenza de' Superiori. Small 8vo, pp. XVI–260, with a figure at the beginning engraved by Antonio Zuliani.

12.—A New General Collection of Voyages and Travels... London : Printed for Thomas Astley, 1745–1747, 4 vols. 4to.

Odoric, IV, p. 620.

13.—Compendio della vita, virtù, morte e miracoli, del b. Odorico da Udine. Udine, Murero, 1758, 8vo.

Valentinelli.

14.—Notizie // delle vite ed opere // scritte da' Letterati del Friuli // raccolte // da Gian-Giuseppe Liruti // Signor de Villafredda, ec. // Accademico nella Società Colombaria // di Firenze, // e dell' Accademia Udinese. // In Venezia // MDCCLX, // appresso Modesto Fenzo, // I, 4to.

Cap. XVII. *Il B. Odorico da Pordenone, altrimente detto da Udine, dell' Ordine de' Frati Minori di S. Francesco*, pp. 274–290.

15.—Storia della Letteratura Italiana del Cavaliere Abate Girolamo Tiraboschi...Tomo V. Dall' anno MCCC. fino all' anno MCCCC. Roma, MDCCLXXXIII, 4to.

Odoric, pp. 105–109.

16.—History of the Voyages and Discoveries made in the North. Translated from the German of John Reinhold Forster, I.U.D. and elucidated by several new and original Maps. London: Printed for G. G. J. & J. Robinson, M.DCC.LXXXVI, 4to.

Odoric, pp. 147–8.

17.—Geschichte der wichtigsten geographischen Entdeckungen bis zur Ankunft der Portugiesen in Japan 1542, von Matthias Christian Sprengel, Professeur der Geschichte in Halle. Zweite vermehrte Auflage. Halle, 1792, small 8vo, pp. 420, without the tab. and the prel. leaves.

See *Odoric*, pp. 340–359. "It is printed with desperate inaccuracy," says Yule, *Cathay*, p. 38.

18.—Historical Account of Discoveries and Travels in Asia, from the earliest ages to the present time. By Hugh Murray... Edinburgh, 1820, 3 vols. 8vo.

Odoric, I, C. IV, pp. 183 seq.

19.—Sacra Rituum Congregatio, Eminentissimo et Reverendissimo Dom. Cardin. Somalia Praefecto et Ponente Utinensi, seu Ordinis Minorum Sancti Francisci, approbat lectiones proprias in officio Beati Odorici Matthiussi, instante Reverendissimo Episcopo Utinensi. Romae, 1822. Ex typis Camerae Apostolicae, folio, pp. 16.

Valentinelli.

20.—History of Maritime and Inland Discovery. By William Desborough Cooley. London, 1830–1, 3 vols. 8vo.

Lardner's *Cabinet Cyclopaedia*.—See Book III.

21.—Ragguaglio breve della vita del B. Odorico Mattiuzzi. Udine, Murero, 1824, in-16.

Valentinelli.

22.—Oderic, appelé vulgairement de Portenau. Par La Renaudière. (*Biographie universelle*, XXXI, p. 162.)

23.—Oderic de Pordenone. Par H. Fisquet. (*Nouvelle Biographie générale*, XXXVIII, col. 469–471.)

An insignificant and erroneous article.

24.—Relation des Mongols ou Tartares par le frère Jean du Plan de Carpin de l'ordre des Frères Mineurs, légat du Saint-Siège apostolique, nonce en Tartarie pendant les années 1245, 1246 et 1247, et archevêque d'Antivari. Première édition complète publiée d'après les manuscrits de Leyde, de Paris et de Londres, et précédée d'une notice sur les anciens voyages de Tartarie en général, et sur celui de Jean du Plan de Carpin en particulier, par M. d'Avezac. (*Recueil de Voyages et de Mémoires publié par la Société de géographie*, IV, Paris, Arthus-Bertrand, 1839, pp. 397–779.)

Oderic Matthiussi, pp. 417–419.

25.—Histoire générale des Missions catholiques depuis le XIIIe siècle jusqu'à nos jours, par M. le Baron Henrion. Paris, Gaume, 1847, 2 vols. large 8vo.

Odoric, I, pp. 111–112.—See in French edition, a long note of Prof. G. del Negro, regarding the Italian translation of this work.

26.—Discorso intorno all' Itinerario del Beato Odorico Matiussi da Udine Missionario Apostolico dell' Ordine de' Minori. Con appendice.

Pub. in Nos. 5 and 6 of the year V of the *Cronaca delle Missioni Francescane* (Roma, 1865). A reply to the anonymous Italian translator of the *Histoire des Missïons catholiques* of Henrion.

M. da Civezza, *Bibl. Sanfrancescana*, No. 194.

27.—Charles MacFarlane.—Romance of Travel: The East. —London, 1847, 2 vols. 8vo.

28.—Le Christianisme en Chine, en Tartarie et au Thibet. By M. Huc...Paris, Gaume frères, 1857–8, 4 vols. 8vo.

Odoric de Frioul, I, pp. 398–411.

29.—Die Missionen in Indien und China im vierzehnten Jahrhundert. (*G. Phillips' und G. Görres Historisch-Politische Blätter für das katholische Deutschland*, München, 1856, 1 Bd.)—I. Die Mission in Meliapor und Tana, pp. 25–38.—II. Die Mission in Columbo, pp 135–152.—III. Die Mission in China, pp. 225–252.—(*Ibid.*, 1856, II Bd.)—IV. Der Missionsbericht des Odoricus von Pordenone, pp. 507–537.—V. Der Reisebericht des Johannes Marignola, pp. 701–719, 793–813.—(*Ibid.*, 1859, 1 Bd.) Die Mission in China, pp. 677–681.

By Prof. F. Kunstmann.

30.—Histoire universelle de l'Église catholique, par l'abbé Rohrbacher—précédée d'une notice biographique et littéraire par Charles Sainte-Foi, augmentée de notes inédites de l'auteur colligées par A. Murcier, ancien élève de l'École des Chartes, et suivie d'un atlas géographique spécialement dressé pour l'ouvrage par A.-H. Dufour. 3e éd. Paris, Gaume, 1857–61, 29 vols. 8vo.

xx, 1858, Odoric de Frioul, pp. 150–152.

31.—Storia universale delle Missioni Francescane del P. Marcellino da Civezza M. O. della provincia di Genova. Vol. III, Roma, Tip. Tiberina, 1859, 8vo, pp. 796.

On Odoric, see chap. XII, pp. 467–519, and the voyage from the Munich Latin MS., No. 903, pp. 739–781.

32.—De // Seraphiensche Palmboom // of // Levens // van de // Heilige en vermaerde Mannen en Vrouwen // uit de dry orden Van S. Franciscus, // door // P. Benignus Fremaut, // Minderbroeder-Recollect. // uitgegeven door // de Minderbroeders-Recollecten der provincie van S. Joseph in België. // Sint-Truiden, Vanwest-Pluymers, 1860–1875. 12 vols. 8vo.

I, 1860, Januarius [14 de Januarius]. *Leven van den zaligen Odoricus van Porto-Naono*, pp. 665–678. (Ex Waddingo et Joanne Bollando, Soc. Jesu.)

33.—L' itinerario del beato Odorico Mattiussi, discorso con appendici. (Nello *Stato del Ginnasio arcivescovile di Udine*, alla fine dell' anno scolastico 1865.) Udine, tip. Jacob e Colmegna, 1865, 8vo, pp. 54.

Per Luigi Fabris.—See *Rivista friulana*, 10 settembre 1865, No. 37.—*Bib. Stor. Friul.*, No. 102.

34.—Storia di Cambanau, di Taid e d' altri luoghi dell' India, narrata dal Beato Odorico del Friuli, anno MCCCXXX. Bologna, Tipi Fava e Garagnani, 1866, 24mo, pp. 48.

"Per le faustissime nozze dell' egregio giovane signor TITO DALLA NOCE colla virtuosa donzella signora ADELAIDE GOLINELLI avvenute nella primavera del MDCCCLXVI."—This little brochure is taken from pp. 311–317 of the third edition of Zambrini's bibliography with the addition of four new chapters.—100 copies printed.—See Zambrini, 4th ed., p. 718.

35.—*Madonna delle Grazie*, Nos. 6, 7 and 8 of 9, 16 and 23 January 1869.

Three short articles devoted to Odoric.

Bib. Stor. Friul., No. 128.

36.—Le Palmier séraphique...par M. Malvoisin...et Mgr. Paul Guérin. Bar-le-Duc, Louis Guérin, 12 vols. 8vo, 1870 seq.

37.—Les Petits Bollandistes...par Mgr. Paul Guérin. Bar-le-Duc, Louis Guérin, 1872, 8vo.

14 January, p. 340, a few lines devoted to Odoric.

38.—Cenni sulla vita e sui viaggi del B° Odorico del Friuli, di Dionigio Largaiolli. (Nella *Cronaca liceale per l' anno 1874–75.*) Catania, tip. Bellini, 1876, 8vo, pp. 58.

Rep. with a few variants, Potenza, tip. Favatà, 1878, 18mo, p. 55.—*Bib. Stor. Friul.*, No. 433.

39.—The Book of Ser Marco Polo, the Venetian...by Colonel Sir Henry Yule...Third edition, revised...by Henri Cordier... London, John Murray, 1903, 2 vols. 8vo.

40.—Il Beato Odorico di Pordenone ed i suoi viaggi : cenni dettati dal Colonello Enrico Yule, Presidente della Società Hakluyt di Londra, quando s' inaugurava in Pordenone il busto di Odorico il giorno 23^{zo} settembre MDCCCLXXXI, br. 8vo, pp. 8.

"Inscritto, colla più grata ed amena ricordanza, ai signori Friulani, Vincenzo Joppi di Udine, e Lorenzo Bianchi di Pordenone."

Italian translation of Count Ugo Balzani.

Printed in London: T. Richards, 37, Great Queen Street, W.C.

Patria del Friuli, 16 sept. 1881, No. 221. (V. Joppi.)—*Revue historique*, XXI, 2, p. 388. (Zahn.)

41.—Odoric. By Henry Yule. (*Encyclopaedia Britannica*, 9th ed., XVII, pp. 728–9.)

An interesting résumé.

42.—Il beato Odorico Mattiussi. (*Tagliamento*, 14 maggio 1881, No. 19.) Pordenone, tip. Gatti, 1881, fol., 2 col.

In the preceding No., 7th May, the *Tagliamento* announced that the communal council, in its sitting of the 4th May, had voted unanimously that a bust of Odoric be erected in the Communal Hall and that the work be entrusted to the sculptor Luigi Minisini.—*Bib. Stor. Friul.*, No. 670.

43. *Il Tagliamento*, periodico settimanale, Anno XI, Pordenone, 23 settembre 1881, n. 38: Pordenone, tip. Gatti, 1881, fol., col. 12.

44.—*Cittadino Italiano*, 25 settembre 1881, No. 215.

Bib. Stor. Friul., No. 669.

45.—Il B. Odorico da Pordenone. Cenni storici. (Dal *Cittadino Italiano* del 23 settembre.) Br. 8vo, pp. 23, Portrait.

Verso of the brochure: Udine.—Tip. Lit. Patronato. An interesting notice published in 1881, for the inauguration of the bust of Odoric at Pordenone, written, I was told at Udine, by Prof. *Giovanni del Negro.*

46.—Dom Foschia.—Il beato Odorico di Udine.—Udine, 1882, 8vo, pp. 26.

47.—Commentarii dei Fatti di Aquileja di Giovanni Candido [Udine, 1884.—Tip. M. Bardusco], br. large 4to, pp. 14.

"Nozze Blum-Levi." Dedication to Giulio Blum signed A. Purasanta, dated: Udine, li 29 ottobre 1884. Contains a valueless notice of the voyages of Odoric.—From Candido's work, edited at Venice in 1544, by Michiele Tramezino, 16mo, pp. 63–68. The original work was published under the title: *Commentariorum Aquilejensium libri octo*, Joannis Candidi Jurisconsulti. Venetiis, per Alexandrum de Bindonibus, 1521, fol. Odoric, ff. XXVI–XXVIII.

48.—Ferd. Blasisch.—Documenti e notizie sulla vita di S. Odorico. Udine, 1884, 8vo, pp. 22.

49.—Histoire du Commerce du Levant au Moyen Age par W. Heyd...Édition française refondue et considérablement augmentée par l'auteur, publiée sous le patronage de la Société de l'Orient latin par Furcy Raynaud. Leipzig, Otto Harrassowitz, 1885–1886, 2 vols. 8vo.

Odoric, II, pp. 132, 151, 220 et seq., 246.

50.—Gli illustri viaggiatori italiani con una Antologia dei loro scritti, per Pietro Amat di S. Filippo. Roma, "Opinione," 1885, 8vo, pp. VIII–548.

Odoric, pp. 19–31.

51.—L'Auréole Séraphique, Vie des Saints et des Bienheureux des trois ordres de Saint-François, par le T. R. P. Léon, Ex-Provincial des Franciscains de l'Observance. Paris, Bloud et Barral, 4 vols. 12mo, n. d. [1886].

Vol. I, pp. 270–7, 3 février, B. Odoric de Pordenone.

52.—Vies des Saints et des Bienheureux de l'ordre de Saint-François dont le culte a été approuvé par l'Église (abrégé de l'*Auréole Séraphique*), par le T. R. P. Léon, Ex-Provincial des Franciscains de l'Observance. Paris, Bloud et Barral, 1887, 12mo.

3 février, Odoric, pp. 11–13.

53.—Untersuchungen über Johann von Mandeville und die Quellen seiner Reisebeschreibung. Von Albert Bovenschen. (*Zeitschrift d. Ges. für Erdkunde zu Berlin*, XXIII Bd., 3 und 4 Hft., No. 135, 136, pp. 177–306.)

54.—"Pro Patria" Alfred Gummá. Le Dondiin et les Philippines Lettres á M. le President de la "Société Géographique de Paris." 16mo, pp. 122.

Printed at Barcelona.

55.—Einundzwanzigstes Programm der Realschule mit Progymnasium zu Leisnig als Einladungsschrift zu den öffentlichen Prüfungen am 3. und 4. April 1895.—Inhalt: (1) Abhandlung des Oberlehrers Max Gnauck: Odorich von Pordenone, ein Orientreisender des 14. Jahrhunderts.—(2) Schulnachrichten, verfasst vom Direktor.—Druck von Herrm. Ulrich in Leisnig. 1895. Progr. Nr. 583. 4to, pp. 55.

56.—Della Patria e della Nazionalità del Beato Odorico da Pordenone, por V. Savi. (Estratto del *Nuovo Archivio Veneto*, tomo XI, parte II, coi tipi dei Fratelli Visentini, Venezia, 1896.)

Nuovo Archivio Veneto, 1896, XI, pp. 301–325.

57.—Hugh Clifford.—Further India...London, 1904, 8vo.

D.—BIBLIOGRAPHICAL WORKS

1.—Biblioteca italiana ossia notizia de' libri rari italiani divisa in quattro parti cioè istoria, poesia, prose, arti e scienze, gia compilata da Niccola Francesco Haym. Edizione corretta, ampliata, e di giudizj intorno alle migliori opere arricchita. Con tavole copiosissime e necessarie.—Milano. Giovanni Silvestri, 1803, 4 vols. 8vo.

2.—Bibliografia del Friuli.—Saggio di Giuseppe Valentinelli socio corrispondente dell' Accademia d' Udine. Edizione sovvenuta dell' Imp. Accademia delle Scienze in Vienna. Venezia, Tipografia del Commercio, 1861, 8vo, pp. VIII–540.

Odoric, pp. 384–5.

3.—Répertoire des Sources historiques du Moyen Âge par Ulysse Chevalier.—*Bio-Bibliographie.* Nouvelle édition refondue, corrigée et considérablement augmentée. Paris, Alphonse Picard et fils, Janvier 1905–Septembre 1907, 2 vols. 8vo.

Odoric, 3402–3403.

4.—Saggio di Bibliografia geografica, storica, etnografica, Sanfrancescana per Fr. Marcellino da Civezza M. O. In Prato, per Ranieri Guasti, editore-libraio. 1879, 8vo, pp. XIV–698.

Odoric, No. 194, p. 148.—465, pp. 433–434.

5.—Le Opere volgari a stampa dei secolo XIII e XIV indicate e descritte da Francesco Zambrini. Quarta Edizione con appendice. Bologna, Nicola Zanichelli, 1884, 8vo, pp. LV–col. 1172–202.

Odoric, col. 714–718, 118.

6.—Società geografica italiana. Studi biografici e bibliografici sulla Storia della Geografia in Italia pubblicati in occasione del III°. Congresso Geografico Internazionale. Volume 1.—Biografia dei Viaggiatori italiani colla bibliografia delle loro opere per P. Amat di S. Filippo. Edizione seconda. Roma, alla sede della Società, 1882, 8vo.

Oderico da Pordenone, pp. 85–98.

7.—BIBLIOTHECA SINICA.—Dictionnaire bibliographique des ouvrages relatifs à l'empire chinois, par Henri Cordier. Paris, E. Guilmoto, 1904–1908, 2 vols. large 8vo.

Vol. III, Odoric, col. 2005–2018.

8.—Accademia di Udine. Bibliografia Storica Friulana dal 1861 al 1882 di Giuseppe Occioni-Bonaffons. Udine, Tip. G.-B. Doretti, 1883, 8vo.

Odoric, Nos. 102, 128, 129, 433, 469, 667, 668, 670, 671, 711.

—dal 1861 al 1885 di Giuseppe Occioni-Bonaffons. Vol. secondo. Udine, Tip. G.-B. Doretti, 1887, 8vo.

Odoric, Nos. 820, 956, 1156.

E.—TEXT OF THIS EDITION

After what has been said about the variations in the different copies of Odoric, it will be obvious that before preparing a translation, it becomes necessary (on the principle of catching your hare before cooking it) to ascertain the text which is to be translated. The determination *verbatim* of a standard text is not possible under the circumstances, but fortunately a large proportion of the variations disappear in translation, as they are not variations in sense. As regards the variations in proper names, in most cases it is possible to deduce from the facts which reading is nearest the truth, though often considerable study has been necessary to ascertain their real indications. Among the variations in other matters, the editor has exercised his judgment in selecting what seemed to be the most probable readings. And where it seemed a pity to omit additional particulars that were curious or interesting, though depending on doubtful or exceptional authority, these have been interpolated into the translation within brackets.

A translation however thus formed requires what the French call "justificative pieces," that the editor's authority for everything may be traced, and that he may not be thought to have developed a new Odoric out of his "moral consciousness." It seemed therefore indispensable to print a Latin text with notes of the collations made.

I had wished to print this text from the copy of Henry of Glatz, the only type of the four already discriminated which never has been printed in full; and a transcript of the Paris MS. (No. 36 above), which was understood to be of this type, was commissioned. By some mistake, or for some unexplained reason, the transcript was made from the *other* Paris

MS. (No. 35 above); and I have therefore been obliged to print this as my Latin text; for the Farsetti MS. in St Mark's (No. 47) is not correct enough for the purpose, and there were stronger reasons against using the Arundel MS. (No. 7), the only other one available to me which is not already in print. It did not suit the object to print an Italian text only, or the St Mark's MS. (Italian No. 65 above) would have been unexceptional.

To the Latin text, however, I have added the Italian of the Florence Palatine MS. In introducing this version, I feel tempted to borrow a formula from a late venerable personage, who presented a newly married lady to his friends as selected "not for her looks, as they saw, but because she was good." The MS. is indeed in the basest style, and has neither looks nor goodness to recommend it. But it is eminently *curious*, as containing so many remarkable passages which appear in no other copy of Odoric, and when one is trying to dispose of Odoric once for all it seems worthy of print. The most notable passages in which the *Minor Ramusian* deviates from this, as well as from the Latin copies, are brought forward in the notes to this version. In printing it, what seemed mere vulgarisms of spelling, such as *rengno* for *regno*, *pripristeli* for *pipistrelli*, have not been followed.

In the comparison of the Latin copies a word by word collation has been out of the question, but it has been intended to record all important variations of proper names, all important variations of sense, and such variations of mere expression as there seemed any sufficient reason for noting.

The subdivision of the narrative into chapters is in all the MSS. very various, irregular and capricious. I have made a new division, assigning short headings in my translation, and for reasons of obvious convenience have extended this also to the Latin and Italian texts. It is to be understood, therefore, that the marginal headings of chapters in these are interpolations, and no part of the originals[1].

[1] I have kept the text and the divisions of Sir Henry Yule; also most of his notes. I have added a good many various readings at the foot of the pages, and a number of new notes to bring the book up to the science of the present day.—H. C.

F.—LIST OF ABBREVIATIONS USED TO INDICATE THE COPIES

A.S., or BOLL. Printed Text of the *Acta Sanctorum*.—See No. 8, p. 80.

BERLIN. Latin Manuscript of the Royal Library of Berlin.—See No. 13–13–1, p. 44.

B.N., or B.N., Lat. 2584. (The printed Text.) Latin MS. of the National Library of Paris, printed in *Cathay* and in this edition.—See No. 35–35–1, p. 51.

B.N., lat. 3195, or PAR. 2. Latin MS. of the National Library of Paris, No. 3195.—See No. 36–36–2, p. 52.

BOLL., or A.S. See A.S., *supra*.—See No. 8, p. 80.

CIV., or M. da CIV. Latin Text of Munich printed by Marcellino da Civezza.—See No. 32–32–2, p. 50.

DOM. Italian Text printed by Domenichelli.—See No. 13, p. 82.

FAR. or FARS. Latin MS. of the Marciana at Venice, used in this edition.—See No. 47–47–8, p. 56.

FR. 1380. French MS. 1380, of the National Library of Paris.—See No. 71–3–1, p. 68.

FR. 2810. French MS. 2810, of the National Library of Paris.—See No. 72–4–2, p. 69.

HAK. Hakluyt's printed Latin Text.—See No. 5, p. 78.

J. de V. MS. of the French translation of Jean de Vignay, British Museum.—See No. 69–1–1, p. 67.

J. ST D. Printed Text by Jean Saint-Denys.—See No. 2, p. 76.

M. da C., or CIV. See CIV., *supra*.—See No. 32–32–2, p. 50.

MAGL. Italian Text of Florence.—See No. 55–5–3, p. 61.

MARC. or MAR. Italian Text of the Marciana, published by Domenichelli.—See No. 65–15–13, p. 64.

MUN. Latin Text of the Munich Library.—See No. 33–33–3, p. 51.

MUS. British Museum, Latin MS. Arundel Coll.—See No. 7–7–7, p. 42.

PAL. Italian MS. of Florence, published by Yule and in this edition.—See No. 54–4–2, p. 60.

RAM. A., or RAM. First Italian Text of Ramusio.—See No. 3, p. 77.

RAM. B., or MIN. RAM. Second Italian Text of Ramusio.—See No. 4, p. 78.

UT. Venni's Printed Collation of Udine MS.—See No. 7, p. 78.

VEN. Venni's printed Latin Text.—See No. 7, p. 78.

VIENNA. Latin Text of the Imperial Library of Vienna.—See No. 27–27–6, p. 49.

WOLF. 40. Latin Text of the Ducal Library of Wolfenbüttel.—See No. 17–17–5, p. 47.

WOLF. 41. Latin Text of the Ducal Library of Wolfenbüttel.—See No. 18–18–6, p. 47.

THE EASTERN PARTS OF THE WORLD DESCRIBED,

BY

FRIAR ODORIC THE BOHEMIAN, OF FRIULI, IN THE PROVINCE OF SAINT ANTHONY

1. What the Friar saw at Trebizond and in the Greater Armenia.

ALBEIT many other stories of sundry kinds concerning the customs and peculiarities of different parts of this world have been related by a variety of persons, yet would I have you to know that I also, Friar Odoric of Friuli, can truly rehearse many great marvels which I did hear and see when, according to my wish, I crossed the sea and visited the countries of the unbelievers in order to win some harvest of souls [and this I did with the leave of my superiors, who have power to grant it by the rules of our Order][1].

[Wherefore I purpose to relate briefly and compendiously under sundry chapters of this little work a multitude of the things which I have seen and heard in the East and the North and the South. Of all I purpose not to speak, though I shall be the first to tell of many which will seem to a number of people past belief. Nor, indeed, could I myself have believed these things, had I not heard them with my own ears or seen the like myself. Fourteen years and a half, in the habit of Francis, that blessed confessor of

[1] BOLL.

Christ, I sojourned in those parts of the world. And now being at Padua, I have here compiled this little work at the request of the reverend Friar Guidotto, the minister of the province of Saint Anthony. If, then, the studious reader shall find anything good in it, let him ascribe that to the divine bounty and not to my poor skill. And if he find anything too hard for belief, and wherein he judgeth me to stray from truth, let him remark thereon with a student's charity, and not with insolent bitterness and spiteful snarling[1].]

First, then, [going with the galleys from Venice[2]] I crossed over the Greater Sea[3], and so passed to TREBIZOND[4], which was of old called Pontus. This city is situated passing well, and is a haven[5] for the Persians, Medes, and all the people on the further side of the sea[6]. And in this country I saw a very pretty sight [which I am the more bold

[1] FAR.

[2] MIN. RAM., which also specifies April 1318 as the time of his departure. Giov. da Uzzano in the next century says the galleys for Romania and Trebizond used to leave Venice between the 8th and 20th of July. (*Della Decima*, iv, 104.)

[3] [VEN., Mare majus.—RAM. A., Mar maggior.—RAM. B., Mare maggiore.—DOM., Mare grande, Mare maius.] *Mare Majus*, as the Euxine was usually called by the Franks in Odoric's time and long after. It is so called (*M. Maggiore*) by Marco Polo in the preceding century, by Haiton the Armenian, by Barbaro in the following century, and even (*Mer Majour*) by Vincent Le Blanc at the beginning of the seventeenth. Carpini and Ricold Montecroce have Mare *Magnum*; Rubruquis, "the Sea of Pontus, commonly called *Mare Majus*," the former name also being given by Edrisi in the shape of *Buntus*.

The title *Greater* was no doubt given at Constantinople with reference to the Propontis, as several have suggested. Marsden aptly quotes the like title given by the Hebrews to the Mediterranean.

Mandeville, like Jordanus, uses Mare *Maurum*; *μαυρός* having in Byzantine and modern Greek the sense of *Black*; and this we find already in plain Latin used by Paschal of Vittoria, and indeed by Jordanus himself (Mare *Nigrum*).

[4] [VEN., Trepessundam.—RAM., Trabisonda.]

[5] *Scala*, which appears still to be the technical word for a trading port in those seas, as well as in Italy. [*Scala*, ladder; a ladder being used to land; French *escale*; cf. Littré, *Diction.*]

[6] [J. V.—"Et est une entrée de la terre des Perses, des Medes et de moult d'autres regions qui sont outre mer."]

to tell, because many persons with whom I have spoken in Venice assure me that they have seen the like][1]. I beheld a certain man[2] taking about with him more than four thousand[3] partridges. For as the man went along the ground, the partridges followed him flying in the air. These partridges he was then taking to a certain castle which is called ZEGANA[4], distant three days' journey from Trebizond, [where they dig copper and crystal][5]. And the way with these partridges was this, that whenever the man wanted to lie down or go to sleep, they all gathered about him like chickens about a hen. And in this manner he took them along to Trebizond, to the palace of the emperor[6]; and he, when they were thus brought before him, took as many partridges as he desired; but the rest of them the man led back to the place whence he had first brought them[7].

[1] MIN. RAM.

[2] ["Barbuto e di feroce aspetto, che menaua con lui circa due mila Perdici." MIN. RAM.]

[3] *French text*: 3000.—J. V., 4000.

[4] [MARCO POLO, Geneza, Ganeza.—VEN., FR. TEXT, Zanega.—DOM. B., Canega.—DOM. A., CIV., Tegena.—FARS., Tanegar.—BOLL., Tegana.—RAM. A., Zanga.—RAM. B., Zanicco.—J. V., Canege.] *Ziganah* is twelve leagues from Trebizond on the road to Erzrum, and gives name to a pass called the Ziganah Dagh. Clavijo, on the *third day* from Trebizond, encamped near a "castle called Sigana, on the top of a high rock, and belonging to a Greek knight" (Curzon's *Armenia*, pp. 31, 173, 175; Brant's Map in *J. R. Geog. Soc.*, vi; *Journ. Asiat.*, 1st series, ix, 228; Markham's *Clavijo*, HAK. SOC., p. 65). Some of the old popular Italian versions of Marco Polo have this partridge story interpolated therein.

[5] PAL. has "silver and crystal." The whole of the Valley of the Karsput River south of Ziganah abounds in ores of copper and lead. There are also silver-mines, as mentioned by Polo. (*Brant.*, u. s., p. 221.)

[6] Alexius II, of the house called "Grand-Comnenus," reigned at this time (1297–1330) independently and prosperously over the long strip of coast called the empire of Trebizond. This state endured till 1460 [when it was destroyed by Mohammed II]. (*Finlay's H. of Greece* (Medieval) *and of the Emp. of Trebizond*, 1851), [and J. C. Falmerayer, *Gesch. d. Kaiserthums von Trapezunt*, München, 1827, pp. 158 seq.].

[7] This is one of the stories which have been accounted most absurd in Odoric's narrative. Yet the accurate Tournefort, after telling how the peasants in Scio keep tame partridges which are sent out to feed

In this same city (of Trebizond) is deposited the body of Athanasius, over one of the gates of the city; of him, that is, that made the creed which beginneth **Quicunque vult salvus esse**[1]. Departing thence, I came into Armenia the Greater, to a certain city which is called ARZIRON[2], which

every day like flocks of sheep under the charge of a public keeper, to whose whistle they come readily, goes on to say: "I have seen a man in Provence in the neighbourhood of Grasse, who used to take whole flocks of partridges out to the fields, and made them come to his call; he would take hold of them, put them in his bosom, and then send them off again to feed with the others." *Voyage du Levant* (Lyon, 1727), ii, 79. Precisely the same account of the partridges at Scio is given at an earlier date in *Busbequii Epist.*, Amsterd., 1660, p. 164. ["Ce ne sais je pas se il le faisoit par art ou par viande." JEAN DE VIGNAY.]

[1] [*French Text*, En ceste cité.—J. V. "Sur la porte de cele cité."—VEN. "Supra ipsius portam civitatis."] I find no confirmation of this. Venni says the *Acta Sanctorum* contain no allusion to the story. [Migne, in his *Patrologia*, places this creed among the *Spuria*.] The body of Athanasius [who died 2nd May, 373] was buried at Alexandria, but afterwards transferred to Constantinople and laid in a church bearing his name. On the capture of the city the relics were said to have been carried to Venice and solemnly placed in the church of Sta. Croce della Giudecca. (*Venni*, 87.)

Can this have to do with Odoric's statement? "Over one of the principal gates (of Trebizond) is a long inscription, which refers to a Christian bishop and one of the emperors of Constantinople. It is evidently not in its original position." (*Brant.*, u. s., p. 189.)

[2] [VEN.—DOM. B., Arziron.—DOM. A., Carztron.—RAM. A., Acron.—RAM. B., Orzaloni.—BOLL., Caricon.—FARS., Arzirai.—CIV., Carztron.] Erzrum, corrupted from *Arzan-al-Rum*, or Roman Arzan, was taken with pillage and havoc by [Chinghiz Khan and Timur, but neither kept it long. It was named *Garine*, then *Theodosiopolis*, in honour of Theodosius the Great; the present name was given by the Seljukid Turks, and it means "Roman Country."] Even in Tournefort's time the Franks commonly pronounced the name Erzeron. Though not the highest city, even of the old world, it stands at a height of some 7,000 feet above the sea, and is noted for the severity of its winters, insomuch that a late Italian traveller calls it the Siberia of the Ottoman Empire. In 1855–56 the centigrade thermometer sunk to 35° below 0°. Sir J. Sheil saw a heavy snowstorm at Erzrum in July. "The weather as a general rule," says Curzon, "may be considered as on the way from bad to worse." Fruit does not grow, but great quantities of "victual," *i.e.*, of corn and meal, are brought from more genial regions, as it is the place where the great caravans between Persia and Turkey recruit their stores. (*Curzon*, pp. 36, 51, 115, 117, 141; Lady Sheil's *Glimpses of Life, etc., in Persia*; De' Bianchi, *V. in Armenia*, etc., 1863; *Tournefort*, iii, 126.) The Franciscans at this time had a convent at Erzrum, in the custodia of Kars. [Known in their Annals under the name of *Alzarome* or *Alcarone*.]

in time long past was a fine and most wealthy city, and it would have been so unto this day but for the Tartars and the Saracens, who have done it much damage. It aboundeth greatly in bread and flesh, and many other kinds of victual, but not in wine or fruits. For the city is mighty cold, and folk say that it is the highest city that is at this day inhabited on the whole face of the earth. But it hath most excellent water, the reason whereof seems to be that the springs of this water are derived from the River Euphrates[1], which floweth at about one day's journey from the city[2]. And this city is just midway to Tauris[3].

Departing from it[4], I came to a certain hill which is called SARBISACALO[5]; and in that country is the

[1] ["A flumine Eufrate qui fuit de paradyso quo distat ab hac civitate unā dietā." Munich, MS. 21259.]

[2] "The town......is on a sort of peninsula formed by the sources of Euphrates. The first of these flows at a day's journey from the city." (*Tournefort*, iii, 114.)

[3] MIN. RAM., and PAL. insert here a strange and unseemly story which is in none of the Latin copies. ["Oue poco inanti era morta vna ricchissima donna, la quale fece testamento, e fra l' altre cose lassò, che de suoi beni si fabricasse vn monastero di meretrici delle piu belle giouani del paese: e di detti beni della defunta queste donne fussero ben vestite, & adornate, secondo loro vsanza, e ben seruite, cosi nel vestire, come nel mangiare: le quali erano obligate, senza alcuna mercede, di sodisfare tutti coloro, da quali fussero richieste. E se pure vi fusse tra loro alcuna, che non hauesse sodisfatto a quei che l' hauessino richiesta, e coloro se ne fussero lamentati, subito la donna fusse mandata via da detto monastero, e priua di tutto quanto haueua in compagnia di quelle. Di che volendo noi saper la cagione: E perche hauessi fatto fare tal cosa doppo morte la detta donna, ci fu riposto, per impetrar misericordia della anima sua, & di suoi peccati dal Dio suo, che ella adoraua."

Abridged in the Florentine Italian MS., in our Appendix.]

[4] [VENNI remarks in his notes, p. 91, that at Erzrum, at the time of Odoric, there was a convent of friars minor known in their Annals under the name of *Alzarome* or *Alcarone*.]

[5] [RAM. A., *Sollisaculo*.—DOM. A., *Sabisorbolo*.—VEN., HAK., *Sobissacelo*.—FARS., *Bobis Sachalo*.—CIV., *Sabisorbolo*.—BOLL., *Sarbisarbolo*.] This puzzling name occurs also in Balducci Pegolotti's detail of stages on the road to Tauris, under the form of *Sermessacalo*. I can only suggest that these Italian corruptions contain the name of the station of *Hassan-Kala'a*, some twenty-four miles from Erzrum, near where the roads to Kars and Tabriz separate, perhaps under some such form as *Serai-Hassan-Kala'a*. It was once a considerable place, and the site of one of the Genoese castles which protected

mountain[1] whereon is Noah's Ark. And I would fain have ascended it, if my companions would have waited for me. But the folk of the country told us that no one ever could ascend the mountain, for this, as it is said, hath seemed not to be the pleasure of the Most High[2].

2. Concerning the City of Tauris and the City of Soldania, where dwelleth the Persian Emperor.

From that country I passed to TAURIS, a great city and a royal, which anciently was called Susis[3], and was the city of the King Ahasuerus[4]. In it they say the Arbor Secco

the road from Trebizond. There are also hot springs at the place. (*Brant.*, u.s., p. 230.) The name *may* however contain the Armenian *Surp* or *Surpazan*, holy.

[1] [FRENCH, "Mont Harach."—RAM. A., "Il monte Gordico."]

[2] MIN. RAM. "For the mountain is most holy, and moreover is inaccessible on account of the deep snow that covers at least two-thirds of it."

On Ararat, see note to *Jordanus*, p. 3. Rubruquis gives a curious popular reason why no one should ascend the mountain (p. 387). Haiton says that though nobody dares mount because of the snow, yet something black appears on the top which is vulgarly called Noah's Ark. The usual Mussulman tradition places the grounding of the Ark not on Armenian Ararat, but on the Jibul Judi in Kurdistan, whence Benj. of Tudela says "Omar Ben Khatab removed the Ark from the summit and made a mosque of it" (p. 93). Sir H. Rawlinson considers Judi to be much higher than Demawend, and as Demawend is believed to be fully 4,000 feet higher than Ararat, the claims of Judi to be the mountain of the Ark are very intelligible. (See President's Address in *Jour. R. Geog. Soc.*, xxix, p. clxx.) [The first European to ascend the Ararat was Prof. Parrot, of Dorpat (1829).]

[3] ["Quae Suors antiquitus vocabatur." ACT. S.—"Que Suisis antiquitus dicebatur. Hec Suisis fuit terra regis Asueri."—VENNI.]

[4] "And on the way I passed the Red River, where Alexander routed Darius the King of Asia; and in that city we have two convents." *Pal.* It is correct that the Franciscans had two convents in Tauris (*Wadding*). Respecting the Red River (*Fiume Rosso*), see note to Pegolotti *infra*. *Tauris* (*Tabriz*), the chief city of Azerbaijan, was the capital of more than one dynasty, and throughout the middle ages a chief point of contact and trade between the Latin and Oriental worlds. It has been identified not only with Shushan of Esther, and the Achmetha of the Apocrypha, but with the northern Ecbatana and half a dozen other ancient cities of fame. Rawlinson, however, considers it not to be older than the third century (*Chardin*, Amsterd., 1735, i, 258; *Journ. Asiat. S.* ii, iv, 117; *J. R. G. S.*, x, 109). [The destruction of Baghdad by Hulaku made Tabriz the great commercial and political city of Asia, and diverted the route of Indian products

existeth in a mosque[1], that is to say, in a church of the Saracens[2]. And this is a nobler city and a better for merchandise than any other which at this day existeth in the

from the Mediterranean to the Euxine.] There are now no traces of magnificence at Tabriz, though it was still in splendour in the seventeenth century (see note in Jordanus, p. 7). Tauris was made the See of a Roman bishop (William, de Cigiis) in 1329, and a successor [Franc. Cinquinus] is traced as late as the following century [1380–84] (*Le Quien*).

[1] [Probably the mosque built by Gazan.]

[2] The Arbor Secco is repeatedly spoken of by Marco Polo, especially as existing in north-east Persia. Marsden (p. 111) identifies it with the *chínár* or plane tree, observing that "the epithet seems to imply nothing more than this; that when the form of the fruit promises an edible nut, the stranger who gathers it is disappointed on finding no perceptible contents, or only a dry and tasteless seed." This is accepted by later commentators; but none explain the evident interest with which Marco refers to it, or why the *Christians* should be specified as giving it this peculiar name. It is clear that the tree was the subject of some Christian legend. This I have not met with in full, but the following passage from Mandeville throws some light upon it. At Mamre, he says, "there is an oak tree which the Saracens call *Dirpe*, which is of Abraham's time, and people call it the *Dry tree*. They say that it has been there since the beginning of the world, and that it was once green, and bore leaves till the time that our Lord died on the cross, and then it died...and there is a prophecy that a lord, a prince of the west side of the world, shall win the Land of Promise, *i.e.*, the Holy Land, with the help of the Christians, and he shall cause mass to be performed under that dry tree, and then the tree shall become green, and bear both fruit and leaves" (p. 162).

The *Arbor Secco* is sprinkled about Central Asia by Fra Mauro, in his celebrated map, now in the Sala dello Scudo at Venice.

Clavijo, in the beginning of the next century, mentions the *Arbor Secco* at Tauris, as still standing in the street "near an open space," and tells a story (in which there is some hiatus) about it in connection with a certain bishop who came to convert the city.

The stories of the dry tree were perhaps spun out of the words of the Vulgate in Ezekiel xvii, 24, "*Humiliavi lignum sublime et exaltavi lignum humile; et siccavi lignum viride*, et frondere feci lignum aridum."

Polo it will be remembered gives a topographical sense to *Arbor Secco* in Persia. Lazari, the late Venetian editor, ingeniously suggests that he may have meant *Elborz-Kuh*, Mount Elborz, near which his *Arbor Secco* certainly lay. [Yule in his *Marco Polo*, myself in my own edition of Odoric, have discussed at length the problem of the *Arbor Secco*, and I do not think it necessary to open the question again, but I should mention a paper published in the *Journal of the R. Asiat. Soc.*, Jan. 1909, in which Gen. Houtum-Schindler comes to the conclusion that Marco Polo's tree is not the "Sun-Tree," but the cypress of Zoroaster; "Marco Polo's *arbre sol* and *arbre seul* stand for the Persian *dirakht i sol*, *i.e.*, the cypress-tree."]

world. For there is not on the face of the earth any kind of provision, or any species of goods, but you will find great store thereof at Tauris. It is admirable for situation, and so opulent a city that you would scarcely believe the things to be found there; for the whole world, almost, hath dealings with that city for merchandise. And the Christians will tell you that the emperor[1] there hath more revenue from that one city than the king of France hath from his whole realm. Near that city is a mountain of salt, which furnisheth great store of salt for the whole place. And of this salt taketh every man as much as he listeth, and payeth nothing to any man[2]. In that city, also, there dwell many Christians of every description, but the Saracens have the rule over them in all things. And there are many things else to be said of that city, but it would take too long to relate them.

Departing from this city of Tauris, I travelled for ten days, and reached a certain city called SOLDANIA[3], in which

[1] The "Emperor of Persia" at this time was the son of Mohammed Khudabendeh, Abu Said Bahádur Khán, the last of the Mongol dynasty who had real power; he died 13 Rebi aul akhir 736.

[2] I do not find recent mention of this salt mine. But Ricold de Montecroce, in entering Persia from this side, speaks with wonder of its mountains of salt, which had to be quarried like stone and broken with iron tools; whilst the Arabian geographer Bakui notices specifically at Tabriz "a mountain of salt, which is extracted in blocks," and Chardin also speaks of an important salt mine close to the city. (*Peregrin. Quat.*, p. 122; *Notices et Extraits*, ii, 477; *Chardin*, i, 258.)

[3] Sultâniah was built as a royal residence by [Arghún and finished by] Oljaïtu, son of Arghún, the eighth of the Mongol Khans of Persia, in 1305. Long after the destruction of the city by Timur, indeed into the seventeenth century, the tomb of Oljaïtu was still magnificent, and especially noted for its colossal gates of damasked steel. The city was reoccupied by some of the Persian kings in the sixteenth century, till Shah Abbas transferred the seat of government to Ispahan. The ruins were of vast extent in Chardin's time. The present Persian dynasty has again adopted Sultâniah as a summer residence. Pope John XXII set up an archbishopric at Sultâniah in 1318, in favour of Francis of Perugia, a Dominican, and the series of archbishops is traced down to 1425, [with Thomas de Abaraner occupying the See]. (*Deguignes*, iv, 277, 279; Barbaro in *Ramus.*, ii, 105; *Chardin*, i, 271; *Le Quien*, iii, 1359–1368; De Sacy in *Mém. de l'Acad. des Inscr.*, vi, 503 *seq.*)

dwelleth the emperor of the Persians in the summer season[1]. But in the winter he goeth to a certain other place [called Axam][2] which is on the sea called the sea of Bacuc[3]. This city (of Soldania) is a great one, and a cool place, with an excellent supply of water, and many costly wares are brought thither for sale[4].

[1] ["Nella quale à un luogo de' Frati Predicatori, e uno de' Frati Minori." PAL.]

[2] BOLL.

[3] The Caspian was very generally called so in the middle ages, from Baku, the chief port on the western shore. The archives of Genoa contain a curious document relating how, in 1374, one Lucchinus Tarigus of that city, with certain comrades as penniless as himself, started from Caffa with a *fusta* or light galley, which they took up the Don, and dragged sixty miles overland to the Edil (Volga), and so descended to the *Sea of Bacu*, which they scoured, taking many prizes and much plunder, with which they returned, abandoning their vessel. On their way back, however, the heroes of this surpassing feat of buccaneering were taken and stript of much of their gains. (Gräberg de Hemso, *Annali di Geog. e di Stattist.*, ii, 290.) [See Yule's *Marco Polo*, i, p. 59. In the French version of Odoric this sea is called Sea of Bascon. The latter name is a corruption of Abeskun, a small town and island in the S.E. corner of the Caspian Sea, not far from Ashurada.]

The Bollandist version says the winter quarter of the Emperor on the sea was called *Axam*. The usual winter resort of the Il-Khans was the plain of Moghan, on the Caspian, near the mouth of the Kur, which had been the quarter to which the hosts of their predecessors used to retire after their annual ravages. Axam (Asham?) might however be Aujan, not far from Tabriz, which was often the spring and winter camp of the later Il-Khans, the Hujan of Clavijo, and where Gazan Khan built a fine city (*D'Ohsson*, v, 277; Quatremère's *Rashid*, pp. 21-23). But in that case the mention of the sea of Baku is a mistake. If not, it may perhaps be *Actam*, which is several times mentioned in the life of Timur, as a place on the plain of Moghan where he used to pitch, especially for great hunting matches. (*Chereffeddin*, by Pétis de la Croix, ii, 390; iii, 208, 398; *D'Ohsson*, iv, 151, 483.)

[4] ["Ce n'est my Somdoma ly une des V citez sur lesquelles Dieux fist plouvoir feu et souffre en vengence de pechié contre nature qui regnoit en eulx comme dit la Sainte Escripture. Car ces V villes furent jadis en la Terre Sainte de promission, en ce lieu qui est ore la Mer Morte. Et ceste Somdoma dont nous parlons si siet ens ou royaume de Persie." JEAN LE LONG.—This passage is omitted in ACT. S. and in RAM. A.]

3. Concerning the City of the Magi; also of the Sea of Sand, and of the Land of Huz.

Departing from this city with a caravan, that is to say with a certain company, I proceeded in the direction of Upper India, and after travelling that way for many days I halted at the city of the three Magi, which is called CASSAN, a royal city and of great repute[1]. But the Tartars have greatly destroyed it. It is a city which aboundeth greatly in bread and wine, and in many other good things. From this city to Jerusalem, (whither the Magi found their way, not surely by human strength but by Divine strength working by miracle, seeing how quickly they went[2]), is a good fifty days'[3] journey. And there be many other things with regard to that city which it boots not much to rehearse[4].

[1] Instead of this, PAL. has: "I came to the city of SABA, the place whence the three Magi came."

[2] ["Li troy Roy qui de ceste cité de Cassan furent en XIII journées amené en Jherusalem par vertu divine et non humaine." JEAN LE LONG.]

[3] ["Piu di LX."—MIN. RAM.—"Sessanta giornate."—PAL.]

[4] Qashân, a city of Persia, still tolerably flourishing, standing about halfway between Ispahan and Tehran, and also about halfway between Sultâniah and Yezd, long noted for its brocades and velvets, and also for its scorpions [and its fine pottery, called *Qaschi*].

Sir T. Herbert alludes to the story of the Magi coming from Qashân, but as he quotes Odoric I suspect his knowledge was derived from him only. For it is remarkable that in the Palatine and Minor Ramusian versions of Odoric, it is at SABA, and not at Qashân, that he speaks of the Magi. And this agrees with Marco Polo, who places at *Sava* the origin and sepulchres of the three kings. One he says was King of Sava, another of Ava, the third of the castle of the fire-worshippers. ["Marco Polo states that he 'found a village there which goes by the name of Cala Ataperistan (*i.e. Ḳalʿah-i Atashparastān*), which is as much as to say "The Castle of the Fire-Worshippers." And the name is rightly applied, for the people there do worship fire!' In an article entitled *The Magi in Marco Polo* [*Jour. Am. Or. Soc.*, 26. 79–83] I have given various reasons for identifying the so-called 'Castle of the Fire-Worshippers' with Kaschan, which Odoric mentions, or a village in its vicinity, the only rival to the claim being the town of Naïn, whose Gabar Castle has already been mentioned above." (Jackson, *Persia*, p. 413.)] Both Saba and Ava still exist between Sultâniah and Qashân, or at least their names and remains do. They retain no traditions now about the kings. (Cf. A. V. Williams Jackson, *Persia*, pp. 412–413.)

Herbert observes that various authors have brought the Magi from Babylon, Shushan, Hormuz, and Ceylon, to which we may add that

Passing thence I travelled to a certain city called IEST[1], [which is the furthest city of Persia towards India[2]], from which the Sea of Sand is but one day distant. Now that sea is a wondrous thing, and right perilous[3]. [And there were none of us who desired to enter on that sea. For it is all of dry sand without the slightest moisture. And it shifteth as the sea doth when in storm, now hither, now thither, and as it shifteth it maketh waves in like manner as the sea doth; so that countless people travelling thereon

Armenian tradition brings them from Lake Van, Haiton the Armenian from Chinese Tartary, and John de' Marignolli from the Indian Archipelago. It was impossible to *bring* the wise men of the East from Europe, so they were *taken* there after death, surely by the strangest fable ever invented!

It is most likely that the location of the wise men at Saba in Persia rose out of a misapplication of Psalm lxxii, 10: "*The kings of Tarshish and the Isles shall bring presents: the kings of Sheba and Seba shall offer gifts.*" And it was probably through some mistake in dictation that all the versions of Odoric but the two mentioned refer the Magi to Qashân instead of Saba. (*Chardin*, i, 297, 300, 301; *Herbert's Travels*; *Haiton*, ch. ii; *Assemanni*, p. 750; *Abbott* in *J. R. G. S.*, xxv, p. 6.)

[1] Yezd, occupying an oasis in the great Persian desert, is mentioned by Barbaro in the following century as a most industrious place, flourishing by its silk and cotton manufactures, and supplying with these a large part of Asia. [Heyd, *Commerce du Levant*, II, p. 109, says the inhabitants of Yezd wove the finest silk of Taberistan.—Marco Polo calls this silk *Yasdi.*] These manufactures still continue. Many important caravan routes converge at Yezd, whilst the desert has given it security, and thus it has become a considerable mart.

The figs [called *misqali*], pomegranates, grapes, and melons of the oasis are noted. The small raisins, not very much larger than Greek currants, are well known in India, into which they are largely imported under the name of *Kishmis*; perhaps from the island of Kais or Kish [*Quisci*, of Marco Polo, I, pp. 64–5; II, p. 453], from which the trade to India was conducted?

Yezd is regarded as holy by the Mussulmans; a sanctity perhaps borrowed from the fire-worshippers who still linger here in degradation and scanty numbers. (*Ramusio*, ii, 106; *Ritter*, viii, 265–270; *J. R. A. S.*, viii, 349.)

[2] From MIN. RAM.

[3] "Quitting Yezd at the end of April, our road ran across a sandy tract, which was, however, cultivated in parts, to Hujetabád, where a fine *caravanserai* and reservoir for water had been recently constructed. All round was a sea of sand, which the worthy Odoricus describes as 'une mer moult marveilleuse et moult perilleuse.' It is interesting to conjecture in what terms he would have commented on the Lut. A year later a European lost his way in this waste, and was obliged to walk about all night, to avoid being frozen." (P. M. Sykes, *Ten Thousand Miles in Persia*, p. 155.)

have been overwhelmed and drowned and buried in those sands. For when blown about and buffeted by the winds, they are raised into hills, now in this place, now in that, according as the wind chanceth to blow[1].] In this city of Iest there is very great store of victuals and all other good things that you can mention; but especially is found there great plenty of figs; and raisins also, green as grass and very small, are found there in richer profusion than in any other part of the world. This is the third best city which the Emperor of the Persians possesses in his whole realm. The Saracens say of it that no Christian is ever able to live in it beyond one year. And there are many other matters there.

Departing thence, and passing by many cities and towns, I came to a certain city by name COMERUM[2], which formerly was a great city, and in the olden time did great scathe to the Romans. The compass of its walls is a good fifty[3] miles and there be therein palaces yet standing entire, but

[1] From MIN. RAM. Whatever may be the exaggeration in this interpolated passage, as regards the Persian desert, the absolute extravagance of the account will seem less to those who will refer to the description by Baron Wrede of the desert in Southern Arabia, called "The Sea of Saffi," from a king who is said to have perished with his army therein (*J. R. G. S.*, xiv, p. 110–111). Tavernier also speaks of the danger of being lost in the desert of Yezd, on account of the mobility of the sand.

[2] The readings of this name are very various (see Latin text). But both Odoric's description and the manner in which I understand his route, seem to identify the remains of which he speaks with those of Persepolis. ["The earliest mention of the Persepolitan ruins, of which I am aware by a European writer, is that of Friar Odoricus." Curzon, *Persia*, II, p. 130.] The name *Comerum* will then probably represent the *grossa villa* of *Camara*, at which Barbaro places the ruins, and this is perhaps the same with the *Kinara* of Rich. [But Barbaro saw in Persepolis a work of Hebrew origin, instead of the ruins of Cyrus' Palace.] The great platform and columns of the palace, probably then more perfect than now, and the vast circuit assigned to the ruins by Persian tradition, varying from twelve to forty-four parasangs (forty to a hundred and fifty miles, the former estimate not exaggerated if the remains in that neighbourhood be supposed within the compass of one city), answer well to the brief words of our traveller.

[3] ["Ejus autem muri benè quadraginta milliarium sunt capaces." —BOLL.]

without inhabitants. It aboundeth however in many kinds of victual.

Leaving this and going on through many towns and cities I reached the city called HUZ[1], which abounds in all kinds of victuals, and is beautifully situated[2]. For near this city are mountains, which afford in great abundance the finest of pastures for cattle. There also is found manna of better quality and in greater abundance than in any part of the world. In that country also you can get four good partridges for less than a Venetian groat. In those parts also you see very comely elders; and 'tis the custom there for the men to knit and spin, and not the women. And this land adjoineth the extremity of Chaldæa towards the North[3].

[1] Some copies have "the land (or city) of Job"; others "the land of Job, called Huz" (see Latin text).—[Ur.—BOLL.]

[2] The Huz of Odoric I at first supposed to be Ahwáz (or Hawáz), or some other city of Khuzistan. Assemanni in Latin calls that country *Huzia*, and sometimes *Huzitis*; whilst Magini in Italian calls it *Cus*. Job's name, which appears in many copies, is probably an interpolation suggested by the name of the country. However, Chardin tells us that Mayn, north-west of Shiraz, was pointed out as the residence of Job; and probably the nearest approximation in modern times to the Patriarch's wealth in cattle is to be found amongst the nomad chiefs of Persia. It is, however, more probable that the Huz of Odoric is the *Hazah* of Eastern writers, frequently coupled with Mosul, and identified by Assemanni with *Adiabene* (see *Assemanni*, pp. 5, 11, 12, 13, 209, 710). This would certainly be more consistent with the accuracy of the last clause of the chapter.

[3] I suppose Odoric to pass through a part of the hill country of Luristan or the regions adjoining, if he does not indeed proceed north as far as Mosul, before descending into Chaldæa. The fine hill pastures, abundant manna, profusion of partridges, and fine old men ("many of them," says an authority quoted by Ritter, "attaining a hundred years in full possession of their bodily and mental faculties"), are all characteristic of the mountains of Kurdistan, embracing the Huz of Odoric according to the second interpretation just given, though I can find little of a specific kind on record as to the hill countries of Khuzistan and Luristan. The knitting and spinning of the men I do not find anywhere mentioned; it is a well-known circumstance in the Himalayan villages. (*Ritter*, ix, 611, 622; *J. R. G. S.* ix, 100, 104, etc.)

4. Fr. Odoric treateth of the manners of the people of Chaldæa; of India within land; and of Ormes.

Departing thence I went into CHALDÆA[1], which is a great kingdom, and as I went thither I passed by the Tower of Babel, which is distant perchance four days' journey from (the city[2]). And in this land of Chaldæa they have a language of their own[3]; and the men are comely, but the women in sooth of an ill favour[4]. The men indeed go smartly dressed and decked as our women go here, and on their heads they wear a kind of fillet of gold and pearls; whilst the women have nothing on them but a miserable shift reaching to the knees, and with sleeves so long and wide that they[5] sweep the ground. And they go barefoot with drawers[6] hanging about their feet, and their hair

[1] Though he calls Chaldæa a great kingdom, he would appear to mean the city of Baghdad. The peculiar language would be Arabic. Hitherto he has been in countries that speak Persian chiefly.

[2] *Ab eâ*, i.e., *Chaldæâ*, showing that Baghdad is meant, which is about sixty miles from the Birs Nimrud, and somewhat less from the ruins of Babylon. Probably the mass called *Babel* at the latter is Odoric's Tower (see note to Marignolli *infra*). It is not clear, however, how Odoric should have come by this to Baghdad. [Dieulafoy's Itinerary might give the explanation: Baghdad, Amarah, Dizful, Susa, Shuster, Ahwáz.]

[3] ["Nella detta Caldea est vero idioma Caldeo. Qual noi chiamamo lingua caldea."—RAM. A.]

[4] In countries where Mahommedan manners prevail, and now including India, the women in the streets have a much meaner appearance than the men, because women of the better class are so little seen. Of the women of Baghdad Ker Porter says: "The humbler females generally move abroad with faces totally unveiled, having a handkerchief rolled round their heads, from beneath which their hair hangs down over their shoulders; their garment is of a shift form reaching to their ankles, open before, and of a grey colour. Their feet are completely naked." (*Travels*, ii, 268.)

[5] "[Sorabules en caldien, sont braies en françois."—JEAN LE LONG.]

[6] *Sarabulas* is the word in the Latin, Anglo-Indicé *paijámas*. The term appears in various forms in Ducange as meaning *braccæ*, and is derived from a Chaldee word, which has been adopted into the Vulgate in *Daniel*, iii, 94. Ducange does not specify the word, but I suppose it is the counterpart of the Arabic *Sarwál*, plural *Saráwal*, better known in India under the Persian form *Shalwár*, and from which in its former shape the Spaniards have made *Zaraguelles*. (See Dozy,

neither plaited nor braided, but in complete dishevelment; and as here among us the men[1] go first and the women follow, so there the women have to go before the men. [Here I saw a young man who was taking to wife a beautiful young woman, and she was accompanied by other beautiful maidens, who were weeping and wailing, whilst the young bridegroom stood by in very gay clothes, with his head hanging down. And by and bye the young man mounted his ass, and the bride followed him barefoot and wretchedly dressed, and holding by the ass, and her father went behind blessing them until they reached the husband's house[2].] And many other matters there be in this city which it booteth not greatly to detail.

So going thence I came to inland India[3], a region which the Tartars have greatly wasted[4]. And there you find people[5] who live almost entirely on dates, and you get

Dict. des Vêtements chez les Arabes, p. 233.) Ricold Montecroce says the Nestorians thought the sacrament profaned if any one entered with the head covered or without *Sorrabula.* Whereon his German editor says: "Soccabula *fortasse sunt socci, calceorum genus. Ducangium frustra consului, qui nec* Sorrabula *habeat nec* Soccabula" (*Peregrin. Med. Æv.* IV, etc., Lipsiæ, 1864, p. 129.) But if he had given *Ducangius* a little more tether in spelling he would have found not only *Sarabula*, but *Serabula*, *Saraballa*, *Sarabella*, *Sarabola*, *Sarabara*, and yet more! The Bollandist Odoric has *Scrobullas*, a sheer error; but Ducange has inserted it as *muliebris vestis* on that authority. [Arabic, *serwal*; it is the *séroual* of the French "zouaves."]

1 ["les vallés."—J. LE LONG.]

2 From MIN. RAM.

3 ["Inde la maiour."—J. LE LONG.]

4 "*India quæ est infra terram.* The *infra* is to be taken in the Italian sense. It is plain that he means some region adjoining the Persian Gulf, and the following extract illustrates the matter more precisely: 'The Talmudic writers...confounded Obillah [on the Lower Euphrates] with the Mosaic Havilah...and thus rendered Havilah everywhere by *Hindeki* or India, precisely as the early Arabs state that Obillah is also called Hind or India; and as the people of Basrah still constantly speak of the districts at the mouth of the river as Hind, from the circumstance of their being the nearest points to India, and the places where the vessels from India rendezvous.'" (Sir H. Rawlinson, in *J. R. G. S.*, xxvii, 186.) Mas'udi mentions that at the time of the Mahomedan conquest the country about Basrah was called *Arz-ul-Hind*, "The Land of India." (*Prairies d'Or*, iv, 225.)

5 ["Sunt homines pulcri."—BOLL.]

forty-two pounds of dates for less than a groat[1]; and so of many other things[2].

Quitting this India and traversing many places, I came to the Ocean Sea. And the first city on it that I reached is called ORMES, a city strongly fenced and abounding in costly wares[3]. [The city is on an island some five miles distant from the main; and on it there grows no tree, and there is no fresh water. There is indeed great plenty of bread and fish and flesh. But it is not a healthy place nor safe for life, and the heat is something incredible. The people both men and women are all very tall. And where I passed by one day there was one just dead; and they had got together all the players in the place, and they set the dead man on his bed in the middle of the house, whilst two women danced round about him, and the players played on their cymbals and other instruments of music. Then two of the women took hold of the dead man, embracing him and chaunting his praises, and the other women stood up one after another and took a pipe and piped on it awhile, and when one had done piping she sat down; and so they went on all night. And in the morning they carried him to the tomb[4].]

[1] ["Vnos grossus Venetus."—BOLL.]

[2] Edrisi, two centuries before, relates that five hundred rotoli of dates were to be had at Basrah for a *dînâr*, according to the report of merchants who were there in 1141 (*Fr. Trans.*, i, 368).

[3] Hormuz, at this time and long after, a great entrepôt of Indian trade, situated on a barren island near the mouth of the Persian Gulf, and apparently representing the ancient Armuza which stood on the mainland opposite, and appears in Ptolemy. (An *island*, Armuza, is also shown in some copies at least of the Ptolemaic maps, though not in the text.) The place, therefore, cannot have derived its name, as D'Herbelot says, from Hormisdas, son of Sapor. It now belongs to the Sultan of Oman (Maskat), and gives him a revenue from the salt which it produces. Hormuz on the mainland still flourished at the end of the tenth century, and the date of its transfer to the island seems uncertain.—See *Marco Polo*, I, p. 110 *n*.

[4] This passage is only in the PAL. An account of the ceremonies of a wake at Baghdad very like this is given by Tavernier.

Here follows in all the Latin MSS. an untranslatable statement of the marvellous effects of the heat at Hormuz. It seems like a

5. Of ships that have no iron in their frame; and in such an one Fr. Odoric passeth to Tana in India.

In this country men make use of a kind of vessel which they call *Jase*[1], which is fastened only with stitching of

confusion of some complaint like hernia with the *guinea-worm*, which did prevail at Hormuz, or as if some one had hoaxed the friar as to the nature of the latter malady. It is worthy of note that Mandeville here omits this statement of Odoric's and substitutes another as to the inhabitants being obliged by the heat to sleep in water, which he does *not* seem to have copied from Polo. This custom prevailed long after, and is mentioned by Peter della Valle among others. Even monks followed it in his day. *Punkahs* of our Anglo-Indian fashion were already in use at Hormuz in the end of the sixteenth century. Linschoten calls them *cattaventos* (*Polo*, ii, 14 ; *Pietro della Valle*, ed. Brighton, 1843, ii, 471 ; *Linschoten*, p. 16). [Yule is here mistaken ; Mandeville mentions the same effects of the heat at Hormuz : " Item lem vait parmi Ynde par mointes diuerses contrees iusques à la grant mer Occiane ; et puis troeue homme vne isle qad noun Crynes, ou ly marchantz de Venise, de Ianewe et des autres marcheez y vont souent pur marchandises achater. Mes y fait si grand chaud en celle isle qe pur la grande destresse de chaleure ly perpendicles del homme, *i.e.* testiculi, issent hors de corps, pendantz iusqes a my iambe, pur la grande dissolucioun du corps. Mes les gentz du pais et cils qui sciuent la nature se font lier mult estreitment et se fond oinder de oignement restrinctif et refrigeratif pur les retenir en corps, ou autrement ils ne purroient viure ne durer." *Warner ed.*, p. 81.—Warner mentions Yule's omission, p. 197.

The Latin text of this passage is given in the appendix. Here is the French text of Odoric : "En ce pays fait si tres grant chault que les tresmoins des hommes leur issent du corps et leur pendent par dessoubs jusques aux genoulx ou jusques en my jambe. Et se il veulent vivre il convient qe il se oingnent d'une maniere de froit oingnement fait à ce ou autrement ils mourroient de chault. Et quant ilz se sont oingt de cest oingnement, ilz mettent leurs tresmoings en sachez propres à ce, et les sourlièvrent et loient ces sachez à leurs rains."]

[1] *Jaház* (*Pers.*), a ship. [This is the Arabic *Djehaz.*]

In his chapter on Hormuz, Marco Polo says (I, p. 108): "Their ships are wretched affairs, and many of them get lost ; for they have no iron fastenings, and are only stitched together with twine made from the husk of the Indian nut. They beat this husk until it becomes like horse-hair, and from that they spin twine, and with this stitch the planks of the ships together. It keeps well, and is not corroded by the sea-water, but it will not stand well in a storm. The ships are not pitched, but are rubbed with fish-oil. They have one mast, one sail, and one rudder, and have no deck, but only a cover spread over the cargo when loaded. This cover consists of hides, and on the top of these hides they put the horses which they take to India for sale. They have no iron to make nails of, and for this reason they use only wooden trenails in their shipbuilding, and then stitch the planks with twine as I have told you. Hence 'tis a perilous business to go a voyage in one of those ships, and many of them are lost, for in that

twine. On one of these vessels I embarked, and I could find no iron at all therein[1]. And having thus embarked, I passed over in twenty-eight days to TANA[2], where for the faith of Christ four of our Minor Friars had suffered a glorious martyrdom. The city is excellent in position, and hath great store of bread and wine[3], and aboundeth in trees. This was a great place in days of old, for it was the city of King Porus[4], who waged so great a battle with King Alexander. The people thereof are idolaters[5], for they worship fire, and serpents, and trees also. The land is under the dominion of the Saracens, who have taken it by

Sea of India the storms are often terrible." These ships are also spoken of by Jordanus and Montecorvino. See *Marco Polo*, I, p. 117, note. Oriental legends say that no iron can be used in the ships navigating the seas of Asia owing to loadstones. Cf. an interesting article of René Basset, *La Montagne d'Aimant*, *Revue des Traditions populaires*, July 1894, pp. 377–380.

[1] ["In quo nullum fratrum ! ! potui reperire."—BOLL.]

[2] Thána, an ancient city on the landward side of the island of Salsette, once the capital of Konkan and a haven of importance, but long superseded by Bombay ; it is mentioned as a cotton port by Marco Polo. [II, pp, 395, 396 n.]

How Porus was brought to these parts it is hard to say. But Gasparo Balbi (1580), speaking of the Cave of Elephanta "at Cape Bombain," says that it was formed by Alexander the Great to mark his furthest conquest. This may have been a current Mahomedan story, and might account for Porus being translated to Tana.

[3] "Di quindi navicammo per lo mare oceano venti otto di ; poi pervenimmo in Tana, la quale fu cittade del Re Porro ; la quale terra è posta in buon luogo, ed a grande abondanza di vittuaglia, espezialmente di burro, di *susuan* [sisamo ?], e riso. Quivi sono molti diversi animali, leoni neri, e pipistrelli grandi come anitre, topi grandi come cani communi, nè non sono presi da gatti ma da cani per la loro grandeza. In questa terra sono idolatrici, ma 'l signore adorano i saracini il bue e dicono ch' egli è il grande Idio, e non mangiano carne di bue, e lavorano col buese i anni, il settimo anno i lasciano libero. Prendono anche dello sterco del bue, e pongolosi a la faccia, e dicono da indi inanzi che sono santificati."—PAL.

[4] ["Nam fuit ciuitas Regis Ponti vel Parti Regis."—BOLL. who add in a note : "Imo Pori, ut alij."]

[5] "La gente è idolatra, e adora il bue, della cui carne non ne mangierebbeno per qual siuoglia cosa del mondo. Mogli fanno ben lauorar la terra : Pero giunti che sono al sesto anno, li lasciano andar via doue loro piace, egli adorano in ogniloco, che se gli fanno in contro. E del loro sterco, se n' vngono il viso, credendo eglino allhora esser santificaté."—MIN. RAM.

force of arms, and they are now subject to the Empire of DILI[1].

Here be found sundry kinds of beasts, and especially black lions in very great numbers, besides monkeys and baboons, and bats as big as pigeons are here. There be also rats as big as here are our dogs called *scherpi*[2]. And

[1] I have ventured here, in justice to Odoric, to restore this name as I believe he really employed it. It is in the Latin text "*subjacentes Daldili.*" Odoric, doubtless, in his dictation, said "*sotto la signoria del Dili.*" Thus, in Fra Mauro's map, we find tolerably well placed, "DELI *cittade grandissima,*" and the rubric attached, "*Questa cittade nobilissima za dominava tuto el Paese* DEL DELI *over India Prima,*" and again to the city of *Here* (Herat), "*Quella era za sotto la Signoria* DEL DELI," etc.

The same kind of fusion and confusion which has created a King Daldili has led to many other strange perversions. The ancient Malabar port and point of *Hili* survives in our maps only as Mount *Deli.* Marco Polo is made to call Lahore the city of *Dilivar*, and the Cilician port of Aias—*Laias*; whilst the name of King D'or, by which (according to Marsden's happy suggestion) he translated the title of the Chinese *Kin* or *Golden* Dynasty, appeared in the Latin editions as *Darius.* So we shall afterwards find that the Tartar name *Talai*, which Odoric gives to the Yang tze kiang, becomes in most MSS. *Doltalay*; and in the English Mandeville we find the land of Dengadda and the Lake of Dasfetidee, for Engaddi and Asphaltites. An analogous case to that of King Daldili also occurs in the city where I write this. An English Archbishop of Palermo, whose name is believed to have been Walter (o' the) Mill, has been handed down as *Gualterus Ofamilius.*

A reverse process also is often found to have taken place. The Arabs have made the Lazarus of the Gospel into *'Azár*; we often see Germany spoken of in Italy as *La Magna*; and from the Portuguese *Laranja*, a corruption of the Indian *Naranja*, we have got our English *Orange*, and the modern Latin form (implying a false etymology) *Aurantia.*

[With regard to the dominion of the Saracens, we may observe that the house of Khilijé, founded by Jalál-ud-din who succeeded to the throne of Delhi lasted from 1290 to 1320; Alá-ud-din, the nephew and successor of Jalál-ud-din, extended the Mohammedan power at the expense of the Solankis of Gujarát (1297), of the Yádavas of Devagiri, on the east, on the very coast of Tána, and of the Hoysalas of Dvàrasamudra, in the south; in 1318, a short time before the arrival of Odoric, Harapâla, the last of the sovereigns of Devagiri, revolted, was captured and skinned alive by Múbarik, successor of Alá-ud-din. The house of Khilijé was replaced by a Túrkí slave, leader of a rebellion, Ghiyás-ud-din Tughlak, who founded the Tughlak dynasty (1320–1414). It is evident from Odoric's testimonial that—if rebellions were constant inland—the maritime emporia were kept in order by the Musulman governors.—H. C.]

[2] This word is written also *scepi*, *depi*, *scoipi*, *sarpi*, etc., because (it may be supposed) the transcribers, like the present editor, could make nothing of it.

for this reason rats are there caught by dogs, for the mousers or cats are of no use for that[1]. In this country every man hath before his house a plant of twigs as thick as a pillar would be here, and this never withers as long as it gets water. And many other strange things are there which it would be pretty to hear tell[2].

[The women go naked there, and when a woman is married she is set on a horse, and the husband gets on the crupper and holds a knife pointed at her throat; and they have nothing on except a high cap on their head like a mitre, wrought with white flowers, and all the maidens of the place go singing in a row in front of them till they reach the house, and there the bride and bridegroom are left alone, and when they get up in the morning they go naked as before[3].]

["Qui viddi vno Leon grande, e negrissimo, alla guisa di vn bufalo: e viddi le nottole, o vogliam dire uespertiglioni, come sono le anatre di qui da noi. E topi, chiamati Sorici di Faraone, che sono grandi come uolpi, e ue ne sono vu infinità grande, e peggiori de cani mordenti: il paese è di Saracini."—(MIN. RAM.)

I have no doubt that this passage refers to the mangouste or ichneumon (*Herpestes ichneumon*) formerly found in this part of Asia as well as in Egypt where it was venerated.—*H. C.*—See *Marco Polo*, I, p. 254, note 3.]

[1] As to the great bats and rats enough has been said in the notes to Jordanus (pp. 19, 29).

The word which I have translated *bats* is *noctuæ*, but I think *bats* are meant. *Nottola* in Italian means not an owl but a bat; and the MIN. RAM. and PAL. confirm this. They also say "as big as our ducks," which is more germane than *pigeons*. The "black lions" are tigers, we may presume. Polo always calls tigers *lions*. *Nigri leones*, apparently for tigers, will be found in the Latin translation of Arabshah's *Life of Timur*, i, p. 466. [See note, *supra*.]

[2] This passage must have been mangled in the dictation. But it is evident that what is spoken of is the sacred *Tulasi* or Basil (*Ocymum Sanctum*). The following extract describes intelligibly and correctly what Odoric's amanuensis apparently did not understand. "Almost all the Hindus...adore a plant like our *Basilico Gentile*, but of more pungent odour....Everyone before his house has a little altar, girt with a wall half an ell high, in the middle of which they erect certain pedestals like little towers, and in these the shrub is grown. They recite their prayers daily before it, with repeated prostrations, sprinklings of water, etc. There are also many of these maintained at the bathing places, and in the courts of their pagodas." (*Vincenzo Maria*, p. 300; see also Ward's *Hindoos*, iii, 203.)

[3] From MIN. RAM.

[In this country there are trees which give wine which they call *loahc*[1], and which is very intoxicating. And here they do not bury the dead, but carry them with great pomp to the fields, and cast them to the beasts and birds to be devoured. And they have here very fine oxen; which have horns a good half pace in length [girth?], and have a hump on the back like a camel. And from this city to Panche [Paroche?] is fourteen days' journey[2].] And it was in this place called Tana, as I have said before, that the four Minor Friars suffered a glorious martyrdom for the faith of Christ, and it took place after the manner following[3].

6. History of the martyrdom of the four Friars in the city of Tana.

When the friars aforesaid were at Ormes they made a bargain for a certain ship to take them to Polumbum, but being once on board they were taken against their will to Tana. Here there be fifteen houses of Christians, that is to say of Nestorians, who are schismatics and heretics. And the friars having thus come hither, found harbour in the house of one of those Christians. And whilst they were staying there, one day there arose a quarrel between the good man of the house and his wife, and in the evening he gave her a sound beating. And in the morning the woman went and made a complaint of the beating to the *Cadi*, *i.e.*, in their tongue the Bishop. And the cadi having asked her if she had any proof of what she alleged, she answered that she could well prove it, "For," quoth she,

[1] This may be the term which is used by the old materia medica writers for an essence or extract, *Lohoc* and *Loch*. It is doubtless, as suggested by Mr Badger, the Arabic *Rúhh*, generally pronounced *Rúahh*, a spirit, an essence.

[2] From PAL.

[3] ["Occisi sunt Kalendis Aprilis tres, Fr. Thomas de Tolentino, Fr. Jacobus de Paduâ et Fr. Demetrius Laicus: triduo post Fr. Petrus de Senis an. Ch. 1321." (*A. S.*, note, xiv Jan.)]

"there were four Frank Rabbans[1]," (which is to say in our tongue four men of a religious order) "there in the house when he handled me thus. Question them and they will tell you the truth." And when the woman said this, there was a certain man of Alexandria there present who begged the cadi to send for them, saying that they were men of great learning and knowledge in the Scriptures, and that it would be good to have a dispute with them concerning religion. The cadi, hearing this, sent for them. And so when those brethren were brought before him, to wit, Friar Thomas of Tolentino in the March of Ancona[2], Friar

[1] *Rabban*, "*my master*," is the usual address to a monk in the Syrian church (*Assem.*, p. 537). [From *rabb* (*hebr.*), master, doctor.]

[2] Thomas of Tolentino was a venerable soldier of his Order, whose name occurs several times in its annals. He had been twice in the preceding century imprisoned by his superiors for his unwelcome zeal in urging observance of the vow of poverty, and in disputing the Pope's authority to relax this obligation. Wadding says he suffered in his sixtieth year, but as his first imprisonment took place in 1275, and his death in 1321 or 1322, he must have attained nearly if not quite threescore and ten.

Raymund Fitz-Geoffry becoming general of the order in 1290, and finding Thomas and his friends in durance, released them with good words, but to prevent further trouble with their zeal, sent them on a mission to Armenia (i.e. Lesser Armenia, or Cilicia) the king of which country had invited a party of friars. In 1292 the king, apparently Hethum or Hayton II, sent Thomas and another monk to the kings of France and England to beg help against the Saracens. Again in 1302 he came to Europe to ask aid for the missionary work in which he was engaged, as holding out great promise of success. He obtained twelve chosen friars, and departed with them.

In 1307, Thomas, who had been preaching in Tartary, returned to the Papal Court, and gave the Pope an account of the success of John of Monte Corvino and others, a report which apparently led to the nomination of that missionary as Archbishop of Cambalec. As Thomas was himself the bearer of a letter from Monte Corvino, it is *possible* that he had been as far as Cathay himself. He probably returned to the east with the bishops who were then appointed to act under the archbishop in Cathay (see preface to Letters of Monte Corvino in this collection), but I trace him no more till he accompanied Jordanus to India and suffered at Tana as the text relates.

Though Odoric claims to have carried the bones of all his martyred brethren to China, the (alleged) skull of Thomas was afterwards brought from India to Italy, and was in the 17th century preserved, as it may be still, at his native place Tolentino. His feast also was celebrated by his townsmen, who held a fair on that day. (*Wadding*, v, 211, 236, 291; vi, 353 and seq.; ix, 181; *Acta Sanctorum*, 1st April.)

Nothing seems to be known of the three other friars beyond what

James of Padua, and Friar Demetrius, a Georgian lay brother good at the tongues, (Friar Peter of Sienna being left at home to take care of their things), the cadi began at once to dispute with them about our Faith. And when the infidels disputed with them in this manner, alleging that Christ was mere man and not God, Friar Thomas took it in hand, and proved by arguments and instances that He was God and Man in one, and so confounded the Saracens that they were absolutely unable to maintain the contrary.

7. The same continued.

Then the Cadi seeing himself thus put to confusion by them before the whole people, began to call out with a loud voice: "But what sayest thou of Machomet? What sayest thou of Machomet?" For such is the wont of the Saracens, that when they cannot maintain their cause with arguments, they take to maintaining it with swords and fists. And as the Cadi thus questioned Friar Thomas, the brethren answered saying: "We have proved to thee by arguments and instances that Christ who delivered a religion to the world was true God and Man, and since him Machomet hath come and hath delivered a religion which is contrary to the former. If thou be wise then well mayst thou wot what to think of him." Then the Cadi and the other Saracens only shouted the louder: "But again what sayest thou of Machomet?" Then Friar Thomas replied: "Since ye can only repeat *What do I say of him*, I should blush to refuse the reply ye seek. I reply then, and tell you that Machomet is the son of perdition, and hath his

their names tell. The account in Wadding, derived from the letter of one Francis of Pisa, is substantially the same as that in the text. It calls the lay brother Demetrius of *Teflis*. On the cloister wall of St Anthony's at Padua I have seen a rude fresco of Friar James, with a symbol of decapitation, and the label, *S• Jacobus Martyr Patavinus*. [Petrus of Sienna=Sena Julia; Demetrius of Tiflis, in Georgia, Interpreter; cf. Venni, pp. 107–108.]

place in hell with the devil his father, and not he only but all such as follow and keep his law, false as it is, and pestilent and accursed, hostile to God and the salvation of souls." And when the Saracens heard this they all began to shout with a loud voice together: "Let him die; Let him die, for he hath blasphemed the Prophet!" And then they took the friars and bound them there in the sun, that they might die a dreadful death by the intense heat. For there the heat is so great that if one shall stand [bareheaded] in the sun for the space of a single mass he will die outright. Yet there they abode in the sun praising and glorifying God from the third until the ninth hour, cheerful and unscathed. And when the Saracens saw this they took counsel together, and came to the brethren, saying: "We mean to kindle a great blazing fire, and to cast you into it. And if the doctrine ye hold be true the fire will not burn you, but if it be false and evil ye shall be utterly consumed."

Then the brethren answered, saying: "We are ready, O Cadi, to go into the fire and into prison, or to endure whatever thou canst inflict on us for our religion; and ready thou shalt ever find us. But this one thing thou oughtest to know, that if the fire consume us, think not this cometh from (the fault of) our religion, but only from our sins, seeing that on account of our sins God may well let us burn. And for all that, our religion is not the less good and perfect as anything in the world ever can be; nor is there in the world any other faith whereby men may be saved but this."

8. The same history continued.

And as order was thus being taken for the burning of the friars, the report thereof spread like lightning throughout the whole city; and from the said city great and small, men and women, flocked together to see what should come of it. But the brethren were meanwhile brought out to the *Medan*[1] *i.e.*, the piazza of the city, where an exceeding great fire had been kindled. And Friar Thomas went forward to cast himself into the fire, but as he did so a certain Saracen caught him by the hood, saying: "Nay, thou shalt not go, for thou art old, and mayest have upon thee some crafty device whereby the fire could not burn thee; so let another than thou go in!" Then incontinently four Saracens laid violent hands on Friar James of Padua in order to cast him into the fire; but he said to them, "Suffer me and I will of my own free will cast myself in." But they, heeding not what he said, straightway threw him into it. And when they had done so, and he was there abiding in the fire, it blazed so high and far abroad that no one was able to see him, but they heard his voice continually invoking the name of the Blessed Virgin. And when the fire was quite spent, there was Friar James standing on the embers, joyous and exultant, with his hands raised to heaven making the sign of the cross, and with sound mind and pure heart praising the Lord without ceasing. And though the fire had been so great the slightest hurt or burn could not be found upon him. And when the people saw this they began to call out with one consent, "They are saints! They are saints! 'Tis sin to do them hurt. And we see that in truth their religion is good and holy." And when they had said thus, Friar James was called forth from the fire, and came out sound and unhurt. And when the Cadi saw this, he too began to cry out saying: "He is no saint! he is no saint!. But the reason why he is not burnt is that he hath on his back a garment from the land of Abraham[2]. Wherefore let him be stript naked and so cast into the fire!"

[1] *Maidán.* We generally employ this word in India for an open plain, or the esplanade outside a city; but in Western Asia it seems to be used specially for the public square or piazza (in the Italian sense) of a city, as here.

[2] The tradition respecting Abraham's being cast into a fire by

And that this might be done effectually then came some villains of Saracens, and kindled a fire twice as great as before. And then they stript Friar James, and washed him, and anointed him copiously with oil, and that the fire might blaze more fiercely and burn up the friar the faster, they poured great quantities of oil upon the pile of wood, and then flung Friar James with a forcible fling into the middle of it. And the Friars Thomas and Demetrius abode without upon their knees, engaged fervently and instantly in prayer. And thus also Friar James came forth a second time without hurt as he had done before.

9. The same history continued.

And when the people saw this they shouted again with one consent: "'Tis a sin! 'Tis a sin to hurt them, for saints they be!" And so there was a very great noise among the people. And on seeing this second miracle the Melic, i.e. the podesta of the city[1], called to him Friar James, and made him put on his clothes, and said: "Go, brethren, with the grace of God, for ye shall suffer no harm at our hands. For we see well that ye are good and holy men; and that your religion is good and holy and true, we see past question. But to provide the better for your safety we counsel you to quit this place as speedily as ye may; for the Cadi will do his uttermost and spare no pains to take your lives."

Nimrod for his contempt of idol worship is well known, and may be read at length in *Weil's Biblical Legends*, both in its Jewish and Mussulman shapes. The legend forms the subject of one of the great frescoes in the Campo Santo at Pisa. [Cf. GEN. xv, 7.—ISAIAH, xxix, 22.]

[1] "*Lomelic, scilicet Potestas.*" The Kotwal. Ibn Batuta about this time tells us that the title *Malik* (King) was used by the Mahomedans of India, where the people of Egypt would use *Amir*. However, in Egypt in 1384, the Italian Frescobaldi tells us that the Governor of Alexandria was called *Lamelech* (Al Malik). [*Melik* ملك, governor; under the mongol dynasty, this title was given to the collector of taxes.]

While he was thus speaking it was about the hour of complines, and the whole people, idolaters and others, were standing about in a state of awe and astonishment, saying: "We have seen from these men things so great and marvellous, that we know not what law we ought to follow and keep." And as they thus spake, the Melic caused those three friars to be taken and conveyed away across a certain arm of the sea that was at a little distance from the city, and where there was a certain suburb[1], whither the man in whose house they had been lodged accompanied them, and so they found harbour in the house of a certain idolater. And whilst they abode there the Cadi went to the Melic and said: "What are we about? for the law of Machomet is going to destruction unless something else be done. For these Frank Rabbans will now go preaching through the whole country, and as they have done such great marvels here which the whole of the people have seen, all will be converted to them, and so the law of Machomet will lose all power. And that this be not so there is a thing you ought to consider, and that is that Machomet hath ordered in the Alchoran (i.e. in his law) that if any one shall slay a Christian he shall have as much merit as if he had gone to Mecha." (Now ye must know that Alchoran is the law of the Saracens as the Gospel is the law of the Christians; and Mecha is the place where Machomet is buried, and the Saracens go there on pilgrimage just as Christians go to the Sepulchre[2].)

Then the Melic answered the Cadi: "Go then and do as thou wilt."

[1] The narrative of Francis of Pisa, quoted in Wadding's Annals, says here: "*ad oppidum situm ex aliâ parte fluminis seu marini brachii quo civitas circumcingitur.*" These are touches from real knowledge. Tana stands on a river-like arm of the sea separating Salsette from the main, and now crossed by a railway bridge.

[2] It is curious how persistently the error of Mahomed's being buried at Mecca was repeated. Even Mandeville (?), who had served the Saracens in Egypt, repeats it.

10. The same history continued.

And when he had thus spoken the Cadi immediately took four armed men and sent them to slay the friars. But by the time these men had crossed the water it was night, and so at that late hour they could not find them. And now the Melic caused all the Christians who were in the city to be seized and put in prison. But when midnight was come the friars got up to say matins, and so the men who had been sent to slay them discovered where they were, and took them away outside the town beneath a certain tree, and said to them: "Ye must know that we have orders from the Cadi and the Melic to slay you; and we are reluctant to do it, for ye are good and holy men. But we can do no otherwise. For if we do not their behests we and all our children and our wives shall die!" And the friars answered them saying: "Since ye come hither that we through death temporal may attain to life eternal, do that which ye are bidden. For we are ready to bear manfully whatever tortures ye may inflict on us for our religion and for the love of Jesus Christ our Lord." And when they answered with this boldness and constancy, that Christian who had joined their company got into deep altercation with those four evil men. For he spake to them in this wise, saying: "Had I but a sword I would hinder your doing this, or ye should slay me along with them." Then they caused the friars to strip. And straightway Friar Thomas, joining his hands in the sign of the cross, suffered first, his head being cut off. And one of them then smote Friar James on the head and clove him to the eyes, and then immediately cut his head off. Friar Demetrius also first received a desperate stab in the breast and then his head was cut off. And as they thus rendered their souls to God in martyrdom, straightway the air was illuminated, and it became so bright that all were stricken with amazement, and at the same time the moon waxed wonderfully light and lustrous. And after this there were so great thunderings, lightnings, and flashings of fire, that almost all thought their end was come. And that ship which ought to have taken them to Polumbum, but carried them to Tana against their will, went to the bottom, so that nothing ever was known of her or her crew.

11. The same continued.

And in the morning the Cadi sent to the house to take possession of the friars' gear; they found there Peter of Sienna, the comrade of the other three friars, and took him to the Cadi. So the Cadi and other Saracens addressed him, and made him promises of great things if he would deny the faith, and confess that of Machomet. But he only ridiculed them and scorned their proposals in a way that made them marvel. So they began torturing him, and did so from morning until noon with sundry kinds of tortures. But he remained ever unshaken and firm in the faith, and manfully demolishing their doctrine, and showing it to be false. And when the Saracens saw that he was not to be turned from his purpose, they hung him up to a certain tree, and there he remained from the ninth hour until night. But when night fell they took him down from the tree quite unhurt, and when they saw it was so, they clove him in sunder, and in the morning no trace of him was to be found. But it was revealed to a person worthy of belief that God had concealed his body till in due season He should be pleased to disclose it[1].

[1] There are different statements as to the date of the martyrdom of these four friars. Wadding puts it under 1321, the *Acta Sanctorum* under 1322. [See note, p. 117.] The editors of the latter urge the authority of a MS. of Odoric's narrative of the circumstances, which had been communicated to them, and which named the Kalends of April as the day, combined with the assertion of Jordanus (see letter in this collection) that it was on the Thursday of the week before Palm Sunday, a combination which would fix the date to 1322. This, however, is inconsistent with the positive evidence of Jordanus in his

And that God might make manifest that their souls had inherited the Kingdom of heaven, on that very day when these blessed friars became glorious martyrs, that Melic had fallen asleep, and as he thus lay asleep, lo! there appeared to him those glorious martyrs bright and shining like the sun, and holding swords in their hands, which they brandished over the Melic in such a way as if they would have cloven him asunder. And at this sight the Melic began to roar out, and with his noise brought his whole family running to see what ailed him, and what he would have. And he told them in reply: Those Frank rabbans whom I have caused to be slain have come hither with swords to slay me! And so he sent for the Cadi, to whom he told what had befallen him, and asked his counsel as to what should be done in the matter, for he was convinced that he should perish utterly at their hands. Then the Cadi advised him that he should do some great work of

following letter. For in it, dated Feast of Fabian and Sebastian, 1323—*i.e.*, in our reckoning, 20th January, 1324—he says that he had then been alone for *two years and a half* since he had buried his comrades. Had their death occurred in 1322, the interval would have been only one year and eight months, which no rounding of numbers could convert into two years and a half; whereas if it had occurred in 1321, the interval might naturally have been so spoken of.

It does not appear to be clear that those four friars ever received the official beatification of Rome, though they appear as Beati in the *Acta Sanctorum*. The Order applied to John XXII to have this done, and he intimated approval; but certain schisms and controversies arising in the Order about this time, the matter was lost sight of. According to one author, however, quoted by Wadding, but apparently without much confidence, the beatification was sanctioned by John's successor, and the feast ordered to be celebrated on the Wednesday of Holy Week. ["The Holy See sanctioned the *cultus* of the Martyrs of Tana by a decree of July 10, 1894; by another, of August 14, 1894, the Congregation of Rites granted the recital of an approved Office and Mass for the feast of Blessed Thomas of Tolentino. The addition authorised for insertion in the *Martyrologium Romano-Seraphicum Sanctorum et Beatorum trium Ordinum S. P. N. Francisci* is the following:

"April 6.—Tanae in India beati Thomae a Tolentino Ordinis Minorum, qui cum tribus sociis ejusdem ordinis glorioso pro fide Christi martyrio coronatus est.

"From the Lesson of the Breviary...the date on which the martyrdom took place was the end of April 1321." Medlycott, *India and the Apostle Thomas*, 1905, p. 91 *n*.]

charity on their account, if he would escape from the hands of those murdered men. So he sent straightway for the Christians whom he held in durance, and humbly asked their pardon for what he had caused to be done to them, behaving to them like a fellow and a brother. And besides he ordered that any one who should hurt any of the Christians in future should suffer death. Afterwards also the Melic caused four mosques, i.e. churches, to be built in honour of the Friars, and put Saracen priests in each of them to abide continually.

12. The same history continued.

And when the Emperor of Dili[1] heard that those Friars had undergone such a sentence, he sent and ordered the Melic to be seized and despatched to his presence with his hands bound. Being thus brought before the emperor, and questioned why he had so cruelly put those friars to death, he replied: "I suffered them to die because they sought to overthrow our law, and blasphemed the Prophet." Then the emperor said to him: "Most cruel hound, when thou sawest that God had twice delivered them from the fire how couldst thou dare thus to inflict death upon them?" And having spoken thus, he ordered him with his whole family to be cut in sunder. Such a death therefore as he caused those brethren to undergo to their glory, he himself had now to undergo to his own damnation. And the Cadi hearing of this fled from the city, and from the emperor's dominions.

Now in that country it is the custom never to bury the dead, but bodies are only cast out in the fields, and thus are speedily destroyed and consumed by the excessive heat. So the bodies of these friars lay for fourteen days in the

[1] The Sultan of Dehli at this time must have been Ghiyás-ud-din Tughlak, who assumed the throne in 1320, according to the latest corrections of the Chronology. (See French editor's preface to *Ibn Batuta*, vol. iii, p. xiii, and *supra* p. 115.)

sun, and yet were found quite fresh and undecayed as if on the very day of their glorious martyrdom. And the Christians who were in that place seeing this took the bodies, and caused them to be committed to the tomb[1].

13. How Fr. Odoric took up the bones of the four Friars; and the wonders wrought thereby.

Then I, Friar Odoric, came into those regions, having heard of their glorious martyrdom, and opening their tombs I humbly and devoutly took up their bones. And as God ofttimes worketh great marvels by means of his saints, through these also it pleased him to work powerfully. Thus when I had taken their bones, and wrapt them in fair napkins, and accompanied by one brother of the order and a servant, I was taking them to the house of our friars at a certain place in Upper India[2], I chanced to lodge in the house of a certain man, and when I went to sleep I placed those bones, or sacred reliques rather as I would call them, under my head. And as I thus slept the house was suddenly set fire to by the Saracens, that they might bring about my death by acclamation of the people. For this is the emperor's command, that any whose house is burnt shall suffer death[3]. The house then being on fire my

[1] It is remarkable that Odoric seems purposely to avoid all mention of Jordanus in connection with this, though we know that it was he who carried off the bodies and buried them at Supera. (*Friar Jord.*, p. vii.)

[2] Upper India with Odoric is China.

[3] This passage is very obscure in all the copies that have it. ["Ainsi que je m'en aloie portant ces reliques de ces freres martirs dessus dis, je fu hostellez en une maison et quant je alay dormir je mis ces reliques dessoubs mon chief; moy ainsi dormant vinrent Sarrazin ainsi criant commandement est de la majesté imperial que ceste maison soit arse et tous ceulx que nous y trouverons dedens. A ce mot, mes compaignons et les autres de l'ostel s'enfouirent par peur du commandement et me laisserent seul avec ces saintes reliques. Tantost ces Sarrazins bouterent le feu en ceste maison. Le feu fut moult grans et aspres tout environ moy et fut la maison arse de tous costez, fors seulement ce lieu ouquel je gisoit avec ces saintes reliques. Celle chambre n'eult oncques garde, comment que le feu fust si grant tout environ."—FRENCH TEXT.]

comrade and the servant made their escape from it, leaving me in it with those bones. And I took the bones of the brethren, and seeking help from God I crouched into a corner of the burning house. And three corners thereof were consumed, and that one only was left in which I was abiding. And as I sat there the fire was over my head, doing me no harm and not burning the corner of the house. And as long as I continued there with the bones, the fire never came lower but hung over me like an atmosphere. But as soon as I quitted the house it was entirely destroyed and many others adjoining besides. And so I escaped scatheless.

14. The same continued.

Another such thing happened to me also on that journey. For as I went by sea with those bones, towards a certain city called Polumbum (where groweth the pepper in great store) the wind failed us utterly[1]. Then the idolaters came

[1] This is undoubtedly the Columbum of Jordanus and John de' Marignolli, Kulam [Kollam, Koilam], or the modern Quilon [Kollam], though it is not easy to see how the P got into all, or nearly all, the MSS. of Odoric, unless the error occurred in the first transcription.

In the preface to the translation of Jordanus, the high authority of Professor H. H. Wilson was quoted for the fact that Kulam dated only from the ninth century. But the era there alluded to may have been that of a *re*-foundation, an event often prominent in eastern annals, and which is found in the adjoining state of Cochin furnishing an era called the "New Foundation" (corresponding to A.D. 1341). For there seems reason to believe the city of Kulam to be more ancient than the time named. There is in *Assemani* (iii, pt. ii, p. 437), a letter from the Nestorian Patriarch, Jesujabus of Adiabene, who died in 660, addressed to Simon Metropolitan of Fars, which complains of his grievous neglect of duty, and alleges that in consequence not only is India, "*which extends from the coast of the kingdom of Fars to* COLON, *a distance of* 1200 *parasangs*, deprived of a regular ministry, but Fars itself is lying in darkness." This Colon is, I suppose, Kulam. [Quilon is "one of the oldest towns on the coast, from whose re-foundation in 1019 A.D., Travancore reckons its era." (Hunter, *Gaz.*, xi, p. 339.)]

I find that Professor Kunstmann of Munich, in his Essays on the Medieval Missions, has taken up the view that Columbum lay upon the east side of Cape Comorin, and was identical with the Cael of Marco Polo. I do not, however, find any material ground alleged for this easterly position, except that it is so represented in the Catalan Map of 1375. This I cannot think of great weight against the chain

beseeching their gods to give them a fair wind; which however was all to no purpose. Next came the Saracens, and wrought greatly to have a wind granted to them; but neither had they anything for all their prayers. Whereupon they enjoined on my comrade and me that we should pour forth our prayers to our God to bestow it upon us. And if this took effect the greatest honour would be shown us. And the skipper said to me, speaking in the Armenian tongue, that others might not understand: "If we cannot have a wind we shall cast those bones of yours into the

of evidence for its identity with Quilon, adduced in my preface to Jordanus, whilst the passage in Marco Polo which is therein alluded to, may very probably have misled the geographer. When Giovanni da Empoli in 1503 describes the first visit of the Portuguese to *Colom*, and the delight of the Christians called *Nazzareni* to receive them, who can doubt that these are the Columbum and the Nasçarini of Jordanus? And Marignolli tells us precisely that Columbum was in Mynibar (Malabar), which he as precisely distinguishes from Maabar where St Thomas lay, *i.e.* the east side of the Peninsula.

I suspect it will be found that the form Columbum or Columbo, as applied to Quilon, is founded on some form of the name Kulam formerly in use among the merchants and navigators of the Indian Seas. Sir Emerson Tennent tells us of a Hebrew MS. in the possession of the Cochin Jews, which in speaking of Sri Perumal the famous King of Malabar, says his rule extended *from Goa to Columbo*. This, Tennent takes for Columbo in Ceylon, but as Goa and Quilon would with tolerable precision form the Dan and Beersheba of the Malabar coast, I have little doubt that Quilon is the place meant.

Columbum was often represented as an island, but this must not be taken for Ceylon. Thus Pegolotti (pp. 359, 360) speaks of the "Columbine ginger which was the produce of the Island of Columbo of India." The World-Map in the Portulano of Andrea Bianco, in St Mark's library at Venice, also shows opposite the south-west corner of India the "*Ixola di Colonbi*," whilst Fra Mauro's great map has also "*Isola Colombo*," placed to the *east* of India, and noted in the rubric for its pepper, great resort of merchants, and black lions (*i.e.* tigers). [Jordanus of Séverac was elected titular bishop of the see of Columbum on the 21st of August 1329 by a bull of Pope John XXII, dated Avignon, 9th August 1329.]

[Yule writes (*Marco Polo*, ii, p. 377 *n.*): "The form *Columbum* is accounted for by an inscription, published by the Prince of Travancore (*Ind. Antiq.*, ii, 360) which shows that the city was called in Sanskrit *Kolamba*. May not the real etymology be Sansk. *Kolam*, 'Black Pepper'?" Dr Caldwell makes a few remarks on this suggestion, one to the effect: "I fancy *Kôla*, a name for pepper in Sanskrit, may be derived from the name of the country *Kôlam*, North Malabar, which is much more celebrated for its pepper than the country about Quilon. This *Kôlam*, though resembling *Kollam*, is really a separate word, and never confounded with the latter by the natives." *M. Polo*, *l. c.*]

sea." Then my comrade and I made prayers to God Himself, but seeing that still there was no wind to be had we began to promise ever so many masses in honour of the blessed Virgin if we could but have a wind; but even so we could not obtain any wind at all. So then I took one of those bones and gave it to our servant, and told him to go to the bow of the ship with haste and cast it into the sea. Then when the bone was so cast into the sea straightway a most favourable wind arose which never failed until it brought us into harbour; and thus we got thither safely through the merits of those friars[1].

15. The same continued.

And when we were there in harbour at Polumbum we embarked on board another ship called a junk, and went as has already been said to Upper India, to a certain city called Zaiton, in which our friars have two houses, in order there to deposit those sacred reliques. Now on board that ship there were good seven hundred souls, what with sailors and with merchants. And the idolaters have this custom, that before they enter port they make search throughout the whole vessel to ascertain what is on board; and if any

[1] Centuries later we find a man of considerable intelligence, Father Ripa, relating how, on his voyage to China, he went through just such a process as this with a "holy Candle," whatever that may be, and he believed that the ship was saved thereby. Years afterwards also, on his return to Europe, he repeats this operation with an Agnus Dei, and with similar success. (*Mem. of F. Ripa*, pp. 31, 139.)

Wadding relates additional wonders as wrought by the reliques of those friars, which are interesting for other reasons than the value of the alleged miracles. One story tells how Giovannino, son of Ugolino of Pisa, a merchant, having been lucky enough to appropriate the head of one of the martyrs, saved his ship when attacked by pirates, by holding out this head as a buckler, whilst his two consorts were captured. Friar Jordanus also cured the young Genoese, who had helped him to bury the bodies, of a bad dysentery, by help of a tooth of Thomas of Tolentino. He deposited a part of the relics in the house of his order at Sultaniah, and these gave rise to further marvels. But let it be noted that neither these stories nor the miracles alleged to have attended the slaughter of the friars rest on anything that has come down to us from Jordanus himself.

dead men's bones should be found they would straightway cast them into the sea, for they say that to have such things on board involves great peril of death[1]. Though they did accordingly make this diligent search, and though the bones were there in a great quantity, yet they never did get any inkling of them. And so by God's permission we brought them safely to the house of our brethren, and there they were worthily deposited with honour and great worship. And by means of these sainted friars doth Almighty God still work many other wonders; and this is held true by both Pagans and Saracens. For when they are caught by any disease, they go and take of the earth of the place where the friars were slain, and wash it in water, and then drink the water, and so are immediately freed from all their ailments[2].

16. Fr. Odoric is done with the four friars; and now he telleth of the kingdom of Minibar and how pepper is got.

And now that ye may know how pepper is got, let me tell you that it groweth in a certain empire whereunto I came to land, the name whereof is MINIBAR[3], and it groweth

[1] This no doubt refers to the strict examination of papers and cargo on arrival of a ship in China, respecting which Ibn Batuta gives details after his manner; see his Voyage to China, *infra*.

[2] We are told that the Christians of Malabar used to prepare their holy water by mixing some particles of earth from the tomb of the apostle Thomas. See also the healing power ascribed by M. Polo to earth from that shrine. [" The use of the earth from the tomb of St Thomas for miraculous cures is mentioned also by John Marignolli, who was there about 1348–1349. Assemani gives a special formula of the Nestorians for use in the application of this dust, which was administered to the sick in place of the unction of the Catholics. The Abyssinians make a similar use of the earth, from the tomb of their national Saint Tekla Haimanot. And the Shfahs, on solemn occasions partake of water in which has been mingled the dust of Kerbela. Fa-hian tells that the people of Magadha did the like, for the cure of headache, with earth from the place were lay the body of Kasyapa, a former Buddha."] (*Padre Paolino di S. Bart.*, p. 136; M. Polo, ii, pp. 354, 356 *n.*)

[3] [" Poi veni per lo mare Oceano quaranta giornate, e pervenni a lo' mperio di Pirabar dove nasce il pepe."—PAL.]

Minibar is Malabar, and seems to have been an old Arabic form

nowhere else in the world but there. And the forest in which the pepper groweth extendeth for a good eighteen days' journey, and in that forest there be two cities, the one whereof is called FLANDRINA and the other CYNGILIN[1].

of that name. It is the same that we shall find in Marignolli. Edrisi has *al-Manîbâr*, so has Abulfeda; and a Turkish work translated by Von Hammer for the *Bengal Journal*, has *Monebâr*. Ibn Batuta and Kazwini write *al-Malîbâr*, Bakui has *Malibar*, and Fra Mauro *Milibar*. (*Jaubert's Edrisi*, i, 175; *Abulfeda* in *Reinaud* and *Gildemeister*, p. 188, comparing p. 45 of the Arabic; *Notices et Extraits*, ii, 389; *Journal A. S. Beng.* v, pp. 458, 461; and see *D'Herbelot* in v. *Manibar*.) [Marco Polo says, ii, p. 589: "There is in this kingdom a great quantity of pepper, and ginger, and cinnamon, and turbit, and of nuts of India." Heyd, *Commerce du Levant*, ii, pp. 659–660, writes that it was well known in former times that Malabar was the very country of pepper; he quotes the *Periplus* of Arrian, and Cosmas; he adds that the ancient Arabs did not ignore where the pepper they received through Sirâf or Aden came from; early, among them, the name of Malabar was synonymous of country of pepper.]

[1] [RAM. A, Alandrina.—PAL., Filandria.—FRENCH TEXT, Flanderne, Frandrine.—RAM. A, Ziniglin.—PAL., Sigli.—FR. TEXT, Singulir, Singulum.] *Flandrina*, as has been pointed out in a note on Jordanus (p. 40), is doubtless the Fandaraina of Ibn Batuta, and the Pandarani of the Ramusian geographer. It is found as Fandaraina (also miswritten Kandaraina) in Edrisi, and is probably the Bandinánah (for Bandiránah) of Abdarrazzak. It has vanished from the maps, but stood about sixteen miles north of Calicut [it is Pandarani or Pantaláni]. *Cyngilin* is a greater difficulty. It is, however, evidently identical with the *Cynkali* of Marignolli, with the *Singugli* of Jordanus (p. 40), which that author mentions as a kingdom between Calicut and Quilon, with *Jangli* (which I doubt not should be read *Chinkali*) of Rashiduddin, and perhaps with the Gingala of Benjamin of Tudela. And it is unquestionably the *Shinkala* or *Shinkali* of Abulfeda (see *Gildemeister*, p. 185, and Arab. text, p. 41), which he couples with Shâliyat, as two cities of Malabar, *one of which was inhabited by Jews*, though his informant knew not which. Shâliyat, also mentioned under that name by Ibn Batuta, and called by the European navigators Chalia and Chale, was the port next below Calicut, and the next to that again, of any importance, was *Cranganor*. Now Assemani tells us incidentally (p. 440—see also p. 732): "SCIGLA (*i.e.* Shigla or Shikala = Shinkala of Abulfeda) *alias et* Chrongalor *vocatur ea quam* Cranganoriam *dicimus Malabariæ urbem, ut testatur idem Jacobus Indiarum episcopus, ad calcem Testamenti Novi ab ipso exarati...anno Christi* 1510," etc. Cynkali or Cyncilim or Shinkala, then, is CRANGANOR, the seat of one of the old Malabar principalities, and famous in the early traditions of both Jews and Christians on that coast. It was there that, according to the former, the black Jews of the tribe of Manasseh first settled and abode for more than one thousand years; it was there that St. Thomas is said to have first preached on the shores of India; and there also the Mahomedans were first allowed to settle and build a mosque. Barbosa, in the beginning of the sixteenth century, notices *Crangulor* as occupied by a varied population of "Gentiles,

In the city of Flandrina some of the inhabitants are Jews[1]

Moors, Indians (?), Jews, and Christians of St. Thomas." (*J. R. A. Soc.*, i, 173, 174; *Sir H. M. Elliot, Historians of Muham., India*, p. 43; *Lassen*, iv, 256; *Ramusio*, i, 311.) It is true that Odoric says in the text that the Jews and Christians lived in Flandrina, but what follows shows that there is some confusion, and that he means either that Jews and Christians lived in both cities, or Jews in the one and Christians in the other. [*Cranganore = Kodungalùr = Kodungalùr Singulyi*, a town of the state of Cochin, Madras. "Tradition assigns to it the double honour of having been the first field of Saint Thomas' labours (A.D. 52 ?) in India, and the seat of Cherumán Perumál's government (A.D. 341). The visit of Saint Thomas must be regarded as mythical. But it is certain that the Syrian Church was firmly established here before the 9th century (Burnell), and probably the Jews' settlement was still earlier. The latter, in fact, claim to hold grants dated 378 A.D. The cruelty of the Portuguese, and their Goa Inquisition, drove most of the Jews to Cochin. Up to 1314, when the Vypín harbour was formed, the only opening in the backwater, and outlet for the Periyár, was at Kodungalúr, which must at that time have been the best harbour on the coast. Dr Day says: The Cranganore (Kodungalúr) Division has been the scene of most momentous changes in times gone by. Here the Jew and the Christian obtained a footing, and founded towns before the Portuguese landed in India." (Hunter's *Imp. Gaz. of India*, 2d ed., viii, pp. 240–1.)—Heyd, ii, p. 661, would prefer "Kayam-Koulam" to *Cranganore* for *Singulir*.]

To these notices of Cyncilim, I may add that the Chinese annals also mention *Sengkili*, as one of the Western Kingdoms which sent tribute (*i.e.* envoys and presents) to Kúblái; and as it is coupled with other countries which may be identified with Ma'bar and Somnath, it is highly probable that Shinkali or Cranganor is intended (see the passage quoted in the preliminary essay to this volume). [Marco Polo, speaking of the Kingdom of Melibar, says, ii, p. 390: "Ships come hither from many quarters, but especially from the great province of Manzi. Coarse spices are exported hence both to Manzy and to the west...." Yule adds the following remarks, *M. Polo*, ii, p. 391 *n.*: "I have been unable to find anything definite as to the date of the cessation of this Chinese navigation to Malabar, but I believe it may be placed about the beginning of the 15th century. The most distinct allusion to it that I am aware of is in the information of Joseph of Cranganore, in the *Novus Orbis* (ed. of 1555, p. 208)." Yule quotes also an account of the Voyages of Da Gama by Gasper Correa and goes on saying: "It is probable that both these stories must be referred to those extensive expeditions to the western countries with the object of restoring Chinese influence which were despatched by the Ming Emperor Ch'êng Tsu (or Yung-lo), about 1406, and one of which seems actually to have brought *Ceylon* under a partial subjection to China, which endured half a century."]

[1] The Jews of Malabar were and are distinguished into black and white. The former are much more assimilated to the Hindu natives, and are regarded as inferiors by the latter. Thirty years ago, the white Jews were reduced to about two hundred, living in Mattancheri, a suburb of Cochin, in which the black Jews also had a separate synagogue. The great body of the black Jews inhabited towns in the interior, and had many other synagogues. The tradition of these

and some are Christians[1]; and between those two cities

latter was that they were part of the tribe of Manasseh carried captive by Nebuchadnezzar, who emigrated at a later period to Cranganore. The white Jews believe themselves to have come soon after the destruction of Jerusalem. ["In A.D. 68 a number of Jews, fleeing from Roman persecution, seem to have taken refuge amongst the friendly coast-people of South India, and to have settled in Malabar." (*Imp. Gaz. India*, New ed., ii, 1909, p. 326.)] A grant in favour of the Jews, by a native king in Malabar, is said to date from A.D. 231. Firishta testifies to their presence when the first Mahomedans settled on the coast.

Padre Paolino, towards the end of last century, estimated the Jews of Mattancheri, Mutlam, and Kayan Kulam at between 15,000 and 20,000. (*J. R. A. Soc.*, i, 173, and vi, p. 6; P. Paolino di S. Bartolomeo, *Viaggi*, p. 109; Briggs's *Firishta*, iv, 532, quoted by *Ritter*.)

["In 1807," says Walter Hamilton, *East-India Gazetteer*, 2d ed., 1828, i, p. 425, "the population of Jews in Cochin and its vicinity was as follows:—White Jews 223; black Jews 720; at places in the country 586; total 1529 persons." The Census taken on the 17th February 1881 gives a total of 1249 Jews.—Cf. on the Cochin Jews, *Revue du Monde musulman*, Mai 1909, pp. 39-44.—With regard to the Copper charter see the *Madras Journal*, xiii, pt ii, p. 12 and Burnell in *Ind. Antiq.*, iii, p. 315. Yule quotes the following passage (*Hobson-Jobson*): 'c. 774 A.D.'—We have given as eternal possession to Iravi Corttan, the lord of the town, the brokerage and due customs...namely within the river-mouth of Codangalur? Also: 'c. 1570.'—...prior to the introduction of Islamism into this country, a party of Jews and Christians had found their way to a city of Malabar called Cadungaloor." (*Tohfat-ul-Mujahideen*, 47.)]

[1] Some slight account of the present state of the Malabar Christians will be found in a work lately published by the Rev. G. B. Howard, formerly a chaplain in those parts. It is some satisfaction to learn from this book that the Christians have not greatly diminished in number since the beginning of the sixteenth century, when the Nestorian Bishop Jaballaha reported them as consisting of 30,000 families —say 150,000 souls. For Mr Howard states the last estimate of the Syrian Christians in Travancore and Cochin to be 116,483; whilst those of the Syro-Roman Church, who ought, perhaps, to be taken into account, are reckoned at 117,000 more. It is also pleasant to learn that the Syrian Christians are still held in respect by their heathen neighbours, and still retain that character "as a sensible honest people, remarkable for modesty and truth," to which a long chain of witnesses has borne testimony. One of these is the Carmelite P. Vincenzo Maria, who was sent from Rome in the middle of the seventeenth century to bring dissidents into the Roman pen; and his evidence is distinct as to their sobriety, courage, and superiority to the ordinary "Gentiles" in disposition, intellect, and manners. At the same time, he vividly depicts their Asiatic traits, their flattery, fluent talk, ceremonies, politeness, and prolixity.

These things are pleasant to hear of, but almost everything else in their history for three hundred and fifty years is painful. The contact of Eastern and Western, even when there are none of the more selfish interests in collision, oftener breeds evil than good. The relations of

there is always internal war, but the result is always that the Christians beat and overcome the Jews.

Now, in this country they get the pepper in this manner. First, then, it groweth on plants which have leaves like ivy, and these are planted against tall trees as our vines are here, and bear fruit just like bunches of grapes; and this fruit is borne in such quantities that they seem like to break under it. And when the fruit is ripe it is of a green colour, and 'tis gathered just as grapes are gathered at the vintage, and then put in the sun to dry. And when it is dried it is stored in jars[1] [and of the fresh pepper also they make a confection, of which I had to eat, and plenty of it[2]]. And in this forest also there be rivers in which be many evil crocodiles, *i.e.* serpents. [And there be many other kinds of serpents in the forest, which the men burn by kindling tow and straw, and so they are enabled to go safely to gather pepper[3].] [And here there be lions in great numbers, and a variety of beasts which are not found in our Frank countries. And here they burn the brazil-wood for fuel, and in the woods are numbers of wild peacocks[4].]

At the extremity of that forest, towards the south, there

the English Church with the Syrian, initiated with the best feelings on one side, and welcomed on the other, have ended only in disappointment and mutual offence. And as regards Her of Rome, scarcely anything in all her history is more odious than her conduct to the churches of Malabar. Did ever discovery seem more calculated to draw out brotherly kindness than when the Portuguese, emerging from their dim and venturous navigation, lighted on this isolated Christian flock? And the result to that flock was persecution, strife, and misery, from which they have never recovered. (*The Christians of St Thomas and their Liturgies, by the Rev. G. B. Howard, etc.*, 1864; *Assemani*, p. 450; *P. Vincenzo Maria*, pp. 139, 143, and seq.)

[1] [FR. TEXT: "Ilz les mettent en sauf."]

[2] [PAL.: "E del pepe ricente fanno composto e io ne mangiai, ed ebbine assai."]

[3] From PAL.

[4] From HAK. and MUS. Marignolli has a mild sneer directed probably at Odoric's talk about the pepper "forest"; apparently the latter did not stay any time in Malabar, and he probably derived his information from harbour gossip.

is a certain city which is called Polumbum, in which is grown better ginger than anywhere else in the world[1]. And the variety and abundance of wares for sale in that city is so great that it would seem past belief to many folk.

17. Fr. Odoric discourseth of the manners of the idolaters of Polumbum.

[Here all the people go naked, only they wear a cloth just enough to cover their nakedness, which they tie behind[2].] All the people of this country worship the ox for their god [and they eat not his flesh[3]]; for they say that he is, as it were, a sacred creature. Six years they make him to work for them, and the seventh year they give him rest from all labour, and turn him out in some appointed public place, declaring him thenceforward to be a consecrated animal[4]. And they observe the following abominable

[1] Ginger is classed by Pegolotti as "*Belledi*, which is found in many places in India [Ar. *Balladi* or country *ginger*], *Colombino, and Mecchino*," the two last from the countries producing them; *viz.*, Colombo of India, *i.e.* our Columbum or Kulam, and the territories of Mecca. [A century later, in G. da Uzzano, we still find the *Colombino* and *Belladi* ginger.—Yule, *M. Polo*, ii, p. 381 *n.* "Good ginger also grows here [Coilum], and it is known by the same name of *Coilumin* after the country." *Marco Polo*, ii, p. 375.]

Pegolotti speaks of a kind of Brazil wood (*Verzino*) which was called *Colomni* or *Colombino*, no doubt from the same place; and of cinnamon also with the same epithet. (*Della decima*, iii, pp. 210, 296, 308, 359–360, &c.) [From *Marco Polo*, ii, p. 375: "A great deal of brazil is got here [Coilum] which is called *brazil Coilumin* from the country which produces it; 'tis of very fine quality." The brazil-wood of Kaulam appears in the Commercial Handbook of Pegolotti (*circa* 1340) as *Verzino Colombino*, and under the same name in that of Giov. d' Uzzano a century later. Pegolotti in one passage details kinds of brazil under the names of *Verzino salvatico*, *dimestico*, and *columbino*. In another passage, where he enters into particulars as to the respective values of different qualities, he names three kinds, as *Colomni*, *Ameri*, and *Seni*, of which the *Colomni* (or Colombino) was worth a sixth more than the *Ameri* and three times as much as the *Seni*.—Yule, *M. Polo*, ii, p. 380 *n.*]

[2] [PAL.: "Quivi vanno tutti ignudi, salvo che portano un panno innanzi a la vergogna istremo (?) e legalosi di dietro."]

[3] From PAL.

[4] This fuller explanation is from MUS. The copies which I am generally following (PAR. and VEN.) have simply *positus est in communi*. The custom of setting free bulls to roam at large, as offerings

superstition. Every morning they take two basins of gold or silver, and when the ox is brought from the stall they put these under him and catch his urine in one and his dung in the other. With the former they wash their faces, and with the latter they daub themselves, first on the middle of the forehead; secondly, on the balls of both cheeks; and, lastly, in the middle of the chest. And when they have thus anointed themselves in four places they consider themselves to be sanctified (for the day). Thus do the common people; and thus do the king and queen likewise.

They worship also another idol, which is half man and half ox. And this idol giveth responses out of its mouth, and ofttimes demandeth the blood of forty virgins to be given to it. For men and women there vow their sons and their daughters to that idol, just as here they vow to place them in some religious order. And in this manner many perish.

And many other things are done by that people which it would be abomination even to write or to hear of, and many other things be there produced and grown, which it booteth little to relate[1]. But the idolaters of this realm

I believe to Siva, is here alluded to. They are known among Anglo-Indians as "Brahmini bulls," and, having the run of the bazars, are always fat. In Calcutta, where they were a dangerous nuisance, they used to be laid hold of by the police and yoked in the dust cart.

What follows about cow-worship is little, if at all, exaggerated, as may be seen by reference to Abbé Dubois (pp. 29, etc.).

[1] PAL. has: "*And in this land there be trees that produce honey, and 'tis as good as is in the world. And there be others that give wine, and others that give wool wherewith cords and cables of all kinds are made. And there be also trees which produce fruits so big that two will be a load for a strong man. And when they come to be eaten* conviene che altri s' unga le mani e la bocca, (?) *and they are of a fragrant odour and very savoury; the fruit is called* chabassi." [The wool-bearing tree in this doubtful passage is a reference to the coir or coco-nut fibre, I think, rather than to cotton. The large fruit, fragrant and savoury, is the jack, I doubt not, but the name *chabassi* is probably corrupted.] "*And here I heard tell that there be trees which bear men and women like fruit upon them. They are about a cubit in measurement, and are fixed in the tree up to the navel, and there they be; and when the wind blows they be fresh, but when it does not blow they are*

have one detestable custom (that I must mention). For when any man dies, they burn him, and if he leave a wife they burn her alive with him, saying that she ought to go and keep her husband company in the other world. But if the woman have sons by her husband she may abide with them, an she will. And, on the other hand, if the wife die there is no law to impose the like on him; but he, if he likes, can take another wife[1]. It is also customary there

all dried up. This I saw not in sooth, but I heard it told by people who had seen it." Here again we have a genuine Oriental story, related by several Arab geographers of the island of *Wak-wak* in the Southern Ocean (*e.g.* see Bakui in *Not. et Ext.*, ii, 399). Al Biruni denies that the island is called so, "as is vulgarly believed, because of a fruit having the form of a human head which cries *Wak! Wak!*" (*Journ. Asiat.* S. iv, t. iv, p. 266). And Edrisi declines to repeat the "incredible story" related by Masudi on the subject, with the pious reservation, "But all things are in the power of the Most High" (i, 92). [Cf. *Madagascar et les îles Uâq-Uâq* par M. Gabriel Ferrand (*Journ. Asiat.*, Mai–Juin 1904, pp. 489–509).—Ed. Chavannes (*T'oung Pao*, 1904, pp. 484–7.—G. Ferrand.—*L'arbre merveilleux.* (*J. Asiat.*, Nov.–Déc. 1907, pp. 483–494.)—The text of PAL. runs as follows: "In questa terra sono albori che conducono [producono?] mele, ed è del buono del mondo. Sonvi altri albori che producono vino ed albori che producono lana di che si fa tutto corde e funi, e sonvi albori che producono frutti che di due sarebe carico un forte uomo, e quando si vengono a manicare conviene che altri s' unga le mani e la boca, e sono odorifili e molti saporiti e chiamansi frutto *chabassi*. Quivi udi dire che sono albori che producono uomini e femmine a modo di frutti, e sono di grandezza un gomito, e sono fitti nell' albore insino al bellico, e cosi istanno; e quando trae vento e sono freschi, e quando non, pare che si seccano. Questo non vidi io, ma udilo dire a persone che l' aveano veduto."—This fruit is the jack or *kadhil Artocarpus integrifolia*. We read in Baber's *Memoirs* by Leyden and Erskine, 325: "Another is the *kadhil*. This has a very bad look and flavour (odour?). It looks like a sheep's stomach stuffed and made into a haggis. It has a sweet sickly taste. Within it are stones like a filbert....The fruit is very adhesive, and on account of this adhesive quality many rub their mouths with oil before eating them. They grow not only from the branches and trunk, but from its root. You would say that the tree was all hung round with haggises." Yule remarks (*Hobson-Jobson*): "Here *kadhil* represents the Hind. name *kaṭhal*. The practice of oiling the lips on account of the 'adhesive quality' (or as modern mortals would call it 'stickiness') of the jack, is still usual among natives, and it is the cause of a proverb on premature precautions: *Gāch'h meṅ Kaṭhal, honṭh meṅ tel!* 'You have oiled your lips whilst the jack still hangs on the tree'!"]

[1] Mr Elphinstone says: "The practice of Suttee is by no means universal in India. It never occurs to the south of the River Kishna." But this absolute statement certainly conveys an erroneous impression. Marco Polo states the practice of Southern India just as Odoric does,

for the women to drink wine and not the men. The women also have their foreheads shaven, whilst the men shave not the beard[1]. And there be many other marvellous and beastly customs which 'tis just as well not to write.

whilst in 1580, Gasparo Balbi, an accurate and unimaginative traveller, describes with seeming truth a suttee which he witnessed at Negapatam, and speaks of the custom as common. In the middle of the seventeenth century, P. Vincenzo, the Procurator-General of the Carmelites, says it was especially common in Canara; whilst he was told that on the death of the Naik of Madura 11,000 women had offered themselves to the flames! These 11,000 suttees may have been as mythical as the 11,000 virgins of Cologne, but they prove the practice. And in the beginning of the last century it continued to be extremely prevalent in that region. P. Martin, in a letter from Marawar (or Ramnad, opposite Ceylon), dated in 1713, mentions three cases then recent, in which respectively forty-five, seventeen, and twelve women had performed suttee on the death of the husbands, princes of that state. The widow of the Raja of Trichinopoly, being left pregnant, burnt herself after delivery. (Elphinstone's *H. of India*, p. 190; *M. Polo*, iii, 20; *Viaggio di Gasparo Balbi*, f. 83; *P. Vincenzo*, p. 322; *Lettres Édifiantes*, ed. Lyon, 1819, vii, 73, 75.) Suttees still occur in spite of our prohibition, and not very unfrequently, both in our own territory and in the native states. [" Suttee is a Brahmanical rite, and there is a Sanskrit ritual in existence (see *Classified Index to the Tanjore MSS.*, p. 135 *a*). It was introduced into Southern India with the Brahman civilisation, and was prevalent there chiefly in the strictly Brahmanical Kingdom of Vijayanagar, and among the Mahrattas. In Malabar, the most primitive part of S. India, the rite is forbidden (*Anāchāranirṇaya*, v, 26). The cases mentioned by Teixeira, and in the *Lettres Édifiantes*, occurred at Tanjore and Madura. A (Mahratta) Brahman at Tanjore told one of the present writers that he had to perform commemorative funeral rites for his grandfather and grandmother on the same day, and this indicated that his grandmother had been a sati." Yule, *Hobson-Jobson*.]

Ramusio quotes Propertius on suttee. I borrow a few lines, showing how familiar this still-enduring Indian practice was to the Romans nineteen hundred years ago:—

——— Uxorum fusis stat pia turba comis;
Et certamen habet lædi, quæ viva sequatur
Conjugium; pudor est non licuisse mori.
Ardent victrices, et flammæ pectora præbent,
Imponuntque suis ora perusta viris.

[1] This reasonable reading is from Venni's originals only. I have overlooked it in the Appendix, where the strange readings of other copies will be seen. ["Mulieres etiam faciunt sibi abradi frontem et barbam homines non." VEN., p. 57.]

18. Concerning the kingdom of Mobar, where lieth the body of St. Thomas.

From this realm 'tis a journey of ten days to another realm which is called MOBAR[1], and this is very great, and hath under it many cities and towns. And in this realm is laid the body of the Blessed Thomas the Apostle[2]. His church

[1] The Coromandel region; see note to Jordanus, p. 19. It is possible that the Arabic name (*Ma'abar*, *Ma'băr*, the passage or ferry) was, as some one has suggested, originally a corruption of Marawar, the name of the Hindu state which adjoined Adam's Bridge, and the chief of which state was called *Setu Pati*, "the lord of the bridge." Such corruptions are often twisted for the sake of an apparent etymology among Orientals, and also among Occidentals. Thus in India the English word *receipt* is converted into *Rasíd*, and understood by many as deriving its meaning from the Pers. *Rasídan*, to arrive. *Jerusalem* artichokes afford a Western instance.

Marawar, or Marava, on the other hand, is perhaps also the Marulló of Cosmas Indicopleustes, which was on the continent adjoining Ceylon and produced conch-shells. I know not if the obvious suggestion has been put forward that the pearl fisheries in this vicinity originated the Pers. *Marwárid*, from which we get *Margarita*.

Ritter puts Ma'abar on the west coast, and Lassen (iv, 888) says that the name with Ibn Batuta signifies the southernmost part of the Malabar coast, but both learned authors are certainly wrong. Kunstmann again says: "it has been recently pointed out that the name applies neither specially to the south-west coast nor to the south-east, but to the whole southern apex of the peninsula." I do not know what evidence can be alleged. All use of it that I have seen is clear for its being the south-east coast, as Abulfeda precisely says, commencing from Cape Comorin. [Maabar extended from Cape Comorin to Nellore.] (See *Gildemeister*, pp. 56 and 185.) [The name does not appear in Edrisi, nor, I believe, in any of the older geographers, and the earliest use of it that I am aware of is in Abdallatif's account of Egypt, a work written about 1203–1204. (De Sacy, *Relat. de l'Égypte*, p. 31). Yule, *M. Polo*, ii, pp. 332–3.] ["When you leave the Island of Seilan and sail westward about 60 miles, you come to the great province of MAABAR which is styled INDIA THE GREATER; it is best of all the Indies and is on the mainland." *M. Polo*, ii, p. 331.]

[2] [As vague as Polo's is Odoric's indication of the position of the Shrine of St Thomas. Yule says Polo's "is the first geographical indication of it that I know of, save one. At the very time of Polo's homeward voyage, John of Monte Corvino on his way to China spent thirteen months in Maabar, and in a letter thence in 1292–1293 he speaks of the Church of St Thomas there, having buried in it the companion of his travels, Friar Nicholas of Pistoia."

There are two St Thomas's Mounts, the Great or Mount St Thomas where the Apostle expired, and a stone slab with a Pehlevi inscription and a cross were discovered in 1547 about six miles from Mailapúr, and the Little Mount where the Apostle was attacked and wounded two miles from San Tomé. "The Portuguese ignored the ancient translation of the Saint's remains to Edessa, and in 1522, under the

is filled with idols, and beside it are some fifteen houses of the Nestorians, that is to say Christians, but vile and pestilent heretics. There is likewise in this kingdom a certain wonderful idol, which all the provinces of India greatly revere. It is as big as St. Christopher[1] is commonly represented by the painters, and it is entirely of gold, seated on a great throne, which is also of gold. And round its neck

Viceroyalty of Duarte Menezes, a commission was sent to Mailapúr, or San Tomé as they called it, to search for the body. The narrative states circumstantially that the Apostle's bones were found, besides those of the king whom he had converted, etc. The supposed relics were transferred to Goa, where they are still preserved in the Church of St. Thomas in that city." (Yule, *M. Polo*, ii, p. 358.) "The traditional site of the Apostle's Tomb, now adjacent to the sea shore, has recently come to be enclosed in the crypt of the new Cathedral of San Thomé." (Medlycott, p. 123.) With reference to the passage of Odoric: "His church is filled with idols," M. Barth (*Revue Critique*, 13th March, 1893, pp. 200–1), says it was really a Hindu Temple, and seems to refer to the Mailapúr sanctuary, where, from a long time, stood the temple of Mayilâ devî which, to this date, is near the Christian Cathedral; M. Barth also points out that the place where tradition located the death and the tomb of the Apostle was occupied by the Unfaithful, a fact which could not have been possible on the other coast, where the Christians were more powerful and better organized in Malabar. It must not be forgotten that for about a dozen years this Coromandel Coast was under the rule of the Emperor of Delhi. We speak of St. Thomas in the *Recollections of John de' Marignolli*, in the third volume of this edition of *Cathay*. See *Notes d'épigraphie indienne* par M. E. Senart. (*Journ. Asiat.*, Fév.–Mars 1890, pp. 125–129).—*Saint Thomas, Gondopharès et Mazdeo* par M. Sylvain Lévi. (*Ibid.*, Janv.–Fév. 1897, pp. 27–42).—Marquart, *Die Chronologie des alttürkischen Inschriften.* Leipzig, 1898, and *D. Z. M. G.*, xlix, 642.—*The Connection of St. Thomas the Apostle with India*, by W. R. Philipps. (*Indian Antiq.*, 1903, Jan., pp. 1–15; April, pp. 145–160.) Mr. Philipps comes to the conclusion: "There is no evidence at all that the place where St. Thomas was martyred was in Southern India; and all the indications point in another direction."—"We have no indication whatever, earlier than that given by Marco Polo, who died 1324, that there ever was even a tradition that St. Thomas was buried in Southern India." (April, p. 151.)—A. E. Medlycott, Bishop of Tricomia, *India and the Apostle Thomas, An inquiry. With a critical analysis of the Acta Thomae.* London, David Nutt, 1905, 8vo.]

[1] [It is very natural that the image of Saint Christopher be present to the mind of Odoric, as this giant, universally honoured during the Middle Ages, was particularly so at Padua: the church *degli Eremitani*, of which the choir began to be rebuilt in 1264, was in the hands of the architects at the beginning of the xivth century (1306) and later on it was in this very church that Mantegna, Buono da Forli and Ansuino da Forli, were to paint the lives of Saint James and of Saint Christopher.]

it hath a collar of gems of immense value[1]. And the church of this idol is also of pure gold, roof (and walls) and pavement[2]. People come to say their prayers to the idol from great distances, just as Christian folk go from far on pilgrimage to St. Peter's[3]. And the manner of those who come is thus:—Some travel with a halter round their necks; and some with their hands upon a board, which is tied to their necks; others with a knife stuck in the arm, which they never remove until they arrive before the idol, so that the arm is then all in a slough[4]. And some have quite a different way of doing. For these as they start from their houses take three steps, and at the fourth they make a prostration at full length upon the ground. And then they take a thurible and incense the whole length of that prostration. And thus they do continually until they reach the idol, so that sometimes when they go through this operation it taketh a very great while before they do reach the idol. But when those who are going along in this way wish to turn aside to do anything, they make a mark there to show how far they have gone, and so they (come back upon this, and) continue until they reach the idol[5].

[1] ["Et siet en un tabernacle d'or fin." FRENCH TEXT.]

[2] Pure gold *leaf* perhaps. From what we see in Burma, where many obsolete Indian practices have been preserved by Buddhism, we may judge that extensive gilding of sacred buildings was formerly much more common than it is now. An Indian example is still familiar in the Sikh sanctuary at Amritsar. There were, however, temples of enormous wealth in this part of India. A few years before, the soldiers of Ala-eddin King of Dehli had carried off a fabulous booty of gold and jewels from the temples of Dwara-Samudra and Ma'abar. (Briggs's *Firishta*, i, 373.)

[3] ["Comme cy nous Crestiens vont a Saint Jaques en Galice, ou a Saint Pierre ou a Saint Pol a Romme." FRENCH TEXT.]

[4] ["Pluseurs autres sans comparoison plus sot et qui cuident estre trop plus devot que les autres sacrefient leurs fieulz et leurs filles a ceste ydole comme a leur propre dieu souverain. Et quant ilz ont ainsi leurs enfans murdris devant celle ydole, ilz l'espersent du sang comme Crestien font les asperges d'eaue benoite, cilz de la ville et qui sont assez pres de cest temple manant." FRENCH TEXT.]

[5] The word *venia* used here is a technical term in the Roman

19. Concerning other customs of the Idolaters.

And hard by the church of this idol there is a lake, made by hand, into which the pilgrims who come thither cast gold or silver or precious stones, in honour of the idol, and towards the maintenance of the church, so that much gold and silver and many precious stones have been accumulated therein. And thus when it is desired to do any work upon the church, they make search in the lake and find all that hath been cast into it[1].

But annually on the recurrence of the day when that idol was made, the folk of the country come and take it down, and put it on a fine chariot; and then the king and queen and all the pilgrims, and the whole body of the people[2], join together and draw it forth from the church with loud singing of songs and all kinds of music; and

church for a prostration in worship, but being unfamiliar it has perplexed the copyists. It is, however, clearly explained by the parallel passage in PAL., "*si stende in terra boccone.*" The performance described is a well-known penance both of Hindus and Tibetan Buddhists. The newspapers lately contained a striking notice of penances of this kind in the Deccan. Omitting the incense the account is almost Odoric's. One man had come 450 miles measuring his length continuously at the rate of about a mile a day. (*Allen's Indian Mail*, Oct. 11th, 1864, p. 782.)

[1] PAL. has: *and they call that place* Celai *in their tongue.* There is a like story in Mas'udi regarding the Maharajah of the Isles. His palace was over a tank, which communicated with the sea. Every morning the treasurer threw in a golden ingot. At the king's death the accumulation was taken out and divided among his dependents and the poor. (*Paris trans.*, 1861, i, 175.) Odoric's story is corroborated by the *Masálak-el-Absár*, which says that among the towns in the south of India conquered by Mahomed Tughlák (a few years after Odoric's visit) was one standing by a lake in the middle of which was an idol-temple which enjoyed a great reputation in that country, and into which the people used continually to cast their offerings. After the capture of the city the Sultan caused the lake to be drained and the wealth which he found accumulated in it sufficed to load two hundred elephants and several thousand oxen. (*Not. et Extraits*, xiii, 220, 221.)

[2] PAL. has: *The Emperor, and their Pope and other priests, which are called* Tuin, etc. It is curious to find this word used here. It was the name, or one of the names, which the *Mongols* applied to the Buddhist priests. (See *Rubruquis*, p. 352, and *D'Ohsson*, ii, 264.) [See Rockhill's *Rubruck*, p. 159 *n.*]

many maidens go before it by two and two chaunting in a marvellous manner. And many pilgrims who have come to this feast cast themselves under the chariot, so that its wheels may go over them, saying that they desire to die for their God. And the car passes over them, and crushes and cuts them in sunder, and so they perish on the spot. And after this fashion they drag the idol to a certain customary place, and then they drag him back to where he was formerly, with singing and playing as before. And thus not a year passes but there perish more than five hundred men in this manner; and their bodies they burn, declaring that they are holy, having thus devoted themselves to death for their God[1].

And another custom they have of this kind. One will come saying: "I desire to sacrifice myself for my God?" And then his friends and kinsfolk, and all the players of the country, assemble together to make a feast for him who is determined to die for his God. And they hang round his neck five very sharp knives, and lead him thus to the presence of the idol with loud songs. Then he takes one of those sharp knives and calls out with a loud voice: "Thus I cut my flesh for my God"; and cutting a piece of his flesh wherever he may choose, he casteth it in the face of the idol; and saying again: "I devote myself to die for my God," he endeth by slaying himself there. And straightway they take his body and burn it, for they look on him as a saint, having thus slain himself for his idol. And many other things greatly to be marvelled at are done by these people, which are by no means to be written.

But the king of this island[2] or province is passing rich

[1] One might think Odoric had got to Juggurnath. But this practice was not peculiar to Orissa. (See *Dubois*, pp. 413, 414; and *Gasp. Balbi*, f. 84, etc.) A gross instance, involving three victims, has recently been reported within a few miles of Calcutta. (See Allen's *Indian Mail* of August 15th, 1864.)

[2] This is the only time that Odoric makes a mistake of this kind. Mandeville (?) makes islands of nearly all the Eastern regions. It has

in gold and silver and precious stones. And in this island are found as great store of good pearls as in any part of the world. And so of many other things which are found in this island, which it would take too long to write.

20. Concerning the country called Lamori, where the pole star is hidden; and also of Sumoltra.

Departing from this region towards the south across the ocean sea, I came[1] in fifty days[2] to a certain country called LAMORI[3], in which I began to lose sight of the north star,

been noticed in a previous note that some of the mapmakers made Columbum an island. This probably came first from the loose use, by the Arabs, of the word *Jazírah*, which means properly an island (see note to Ibn Batuta). But it is worthy of remark that Linschoten, who could not have said it through ignorance, calls China "*la dernière isle de la navigation orientale.*" Was the word then used for *a place reached by sea*?

[1] [" Per il mar oceano ventigiorni nauigando." RAM. A.]

[2] [FARS., xv dietis.—PAL., xl giornate.]

[3] Lamori is no doubt the Lambri of Marco Polo and De Barros, the Lámúrí of Rashíduddín, and the Al-Rami, Ramin, and Ramni of Edrisi and other Arabian geographers, who extend the term to the whole island of Sumatra. Lambri is mentioned also by the Malay annalists. [It is also the *Lan-wou-li*, of the Chinese.] It appears to have lain near the north-west end of the island, and being on that account probably the first port of Sumatra known to the Arabs, naturally gave its name to the whole. I believe the exact position is not now known, but the list of kingdoms in Murray's *Polo*, pt. iii, ch. xiv, places it south of Daya.

[Mr W. P. Groeneveldt in his *Notes on the Malay Archipelago*, 1877, after quoting two Chinese works *Ying-yai Shêng-lan* (1416) and the *History of the Ming dynasty*, Book 325, writes, p. 100: "According to the two last extracts, Lambri must have been situated on the north-western corner of the island of Sumatra, on or near the spot of the present Achin: we see that it was bounded by the sea on the north and the west, and that the Indian ocean was called after this insignificant place, because it was considered to begin there. Moreover the small island at half a day's distance, called Hat-island, perfectly agrees with the small islands Bras or Nasi, lying off Achin, and of which the former, with its newly erected lighthouse, is a landmark for modern navigation, just what it is said in our text to have been for the natives then. We venture to think that the much discussed situation of Marco Polo's Lambri is definitely settled herewith."]

[Captain M. J. C. Lucardie mentions a village called Lamreh, situated at Atjeh, near Tungkup, in the xxvi. Mukim, which might be a remnant of the country of Lâmeri. (*Merveilles de L'Inde*, p. 235.)]

Pegolotti speaks of cinnamon of *Ameri*, which is perhaps intended for the same word (Lamori, L'Amori, Ameri). *Pegol.* p. 361.

as the earth intercepted it. And in that country the heat is so excessive that all the folk there, both men and women. go naked, not clothing themselves in any wise[1]. And they mocked much at me on this matter, saying that God made Adam naked, but I must needs go against His will and wear clothes. Now, in that country all the women be in common ; and no one there can say, this is my wife, or this is my husband! But when a woman beareth a boy or a girl she giveth the child to whom she listeth of those with whom she hath consorted, and calleth him the father[2].

[1] PAL. *Unless it be that some women when they be near child-bearing wear the leaf of a tree to cover their nakedness, and tie it on with a strip of bark.*

[Ibn Khordâdhbeh (trad. de Goeje, p. 44) mentions at Râmny "in the forests men who go naked and whose language is an unintelligible whistling"; Edrisi (trad. Jaubert, pp. 75–6) has the same remark. Cf. G. Ferrand, *Les îles Râmny, Lâmery, Wâkwâk, Komor des Géographes Arabes et Madagascar.* (*Journ. Asiat.*, Nov.–Déc. 1907, pp. 433 *seq.*)].

[2] [E. Westermarck, in *The History of Human Marriage*, 2d ed., 1894, writes, pp. 54–5: "The Lubus of Sumatra, the Olo Ot, together with a few other tribes of Borneo, the Poggi Islanders, the Orang Sakai of Malacca, and the mountaineers of Peling, east of Celebes, are by Professor Wilken stated to be entirely without marriage. The same is said by Professor Bastian to be the case with the Keriahs, Kurumbas, Chittagong tribes, Guaycurûs, Kutchin Indians, and Arawaks. He states, too, that the Jolah on the island of St Mary, according to Hewett, possess their women in common, and that, according to Magalhães, the like is true of the Cahyapos in Matto Grosso. We read in Dapper's old book on Africa, that certain negro tribes had neither law, nor religion, nor any proper names, and possessed their wives in common."

Skeat and Blagden, *Pagan Races of the Malay Peninsula*, ii, p. 68, quoting A. G. Campbell, say "that the women of the 'Cape Tribe' ('Orang Tanjong,' Sakai of Selangor) were allowed to have more than one husband, and that one woman who lived at Bandar Kanching formerly had four. These women (he adds) used to seek their own husbands."

They also, *l.c.*, p. 56, mention an observation from Miklucho-Maclay who "heard from Malays and members of the Catholic Mission at Malacca that communal marriage existed among the Sakai (*sic*, ? Mantra). Some days or weeks after marriage the girl was said to leave her husband with his consent and take up with the men of his family in turn. She then came back to her husband, but kept up these irregular liaisons, which were regulated by chance and her own wishes." They add that this notice from the *J. R. As. Soc., St. Br.*, No. 2, p. 215 "is the only notice of such a custom, and resting as it does on second-hand evidence or worse, cannot be accepted without due corroboration."]

The whole of the land likewise is in common; and no one can say with truth, this or that part of the land is mine. But they have houses of their own, and not in common[1].

It is an evil and a pestilent generation, and they eat man's flesh there just as we eat beef here. Yet the country in itself is excellent, and hath great store of flesh-meats, and of wheat and of rice; and they have much gold also, and lign-aloes, and camphor, and many other things which are produced there[2]. And merchants come to this island from far, bringing children with them to sell like cattle to those infidels[3], who buy them and slaughter them in the

[1] I cannot point out any region of Sumatra of which all these strange stories are true. But Odoric did not invent them, though it may be doubted if he *witnessed* all that he tells here. The community of women is positively asserted to exist among the Poggy or Pagi Islanders off the west coast of Sumatra, whilst their clothing is the merest strip of bark cloth; and *they* have not even individual houses. Such a state of things may have been found on the main island of Sumatra five hundred and fifty years ago. Very strange things *have* been found there even in our own day. (For Pagi Islanders see *Tijdschrift voor Indische Taal-Land-en-Volken Kunde*, second year, No. 4.)

["Cest pais est tout commun, si que nulz ne pu dire ceste terre ou ceste maison est mienne. Pou de choses ont ilz en especial. Ceste terre est tres bonne, car il y a tres grand plante de chars, de blés, de ris, d'or, de clous de girofle et de tous autres biens." FRENCH TEXT.

"Il sito di questa terra é molto buono, abondeuole si di carne, di biada, & di riso, come ancora d' oro, di legna, di Aloe, di canfora copioso, ma habitato da genti crudeli, & pessime." RAM. A.]

[2] ["In this country (Lambri) cows, buffaloes, goats, fowls, ducks, vegetables and rice are all scarce, but fish and shrimps are very cheap." (The Chinese work *Ying-yai Shêng-lan* (1416) quoted by Groeneveldt, *Notes*, p. 98.)]

[3] This from VEN. PAR. has *men*; HAK. *fat men*; PAL. *white men*; *for black men, like themselves, they eat not.*

["Quivi eziando mangiano le carni umani, e Saracini vi recano de l' altre provincie gli uomini e vendogli loro in mercatanzia; *e sono mangiati da coloro e sono uomini bianchi, che de' neri come sono eglino non mangiano.* E sono uomini fieri in battaglia e vanno a la battaglia ignudi, salvo que portano in braccio uno iscudo che gli quoprono insino a piedi. E se prendono alcuno nella battaglia si lo mangiano." PAL.

"Ad hanc insulam de longinquis veniunt mercatores portantes infantes, ipsosque more bestiarum vendentes hiis *infidelibus*, qui eos interficiunt in macello." VEN.]

["L'île de Ramny produit de nombreux éléphants, ainsi que le bois de brésil (*baccam*) et le bambou (*khayzoran*). On y remarque une peuplade qui mange les hommes. Cette île est mouillée par deux

shambles and eat them[1]. And so with many other things both good and bad, which I have not written.

In this same island towards the south is another kingdom by name SUMOLTRA[2], in which is a singular generation

mers, la mer de Herkend et celle de Schelaheth." (*Relat. des Voy. faits par les Arabes et les Persans*, I, pp. 6–8.)]

[1] Gold, aloeswood, and camphor, are all true products of Sumatra; so also is cannibalism, though we must expect from Odoric, in regard to such stories, no more than that he repeat them in the current form.

Here is a specimen of the modern *evidence*:—"Persons caught in housebreaking or highway robbery, are publicly executed and immediately eaten......A man taken in adultery may be eaten piecemeal without being first deprived of life......Twelve months before, twenty persons were eaten in one day, in a village where the authors resided. Prisoners taken in a great war (not a mere broil) were allowed to be eaten." (*Burton and Ward*, in *Trans. R. As. Soc.*, i, 506, 507; see also *Jour. R. As. Soc.*, ii. 49; *Crawfurd's Dict. of Indian Islands*, art. *Batak*; and *Marsden's H. of Sumatra*, 1811, p. 392.)

Here is a specimen of the modern *current stories*:—"Some years ago a Battak servant of a gentleman in Malacca, on seeing his master's child washed, made the following remark:—'In our country it would not be necessary to wash that child; he might be roasted at once.'" (*Moor's Notices of the Ind. Archip.*, p. 117.)

[2] [VEN., RAM. A, DOM., Sumoltra.—CIV., Summoltra.—B. N., Sumolchra.—HAK., Sumolcra.—BOLL., Zumptloc.—FARS., Simultam or Simultra.—ARUNDEL, Simoltra sive Sumolara.—PAL., Sumetra.] Odoric may have the credit of being the first western traveller to give the name of Sumatra so distinctly, though I have little doubt that the Samara or Samarcha of Polo means the same place, and was probably uttered by him correctly enough. The city of Samudra, the name of which has extended (no one well knows how) to the whole island, is frequently mentioned in the Malay annals, and its king became Mussulman under the name of Malik-al-Sálah about Odoric's time, or a little before. It is believed to have stood between Pasei and Pedir, near the place now called Samarlanga. I do not know whether the tattooing described by Odoric is still practised by any nation of Sumatra, but among the Pagi islanders off the west coast, it is carried to a higher degree of elaboration than perhaps anywhere in the world, and it is practised on both sexes. It is also found among the more civilised people of Nyas on the same coast.

["The King of Nakur is also called the king of the Tattoed Faces. His country is situated at the west of Sumatra and consists only of one mountain-village; his people tattoo their faces with three pointed green figures, and for this reason he is called the king of the Tattoed Faces." Groeneveldt, *Notes*, p. 96, from the *Ying-yai Shêng-lan* (1416).

"The country of the Tattoed Faces borders on Sumatra and extends as far as the sea of Lambri.......The men tattoo their faces with representations of flowers and animals; their hair hangs loose and the upper part of the body is naked, the lower part being covered with a single piece of cloth. The women wear a coloured piece of

of people; for they brand themselves on the face with a little hot iron in some twelve places[1]; and this is done by men and women both. And these folk are always at war with the others[2] who go naked. In this country there is great abundance of produce; [it is a great market for pigs and fowls and for butter and rice, and they have also the excellent fruit called *mussi*. And here also gold and tin are found in great abundance[3]].

And near this country is another realm called RESENGO, towards the south[4]. Many things are there produced whereof I do not write.

cloth and have their hair in a knot behind the head. The country is rich in cattle, goats, fowls and ducks." Groeneveldt, *Notes*, p. 97, from the *Hsing-ch'a Shêng-lan* (1436).]

[1] ["en pluseurs lieux." FRENCH TEXT.]

[2] ["à ceulz de Lamorj." FRENCH TEXT.]

[3] From PAL. This passage notices the tin, which is so prominent a product of the Malay countries. *Mussi* is, I presume, the (Ar.) *Mauz* [from Skt. *Mocha*] or plantain. [*Musa Sapientum*.]

["The fruits are plantains, sugarcane, mangoustine, nangka, etc. There is one kind called by the natives durian, 8 or 9 inches long and with sharp points on its surface; when it is ripe it divides into 5 or 6 parts and when opened smells like rotten beef; it has large kernels covered with a juicy and white pulp, fourteen or fifteen in number and very sweet and nice; when the kernels are roasted they taste like chestnuts. Citrons are abundant throughout the whole year; they are not very sour and can be kept a long time without rotting. There is a kind of mango, called by the natives *yam-pa*; it is like a pear, but a little longer and has a green skin; its smell is very strong and when eaten the skin is removed and slices of the pulp are cut off; it is sour and sweet, very nice, and the kernel has the size of a fowl's egg." Groeneveldt, *Notes*, pp. 86–87, from the *Ying-yai Shêng-lan* (1416).]

[Marco Polo who calls Sumatra *Java the Less* says (ii, p. 384): "The Island hath great abundance of treasure, with costly spices, lign-aloes and spikenard and many others that never come into our parts." The production of gold at Sumatra is a fact well-known long ago.

"This place is visited by many native ships and the trade in native articles is very important; the money used are coins of gold and tin. The golden coins are called *dinar* and contain seven-tenths of pure gold; they are round....In trading they make much use of tin money." Groeneveldt, *Notes*, p. 87, from the *Ying-yai Shêng-lan* (1416).]

[4] It seems fair to adopt the one intelligible reading of a proper name among many of which nothing can be made, especially when that one is so unlikely to be the result of accident as here. Resengo I take to be the territory of the REJANG, "one of the most civilised nations of

21. The friar speaketh of the excellent island called Java.

In the neighbourhood of that realm is a great island, JAVA by name[1], which hath a compass of a good three

Sumatra, having a peculiar language in an original written character" (*Crawfurd* in voce). The old British settlement of Bencoolen, which we held for one hundred and forty years to little profit, but which had William Dampier for its gunner, and Raffles for its governor, lay in the Rejang territory. [The passage relating to *Resengo* is not to be found in all the texts : CIV., Recemgo.—VENNI, Bothonigo, of which he made Borneo.—B. N., Rotemgo.—BOLL., Resengo.—ARUND., Boteingo.—DOM., Botenigo.

"Nel medesimo paese di Lamori verso il mezo giorno, e' vn' altro regno, chiamato Sumoltra, di molte cose copioso, nel qual sì gli huomini, come le donne, usano in circa dodeci parte della faccia con vn ferretto caldo segnarsi : & questi continuamente fanno guerra con quelli che vanno nudi. Vicino alqual v' e vn' altro Regno, chiamato Botterigo. Doue nascono molte cose, quali non scriuo." (RAM. A.)

"In hac eadem insula versus meridiem est aliud regnum nomine Sumoltra. In quo est generatio quedam singularis. Signant enim se ferro calido. Parvo bene in XII locis faciei. Et hoc tam homines quam mulieres. Hii semper gerunt cum nudis bellum. Et est hic maxima rerum copia." (VENNI.) And after: "Penes hanc patriā ē regnū nōie Botenigo ṽsus meridiem." (MUN.)]

[1] [RAM. A., Iana.—FARS., ARUND., B. N. 1380, Jana.—FRENCH TEXT, Fana.] Whatever doubts may have been raised as to the Java Major of Polo, this of Odoric is the true Java. The circuit, indeed, of three thousand miles is vastly exaggerated; it is the same which Polo and Conti ascribe to their Java Major, and was no doubt the traditional assertion of the Arab sailors, who never visited the south of the island, and probably had extravagant notions of its extension in that direction, as we know that later voyagers had.

[With reference to the name *Java*, Yule remarks (*Hobson-Jobson*) "that the terms *Jāwa*, *Jāwi* were applied by the Arabs to the Archipelago generally, and often with specific reference to Sumatra. Prof. Kern, in a paper to which we are largely indebted, has indicated that this larger application of the term was originally Indian. He has discussed it in connection with the terms 'Golden and Silver Islands' (*Suvarṇa dvīpa* and *Rūpya dvīpa*), which occurs in the quotation from the *Rāmāyana*, and elsewhere in Sanskrit literature, and which evidently were the basis of the Chrysē and Argyrē, which take various forms in the writings of the Greek and Roman geographers. We cannot give the details of his discussion, but his condensed conclusions are as follows :—(1) *Suvarṇa-dvīpa* and *Yava-dvīpa* were according to the prevalent representations the same; (2) two names of islands originally distinct were confounded with one another; (3) *Suvarṇa-dvīpa* in its proper meaning is Sumatra, *Yava-dvīpa* in its proper meaning is Java; (4) Sumatra, or a part of it, and Java were regarded as one whole, doubtless because they were politically united; (5) By *Yava-koṭi* was indicated the east point of Java."]

Though Odoric's statements are vague and superficial, and the history of Java is excessively perplexed at this period, there are some

thousand miles. And the king of it hath subject to himself seven crowned kings. Now this island is populous

positive landmarks to be discerned, by which, in a degree, our traveller's narrative is verified.

A powerful dynasty about this time existed in Java, and in an inscription of ascertained date (A.D. 1294) the king Uttungadewa claims to have subjected *five kings*, and to be sovereign of the whole island (Jawa-dwipa). Nearly to the same date attaches the history of two unsuccessful expeditions dispatched by Kúbláí Khan to Java, one to claim homage and tribute, in which his envoy was handled much as king David's envoys were treated by the children of Ammon, and a second to avenge this insult, but which ended, after various events, in the expulsion of the Mongol force with loss and ignominy.

It must, I fear, be quite uncertain where the royal residence was, which Odoric describes in such glowing terms; for though Majapahit, in the eastern part of the island, was the seat of the most powerful sovereigns from a date believed to be somewhat later than our traveller's time till the establishment of Mahomedanism one hundred and fifty years afterwards, the king abovenamed appears to have had his abode near Pajajaran in the West.

[Marco Polo, ii, p. 272, says: "And I can assure you the Great Kaan never could get possession of this Island, on account of its great distance and the great expense of an expedition thither." This was not true a short time after, for Kúbláí having sent an ambassador, the Chinese Mêng K'i, to claim the homage of the Javanese sovereign, the man was sent back with his face branded like a thief's. From the Chinese works translated by Groeneveldt, *Notes*, we have full information on this fact. We read in the *Yuan-shi* (Bk. 210), that "Java is situated beyond the sea and further away than Champa; when one embarks at Ts'wan-chau and goes southward, he first comes to Champa and afterwards to this country." It appears that when his envoy Mêng-K'i had been branded on the face, Kúbláí, in 1292, appointed Shih-pi a native of Po-yeh, district Li-chau, Pao-ting fu, Chih-li province, Commander of the expedition to Java, whilst Ike-Mese, a Uighúr, and Kan-Hsing, a man from Ts'ai-chau (Ho-nan) were appointed to assist him. Mr Groeneveldt has translated the accounts of these three officers. In the *Ming-shi* (Bk. 324) we read: "Java is situated at the south-west of Champa. In the time of the Emperor Kúbláí of the Yuan Dynasty, Mêng-K'i was sent there as an envoy and had his face cut, on which Kúbláí sent a large army which subdued the country and then came back." (*L. c.*, p. 34.) The prince guilty of this insult was the King of Tumapel "in the eastern part of the island Java, whose country was called Java par excellence by the Chinese, because it was in this part of the island they chiefly traded." (*L. c.*, p. 32.)—Cf. Pelliot, *Bull. École Ext. Orient*, iv, 1904, p. 320, on the relations between China and Java.]

There is nothing improbable in Odoric's description of the palace, if we remember that gold leaf glitters as much as gold plate. The vivid imagination of these old travellers would have seen almost similar golden glories in the palaces and monasteries of Amarapura as they have existed in our own day; and the walls and corridors sculptured in relief with court-scenes and battle-scenes, are precisely what we do find, on a vastly extensive scale, in the galleries of the

exceedingly, and is the second[1] best of all islands that exist. For in it grow camphor, cubebs, cardamoms[2], nutmegs, and

great Buddhistic monument Boro Bodor, completed, according to Crawfurd, about twenty years after our traveller's visit to the island. That the bas-reliefs of Boro Bodor were gilt, or were intended to be gilt, I have not the slightest doubt. I do not remember whether the halo or glory round sacred heads, to which Odoric refers, is to be found round those sculptures; but it is essentially a Buddhist feature. Burnes mentions it on the paintings behind the great idols at Bamian; and I have seen examples of figures so glorified in some of the ancient temples at Pagàn on the Irawadi, which were very striking from their resemblance to Byzantine Apostles. (*Lassen*, iv, 482; *Walckenaer*, *Sur la chronologie*, *etc. des Javanais* in Mém. Acad. Inscript. 1842, xv, 224; *Gaubil*, *H. de Gentchis Can*, *etc.*, pp. 217–219.) As to golden palaces, however, see Polybius's account of that at Ecbatana, quoted by Rawlinson (*Herodotus*, i, p. 194).

[Regarding Chipangu (Japan), Marco Polo says, ii, pp. 253–4: "I will tell you a wonderful thing about the Palace of the Lord of that Island. You must know that he hath a great Palace which is entirely roofed with fine gold, just as our churches are roofed with lead, insomuch that it would scarcely be possible to estimate its value. Moreover, all the pavement of the Palace, and the floors of its chambers, are entirely of gold, in plates like slabs of stone, a good two fingers thick; and the windows also are of gold, so that altogether the richness of this Palace is past all bounds and all belief." Doubtless an old "yarn" as Yule puts it.]

[1] [FARS., "tertia melior."—BOLL., "est de melioribus Indiae una."]

[2] The word here translated cardamoms is *Melegetæ*, for which no other concise rendering seems practicable. One Italian dictionary indeed (*Vocab. Universale Italiano*) does give *cardamomo* as the explanation of *Meleghette*; whilst Ducange gives nothing more precise than *floris species*, quoting this passage from Odoric, and another from Rolandus Patavinus out of Muratori, in which last *Meleghetæ* are coupled with camphor, cummin, cloves, and *cardamons*. This, therefore, shows that the two were not properly identical. In two passages also of Pegolotti, I find *cardamomi* and *meleghette* mentioned at short intervals, as if they were different species. And in the book of G. da Uzzano (*Della Decima* iv) *Meleghette* and *Meleaghette* appear repeatedly, and as distinct from cardamoms. In yet another passage of Pegolotti we have "meleghette *o vuoli ti dire Noci sarche o in grano o in polvere che fussero*," which might settle what was meant by meleghette in the 14th century, if one could only tell what *noci sarche* may be!

In later times the name has been applied (*Mellighetta*, *Malagueta*, *Manighetta*) sometimes to two kindred species of amomum exported from different parts of the West African coast (*Am. Granum Paradasi* and *Am. Melegueta*), and sometimes to a quite different article, the seeds of the *Unona Ethiopica* or Ethiopic Pepper. It appears to be one of the former which Gerarde and Mattioli describes as the greater cardamoms or melegette, for Gerarde states they were said to come from "Ginny," and were called in England "Graines of Paradise." The author of the article *Melligetta* in Rees's Cyclopædia however asserts that the *Cardamomum majus* of the old botanists came from

many other precious spices[1]. It hath also very great store of all victuals save wine[2].

The king of this island hath a palace which is truly marvellous. For it is very great[3], and hath very great

Madagascar, and we find Andrea Corsali praising the *meleghetta* of that island. All this does not tend to clear up the subject, which seems densely entangled.

Martin Behaim, the celebrated cosmographer of the 15th century, is found among his other occupations voyaging to the coast of Africa for *Malagueta*, and Columbus calls the whole coast of Guinea *Costa di Maniguetta*. According to Humboldt, from whom the two last facts are borrowed, the malagueta used to come across the Sahra to the north coast, and was largely exported to Antwerp. This however was perhaps rather the Ethiopic pepper than the Grains of Paradise. Mattioli derives the name from the resemblance of the grains to those of Indian millet, called *melega* in some parts of Italy. But Humboldt connects it with *molago*, a Malabar name of pepper proper; and Zedler's *Lexicon* with Melega, "a city of Africa."

There are several Asiatic species of amomum, producing aromatics resembling more or less the true cardamomum of Malabar (*Elettaria cardamomum*), two of which (*A. Cardamomum* and *A. Maximum*) are found in Java, and one of these may be the *melegeta* of Odoric, if indeed any precision is to be looked for.

(*Pegolotti* in *Della Decima*, iii, pp. 57, 114, 296–7; *Ramusio*, i, f. 115 v, and 178; *Mattioli*, *Discorsi ne' Sei Libri di Dioscoride*, ed. Ven. 1744, p. 24; *Gerarde's Herball*, ed. 1633, p. 1542; *Humboldt*, *Examen critique*, etc., i, 257 *seq.*; *English Cyclopædia*, Arts and Sciences, Art. *Cardamom*, and Nat. Hist. Articles *Amomum* and *Unona*; *Rees's Cyc.*, vol. xxiii.)

[In my own edition of Odoric, I have given a long note on these products which I think useless to repeat here. Cf. *L'Origine de la Melaguette et les Dieppois* par Edouard Le Corbeiller (*Bul. Soc. Géog.*, Paris, 1893, pp. 390–8).]

[1] ["The Island is of surpassing wealth, producing black pepper, nutmegs, spikenard, galingale, cubebs, cloves, and all other kinds of spices." *Marco Polo*, ii, p. 272.]

[2] ["In ipsa enim nascitur camphora, cubebe, melegete, nuces muschate, multeque alie species preciosse, in ea est maxima copia victualium preterquam vini." (VENNI.)—"In ipsa enim nascuntur cubebae, melegetae, nucesque muscatae, multaeque aliae species pretiosae. In eâ est copia magna victualium preterquam vini." (B. N.)—"In ipsa nascitur camphora cubebe, crescunt ibi melegote nucesque muscatae et multae species praeciosae. Illic est copia victualium praeter vinum." (CIV.)—"In ipsâ nascitur camphora, cubebae crescunt, & melegetae, nucesque musquatae, & multae species pretiosae." (BOLL.)—"Nella quale nasce la câfora, le cubebe, le melegete, le noci moscate, & molte altre specie similmente pretiose, è finalmente grassa di tutte le cose al viuere dell' huomo necessarie, eccetto che di vino." (RAM. A.)]

[3] [BOLL., "quod multis impossibile videretur."—CIV., "quod...videtur."]

staircases, broad and lofty, and the steps thereof are of gold and silver alternately. Likewise the pavement of the palace hath one tile of gold and the other of silver, and the wall of the same is on the inside plated all over with plates of gold, on which are sculptured knights all of gold, which have great golden circles round their heads, such as we give in these parts to the figures of saints[1]. And these circles are all beset with precious stones. Moreover, the ceiling is all of pure gold, and to speak briefly, this palace is richer and finer than any existing at this day in the world.

Now the Great Khan of Cathay[2] many a time engaged in war with this king; but this king always vanquished and got the better of him. And many other things there be which I write not.

22. Of the land called Thalamasin, and of the trees that give flour, and other marvels.

Near to this country is another which is called PANTEN[3], but others call it THALAMASYN[4], the king whereof hath many islands under him[5]. Here be found trees that

[1] ["Sicut apud sanctorum diademata describuntur." (CIV.)—"Sicut hic facimus sanctis nostris." (VENNI.)—"Si come qui l' imagine di nostri tengano." (RAM. A.)]

[2] [VENNI, Chaam.—B. N., Canis.—HAK., Canis de Katay.—CIV., Chan tamen magnus Chatay.—BOLL., Can autem magnus Catay.]

[3] [VEN., HAK., Panten.—FARS., Panthen.—PAL., Panthe.—RAM. A., CIV., Paten.—BOLL., Pacen.—B. N., Patem.—FRENCH TEXT, Natem; fr. 1380, Naten.]

[4] [BOLL., CIV., Thalamasym.—ARUND., Thalamasim.—B. N., Talamasim.—FARS., Thamalsi.—PAL., Talamosa.—VEN., Malamasin.—RAM. A., Malamasmi.]

[5] There are many places which might be supposed to answer in sound to the first of these names, Bantam, Bintang, Bandan, Patani, etc., but no one of them has a good claim to identification with it. And the probable meanings of the word have so large an application, as my respected friend Mr. Crawfurd tells me (in Malay, *Pantai* or *Pante*, shore or beach, *Pantan* or *Pantian*, a place on the beach; Javanese, *Panti*, a dwelling, etc.), that they point to no definite locality. Thala Masyn, the same authority considers to be probably intended for (Malay or Javanese) *Talaga Masin*, "The Salt Lake," though

produce flour, and some that produce honey, others that

with the remark that he knows of no place so called in the Archipelago. (Might it not stand for *Tanamasin*, "Salt Land"?)

What, then, are the characteristics of the region to which Odoric gives these names? They are as follows:—That it lies between Java and Champa; that it produces sago and toddy palms; a virulent vegetable poison and great bamboos and rattans; the use of amulets inserted under the skin; the use of the sumpitan or blow-pipe; and its adjacency to the Southern Ocean. All these characters but the last apply to nearly the whole Archipelago. The last appears to confine our choice to the southern part of Borneo, Celebes, and the Moluccas. It is not improbable that Banjarmasin (*Banjar*, Order, Array, *Masin*, Salt, generally rendered *Salt Garden*) is meant. This was established as a semi-civilised state in the eleventh century, and was tributary to Majapahit in the flourishing time of that monarchy.

I may mention, however, as suggestive for further examination, that in Stieler's *Hand-Atlas*, a river-delta which is shown on the coast of Biru in the east of Borneo is marked *Panteh*; and that Crawfurd's own map in his *Dict. of the Indian Islands* marks almost at the same spot a place called *Talysian*. Again, that the emporium of Cambodian trade three centuries ago was called *Ponteamas*, which has also some resemblance to a combination of the names assigned by Odoric. And, lastly, that in Extracts of the Japanese Encyclopædia, given by Rémusat, there occurs, in a list of foreign countries, the name of *Tanmaling*, as that of a region ten days south of Cambodia. It is moreover followed in the list by *Kwawa* or Java, so that it would appear to hold the same position in regard to those two countries that Odoric's Panten does. (*Rémusat, Mél. As.*, ii, 166.)

[Col. G. E. Gerini published in the *J. R. A. S.*, July 1905, pp. 485–511 a paper on the *Nāgarakretāgama*, a Javanese poem composed by a native bard named Prapañca, in honour of his sovereign Hayam Wuruk (1350–1389), the greatest ruler of Mājapāhit. He upsets all the theories accepted hitherto regarding *Panten*. The southernmost portion of the Malay Peninsula is known as the *Malaya* or *Malayu* country (Tānah Malāyu) = Chinese *Ma-li-yü-êrh* = *Malāyur* = *Maluir* of Marco Polo, witness the river *Malāyu* (*Sungei Malāyu*) still so called, and the village *Bentan*, both lying there (ignored by all Col. Gerini's predecessors) on the northern shore of the Old Singapore Strait. Col. Gerini writes (p. 509): "There exists to this day a village *Bentam* on the mainland side of Singapore Strait, right opposite the mouth of the Sungei Selitar, on the northern shore of Singapore Island, it is not likely that both travellers [Polo and Odoric] mistook the coast of the Malay Peninsula for an island. The island of *Pentam*, *Paten*, or *Pantem* must therefore be the *Be-Tūmah* (Island) of the Arab Navigators, the *Tamasak* Island of the Malays; and, in short, the Singapore Island of our day." He adds: "The island of *Pentam* cannot be either Batang or Bitang, the latter of which is likewise mentioned by Marco Polo under the same name of *Pentam*, but 60 + 30 = 90 miles before reaching the former. Batang, girt all round by dangerous reefs, is inaccessible except to small boats. So is Bintang, with the exception of its south-western side, where is now Riāu, and where, a little further towards the north, was the settlement at which the chief of the island resided in the fourteenth century. There was no reason for Marco Polo's junk to take that roundabout

produce wine[1], and others a poison the most deadly that existeth in the world. For there is no antidote to it known except one; and that is that if any one hath imbibed that poison he shall take of *stercus humanum* and dilute it with water, and of this potion shall he drink, and so shall he be absolutely quit of the poison[2]. [And the men of this

way in order to call at such, doubtlessly insignificant place. And the channel (*i.e.* Rhio Strait) has far more than four paces' depth of water, whereas there are no more than two fathoms at the western entrance to the Old Singapore Strait."

Marco Polo says (ii, p. 280): "Throughout this distance [from Pentam] there is but four paces' depth of water, so that great ships in passing this channel have to lift their rudders, for they draw nearly as much water as that." Gerini remarks that it is unmistakably the *Old Singapore Strait* and that there is no channel so shallow throughout all those parts except among reefs." The *Old Strait* or *Silat Tebrau*, says N. B. Dennys, *Descriptive Dict. of British Malaya*, separating Singapore from Johore; before the settlement of the former, this was the only known route to China; it is generally about a mile broad, but in some parts little more than three furlongs. Crawfurd went through it in a ship of 400 tons, and found the passage tedious but safe."—Most of Sinologists, Beal, Chavannes, Pelliot, *Bull. École Ext. Orient*, iv, 1904, pp. 321–322, 323–324, 332–333, 341, 347, place the Malaiur of Marco Polo at Palambang in Sumatra.]

[1] As in India, so in the islands, various palms furnish sugar and toddy. But the most important provision of these in the Archipelago comes from the Sagwire or Aren (*Borassus Gomuti*). Herodotus uses the same expressions, *wine* and *honey*, in speaking of the produce of the date-palm. *Honey* in this way probably indicates the molasses or uncrystallised sugar. Thus we find Pegolotti (p. 64) distinguish between "*Mele d'ape, Mele di Cannamele*, and *Mele di Carrubi*," "bees' honey, cane honey, and carob honey." [See my edition of *Odoric*, pp. 179–180.]

[2] The poisons of the Archipelago are famous, and have given rise to the fables of the upas. Dalton, in his account of the Kayans of Borneo, speaks of a man dying in four minutes from a poisoned arrow-wound in the hand. The arrow-poison used in Cambodia is said sometimes to kill an elephant in a few minutes. (*Moor's Notices of the Indian Arch.*; *J. R. G. S.*, xxx, p. 196.)

The antidote to this poison mentioned in the text is the same that is used in Abyssinia for snake-bites. At least, so the Abyssinian Abba Gregory told Ludolf: "*nam excrementis humanis in aqua desumptis curari dicebat*," and Ludolf adds: "*Quod remedium Panthera forte homines docuit, quæ si carnem a venatoribus aconito perfricatam voraverit, merda humana sibi medetur.*" (*Hist. Æthiop.*, lib. i, c. 13, § 8, 9.)

[On poisons, see the following note.—In the catalogue of the Dutch Colonial Exhibition at Amsterdam, 1883, group 11, p. 82, we find a note on these poisons: those that are most in use for hunting are the *Wali-kambing* or *Kala-kambing* (*Sarcobolus Spanoghei* [and *dichotomus*?] asclepiad., Miquel, *Flore des I. néerl.* ii, 502), and some strynach., particularly the *Shetik* (*Strychnos tieute*, Miq., ii, 381) to

country being nearly all rovers, when they go to battle they carry every man a cane in the hand about a fathom in length, and put into one end of it an iron bodkin poisoned with this poison, and when they blow into the cane, the bodkin flieth and striketh whom they list, and those who are thus stricken incontinently die[1].]

But, as for the trees that produce flour, 'tis after this fashion. These are thick, but not of any great height[2];

which is often given the better-known name of *Wali-kambing*, as well as to some menispermac., the *Brata-wali* and the *Anda-wali* (*Tinospora crispa* and *Anamirta Cocculus*, Miq., i, 77 and 78). The poison most in use is the first on the list, the true *Wali-kambing*: it is less violent than the *Shetik*, and the tiger has less suspicion of its presence. Moreover the flesh of the animal killed by this poison can be eaten, which is not the case for the other one, and they care for this property because tiger's flesh is considered as being fortifying and anti-rheumatismal.]

1 From PAL. This is a remarkable passage from the Palatine MS., and is, I suppose, the earliest mention of the *sumpit* or blow-pipe of the aborigines of the Archipelago. The length stated is a *braccio*, which I have rendered *fathom*, as nearest the truth, a meaning which the word seems to have in sea phraseology.

[PAL.: "E quelli uomini sono quasi tutti corsali, e quando vanno a battaglia portano ciascuno una canna in mano, di lunghezza d' un braccio e pongono in capo de la canna uno ago di ferro atossiato in quel veleno, e sofiano nella canna e l' ago vola e percuotolo dove vogliono, e' ncontinente quelli ch è percosso muore. M' a egli hanno le tina piene di sterco d' uomo e una iscodella di sterco guarisce l' uomo da queste cotali ponture."

Sumpītan, a "narrow thing," Malay, from *sumpit*, "narrow," "strait."—Cf. Ling Roth, *Natives of Sarawak and Brit. N. Borneo*, ii, pp. 184 *seq*. Dennys, *Des. Dict. of Brit. Malaya*, writes: "Usually made of *Kayu jati*, *Kayu dammar laut*, or *Bulu timiang*, a species of bamboo ....The *sumpitan* of the aborigines of the Peninsula, unlike that of the Dyaks, which is bored in solid wood, consists of two *timiang* bamboos, one within the other. The darts or arrows (*damak*) are made of the stem of the *bertam* leaf, 10 inches in length and 1/16th in diameter at the base, whence they taper to a very fine point. The base is inserted into a cane of *Kayu tutu* (which is very light and porous) so as to fit the bore, while the point is dipped for nearly an inch in *ipoh* poison, said to be made by taking *ipoh* root and wood limes and *tuba*, the whole being bruised, boiled and strained. Arsenic is then added, and other drugs are sometimes mixed with it. The preparation has the consistency of *chandu*. A nick is cut below the poison to ensure the head of the arrow breaking off in the wood." Dennys gives also from the *Journ. St. Br. R. As. Soc.* a different account of the poison from a writer who says that "the chief ingredient of this poison is the juice of the well-known Upas tree of the Javanese, the *Antiaris toxicaria*."]

2 [" Les arbres sont grans et haulz et larges." FRENCH TEXT.]

they are cut into with an axe round about the foot of the stem, so that a certain liquor flows from them resembling size. Now this is put into bags made of leaves, and put for fifteen days in the sun; and after that space of time a flour is found to have formed from the liquor. This they steep for two days in sea-water, and then wash it with fresh water. And the result is the best paste in the world, from which they make whatever they choose, cates of sorts and excellent bread, of which I friar Odoric have eaten: for all these things have I seen with mine own eyes. And this kind of bread is white outside, but inside it is somewhat blackish[1].

By the coast of this country towards the south is the

[1] ["Hic vero panis exterius pulcher, interius aliquantulum niger apparet." CIV.—"Il est au dehors un pou noir, mais dedens il est tres bel et tres blanc."—FRENCH TEXT.]

Though Odoric's account of sago is incorrect, I think it is that of an eye-witness who did not clearly understand what he saw. The palm is a good deal thicker than the coco-palm, but not nearly so tall. The trunk is cut down and lopped; a strip is then removed from the upper side, exposing the pith, which is hewn out with an adze of stone or bamboo. It is then carried to a stream, washed and strained into troughs made of the sago-trunk, and in that the starchy matter deposits. This is packed away in conical baskets made of the sago-leaves (the *sacci de foliis facti* of our author), and this is the raw sago of commerce.

In some parts of New Guinea the sago pith is filled into a house with an open floor, and trampled with water till it flows through into troughs made of the sago-trunk which are placed below. It is thus intelligible how the friar supposed the sago to flow in a starchy state (*in modum collæ*) from the stem.

The Chinese at Singapore pass this crude sago through several additional processes to produce the granulated sago of our markets.

Raw sago boiled with a little water forms a starchy mass eaten with chopsticks. More commonly it is baked into cakes in small clay pans. Fresh from the baking, these are said to taste like hot rolls.

The total cost of a sago tree, and labour in preparing the sago, is about twelve shillings; and this feeds a man twelve months. But Mr. Wallace justly remarks that this excessive cheapness is no blessing. Industry is not acquired; labour is distasteful, and sago eaters have generally the most wretched of huts and clothing. (*Wallace* in *J. R. G. S.*, xxxii; *Journ. of Ind. Archip.* iii, 288—also *A. R. Wallace's Malay Archipelago*, 1869, ii, pp. 118–121.)

[Marco Polo says, ii, p. 300, *Fansur*: "And I will tell you another great marvel. They have a kind of trees that produce flour, and excellent flour it is for food. These trees are very tall and thick, but have a very thin bark, and inside the bark they are crammed with flour. And I tell you that Messer Marco Polo, who witnessed all this,

sea called the Dead Sea, the water whereof runneth ever towards the south, and if any one falleth into that water he is never found more. [And if the shipmen go but a little way from the shore they are carried rapidly downwards and never return again. And no one knoweth whither they are carried, and many have thus passed away, and it hath never been known what became of them[1].]

In this country also there be canes or reeds like great trees, and full sixty paces in length. There be also canes of another kind which are called *Cassan*[2], and these always grow along the ground like what we call dog's grass, and at each of their knots they send out roots, and in such wise extend themselves for a good mile in length[3]. And in

related how he and his party did sundry times partake of this flour made into bread, and found it excellent."

Sago Palm = *Sagus Rhumphiana* and *S. Lævis* (DENNYS).—"From Malay sāgū. The farinaceous pith taken out of the stem of several species of a particular genus of palm, especially *Metroxylon laeve*, Mart., and *M. Rumphii*, Willd., found in every part of the Indian Archipelago, including the Philippines, wherever there is proper soil." (*Hobson-Jobson*).]

[1] ["Ed egli è tutto il contrario, che 'l mare pende e corre si forte ch' è incredibile, e se marinai si partono punto dallito vanno discendo, e non tornano mai. E non è alcuno che sapiano dove si vadono, e molti sono costi iti e non seppono mai che se ne fossono. E la nave nostra fuè in grande pericolo, andando quindi, se non se che Idio ci aiutoe miracolosamente." PAL.] De Barros says that the natives believed that whoever should proceed beyond the Straits of Bali to the South, would be hurried away by strong currents, so as never to return. (*Major's Early Voyages to Terra Australis*, HAK. SOC., p. lv.) And Fra Mauro, towards the south-east of India, has the notification, "that ships sailing towards the south, which allow themselves to approach the Dim Islands (*Isole Perse*) will be carried by the currents into the Darkness, and once entered into those regions, through the density of the air, and of the tenacious waters, they must perish." Similar rubrics occur elsewhere towards the south.

The term Νεκρὸν is applied by Agathemerus to the Arctic Sea, and perhaps some notion of the Antarctic was involved in the like term heard of by Odoric. (See *Hudson*, *Geog. Gr. Minores*, ii, 56.)

[2] [B. N., CIV., VEN., Casan.—FARS., Cassam.—MUN., Casan, Cassan.—PAL., Cansalle.—RAM. A., Casar.—ARUND., Cassali ex quibus in apotecariis inveniuntur cassia fistulae (absurd!).—FRENCH TEXT, Cassay.]

[3] PAL. "These are not, however, of any great thickness, but much about the same as the canes in our Frank countries." ["In hac etiam contrata sunt canaveriae seu arundines longae bene pluribus lx passibus,

these canes are found certain stones which be such that if any man wear one of them upon his person he can never be hurt or wounded by iron in any shape, and so for the most part the men of that country do wear such stones upon them[1]. And when their boys are still young they take them and make a little cut in the arm and insert one of these stones, to be a safeguard against any wound by steel. And the little wound thus made in the boy's arm is speedily healed by applying to it the powder of a certain fish[2].

magnae ut arbores." B. N.—"Sunt etiam in hac contracta canne varie longe plus 60 passibus magne ut arbores." VEN.—"Une manière de roseaulz aussi grans comme grans arbres, et sont ces roseaulz si grans que ilz ont bien quarante audains de long." FRENCH TEXT.] *Cassan* is the reading of the majority of copies, which may be a mistake for either *Cassar*, representing *Khaizurán* (Arab.), a bamboo, (and Casar is the reading in Ramusio), or for *Cassab* (Arab. *Qassab*) a cane in general. But in any case there seems to be confusion. The first canes like trees, etc., are certainly bamboos ; the *Cassan*, which runs along the ground for a mile, is certainly a Rattan. But the striking out roots at the knots appears to be a feature taken from certain kinds of bamboo, and the stones of which he goes on to speak, must be the siliceous concretions (*Tabashír*) found in the *bamboo*, though perhaps they have been confounded with the bezoar stone, which has always been a notable product of Borneo, and is still an article of trade there.

The largest known bamboos (*B. Maxima*) are found in the Malay islands and Cambodia. They reach to eighty and one hundred feet in length. In Pegu I have seen them close upon, if not quite, ten inches in diameter. Gosse quotes from Rumphius a rattan of twelve hundred feet in length. I cannot get nearer to Odoric's mile. (*Rom. of Nat. Hist.*, p. 130.)

["Le *rotin*, *panjalin*, que donne le *Calamus*, *spec. div.*, est resté à peu près complètement produit forestier. Ni le rotin de Palembang, dont on fait des *piques* et des *cannes*, ni celui de Banjermasin, mince, flexible, qui sert de *liens*, et qu'on tresse pour les *meubles* et les *nattes*, ni le rotin à *cordes* de Java, ni celui des *cables d'ancres tressés* des Moluques, ne sont des produits de la culture. Tant le commerce européen que celui des indigènes et l'exportatión ont dans le rotin un article toujours demandé, toujours courant dans ses nombreuses variétés." *Cat. Sec. colon. néerl.*, 1883, gr. ii, p. 189.]

[1] PAL. "And when looking for these stones they strike every cane with steel, and if the steel cannot cut it then they search that cane for the stone, getting a piece of wood of the hardest and sharpest, with which they hack and hew until they come at the stone."

[2] ["Quivi nasce un pesce ch' à cotale natura che quando altri pigliase questo pesce e ricideselo in più parti e una di queste parti si racozi e tochi l' altra incontinente si rapica insieme e saldasi come se mai non v' avesse ; avuto niente. Di questo pesce fanno seccare e

And thus through the great virtue of those stones the men who wear them become potent in battle and great corsairs at sea. But those who from being shipmen on that sea have suffered at their hands, have found out a remedy for the mischief. For they carry as weapons of offence sharp stakes of very hard wood[1], and arrows likewise that have no iron on the points; and as those corsairs are but poorly harnessed the shipmen are able to wound and pierce them through with these wooden weapons, and by this device they succeed in defending themselves most manfully[2].

Of these canes called *Cassan* they make sails for their

fannone polvere, e portala con loro duunche vanno in battaglia, e pongosela i loro ferite e'ncontinente salda."—PAL.

"Cujus nomen ignoro."—HAK., ARUND.]

1 [" Nam ipsi portant propugnacula seu palos acutissimos de uno fortissimo ligno, portant[que] sagittas cum (!) ferro." B. N.—"Absque ferro." VEN.—"Sine ferro." FARS.—"Lances et de sajettes sans fer." FRENCH TEXT.]

2 The Burmese formerly used to insert pellets of gold under the skin in order to render them invulnerable. But Marco Polo specifically speaks of these "consecrated stones in the arm between the skin and the flesh," in a story about Japan; and Conti mentions the amulet so used in Java Major, as a piece of an iron rod which is found in the middle of certain rare trees. (*Mission to Ava*, 1855, p. 208; *Polo*, iii, 2; *Conti* (HAK. SOC.), p. 32.)

[I have no doubt that this refers to *Bezoar*, a corruption of Persian *pādzahr*, "pellens venenum," or *pāzahr*. Marcel Devic, Supp. to Littré's *Dict.*, derives it from the Arabic *bādizahr* or *bāzahr*, from the Persian *pād-zehr*. Borneo has always been famed for that stone. "E os mâttos produze grossa madeira, onde se criaó elephantes, badas, tigres arymos, antas e grandes cobras e bogiôs de pedra *bazar*, e todo genero de montarya e volatilia e muy formosos paçaros de canto de suave armonia." *Godinho de Eredia*, f. 10 v°.—Cf. the French edition of Odoric.]

Dalton says the Dyaks of Borneo have a defensive armour of leather which is proof against arrow, spear, and sword. This may have to do with the story of these invulnerables. But we find St. John alluding to a belief among the Malays of Borneo that by certain ceremonies they can render themselves invulnerable, though he does not specify what the process is. There is such a class of invulnerables also in Fiji. The use in the Archipelago of lances, etc., of cane and wood hardened in the fire is mentioned by Pigafetta. Such arms were used by the islanders of Matan, in a fray with whom the great Magellan fell. (*Crawfurd's Desc. Dict.*, 139; *J. R. G. S.*, xxvii, 251; *Pigafetta* (Milan ed.), p. 97; *Life in the Forests of the Far East*, i, 134.)

ships, dishes[1], houses, and a vast number of other things of the greatest utility to them. And many other matters there be in that country which it would cause great astonishment to read or hear tell of; wherefore I am not careful to write them at present.

23. How the King of Zampa keepeth many elephants and many wives.

At a distance of many days[2] from this kingdom is another which is called Zampa[3], and 'tis a very fine country, having great store of victuals and of all good things. The king of the country, it was said when I was there, had, what

[1] *Sestoria*, perhaps for *sessoria*=either *seats* or *dishes*. Or it may be for *sextaria*—measures for corn (It. *sestieri*).

[2] ["Ab isto regno per multas dietas." B.N.—"Ab hoc regno distans per dietas multas." VEN.]

[3] [VEN., Zampa.—PAL., CIV., RAM. A., Zapa.—HAK., DOM., B. N., Campa.—FARS, Canpa or Carpa.—MUN., Capa.—FRENCH TEXT, Campe.—Venni takes it for Zipangu (Japan!).]

The Cianba and Ziamba of Polo, the Sanf of the Arabian geographers (as Mr. Lane I believe first pointed out), the Champa of Jordanus, the Tsiompa and Champa of our modern maps, to the south of Cochin China, of which it now forms a part. Rémusat appears to consider that in the middle ages Cochin China was included in Champa.

Many of the copies read *Campa*, and this (Campaa) is the form in which the name appears in old Portuguese writers, and in Pigafetta (in Ramusio; the Milan Pigafetta has Chiempa). Probably Çampa was the intended form in these cases.

Champa [in Sansk. *Campā*] was the name of an ancient Buddhist royal city on the Ganges, near the modern Bhágalpúr, and was probably adopted by the Indo-Chinese country after its conversion to Buddhism according to the practice so generally followed in Indo-China and the great islands.

[Champa was on the coast of Annam, the Binh-Thuan province showing more particularly what remains of the ancient kingdom. In a Chinese work published in the 14th century, by an Annamite, under the title of *Ngan-nan chi lio*, and translated into French by M. Sainson (1896), we read (p. 397): "Elephants are found only in Lin-y; this is the country which became Champa. It is the habit to have burdens carried by elephants; this country is to-day the Pu-cheng province." M. Sainson adds in a note that Pu-cheng, in Annamite Bó chánh quân, is to-day Quang-binh, and that, in this country, was placed the first capital (Dong-hoi) of the future kingdom of Champa thrown later down to the south. In 1471, the King of Tong-King, Lê Thanh-tong, conquered the country. Cf. *Marco Polo*, ii, pp. 268–271, and the French edition of Odoric. See in *T'oung pao* from May 1910, a series of articles by G. Maspero on *Le Royaume de Champa*. Lin-y is old Champa.]

with sons and with daughters, a good two hundred[1] children; for he hath many wives and other women whom he keepeth[2]. This king hath also fourteen thousand[3] tame elephants, which he made to be kept and tended by his boors as here oxen and various other animals are kept in partnership[4]. [And other folk keep elephants there just as commonly as we keep oxen here[5].]

And in that country there is one thing which is really wonderful. For every species of fish that is in the sea visits that country in such vast numbers that at the time of their coming the sea seems to consist of nothing else but fish. And when they get near the beach they leap ashore, and then the folk come and gather them as many as they list. And so these fish continue coming ashore for two or

[1] [HAK., 300.]

[2] ["In the year of Christ 1285, Messer Marco Polo was in that country, and at that time the King had, between sons and daughters, 326 children, of whom at least 150 were men fit to carry arms." *Marco Polo*, ii, p. 268.]

A Chinese account of the adjoining *Chinla* or Cambodia, translated by Rémusat, says the king of that country had five wives, and from three thousand to five thousand concubines. (*Nouv. Mélanges As.* i, 71.) The late well-known king of Persia, Futteh Ali Shah, left behind him nearly three thousand direct descendants, and his son Sheikh Ali Mirza used to ride attended by a body guard of *sixty* sons of his own. (*Rawlinson's Herodotus*, i, 221.)

[3] [ARUNDEL, xiii millia.]

[4] "*Sicut...tenentur ad* Socedam." Ital. *Soccità*, the name for a sort of *métairie* in cattle-keeping, the cattle being tended for the owners on a division of profits.

Cambodia and the adjoining regions abound in domesticated elephants to a degree unknown elsewhere in Asia. See Jordanus and note (HAK. SOC.) p. 37; also Ibn Batuta in this collection *infra*; *Rémusat* in the article just quoted; *J. R. G. S.* xxvii, 93, 105, and xxxii, p. 146.

[Marco Polo, ii, pp. 267 and 268, says: "The people are Idolaters and pay a yearly tribute to the Great Kaan, which consists of elephants and nothing but elephants...." "There are very great numbers of elephants in this kingdom." In a paper in *Exc. et Recon.*, No. 24, 1885, p. 235, Aymonier says about the Binh Thuan province: "Les éléphants également très nombreux, ne fuient ni n'attaquent l'homme qui les rencontrera souvent, en voyageant du côté des montagnes. Ces animaux dévastent les plantations et prennent la fuite quand le propriétaire les chasse."]

[5] PAL.

three days together. And then a second species of fishes comes and does the same as the first; and so with the other species each in turn and in order until the last; and this they do but once in the year. And when you ask the folk of that country how this comes about, they tell you in reply that the fish come and act in that fashion in order to pay homage to their emperor[1].

In that country also I saw a tortoise bigger in compass thán the dome of St. Anthony's church in Padua[2]. And

[1] I have not been able to trace the original basis of this mythical story. Indeed very little is to be known from any books accessible to me of the coast of Champa. But perhaps this passage from Duhalde may throw a little light on the matter. "Dans la province de Kiangnan on voit surtout de gros poissons venant de la mer, ou du Fleuve Jaune, qui se jettent dans des vastes plaines toutes couvertes d'eau; tout y est disposé de telle sorte que les eaux s'écoulent aussitôt qu'ils y sont entrés. Ces poissons demeurant à sec, on les prend sans peine," etc. (ii, 140.)

[Pauthier remarks, *Marco Polo*, p. 557, note: "Cette histoire des poissons, racontée si naïvement par le frère Oderic, expliquerait peut-être l'origine du nom de *Cyamba* ou *Ciampa* donné à ce pays, car, dans la langue télingana, de la côte de Coromandel, le poisson se nomme *Champa*."

With regard to this legend, Abel Des Michels writes, *Luc Van tiên*, p. 66, note: "Dans la province de Thái Nguyên (Tong King) est un golfe où se trouve un grand rocher au pied duquel un jeu de la nature a formé trois degrés assez hauts, et disposés comme les marches d'un escalier. D'après une croyance populaire, l'on verrait tous les ans, à des époques déterminées, plusieurs espèces de poissons s'y réunir et lutter à qui bondira par dessus. Ceux qui seraient assez heureux pour arriver jusqu'au degré le plus élevé, seraient, après y avoir séjourné un certain temps sans prendre aucune nourriture, transformés en animaux terrestres. A ces époques fixes, connues des habitants, un grand nombre d'entre eux s'y rendraient pour ramasser les poissons qui, ne pouvant franchir les trois degrés, se brisent la tête contre le rocher." In China, there is a legend of sturgeons ascending every year the Yellow River at the third moon and that those who are successful in crossing the rapids of Lung-men become dragons (*lung*). No doubt this phenomenon is but the natural fact altered into a legend of the ascent up river of some kind of fish to make their roe. Perhaps this fish is the alose, the *sam laï*, so appreciated in the Far East, which enter the rivers in May and leave in September to return to sea.]

[2] ["En ceste contrée vy je une lymace qui estoit si grande que ce estoit merveille. Elle estoit plus grande que le clochier Saint-Martin de Padue, se il feult ainsi tournez comme maison de lymace." FRENCH TEXT.—This is the only text having *Saint Martin* instead of *St. Anthony*.]

["There is a kingdom twenty days journey from Cathay, of which

many other like things be there, which unless they were seen would be past belief; wherefore I care not to write them[1].

When a married man dies in this country his body is burned, and his living wife along with it. For they say that she should go to keep company with her husband in the other world also[2].

the king and all the inhabitants are Christians, but heretics, being said to be Nestorians....He asserted that their churches were larger and more ornamented than ours, and were constructed entirely of tortoise-shell." *Nicolò Conti*, in Major, p. 33.—"Testudinibus tantum structas asseverabat" says the Latin Text, p. 148.]

[1] O friar! The smallest of St. Anthony's many domes is about forty feet in diameter. On big tortoises see *Tennent's Ceylon*, i, 190; *Mr. Major* in introd. to *India in the 15th cent.* p. xliii; and *Mr. Badger on Varthema*, p. 240. But I do not understand the use these gentlemen make of Falconer and Cautley's fossil monsters. *They* did not flourish in the middle ages.

Vincent le Blanc (who is very bad authority) says that many houses in Pegu were gilt and roofed with tortoise-shell, not with *a* shell. It is possible that Odoric may have seen a temple so roofed, and taken it for a single shell. But I believe the probable *rationale* of the story is that which I have given in the introductory notice of Odoric, p. 27. The largest turtle that I can find mentioned on modern authority had a carapace of about seven feet in length. (*Eng. Cyc.* Art. *Chelonia.*)

[VENNI, Not. 44, p. 118, adds to the exaggeration of Odoric: "Della smisurata grandezza delle Testuggini Indiane rammentata dal Beato favella a lungo il citato Oviedo, ed altri Viaggiatori, dicendo, che una di esse basta a coprire colla scorza superiore una casa ordinaria."

The Arabs tell also stories of big tortoises. Cf. *Livre des Merveilles de l'Inde*, Leiden, 1883, pp. 36–37.

There was a letter in the *Standard* of July 9, 1895, on the gigantic land tortoises indigenous to the Aldabra group of the Seychelles Archipelago.—See also *le Monde illustré*, 7th Dec. 1895, and *l'Illustration*, 18th Jan. 1896.

M. Romanet du Caillaud took great pains in the *Comptes rendus* of the Soc. de Géog. Paris, 1896, pp. 162–4, to prove that *testitudo* in Odoric does not mean a tortoise but an arch-roof!

Mandeville relates Odoric's story and Mr. Warner points out, p. viii, that while the French texts of both change the tortoises of the latin texts into "limaces," the English text gives also *snails* (*snyles*): "I may point out also to the singular fact that, whereas in repeating Odoric of Pordenone's account of giant tortoises in the Indian Seas the French text transform them into snails, the Latin retains Odoric's own term "testudines."]

[2] [CIV., "in alio saeculo."—VEN., "in alio mundo."]

["Quant aucuns homs meurt en ce pays on ensevelist sa femme

24. Of the island of Nicoveran, where the men have dogs' faces[1].

Departing from that country and sailing towards the south over the Ocean Sea[2], I found many islands and

avec lui, car ilz dient que drois est que elle demeure avec lui en l'autre siècle." FRENCH TEXT.—"Cum vir uxoratus in hac contracta moritur comburitur eius corpus una cum uxore viva. quod ideo faciunt, quia dicunt ipsam cum marito ire ut in alio mundo similiter conversetur cum eo." VENNI.]

This story is a proof of the veracity of Odoric. Incineration has been and is still practised in these countries. Bouillevaux, *L'Annam et le Cambodge*, 1874, p. 243, writes: "Au Chiêm-thành, les épouses du roi après la mort de leur seigneur et maître, doivent monter sur le bûcher."—E. Aymonier, *Les Tchames*, 1891, pp. 57–8, witnessed in 1884 the cremation of a lady of quality. He says: "La crémation est généralement pratiquée chez les Tchames païens. N'en sont exceptés que les enfants morts avant l'âge de raison, ainsi que les cadavres des gens pauvres dont le famille n'a pas les moyens de subvenir aux frais d'une cérémonie que les usages rendent très coûteuse; alors l'inhumation a lieu sans prêtres, la tête est placée du côté du sud. Aux yeux des Tchames la crémation, indispensable pour tout adulte, détruit la chair et les péchés, la corruption physique et la corruption morale."—Tru'o'ng viñh-ký, *Cours d'histoire annamite*, i, p. 97, relates: "Le roi son mari mourut l'année même, et la loi voulait qu'à l'instar des sutties de l'Inde elle montât sur le bûcher qui allait consumer les restes de son royal époux." Recently Ant. Cabaton, *Les Chams*, 1901, gives also an account of this ceremony, pp. 47–48: The dead is placed upon the funeral pile, which may be made with any sort of wood, with his arms, clothings, and jewels; then he is served a last meal, that is to say with the help of a sword some rice is placed under the tongue, and after his wives, relations and servants have knelt before him for the last time, the body is covered up, the fire is lit and the priests place on the pile their hataṃ furnished with candles. When all has been consumed, a man, who bears for the nonce the name of Pô Damön or Master of Regrets, remains at the mortuary house which he curses; then he adjures the dead man not to come back and torment his family. When the cremation is over the relations offer a meal to those present after begging the Pô Damön the ritual permission to reinstate the house. After the incineration, the central part of the frontal bone (*thĕi*) is collected and broken into nine pieces of the size of a cash; they constitute the *noble bones*. The nine pieces are enclosed in a box made of gold, silver, or generally of copper, called kloṇ. The box is buried at the foot of a tree and the spot is marked with a stone.—In the *Bull. de l'École d'Ext. Orient*, iii, 3, 1903, there is a very exact account by a missionary, Father E. M. Durand, of cremation under the title of *Notes sur une crémation chez les Chams* which begins with the saying well known in Binh-thuân: "*Čam mötai lwai bruk bloḥ čuḥ; Bani mötai page byör harei dar.* Après la mort d'un Cham, on laisse son cadavre se décomposer, puis on le brûle; après la mort d'un Bani [Mohamedan], on enterre son cadavre dès la première heure du jour."]

[1] [VENNI.—De insula Nicuueran ubi Cinocofuli.]

[2] ["Recedens et navigans per mare Oceanum." B.N.—"Navigans

countries, whereamong was one called NICOVERAN[1]. And

per mare oceanum." CIV.—"Nauigando per lo mare Oceano, verso il Nirisi." RAM. B.]

[1] [2810 fr., Nichonieran.—B.N., Sacimeram.—VEN., Nicuueran.—FARS., Nichovera.—PAL., Nichoverra, Nichovera.—RAM. B., Nicouerra.—DOM., Nicuvera.—CIV., Nicimeram.—RAM. A., Hicunera.—HAK., Moumoran.—ARUND., Mochimoran.—BOLL., Insimezan.—MUN., speaks of the island without naming it.]

The name no doubt is that of the Nicobar Islands, and is the same as that used by Polo. But there seems to be no feature of the narrative, except the nakedness of the people, appropriate to those islands. The whole chapter is an anomalous jumble. The Dog-faces belong, according to the usual story of the period, to the Andaman Islands; the miniature ox worn on the forehead seems derived from one of Marco's chapters on Maabar; the king's great ruby appertains to Ceylon, in connexion with which it has been celebrated by Marco, Haiton, Jordanus and Ibn Batuta; whilst the great shield covering the whole body is a genuine feature of the wilder islands of the Archipelago, being found for example upon Nyas, among the Dayaks, the more uncivilised races of the Moluccas, and on Formosa. Cannibalism is also a genuine feature characterising other races of the Archipelago besides the Battaks of whom we have spoken. Dalton, speaking of his own entertainer, the Raja of Selgie, a chief of Kayans in Borneo, says: "Should the Raja want flesh (on a war expedition)...one of the followers is killed, which not only provides a meal, but a head to boot." (*Moor's Notices*, p. 49.)

The concluding passage of this account of the Dog-heads curiously coincides with one in Ctesias, who says of the Cynocephali, that "they are just in their dealings and hurt no man" (*Baehr's* edition of *Ctesiæ Reliq.*, pp. 253 and 362). Regarding the probable origin of stories of Dog-faces, see note on Ibn Batuta, *infra.*

[Marco Polo says (ii, p. 306): "In this Island they have no king nor chief, but live like beasts. And I tell you they go all naked, both men and women, and do not use the slightest covering of any kind. They are Idolaters." Mr. G. Phillips says (*J. R. A. S.*, July 1895, p. 529) that the name Ts'ui-lan given to the Nicobars by the Chinese is, he has but little doubt, "a corruption of Nocueran, the name given by Marco Polo to the group. The characters Tsui-lan are pronounced Ch'ui-lan in Amoy, out of which it is easy to make Cueran. The Chinese omitted the initial syllable and called them the Cueran Islands, while Marco Polo called them the Nocueran Islands." Schlegel, *T'oung pao*, ix, pp. 182–190, thinks that the Andaman Islands are alone represented by Ts'ui-lan; the Nicobar being the old country of the Lo-ch'a, and in modern time, *Mao-shan* "Hat Island." Pelliot, *Bull. École Ext. Orient*, iv, 1904, pp. 354–5, is inclined to accept Phillips' opinion. He says that Mao-shan is one island, not a group of islands; it is not proved that the country of the Lo-ch'a is the Nicobar Islands; the name of *Lo-hing-man*, Naked Barbarians, is, contrary to Schlegel's opinion, given to the Nicobar as well as to the Andaman people; the name of Andaman appears in Chinese for the first time during the XIIIth century in Chao Ju-kwa under the form *Yen-t'o-man*; Chao Ju-kwa specifies that going from Lambri (Sumatra) to Ceylon, it is an unfavourable wind which makes ships drift towards these islands; on the other hand, texts show that the Ts'ui-lan islands

this is a great isle, having a compass of a good 2,000 miles[1], and both the men and the women there have faces like dogs[2]. And these people worship the ox as their god, wherefore they always wear upon the forehead an ox made of gold or silver, in token that he is their god. All the folk of that country, whether men or women, go naked[3], wearing nothing in the world but an handkerchief[4] to cover their shame. They be stalwart men and stout in battle, going forth to war naked as they are with only a shield that covers them from head to foot. And if they hap to take any one in war who cannot produce money to ransom himself withal they do straightway eat him. But if they can get money from him they let him go.

And the king of that country[5] weareth round his neck a string of three hundred very big pearls[6], for that he maketh to his gods daily three hundred prayers. He carrieth also in his hand a certain precious stone called a ruby, a good span in length and breadth, so that when he hath this stone in his hand it shows like a flame of fire. And this, it is said, is the most noble and valuable[7] gem that existeth at this day in the world, and the great

were on the usual route from Sumatra to Ceylon.—Gerini, *Researches*, p. 396, considers that *Ts'ui-lan shan* is but the phonetic transcript of *Tilan-chong* Island, the north-easternmost of the Nicobars.—See Hirth and Rockhill's *Chau Ju-kwa*, p. 12 *n.*—Sansk. *nārikera*, "cocoanuts" is found in Necuveram.

Cf. our Notes in *Marco Polo*; there is a long account of the dog-headed barbarians in our French edition of Odoric.]

1 [B.N., CIV., RAM. A. and B., etc., 2000 miles.—VEN., duo milliariorum.—2810 fr., 2 milles.]

2 [RAM. A does not mention the dog-headed men.]

3 ["Gli huomini sono grandi communemente, e fortissimi. La maggior parte del tempo fanno guerra." RAM. B.]

4 [B.N., VEN., toaleam.—CIV., thoalia.—PAL., tovagliuola.—HAK., ARUND., "unum pannum lineum."]

5 MIN. RAM. "Of these beasts." ["E'l re di queste bestie."]

6 [B.N., PAL., VEN., DOM., 300 pearls.—ARUNDEL, CC.—RAM. A., trecento perle grosse.—RAM. B., trecento perle grosse *e bianche.*—MUN., "Rex istorum portat appensas ad collū bene trecentas margaritas et rosas."]

7 [2810 fr., riche.]

emperor of the Tartars of Cathay hath never been able to get it into his possession either by force or by money, or by any device whatever[1]. This king attends to justice and maintains it[2], and throughout his realm all men may fare safely. And there be many other things in this kingdom that I care not to write of.

25. Concerning the island of Sillan, and the marvels thereof.

There is also another island called SILLAN[3], which hath a compass of good 2,000 miles[4]. There be found therein an infinite number of serpents[5], and many other wild

1 ["Verumptamen magnus imperator Tartarorum Cathaii illum lapidem preciosum nec vi, nec pecunia nec etiam ingenio unquam habere potuit. In hac etiam contratâ ipse rex bene justitiam tenet et observat, unde per totum suum regnum quilibet potest ire securus. Multa etiam in hac contrata sunt quae etiam ego scribere non curo." B.N.

"Veruntamen magnus imperator Tartarorum Chatay hunc lapidem ab ipso Rege nec vi nec praecio, vel aliquo umquam ingenio potuit obtinere. Rex etiam iste est bonus iusticiarius, et terram suam bene pacificat et gubernat. Unde quilibet potest in regno suo secure omni tempore ambulare." CIV.]

2 MIN. RAM. "Albeit he is an idolater and hath a face like a dog's." ["Il Re benche sia idololatra, e col viso rassembri vn cane."]

3 [CIV., 2810 fr., Silan.—RAM. A., FARS., Silam.—PAL., Silan and Sillia.—VEN., DOM., Sillam.—B.N., Sillan.—ARUND., Salam.—HAK., Ceilan.—RAM. B. does not mention Ceylon.]

We need not wonder at the dimensions ascribed to Ceylon, when the same have in the preceding chapter been assigned to Nicobar. But the persistence of marine tradition in exaggerating the size of Ceylon, in the face of facts tolerably manifest, is curious. The examples may be seen in *Sir Emerson Tennent's Ceylon*, ch. i.

[Marco Polo says, ii, p. 312: "You must know that it has a compass of 2400 miles, but in old times it was greater still, for it then had a circuit of about 3600 miles, as you find in the charts of the mariners of those seas. But the north wind there blows with such strength that it has caused the sea to submerge a large part of the Island; and that is the reason why it is not so big now as it used to be." See *Marco Polo*, ii, p. 314 *n.*, for the origin of the word Ceylon. The native kings of this period were Pandita Prakama Bahu II, who reigned from 1267 to 1301 at Dambadenia, about 40 miles north-north-east of Columbo (Marco Polo's time), Vijaya Bahu IV, 1301–1303; Bhuwaneka Bahu I (1303–1314); Prakama Bahu III (1314–1319); Bhuwaneka Bahu II (1319).]

4 [DE BACKER and 2810 fr., deux cens milles.]

5 [On serpents, cf. French ed. of Odoric, p. 224 *note*; and on elephants, *ibid.*, p. 225 *note*.]

animals in great numbers, especially elephants[1]. In this country also there is an exceeding great mountain, of which the folk relate that it was upon it that Adam mourned for his son one hundred years[2]. In the midst[3] of this mountain is a certain beautiful level place, in which there is a lake of no great size, but having a great depth of water. This they say was derived from the tears shed by Adam and Eve[4]; but I do not believe that to be the truth, seeing that the water naturally springs from the soil[5].

The bottom of this pool is full of precious stones, and the water greatly aboundeth in leeches. The king taketh not those gems for himself, but for the good of his soul once or twice a-year he suffereth the poor to search the water, and take away whatever stones they can find[6]. But that they may be able to enter the water in safety they take lemons[7] and bruise them well, and then copiously

[1] ["Ed avi una generazione di serpenti ch' anno collo di cavallo e capo di serpente e corpo di cane e coda di serpente ed anno quatro piedi e sono grandi come buoi e piccoli com' asini." PAL.]

[2] ["Adam planxit filium suum Cannis." VEN., B.N.—"Luserit Adam filium suum Cannis." CIV.—"Adam pianse al figliolo Cain." DOM.—"500 annis." HAK.—"Adam et Eve plourerent leurs pechiez C ans." FRENCH TEXT.]

[3] VEN. has "at the summit of the mountain," but the text is better. ["In montis cuius cacumine." VEN.—"In supremo huius montis." CIV.—"Au milieu de ceste montaigne." FRENCH TEXT.]

[4] ["Dicunt esse lacrimas, quas fudit Adam et Eva pro filio suo Abel." CIV.]

[5] This "*pulchra planities*" and lake are afterwards spoken of by Marignolli also (v. *infra*) where some further remarks as to the place intended will be found. Ibn Batuta also speaks of a pool below the mountain from which gems were extracted. The chief gem locality in Ceylon is still one at a short distance from the base of Adam's Peak, and *gem-fishery* is the term applied to the search by Pridham. "The tears flowed in such torrents from Adam's eyes that those of his right eye started the Euphrates, while those of his left set the Tigris in motion." (*Weil's Biblical Legends of the Mussulmans*, p. 16.)

[6] ["Istos lapides non tollit ipse Rex, sed pro salute sua semel et quinque bis in anno pauperibus terrae dimittit, ut ex iis lapidibus eorum inopia sublevatur." CIV.]

[7] UTIN. and RAM. have "take *bavoyr*, *i.e.*, a certain fruit, which they bruise," etc. This *may* be intended for some Persian word There is *bajúra*, a citron. [PAL., lunbors.]

anoint the whole body therewith, and after that when they dive into the water the leeches do not meddle with them. And so it is that the poor folk go down into the pool and carry off precious stones if they can find them[1].

The water which comes down from the mountain issues forth by this lake. And the finest rubies are dug there; good diamonds too are found and many other good stones[2]. And where that water descends into the sea there be found fine pearls. Wherefore the saying goes that this king hath more precious stones than any other king in the world.

In this island there be sundry kinds of animals, both of birds and other creatures; and the country folk say that the wild beasts never hurt a foreigner, but only those who are natives of the island. There be also certain birds as

[1] There *are* water-leeches in Ceylon, which are annoying to cattle chiefly, by entering their nostrils; but the land-leeches are the great pest of the island. See a fearful picture in Tennent (i, 304). Ibn Batuta, on his ascent to the Peak, says:—"Here we saw the *flying leech*, which the natives call *zulú*. It holds on by the trees and grass near water, and when a man comes near it drops upon him... *The natives take care to keep ready a lemon* and to squeeze its juice upon the leech," etc. This name of the *flying leech*, implying the power ascribed to it of springing upon a passing victim, has come down to our time (see *Heber's Journals*, ed. 1844, ii, 167). Tennent also corroborates Odoric's mention of lemon-juice as the Ceylonese remedy for leech-bites; and so does Robert Knox (first edition, p. 25).

[2] There are no diamonds in Ceylon, but some of the Arabian geographers *say* that there are. The gems were a royal monopoly under the native dynasties. (*Tennent*, i, 38.) [On pearls, see *Chau Ju-kua*, pp. 229, 230.]

["This mountain [Adam's Peak] abounds with rubies of all kinds and other precious stones. These gems are being continually washed out of the ground by heavy rains, and are sought for and found in the sand carried down the hill by the torrents. It is currently reported among the people, that these precious stones are the congealed tears of Buddha." (*Ma-Huan*, trans. by Phillips, p. 213.)

In the Chinese work *Cho keng lu*, containing notes on different matters referring to the time of the Mongol dynasty, in ch. vii, entitled *Hwui hwui shi t'ou* ("Precious Stones of the Mohammedans") among the four kinds of red stones is mentioned the *si-la-ni* of a dark red colour; *si-la-ni*, as Dr Bretschneider observes (*Med. Res.*, i, p. 174), means probably "from Ceylon." The name for ruby in China is now-a-days *hung-pao-shi*, "red precious stone." (*Ibid.*, p. 173.) Cf. *Marco Polo*, ii, p. 316 *n.*]

big as geese, which have two heads[1]. And this island hath also great store of victuals, and of many other good things whereof I do not write.

26. Of the island called Dondin and the evil manners there.

Departing from that island and going towards the south, I landed at a certain great island which is called DONDIN[2],

[1] [FARS., "mille capita"!] The history of this bird with two heads is a good example of the gradual resolution of a fable.

In 1330 Odoric tells of a bird, as big as a goose, with *two heads*.

In 1672 P. Vincenzo Maria describes a bird, also as big as a goose, but with *two beaks*, the two being perfectly distinct, one going up and the other down; with the upper one he crows or croaks, with the lower he feeds, etc. (*Viaggio*, p. 401.)

In 1796 Padre Paolino, who is usually more accurate, retrogrades; for he calls the bird "as big as an ostrich." According to him, this bird, living on high mountains where water is scarce, has the second beak as a reservoir for a supply of water. He says the Portuguese call it *Passaro di duos bicos*. (*Viag.*, p. 153.)

Lastly, Lieut. Charles White describes the same bird in the *Asiatic Researches*: "It has a large double beak, or a large beak surmounted by a horn-like shaped mandible," etc. (*Asiat. Res.*, iv, 401.) The bird is a hornbill, of which there are various species having casques or protuberances on the top of the bill, the office of which does not appear to be ascertained. How easy here to call Odoric a liar! but how unjust, when the matter has been explained.

[This is the *calao* (hornbill; lat., *buceros rhinoceros, buceros pica*). Cf. Odoric, French ed., p. 234 *note*.]

[2] [B.N., VEN., Dondin.—ARUND., BOLL., CIV., Dodyn.—PAL., Dodin.—DOM., Dodim.—HAK., Bodin.—RAM. A., Dadin.—RAM. B., Diddi.—FRENCH TEXT, Dondiin.]

Much of what has been said on the chapter about Necuveran applies here. These two narratives are destitute, it seems to me, of the appearance of being drawn from experience. I cannot identify Dondin with any known island, nor trace the etymology which the traveller assigns to the name. But it is just possible that Dondin or Dandin might be a misread contraction of Isola *D'Andiman* (ꝺ'anꝺīn?). [Schlegel, *T'oung-pao*, x, pp. 459–463, thought that Tan-tan might apply to Dondin, but this theory has no foundation whatever. Cf. Pelliot, *Bull. École Ext. Orient*, iv, 1904, p. 285.] Stories like that related here, about the treatment of the sick or the aged were told in old times (as by Herodotus) of the Paddæi and other people, and are still very rife in the East in regard to certain races, just as stories of men with tails are, but the alleged locality shifts with the horizon. "I was informed," says Raffles, of the Battaks, "that formerly it was usual for the people to eat their parents who were too old for work. The old people selected the horizontal branch of a tree, and quietly suspended themselves by their hands, whilst their children and neighbours, forming a circle, danced round them, crying out, '*When the fruit is ripe it will fall.*' This practice took place during the

and this signifieth the same as "Unclean." They who dwell in that island are an evil generation, who devour raw flesh[1] and every other kind of filth. They have also among them an abominable custom; for the father will eat the son, the son the father, the wife will eat the husband, or the husband the wife. And 'tis in this way:—Suppose that the father of some one is ill. The son goeth then to the astrologer or priest (for 'tis the same), and sayeth thus:—"Sir, go, I pray, and inquire of our God whether my father shall be healed of this infirmity or shall die of it." Then the priest and he whose father is ill go both unto the idol, which is made of gold or silver, and make a prayer to it, and say:—

season of limes, when salt and pepper were plenty, and as soon as the victims became fatigued and could hold on no longer they fell down, when all hands cut them up and made a hearty meal of them." (*Memoirs*, p. 427.) Gasparo Balbi tells the same story of the same people, not omitting the salt and pepper, and so does a notice in Moor. And I have heard it almost exactly as told by Raffles, from a native of Arakan, when I was travelling in that country in 1853, the alleged actors being some of the wild tribes then to the north-east of us. Something similar is related by Edward Barbosa of a tribe in the interior of Siam. Vincent Le Blanc says he was assured by the people of Pulowé that the islanders of Sumatra eat their dead, "but we found it quite the contrary," he goes on, "and saw them buried." He nevertheless tells the same story as true, of an island called *Pulovois* (apparently imaginary) south of the Maldives.

The custom, or its allegation, is not confined to the old world. Tribes (*e.g.*), both of Brazil and of Vancouver's Island, are stated to have been in the habit of putting sick relatives to death, when the conjuror or medicine-man despaired of recovery. And the Brazilian tribe *ate* the bodies of those who were thus given over.

The particular story related by Odoric is evidently the same as that told by Marco Polo of "the kingdom of Dragoian" in the island of Java Minor or Sumatra. The situation of Dragoian has been much disputed, but if Marco's kingdoms were, as they seem, recounted in geographical succession, it must have been nearly coincident with Achin. And it is worth noticing that Balbi ascribes this cannibalism to the kingdom of the "Rey del Dagin," which he afterwards lets us see is meant for Achin. Can Odoric mean the same place by Dondin?

[M. Romanet du Caillaud, *Ctes. rendus Soc. Géog.*, 1896, p. 117, writes that, in his opinion, under the name of Dondin, Odoric includes the whole of the Indian archipelago from Sumatra to the Philippine Islands included. Señor D. A. Gummá y Marti, l.c., p. 173, answers that Odoric never went to the Philippine Islands, which is true, and that Dondin includes Ceylon, some of the Sunda islands, perhaps Borneo, and Hai-nan. All this is sheer nonsense.]

[1] [RAM. A., "si humana."]

"Lord, thou art our God! and as our God we adore thee! Answer to that we ask of thee! Such an one is ailing grievously; must he die, or shall he be delivered from his ailment? We ask thee!" Then the demon replies by the mouth of the idol, and says:—"Thy father shall not die, but shall be freed from that ailment. And thou must do such and such things and so he shall recover." And so the demon shows the man all that he is to do for his father's recovery; and he returneth to his father accordingly, and tendeth him diligently until he be entirely recovered. But if the demon reply that the father will die, then the priest goeth to him and putteth a linen cloth[1] over his mouth, and so suffocateth him and he dieth. And when they have thus slain him, they cut him in pieces, and invite all their friends and relations and all the players[2] of the country round about to come to the eating of him, and eat him they do, with singing of songs and great merrymaking. But they save his bones and bury them underground with great solemnity[3]. And any of the relatives who have not been invited to this wedding feast (as it were) deem themselves to have been grievously slighted[4].

I[5] rebuked these people sharply for so acting, saying to them:—"Why do ye act thus against all reason? Why, were a dog slain and put before another dog he would by no means eat thereof; and why should you do thus, who

[1] [RAM. A., un paño.—RAM. B., PAL., DOM., panno.—VEN., pannum linum.—CIV., pannum.—FRENCH TEXT, Pomme, which is an obvious mistake for *pagne*.]

[2] [RAM. A., buffoni.—CIV., cum hystrionibus.—B.N., hystriones.—VEN., jaculatores.]

[3] [VEN., "Eius tamen ossa occipiunt, ipsa sub terra cum magna solemnitate sepelliunt."—CIV., "Post haec occipientes ossa sepulturae tradunt, cum magna sollemnitate."—RAM. A., "Le ossa del quale poi con grande solēnita sotterano."—RAM. B., "E dell' ossa si fan certe cerimonie e poi sono sotterrate."

[4] MIN. RAM. "And the kinsfolk rejoice when any one gets ill, in hope of eating him and having a merrymaking." ["E quasi sono lieti quando alcuno s' inferma per posser lo mangiare, e farne festa."]

[5] [CIV., etc., "Ego frater Odericus."]

seem to be men endowed with reason?" And their answer was:—"We do this lest the flesh of the dead should be eaten of worms; for if the worms should eat his flesh his soul would suffer grievous pains[1]; we eat his flesh therefore that his soul suffer not." And so, let me say what I would, they would not believe otherwise nor quit that custom of theirs.

27. A word in brief of India and the isles thereof.

And there be many other strange things in those parts which I write not, for unless a man should see them he never could believe them. For in the whole world there be no such marvels as in that realm (of India). What things I have written are only such as I was certain of, and such as I cannot doubt but they are as I have related them.

And as regards this India[2] I have inquired from many who have knowledge of the matter, and they all assured me as with one voice that it includeth in its limits a good twenty-four thousand[3] islands, in which there are sixty-four[4] crowned kings. And the greater part of these islands is well peopled. So here I have done with this India, and will say no more thereof; but I will now tell you somewhat of Upper India.

28. Friar Odoric cometh to Upper India[5] and the Province of Manzi, and discourseth of them.

Ye shall know then that after I had sailed eastward over the Ocean Sea for many days I came to that noble

[1] MIN. RAM. "For that God, offended at the stink, would refuse them admittance into his glory." ["Di modo che Iddio offeso dalla puzza non gli riceuerebbe nella gloria sua."]

[2] [CIV., "De magnitudine huius inferioris Indiae."—RAM. A., PAL., "questa India."]

[3] [VEN., 24 milia.—CIV., 24 millia.—RAM. A., vintiquattro mila isole.—HAK., 4400!]

[4] [VEN. and CIV., sexaginta quatuor reges.—RAM. A., PAL., sessantaquattro Re.—2810 fr., VIII.]

[5] ["E con questo faccio fine di scriuere altro dell' India inferiore: al presente intendo solamente dire della superiore." RAM. A.—"De hac India dicta sufficiant ut ad superiorem Indiam me traducam." VEN.]

province[1] MANZI[2], which we call Upper India[3]. And as

1 [RAM. A., "Venni in vna nobile & grande prouincia."—B.N., nobilem provinciam.]

2 [A.S., Manzy.—RAM. A., B.N., VEN., FARS., PAL., CIV., Manzi.—CIV., Manza.—B.N., Mansi.—HAK., Manci.—DOM., Mati.—RAM. B., Mangi.]

"Manzi," says Klaproth, "is the Chinese word *Man-tsu*, by which the people and country of Southern China were designated during the supremacy of the Mongols." Davis says the name, which he writes *Mantze*, was originally applied by the Chinese to the *barbarians* of the south. And Magaillans, giving the same account of the original meaning, tells us that in his own time (the latter part of the seventeenth century) the term *Mantzu*, or barbarians, was applied by the Tartars scoffingly to the Chinese. This is perhaps copied from Martini, who says the same. It is, therefore, a mistake to suppose, as has been put forward by Assemani and others, that Manzi or Mangi is a corruption of the Machin and Masin of the Persians and Arabs. These last are merely modifications of the Sanscrit *Maha Chin*, Magna China. But it seems probable that a confusion did take place between the two words; for in the history of Rashideddin (as probably in other Mahomedan writers) *Machin* is sometimes used for *Manzi*, as the special name of Southern China. (*Journ. As.*, ii, sér. xi, 337, 341, 343; *Davis's Chinese*, i, 180; *Baldello*, i, 29; Martini, *Atlas Sinensis*.) Pauthier, it should be added, gives quite a different explanation of Manzi. He says that Fukien was formerly called the principality of *Mán*, a name still applied in poetry. Hence the subjects of the Sung Emperors were called by the Northern Chinese *Mán-jin*, or Men of Mán (*op. inf. cit.*, p. 117). But M. Pauthier seems to have now abandoned this opinion; see his fine new edition of Polo, p. lvii.

[Before the Mongols Chinghizkhanides once more became sole masters of China, the Middle Kingdom was ruled, in the North, by the Niu-chen Tartars or Kin, reigning at Yen-king (Pe-king), in the South, by the Chinese of the Sung Dynasty, with Lin-ngan (Hang-chau) as their capital, in the Cheh-kiang province. Northern China was designated as *Kitaï*, from the K'i-tan Tartars or Leao, still in use by the Russians, Китай, the Greeks, Κιτάϊα, and the Turks, *Khitài*, hence the name CATHAY; these northern men called the southern inhabitants of China Barbarians, *Man*, or Sons of Barbarians, *Man-tzu* or *Man-tze*, hence MANGI and MANZI; it is true the latter retaliated by calling their northern foe *Pe-taï*, "Fools of the North."—Dr. G. Schlegel has given a note on this word in *Notes and Queries on China and Japan*, i, p. 91; it is not to the point: there is every reason to believe that Odoric and Marco Polo (the latter resided at Yang-chau) heard the word *Mangi* not only at Zaytún, but in many other places.]

[RAM. B., "In molte parti di detta prouincia viddi più stretta la gente, che non e' a Vinetia al tempo dell' Ascensione."—MUN. mentions: "videlz Venecij. Januensibus. Neapoli. Brundusie."]

3 As late as the seventeenth century we find Martini, in his *Atlas Sinensis*, calling China *Asia Superior*.

[RAM. A., DOM., India superiore.—RAM. B., PAL., India di Sopra.—B.N., VEN., "quam Indiam vocamus superiorem."]

to that India I made diligent inquiry from Christians, Saracens, and idolaters, and from all the great Khan's officers, and they all told me, with one consent as it were, that the province of Manzi[1] hath two thousand great cities[2]; cities I mean of such magnitude that neither Treviso nor Vicenza[3] would be entitled to be numbered among them[4]. Indeed in that country the number of the people is so great that among us here it would be deemed incredible; [and in many parts I have seen the population more dense than the crowds you see at Venice on the Ascension Day][5]. And the land hath great store of bread, of wine, of rice, of flesh, and of fish of sorts, and of all manner of victuals whatever that are used by mankind.

[1] [1380 fr., Mongin.—2810 fr., Mangy.]

[2] [DOM., "due cento grandi città."]

[3] [B.N., VEN., Trevisium neque Vincencia.—A.S., Taruisium & Vincentia.—CIV., Tervisum et Vincencia.—RAM. B., Vicenza, o Triuigi.—RAM. A., Venetia, ne altra città.—MUN., "talesq; nec Vincentia n^c Teruisiū que sūt maiores q^m Ezlinga si ponerat."]

[4] So Wassaf says: "China possesses besides Khanzai, four hundred considerable cities, of which the smallest surpasses Baghdad and Shiraz." (*D'Ohsson*, ii, 418.) There is great exaggeration in Odoric's statement. The number of cities of different classes in China (which includes much more than Manzi) is, according to modern official statements, as follows:—

Fu, or chief cities of Prefectures	182
Chau, " " of circles	134
Hien, " " of districts	1281
Other cities	112
Total,	1709

(From *Pauthier*, *Chine Moderne*, p. 129.)

[Father Magaillans, *Nouv. Relat. de la Chine*, pp. 92—93, reckons 4402 walled cities in China.—Archdeacon J. H. Gray, *China*, 1878, i, p. 5: "The eighteen provinces of China proper, in their collective capacity, contain upwards of four thousand walled cities."]

[5] The feast of the Ascension was the first day of the great fair at Venice, in the middle ages one of the greatest fairs in the world. Like the fairs in India it combined religion and trade, for many then came as pilgrims either to visit the relics of the saints at Venice, or to take passage for the shrines beyond sea, such as Loretto, Rome, Compostella, or Jerusalem. On the Ascension Day also took place the celebrated espousals of the Adriatic. Semedo likewise compares the throng habitually encountered in China to that of great public festivals in Europe. (*Rel. della Cina*, 1643, p. 7.)

And all the people of this country are traders and artificers[1], and no man ever seeketh alms, however poor he be, as long as he can do anything with his own hands to help himself[2]. [But those who are fallen into indigence and infirmity are well looked after and provided with necessaries[3].]

The men, as to their bodily aspect, are comely enough, but colourless, having beards of long straggling hairs like mousers,—cats I mean. And as for the women, they are the most beautiful in the world!

29. Of the great city Censcalan[4].

The first city to which I came in this country was called CENSCALAN[5], and 'tis a city as big as three

[1] [VEN., artiste.]

[2] Davis notices the "cheerful industry" of the Chinese as a characteristic which is "the first to strike all visitors of China." (*Chinese*, i, 200.)

[3] [MIN. RAM., "E non ui é chi vada cercando la limosina. Perche o poueri o infermi sono ben gouernati, e prouisti delle cose necessarie. Gli huomini sono tutti vgualmente grandi, e pallidi con i peli della barba irti, & male composti alla guisa delle capre. Le donne sono bellissime."—Cf. RAM. A.—PAL., "Le più belle del mondo."—B. N., "Mulieres vero pulcherrimae de mundo."—VEN., "Pulcerime sunt de mundo."—A. S., "Mulieres nimiùm sunt formosae."—CIV., "Mulieres vero nimium sunt formosae."]

[4] [FARS., Censcalam.—DOM., Censscanlan.—B. N., Censcolan.—HAK., Censkalon.—RAM. A., Ceuscala.—VEN., Conscala.—RAM. B., Tescol.—MUN., Tascalan.—PAL., Teschalan.—CIV., Senstalay.—A. S., Soustalay.]

[5] This name, which is grievously mangled in most of the MSS. and editions of Odoric, is the *Cynkalan* of Marignolli, the *Sínkalán* of Ibn Batuta, the *Chínkalán* of Rashideddin and Wassaf the Persian historians of the Mongols, and represents, I believe, without doubt the modern Canton. Odoric's description of it as the first port reached by him, with its great estuary and vast amount of shipping, points to this identification. Ibn Batuta tells us the great junks for the Indian trade were built only at Zaitún and at Sínkalán. Now Zaitún, Canton, and Kanfu are known to have been the three ports for Indian trade; and of the first Ibn Batuta speaks by this name—he speaks of *Khansá*, of which Khanfu was probably the port, though the names were interchanged by the Arabs—but does not mention Canton unless it be Sínkalán. He also speaks more than once of the space from Khanbaliq to Sínkalán, as of the Dan and Beersheba of China, whilst

Venices[1]. It is one day's voyage from the sea[2], standing upon a certain river, the water whereof is derived from the sea, and extendeth twelve days' journey into the land[3]. The whole population of this city, as well as of all Manzi and Upper India, worship idols. And this city hath shipping so great and vast in amount that to some it would seem well nigh incredible[4]. Indeed all Italy hath not the amount of craft that this one city hath[5]. And here you can buy three

the latter city is said to adjoin barbarous and cannibal tribes. All this points to Canton. Rashideddin too indicates its position as south of the port of Zaitún.

Cincalan will also be found in its proper place, i.e. as the first port of China from the south, in the extraordinary Catalan map of 1375.

The name I have no doubt is Persian, with the meaning ascribed to it by Marignolli, "*Great China*," and is, therefore, simply a translation of Mahachín. This would consist with the practice which seems to have prevailed among the Arab seafarers of giving a chief city the name of the country to which it belonged, a practice which probably originated that city of Bengala which has given so much trouble to geographers. Indeed, I find that Rashid and Al Biruni distinctly apply the name Mahachin to a city, no doubt Canton.

Though Zaitún and Kanfu (the ancient port of King sé or Hangchau fu) appear to have been the havens most frequented by western trade under the Mongol dynasty, Canton was a very early resort of the Arabs and Persians. In 758 they were numerous enough to master and pillage and burn the city. (See *Marignolli* infrà; *Ibn Batuta*, iv, 92, 255, 268, 274; *D'Ohsson*, 418, 638; *Deguignes*, i, 59; *Elliot's Historians of M. India*, p. 46; and *Sprenger*, *Post-und-Reiserouten des Orients*, p. 90.)

[The singular name is but a corruption of صين كيالن *Sin Kîlan*, given by the Mohammedans to Canton.]

[1] [MUN., "Magnitudo eius benè equipollet tribus Vincentijs que ut puto maior q^m sit Spira, Wormacia, Moguncia."]

[2] [VEN., "Prima civitas quam inveni vocatur Conscalan que est in triplo maior Vincencia distans a mari per dietam unam."]

[3] This is very obscure; "*cujus aqua propter ipsum mare ascendit ultra terram bene xii dietis.*" I have translated as if the tidal flow were alluded to, but with great doubt as to the meaning. Hakluyt's translation runs, "the water whereof, near unto the mouth where it exonerateth itself into the sea, doth overflow the land for the space of twelve days' journey." It may be a reference to the breadth of the estuary, which is about eighty miles at the mouth. But the passage seems corrupt in all copies.

[4] [A. S., "Ciuitas autem ista sola plus habet de nauigio & mercationibus, quàm tota Italia posset habere."]

[5] "Hundreds of thousands" of boats, says Fortune. "In the river and port alone," says Linschoten, "there is more craft of different

hundred pounds of fresh ginger for less than a groat[1]! The geese too are bigger and finer and cheaper[2] than anywhere in the world[3]. For one of them is as big as two of ours[4], and 'tis all white as milk, but has a bone on the top of its head about the size of an egg, which is of a blood colour; whilst under its throat it has a skin hanging down for half a span[5]. And these geese are as fat as fat can be,

kinds (*barques et frégates*) than in the whole of Spain." (*Three Years' Wanderings*, p. 148; *Linsch.*, p. 40.)

[1] MIN. RAM. has "700 lbs. for a ducat." "E per vn ducato viddi dar 700 libre de Zenzeuero verde, e fresco."—DOM., "Tre libre di giengievo."—PAL., "In questa cittade s' à per meno d' un Viniziano ben trecento lib. di gengiovo fresco."—A. S., "In hac etiam ciuitate benè *centum* librae zinziberis recentis possunt haberi vno minori grosso Veneto."]

[Canton is well-known for its ginger, *Kan-kiang*; the Chinese make very good preserve with it.]

[2] "*In meliori foro*," a dog-latinism which Venni does not seem to have understood, for he proposes to read "*meliori formâ*." Yet the Italians have *buon mercato*, as the French have *meilleur marché*, and our old English had *good cheap*, though we have cut it down into an elliptical adjective. The old translation of Mendoza says on the same matter, which continued to strike visitors to a much later date: "All things is so good cheape that almost it seemeth they sell them for nothing." Early in last century from 3d. to 6d. a head covered the expenses of Ripa's party for a good dinner, supper, and lodging. (*Major's* edit. of *Mendoza*, HAK. SOC. i, 12; *Father Ripa*, p. 133.)

[3] B. N., "Sunt majores et pulchriores anseres ac melius forum."—VEN., "In meliori foro."]

[4] [RAM. B., "maggiori tre uolte delle nostre."]

[5] This description of Odoric's agrees almost precisely with the following: "*Anser Cygnoides*, the Guinea goose...approaching in size to the swan...it has a fleshy tubercle rising from the base of the bill... and a pendant skin in the form of a pouch under the throat....The beak and tubercle are reddish," etc. (*Nouveau Dict. de l'Hist. Naturelle*, Paris, 1817, tom. xxiii.) I am told on excellent authority that the modern domestic goose of China has *not* the pendant skin, though it certainly has the knob or tubercle. Yet Odoric's evidence is curiously precise.

A zoological friend of mine, E. H. Giglioli, attached to the Italian expedition of circumnavigation, writes to me from Singapore (May 18th, 1866), that among a flock of "knobbed" geese in the Chinese quarter there he had seen one "with a well-developed membrane hanging under its beak." So that Odoric's account can be justified.

[Father David, *Oiseaux de la Chine*, p. 493, confirms this evidence; he says the male *anser cygnoides* has a horny tubercle in the frontal region; moreover he wrote to me that in a domesticated state, the goose has also a pendant skin (Jabot).—"The goose market which is held daily at Canton, in the street called Luen-hing Kai, is almost as

yet one of them well dressed and seasoned you shall have there for less than a groat. And as it is with the geese, so also with the ducks[1] and fowls; they are so big that you would think them perfectly marvellous.

Here too there be serpents bigger than anywhere else in the world, many of which are taken and eaten with great relish. These serpents [have quite a fragrant odour and][2] form a dish so fashionable that if a man were to give a dinner and not have one of these serpents on his table, he would be thought to have done nothing[3]. In short this city hath a great abundance of all possible kinds of victual.

large as the annual goose fair for which Nottingham is so famous. Flat-bottomed boats discharge large numbers of these birds, at the wharf immediately in front of the market. I have seen no fewer than three hundred geese removed from one boat, several others, each containing an equal number, awaiting their turn alongside the wharf." Gray, *China*, ii, pp. 186–7.]

[1] [Father Armand David wrote to me that the Chinese possess but the vulgar duck, *Anas boschas*, and its varieties.]

[2] MIN. RAM. ["E gli paiono odoriferi."]

[3] Conti speaks of the large pythons of the Burmese forests as being greatly prized for food. But, more precisely, Chinese authors quoted by Klaproth speak of a great snake called *Nan-che* or southern serpent, from being found only south of the great chain of Southern China (therefore in Kwang tung and the adjacent provinces), which is hunted and sold at a great price, the flavour of the flesh being in such high estimation. (*Journ. As.*, sér. 2, ii, 118.) Till I found this I suspected some mistake on Odoric's part, his expressions so closely resemble those of a later ecclesiastic in speaking of swallow-nest soup: "No entertainment without this dish; if it is wanting the best is wanting; and without it no dinner can be deemed in worthy style." (*P. Marini*, quoted by Kircher, *China Illust.*, 199.)

[Marco Polo, in the Province of Carajan, says, ii, p. 76: "In this province are found snakes and great serpents of such vast size as to strike fear into those who see them...they also sell the flesh of this serpent, for it is excellent eating, and the people are very fond of it." Yule, p. 81, writes that it cannot be doubted that Marco's serpents here are crocodiles.—"According to Chinese notions, Han Yü, the St Patrick of China, having persuaded the alligators in China, that he was all-powerful, induced the stupid saurians to migrate to Ngo Hu or 'Alligators' Lake in the Kwang-tung province." *North-China Herald*, 5th July 1895, p. 5.]

30. Concerning the noble city called Zayton; and how the folk thereof regale their gods.

Departing from that district, and passing through many cities and towns, I came[1] to a certain noble city which is called ZAYTON[2], where we friars minor have two houses[3];

[1] [PAL., per xxxvi giornate.—RAM. B., nauigammo 27 giornate.]

[2] [B. N., Zayton.—DOM., Zaiton.—CIV., Zaycon.—RAM. A., Zaton.—RAM. B., Zanton.—PAL., Zataiton.—BOLL., Saiton.—ARUND., Kaycon.—FARS., Caicham.—HAK., Kaitam.—FRENCH TEXT, Cartan, Catan.]

Zayton, Zaitún, Zeithum, Çayton, the great port of Chinese trade with the west in the middle ages; that from which Polo sailed on his memorable voyage; that at which Ibn Batuta landed, and from which Marignolli sailed for India, is mentioned by nearly all the authors who speak of China up to the fourteenth century inclusive. A veil falls between China and Europe on the expulsion of the Mongols, and when it rises in the sixteenth century, Zayton has disappeared.

Martini had hinted, and De Guignes had conjectured, that Polo's Zeithum was the port of Ts' wan-chau fu, in the province of Fu-kien. It remained for Klaproth to show from the Imperial Geography that the port in question was originally called *Tseu-thung*, the corruption of which to Zeithum and Zaytún would be easy.

From this port sailed the expeditions of the Mongol sovereign against Java and Japan, and for a time after the rediscovery of China it was one of the harbours frequented by the Portuguese, under the name of *Chinceo*; that of Zaytún having passed away from common use, though it is not unlikely that an Arab or Malay skipper could have pointed out the place so called. (*Martini*, in Thévenot, iii (1666), p. 155; *De Guignes*, iv, 169, 180; *Klapr.*, *Mém.* ii, 200 and *seq.*; *Polo*, II, 234 *seq.*; *Hakluyt* (reprint), ii, 546.)

[I think it would be fastidious to re-open the controversy regarding the respective claims of Chang-chau and Ts'wan-chau to be Zaytún. It will be remembered that the late George Phillips held for the former, and he had given many proofs of the importance of Chang-chau at the time of the Mongol dynasty, but the weak point of his discussion was his theory about Fu-chau. Drawing from Chinese sources, Dr. F. Hirth, writes that "to start for foreign countries one must embark at Ts'wan-chau, and then go to the sea of Ts'i-chau (Paracels), through the Tai-hsü pass; coming back he must look to Kwen-lun (Pulo Condor)." Cf. *Marco Polo*, ii, p. 194.—This passage in itself would be almost sufficient to show that Zaytún = Ts'wan-chau. However the question has been fully treated in my edition of *Odoric* and in *Marco Polo*, ii, pp. 237–242.]

[3] See both of these establishments spoken of by Bishop Andrew of Zaytún in a letter below, which was written [January 1326] a year or two after Odoric's visit. [In his letter Bishop Andrew speaks of the Tana Martyrs, but does not say that Odoric brought their bones to Zaytún.] John Marignolli mentions a third house in his time, twenty years later.

and there I deposited the bones[1] of our friars who suffered martyrdom for the faith of Jesus Christ.

In this city is great plenty of all things that are needful for human subsistence[2]. For example you can get three[3] pounds and eight ounces of sugar[4] for less than half a groat[5]. The city is[6] twice as great as Bologna[7], and in it are many monasteries of devotees, idol worshippers every man of them. In one of those monasteries which I visited there were three thousand monks and eleven thousand idols[8]. And one of those idols, which seemed to be smaller than the rest was as big as St. Christopher might be[9].

1 [FRENCH TEXT: "Je portay ces III corps sains desquelx nous avons fait cy devant mention des III frères meneurs qui furent martirisiez en la cité de Cana."—CIV. has "quatuor" instead of III.]

2 [HAK., pro lenissimo foro.]

3 [FRENCH TEXT, IIII livres.—B. N., CIV., tres.]

4 [CIV., BOLL., *zinziberis* instead of *zuchari*.]

5 [FRENCH TEXT, un demi gros.—PAL., per un grosso.—RAM. B., per vn soldo.]

6 [ARUND., ut fideliter assero.]

7 MIN. RAM.: "Men and women, both, are of pleasing manners, handsome and courteous, especially to foreigners."

["Huomini e donne sono piaceuoli, e belli, e cortesi, massime a forastieri."]

[PAL., RAM. A. et B., Bologna.—B. N., CIV., Bononia.—FRENCH TEXT, Romme.]

8 Far greater numbers of monks are ascribed by Fa hian to monasteries of Ceylon in his day, and by Huc to Tibetan monasteries in our own. The great establishment at Pooto, an island of the Chusan Archipelago, had three thousand monks in the beginning of the last century, and even in her modern decay, in our own day, had two thousand monks, with idols innumerable (*Astley*, iv, 43; *Davis*, ii, 189). The Dutch embassy of 1655 speaks of a famous temple near Nan king, which had ten thousand images. But most of these were small. The monastery visited by Odoric at Zaitún, or Ts'wan-chau, was probably that called the *Water-Lily*, founded [under the T'ang Dynasty, during the K'aï Yuan period (713–742)], and still magnificent, boasting two great seven-storied towers. (See *Chine Moderne*, p. 117.)

9 "The picture of St. Christopher, that is of a man of giant-like stature, bearing upon his shoulders our Saviour Christ, and with a staff in his hand wading through the water, is known unto children, common over all Europe, not only as a sign unto houses, but is described in many churches, and stands colossus-like in the entrance of Notre Dame." (*Sir T. Brown*, *Vulgar Errors*, ii, 52.) [See note in my ed. of *Odoric*, pp. 130–133, 284.]

St. Christopher, I suppose, may be taken at nine to twelve feet

I went thither at the hour fixed for feeding their idols, that I might witness it; and the fashion thereof is this: All the dishes which they offer to be eaten are piping hot[1] so that the smoke riseth up in the face of the idols, and this they consider to be the idols' refection. But all else they keep for themselves and gobble up. And after such fashion as this they reckon that they feed their gods well[2].

The place is one of the best in the world, and that as regards its provision for the body of man. Many other things indeed might be related of this place, but I will not write more about them at present.

31. The friar telleth of the city Fuzo and its marvels; also of rare fashions of fishing.

Thence I passed eastward to a certain city called FUZO[3],

high. But many of the Chinese Buddhas are from thirty to forty feet in height.

[B. N., "In uno autem istorum monasteriorum ego fui in quo bene erant tria millia religiosorum habentium XI millia ydola; et unum illorum ydolorum quod minus aliis esse videbatur erat bene ita magnum esset sicut Sanctus Christophorus."—CIV., "Multa sunt monasteria religiosorum idola colencium. Et in uno monasterio ego fui, in quo erant tria millia religiosorum illorum, qui sub cura sua habebant undecim millia idolorum. Et quod minus inter illa videbatur, ita magnum erat sicut Christoforus depingitur apud nos."—PAL., "Sonci molti munasteri di religiosi di l' idolatri, ne' quali sono ben dumilia riligiosi, ed anno bene XI^{m} d' idoli. E 'l minore è a modo d' un grande san Christofano...."—RAM. B., "Sono in questa terra molti monasteri, & idololatrice: auisandoui che ui sono piu di 3000 idoli: & il minore è due uolte piu grande d' un huomo, & sono d' oro, o d' argento, o d' altri metalli lauorati."—FRENCH TEXT: "Il y a pluseurs abbaies de religieux ydolatrez, car tout le peuple est communément ydolatre, dont le souverain de tous leurs ydoles ilz font aussi grant comme nous faisons ici saint Christofle."]

1 [HAK., ARUND., calidissima et fumigantia.—FRENCH TEXT, très chaudes et boullans.]

2 "The principal hall in the house was set in order, a large table was placed in the centre, and shortly afterwards covered with small dishes filled with the various articles commonly used as food by the Chinese. All these were of the very best....Candles were lighted, and columns of smoke and fragrant odours began to rise from the incense which was burning on the table....By and bye, when the gods were supposed to have finished their repast, all the articles of food were removed from the table, cut up, and consumed by people connected with the family." (*Fortune's Three Years Wanderings*, p. 190.)

3 [VEN., DOM., Fuzo.—B. N., Fucho.—HAK., Fuko.—ARUND.,

which hath a compass of good thirty miles[1]. And here be seen the biggest cocks in the world. And there be hens also that are white as snow, and have no feathers, but have wool only upon them, like sheep[2]. The city is a mighty fine one, and standeth upon the sea[3].

Fuco.—FARS., Fuc.—PAL., Fozzo.—RAM. B., Foggia.—RAM. A., Fluzo. —A. S., Suctio.—CIV., Sucho, quae in circuitu viginta miliaria dicitur habere.]

Undoubtedly Fu-chau, capital of Fu-kien province, one of the most wealthy and populous cities in China.

[Marco Polo, ii, p. 231, says: "Now this city of Fuju is the key of the kingdom which is called *Chonka*, and which is one of the nine great divisions of Manzi. The city is a seat of great trade and great manufactures. The people are Idolaters and subject to the Great Kaan. And a large garrison is maintained there by that prince to keep the kingdom in peace and subjection. For the city is one which is apt to revolt on very slight provocation. There flows through the middle of this city a great river, which is about a mile in width, and many ships are built at the city which are launched upon this river. Enormous quantities of sugar are made there, and there is a great traffic in pearls and precious stones. For many ships in India come to these parts bringing many merchants who traffic about the Isles of the Indies. For this city is, as I must tell you, in the vicinity of the Ocean Port of Zayton...." According to the late Mr. Phillips, Fuju is Ts'wan-chau, which view I do not accept; see Zaytún, p. 183.]

[1] [The French Text omits this sentence.]

[2] [RAM. B., "Di qui partendo verso oriente, giunsi in vna città, che e sopra il mare, grande più di 30 miglia, chiamata Foggia, i Galli sono grandissimi: le galline bianchissime, & in vece di piume sono vestite di lana, come pecore."—B. N., "De hac contrata veni versus orientem ad unam civitatem quae vocatur Fucho, quae bene circuit per XXX miliaria, in qua sunt majores galli qui sunt in mundo. Gallinae vero sunt albae ut nix, non habentes pennas sed solum lanam ut pecus sunt portantes."]

Phasianus Lanatus, *Gallus Lanatus*, Coq à duvet, or Silk fowl. Kircher thus describes them, out of Martini: "Woolly hens, the wool of which is much like that of sheep. They are small, with very short legs, but courageous, and much petted by the women." He adds: "It is generally owned that the wool of these hens cannot be woven into cloth (!) except it be first steeped in a lye, of which I have the secret." (*China Illust.* 196.) Martini is speaking of Sze-ch'wan, but Polo also speaks of these fowls in Fu-kien as "hens that have no feathers, but skins like a cat," i.e. an Angora or Persian cat, a race of which Martini mentions in China. "It is this breed which gave rise in 1766 to the fable of the fowl-rabbit, which was shown at Brussels as the produce of a rabbit and a common hen." (*Nouv. Dict. de l'Histoire Naturelle*, vol. vii.)

[The *Gallus Lanatus* is but a race of the *Gallus ferrugineus* from which come probably all the hens of the world; this Chinese variety, by its domestication, is more delicate than the others and is very prolific.]

[3] [Sentence omitted in the French text.]

Departing thence and travelling for eighteen days, I passed through many cities and towns, and witnessed a great variety of things. And as I travelled thus I came to a certain great mountain. And on the one side all the animals that dwell there are black, and the men and women have a very strange way of living. But on the other side all the animals are white, and the men and women have a quite different way of living from the others[1]. All the

[1] [BOLL., "In cuius latere nigra animalia morabantur; ex alio autem latere eiusdem montis animalia sunt alba."—CIV., "In cuius latere magna animalia morabantur, ex alio autem latere eiusdem montis...animalia fuerunt alba."—RAM. B., "E peruenimmo ad vn monte altissimo nel qual mi parue veder cosa strana, che da quel lito, doue noi discēdessemo, io viddi huomini, le donne, & bestie tutti negrissimi piu che carboni spenti, & da l' altro lato verso Oriente erano tutti huomini, e donne, e bestie bianchissimi: ma l' vna parte, e l' altra mi pareua che viuessino, e vestisseno come bestie."]

"Though on both one side and the other methought they lived and dressed in a beastly manner." MIN. RAM. It is difficult to explain precisely what this theory means, but doubtless the range of mountains [called Nan Shan] was that which separates Fu-kien from the rest of the empire, and which Odoric may have crossed either northwards into Che-Kiang, or westwards into Kiang-si, which last we shall see was the route followed by Ibn Batuta in going to King se or Hang-chau fu.

The differences between the races on the two sides of the mountain probably point to the friar's having passed a part occupied by the Meau-tze or other aboriginal tribes. These do not now extend so far east, but what Polo says of savage cannibals with blue-painted (i.e. tattooed) faces in Fu-kien, seems to imply that they did so in his time; and some observations of Sir John Davis's corroborate this (*Polo*, i, 78; *Chinese, supp. vol.* p. 260). And in the modern Chinese census one class of population in a district of the province of Canton appear as *Blacks* (*Chine Mod.*, p. 167). Indeed Semedo (about 1632) says there was still an independent kingdom, presumably of the Meau-tze, in the mountains dividing Fu-kien, Canton, and Kiang-si, viz., those of which Odoric speaks (*Rel. della Cina*, p. 19).

The habits and appearances of those races would, no doubt, stand in strong contrast to those of the Chinese, who call them *Dogmen* and *Wolfmen*. The "barrel of horn" worn on the head may perhaps be identified with the grotesque coiffure of the Meau-tze women, described by Duhalde as "a light board, more than a foot long and five or six inches wide, which they cover with their hair, and fix it with wax, so that they seem to have a hair hat on. They can't rest the head nor lie down, except by putting something under the neck, and they are obliged constantly to twist the head right or left in passing along the forest paths. And the business of combing the hair is a still greater difficulty; they must then hold their heads for hours by the fire to melt the wax," etc.

The description of this head-dress in the *Minor Ramusian* version, however, rather recalls that of the wooden sugar-loaf head-dress worn

married women there wear on their heads a great barrel of horn[1], that they may be known to be married[2].

Passing hence, and travelling for eighteen days more, through many cities and towns, I came to a certain great river[3], and I tarried at a certain city [called Belsa][4] which

by the Druze women; and it is curious in connexion with this to remember the Chinese origin of the Druzes, which their traditions maintain (see Mr. Cyril Graham on the Druzes of Bashan, in *J.R.G.S.*). Hiuen Tsang describes a horn of some three feet in height as worn by the married women of *Himatala*, apparently a district of Upper Badakhshan. (*Vie de H.T.*, p. 269.)

[Dr. D. J. Macgowan in his *Note on the Chihkiang Miautsz'*, in the *Journ. of the North China B. Roy. As. Soc.*, N. S., vi, p. 124, crossing the hilly country between Kin hwa fu and Chu Chau fu, writes: "In 1859 I crossed with a fellow traveller the mountains which divide the departments of Kin hwa and Chi-chau, in one of the glens of which we met a party of women whose extraordinary habiliments attracted our attention. They were evidently out on a holiday ramble which their full-sized unbound feet (so unlike those of their Chinese sisters), enabled them to enjoy. They wore their hair folded towards the forehead in the form of an arch, from which was suspended by a silver chain a silver plate, isoceles shape, rounded at the angles, and inscribed with felicitous characters, as "longevity," "happiness," and the like. These were amulets. As I merely regarded them as a hill clan, and as they were extremely timid, I made no attempt to interrogate them. On descending the valley, however, I made inquiries concerning them and was informed they were Miautsz'; that they lived secluded in the recesses of the adjacent mountains, conforming to a considerable extent to the customs of the neighbouring country; the men presenting no peculiarity in dress."]

[1] [B. N., barile de cornu.—RAM. A., un gran barile di corna.—Fr. 1380, couronne.]

[2] MIN. RAM. has "wear on the head, in the middle of the forehead, a horn of wood covered with skin, and more than two spans in length." ["Le donne maritate portano in testa vn corno di legno couerto di pelle, lungo piu di due spanne, a mezzo la fronte."—FRENCH TEXT: "Les dames mariées y portent une corne sur leur chief et par celle corne recognoist-on les dames mariées des autres."]

[3] [Odoric having just crossed the Nan Shan range, on his way to Hang-chau, is in the Che-Kiang province, and the great river mentioned by him is very probably the Ts'ien t'ang River.]

[4] I suppose it is not possible to determine the city on a great river where Odoric saw the fishing cormorants. Even if the name *Belsa* given in the *Min. Ram.* be genuine, I find nothing nearer it than Wen-chau in Che-Kiang, and it is doubtful if Odoric's route could have lain that way.

The story of the fishing birds is a perfectly accurate account of the practice, as it still exists in China, and is described by Duhalde, Staunton (these two give plates of the operation), Mendoza, Martini, Father Ripa, Davis, Fortune, and many more. The last-named author says the bird "is as docile as a dog; he swims after his master, and

hath a bridge[1] across that river. And at the head of the bridge was a hostel in which I was entertained[2]. And

allows himself to be pulled into the sanpan, where he disgorges his prey, and again resumes his labours. And what is more wonderful still, if one of the cormorants gets hold of a fish of a large size, so large that he would have some difficulty in taking it to the boat, some of the others haste to his assistance," etc. (*Three years' Wand.*, p. 110.) Fortune procured specimens to carry home, but could not bring them alive to England. The price in China was from six to eight dollars a pair.

The bird, which is called by the Chinese, with contempt for generic accuracy, "Fishing Hawk," or "Fishing Duck," is a cormorant, and has been termed *Phalacrocorax sinensis*, as differing from the English species (*Ph. Carbo*). I learn however that Mr. Swinhoe considers it to be only a variety produced by domestication. The English bird was formerly used for fishing both in England and in Holland quite in the Chinese way. Charles II had a *master of the cormorants.* (*Knight's Mus. of Animated Nature*, ii, 781.)

[This refers of course to Cormorant fishing, very much in favour in this very province of Che-Kiang. Cf. French ed. of Odoric, note, pp. 290-6.—In *The Special Cat. of the Chinese Col. Int. Fisheries Exhib.*, Lond., 1883, p. 46, we read: "Many are the ways used in this province for catching fish of all kinds in the rivers, lakes, and canals, but none of them are more curious than the cormorant fishing, which may be seen everywhere about Ningpo. Certain places are noted for the excellence of the birds which are bred and trained there; amongst these we may name Fênghua and Shaohsing. The most celebrated place, however, is a small town called T'anghsichên, 50 *li* north-west of Hang-chau, the people of which are currently believed to possess a secret in cormorant-rearing which gives them special success. The cormorant's book name is *Lu tzŭ*, and the common name is *Yü ying*, "fish hawk," or *Yü ya*, "fish crow."]

[1] [RAM. A., di marmo.]

[2] MIN. RAM. This edition has in this passage an exceedingly curious variation, difficult to account for. It runs thus: "Mine host ...took us to one side of the bridge where the river was wider, and there we found many boats, and there was one of them employed in fishing by aid of a certain fish called *Marigione.* The host had another such, and this he took and kept it by a cord attached to a fine collar. And this indeed is a creature that we have seen in our own seas, where many call it the *sea-calf.* It had the muzzle and neck like a fox's, and the forepaws like a dog's, but the toes longer, and the hind feet like a duck's, and the tail with the rest of the body like a fish's. Mine host made him go in the water, and he began to catch quantities of fish with his mouth, always depositing them in the boat. And I swear that in less than two hours he had filled more than two big baskets," etc. [" E lo hostieri p darci piacere, ci disse, se noi voleuamo ueder pescare, e menocci al lato del ponte, doue il fiume era piu largo: la oue erano molte barche, & eracene una, che pescaua con un pesce, che loro chiamano marigione. E l' hoste ne haueua un' altro, e quello tolse, e teneualo con vna corda messa in vna bella collana: e ben vero che noi ne haueuamo ueduti ne' nostri paesi assai: e molti lo chiamano Veglio marino. Questa bestia hauea il muso, e 'l collo com' vna volpe,

mine host, wishing to gratify me, said: "If thou wouldst like to see good fishing, come with me." And so he led me upon the bridge, and I looked and saw in some boats of his that were there certain water-fowl[1] tied upon perches. And these he now tied with a cord round the throat that they might not be able to swallow the fish which they caught. Next he proceeded to put three great baskets[2] into a boat, one at each end and the third in the middle, and then he let the water-fowl loose. Straightway they began to dive into the water, catching great numbers of fish, and ever as they caught them putting them of their own accord into the baskets, so that before long all the three baskets were full. And mine host then took the cord off their necks and let them dive again to catch fish for their own food. And when they had thus fed they returned to their perches and were tied up as before. And some of those fish I had for my dinner.

After departing thence and travelling for many days, I witnessed another fashion of fishing. The men this time were in a boat, wherein they had a tub full of hot water; and they were naked, and had each of them a bag slung

& i piedi dauanti com' vn cane, ma hauea le dita piû longhe, & i piedi di dietro com un' oca, e la coda col resto del busto come un pesce: quale l' hoste lo mando giù nel fiume: & egli cacciatosi dentro cominciò a prendere di molto pesce con la bocca tutta via mettendolo nella barca. E giuro che in meno di due hore n' empì piu di dui cestoni: e similmente fecero gli altri pescatori: quando poi non volean piu pescare, lasciauano la bestia nell' acqua, accioche andasse a pascerci: e quando era ben pasciuta, ritornaua ciascuna al suo pescatore, come cosa domestica."

RAM. A. is much shorter: "Nel capo d' esso [ponte era] una casa di un pescatore, doue allogiai: qual, volendo darmi alquanto spasso, mi disse: che se voleuo andar seco, a uedere vn bel pescare."]

Apollonius related that he had seen at Ægæ, near Issus, a female *phoca*, which was kept for fishing purposes. And the authority quoted in the preceding note [*Knight*], says the seal may be taught to assist in fishing. So probably the story was altered by some one aware of these facts about the seal, but indisposed to believe in the cormorants, and the use of the word *marigione*, apparently for *marangone* "a diver," appears to be a trace of the unaltered narrative.

[1] [Fr. Text, plungons.]

[2] [Fr. 1380, IIII questes.]

over his shoulder. Now they dived under water [for half a quarter of an hour or so][1], and caught the fish with their hands, stowing them in those bags that they had. And when they came up again they emptied the bags into the boat, whilst they themselves got into the tub of hot water[2], and others went in their turn and did as the first; and so great numbers of fish were taken[3].

[1] MIN. RAM. [Per un ottauo d' hora in circa.]

[2] [B.N., se ponentes.—VEN., ponebant.—CIV., se ponebant.—ARUND., balnearunt.]

[3] [RAM. B., "Stauano gli huomini tutti nudi in barca, e ciascuno haueua un sacchetto a torno, e buttauasi in acqua per un *ottauo d' hora* in circa, e prendeua del pesce con mano, mettendolo in sacchetto, e poi tornaua in barca: & incontinente si metteua in una tina d' acqua calda, & un' altra volta poi si buttauano in acqua, a pigliar del pesce."

The A.S. do not mention any fishing, and HAK. does not speak of the second manner.]

Fortune describes this mode of fishing also. "The fisherman," he says, "is literally amphibious. He is to be seen perfectly naked, half walking, half swimming; now he raises his arms and hands above his head, and, bringing them down, strikes a sharp blow upon the water, making a loud and splashing noise. His feet are not idle: they warn him that a fish is at hand, and they are now feeling for him amongst the mud at the bottom of the pond. The next moment the fisherman has disappeared...he appears rubbing his face and eyes with one hand, and in the other the poor little fish which he has just captured. It is immediately placed safely in his basket, and the work goes on as before." He says nothing of the tub of hot water (p. 109).

[This passage of Dabry's *Pisciculture en Chine*, pp. 170–1, will make clear this text: "A la fin de l'automne, et au commencement de l'hiver, c'est-à-dire pendant les dixième, onzième, douzième et premières lunes, quelques espèces de poissons aiment à rester blottis sous les pierres ou les éminences de terre qui s'élèvent au milieu des eaux. Les pêcheurs qui connaissent ces sortes de réservoirs, dans lesquels la température descend moins bas que dans les endroits non abrités, en profitent pour y prendre à la main cinq ou six espèces de poissons, tels que *yong-yu* (Hypophthalmichtys Simoni), *ky-yu* (Siniperca), *nien-yu* (Silurus Xansthosteus), *houang-chang-yu* (Peltobagrus calvarius). Comme ces trous sont généralement à des profondeurs assez considérables, le pêcheur est obligé de plonger pour les découvrir; il porte attaché autour de ses reins un petit filet, en forme de panier, dans lequel il met le poisson qu'il est parvenu à saisir avec ses mains; lorsque celui-çi est très gluant, le pêcheur le serre entre le pouce, le médium et l'annulaire formant ainsi une véritable pince. Quand le poisson est armé d'ailerons et de nageoires dangereuses, il le saisit sous le ventre et évite ainsi de se blesser. Chaque pêcheur, à tour de rôle (ils sont ordinairement quatre associés), plonge trois fois par demi-heure; aussitôt sorti de l'eau, il vient se réchauffer près du feu que l'on entretient continuellement sur le bâteau. Les jours où le

32. Concerning the city of Cansay, which is the greatest city on earth[1].

Departing thence, I came unto the city of Cansay, a name which signifieth "*the City of Heaven*[2]." And 'tis the

froid est trop considérable, on ne plonge pas. Quelquefois, après une grande fatigue, le pêcheur éprouve de violentes hémorrhagies."]

[1] [B.N., de civitate Cansaiâ.—VIENNA, de civitate Cansana.—RAM. A., Cansay.—PAL., Chansay.—VEN., Campsay, of which he wrongly makes *Nanking*, p. 123.—A. S., Chamsana.—CIV., Ahamsane.—DOM., Cansave.—RAM. B., Guinzai.—Fr. 2810, Casaie.—FRENCH TEXT, De la cité Casay la grande, alias Catusaie.]

[This chapter on Hang-chau is one of the most important of Odoric's Travels; we may refer the reader to Yule-Cordier's *Marco Polo*, Cordier's *Odoric*, the papers by Vissière and Hirth mentioned in the notes and especially Bishop Moule's *Notes on Col. Yule's Edition of Marco Polo* (*Journ. N. C. B. R. As. Soc.*, ix, 1874, p. 1), *Notes on Hangchow past and present* [1889], a second edition of which was published in 1907.]

[2] Cansay or Campsay is, of course, the Quinsai of Marco Polo (see his more detailed account of its marvels), the modern Hang-chau-fu, called at that time properly Lin-ngan [a name given by the Sung Emperor Kao-tsung, 1127–1162, when he was compelled, 1129, by the Kin Tartars, to remove his capital from K'ai fung, in Ho-nan, to Che-kiang], but also popularly *King-sze*, Seat of the Court or Capital (the term now officially applied to Pe-king), from its having been the seat of the Sung dynasty from 1127 to 1276, when the city was captured by the Mongols, when Northern China was in the hands of the *Kin*, or Niu-chen Tartars and afterwards of the house of Chinghiz. That is, as Odoric expresses it: "it was the royal city in which the Kings of Manzi formerly dwelt." The city is mentioned under various forms of the same name, representing the King sze of the Chinese, by Marignolli, Pegolotti, Ibn Batuta and other Arabic and Persian writers. It seems to have retained the name, indeed, centuries after it ceased to be a capital. For it is marked *Camse* in Carletti's transcription of the name in the *Chinese Atlas* (dated 1595) which he brought home in 1603, and which is now in the Magliabecchian Library. (*Baldello Boni*, i, cxiii, cxxi.)

The interpretation of the name as City of Heaven, given by Polo as well as Odoric, was probably current among the Western Asiatics in the ports of China, and may have grown out of the proverb quoted by Duhalde, Davis, and others: "*Above is Paradise, but Su-chau and Hang-chau are here below.*" The glories of these sister cities have vanished under the barbarities of T'aï-p'ing occupation and imperial re-conquest, but they existed till these recent events with no vast diminution of wealth and splendour. The most enthusiastic corroboration, in comparatively modern times, of Marco Polo's details, is probably that of Father Martini in the *Atlas Sinensis*. He even stands up, on a certain latitude of interpretation, for the ten thousand bridges, which meet with no corroboration from modern official works; the Imperial Geography, quoted in *Chine Moderne*, mentioning only two as worthy of note. But Ibn Batuta's account in the present

greatest city in the whole world, [so great indeed that I should scarcely venture to tell of it, but that I have met at Venice

volume may be compared with Odoric's, and also the following from Wassaf, one of the Persian historians of the Mongols. "Khanzai," he says, "is the greatest city of China, having nearly twenty-four farsangs of compass. Its houses are of wood, adorned with beautiful paintings. From one end to the other there is a distance of three posts. Most of the streets have a length of three farsangs. The city contains sixty-four squares bordered with houses uniformly built. The produce of the salt duty amounts daily to 700 *balish* of paper money. One may judge of the great number of its artizans by that of the working dyers, for of these there are 30,000. The garrison amounts to seven *tománs* (70,000). The census lets us know that there are seventy *tománs* of families taxed. There are seven hundred temples, which look like fortified castles; all full of monks. There are three hundred and sixty bridges [the number which Odoric assigns to Nanking]. An innumerable multitude of boats of all sizes serve for communication. One finds there a prodigious concourse of strangers of all countries on earth, merchants and others. Such is the capital." (In *D'Ohsson*, ii, 417.) Extracts of other accounts of Quinsai or Khansa from Arabic and Persian authors are given by Quatremère (*Introd. to Rashideddin*, pp. lxxxvii *seq.*).

[Marco Polo affirms: "the city of Kinsay to be so great that it hath an hundred miles of compass. And there are in it twelve thousand bridges of stone, for the most part so lofty that a great fleet could pass beneath them. And let no man marvel that there are so many bridges, for you see the whole city stands as it were in the water and surrounded by water, so that a great many bridges are required to give free passage about it....Since the Great Kaan occupied the city he has ordained that each of the 12,000 bridges should be provided with a guard of ten men, in case of any disturbance, or of any being so rash as to plot treason or insurrection against him."

The 100 *miles* of Marco Polo and of Odoric may stand for 100 *li*. "The wall existing in the Sung Dynasty was repaired or perhaps rebuilt after great rains about A.D. 1159. The Yung Kin gate certainly, and the Li-shê probably, existed before this date, and it is possible that the wall was substantially the same as the original wall of the Sui dynasty. There are, however, indications that that early wall did not include the Fêng-hwang hill." (Moule, *Hangchow*, 1907, p. 55.) Referring to Mr. E. H. Parker's travels in Che-kiang, Mr. Moule wrote in the *Journal of the China Br. Roy. Asiat. Soc.*, xx, 1885, p. 55: "Hangchow is described as having a circuit of from 20 to 25 miles. Now whether we take this as meaning English miles, or Chinese *li*, the computation is equally misleading. The circuit of the walls of Hangchow is given by the latest survey as 36 *li* and 90 paces; or about 12 English miles....Six hundred years ago, in the time of the great Venetian, the circuit of Hangchow was given as 100 *miles*, evidently Chinese *li*, or about 30 English miles; and the city walls are known to have stretched in those days to the S.W. far beyond the present boundary; and they included several of the neighbouring hills." Cf. *Marco Polo*, 3rd ed., ii, pp. 193–4.

Mr. Moule says (*Jour. N. C. B. R. As. Soc.*, ix, 1875, p. 7): "The Bridges, neither of the Sung Map, nor of the existing city, will justify Marco's number [the same as Odoric's]. Some of them, especially

people in plenty who have been there][1]. It is a good hundred miles in compass, and there is not in it a span of ground which is not well peopled. And many a tenement is there which shall have ten or twelve households[2] comprised in it[3]. And there be also great suburbs which contain a greater population than even the city itself. For the city hath twelve[4] chief gates, and from each of them cities extend to

outside the present north wall, are lofty enough for large river junks to carry their masts in passing them; but all told, they seem never to have numbered more than from one to two hundred."]

[Dr. F. Hirth, in a paper published in the *T'oung pao*, v, pp. 386–390 (*Ueber den Schiffverkehr von Kinsay zu Marco Polo's Zeit*), has some interesting notes on the maritime trade of Hang-chau, collected from a work in twenty books, kept at the Berlin Royal Library, in which is to be found a description of Hang-chau under the title of *Mêng-liang-lu*, published in 1274 by Wu Tzu-mu, himself a native of this city: there are various classes of sea-going vessels; large boats measuring 5000 *liao* and carrying from five to six hundred passengers; smaller boats measuring from 2 to 1000 *liao* and carrying from two to three hundred passengers; there are small fast boats called *tsuan-fêng*, "wind-breaker," with six or eight oarsmen, which can carry easily 100 passengers, and are generally used for fishing; sampans are not taken into account."]

[1] MIN. RAM. ["Arriuãmo in vna città marauigliosa detta Guinzai ...questa città e la maggiore che sia in tutto 'l mondo, & e si grande, che a pena ardisco di dir lo: *Ma ho ben trouate in Vinetia assai persone, che ui sono state.*"—A.S., "Omni aliâ quam conspexi."—CIV., "Haec maior est omnium aliarum quam conspexi."—RAM. A., "Venni doppo questo in vna città, domandata Cansay, che appresso noi vuol dire città, celestiale, di pane, di vino, di carne, di porco, di riso, & finalmente di tutte quelle cose, che sono all' humano vso necessarie, copiosa, & ancora di mercantie grandi, & nobilissima, questa è la maggior città, che sia hoggi al mondo."]

[2] [PAL., dieci e dodici.—A.S., "decem vel duodecim suppellectibiles, id est familias."—FRENCH TEXT, "Et si y a maintes maisons esquelles il y a x mainages ou plus."]

[3] This is absurdly converted in HAK. into "houses having ten or twelve stories, one above another"; a circumstance which Chinese habits notoriously contradict. The real reference is probably to the Chinese mode of living, which Davis calls "a universal system of clubbing upon the most economical plan. The Emperor observes in the Sacred Institutions that nine generations once lived under the same roof, and that in the family of Chang-she of Kiang-chau seven hundred partook of the same daily repast" (iii, 162). I must add, however, that I find the *Masálak-al-Absár*, quoted by Quatremère (*Rashideddin*, p. lxxxviii), says the houses of Khansa "*have five stories.*"

[4] [French 1380 gives X gates, but Fr. 2810, and all the other MSS., PAL., CIV., DOM., VEN., A.S., etc., give twelve gates.]

[Under the Sung dynasty, Kao-tsung period (1127–1162), the gates

a distance of some eight miles, each one greater than Venice is or Padua[1]. So that you may for six or seven days travel continually about one of these suburbs, and yet shall you seem to have gone but a very little way.

This city is situated upon lagoons of standing water [with canals][2] like the city of Venice[3]. And it hath more than twelve thousand bridges[4], on each of which are stationed guards guarding the city on behalf of the great Khan. And at the side of this city there flows a river near which it is built like Ferrara by the Po, for it is longer than it is broad[5].

I made diligent inquiry regarding the city, and asked questions of Christians, Saracens, idolaters, and everybody else, and they all agreed as with one voice that it had a circuit of one hundred miles[6]. And they have an

were thirteen: on the east: Kan shan, Tung Ts'ing, Ts'ung-sin, Sin, Pao-ngan, Hou-ch'ao, Pien; on the south: Li-she; on the west: Ts'ien hu, Ts'ing-po, Yung-kin, Ts'ien-t'ang; on the north: Yû-hang.

Three gates were closed in 1370. (Moule, *Journ. N. China Br. Roy. As. Soc.*, ix, 1875, p. 12; *Notes on Hangchow*, 1907, p. 56.)]

[1] [PAL., Padova o Vinegia.—B.N., A.S., Civitas Venetiarum et Padua.—CIV., Civitas Veneciarum et Pudua.—DOM., Vinegia o Padoa.—RAM. A., Venetia, & Padoua.—FRENCH TEXT, Venise.]

[2] MIN. RAM.

[3] [PAL., "in aqua di lagune a modo di Vinegia."—B.N., CIV., "in aquis lacunarum...sicut civitas Venetiarum."—RAM. B., "e fatto lagune, *per certi canali*, come sono a Vinetia."—FRENCH TEXT, "Ceste cité est assise en bas terroir, entre lacs, mares, et estancs, ainsi que la cité de Venise."]

[4] MIN. RAM. makes Odoric take an oath to this. ["O uero lagune hanno porte, che *per Dio uero*, sono di certo di piu di diece miglia."—RAM. A., 11,000 porti.—FRENCH TEXT, "Si y a plus de XII mille pons, et à chascun pont a gens qui le gardent de part le grant Kaan."]

[5] [B.N., "Flumen juxta quod sita est civitas ista, sicut Ferraria ipsa manet."—VEN., A.S., sicut Ferraria juxta Padum.—CIV., Ferraria super Padum.—RAM. A., si come in Ferrara.—FRENCH TEXT, "A un lez de la ville, cuert un très grand fleuve, et pour ce est ceste cité plus longue que large."]

The Arabic work *Masālāk-al-Absār* says "the city of Khansa extends in length the space of a whole day's journey, and in breadth the space of a half-day's journey." (In *Quatremère's Rashideddin*, p. lxxxviii.)

[The river alluded to is the Ts'ien T'ang kiang, famous by its bore.]

[6] [FRENCH TEXT, "Tous me dirent que ceste cité a plus de C

edict from their Lord that every fire shall pay to the great Khan annually[1] a tax of one *balis*, i.e. of five pieces of paper like silk[2], a sum equal to one florin and a half[3].

milles de tour, sanz les fourbours et ces XII citez susdittes, qui sont à VIII milles au dehors de chascune porte, et si est toute subgette au seigneur le grant Kaan qui en lève si grand avoir que c'est merveilles."]

[1] [FRENCH TEXT, "Car chascun feu lui paye tous les ans V *cacques de coton* qui bien valent là un fiourin et demi; mais tant y a que X ou XI mainages ne font que un feu; au payer, le nombre des feux de la ville monte à IIII^xx^ V tumans de ceulz de leur loy, et IIII tumans de Sarrazins, qui en tout font IIII^xx^ IX tumans, dont un tuman vault X^m^ feux."—*cacques de coton* is absurd.]

[2] [Odoric says that one *balis*=one florin and a half. L. Cibrario writes, *Dict. de la Conversation*, that at the end of the XIVth century, there were several kinds of florins varying in price from 12 francs 80 c. to 10 fr. 93. In the French edition of Odoric, I came to the conclusion that every fire paid to the great Khan a sum varying from 18 fr. 87 c. to 16 fr. 40; the actual equivalent would be five times as much.]

[3] [PAL., "bastise, ciò cinque carte bambagine."—B.N., "balis..., id est quinque cartas ad instar bombicis."—CIV., "ballis id est quinque cartas bombicis."—MUN., basis.—RAM. A., bastagne.—The whole of this passage is left out in the A.S.]

A note on the Chinese paper currency will be found in the comment on Pegolotti. In the meantime there is something to be said about the term *balis* which Odoric applies to it, or rather to a certain sum estimated in that currency. It is a genuine word, applied by the Western Asiatics in the same way. We shall meet with it in Pegolotti under the form *balish* (*balisci*), and in Ibn Batuta as *bálisht*, plural *bawálisht*, identical in spelling with a word which he uses elsewhere for a kind of cushion. Two questions arise about the word; Whence is it? and what value did it indicate?

As to the first, my friend Mr. Badger writes: "If corrupted from an Arabic word, which is not improbable, I take this to be *fals*, a small coin, money; a term in common use throughout the East, but vulgarly pronounced *fils*. According to the author of the Kâmus it also signifies *sigillo impressa charta in collo pendens, quo tributarium esse significabatur*. Perhaps this term was similarly applied to the stamped paper money of the Tartar dynasty." This is *almost* satisfactory, but does not quite carry conviction, both because we find Arabic authors like Ibn Batuta using *bálisht* as a distinct word, and because its meaning seems to have been that of a certain sum or monetary unit, apart from any connexion with paper currency. The Arabic *fals*, according to Reinaud (*Mém. de l'Acad. des Insc.*, xviii, 237), is merely a corruption of *obolus*, representing copper coin, as *dirhem* from drachma represents silver coin, and *dínár* from denarius gold. It seems therefore unlikely that it should be applied to a large sum of gold or silver. Ibn Batuta tells us that "*bálisht* means the same as a dínár or piece of gold with us," whilst we find that Shah Rokh's embassy to the Ming Emperor in 1420 receives, amongst other presents, *eight balish of silver*. Another of the presents is five thousand *chao*, which was the genuine Chinese name for the paper money. In a story about certain merchants, related by Gregory Abulpharagius in connexion with the invasion of Turkestan by Chinghiz, we find the Khan ordering one *balish of gold* to be paid for each piece of gold brocade, and two *balish of silver* for each piece of muslin. We are told also that Húlakú deposited his treasures in a castle on Lake Urumia, after casting his gold into *balish*.

D'Ohsson does not explain the word, but he quotes three valuations of it from Persian historians. The author of *Tarikh Jahan Kushai* (d. 1282) says that the balish, whether of gold or silver, was a weight of five hundred *mithkals*. Wassaf, in the beginning of the fourteenth century, says the balish of gold was equal to two thousand dínárs; the balish of silver, two hundred dínárs; and the balish cháo, or of paper money, was but ten dínárs. The author of *Rozát ul Janát*, written in the fifteenth century, estimated the balish of gold at five hundred dínárs. I may add that the author of the *Livre du Grant Caan*, a contemporary of Odoric, says the *balisme* of gold was equal to one thousand golden florins. Pétis de la Croix says (but I do not know on what authority) that a balish of gold was worth seventy-five golden dínárs, and adds that in short a balish was what in his own day was in Turkey called a *purse*. (*Vie de Genghiz Can*, Ital. tr. Ven., 1737, p. 195.)

With regard to the paper *balish*, Ibn Batuta tells us only that *twenty-five* notes went to it, whilst Odoric says *five* notes went to it, and that it was worth a florin and a half, i.e. about fourteen shillings. Pegolotti says four balish were worth a *sommo*, and that was worth about five florins. This would make the balish about twelve shillings.

It would seem from these various statements that the value of the metallic *balish* had varied, though perhaps a weight of five hundred *mithkals* was its original standard. The difference in value of the paper and silver *balish* was probably entirely due to the depreciation of paper caused by the excessive issues and strange financial pranks of the Mongol emperors, including the great Kúblái himself.

Freytag's *Lexicon* gives the word and explains it as a Tartar designation for a certain great sum of gold or silver, but offers no etymology. Richardson gives "BALISH, P., *a cushion or pillow, bedding, a staple.* A certain weight of gold; *from* balídan, *to extend, spread, reach, overtake*; to match or equal, *to grow long, to ripen,*" etc.; and also "BALISHE, *a little cushion put on a saddle, which it resembles in shape.*" Now may not the balish have been an ingot of gold or silver resembling in form such a cushion, or some other object of like name? For instance, Richardson also gives "BALIK, *a shoe or slipper*"; and we find in Barrow's account of the presents given at the Chinese court to Lord Macartney's suite, that, as in the case of their Persian predecessors centuries before, a part consisted of ingots of silver, and these were "cast in the form of a Tartar shoe [*Yuen-pao*], each being about an ounce in weight."...More about *balish* is to be seen, I find, in Quatremère's notes on Rashideddin, pp. 320–21.

["Le *balich* d'or ou d'argent," says C. Schefer, *Chrestomathie persane*, ii, p. 155, "était une monnaie de compte. Les lexicographes persans nous disent que le balich était un lingot du poids de cinq cents miçqals. Ala Eddin auquel cette définition est empruntée, nous apprend que de son temps, le balich d'argent avait la valeur de 75 dinars (*roukny*), chacun ayant le poids de quatre dangs. Le dinar Roukny était la pièce d'or frappée au nom de Roukn Eddin de la dynastie de Kharezmchâh. Wassaf dit, à la fin du chapitre consacré à l'avènement au trône de Qoubilay Qaân, que le balich d'or valait deux

And their way of managing is this, that ten or twelve households[1] will unite to have one fire, and so pay for one fire only[2]. Now of these fires there are reckoned eighty-five *tumans*[3], and with four more of Saracens[4], making eighty-

mille dinars, le balich d'argent, deux cents dinars, et le balich *tchao*, ou en papier-monnaie, dix dinars. Plus tard, le balich d'or ne valut plus que huit dinars et deux dangs et le balich d'argent huit dirhems et deux dangs."]

[See Yule, *Hobson Jobson*, s.v. "Shoe" and "Tael," and N. Elias' *Tarikh-i-Rashidi*, p. 256 *n.*]

[1] [FRENCH TEXT, X ou XI mainages.]

[2] The term "fires" (*ignes*) used by Odoric is technically correct, or nearly so. The official word used in the Chinese census is *yen-hu*, literally *fires-doors*. Persons called *Pao-kia*, or "chiefs of ten fires," are appointed to collect the numbers of their tithing, and this may have been misunderstood by Odoric. (See *Chine Moderne*, p. 167.)

[This may be an explanation of this passage; Pauthier writes, *Chine moderne*, p. 167: "Pour établir le chiffre exact de la population de chaque province, le gouverneur et le lieutenant-gouverneur font recueillir dans tous les lieux qui sont de leur ressort, par des préposés nommés *Paò-kiâ* ou *chefs de dix feux*, les chiffres portés sur les tablettes en bois attachées aux portes des maisons (*mên pâi-tsè*), pour avoir le nombre réel des personnes qui les habitent."

According to the *Yuan shi*, quoted by Pauthier, *Marco Polo*, p. 492, there were in 1290 in the circuit of Hang-chau 360,850 Heads of Families and 1,834,719 women, old men and children.]

[3] *Tuman* in the Mongol language signifies ten thousand. It was borrowed by the Persians and Arabs, and with them means a weight or sum of money, originally equal to ten thousand *mithkals* or Arab drachms of silver. "The Mogols and Khwaresmians often use the word for ten thousand men, and say (e.g.) that the city of Samarkand affords seven *tumans*, i.e. seventy thousand men capable of bearing arms." (*D'Herbelot* in voce.)

Polo reckons the population of Quinsai at one hundred and sixty tumans of fires, but he does not add Odoric's exaggeration about each fire representing ten or twelve families.

["Moreover, I must tell you that in this city there are 160 tomans of fire, or in other words 160 tomans of houses. Now I shall tell you that the toman is 10,000, so that you can reckon the total as altogether 1,600,000 houses, among which are a great number of rich palaces." *Marco Polo*, ii, p. 192.]

[4] Fires of the *Hwei Hwei* or Mahomedans appear as a separate class also in the modern Chinese census. (*Chine Mod.*, p. 166.)

[In the heart of Hang-chau, one of the bridges spanning the canal which divides into two parts the walled city from north to south is called *Hwei Hwei k'iao* (Bridge of the Mohamedans) or *Hwei Hwei Sin k'iao* (New Bridge of the Mohamedans) while its literary name is *Tsi Shan k'iao* (Bridge of Accumulated Wealth); it is situated between the *Tsien k'iao* on the south and the *Fung lo k'iao* on the north. Near the *Tsi Shan k'iao* was a mosk and near the *Tsien k'iao*, at the time of the Yuen, there existed Eight Pavilions (*Pa kien lew*) inhabited by wealthy Mussulmans. Mohammedans from Arabia and

nine[1] *tumans.* Now one tuman is equal to ten thousand fires[2]. And besides these there are the Christians[3] and the merchants and others only passing through the country.

This being so, I greatly marvelled how such numbers of human bodies could manage to dwell in one place, and yet there is always there great plenty of bread and pork[4], and rice and wine, which wine is otherwise called *Bigni*[5], and is reputed a noble drink ; and indeed great abundance of all other victuals is found there.

Turkestan were sent by the Yuen to Hang-chau ; they had prominent noses, did not eat pork and were called *So mu chung* (Coloured-eye race). Vissière, *Rev. du Monde Musulman*, March, 1913.]

[1] [RAM. A., 90.]

[2] [RAM. B., "E mi fu detto, che ciascuna casa paga l' anno al Signore vn bastagne, che val vn ducato, e mezzo : e dieci fameglie fanno vn fuoco per focolaro, questi focolari della terra sono 85 & ogni focolaro è dieci mila fochi, & ogni foco è communemente 10 famiglie : e questo è solamente de' Saracini, tutti il resto è di Christiani, e mercadanti, & altre genti forastiere che sono dieci volte piu di Saracini."]

[3] [Marco Polo, II, p. 192, says : "There is one church only, belonging to the Nestorian Christians." It was one of the seven churches built in China by Mar Sarghis, called *Ta p'u hing sze* (Great Temple of Universal Success) or *Yang yi Hu-mu-la*, near the *Tsien-k'iao men.* Cf. *Marco Polo*, II, p. 177 ; Vissière, *Rev. du Monde Musulman*, March 1913, p. 8.]

[4] [B. N., VEN., carnium de porco.—FRENCH TEXT, char.]

[5] [Fr. 2810, bygun.—FRENCH TEXT, *bigum.*—VEN., bigini.—B. N., vigim.]

In calling this Chinese liquor *wine*, Odoric does the same as many later travellers. Before his time Rubruquis says he could not distinguish it except by the smell from the best wine of Auxerre (*Vinum Autisiodorense, qu.* of the Chablis kind ?). Ysbrandt Ides says when kept a year or two it very much resembled in colour, taste, and strength the best Rhenish. Father Ripa : " Rice is bruised and compressed into solid cakes. When used these cakes are broken and put into vessels with hot water and fermented. The liquor thus produced might be mistaken for excellent grape-wine. It is made sweet or acid at pleasure by the addition of certain herbs during the fermentation, and a colour is given to it as required." John Bell of Antermony calls it "clear and strong as Canary." A modern traveller's description quoted by Davis compares it to Madeira in colour, and a little in taste. (*Rubruq.*, 299 ; *Astley*, iii, 567 ; *Father Ripa*, p. 51 ; *Davis*, ii, 21.)

This liquor was called by the Mongols *darassun*, the *terracina* of Rubruquis. The word *bigini* or *bignii* is probably the Persian *bagni*, " malt liquor or beer," though this is not a good description of the Chinese beverage. This word *bagni* is applied by some of the people of the Caucasus to their own beer (which Klaproth says is very like London porter), and might be used by the Alans, with whom, as

33. Of the marvellous sight that Friar Odoric beheld in a certain monastery of the idolaters.

This is the royal city in which the king of Manzi[1] formerly dwelt. And four[2] of our friars that were in that city had converted a man[3] that was in authority there, in whose house I was entertained. And he said to me one day: "*Atha* (which

disciples of the old Archbishop John, Odoric would be much in contact whilst at Cambalec. (*Richardson's Pers. Dict.*; *Klaproth*, *Voy. au Caucase*, i, 243.)

[Schlegel, *T'oung-pao*, Sept. 1891, says that in the "Ancient Informations of *K'io-wei*," there is a complete list of the celebrated wines of China, and that he finds for Hang-chau the wine "Bamboo-leaves Green," the "Fragrant Saphire" and the "White Wine," but that Odoric's wine is probably the liquor made with the date *Mi-yin* (in ancient times, pronounced *Bi-im*).

This passage may refer to rice wine in use among the Mongols who called it *tarassun*, the *terracina* of Rubruck, *cervisia* (beer) *de risio*. Rockhill says however that "here Chinese rice made wine, or *Shao hing chiu*, is meant. There is another stronger liquor distilled from millet, and called *shao chiu*; in Anglo-Chinese, *samshu*. Mongols call it *araka*, *arrak*, and *arreki*. Ma Tuan-lin (bk. 327) says that the Moho (the early Nu-chên Tartars) drank rice wine (*mi chiu*), but I fancy that they, like the Mongols, got it from the Chinese." (*William of Rubruck*, pp. 166-7, note.)

Speaking of the shops of Kinsay, Marco Polo says (ii, p. 202): "Some of these shops are entirely devoted to the sale of wine made from rice and spices, which is constantly made fresh and fresh, and is sold very cheap." He had said just before: "Neither grapes nor wine are produced there, but very good raisins are brought from abroad, and wine likewise. The natives, however, do not much care about wine, being used to that kind of their own made from rice and spices."

Dr. E. Bretschneider (*Botanicon sinicum*, ii, pp. 154 seq.) has an interesting note on the use of intoxicating beverages prepared from the grains of cereals. "The invention of wine or spirits in China is generally ascribed to a certain Iti, who lived in the time of the Emperor Yü. According to others the inventor of wine was Tu K'ang."..."In Middle and South China glutinous rice is more generally used. This rice is employed for the fabrication of the much-esteemed wine of Shao-hing, a city of Che-kiang." This confirms Rockhill's note.

Marco Polo has a chapter (i, p. 441) *Concerning the Rice-Wine drunk by the people of Cathay*: "Most of the people of Cathay drink wine of the kind that I shall now describe. It is a liquor which they brew of rice with a quantity of excellent spice, in such fashion that it makes better drink than any other kind of wine; it is not only good, but clear and pleasing to the eye. And being very hot stuff, it makes one drunk sooner than any other wine."]

[1] [Fr. 1380, Mangin.] [2] [French Text, III freres.]

[3] [Ram. B., "Doue è vn luogo di frati minori, che conuertirono vn grandissimo barone."]

is to say *Father*)[1] wilt thou come and see the place?" And when I said that I would willingly go, we got into a boat, and went[2] to a certain great monastery[3] of the people of the

[1] [B. N., RAM. A., DOM., Atha.—RAM. B., Acta.—FRENCH TEXT, MUN., Acha.—VEN., Archa.—A. S., CIV., Ara.—PAL., Atta.]

Atha is a Turkish word signifying, as Odoric says, *father*. Taking it in connection with *Rabban*, which occurs just below, it may be noted that in 1288 there came on a mission from the Ilkhan of Persia to the court of France, a certain Nestorian Bishop, who is termed by the chroniclers *Rabban Ata*. Rémusat observes that this is probably no proper name, but the union of two titles in different languages, and cites a certain Syrian priest at the court of Okkodai Khan who was called by the sovereign *Ata*, father, and by the courtiers *Rabban*, master. (*Mém. de l'Acad. des Insc.*, vii, 359.)

It is curious that Ibn Batuta should quote this Turkish word *Atha* as being commonly addressed to old men in this very city of Cansai (iv, 288).

[Quatremère, *Hist. des Mongols*, i, p. xxxviii, note, observes that Odoric's narrative is here slightly inexact, and that his word *acha* does not mean *father*, but *eldest brother*. At times, the *khan* would merely take the title of elder brother, *âka*, "which is somewhat simple and patriarchal." (Quatremère, *l.c.*, p. 86, note.) The Chinese give an idea of respect, of friendship, to the expression of elder brother, *kô*: *kô kô*, *ta-kô*, *Kô-tze*, my elder brother; *lao kô*, respectable Sir.]

[2] [B. N., "Et sibi semel dixi me velle ire, unde ascendimus unam barcham et sic ivimus ad unum magnum illorum monasteriorum quae ibi erant."—CIV., "Ascendimus simul in unam barcham."]

[3] [PAL., Al munistero di Rabani.]

The monastery which they visited in a boat was probably on the lake called *Si-hu* ("Western Lake"), of which, with the temples, monasteries, gardens, and palaces which bordered it, Polo gives a brilliant account, confirmed by Martini and Alvaro Semedo, and to some considerable extent in later times by Barrow. (*Autobiog.*, p. 104.)

["Inside the city," says Marco Polo, ii, pp. 186–7, "there is a Lake which has a compass of some 30 miles: and all round it are erected beautiful palaces and mansions, of the richest and most exquisite structure that you can imagine, belonging to the nobles of the city. There are also on its shores many abbeys and churches of the Idolaters. In the middle of the Lake are two Islands, on each of which stands a rich, beautiful and spacious edifice, furnished in such style as to seem fit for the palace of an Emperor. And when any one of the citizens desired to hold a marriage feast, or to give any other entertainment, it used to be done at one of these palaces. And everything would be found there ready to order, such as silver plate, trenchers, and dishes [napkins and table-cloths], and whatever else was needful. The King made this provision for the gratification of his people, and the place was open to every one who desired to give an entertainment. [Sometimes there would be at these palaces an hundred different parties; some holding a banquet, others celebrating a wedding; and yet all would find good accommodation in the different apartments and pavilions, and that in so well ordered a manner that one party was never in the way of another."]

country [which was called THEBE][1]. And he called to him one of their monks, saying: "Seest here this *Franki Rabban*? (which meaneth this Frank monk). He cometh from where the sun sets, and goeth now to Cambalech to pray for the life of the great Khan[2]. Show him therefore, prithee, something worth seeing, so that if he get back to his own country he may be able to say, I have seen such and such strange things in Cansai!" And the monk replied that he would do so with pleasure.

So he took two great buckets full of scraps from the table, and opening the door of a certain shrubbery which was there we went therein. Now in this shrubbery there is a little hill covered with pleasant trees [and all full of grottoes][3]. And as we stood there he took a gong[4], and began to beat upon it, and at the sound[5] a multitude of animals of divers kinds began to come down from the hill, such as apes, monkeys, and many other animals having faces like men[6], to the number of some three thousand[7], and took up their places round

[1] MIN. RAM. ["Salimmo in vna barchetta, e mi menò in *un monastero chiamata* THEBE."]

[2] [B. N., Et nunc vadit Cambaleth.—PAL., E vae a Chanbalu.—DOM., Va a Cambalec.—VEN., A. S., Cambalech.—RAM. A., Cabalec.—FRENCH TEXT, "Est du bout et de la fin du monde là où le soleil se escousse est venus en ce pais pour la vie et le salut de nostre Kaan."]

[3] [VEN., B. N., CIV., A. S., plenus arboribus amoenis.—PAL., ch' era pieno d' albori.—DOM., pieno d' alberi dilettevoli.—RAM. B., "un monticello *tutto pien di cauerne*, & intorno intorno d' alberi fruttiferi."]

[4] [PAL., DOM., RAM. B., cembalo.—RAM. A., CIV., cimbalo.—B. N., cimballum.—VEN., timpanum.—A. S., tintinnabulo.]

Cimbalum. No doubt *gong* is the proper thing, though perhaps not the proper word to put into Odoric's mouth.

[5] [RAM. B., "& subito viddi cosa piu marauigliosa, che hauessi mai visto per viaggio."]

[6] [Fr. 2810, bestelettes.—FRENCH TEXT, "III mille bestes qui toutes avoient les visages comme gens ainsi que ont les marmotes."—RAM. B., "Le migliaia di bestie saluatiche le piu diuerse, e strane, che mai piu fussino vedute: fra quali conobbi gatti saluatichi, martarelli, scimie, maimoni, volpi, lupi, spinosi: & erano bestie cornute con viso humano, e altri assai diuersi, ma la piu parte haueano viso humano."—B. N., "Symiae, catti, maymones."—CIV., "Simeae, cathi et maymones."—VEN., "Symie gati maymones."]

[7] [Fr. 2810, 200,000.—DE BACKER, II. C. mille bestelettes.—A. S., ad tria millia circa.]

about him in regular ranks. And when they were thus ranged round about him, he put down the vessels before them and fed them as fast as he was able. And when they had been fed he began again to beat the gong, and all returned to their retreats. So I, laughing heartily[1], began to say: "Tell me, prithee, what this meaneth?" And he answered: "These animals be the souls of gentlemen, which we feed in this fashion for the love of God!" But quoth I: "No souls be these, but brute beasts of sundry kinds." And he said: "No, forsooth, they be nought else but the souls of gentlemen. For if a man be noble his soul entereth the form of some one of these noble animals; but the souls of boors enter the forms of baser animals and dwell therein!" And say what I list against it, nought else would he believe[2].

[1] [CIV., "Ego autem multum ridens illi seni dixi."—VEN., "Tunc multum ridere cepi dicens."—FRENCH TEXT, "Je en eus grant merveille."]

[2] That this exhibition really took place and was well known to travellers in China, is obvious from the allusion which John Marignolli makes to it (*infra*).

[Here is a confirmation of Odoric's relation: In the French edition of Odoric, I have reproduced, pp. 337–339, the following note of the Right Rev. G. E. Moule, bishop of Hang-chau, sent to me by Sir H. Yule, who had printed it in the *Geographical Magazine*, Lond., 1875, pp. 137–8:

"Extract from the *Si-Hu Che* [Topography of the Western Lake], sect. vi, fol. 19.

"*Apes' call Grotto*, at the foot of Fei-lai Hill. This grotto has a passage leading all the way to *T'ian-chuh* (India). Under the Sung there was a monk called Che-yih, good at whistling, who used to keep apes among the hills. When he went down to the stream and gave a long whistle, every one of the apes would assemble. They called him 'Father of Apes.'

"Fei-lai Hill is a rocky hill, perhaps 80 to 100 feet above the plain, within the precints of Linyin Convent, one of the most famous of those among the hills west of the Si-hu. The convent is said to have been built early in the Sung period, by a monk from India, who, walking there with his white ape, thought the place so much like his home in India that he called it after his old convent, *Lin-tsiu* (Spirit Eagle), changed afterwards to *Lin-yin* (Spirit Retreat), and vowed that the grottoed rock must have "flown hither" (*Fei-lai*) from India. It is added that the ape thought so too! Whether this means that he betook himself naturally to the peaks and caverns, I do not know. It is certain that there is a strong flavour of apes about the traditional notices and poetical quotations which make up most of the topographical chapter on this Lin-yin convent. Only the other day a monk told me that the

But if anyone should desire to tell all the vastness and great marvels of this city, a good quire of stationery[1] would not hold the matter I trow. For 'tis the greatest and noblest city, and the finest for merchandize, that the whole world containeth.

34. Of the city called Chilenfu, and of the great river Talay, and of certain Pygmies.

Departing from that city and travelling for six days, I arrived at another great[2] city called CHILENFU[3], the walls

apes had been seen on the rocks within this twelve month. No animals are now kept there except a few goats. There are plenty of squirrels in the trees. The great emporium of animals privileged on Buddhist (transmigration) principles, is further off, at "Cloud-Lodge-Convent!" (*Yun-tsi-she*) where cattle, swine, etc., are offered by devotees, and fed by the monks in privileged idleness.

"I cannot hear that apes or any other wild animals are treated in this way. Nor can I find 'poor gentlemen,' or metempsychosis, in any form to be specially connected with the apes either of tradition or of the present time. At one of the chief convents in this province, three days' journey from hence (*T'ian Muh*, Eye of Heaven Convent), there are said to be many apes or monkeys, wild and somewhat formidable.

"For the rest, I think Lin-yin and the Fei-lai Hill probably were the object of Odoric's excursion, since, though not on the lake shores, they are often visited by crossing the lake, and walking thence 1 or 2 miles through the woodland." What *Thebe* is I cannot tell. If Odoric wrote badly is it possibly *Phé-lé*=Fei-lai?" (*G. E. M.*)

[The French sinologue A. VISSIÈRE in a relation of *Une visite à l'ancienne capitale du Manzi* (*Bul. Soc. Géog. comm. Paris*, T. xxiii, 1901, p. 113) after speaking of the *Monasteries* of the Si-hu, writes: "Si les singes du Fei-lai-fong paraissent avoir disparu de nos jours, ils ont laissé de nombreux souvenirs. Le *Pic du singe blanc*, la *Grotte où l'on appelle les singes* et la *Terrasse où l'on nourrissait les singes*, sont autant de témoins de leur importance passée, subsistant aujourd'hui et qui viennent corroborer les données précises des historiens chinois."]

[1] *Unus bonus quaternus stationis hæc talia tenere non posset.* This use of the word *statio* for paper, though so directly leading to our use of the word *stationer*, does not occur among thirteen significations of *statio* in the modern Paris edition of Ducange.

[2] [RAM. B., bellissima città.—A. S., bene muratam.]

[3] [FRENCH TEXT; FR. 2810, Gilenfo.—DOM., Chilenfo.—VEN., Chilemfo. — CIV., Chilefo. — B. N., Chilenfu.—ARUND., Chilefu or Chilenfu.—FARS., Chilopho or Chilepho.—HAK., Chilenzo.—PAL., Chilensi.—RAM. B., Chilense.—RAM. A., Chileraphe.—A. S. Chyleso.]

The city of Chilenfu is undoubtedly Nan-king, a conclusion at which I had arrived before seeing that Professor Kunstmann had come to the same. Six days is, however, too short an estimate of the distance from Hang-chau, which in a straight line appears to be about 125 miles.

Though the plan of Nan-king in Duhalde does not show its canals and bridges, Martini says expressly of it: "This city has very many bridges of stone, supported on arches"; and again, in speaking of Su-chau, he observes, "that though that city has a great number of bridges all of stone, and some of them magnificent, there are not so many as at the capital of the province." (In *Thévenot*, pp. 120, 124.)

The circuit of the modern walls of Nan-king is about twenty miles; so that if the suburbs were at all extensive the compass of the *town* may have been nearly what Odoric gives. Le Comte calls the circuit of the city forty-eight miles; Gemelli Carreri calls it thirty-six, and quotes others who called it forty. (*Astley*, iii, 553; *Carreri*, *Giro del Mondo.*) The latter also speaks of its canals as *molti e profondi.*

["La ville mesurait alors 15 kil. de tour, et ses murailles, larges de 8 à 15 mètres au sommet, de 15 ou 20 à la base, atteignaient ça et là 10 mètres de hauteur. Elles étaient percées de huit portes; des fossés profonds de 5 m. sur 100 de largeur suivaient les murs à l'extérieur; ils avaient été creusés de 1260 à 1265," under Li Tsung, 5th of the Nan Sung, 14th of the Sung Emperors. *Gaillard*, p. 149.]

[It is well known that Nan-king had been several times the capital of the Empire, for instance under the Wu (3rd cent. A.D.) the Eastern Ts'in (4th cent. A.D.), when it was called Kien Yeh, and the Southern Ts'i; when the Sung were defeated in 1127, Kao Tsung (1127–1163), the first of the Nan Sung Emperors, settled first at Kien k'ang fu, the name given to Nan-king in 1129, and then removed to Yang-chau and after to Lin-ngan (Hang-chau, *vide supra*, p. 192). Kien k'ang remained one year in the hands of the Kin Tartars. After Odoric's time, Nan-king became again the capital of the Empire on the expulsion of the Mongols by the Ming in 1368, and remained so until Yung-lo in 1406 decided upon the transfer of his government to the Northern Capital (Pe-king).]

With regard to the name which our traveller gives the city, it must be noted that *Nan-king* signifies merely "Southern Court"; the name of the city being Kiang-ning-fu. *Kin-ling-fu* is also given by de Mailla as one of the ancient names of Nan-king, and it would appear from Pauthier (*Chine Moderne*, p. 60) that this name, signifying the "Golden Hill," is still in occasional use. [Biot, *Dict. des noms...de l'Empire chinois*, p. 73, mentions *Kin-ling* under the T'ang; this name is also given by Playfair, *Cities and Towns of China*, p. 43.] But perhaps the Chelinfu of Odoric is merely a provincial pronunciation of Kiang-ning-fu, putting *l* for *n*, as we find that the Portuguese in later days called Nan-king *Lankin* and Ningpo *Liampo*, after what was, as we are told, the *Fu-kien* pronunciation. Indeed, in Hakluyt's "Early Reports of China learned through the Portugals," this province of Kiang-nan or Nan-king, "the fift shire of China," as he quaintly calls it, is termed *Chelim*, the very name that we have here. (See Martini in *Thévenot*, p. 120; *Mendez Pinto* passim; *Hakluyt*, l. c.)

It is true that Marco Polo mentions a city of the same name, Quelinfu, also noted for fine stone bridges. But this is *Kien-ning-fu* in the interior of Fu-kien, a region which Odoric has now left far behind. Here, however, we see exactly the same change of letters that we have supposed.

[Wylie, *Notes on Chinese Literature*, p. 48, writes: "The *Kin ling koo kin t'oo k'aou* is a series of 16 plans of the city and neighbourhood of Nanking, from 1000 years before the Christian era, down to the

whereof have a circuit of forty miles[1]. And in it there be some three hundred and sixty stone bridges, finer than the whole world can show[2]. In this city was the first residence of the king of Manzi[3], where he used to dwell. It is very well peopled, and there is such an amount of craft thereat as is right marvellous to behold. The city is planted passing well, and hath great store of all good things.

And quitting this city[4], I came to a certain great river which is called TALAY[5], and this is the greatest river that

Ming dynasty, with a description to each, by Ch'în E, dated 1516. A companion volume entitled *Kin ling t'oô yung*, gives 40 plates of remarkable spots in Nan-king, with a short topographical notice, and a few lines of poetry accompanying each. This was published in 1623." I have not been able to get a copy of this work, but Father Gaillard, S. J., of Zi-ka-wei, has been more fortunate, and in his valuable work: *Nankin d'alors et d'aujourd'hui, Aperçu historique et géographique*, Shang-hai, 1903, 8vo, he has reproduced the 16 or rather 17 plans of the book, and among them the plan of Nan-king under the Nan-Sung, p. 140. The reader should refer to the chapter devoted by Father Gaillard to the Southern Sung, p. 140, and especially to the part of it devoted to the archaeology of Nan-king under the Sung, p. 145; also to the chapter of Yuen dynasty, pp. 152 seq. In 1277 the prefectoral title of *Kien k'ang fu* was altered into *Kien k'ang lu tsung-kwan fu*.]

[1] [RAM. B., piu di quaranta.]

[2] [B. N., 340 ponts.—FRENCH TEXT, XL pons.—DOM., trecento quaranta cinque.—CIV., tercentum sexaginta pontes murati lapidei.—PAL., VEN., 360.—RAM. B., "360 porte tutte lauorate di marmo con intagli bellissimi."—RAM. A., "370 ponti di pictre."—A. S., "quadraginta."]

[3] [B. N., "In hac civitate fuit prima sedes Regis Manzi in qua ipse morari solebat."—CIV., VEN., A. S., "In hac civitate fuit prima sedes Regis Manzi."—DOM., "In questa città fue la prima sedia del re (Mazi) ne la quale egli solea stare."—PAL., "Questa cittade fue la prima sedia del Re de Manzi."—RAM. B., "E dicesi che questa terra fu la prima che hauesse il Re de Mangi."—RAM. A., "Nella quale fu la prima sede del Re Manzo, & nella quale sono circa 370 ponti di pietre, piu belli, che siano al mondo: quiuì ancora è vna sorte di barche per nauigare, di grandezza mirabile."—1380, Magin.]

[4] [PAL., "Di quindi partendomi per tre giornate veni a uno grande fiume de maggiori del mondo che là dove gli è più istretto e largo ben VII miglia."—RAM. B., "Ma perche non vi erano cose degne di merauiglia, poco ui dimorammo, & nauigando trouammo un fiume largo piu di 20 miglia, di cui un ramo passa la tierra, chiamato Piemaronni."]

[5] [VEN., B. N., Talay.—DOM., Talai.—ARUND., HAK., Thalay.—RAM. A., Dotalay.—A. S., Tannay.—VIEN., Thanay.—FARS. gives *Thanai* with the addition quoted by Yule: "de quo scripsit Isidorus 12° libro etymologiarum, a Thano primo rege Sitharum denominatus, qui ex nivosis (?) fluviis descendens determinavit Europam ab Asia et est inter illas partes mundi medias currens, atque in Pontum fluens."

exists in the world. For where it is narrowest it is some seven miles in width[1]. And this river passeth through the land of the Pygmies, or Biduini[2], whose city is called CATHAN, and that is one of the best and finest cities in the world. These pygmies are three spans[3] in height, and they do greater work in cotton[4], as it is called, than any people in the world[5]. And the full-sized men who dwell there

—CIV., Chanay, with this explanation: "Homo est de quo scripsit Isidorus decimo tertio libro Ethymologiarum a Chane primo Rege Scitarum denominatus, qui ex cipheis foliis descendens determinavit Europam ab Asia. Istud flumen currit cum impetu in duas partes mundi; medium est mirae magnitudinis." Fr. 2810, Calay.]

This name in some versions reads *Tanay*, which is a confusion with the better known Tanais or Don (called *Tanay* in the Catalan map), and in others *Doltalay* and the like, a mistake of the kind spoken of in note at p. 115. The great river is of course the Ta-kiang or Yang-tze, and the name given by Odoric (which seems to be mentioned by no other traveller of his time) is the Mongol *Dalai* or *Talai*, "the sea," which lends a figurative title to the Great Lama. That this word was applied as a name to the Kiang by the Mongols, I learn by an incidental quotation (from *Fischer de Origine Tartarorum*, p. 76, cited by J. G. Meinert in his Essay on Marignolli's Travels; see Introd. to Marignolli *infrà*). The use of the word *Dalai* in this way seems, therefore, to be quite parallel to that of *Bahr* as applied by the Arabs to the Nile. So also the Tibetans apply the term *Samandrang* (*Samudra*, "the Ocean") to the Indus and Sutlej (*J.R.G.S.*, xxiii, 34).

[1] [PAL., "Questo fiume passa per mezzo la città Piomario la cui contrada si chiama Chaicho, ch' è delle più belle cittadi del mondo, e delle maggiori."—Fr. 2810, un mille.]

[2] [RAM. A., Pymei.—CIV., bidumii.—B. N., terram pigmeorum scilicet vidinnorum.—DOM., bidorni.—VEN., per medium terre pigmeorum.—VIEN., terram biduinorum.—Fr. 2810, Pumeaux.]

[3] [VEN., tribus spannis.—DOM., tre spanne.—RAM. A., tre spanne o palmi.—CIV., tribus palmis.]

[4] [B. N., "Faciunt magna opera Goton, id est bombicis, quam aliqui homines qui sunt in mundo."—VEN., "Faciunt maiora opera bonbacis quam homines qui sint in mundo."—CIV., "Et tamen faciunt maiora opera goton, id est bombacis, quam aliqui homines in hoc mundo."]

[5] [VIEN., Cathan.—CIV., Catan.—DOM., Chacan.—B. N., Chathan. VEN., Cacham.—PAL., Chaicho.—MUN., Kakan.—RAM. A., Tacchara. —Fr. 2810, Chaam.]

The *Cathan* of the text is only one out of many readings, but it is that to which the others seem to point. It may be Khoten that is meant, if it is worth while to connect any real name with this legend. But the fine cotton was an element nearer at hand, as the western part of the province of Kiang-nan was noted for its enormous production of cotton cloth.

[In the Ngan-hwei province there is a town called Su-sung which beget sons who are more than half of them like those pygmies who are so small. The women are wedded[1] in their fifth year, and so there are born and begotten of these

was named Kao-t'ang under the Liang Dynasty. Does it refer to our Cathan? Cf. Biot, *Dict.*, p. 348; Playfair, *Dict.*, No. 6677.]

Sir Thomas Brown points out that the stories of pygmies were brought under the shield of Scripture by the Vulgate version of Ezekiel xxvii, 12, *Sed et* Pygmæi *qui erant in turribus tuis*, etc., and goes on afterwards: "Though Paulus Jovius delivers that there are pygmies in Japan, Pigafetta about the Moluccas, and Olaus Magnus placeth them in Greenland, yet wanting frequent confirmation in a matter so confirmable, this affirmation carrieth but slow persuasion." (*Vulgar Errors*, i, 424.)

Though we cannot tell how Odoric got hold of this story, there is a considerable combination of "authorities" to place pygmies in the inland countries west of China. We may cite two of these. Reinaud's Arab voyagers say that in the mountains of China there is a town called *Táyu*, whose inhabitants are pygmies. But the story most in point is contained in a rubric of the Catalan world-map (1375). To the N.W. of Catayo near the Himalayas it represents a combat of pygmies and cranes, with a legend that runs thus: "Here grow little men who have but five palms in length; and though they be little, and not fit for weighty matters, yet be they brave and *clever at weaving*, and at keeping cattle. And know ye that these men have children when they be but twelve years old; and they live commonly to but forty years, and have not a proper age (?). And valiantly they defend themselves from the cranes, and take and eat them. And here endeth the land of Catay." (See *Ctesias* xi, in Didot's edit. 1858; *Pliny* vii, 2; *Rémusat, Nouv. Mél. Asiat.*, i; *Reinaud, Rel. des Voyages, etc.*, p. 47; *Notices et Extraits*, xiv, 141.)

[This is the text of the Catalan Map concerning the pygmies:

"Ací nexen homs pochs quj no han síno. v. palms d'lōchs
e jassia q́ síen pochs | e no aptes a fer coses greus | ells empo son | [forts aptes
a texir ꝛ guardar bestiar | E sapiats q́ aquets homēs con son de XII anys
de aquí auant engenren | ꝛ entro a XL anys comunamēt ujuen | [e no han
prospiatat | E ualentament se defenen de les grues | ꝛ les prenen e les
menjen | Açy feneys la terra del senyor de catayo."]

[I have written a lengthy note on the Pygmies in the French edition of Odoric, pp. 348–355; I refer the reader to it; however I may say that the Chinese Documents are full of information on the *Siao-jen* or dwarfs, and that to this day some sort of negritos are to be found in south-western China.]

[1] [RAM. A., "Quali essendo nell' età di cinque anni si maritano: onde vi nasce, & è tanto il numero di questi, che non si può ne dire, ne numerare: per la lor picciolezza vengono da tutto il mondo nominati, & famosi."]

[VEN., "Hii pigmei formosi sunt tam mares quam femine per magnitudinem suam, & femine nubunt in quinto anno, habent autem hii animam rationalem sicut nos."]

little people a countless number. These pygmies, both male and female, are famous for their small size. But they have rational souls like ourselves[1].

35. Concerning the cities of Iamzai and of Menzu.

And as I travelled upon this river Talay[2], I passed many cities and towns, and I came to a certain city called IAMZAI[3],

[1] This passage is very confused in almost all versions. I have closely followed Ramusio's (larger) which is the most intelligible.

[FRENCH TEXT: "Ces Pymains ont tousjours guerre aux grues et aux cygnes du pays qui là sont plus grans que les Pymains. Et souvent en l'année s'on vont ces Pymains à très grant ost et à très grant multitude contre ces oyseaux et se combatent à eulx aussi cruelment et aussi mortelment comme nulle autre grant peuple ou monde se combatent les uns aux autres. In ceste cité, les Pymains ne labourent point les terres ne les vignes ne telz fortes labeurs, mais ilz font le meilleur ouvraige de coton que on teinst ou monde,—et si ont en leurs citez grandes gens qui labeurent les terres et les vignes et font les autres grandes labeurs; de ces grandes gens se truffent ces Pymains ainsi que nous faisons en ces parties des gens qui sont grant oultre mesure de raison. Le grant Chaan [fait] garder ces Pymains très soingneusement et fait leur ville garnir de tous biens à très grant habundance. Ils sont droitement gens visans raison comme nous."]

[2] [RAM. B., "Di qui vsciti, caminando, e passando vna infinità di città, e castella, giũgessimo in vna città chiamata *Sai*, oue è vn luogo de frati minori."—B. N., "Dum per istud flumen del Talai sic irem transivi per multas civitates et veni ad unam que vocatur *Jamzai*, in qua est unus locus nostrorum fratrum minorum."—HAK., "Indè per illud flumen transiens, veni ad vnam ciuitatē Ianzu...."—FRENCH TEXT, "Quant j'eus regardé cel affaire de ces Pymains, je m'en alay vers une cité qui a nom Jamathay, alias Jansu."]

[3] [B.N., Iamzai and Jamzai.—VEN., Iamzay and Iamzai.—DOM., RAM. A., Iamzai.—PAL., Jamsai.—HAK., Ianzu.—ARUND., Jancus.—A.S., Ianzi.—CIV., Jancy.—FARS., Iantu.—FR. 1380, Jamathoy and Jamathay.]

This great city of Yamzai, which he approaches from Nan-king by the Kiang, is, I think, undoubtedly Yang-chau-fu, the first great city on the canal north of the Kiang, and only a short distance from that river. It is the Yangui of Marco Polo, who was governor there for three years. At an earlier period the province under Yang-chau had comprehended all Kiang-nan and part of Ho-nan and Kiang-si. But it has always continued a place of great trade and population, insomuch that P. Bouvet and his party estimated the latter at two millions!

Martini specifies that the emperor had in this city a revenue office which drew very large sums, *chiefly from the distribution of salt*, there being many salt works to the east of the city.

The city appears as *Iangio* in the Catalan map, almost always surpassing in accuracy of knowledge; whilst in travellers of the

at which our minor friars have a house[1]. And here also be three churches of the Nestorians[2]. This is a noble city, and hath good forty-eight to fifty-eight tumans of fire-places[3], every tuman being ten thousand. In this city are to be had in great abundance all kinds of things on which Christian people live. And the lord of this city hath from salt alone a revenue of five hundred[4] tumans of *balis*; and a *balis*

sixteenth and seventeenth centuries we find *Iamceu* (Trigault), *Iangsé* (Nieuhof), *Yamsé* (Montanus), forms close to that of Odoric. It is probably also the *Yaneku* or *Janku* of Arab writers.

[In Marco Polo's edition, ii, pp. 155–6, I have given two plans of Yang-chau from the *Yang-chau fu ché* (ed. 1733); one bears the title: "The Three Cities under the Sung," and the other: "The Great City under the Sung." The three cities are *Pao yew cheng*, built in 1256, *Sin Pao-cheng* or *Kia cheng*, built after 1256, and *Ta cheng*, the "Great City," built in 1175; in 1357, Ta cheng was rebuilt, and in 1557 it was augmented, taking the place of the three cities; from 553 B.C. until the 12th century, Yang-chau had no less than five enclosures.—Abulfeda (ed. *Guyard*, II, ii, 122) says that Yang-chau is the capital of the Faghfûr of China, and that he is called Tamghâdj-Khan.—According to Pauthier, Yang-chau belonged to the administration of the Chi-li province; the population included 249,466 families and 1,471,194 people including women and children. (*Marc. Pol.*, pp. 466, 467.)]

1 [FR. TEXT. "Une maison et couvent."]

2 [RAM. B., "Qui trouassimo tre belle chiese di Christiani."—B.N., "In hoc etiam sunt tres ecclesiae Nestorinorum, *scilicet virorum religiosorum*."—CIV., "In hac eciam civitate sunt ecclesiae Nestorianorum."—HAK., "In ea tres ecclesiae Nestorianorū."—FR. TEXT, "Si y a pluseurs autres Eglises de religieux, mais ceulz sont nestorins."]

Marco Polo does not mention the Nestorian churches and the Franciscan establishments were all subsequent to his time. (*Duhalde*, i, 69; *Martini in Thévenot*, p. 129, etc.)

[Prof. Pelliot writes to me that a text of 1317 in the *Yuen tien chang* mentions a certain Ngao-la-han [Abraham?] still alive at Yang-chau, who was, according to the text, the son of the founder of the "Church of the Cross of the ärkägün" (*Ye-li-ko-wen she-tze-sze*) of Yang-chau.]

3 [RAM. B., 18 tomani di focolari.—RAM. A., 80 tunne, cioè 80,000 fuochi.—PAL., lviii tomani di focolari.—B.N., "Habens bene xlviii vel lviii tuman ignium."—ARUND., xlviii vel l thumans.—HAK., 48. Thuman ignium.—FRENCH TEXT, "Il y a bien à tout le moins XL, autres dient LII tumans de feux."]

4 [FRENCH TEXT, "L tumans de balisses dont une balisse vault un florin et demi; si que un tuman vault XV mille florins; et non pourquant leurs sires leur fait grâce chascun an de CC tumans affin que en la ville ne soit pas trop grant chierté."—B.N., Quinquaginta milia Tuman balisi.—HAK., "50 Thuman balisi, & valet balisus vnum florenū cum dimidio: Ita quòd vnum Thuman facit 15. millia florenorum, vnā tamen gratiam facit dominus populo, quia dimittit ei,

being worth a florin and a half, thus a tuman maketh fifteen thousand florins. But as a grace to this people the said lord made a remission to them of two hundred tumans, lest distress should be created[1].

There is a custom in this city that if any one desire to give a great dinner or entertainment to his friends he goes to one of the hostels which are established for this very purpose, and saith to the host thereof: "Make me a dinner for such a number of my friends, and I propose to expend such and such a sum upon it." Then the host does exactly as ordered, and the guests are better served than they would have been in the entertainer's own house[2].

This city hath also a vast amount of shipping.

About ten miles from this city, towards the mouth of that great river Talay, there is a certain other city called MENZU[3]. This city hath shipping finer and more numerous peradventure than any other city in the world. And all the

ne sit caristia in eo, 200. Thuman."—RAM. A., "Rendita 50 tunne di balassi, cioè numero de 750,000 fiorini, essendo che pur habbiamo detto, che ogni balasso importa il valore de vn fiorino & mezzo delli nostri: Ma, accioche per il pagare di una tanta summa di denari detta città non patisse disaggio, & impouerisse: il detto Signore gli lassaua dugento tunne."]

[1] The numbers in this paragraph seem corrupt in all the MSS. For some state the revenue at fifty tumans of balish, others at fifty thousand tumans, whilst all state the *remission* at two hundred tumans. As this would exceed the whole amount in the first reading, and be a too insignificant fraction of the second, I have thought that *five hundred tumans* must have been the true reading of the amount of revenue. At Odoric's estimate of the balish this would be equal to about £3,400,000. According to a statement quoted by Pauthier the Chinese revenue from salt in 1753 was equivalent to about £1,779,372 (*Chine Moderne*, p. 195).

[2] [HAK., "& per illum modum meliùs conuiuant amici in pluribus hospitijs quam facerent in vno." [*sic*]]

[3] [B.N., PAL., VEN., Menzu.—DOM., Mezu.—CIV., Mency.—A.S., Mensy.—ARUND., Mencu. — FARS., Menchu. — HAK., Montu. — RAM. A., Meugu.]

I believe that Odoric's expression, "*in capite hujus fluminis,*" is correctly rendered above, though our inconsistent idiom puts a river's head and its mouth at opposite extremities. Thus Polo says of the same great river (Ramusian edition), "*E per lunghezza fine dove* mette capo *nel mare Oceano,*" etc. And Barbaro says of the Erdil or Volga, "*il quale* mette capo *nel Mar di Bachu.*" Fra Mauro,

vessels are as white as snow, being coated with whitewash[1]. And on board of them you find halls and taverns and many other conveniences, as handsome and well ordered as are anywhere to be found. Indeed it is something hard to believe when you hear of, or even when you see, the vast scale of the shipping in those parts[2].

36. Of the river Caramoran; and of certain other cities visited by Friar Odoric.

Quitting that city and travelling by fresh water channels, I passed many cities and towns, and after eight[3] days I came to a certain city named LENZIN[4], which standeth on a river

however, has not understood it so; for though here evidently making use of Odoric, he has put the name of Menzu *up* the river from Iamzai.

The distance and direction assigned would bring us to about Chin-kiang-fu, which was indeed celebrated for the vast numbers of vessels that used to be gathered there. But it does not seem to have borne any name resembling Menzu.

[I believe that Odoric refers to Chin-kiang, though this place has kept the same name since the Sung dynasty.]

The fact is, that Mingchu (or Menzu in Odoric's spelling) is the old name of Ningpo, and there can be little doubt that there is some mistake in the text as to the position assigned to it. Perhaps Odoric was here speaking only from hearsay, and had not visited the place himself. *Mingio* appears in the Catalan map as the next seaport northward from Zaytún. (See *Biot*, *Diction. des Noms Anciens et Mod. compris dans l'Empire Chinois.*)

1 "*Gesso depicta.*" The Chinese caulk with "a kind of composition of lime, oil, or rather rosin which distils from the tree called *tongshu*, and okam of Bambu. When the stuff is dry one would take it for lime, which is the chief ingredient, and nothing else." (*Astley*, iv, 128.) [See *Marco Polo*, II, p. 250, and *note* 4, p. 251.]

2 Two examples are worth quoting of the view taken by more modern travellers of the vast amount of craft. One party of missionaries estimated that the vessels of all sizes which they met on the canal would suffice to build a bridge from Macao to Goa. (*Astley*, iv, 109.) And Barrow calculated that there were at the single city of Nan-c'ang fu, south of the Poyang Lake, 100,000 tons of a class of vessels averaging 250 tons, besides multitudes of smaller craft. (*Autobiog.*, p. 107.)

3 [B.N., "Ab ista civitate recedens et transiens per iiii dietas per multas terras et civitates per aquam dulcem, veni ad quamdam civitatem quae vocatur Lenzin."]

4 [DOM., B.N., Lenzin.—VEN., Lenzi.—ARUND., Lencyn.—FARS., Lencim.—A.S., Lensium.—CIV:, Lencui.—HAK., Lencym.—RAM. A., Benzin.—PAL., Launcj.—RAM. B., Laurenza.—FRENCH TEXT, Lancerny.—French 2810, Lanterny.]

called CARAMORAN[1]. This river passeth through the very midst of Cathay, and doth great damage to that country when it breaks its banks, just as the Po does by

[1] [B.N., PAL., VEN., HAK., DOM., Caramoram.—CIV., Canamoran.—MAGL., Charamorani.—RAM. A., Caramoraz.—FARS., Tharamoram.—A.S., Tharamorim.—Fr. 2810, Caramarion.—FRENCH TEXT, Caramorian.]

Kara-muren (*Mong.*, "the Black River"), called by the Chinese *Hwang Ho* or the Yellow River. The embankment of the river is said to date from the twenty-second century B.C. Its regulation has ever been a source of anxiety to the Chinese Government, and there used to be a tax on the Hong merchants at Canton expressly on account of this object. The will of the Emperor Kia K'ing, who died in 1820, has the following passage:—"The Yellow River has, from the remotest ages, been China's sorrow. Whenever the mouth of the stream has been impeded by sand-banks, it has higher up its banks created alarm by flooding the country," etc. This seems to have been eminently the case in 1855 or 1856, when the stream of the Hwang Ho near the debouchment of the Great Canal was reduced to a few yards in width, the northern banks having given way far up, and the inundations poured over Shan-tung. On this occasion, much of the water was reported to have escaped into the Gulf of Pe Chi-li, which the Chinese believe to have been the original exit. During the reign of the last Mongol Emperor, a project was adopted for restoring it to this channel. The discontent created by this scheme assisted in exciting the movement for the expulsion of the dynasty. (*Davis*, i, 137, 190; *De Guignes*, iv, 216; *J. R. G. S.*, xxviii, 294; see also *Biot* in *Jour. As.*, sér. iv, vols. i and ii.)

Lenzin is Lin-ching, which appears in Berghaus, and in Keith Johnston's Royal Atlas, on the Great Canal very near the 35th degree of latitude. It is plain that Odoric either confounds the canal with the Hwang Ho or takes it for a branch of that river. Indeed, the Chinese official geography quoted in Pauthier's *Chine Moderne* (p. 5), describes a river called the *Yu-hwang-ho*, as traversing Shan-tung and Pe Chi-li, and introducing itself successively into the Y-ho, the Wen-ho, the Wei-ho, the Chang-ho, and the Tien. This must surely be the canal itself, and the name seems to show that it has been in some way identified with the Hwang-ho. [No doubt Odoric is making a confusion between the Hwang-ho and the Yun-ho, the Grand Canal, on the banks of which were built both Lin-t'sing and Ts'i-ning chau. The length of the Grand Canal from Hang-chau to Pe-king is about 3630 *li*. From Chen-kiang on the Yang-tze to Pe-king it is about 2850 *li* long. Cf. D. Gandar, *Canal Impérial*, Shang-hai, 1894.] Lin-ching is also the Linju of Polo, and the Lincegam of Nieuhof.

[This is Lin-t'sing chau on the bank of the Grand Canal; it lost a great deal of its importance during the T'aï P'ing war (1855). Marco Polo calls it Linju and says it is eight days towards the south of Sinju-matu. The Rev. D. Z. Sheffield wrote in 1885 (*Chin. Rec.*, March, 1886, p. 122): "Lin-ching is a city of upwards of 200,000 inhabitants [Richard says 48,000], I should judge. It is on the Grand Canal, at the point of divergence from the Wei river. The people were very civil to us, the merchants often inviting us into their shops.

Ferrara[1]. And as I travelled by that river towards the east, and passed many towns and cities, I came to a certain city which is called SUNZUMATU[2], which hath a greater plenty

From one-fourth to one-third of the population is Mohammedan. There are three large mosques, near the city but in bad repair."]

[From a letter from Father Jose Maria Vila, missionary at Tsi-nan fu, published in the *Missioni Francescane* of Florence, 31st August 1892, M. Romanet du Caillaud (*Cte. rendu Soc. Géog. Paris*, 1893, p. 39) writes that at two leagues from Lin-ts'ing two tombs of franciscan missionaries of the XIVth century have been discovered: on one the name *Bernard* may be read; this Bernard accompanied Odoric, who left him at Lin-ts'ing in charge of a Christian mission existing already; the other was the grave of a franciscan bishop buried in 1387, whose name cannot be deciphered; in his tomb were found a sealed bottle with a MS. which fell to ashes when handled, a small bronze box with an episcopal ring and a pectoral cross with the seal of St. Francis.]

1 [B.N., "Sicut est Padus transiens per Ferrariam."—VEN., "Dum rumpitur sicut facit Padus Ferarie."—CIV., A.S., "Sicut est Padus transiens versus Ferrariam."—FRENCH TEXT, "un grant fleuve qui... passe parmi le royaume de Cathay et y porte moult grant dommaige quant il croist trop et ist hors de son chanel."]

2 [VEN., DOM., B.N., Suzumato.—FARS., A.S., CIV., Sucumat.—HAK., Sumacoto.—ARUND., Sumakoto.—PAL., Sogomerca.—RAM. B., Sunzomaco.—RAM. A., Suzupato.—FRENCH TEXT, Ingarmato.]

There is no doubt this is the Singuimatu of Polo, who nearly always substitutes *gui* for *zu* or *chu*, a Tartar idiom according to Martini (p. 145). *Mat'u* (matheu) signifies a place of river trade; literally a "horse's head," and so a "jetty, [a landing place]." Marsden and Baldelli Boni are probably right in identifying Singuimatu with Lin-tsin-chu, a well known city of Shan-tung, near the junction of the Canal with the Wei River coming from the south-west. I am aware of what Klaproth has written on this subject, identifying the place with that called *Fenchui-nanwang*, where the river Wen-ho, introduced from the north-east, is made to divide its waters north and south in the manner described by Marco. He supposes the name in Polo to be a corrupt transcript of *Fenchui-matheu*, "The Port of the Division of the Waters." I venture to doubt this ingenious suggestion; *first*, because the independent occurrence of the name in Odoric shows that it is not corrupt; *secondly*, because Marco says distinctly that the stream in question comes from the *south*, which corresponds with the Wei and not with the Wen; and, *thirdly*, because we have no evidence adduced that this Fenchui was a place of trade at all; whereas Trigault, Martini, Nieuhof and others concur with later authorities in speaking of Lin ts'in as one of the most important commercial towns of the empire, in accordance with Odoric's notice. *E.g.* Trigautius says:—"Lincinum urbs est e maximis, et commercio celebris in paucis (?), ad eam enim non provincialia solum mercimonia sed e toto quoque regno pervadunt." (*Polo* in *Ram.*, cliii; *Klaproth, Mém. Rel. à l'Asie*, iii, 325; *Trigautii, Exp. Sinensis*, 345; *Martini Atlas Sinensis in loc.*; *Astley*, iii, 418.)

MIN. RAM. places Sunzomatu four days from Pe-king, which would

of silk than perhaps any other place on earth, for when silk there is at its dearest you can still have forty pounds for less than eight groats[1]. There is in the place likewise great store of all kinds of merchandize, and likewise of bread and wine, and all other good things[2]. [And seeing that there were in this place more people than I had seen in any other, when I asked how that came to pass, they told me that it was because the air of the place was so salubrious, insomuch that there were few that died of aught but old age[3].]

37. The Friar reacheth Cambalech, and discourseth thereof, and of the Great Caan's Palace there.

And departing thence, I passed on through many a city and many a town towards the east, until I came to that noble city CAMBALECH[4], an old city of that famous

tend to identify it with T'ien-tsin. But T'ien-tsin is said to be quite modern. (*Biot* in voc.) P.S. I find since writing the above that Pauthier (*Le Livre de Marc Pol*, p. 444) considers the Singui of Polo to be certainly *Thsiningchau*. And if he is right in saying that the vulgar pronunciation of that name would be *Thsinju*, this may well be accepted.

[Pauthier is no doubt right here and Yule has since accepted his theory in *Marco Polo*; this is Ts'i-ning chau along the bank of the Grand Canal. This is the Sinjumatu of Marco Polo (see ii, p. 138 and 139 note). Sir John F. Davis writes that Ts'i-ning chau is a town of considerable dimensions...."The *ma-tow*, or platforms, before the principal boats had ornamental gateways over them....The canal seems to render this an opulent and flourishing place, to judge by the gilded and carved shops, temples, and public offices, along the eastern banks." (*Sketches of China*, i, pp. 255—257.) See *Marco Polo's Sinjumatu* by A. C. Moule. (*T'oung pao*, July 1912, pp. 431–3.)]

1 [DOM., "Quaranta libre [di seta] per meno de otto."—RAM. A., Otto grossi.—RAM. B., vn soldo.—A.S., "octo solidis grossorum minorum."—FRENCH TEXT, "XL livres pesant pour IX gros."]

2 [HAK., "In ea est copia omnium mercimoniorū, & omnium victualium, panis, vini, carnium, piscium, & omnium specierum electarum."]

3 MIN. RAM.

["E perche ui era in questo loco piu gēte, che in niun' altro, che hauessi visto, domandando, donde ciò auuenisse mi fu risposto, p conto che l' aria, & il luogo sono alla generatione molto salutiferi, di modo tale, che pochi sono che muoiono, se nō di vecchizza."]

4 [RAM. B., "E nauigando da quattro giornate, peruenimmo nella nobil città chiamata Cambalù."]

province of CATHAY[1]. The Tartars took the city, and then

[1] [Khân Bâliq خان باليغ, the City of the Khan. VEN., Cambalech.—CIV., Cambalet.—RAM. A., Cabalec.] PEKING. The Chinese capital was still so called by the Turks in the time of P. Ricci, and may probably be called so to this day.

[The Chinese Annals, quoted by Bretschneider, report that in 1121 B.C., a descendant of the celebrated Emperor Hwang-ti was invested with a fief in the north, and that he resided at *Ki*, which city is supposed by the Chinese to have been situated at about the same place where Pe-king now stands. During the Ch'un tsew period (723—481) and the Chau kwo (418—221) the city of Ki is mentioned as the capital of the kingdom of Yen destroyed in the 3rd century B.C. by Shi Hwang-ti. During the T'ang dynasty (618—907), Peking was known under the name of Yu-chau and was captured in 936 by the K'itan or Leao and became their southern capital as *Nan-king*; in 1031, the name was changed to Yen-king; in 1151, Peking received from the fourth Kin sovereign the name of *Chung-tu* or Middle Capital; in 1215 it was captured by Chinghiz and in 1264 Kúblái transferred there the capital of the Empire, but in 1267, he built a new city called since 1271 *Ta-tu* (Great Capital) by the Chinese and *Khan-baliq* by the Mongols to the north-east of the Kin Capital.

Marco Polo says, i, p. 374: "Now there was on that spot in old times a great and noble city called Cambaluc, which is as much as to say in our tongue 'The city of the Emperor.' But the Great Kaan was informed by his Astrologers that this city would prove rebellious, and raise great disorders against his imperial authority. So he caused the present city to be built close beside the old one, with only a river between them. And he caused the people of the old city to be removed to the new town that he had founded; and this is called Taidu."]

This city was abandoned as a royal residence on the expulsion of the Mongol dynasty in 1368 [and the first Ming Emperor, Hung Wu, changed its name into *Pei-p'ing fu*, but in 1409 the third Ming Emperor Yung-lo left his capital *Ying-tien*, or *Nan-king*, and established his court at *Pei p'ing* which became Pe-king; in 1421, all the work was finished.] He built the walls as they now exist, reducing their extent and the number of the gates to nine. This is what is commonly called the *Tartar city* of the present day (called also by the Chinese *Lau-ch'eng* or "Old Town"), which therefore represents the Taydo of Odoric. The ruins of the older Yen-king or Chung-tu were still visible in the time of the Ming, but they were embraced in the new southern city called *Wai-ch'eng* or "Outer Town," the wall of which [28 *li* long] was built in 1543.

The circumference of the present Tartar city appears from the plans to be about fifteen miles. [According to the French astronomers (Fleuriais and Lapied) sent to Peking for the Transit of Venus in December, 1875, the present Tartar City is 23 kil. 55 in circuit, viz. if 1 *li*=575 mètres, 41 *li*; from the north to the south 5400 m.; from east to west 6700 m.; the wall is 13 m. in height and 12 m. in width.] Martini speaks of it as having still twelve gates in his time, but he was almost certainly wrong. It has three on the south side, and two on each of the others. The circuit of the two cities together is about twenty-two miles according to the scale on the plan given by Pauthier,

built another[1] at a distance of half-a-mile[2], which they called TAYDO[3].

This latter city hath twelve gates[4], between every two of which there is a space of two long miles; and betwixt the two cities also there is a good amount of population, the compass of the two together being more than forty miles[5]. Here the Great Khan[6] hath his residence, and hath

though Timkowski states it at forty versts, or 26⅔ miles. But Odoric's dimensions may have been quite correct, for the Tartar city was larger, and there was a space of more than half-a-mile between the two. (*Timkowski*, i, 315, etc., etc.)

[1] [RAM. B., "Gira 24 miglia, & vn' altra appresso a questa meno di un mezzo miglio. Il circuito di ambedue e da 60 miglia. Sono poi tutte dui insieme cerchiata da vn' altra muraglia, che gira in tutto circa 100 miglia."—DOM., "Lo circuito di queste due città circonda più che quaranta miglia."—RAM. A., Cinquanta.]

[2] [A.S., dimidio milliari.]

[3] [VEN., DOM., Taydo.—PAL., Taido.—B.N., CIV., Caydo.—FARS., HAK., Caido.—FRENCH TEXT, Cayto.—A.S., Thayde.]

[4] [Marco Polo says also, ii, p. 374, that "there are 12 gates, and over each gate there is a great and handsome palace, so that there are on each side of the square three gates and five palaces; for (I ought to mention) there is at each angle also a great and handsome palace. In those palaces are vast halls in which are kept the arms of the city garrison." Gaubil and Martini also say that there were 12 gates. "The *Yuen shi*, as well as the *Ch'ue keng lu*, and other works of the Yuen, agree in stating that the capital had *eleven* gates. They are enumerated in the following order. Southern wall: 1. The gate direct south (mid.) was called *Li-cheng men*; 2. The gate direct to the left (east) was called *Wen-ming men*; 3. The gate direct to the right (west) was called *Shun-ch'eng men*.—Eastern wall: 4. The gate direct east (mid.) was called *Ch'ung-jen men*; 5. The gate direct to the south-east was called *Ts'i-hua men*; 6. The gate direct to the north-east was called *Kuang-hi men*.—Western wall: 7. The gate direct west (mid.) was called *Ho-i men*; 8. The gate direct to the south-west was called *P'ing-tse men*; 9. The gate direct to the north-west was called *Su-ts'ing men*.—Northern wall: 10. The gate to the north-west was called *K'ien-te men*; 11. The gate to the north-east was called *An-chen men*." (Bretschneider, *Peking*, pp. 13, 14.) There are now nine gates in the Tartar City.]

[5] [A.S., "Harum civitatum circuitus plus ambit quàm quadraginta milliaria magna."]

[6] I am not sure that a faithful version should not render *Magnus Canis* as the "Great Dog," for in most copies the word is regularly declined, *Canis*, *Cani*, *Canem*, as if he were really a bow-wow. According to Ludolf, an old German translation of Mandeville does introduce the mighty prince as *Der Grosse Hund*. That author thinks that some such *double entente* may have led to the story in Pliny about a people who have a dog for their king, a suggestion which would have

a great palace, the walls of which are some four miles in compass[1]. And within this space be many other fine palaces. [For within the great palace wall is a second enclosure, with a distance between them of perhaps half a bowshot, and in the midst between those two walls are kept his stores and all his slaves; whilst within the inner enclosure dwells the Great Khan with all his family, who are most numerous, so many sons and daughters, sons-in-law, and grandchildren hath he; with such a multitude of wives and councillors and secretaries and servants, that the whole palace of four miles' circuit is inhabited[2].]

And within the enclosure of the great palace there hath been a hill thrown up on which another palace is built, the most beautiful in the whole world. And this whole hill is planted over with trees, wherefrom it hath the name of the *Green Mount*. And at the side of this hill hath been formed a lake [more than a mile round[3]], and a most beautiful bridge built across it[4]. And on this lake there be such multitudes of wild-geese and ducks and swans[5], that it is

been a happy one had the people in question dwelt in the heart of Asia instead of the heart of Africa. (*Ludolf, Supp. to Comm. in Hist. Æthiop.* p. 26.) The familiarity of North Italy with the Can Grande of Verona may have made Odoric and his contemporaries look less strangely on the denomination.

1 [RAM. B., "& ad ogni cãtone è un palazzo doue dimora vno di quattro suo baroni principali."]

2 [MIN. RAM. "E dentro al palazzo grãde è vn' altro circuito di muro, che da vn muro all' altro e forse mezza tirata d' arco, e tra questi muri vi stanno i suoi prouisionati con tutte le sue fameglie: Et nell' altro circuito habita il gran cane con tutti i suoi congiunti, che sono assaissimi cõ tanti figluoli, figluole, generi, de nepoti: con tante moglie, consiglieri, secretarij, e famegli, che tutto il palazzo, che gira 4 miglia, viene ad esser habitato."]

3 [RAM. B., "Che gira piu d' vn miglio."]

4 [RAM. B., "E 'l piu bel põte che nõ ho mai visto il migliore, in considerando il marmo, e l' artificio, che è vna marauiglia."—DOM., un bellissimo ponte.]

5 [RAM. B., "Eran nell' acqua le centinaia dell' anatre, et de assaissimi vccelli, che viuono di pesce, d' ogni sorte, che quel lago produce." —DOM., "Tante oche salvatiche, anitre et cesani."—B.N., "Sunt anseres silvestres, anathes, et cesenae."—CIV., "Silvestres anseres et anete et cessene."]

something to wonder at; so that there is no need for that lord to go from home when he wisheth for sport. Also within the walls are thickets full of sundry sorts of wild animals; so that he can follow the chase when he chooses without ever quitting the domain[1].

The word is in all the best MSS. *Cesani* or *Cesenæ*, for which MUS. substitutes a gloss "*avium aquaticarum*." The word is not to be found in Ducange, or, I believe, any Italian dictionary. It occurs also in some of the MSS. of Marco Polo describing the Khan's falconry as *Cesini*, where others have *Cycni*, and where Baldello Boni considers it a copyist's error for that word. I do not believe it to be so, for I find *Cecini* also coupled with *gruve* or cranes, in a list of poultry and game, etc., in the book of Giovanni da Uzzano on Merchandize. (*Della Decima*, iv, 63.) It is, therefore, almost certainly a word which should be recognised, though most likely it means swans, and so I have rendered it. Indeed the old French Polo just edited by Pauthier has *sesnes* (p. 310).

[1] In this account of the palace we have an instance of true particulars occurring only in the Minor Ramusian version, e.g. the double enceinte. This is mentioned by Polo, and is found in the existing palace, which appears to preserve many of the features of that of the Mongols, though the latter was burnt about thirty years after their fall. Indeed the arrangement of royal enclosures in all the Indo-Chinese countries, including Burma and Java, appears to follow the same traditional rules, probably derived originally from India. The palace at Amarapura, with its square form, its successive enclosures, its masonry basement eight or nine feet from the ground, its hall of gold and vermilion, etc., quite corresponded on a smaller scale with this description.

[Dr. Bretschneider observes "that in the ancient Chinese works, three concentric inclosures are mentioned in connection with the palace. The innermost inclosed the *Ta-nei*, the middle inclosure, called *Kung-ch'eng* or *Hwang-ch'eng*, answering to the wall surrounding the present prohibited city, and was about 6 *li* in circuit. Besides this there was an outer wall (a rampart apparently) 20 *li* in circuit, answering to the wall of the present imperial city (which now has 18 *li* in circuit)." The *Hwang-ch'eng* of the Yuen was measured by imperial order, and found to be 7 *li* in circuit; the wall of the Mongol palace was 6 *li* in circuit, according to the *Ch'ue keng lu*. (Bretschneider, *Peking*, 24.)—Marco Polo's mile could be approximately estimated=2·77 Chinese *li*. (*Ibid.*, p. 24, note.) The common Chinese *li*=360 *pu*, or 180 *chang*, or 1800 *ch'i* (feet); 1 *li*=1894 English feet or 575 mètres; at least according to the old Venice measures quoted in Yule's *Marco Polo*, ii, one pace =5 feet. Beside the common *li*, the Chinese have another *li*, used for measuring fields, which has only 240 *pu* or 1200 *ch'i*. This is the *li* spoken of in the *Ch'ue keng lu*. (*Ibid.*, p. 13, note.)]

The existing Tartar city at Pe-king officially termed *Nei-ch'eng* or "Inner-Town," encloses a second called *Hwang-ch'eng* or "Imperial (yellow) Town," which, no doubt, represents the outer palace of Odoric's day, and that includes a third called *Tseu-kin-ch'eng*, or "Red City," which is the actual residence.

The Green Mount, to which Kúblái, anticipating the experiments

But his own palace in which he dwells is of vast size and splendour. The basement[1] thereof is raised about two paces from the ground, and within there be four-and-twenty columns of gold[2]; and all the walls are hung with skins of red leather, said to be the finest[3] in the world. In the midst of the palace is a certain great jar[4], more than two

of zealous planters in our day, caused remarkable trees of every bulk to be transferred with the earth attaching to their roots, still stands conspicuous within the palace walls of Pekin. "Your eye rests with pleasure upon this round wood-covered hill, rising picturesquely from the middle of the glittering roofs and umbrageous trees within the palace walls." (*Swinhoe, North China Campaign*, p. 353.) It is called by the Chinese *King-Shan*, "Court Mountain," *Wan-Su-Shan*, "Ten thousand years Mount," or *Meï-Shan*, "Coal Hill," the last from the material of which it is traditionally said to be composed, as a reserve store in case of siege. It rises 160 feet above the natural soil, and on it the last Ming Emperor met a miserable end. The lake also (called *Thai-i-chi*) still exists as a swampy hollow; and the "beautiful bridge" is there in decay. (*Polo*, i, 10; *Expéd. de Chine par P. Varin*, 1862; *Davis*, ii, 75; *Timkowski*, ii, 154; *Swinhoe, u.s.*; *Pauthier, Chine Moderne*, p. 19.)

[Marco Polo speaks also of the Green Mount (i, p. 365): "Not only are the trees all green, but the hill itself is all green likewise; and there is nothing to be seen on it that is not green; and hence it is called the *Green Mount*; and in good sooth 'tis named well." The "Green Mount" was an island called *Pai-t'a shan* or *K'ung-hua tao* at the time of the Kin; in 1271, it received the name of *Wan-sui-shan*; it is about 100 feet in height, as is the only hill mentioned by Chinese writers of the Mongol time who refer to the palace grounds. It is not the present *King-shan*, north of the palace, called also *Wan-sui-shan* under the Ming, and now the *Mei-shan* of more recent formation. "I have no doubt," says Bretschneider (*Peking*, p. 35), "that Marco Polo's handsome palace on the top of the Green Mount is the same as the *Kwang-han tien*" of the *Ch'ue keng lu*. It was a hall in which there was a jar of black jade, big enough to hold more than 30 piculs of wine; this jade had white veins, and in accordance with these veins, fish and animals have been carved on the jar. (*Ibid.*, p. 35.) "The *Ku kung i lu*, in describing the *Wan-sui-shan*, praises the beautiful shady green of the vegetation there." (*Ibid.*, p. 37.)]

[1] [CIV., "Cuius pavimentum est duobus passibus elevatum."—DOM., "Del quale la terra è piu alta duo passa."]

[2] [HAK., 14 columnas.—FRENCH TEXT, "XXIIII colompnes toutes de fin or pur."]

[3] [Fr. 2810, belles.—FR. TEXT, nobles.]

[4] [RAM. B., "Vna pigna di pietra pretiosa, & è si fina, si come io intesi, che 'l suo prezzo non lo potrebbono agguagliare *quattro grosse cittadi*."—FRENCH TEXT, "Une grant pigne, c'est-à-dire un pignetaire un grand vaissel là ou on met piment et buvrage."—Bretschneider, *Archaeolog. Res. on Peking*, p. 28, mentions from the *Ch'ue keng lu*: "There is further a *large jar* made of wood and varnished, the inside

paces in height, entirely formed of a certain precious stone called *Merdacas*[1] [and so fine, that I was told its price exceeded the value of four great towns[2]]. It is all hooped round with gold, and in every corner thereof is a dragon[3] represented as in act to strike most fiercely. And this jar hath also fringes of network of great pearls hanging therefrom, and these fringes are a span in breadth. Into this vessel drink is conveyed by certain conduits from the court

lined with silver. A dragon in golden clouds twines around the jar, which is 17 feet in height and holds more than 50 piculs of wine. There is also a jar of jade."]

[1] Certainly the oriental Jade or *Yu* of the Chinese, which stood as high in the estimation of the Mongols, and figures largely in their legends and their poetry. Thus when Chinghiz was proclaimed Khagan on the grassy meadows of the river Kerulan, a certain stone spontaneously flew asunder, and disclosed a great seal of graven jade, which was kept as a palladium by his descendants, and was almost the only thing saved by the last emperor of his house when flying from the Chinese insurgents. (*Schmidt*, pp. 71, 133.)

The Mongol word for jade cited in this authority is *khas*, which is doubtless the termination of the name used in the text.

I cannot say what the first part of that name is. But it is worthy of notice that the mountain near Khotan, which supplies some of the best jade, is called, according to Timkowski, *Mirjái*, or *Kash-tash* (*Turk.* "Jade-rock"). Can Merdacas = *Mirjai-khas*? Further, can the Tartar name have anything to do with the Persian *khás*, "royal, noble"? Crawfurd technically styles the Burmese jade "noble serpentine," and in the narrative of Goës we find the jade of Yarkand spoken of as "*marmoris illius apud Sinas* nobilissimi."

It may be added that Pegolotti names, among various kinds of silk in the Eastern markets, *seta merdachascia*; what does *this* mean? (*Pegolotti*, p. 301.) Since writing these words I find that Freytag's Arab. lexicon has "*Midaqs*; Sericum crudum," found also in Armenian as *Metaks* (*St. Martin* in *Lebeau*, ix, 226), which is, therefore, probably the *seta merdachascia* of Pegolotti, as well as the μέταξα, μέταξις of the Byzantines. It is possible that this word was an Orientalised reflexion of Μηδική which Procopius says had been the old Greek name for silk stuffs?

[VEN., CIV., merdacas.—RAM. A., merdicas.—FARS., DOM., B.N., merdatas.—PAL., medacas.—RAM. B., medecas.—HAK., merdochas.—MAGL., mordacas.—FRENCH TEXT, marthatedes.—I believe this is the name of the contents for the name of the jar. We find in Francis Johnson's *Dict. Persian, Arabic, and English*, Lond., 1852, p. 1161 the Arabic مردقوش *mardakūsh* after the Persian مردهگوش *murda-gosh* "Marjoram, Saffron. A kind of aromatics of a reddish black colour, with which women perfume their combs." I prefer this explanation to Yule's.]

[2] MIN. RAM.

[3] *Serpens*. [FRENCH TEXT, "serpent."—Fr. 2810, "serpent d'or."]

of the palace; and beside it are many golden goblets from which those drink who list.

In the hall of the palace also are many peacocks of gold. And when any of the Tartars wish to amuse their lord then they go one after the other and clap their hands; upon which the peacocks flap their wings, and make as if they would dance. Now this must be done either by diabolic art, or by some engine underground[1].

38. The friar setteth forth the state of the Khan's court.

But when the Lord Khan[2] is seated on his imperial throne, the Queen is placed at his left hand; and a step lower are two others of his women; whilst at the bottom of the steps stand all the other ladies of his family[3]. And all who are married wear upon their heads the foot of a man as it were, a cubit and a half in length, and at the top of that foot there are certain cranes' feathers, the whole foot being set with great pearls[4]; so that if there be in the whole world any fine and large pearls they are to be found in the decorations of those ladies[5].

[1] [B.N., "Hoc autem fit vel arte dyabolica vel ingenio quodam sub terra fit."—HAK., "Et hoc credo factũ arte Magica, vel aliqua cautela subterranea."—CIV., "Hoc autem ut puto fit arte diabolica, vel forte ingenio humano sub terra."—FRENCH TEXT, "Et quant aucuns Tartres veult en ce palais faire aucune feste à son seigneur, il bat les mains ensemble et tantost ces paons espandent les elles et alettent et semble droit que ilz dancent tellement; sont faits cilz paon par science d'homme ou par art de diable."]

[2] [The Great Khans of Odoric's time were the Yuen Emperors Ying Tsung (Che Che, 1321)=Shodibala Gegen and Tai Ting Ti (Tai Ting, 1324; Che Ho, 1328)=Yissun Timur.]

[3] [FRENCH TEXT, "Quant le Grant Caan siet sur son trosne en sa majesté impérial, à son senestre costé siet la royne un degré plus bas que le roy, puis deux autres femmes concubines que li roys tient au tiers degré qui est le plus bas. Et après ces concubines sient les autres dames du sang royal."]

[4] [FRENCH TEXT, "Tous ces piés est d'or aournez et de grosses perles."]

[5] The coiffure of the Tartar married women is thus described by Rubruquis: "They have an ornament for the head called *Bocca* (or *Botta*, perhaps *Bocta*). This is made of the bark of trees or similar light stuff, round, and large enough to require both hands to span it. It

On the right hand of the king is placed his first-born son that shall reign after him; and below stand all who are

is more than a cubit high, and is square above, like the capital of a pillar. The whole affair is covered with silk, and on the top or capital they put in the middle a thin tuft of quills or slender canes, also of a cubit or more. And this tuft is adorned at top with peacock's feathers, and round about with mallard's feathers and precious stones" (p. 232). Carpini describes it in the same way (p. 615). And Ibn Batuta says of a princess of Kipchak: "On her head was a *boghthak*, that is, a high tiara incrusted with jewels, and decked at the apex with peacock's feathers" (ii, 379 and 388). But the only confirmation of Odoric about the "man's foot" that I find is given by Ricold of Montecroce. After telling a story of how the Tartar women helped to gain a great victory he adds: "In memory of this victory the Tartars granted leave to their wives to wear lofty crowns to the height of a cubit or more. But lest the women should wax over proud thereupon, the Tartars also determined that these crowns should at the summit take the form of a foot. And in fact at the top of such a great crown there is as it were a foot over it, as if to maintain a testimony that the women did not win the victory alone, but by help of their husbands, who came to their rescue; and as if it were said to them:—'Crowned though ye be, forget not that ye be under the power of your husbands!' and so by a kind of natural reason they seem to have divined that which is written in the Law of God, '*Sub viri potestate eris.*'" (*Peregrinatores Quatuor*, p. 116.) Notices of relics of this Tartar head-dress still existing are quoted in the *Journ. Asiat.*, sér. iv, tom. x, 169, xvi, 157. It appears from one of these that the name *Bogtac* still indicates the head-dress of women of a certain age among the Circassians and Ossetes.

[Cf. FRENCH EDITION, p. 409.—Vincent de Beauvais (bk. xxix, ch. lxxxv, 421 *b*) describes the *bogtak*, but does not mention it by its name. Rockhill (*Rubruck*, p. 74) makes the following remarks on this subject: "Such high head-dresses seem to have been worn at various times by many Asiatic peoples or tribes; whether they were quite like the Mongol *bogtak* or not I am unable to say. *Wei shu* (bk. 102, 13) speaking of an Uigur people called the Yen-ta, says: 'It was the custom of the Yen-ta for brothers to have the same wife: if a man had no brothers, his wife wore a head-dress (or cap) with but one horn. If he had brothers, she added as many points (or horns) as he had brothers.' Yüan-chuang describes in about the same terms the head-dress of the women of Himatala, who may, by the way, be the Yen-ta of the *Wei shu* (Julien, *Voyages*, ii, 197). The nearest modern approach to the Mongol *bogtak* seems to me to be the high head-dress, covered with bark or red cloth, of the Votiak women of Kasan (Pallas, *Voyages*, v, 32). We find another head-dress of like description, which may owe its origin to the *bogtak*, worn at the present time by the Christian women of Urfah, between Diarbekir and Aleppo (Percy Badger, i, 329). The head-dress of the Kirghiz women, and the high Flemish head-dress called *hennin*, introduced into France by Isabeau de Bavière, should not be omitted in this enumeration." Cf. *Hennins or Conical lady's hats in Asia, China and Europe* by G. Schlegel (*T'oung Pao*, iii, 1892, pp. 422–429). "But in the reign of Jin-tsung of the Sung dynasty (1023–1063), the court ladies made hats and combs

of the blood royal. And there be four scribes also, to take down all the words that the king may utter. And in front of the king stand his barons and others, an innumerable multitude, and nobody dares say a word[1] unless the lord shall address him, except the jesters[2], who may say something to amuse their lord. But even they must not be bold enough to transgress the bounds which the king hath laid down for them.

And before the gates of the palace stand barons as warders, to see that no one touch the threshold of the door; and if they catch anyone doing so they beat him soundly[3].

And when that great lord wishes to make an entertainment he shall have fourteen thousand[4] barons with coronets on their heads waiting upon him at the banquet. And every one of them shall have a coat on his back such that

of white horn; these hats reached a height of *three feet*, and the combs that of *one foot*....During the Mongol dynasty (1206–1367), the royal ladies and legitimate spouses of the great officers all wore *Koo-koo's*. The *Kookoo* was about *two feet* high, and was covered with red silk.... We thus see, that this strange and absurd fashion, invented by the ladies of *Ye-tha*, or Chorasmia, reigned paramount in China from the 11th to the 14th century, notwithstanding imperial edicts against it."—The married women of Phari in Tibet, says Waddell, *Lhasa*, p. 101, "wear a wonderful piece of headgear, a large hoop like the framework of a tall crown, suggestive of the Norwegian bride's hat, and set with a wealth of turquoise, coral, etc."]

[1] [FRENCH TEXT, sorier.—Fr. 2810, sonner.]

[2] [FRENCH TEXT, "excepté les héraux et les menestrelz."]

[3] Marco Polo explains that it was a grievous offence to touch the imperial threshold, and strangers were officially warned of this before their entrance. Rubruquis mentions the same; his comrade got into a scrape for breaking the rule, and was not allowed again to visit the court. Carpini indeed says: "*Si quis calcat limen stationis alicujus ducis* interficitur." (*Polo*, i, 15; *Rub.*, 255, 268; 320, 338; *Carpini*, 625, 741.)

[Mr. Rockhill remarks (*Rubruck*, p. 104): "The prohibition extended to the tent-ropes. The same custom existed among the Fijians, I believe. I may note that it also prevailed in ancient China. It is said of Confucius 'when he was standing he did not occupy the middle of the gate-way; when he passed in or out, he did not tread on the threshold.' (*Lun-yü*, bk. x, ch. iv, 2.)"]

[4] [RAM. B., Quindecimila baroni.—B.N., XIIII milia.—FRENCH TEXT, "IIII^m barons couronnez tous de couronnes d'or qui le servent."]

the pearls[1] on it alone are worth some fifteen thousand florins. And the court is ordered passing well, all being ranked by tens and hundreds and thousands, and all having their duties assigned, standing answerable one to another for any breach either to their own charges or in the charges of those subordinate to them[2].

I, Friar Odoric, was full three years in that city of his, and often present at those festivals of theirs[3]; for we Minor Friars have a place assigned to us at the emperor's court, and we be always in duty bound to go and give him our benison. So I took the opportunity to make diligent inquiry from Christians, Saracens, and all kinds of idolaters, and likewise from our own converts to the faith, of whom there be some who are great barons[4] at that court, and have to do with the king's person only[5]. Now these all told me

[1] [FRENCH TEXT, rubis.]

[2] ["Moreouer, the Emperour of the Tartars hath a wonderfull dominion ouer all his subiects. For no man dare abide in any place, vnles he hath assigned him to be there. Also he himselfe appointeth to his dukes where they should inhabite. Likewise the dukes assigne places vnto euery Millenarie or conductor of a thousand soldiers, the Millenaries vnto each captaine of an 100, the capitaines vnto euery corporall of ten." (Beazley, *Carpini*, p. 120.)]

[3] [MIN. RAM., "in company with the Minor Friars, who have a monastery there; and they used to send us from the court supplies enough for a thousand friars! And, by the true God, there is as great a difference between that prince and those of Italy, as between a very rich man and a beggar." "Et io vi stetti tre anni in compagnia di frati minori, che vi hanno il monastero: doue dalla corte vi veniua tanta robba, che sarebbe stata bastante per mille frati. E per lo Dio vero è tãta differẽza da questo Signore a questi d' Italia, come da vn huomo richissimo ad vn che sia il piu pouero del mondo."—B.N., "Ego frater Odoricus ibi fui bene tribus annis in hac sua. civitate et multotiens in istis suis festis presens fui, nam nos fratres minores in hâc curia suâ habemus locum dêputatum, et nos semper sic oportet ire et dare sibi benedictionem nostram, unde diligenter petii."—A.S., "Ego Fr. Odoricus mansi ibi tribus annis & festis regiis saepius inter fui. Nam nos Fratres Minores...."]

[4] [RAM. B., "Questo Signore teneua da ducento ottanta mila huomini, li quali non attendeuano se non a cani, e caualli, & a tutte le cose, che appartengono alla caccia per seruigio del Signore."]

[5] These great courtiers may have been some of the Christian Alans of whom we hear some years later in connection with the legation of Marignolli.

with one voice as follows: that the king's players alone amount to xiii[1] tumans; that of those others who keep the dogs and wild beasts and fowls there be xv tumans[2]; of leeches[3] to take charge of the royal person there be four hundred idolaters[4], eight Christians, and one Saracen[5]. And all these have from the king's court whatever provision they require[6]. [And there be never more nor fewer, but when one dies another is appointed in his place[7].] As for the rest of the establishment it is past counting. [In short, the court is truly magnificent, and the most perfectly ordered that there is in the world, with barons, gentlemen, servants, secretaries, Christians, Turks, and idolaters, all receiving from the court what they have need of[8].]

39. Of the order of the Great Caan when he journeyeth.

Now, this lord passeth the summer at a certain place

[1] [HAK., 18 thuman.—FARS., 12.—DOM., XIV.]

[2] [B.N., "Alii autem custodientes canes, bestias silvestres, et aves bene XV sunt tuman." Passage omitted in the French Text.]

[3] [CIV., "Sunt Tartari, quatercentum Christiani...."]

[4] [FRENCH TEXT, III[c] ydolâtres.—ARUND., CCC[ti].—RAM. B., 400.—B.N., quadringinti.]

[5] [B.N., unus.—FRENCH TEXT, VII sarrazins.]

[6] The Sultan of Delhi about this time was said to have 10,000 falconers, 1200 musicians, 1200 physicians, and 1000 *poets*! (*Notices et Extraits*, xiii, 185.)

It is not inappropriate to these statistics which Odoric puts forward so solemnly, to refer to a passage in the history of Yesontimur, the Emperor at this time. Alarmed by evil prognostics, he called for an honest report as to what fault in his administration could have excited divine displeasure. The report, after blaming the superstitious cherishing of Bonzes and Fo-worship, goes on: "Whilst the palace is crammed with eunuchs, astrologers, physicians, women, and other idlers, whose entertainment amounts to exorbitant sums, the people are plunged in extreme misery, etc., etc." (*Deguignes*, iv, 206; *Gaubil*, p. 259.)

[7] [MIN. RAM., "Ma morto l' vno in suo loco si mette l' altro."]

[8] [MIN. RAM., "In somma la corte è ordinatissima e magnifica quanto sia per tutto 'l mondo di baroni, gentilhuomini, famegli, agenti, Christiani, Turchi, idololatri: quali tutti hanno dalla corte quel che gli fa di mestieri."]

which is called SANDU[1], situated towards the north[2], and the coolest habitation in the world[3]. But in the winter

[1] [FARS., DOM., ARUND., Sandu.—B.N., Zandu.—RAM. B., Sandoy.—VEN., Sanday.—CIV., Sando.—Fr. 2810, Sandur.—FRENCH TEXT, Sndu.]

The Ciandu or Chandu of Marco Polo, where stood that magnificent park and palace, his description of which set Coleridge a-dreaming (or dreaming that he dreamt) that wonderful poem which tells how

"In Xanadu did Kubla Khan
A stately pleasure-dome decree."

This becomes all the more curious when we are told on an authority of which Coleridge could have known nothing, that the palace was designed to correspond with one which Kúblái *had seen in a dream*, and of which *his memory had retained the plan.*

The place was originally Kai p'ingfu, called by the Tartars Kaiminfu, the Chemenfu (miswritten Clemenfu) of Polo; it stood about 150 *li* beyond the wall, and ten days' journey from Peking. From Kúblái it received the name of *Shang-tu* or "Upper Court"; more than one palace was built in the vicinity, and from 1264, when Kúblái began to visit this district, till the fall of the dynasty, these palaces continued to be frequented by the emperors as summer residences.

In the wail which Ssanang Setzen, the Mongol historian, puts into the mouth of Toghon Temur, the last of the Yuen dynasty, when flying from his throne, the changes of lamentation are rung upon the loss of "My DAÏTU, my capital, my gloriously adorned! my SHANGTU, my cool and delicious summer-seat, pleasure dwelling of the earlier gods!" Cf. *Marco Polo*, i, p. 305.

The ruins of the palace and city existed at the end of the seventeenth century, when they were seen, not described, by Gerbillon in 1691; and the imperial geography of the existing dynasty mentions that those ruins contained an inscription of the reign of Kúblái. The city is stated to be that which appears in D'Anville's map as *Tchao-Naiman-Soumé-hoton.* (*Klaproth's Rashideddin* in *Journ. Asiat.*, 2nd sér., xi, 345–350; *M. Polo, Introd.* 6; i, 24; *DuHalde*, iv; *Deguignes*, i, 296; *Schmidt*, p. 137.)

[Kai-p'ing fu, *Mongolicé* Keibung, is called also *Loan king*, *i.e.* "the capital of the Loan River," according to Palladius. The ruins still exist, and the site is 118 miles in direct line from Chaghan-nor; it was visited in 1872 by Dr. S. W. Bushell, of the British Legation, Peking.

"The Khans usually resorted to Shang-tu in the 4th moon and returned to Pe-king in the 9th. On the 7th day of the 7th moon there were libations performed in honour of the ancestors; a shaman, his face to the north, uttered in a loud voice the names of Chinghiz Khan and of other deceased Khans, and poured mare's milk on the ground. The propitious day for the return journey to Peking was also appointed then." (*Palladius*, p. 26.)]

[2] [RAM. B., Sotto la tramontana.]

[3] [FRENCH TEXT, "Et siet dessus une montaigne dont celle cité est moult froide."]

season he abideth in Cambalech[1]. And when he will ride from the one place[2] to the other this is the order thereof. He hath four[3] armies of horsemen, one of which goeth a day's march in front of him, one at each side, and one a day's march in rear, so that he goeth always, as it were, in the middle of a cross. And marching thus, each army hath its route laid down for it day by day, and findeth at its halts all necessary provender. But his own immediate company hath its order of march thus. The king travelleth in a two-wheeled carriage, in which is formed a very goodly chamber, all of lign-aloes and gold[4], and covered over with great and fine skins, and set with many precious stones. And the carriage is drawn by four elephants, well broken in and harnessed, and also by four splendid horses, richly caparisoned. And alongside go four barons[5], who are called *Cuthe*[6], keeping watch and ward over the chariot that no hurt come to the king[7]. Moreover, he carrieth with

1 [RAM. B., "L' inuerno dimora in vn' altra città caldissima chiamata Cambalù."]

2 [RAM. B., "E di rado il detto Signore colla sua fameglia more di malatthie, se non di vecchiezza."]

3 [FR. 2810, "trois Osts ou quatre."]

4 [PAL., "Tutta di legne d' aloe, ch' è tanto odorifero e prezioso."]

5 [RAM. B., 50 baroni.]

6 [CIV., Chuche.—B.N., Zuche.—FARS., Cuthe.—Fr. 2810, Serigi-nez.—FRENCH TEXT, Strigenes.]

Most read *Zuche* or *Çuche*. This *Cuthe*, which seems best, is in FAR. only.

[*Kin* or *Ju tche* which means mandarin says Rashideddin.]

7 De Mailla and Gaubil relate that there were four Mongol captains who had devoted themselves with singular fidelity to guarding the person of Chinghiz Khan; the descendants of these four Mongols were all employed in the body-guard, and were called the four *Kie-sie* (according to Gaubil *Kuesie*); they were withdrawn from this office only to become ministers of state. (*De Mailla*, *Hist. Gén. de la Chine*, quoted in *Il Milione*, ii, 181; *Gaubil*, p. 6.)

Odoric's four barons undoubtedly were these Kuesie, whom Polo calls *Quesitan*, and the reading *Cuthe* has therefore been preferred to the Zuche of most MSS.

[*Quesitan* or *Keshican* is evidently *Keshikten*. "This is a general Mongol term to designate the Khan's lifeguard. It is derived from the word *Keshik*, meaning a guard by turns; a corps on tour of duty. *Keshik* is one of the archaisms of the Mongol language, for now this word has another meaning in Mongol. Col. Yule has brought together

him in his chariot twelve gerfalcons[1]; so that even as he sits therein upon his chair of state or other seat, if he sees any birds pass he lets fly his hawks at them. And none may dare to approach within a stone's throw of the carriage, unless those whose duty brings them there[2]. And thus it is that the king travelleth.

And so also his women travel, according to their degree; and his heir-apparent travels in similar state.

As for the numbers which the lord hath with him on his progress, 'tis difficult to believe or conceive of them. The number of the troops in those armies that attend the lord is fifty tumans[3], and these are entirely provided with everything by the lord. And if anyone happen to die of those who are enrolled among them, another instantly replaces him; so that the number is always complete[4].

several explanations of the term. It seems to me that among his suppositions the following is the most consistent with the ancient meaning of the word :—

"We find *Kishik* still used at the court of Hindustan, under the great kings of Timur's House, for the corps on tour of duty at the palace....The royal guards in Persia, who watch the King's person at night, are termed *Keshikchi*."

"The Keshikten was divided into a day-watch called *Turgaut* and a night-watch *Kebteul*. The Kebte-ul consisted of pure Mongols, whilst the Turgaut was composed of the sons of the vassal princes and governors of the provinces, and of hostages. The watch of the Khan was changed every three days, and contained 400 men. In 1330 it was reduced to 100 men." (*Palladius*, 42–43. *Marco Polo*, i, pp. 380–1.)

On Tartar Waggons, etc., see *Marco Polo*, i, p. 254.]

[1] [FRENCH TEXT, XII griffons.—RAM. B., Diece Girfalchi.—HAK., "Supra currum sedent duo Gerfalcones albissimi."—Fr. 2810, gerfaux.]

[2] [FRENCH TEXT, "Les gens des contrées par ou li roys doit passer font grans feus à leurs huis et y mettent encens et autres espices bien flairans et font grant fumée afin que li roys ne sente fors que toute bonne oudeur ; et les pluseurs se mettent à genoulz devant lui en mi la rue et lui font révérence."]

[3] [FARS., V^{c}.—HAK., XV Thuman.]

[4] Here MIN. RAM. has the following passage. [And countless is the number of strange beasts that he keeps. Among these were six horses, each of which had six feet and legs. And I saw two very great ostriches, and two smaller ones behind them, that had each two necks and two heads with which they ate; not to mention the wild men who were in the lord's garden, and women all hairy with long grey hair though of human form, which ate apples and drunk drinks such as were supplied to them by the lord's order. And among these were men not bigger than two spans, and these are called *Gomiti*

(Cubits). And in the court I saw men with an eye in the forehead; and these were called *Minocchi* (Monoculi). And at that time there were presented to the lord a pair, male and female, which had a span length of body, with big heads and long legs, and no hands, and which fed themselves with the foot. I also saw a giant about twenty feet high who led two lions, one red and the other black; and another had in charge lionesses and leopards, and such like beasts, with which the lord went hunting stags, wild goats, wolves, boars, bears, and other wild animals. "Le bestie poi di tãte sorti strane sono infinite che lui tiene: fra quali erano sei caualli, che haueano sei piedi e sei gambe per vno: e viddi dui grandissimi struzzi, e dui piccioli dietro di loro cõ dui colli per ciascuno, e dui teste, dalle quali mãgiauano, senza far mentione di altri huomini Saluatichi che stanno nello giardino di detto Signore, e donne tutte pelose di vn pelo grande e bigio, quali han forma humana, e si pascono di poma, & d' altre beuande, che gli ordina il Signore che se gli dia. Fra quali erano huomini non piu grandi di dui spanne, e q̃sti chiamano *Gomiti*. Nella corte ho visto huomini di un' occhio nella fronte, che si chiamauano Minocchi. E a quel tempo furono appresentati al Signore dui, un maschio, & vna femina, quali haueuano vna spanna di busto, colla testa grossa, e le gambe lunghe, e senza mani, e s' imboccauano con uno de i piedi. E uiddi un gigãte grande circa 20 piedi, che menaua dui leoni l' un rosso, & l' altro nero, e l' altro haueua in guardia Leonesse, e Leopardi, e con si fatte bestie andaua il Signore a far caccia a prender cerui, caprioli, lupi, cingiali, orsi, & altre bestie saluatiche."]

Though there is probably interpolation in this passage, and it has not therefore been introduced into the text, there are symptoms of genuineness about it. Even the sagacious Kúblái, the second founder of the dynasty, had a passion for curiosities and sent envoys far and near to procure them. In his day if Napoleon III had turned his attention to the collection of live monsters he would speedily have had a very remarkable gathering, and the influence of the Grand Khan probably extended over a larger area of population than his. As regards some of the monsters mentioned by the writer above, parallels will easily occur to many. I have myself described in print "a woman all hairy," as remarkable as his, though possibly those "in the lord's garden" were only some kind of monkey. I recollect a tame hoolak or black gibbon at a station in India which "ate apples and drunk drinks supplied to it," and was universally called by the natives round the *Jangalí Admí*, or wild man, which indeed is the literal meaning of our *Orang-outang*. And I remember, when a boy, seeing both the Siamese twins and the seven legs of Pin-cushion Jenny, a thorough-bred mare. Miss Biffin not only fed herself with her feet, but threaded her needle and did embroidery work therewith. As to the height of the giants and dwarfs, when very remarkable of their kind they make very exaggerated impressions upon everybody. It is not long since we have ceased to hear from respectable writers of elephants fifteen and eighteen feet high. The *Minocchi*, of course, I give up; they were doubtless factitious, if not fictitious, but the name is not like one that Odoric would give. The names he assigns generally represent some Oriental word; and this is probably an interpolation.

Live monsters are sometimes manufactured, as well as dead ones like Barnum's. I once saw, at Agra, going about as a show, a small bullock which had one or two (apparent) legs and hoofs growing out of its hump. These hung flabbily and boneless, but were certainly, as far as I could judge, vitally united to the flesh of the hump. My

40. The greatness of the Khan's dominion; and how hostels are provided therein; and how news are carried to the lord.

This empire hath been divided by the lord thereof into twelve parts; each one whereof is termed a *Singo*[1]. And of those twelve parts that of Manzi forms one which hath under it two thousand great cities[2]. And, indeed, so vast is that empire of his, that if one wished to visit each of these provinces he would have enough to do for six[3] months; and that exclusive of the islands[4], five thousand in number, which are not comprehended in the number of the twelve provinces. [Moreover, there be four chief ministers to govern the empire of this great lord[5].]

impression (be it just or not) was that they had been *grafted in.* Similar, perhaps, was the calf which Ælian says he saw at Alexandria, with a supernumerary foot hanging useless from the shoulder. (*De Nat. Animal.*, xi, 40.)

[1] [VEN., Singo.—B.N., Syno.—PAL., Siglo.—RAM. A., "Dodici parti nominata ciascuna con il segno de 12. delle quali vna è quella Prouincia di Manzo."—FRENCH TEXT, Strigo.]

"In the whole empire of the Kaan," says Rashideddin, "there are twelve *Sing*." And Klaproth annotates: "This word *Sing* is the Chinese *Sing* or *Ching*, by which is designated a province and its administration." (*As above*, p. 447.)

It is correct that the empire of Cathay was divided, as Odoric says, into twelve great provinces, but not that Manzi constituted only *one* of those provinces. It is true, however, that the one province of Kiang-che embraced all the great cities south of the Kiang which he had visited, except Canton. The twelve provinces as constituted by Kúblái and his successor, will be found stated in an extract from Rashideddin hereafter.

[However, we may state in the meantime that the twelve provinces or *sheng* under the Yuen Dynasty were: Cheng tung, Liao yang, Chung shu, Shen si, Ling Pe (Karakorum), Kan-su, Sze ch'wan, Ho nan Kiang Pe, Kiang che, Kiang si, Hu kwang, Yun nan.—Oxenham, in his *Historic Atlas*, gives only ten provinces, leaving out Cheng tung and Ling Pe.]

[2] [FRENCH TEXT, "le royaume de Mangy ouquel a plus de II^M grosses citez comme dit est par devant."]

[3] [ARUNDEL, V.]

[4] [FRENCH TEXT, grandes et riches.]

[5] MIN. RAM. ["E ui sono proposti quattro che gouernano l' imperio di questo grā Signore."]

This passage from the MIN. RAM. again shows the claims of that version to attention. The four chief governors are the four wazirs whom the Mongols called *Chingsang* (Chin. *Chhingsiang*). These were Mongolian princes, and were aided in their deliberations by four others

And that travellers may have their needs provided for, throughout his whole empire he hath caused houses and courts to be established as hostelries, and these houses are called *Yam*[1]. In these houses is found everything necessary for subsistence, [and for every person who travels throughout those territories, whatever be his condition, it is ordained that he shall have two meals without payment[2]]. And when any matter of news arises in the empire messengers start incontinently at a great pace on horseback for the court; but if the matter be very serious and urgent they set off upon dromedaries. And when they come near those *yam*, hostels or stations, they blow a horn, whereupon mine host of the hostel straightway maketh another messenger get ready; and to him the rider who hath come posting up delivereth the letter, whilst he himself tarrieth for refreshment. And the other taking the letter, maketh haste to the next *yam*, and there doth as did the first. And in this manner the emperor receiveth in the course of one natural day the news of matters from a distance of thirty[3] days' journey[4].

But the despatch of foot runners is otherwise ordered. For certain appointed runners abide continually in certain station-houses called *chidebeo*[5], and these have a girdle with

(*Fanchán*), who were Chinese, Uighurs, or Persians. (See extracts from *Rashideddin*, and notes, *infrà*.)

[Morrison, *Dict.*, Pt. II, Vol. i, p. 70, says: "Chin-seang, a Minister of State, was so called under the Ming Dynasty." According to Mr. E. H. Parker (*China Review*, xxiv, p. 101), *Ching Siang* were abolished in 1395.—Cf. *Marco Polo*, i, pp. 431—433.]

[1] [B.N., "Domus *Yam* vocatur."]

[2] MIN. RAM. ["E ciascuna persona, che facendo viaggio, passa per quei paesi, di qual condition sia è ordinato, che per dui pasti che fa, non paghi nulla."]

[3] [B.N., FARS., HAK., XXX.—FRENCH TEXT, trois.—ARUND., XX.—VEN., "Sic per istum modum in die una naturali nova dictarum trium Imperator habet."]

[4] The MIN. RAM. describes these post-stations as "very high towers." But this seems a confusion arising from some knowledge of the beacon towers mentioned in a note below.

["Per tutto il paese ui sono torri altissime, doue sono assaissime guardie, le quali hanno sempre dui, o tre corni da sonare grandissimi."]

[5] [VEN., B.N., Chidebo.—FRENCH TEXT, Chiribo.]

a number of bells attached to it. Now those stations are distant the one from the other perhaps three miles[1]; and when a runner approaches one of those houses he causes those bells of his to jingle very loudly; on which the other runner in waiting at the station getteth ready in haste, and taking the letter hastens on to another station as fast as he can. And so it goes from runner to runner until it reaches the great Khan himself. And so nothing can happen, in short, throughout the whole empire, but he hath instantly, or at least very speedily, full tidings thereof[2].

[1] [VEN., B.N., "Distat ab alia milliaribus forte tribus."]

[2] With this account of the Chinese posts we may compare that given by Shah-Rokh's ambassadors about a century later. We find in it the *yam* and the *chidebeo* of Odoric both named: "This city (Sokcheu) is the first on passing the frontier of Cathay; thence to Kambálik, the emperor's residence, there are ninety-nine *yams* or post-houses. . . Every *yam* is situated opposite to a city or town, and in the intervals between the *yams* you may count many *kargús* and *kidifús*. The word *kargú* is applied to a tower of some sixty cubits in height, where two men are constantly on duty. The tower is so placed that the next *kargú* is in sight from it; and when any event of importance occurs, like the approach of an enemy's army, the men on watch immediately light a fire, and this being seen from the next *kargú* they make haste to light another. And so the signal passes from one to another, till in the space of one day and night a piece of news passes over a distance of three months' march. Despatches are also sent along without stopping, being passed from hand to hand and from one *kidifu* to another. The word *kidifu* is the name applied to a party of men attached to a station with the following duty. Immediately that a letter or a piece of news reaches them, one who is waiting all ready starts off with it to the next *kidifu*, and so on till it reaches the foot of the imperial throne. The distance from one *kidifu* to another is ten *mereh*; sixteen of which are equal to a *parasang*. The men posted at the *kargú* are ten in number, and are relieved every ten days. But those of the *kidifu* live at their post, building themselves houses there and engaging in agriculture." (From *Notices et Extraits*, xiv, 396.) The *kidifu* is Odoric's *chidebeo*, but I have not been able to make sure of the language or etymology. I may observe however that Ibn Batuta applies to the posts or stages of the foot-runners in India the term *dáwuh* (vol. iii, pp. 96, 145, 191), and the term may possibly be *kad-i-dáwuh* or *kad-dáwuh*, "the house of the runners or foot-post." On the other hand, Martini tells us that the arch which indicated a post station was called in Chinese *P'u*. And the word may be a hybrid, *Kad-i-Pu*, analogous to the equally hybrid *Dak-House* of India. *Kargú* is doubtless connected with the *Karághúl* "Excubitores," and "Viarum Custodes," of Pococke's *Abulpharagius* (363, 369). The double system of horse and foot posts was also found by Ibn Batuta established in India in 1333. The posts of Timur are noticed by Clavijo (p. 105). And

41. Concerning the Khan's great hunting matches[1].

When the Great Khan goes a hunting 'tis thus ordered.

Baber describes his own post between Agra and Cabul, using the word *yam*, but adding that it was called in India *dak-choki*, the term in use in all Northern India to this day. (*Erskine's Baber*, p. 393.) Pauthier thinks *yam* to have been taken from the Chinese *yi-ma*, "horse-post." (*Marc. Pol.*, p. 335.)

[Mr. Rockhill (*Rubruck*, 101, note) says that these post-stations were established by Okkodai in 1234 throughout the Mongol empire. (*D'Ohsson*, ii, 63.) Dr. G. Schlegel (*T'oung Pao*, ii, 1891, 265, note) observes that *iam* is not, as Pauthier supposed, a contraction of *yi-mâ*, horse post-house (*yi-mâ* means post-horse, and Pauthier makes a mistake), but represents the Chinese character 站, pronounced at present *chán*, which means in fact a road station, a post. In Annamite, this character 站 is pronounced *tram*, and it means, according to Bonet's *Dict. Annamite-Français*: "Relais de poste, station de repos." See Bretschneider, *Med. Res.*, i, p. 187, note. Cf. *Marco Polo*, i, p. 437 *n.*]

Burnes was told of the continued existence of both post and fire beacons between Yarkund and Peking. The distance is more than five months' journey as usually travelled, but an express went in thirty-five days, and under very great emergency in fifteen.

The Chinese inns for the lodgment of public officers were, according to Martin, at eighty *li*, or a day's journey apart. According to Magalhaens there were 1145 of these royal inns, or as we should say in India "Government Dak bungalows."

[In my edition of Odoric, p. 419, I wrote that *chidibeo*=*ki-di-fu*, the innkeeper. Schlegel, *T'oung Pao*, Sept. 1891, p. 266, writes that it represents the post-office called *Ki-ti-p'u* (Despatch-office); there is one of these offices at every fifteen miles, and in each there are four messengers and a postmaster. Every messenger is provided with a portfolio, bells, a spear with fringes, three feet of oiled silk, a cover in soft silk for the post parcels, a cap and an overcoat for the rain, a secret red stick, and a return ticket. Cf. Schlegel's *Nederland-Chineesch Woordenboek*, iii, s.v. *Post*.

By the *kargú*, or signal towers, Shah-Rokh's ambassadors meant the Chinese *fung* or *sui* with which fire-signals were given from one tower to another.]

[1] [The FRENCH TEXT contains here the following story, which is not to be found in the other versions:

"Nous avons un nostre frère meneur évesque en l'ostel de l'empereur qui tousdis donne la beneiçon au grant Caan quant il doit chevauchier. Je frère Odric voulz aller avec pour veoir la guise et il m'y mena. Nous alames a procession contre l'empereur qui seoit en un char et portames devant nous une croix sur un hault baston affin que on la puist mieulx veoir et chantames ceste antene: *Veni, Sancte Spiritus.* Quant fusmes venu au char par le comandement

At some twenty[1] days' journey from Cambalech, there is a fine forest of eight[2] days' journey in compass; and in it are such multitudes and varieties of animals as are truly wonderful. All round this forest there be keepers posted on account of the Khan, to take diligent charge thereof; and every third or fourth year he goeth with his people to this forest. On such occasions they first surround the whole forest with beaters, and let slip the dogs[3] and the hawks trained to this sport, and then gradually closing in upon the game, they drive it to a certain fine open spot that there is in the middle of the wood. Here there becomes massed together an extraordinary multitude of wild beasts, such as lions, wild oxen, bears, stags, and a great variety of others[4], and all in a state of the greatest alarm. For there is such a prodigious noise and uproar raised by the birds and the dogs that have been let slip into the wood, that a person cannot hear what his neighbour says; and all the [unfortunate[5]] wild beasts quiver with terror at the disturbance[6]. And when they all have been driven together into that open

du seigneur, car autrement n'y ose nulz approchier comme dit est, li evesques lui donna la beneiçon et li empereur baisa la croix moult devotement; et pour ce que la guise y est telle que nulz n'y ose apparoir devant l'empereur que il ne lui doint aucune chose lui presentasmes un plat d'argent plein de pommes. Il le prist moult agréablement; si en menga lui et ses barons et puis nous fist dire que nous allissons hors de la voie pour la grant route des chevaulx qui le suivoit que nous ne fussions bleciez. Celle meismes guise teinsmes nous en benissant son ainsné filz et la royne et leur donnâmes de noz pommes."]

[1] [FRENCH 2810, XII.]

[2] [FARS., HAK., ARUND., VI.]

[3] MIN. RAM. "And lions and lionesses and other tamed beasts trained to this business."

[4] [B.N., "Sicut sunt leones, cervi, multaque alia tam varia quam diversa."—VEN., Ursi.—CIV., "Ibi ergo boves silvestres, leones, et cervi congregantur, et variarum bestiarum maxima multitudo."]

[5] MIN. RAM. [pouere].

[6] ID. "Like slender reeds shaken by the strong and raging Boreas or Aquilo, both because of what is passing before their eyes, and from their remembrance of being so entrapped before; and so they are near to die of fear."

glade, the Great Khan[1] comes up on three[2] elephants[3] and shoots five arrows at the game. As soon as he has shot, the whole of his retinue do likewise. And when all have shot their arrows (each man's arrows having a token by which they may be discerned), then the Great Emperor causeth to be called out "*Syo!*" which is to say as it were *Quarter*[4]! to the beasts (to wit) that have been driven from the wood. Then [the huntsmen sound the recall, and call in the dogs and hawks from the prey][5] the animals which have escaped with life are allowed to go back into the forest, and all the barons come forward to view the game that has been killed and to recover the arrows that they have shot (which they can well do by the marks on them); and every one has what his arrow has struck. And such is the order of the Khan's hunting[6].

[1] [RAM. B., "& allhora dislaccia i cani, e leoni, e leonesse, & altre bestie fatte domestiche, & accōcie a tal arte, e similmente varie sorti d' vccelli, e la gente si uiene stringendo a poco a poco, e 'l Signore sta nel mezzo della selua, la oue è un prato, che gira un miglio, con quattro huomini armati, & suoi fidati."]

[2] [FRENCH TEXT, II.]

[3] On some kind of litter carried by the elephants it may be supposed. Elephants are rather out of their latitude at Peking; and were not in use by the Mongols, as Polo tells, until Kúbláí's capture of a number in the war with Mien or Ava. A few continued to be kept at the Chinese Court at Timkowski's visit in 1821; I know not if any are still maintained.

[4] [FRENCH TEXT, Syem miran Bibi.—Fr. 2810, siem miram bibi. —CIV., "Syo, id est misericordiam illis bestiis quae salvae remanserunt."]

May possibly be meant for *Pers.* Sheo, *Este! Desine!* (*Meninski*), or *Turkish* Sáo, *Siste!* (*Ib.*)

[My colleagues, the late Pavet de Courteille and M. Houdas suggest that the sentence might be read *Sitt Meryam Bibi.—Miriam* is the Arabic name of the Virgin Mary and *Bibi* means lady in oriental Turkish.]

[5] [RAM. B., "Alla cui voce i cacciatori suonano a raccolta, e chiamano i cani dalla preda, e gli vccelli."]

[6] Father Ripa's account of the Emperor K'ang-hi's hunting in the xviiith century closely resembles this; and so does the historian Mirkhond's of the great hunts maintained by the Mongol sovereigns in accordance with the Yasa or Ordinances of Chinghiz. (*Not. et Extraits*, v, 212.)

42. Concerning the four great feasts that the Khan keepeth.

Every year that emperor keepeth four great feasts, to wit, the day of his birth, that of his circumcision[1], and so forth[2]. To these festivals he summons all his barons and all his players, and all his kinsfolk; and all these have their established places at the festival. But it is especially at the days of his birth and circumcision that he expects all to attend. And when summoned to such a festival all the barons come with their coronets on, whilst the emperor is seated on his throne as has been described above, and all the barons are ranged in order in their appointed places. Now these barons are arrayed in divers colours; for some, who are the first in order, wear green silk; the second are clothed in crimson: the third in yellow. And all these have coronets on their heads, and each holds in his hand a white ivory tablet[3] and wears a golden girdle of half a span in

[1] [The statement of the four feasts from MIN. RAM. is probably more correct. "The first is for his birthday; the second for the day of his coronation; the third for the day of his marriage when he took the Queen to wife; the fourth for the birthday of his first-born son." "Il Signore ogn' anno fa quattro feste. La prima è per il dí della sua natiuità; la seconda è dell' *incoronatione* sua: la terza è del matrimonio, quando menò per moglie la regina: la quarta, è della natiuità del suo primogenito figliuolo." This text is better; circumcision was not practised among the Mongols; coronation is no doubt the word; the last two feasts might be those of Heaven and Earth.] No Mongol Khan of Cathay ever professed Islam, though the Khans of the three Western Empires all adopted it in succession. Buddhism was the state religion of Kúblái and his house from about 1260, when he formally adopted it.

[2] [FRENCH TEXT, "& les II autres pour son ydole."]

[3] [FRENCH TEXT, tables de dens de oliphant.]

Rubruquis, speaking of certain envoys of the Longa nation whom he saw at the court of Karakorum, says: "The principal envoy had in his hand a tablet of polished ivory, about a cubit long by a palm broad, and whenever he addressed the Khan or any other great personage he kept his eyes fixed on this tablet, looking neither right nor left, as if he read there what he had to say" (p. 290). The use of this tablet, called *Kwei*, was a very ancient Chinese etiquette. It is mentioned in De Mailla's version of the Chinese Annals in connexion with Yu, one of the most notable worthies of ancient China, who is said to have flourished B.C. 2286.

[Rockhill writes, *Rubruck*, p. 154 *n.*: "These tablets are called *hu* in Chinese, and were used in China and Korea; in the latter country

breadth; and so they remain standing and silent. And round about them stand the players with their banners and ensigns. And in one corner of a certain great palace abide the philosophers, who keep watch for certain hours and conjunctions[1]; and when the hour and conjunction waited for by the philosophers arrives, one of them calls out with a loud voice, saying: "Prostrate yourselves before the emperor[2] our mighty lord!" And immediately all the barons touch the ground three times with their heads. Then he will call out again: "Rise all of you!" and immediately they get up again. And then they wait for another auspicious moment, and when it comes he will shout out again: "Put your fingers in your ears!" and so they do. And then: "Take them out": and they obey. And then they will abide awhile, and then he will say: "Bolt meal[3]!" and so they go on with a number of other such words of command, which they allege to have a deep import. And there be also many officers to look diligently that none of the barons or of the players are absent. For any one of them who should absent himself

down to quite recent times. They were made of jade, ivory, bamboo, etc., according to the rank of the owner, and were about three feet long. The *hu* was originally used to make memoranda on of the business to be submitted by the bearer to the Emperor, or to write the answers to questions he had had submitted to them."]

[1] [RAM. B., "In vn poggetto di marmo poi stanno tutti i philosophi & astrologi, e tutti, secōdo la loro professione, fanno proua di loro."]

[2] So the Dutch envoys in 1656 were "commanded by a herald to kneel three times, and bow their heads to the ground. After a short pause the herald spoke aloud in Chinese the following words: *Ka Shan*, i.e. 'God hath sent the Emperor!' *Que e*, 'Fall upon your knees'; *Ke e*, 'Stand up!' lastly, *Ko e*, 'Range yourselves on one side'!" The Chinese Kowtow had been fully adopted as the practice of the Mongol court. (*Astley*, iii, 425; 476; 574; *D'Ohsson*, ii, 217.) Odoric is here curiously corroborated by the official account of the Court Ceremonial of the Mongol Emperors, translated by Pauthier in his notes to Polo (p. 290 *seq.*).

[This evidently refers to the *kotow*, knock the head, viz. three kneelings, nine knockings. Pauthier has published the ceremonial of the Court of the Great Khan in the following brochure: *Cérémonial observé dans les fêtes et les grandes réceptions à la cour de Khoubilaï-Khaân, traduit du Chinois.* Paris, 1862, 8vo.]

[3] [FRENCH TEXT, *Buratate farinam.*]

would incur heavy penalties. And when the proper hour and moment for the players comes, then the philosophers say: "Make an entertainment for the lord!" and incontinently they all begin to play on their instruments of every kind, with such a clamour of music and song that 'tis enough to stun you. Then a voice is heard saying: "Silence all!" and they all cease. And after this all those of the famous princely families parade with white horses. And a voice is heard calling: "Such an one of such a family to present so many hundreds of white horses to the lord"; and then some of them come forward saying that they bring two hundred horses (say) to offer to the lord, which are ready before the palace. And 'tis something incredible the number of white horses which are presented to the lord on such an occasion[1]. And then come barons to offer presents of different kinds on behalf of the other barons of the empire; and all the superiors of the monasteries likewise come with presents to the Khan, and are in duty bound to give him their benison. And this also do we Minor Friars. And when all this ceremony has been gone through, then come certain singing men before him, and also certain singing women who sing so sweetly that it is quite delightful to listen to them [and this pleased me most of all[2]]. Then come mummers leading lions whom they cause to salute the lord with a reverence[3]. And jugglers cause cups of gold full of good wine to fly through the air and offer themselves to the lips of all who list to drink of it[4]. Such things and

[1] Polo says 100,000 white horses were presented to the Khan on new year's day. The Tartar chiefs continued, at least to the time of K'ang-hi, to present a tribute of white horses to the emperor. (*Huc and Gabet*, Eng. Tr., 239.)

[2] HAK. ["Tunc accedunt histrionatrices ante dominum dulciter modulantes, *quod mihi plus placuit.*"]

[3] The same is mentioned by Polo, i, 18.

[4] Says Marco: "When the monarch sits at table in his hall of state, and the cups are ten paces distant, full of wine, milk, and other beverages, they cause them by their magical spells to rise from the pavement, and place themselves before the prince, without anyone touching them;

many more are done in that lord's presence. And any account that one can give of the magnificence of that lord, and of the things that are done in his court must seem incredible to those who have not witnessed it.

But no one need wonder at his being able to maintain such an expenditure; for there is nothing spent as money in his whole kingdom but certain pieces of paper which are there current as money, whilst an infinite amount of treasure comes into his hands[1].

43. Concerning a certain melon that produceth a beast like a lamb.

Another passing marvellous thing may be related, which however I saw not myself, but heard from trustworthy persons. For 'tis said that in a certain great kingdom called CADELI[2] there be mountains called the CASPEAN Mountains[3], on which are said to grow certain very large melons[4]. And

this is done in the presence of 10,000 men: and the fact is real and true, without any lie" (i, 24; see also i, 7). This must have been a very ancient Eastern juggle. At the collation given by the Brachmans to the king of their country in presence of Apollonius of Tyana, the company were served by tripods which handed round the wines and dishes spontaneously. (*Philostratus*, Fr. tr. iii, c. 27.)

So Homer also tells of Vulcan's art: *Iliad*, xviii, 373 in Pope's version:

> "That day no common task his labour claimed;
> Full twenty tripods for his hall he framed,
> That placed on living wheels of massy gold
> (Wondrous to tell) instinct with spirit rolled
> From place to place around the blest abodes,
> Self-moved, obedient to the beck of gods."

1 [FRENCH TEXT, "Car pour monnoie ne despent on riens en tout son royaume, fors une manière de brievez qui la vault en tout son pais monnoie."—On Chinese Paper Currency, see *Marco Polo*, i, pp. 426–30 and *Rubruck*, p. 201 *n*. Rubruck says (p. 201) that "the common money of Cathay is a paper of cotton, in length and breadth a palm, and on it they stamp lines like those on the seal of Mangu."]

2 [VEN., Cadeli. — B.N., FARS., DOM., CIV., Caoli. — VIENNA, Caoly.—ARUND., Kaloy.—FRENCH TEXT, Cadili, alias Caloy.]

3 [B.N., lat. 2584, VEN., DOM., Caspei.—CIV., Caspios.—RAM. A., Capesci.—FRENCH TEXT, "unes montaignes lesquelles ilz nomment crispées."]

4 [VEN., mellones. — RAM. A., melloni.—DOM., poponi. — CIV., pepones. —HAK., "In vno regno istius Canis in quo sunt montes

when these be ripe, they burst, and a little beast is found inside like a small lamb[1], so that they have both melons and meat[2]! And though some, peradventure, may find that hard to believe, yet it may be quite true; just as it is true that there be in Ireland[3] trees which produce birds[4]. [And

Kapsei (& dicitur illud regnum Kalor) nascuntur pepones maximi."—FRENCH TEXT, "Ilz dient que en ces montaignes croist pompons merveilleusement grans."]

[1] [CIV., "Intus invenitur bestiola ad modum unius agoli, qui illic pro nobilissimo ferculo reputatur."]

[2] [VEN., "Illas carniculas que sunt ibi."—B.N., "Et illas carniculas quae sunt ibi."—FARS., "Et illae carunculae pro nobilissimo ferculo reputantur."—FRENCH TEXT, "Et mengue on ces pompons et ces bestelettes."]

[3] [B.N., lat. 2584, CIV., Hibernia.—DOM., in (Bernia).—RAM. A., Iberina.—B.N., "In hiberniâ sunt arbores aves facientes."—VEN., "In Ybernia sunt arbores facientes aves."—FARS., "Nam in Imberniâ sunt arbores super aquam quarum folia statim ut cadunt in ipsam aquam mutantur in aves."—CIV., "Quod in Hibernia sunt arbores super aquas, quarum folia statim ut in aquam cadunt in aviculas permutantur."—HAK., "Sicut audiui quòd in mari Hybernico stant arbores supra ripam maris & portant fructum sicut essent cucurbitae, quae certo tempore cadunt in aquam & fiunt aues vocatae Bernakles, & illud est verum."—ARUND., "Hoc cuilibet Hibernicam lęgenti historiam satis patet."—FRENCH TEXT, "Comme des oes qui en Yrlande croissent des arbres."]

[4] The myth of the barnacle geese to which Odoric here refers, and for which he was perhaps indebted to his travelling companion the Irish Friar James, came down to a comparatively recent period in full credit, and even Sir Thomas Brown only ventures to "awake considerations...whether the story be not too much enlarged." The curious history of its origin has been explained by Professor Max Müller in a lecture on mythology.

But the story of the Tartar lamb was also familiar in the seventeenth century, much as that of the sea serpent is now. A full account may be read in J. C. Scaliger. "It is found," he says, "in the lands of the noble Tartar horde called Zavolha. The seed is like that of a melon, but the plant, which is called *Borametz* or the Lamb, grows to the height of about three feet in the form of that animal, with feet, hoofs, ears, etc., complete, only having in lieu of horns two curly locks of hair. If wounded it bleeds; wolves are greedily fond of it; if well grown round with juicy herbage the plant thrives like a lamb in fat pastures; if the grass be cleared away it pines and dies," etc. [J. C. Scaligeri *Exotericarum Exercit. Liber quintus decimus de Subtilitate*..., Lut., 1557, f. 248 *v.*]

Sir T. Brown, after a description which seems to be derived from this of Scaliger's, adds: "And yet, if all this be no more than the shape of a lamb in the flower or seed upon the top of the stalk, as we meet with the forms of bees, flies, and dogs in some others; he hath seen nothing that shall much wonder at it."

The plant about which these fables have gathered seems now to be

here I would make an end of speaking of the Great Khan, for I am certainly unable to tell the thousandth part of

referred to the fern genus *Cibotium*, formerly to *Aspidium*. The *Eng. Cyclopædia* says: "The Rhizoma of *Aspidium Baromez* presents a rude resemblance to an animal. It is covered with a silky down, and when cut into has a soft inside with a reddish, flesh-coloured appearance, sufficient to account for the origin of the fables with regard to its animal nature. It is not improbable that this fern dries up when the grass does, but of course the one has no dependence on the other." [According to the *Dict. des Sciences nat.*, iv, 1816, p. 85, it is the *polypodium barometz*, L.]

The word *baromez* is said to mean *lamb* in Russian [*barántchik* =Tartar Lamb]. The locality of the plant, according to the Cyclopædia, is "an elevated salt plain to the west of the Volga." The Zavolha country to which Scaliger refers it is defined by one of Ramusio's authorities as being between the Caspian, Black Sea, Caucasus, and Volga, whilst another places the tribe between the Volga and the Jaik.

These indications enable us to explain the locus assigned by Odoric to this marvellous plant-animal. The Caspian mountains are of course Caucasus, or some part of it, whilst the kingdom of *Cadeli* is the country on the Ethil, Adil, or Herdil, *i.e.* the Volga. The *c* is constantly substituted for an aspirate by the Italian travellers (*e.g.* Polo's Cormos for Hormuz), whilst the name Athil was sometimes applied to the country on the banks of the Volga, or to the chief city there before the Tartar conquest, at one time the seat of a Chaldean bishop (on this point, see *Le Quien, Oriens Christianus*, ii, 1301). The "Caspian Hills" and the Volga are at some little distance, but that distance does not subtend a great angle from China where Odoric heard the story!

The vegetable curiosity which is the subject of this note, is thus apostrophised by Dr. Darwin:—

> "Cradled in snow, and fanned by Arctic air,
> Shines, gentle BAROMETZ! thy golden hair;
> Rooted in earth each cloven hoof descends,
> And round and round her flexile neck she bends;
> Crops the gray coral-moss, and hoary thyme,
> Or laps with rosy tongue the melting rime.
> Eyes with mute tenderness her distant dam,
> Or seems to bleat, a *Vegetable Lamb*."

See *Loves of the Plants*, 1799, ii, 37–39, which has a plate. Erman, I see, thinks the whole story a mythical view of the cotton plant.

It may be noticed that the Chinese also have their barnacle stories in more than one shape, as related by Martini [*Thévenot*, II, p. 81] and Kircher [*China illustrata*, p. 178].

(*Vulgar Errors*, i, 377, 366; *Eng. Cyc. Nat. Hist.*, sub v. *Aspidium*; *Ramusio*, ii, 71, 76.)

[Cf. on the *Agnus Scythicus* our edition of Odoric;—*The vegetable lamb of Tartary; A curious Fable of the Cotton Plant. To which is added a Sketch of the history of cotton and the cotton trade*....By Henry Lee...Lond., 1887, 8vo.;—G. Schlegel: *The Shui-yang or "Water-sheep" in Chinese accounts from Western Asia and the Agnus Scythicus or Vegetable Lamb of the European Mediaeval Travels.*

what I have seen. In any case I think it best to pass to other matters[1].]

(Cong. Int. Orient. Stockholm, 1889):—F. Hirth: *Trübner's Record*, 3rd s., I, No. 5. Mr. Lee writes, *l.c.*, p. 60: "It seems to me to be clear and indubitable that the fruit which burst when ripe and disclosed within it 'a little lamb' was the cotton pod, and that the soft, white, delicate fleece of 'the Vegetable Lamb of Scythia' was that which we still call 'Cotton Wool.'"—With regard to the name of the mountains, Mr. Lee, here mistaken, says, *l.c.*, p. 11, that it is "probably an error of transcription for 'Caspius.' The mountain of Caspius (now Kasbin) is about eighty miles due south to the Caspian Sea, and in Persian territory, near Teheran."—Bretschneider, *Knowledge of the Ancient Chinese on the Arabs*, p. 24, mentions from Chinese sources "a stuff woven from the hair of sea-sheep and called *hai si pu* (stuff from the western sea)," and he adds: "This is, perhaps, the *Byssus*, a cloth stuff woven up to the present time by the inhabitants of the Mediterranean coast, especially in Southern Italy, from the thread-like excrescences of several sea-shells (especially *Pinua squamosa*)." The *Heu Han Shoo* says: "They have a light stuff which some say is made with the wool of the water-sheep, but which is really manufactured with wild silk-worm cocoons." With regard to this passage Prof. Chavannes has a long note, *T'oung Pao*, 1907, p. 183, in which, while dissociating the water-sheep from the *agnus scythicus*, he says that he does not mean that the *agnus scythicus* is unknown to the Chinese, and he quotes a passage of Chang Sheu-tsie: "Au nord de Ts'in, dans un petit pays qui en dépend, il y a des agneaux qui naissent spontanément dans le sol; en attendant le moment où ils seront sur le point d'éclore, on construit un petit mur tout autour d'eux de peur qu'ils ne soient dévorés par les bêtes féroces. Leur cordon ombilical est rattaché au sol, et, si on le coupe, ils meurent; on frappe donc sur des instruments pour les effrayer; ils crient de peur et leur cordon ombilical se rompt; alors ils se mettent à la recherche de l'eau et des pâturages et se forment en troupeaux." This testimonial, 8th cent. A.D., is the oldest we have of this animal.]

[RAM. A., "Similmente può essere possibile, & vero, che iui si trouassero li predetti melloni."]

[1] MIN. RAM. These words are the conclusion of that version. It makes Odoric say that he *saw* the Tartar lamb at the court of the Khan: "One day among other creatures, I saw a beast as big as a lamb, all white, whiter than snow, and with wool like the skin of a silk-worm when moulting," etc.

["Vn di fra gli altri viddi vna bestia grande come vn' agnello, che era tutta bianca, piu che neue la cui lana rassembraua un bombace, la quale si pelaua. E domandando da i circostanti, che cosa fusse, fummi detto, che era stata donata dal Signore ad un barone, per una carne, che fusse la migliore, e piu utile al corpo humano d' ogn' altra, foggiungendomi che vi è un monte, che ha nome Capsijs, in cui nasconi certi peponi grandi, e quando si fan maturi, si aprono, e n' esce fuori questa bestia. E fummi anche soggionto che nel Reame di Scotia, e d' Inghilterra sono arbori, che producono pomi violati, e tondi alla guisa di una zucca, da quali, quando sono maturi, esce fuora vn' vccello: E questo credo piu, per hauerne hauuto raguaglio da persone d' importanza, e degne di fede, che se l' hauessi visto con i miei propri occhi.

44. The friar, passing from Cathay, describeth sundry lands as of Prester John and others.

Departing from that land of Cathay and travelling westward for fifty days[1] through many cities and towns, I arrived at the country of Prester John[2]; but as regards him not

Ma uoglio qui far fine di dir delle cose del gran Cane, ch' io sarei certo di non poter dir la millesima parte di quanto ho uisto. Tuttauia stimo che sia meglio di passar altroue."]

The allusion to the Irish production is given more fully in HAK. and MUS., with the name *Bernakles*, and the latter MS. adds: "This is perfectly understood by those who have read the *History of Ireland*"; which reminds one of "the great Robinson Crusoe that we read of in history."

[1] [B.N., lat. 2584, L dietis.—ARUND., dietis pluribus.—B.N., lat. 3195, XV dietas.]

[2] [VEN., FARS., Pretezoan.—A.S., Pretesoan.—B.N., lat. 2584, Pretozoan.—CIV., Precezoan.—HAK., ARUND., Pretegoani. — DOM., Prete Gianni.—FRENCH TEXT, prestre Jehan.]

Deferring a notice of Prester John to a later part of this collection, it is here to be remarked that the Prester John's country of the text appears to be the Tenduc of Marco Polo, which he states to have been "the chief seat of Prester John when he ruled over the Tartars," and also the residence of his descendants in their reduced and subordinate position. Klaproth produced Chinese sources to show that *Thiante* or *Thiante-Kiun* was the name of a district or cluster of cities near the Yellow River lying to the north-east of the territory now called that of the Ortus [Ordos] in our maps. This entirely agrees with the indications of Polo, who describes Tenduc between the province of Tangut and Shang-tu, and who in another passage speaks of the Karamoran or Hwang-Ho in its lower course as "coming from the lands of Prester John." It is remarkable that the French version of Odoric by Long John of Ypres gives the land of Prester John the singular name of *Penthexoire*, which has been adopted by Mandeville in his pretended travels. I suspect this name may be genuine, and that it may represent *Tendek-Shahr*.

M. Pauthier, in a pamphlet published in 1862 as a specimen of an edition of Marco Polo, which he had then in the press (and has issued since this went to the printer), though assigning the same substantial position to the Tenduc of Polo, finds somewhat acrimonious fault with Klaproth's identification of the *name* Tenduc with Thiante, because the latter was a denomination belonging to an age long past, the city of Thiante having been destroyed in 960. He himself considers Tenduc to be a corruption of *Tathung*, which was the name of a circle of administration immediately east of that of Ning-hia, embracing a part of the present Ortu territory, and extending to the eastward of the great northern bight of the Hwang Ho. On this one may venture to remark that the more that sources of illustration have been opened, the more accurate Marco's nomenclature (with which such liberties used to be deemed lawful) has proved to be. And it would be hard to believe that he could find no nearer approximation to the sound *Tathung* than that of *Tenduc*. The original of the last may have been some

one hundredth part is true of what is told of him as if it were undeniable[1]. His principal city is called TOZAN[2], and

Tartar appellation not yet discovered. But it is at least conceivable that the old name of Thiante-Kiun, though it had disappeared three centuries before from Chinese official statistics, might have been retained among the Tartars, from whom rather than from the Chinese Marco takes his names of men and places; the city of Thiante when it still stood, having been, according to an authority quoted by Pauthier himself, "*the military post of Tathung.*" And the very passage cited by Klaproth *from a Chinese author of the Mongol era*, describes the Hwang Ho as *passing through the territory of the ancient Chinese city of Thianté.* I may add that Klaproth was quite aware of the denomination Tathung, for a map representing the geography of the Mongol time in his *Tableaux Historiques de l'Asie*, indicates Tathung as the name of a district covering a part of the Ortu country, and extending beyond the Yellow River to the north and north-east.

But neither Klaproth nor Pauthier have noticed Odoric, who here in TOZAN names this identical Tathung as the seat of the Presbytero-Joannides! Tathung, according to Pauthier, is still a department of the Province of Shan-si. Indeed, it appears in Stanford's new map of Asia.

The fifty days assigned by Odoric to his journey from Cambalu is too long if meant as a measure of the distance. This would be some 400 or 450 miles (152 leagues, according to the Imperial Geography cited by Pauthier), and is more fitly put by John Montecorvino at twenty days. The position thus assigned to Prester John's country entirely suits the next step in Odoric's itinerary. Both Gerbillon and Huc note numerous ruined cities in this region, and the Imperial Geography mentions the remains of forty such. (*Klaproth* in *Jour. As.*, i, sér. iv, 299–306; *Ritter*, ii, 248; *Polo*, i, 61, ii, 50; *Astley*, iv, 729, 737; *Huc* and *Gabet*; *Pauthier*, *Le Pays de Tanduc*, etc., *Paris*, 1862, pp. 13–23.)

[I have not altered Yule's note and I shall refer to what he says in *Marco Polo*, i, pp. 285-8 about Tenduc. In this work, *l.c.*, I have given evidence showing that we must look for the city of Tenduc to *Tou Ch'eng* or *Toto Ch'eng*, called *Togto* or *Tokto* by the Mongols. Mr. Rockhill (*Diary*, p. 18 *n.*) says that he cannot but think that Yule overlooked the existence of Togto when he identified Kwei-hwa Ch'eng with Tenduc.]

[VEN., "De hoc Cathay recedens & veniens versus occidens. L dietis per multas civitates & terras..."—HAK., "De isto imperio Katay recessi post tres annos, & transiui 50. dietas versus Occidente."—WOLFENB., 40, "De isto Cataio recedens per plures dietas veni versus occidentem quinquaginta dietas transeundo per multas civitates et terras versus terrā Pretcianis que vocatur *Pentexoria.*"—FRENCH TEXT, "De ce royaume de Caloy [read Cathay], m'en alay vers occident maintes journées, passay maintes terres et citez. Si vins en la terre prestre Jehan et la nomme on l'isle Penthexoire."

FRENCH 2810, Pentexorie qui est.—WOLF., 40; BREMEN, Pentexoria.]

[1] [FRENCH TEXT, "Il n'en est mie la centisme part de ce que on dit comment que soit riche terre et noble pais."]

[2] [VEN., VIEN., Cosan.—WOLFENB., 40, Cosam.—PAL., WOLF., 41,

chief city though it is, Vicenza would be reckoned its superior[1]. He has, however, many other cities under him, and by a standing compact always receives to wife the Great Khan's daughter[2].

Travelling thence for many days I came unto a certain province which is called KANSAN[3], and that is the second

Casan.—HAK., Kosan.—DOM., B.N., lat. 3195, Chosan.—B.N., lat. 2584, Cozoan, Chosan, Casan.—A.S., Tozan.—WOLF., 41, Thozan.—CIV., Rosan.—FRENCH TEXT, "La principale et la maitresse cité a nom Cosan."]

[1] [A.S., "Tozan, quae sola de melioribus est in terrâ."—CIV., "Civitas Rosan vocatur, quae sola est de melioribus in terra."—VEN., "Qua tamen Vicencia melior diceretur. Licet ipsa sit sua civitas principalis."—FRENCH TEXT, "Elle est meilleure et plus grande que Vincensie, mais elle a moult de citez dessoubz lui."]

[2] [VEN., "Semper pro pacto accipit in uxorem filiam magni Chaam."—FRENCH TEXT, "Entre lui et le grant Caan de Cathay a telles convenances et aliances que Prestre Jehan a tousdis à femme la fille du grant Caan et ainsi leurs prédécesseurs a tousjours mais."]

Polo says the Khans often gave their female relations in marriage to the kings of this line (i, p. 239). And other intermarriages were frequent. *E.g.*, the Christian mother of Kuyuk Khan, and Dokuz-khatun the Christian queen of Húlakú, were both princesses of the Kerait royal family, *i.e.*, apparently of Prester John's. The mother of Húlakú was of the same family, and Chinghiz, as well as several of his sons, took wives from it.

[3] [B.N., DOM., Casan.—WOLF., 40, Cassan.—BERLIN, Camsan.—HAK., Kasan.—A.S., Kansan.—CIV., Cansan.—VEN., Chasan.—ARUND., Chosan.—FARS., Consan.—PAL., Chansi.—FRENCH TEXT, Cossam.]

This great and populous province, one of the twelve, abounding in chestnuts and in rhubarb, is undoubtedly the Quengianfu [or Kenjanfu] of Polo, governed in his time by Mangala, the son of Kúblái (i, 39). The Kansan of Odoric and Quengian of Marco represent the name Kenchán or Kenján, which was applied by the Mahomedans, as we gather from Rashid-eddin, to the city of Si-nganfu, and to the province under its government. Previously to 1285 this province embraced not only Shen-si and a large part of Kan-su but the whole of Sze-ch'wan. And I suspect it was of this greater province that Odoric had heard those great dimensions which he states. Sze-ch'wan is noted for its chestnuts (*Martini*, p. 87), and Shensi for rhubarb. (See *Klaproth* in *Jour. As.*, sér. 2, i, 102–3. Cf. *Marco Polo*, ii, pp. 25 seq.)

Odoric's expressions as to the populousness of this territory resemble those of Martini as to the empire in general:—"I have often thought that if the great wall surrounded the whole of China, this great country would be like one great city, full of houses and inhabitants; for you no sooner quit one place closely cultivated and densely peopled, than you find yourself entering another which is equally so" (p. 17).

best province in the world, and the best populated[1]. For where it is most narrow it hath a width of fifty days' journey, and its length is more than sixty[2]. And everywhere it has such a population that when you go forth from the gate of one city you already see the gate of another[3]. And it hath also great store of victuals, but above all of chestnuts. Rhubarb[4] likewise grows in this province, and that in such abundance that you may load an ass with it for less than six groats. And this province is one of the twelve divisions of the empire of the Great Khan[5].

45. Concerning the realm of Tibet, where dwelleth the Pope of the Idolaters.

Quitting this province, I came to a certain great kingdom called TIBET[6], which is on the confines of India Proper[7], and

[1] [VEN., "Deinde per multas dietas perveni ad provinciam quamdam que Chasan dicitur, & est secunda melior provincia & melius habitabilis aliqua huius mundi."—HAK., "Perueni ad vnam provinciam vocatam Kasan ; & haec est secunda melior provincia mundi."—ARUND., "Et spissius ut dicitur civitatibus ornata."—FRENCH TEXT, "C'est une des greigneurs et des meilleurs provinces du monde."]

[2] [FRENCH TEXT, "Et non pourquant est-elle très bien habitée, et espécialment Cassam la cité qui est merveilleusement grande."]

[3] [HAK., "Sicut egomet vidi de multis."]

[4] [B.N., CIV., WOLF., 41, Malus barbarus.—FRENCH TEXT, reobaberen.—FR. 2810, reobabereen.—VEN., reubarbarum.—WOLF., 40, reobarbarus.—DOM., reobarbaro.—HAK. does not mention rhubarb.]

[With regard to rhubarb, *Rheum palmatum*, see *Marco Polo*, i, p. 218 and French edition of Odoric, p. 446. Palladius, *Elucidations of Marco Polo's Travels in North-China*, p. 9, remarks from the *Su-chau chi* that the best rhubarb. with golden flowers in the breaking, is gathered in the province of Sukchur (Su-chau, Kan-Su), district of *Shan-tan*, and that it is equally beneficial to men and beasts, preserving them from the pernicious effects of the heat.]

[5] [DOM., "Questa provincia si è l' una delle sette parti del Gran Cane."]

[6] [WOLF., 41, A.S., PAL., Tibet.—BERLIN, CIV., Tybet.—HAK., Tibek.—ARUND., Tybek.—VEN., DOM., Tibot.—B.N., lat. 2584, Tybot.—WOLF., 40, BREMEN, Riboth.—Fr. 2810, Riboch.—LAT. 3195, Thibocht.—RAM. A., Tiboc.—VIENNA, Zybet.—PRAGUE, Thebet.]

[7] [FRENCH TEXT, "Riboth et marchist à Inde."—FR. 2810, "Riboch qui marchist en Inde."—CIV., A.S., "contiguum est."—B.N., lat. 2584, VEN., "quod ipsi Indie est confine."—RAM. A., "qual confina con essa India."]

[Rockhill, *Rubruck*, p. 151, writes : "The natives call Tibet *Bod*,

is subject to the Great Khan[1]. They have in it great plenty of bread and wine as anywhere in the world. The folk of that country dwell in tents made of black felt[2]. But the chief and royal city[3] is all built with walls of black and white, and all its streets are very well paved[4].

pronounced *Beu*, and Central or Upper Tibet was, and still is, called *Stod Bod*, pronounced *Teu-Beu*, whence the name *Tibet*, *Tebet*, *Tobbat*, and the other forms of the name."]

[1] ["To the Mongols Tibet was known in the Middle Ages under the name of *Tubot*. In the Mongol text of the *Yuen ch'ao pi shi* (Palladius' transl. 148), in one case, the valour and fierceness of the Mongols are compared with those qualities in the dogs of *Tubot*." (Cf. *Marco Polo*, ii, pp. 49–50.)

In the *Yuen shi* Tibet is mentioned under different names. Sometimes the Chinese history of the Mongols uses the ancient name *T'u-fan*. In the Annals, *s.a.* 1251, we read: "Mangu Khan entrusted *Ho-li-dan* with the command of the troops against *T'u-fan*." *Sub anno* 1254 it is stated that Kubilai (who at that time was still the heir-apparent), after subduing the tribes of Yün nan, entered *T'u-fan*, when *So-ho-to*, the ruler of the country, surrendered. Again, *s.a.* 1275: "The prince *A-lu-chi* (seventh son of Kubilai) led an expedition to *T'u-fan*." (Bretschneider, *Med. Research.*, ii, p. 23.)

Cf. *Marco Polo*, ii, p. 46, with regard to the Mongol Conquest.]

[2] [FRENCH TEXT, fuerre noir.—FR. 2810, feutre.—HAK., feltris nigris.—B.N., lat. 2584, "moratur in tentoriis quae ex feltris sunt facta nigris."—VEN., "Gentes ille manent in temptoriis factis ex nigro filtro." —CIV., A.S., "In tentoriis ex filtris magnis factis."]

[Mas'udi, i, p. 350, says that among the Tibetans, some are sedentary and inhabit towns, whilst others live *under the tent*. Huc, *Voy. dans le Tibet*, ii, p. 158, 5th ed., speaking of the Si-fan or Eastern Tibetans, say that they are nomadic, and do not live in *felt-covered yurts*. The large tents they build with black linen are generally hexagonal.]

[3] [FRENCH TEXT, "maistre cité."—WOLF. 40, "Tota sua civitas regalis et principalis ex lapidibus albis et nigris facta est."—ARUND., "Ex lapidibus albis et nigris ut scaccarium dispositis et curiose compositis pulcherrime est murata."—RAM. A., "Et la regale & principal città sua è fatta di mura bianche, & negre."]

[4] This no doubt was Lhásá. The only account of that city that I know is so unsatisfactory (Huc and Gabet's) that no picture of any distinctness can be formed from it. They say the chief streets are broad, well laid out, and tolerably clean, but do not specify if they are paved. I know not if it is worth while to refer to their account of a suburb in which the walls of the houses were inlaid with black and white horns of sheep and oxen, arranged in fantastic designs. I may observe, however, that the ordinary way of building lofty houses in the higher Himalaya, and probably in Tibet, is with large longitudinal timbers inserted at frequent and regular intervals. The stone-work is generally whitewashed, whilst the timber darkens with age, and some photographs of this style of building which I have lately seen give quite the impression of alternate bands of black and white material.

[Montgomerie, *l.c.*, p. 168, writes: "The city of Lhásá is circular,

In this city[1] no one shall dare to shed the blood of

with a circumference of 2½ miles. In the centre of the city stands a very large temple, called by three different names, viz., Máchindránáth, Jo, and Phokpochengrá. This temple is surrounded by bazars and shops, kept by Lhásá, Kashmiri, Ledáki, Azimabad, and Nepalese merchants, a number of whom are Mahommedans. Chinese tradesmen are numerous here also. The city stands in a tolerably level plain surrounded by mountains, the level or open ground extending about 6 miles on the east, 7 on the west, 4 on the south, and 3 on the north."]

A fatality has attended the accounts of Lhásá that *should* have been. Grueber and Dorville, who were there in 1661, give no account of the city. Father Desideri who travelled thither by Ladakh in 1715-16, a route not known to have been travelled by any second European in modern times, gives no detail of his journey beyond Ladakh, and says nothing of Lhásá [where he remained until 1729]. The journal of Samuel Van de Putte, a Dutchman who in the time of the Emperor Yung-Cheng reached Lhásá from India, acquired the language and the friendship of the Lamas, and accompanied a deputation of them to Pe-king, was never published, and appears to have perished. Nothing tangible is to be got out of the notices of Giorgi in the *Alphabetum Tibetanum*. Thomas Manning, an Englishman who reached Lhása from Calcutta in 1811, was arrested and sent back by the Chinese, and died without publishing any particulars of his journey. For nearly thirty years the spirit of geographical exploration has been at a sadly low ebb in India; may it revive before foreign nations snatch the honour from us of solving such problems as the true course of the great river of Tibet, and the latitude of Lhásá, the last uncertain to the extent of *more than a whole degree*. (*Kircher, Ch. Illust.; Lettres Édifiantes*, vol. xv; *Jour. As.*, 2de Sér., x, 322, and xiv, 191; *Prinsep's Tibet, Tartary and Mongolia*, 1851; C. R. Markham, *Mission of George Bogle to Tibet*, Lond., 1876.)

[French Text, "rues bien pavées."—Hak., "Principalis ciuitas sua murata est pulcherrimè ex lapidibus albissimis & nigerrimis interescalariter dispositis & curiosè compositis, & *omnes viae eius optimè pauatae*."—B.N., lat. 2584, "Sunt optime scelatae."—Ven., "Omnesque eius vie optime sillixate."—Civ., "Omnes viae eius sunt optimae."—Dom., "Tutte le vie di quella sono tutte perfettamente mattonate."—Ram. A., "Le vie di quella sono salizate."—Lieut.-Col. L. A. Waddell, in *Lhasa and its Mysteries*, Lond., 1905, writes, pp. 425–6: "As to Friar Odoric's alleged visit, as the first European to enter Lhasa, it seems to me very doubtful whether the city he visited in the fourteenth century A.D. could have been this one at all, as his description of the place is so different from Lhasa as we now find it.... Now none of the streets of Lhasa are paved, although plenty of stones are locally available for the purpose, and it seems unlikely that a city which was formerly 'very well paved' should have so entirely given up this practice and left no trace of it. The only parti-colouring of walls now in vogue is the transverse band of dull maroon along the line of beams on the eaves. I saw hereabouts none of those vertically banded houses with stripes of blue, red, and white that were so conspicuous in the Gyantsé and Ralung valleys."]

[1] [French Text, "Elle est appelée Gota."—J. de St Denys,

any[1], whether man or beast, for the reverence they bear a certain idol which is there worshipped. In that city dwelleth the *Abassi*[2], i.e. in their tongue the Pope[3], who is the head of all the idolaters, and who has the disposal of all their benefices such as they are after their manner[4].

"Goutta."—The other texts do not give any name; there is no city called *Gota*; it may be for *Bod*.]

[1] [With regard to this sentence, the well-known missionary Desgodins writes to his brother from Yer-ka-lo, 27th August, 1878: "Il pouvait en être ainsi au XIVe siècle; mais, depuis ce temps, le bouddhisme de L'Hassa s'est bien relâché de sa rigueur; car, non seulement on y tue assez d'animaux pour bâtir un quartier en cornes de moutons et de bœufs, mais on y tue les coupables et même les suspects. Trop souvent encore, les lamas se font la guerre entre eux, non à coup d'arguments théologiques, mais bien à coups de sabres et de fusils." (*Missions catholiques*, xi, 1879, p. 83.)]

[2] [HAK., BERLIN, ARUND., CIV., Abassi.—A.S., Abbassi.—VIENNA, abasi.—MUNICH, Batssi.—FR. 2810, le bassi.—FR. TEXT, l'obassy.—WOLF., 41, lo abissi.—WOLF., 40, lobessi.—B.N., lat. 2584, VEN., Lo abassi.—PAL., Atassi.—DOM., lo Abiffo.—RAM. A., Alfabi.—J. DE ST D., lobasse.]

[3] [HAK., "Papa eorum, qui est caput & princeps omnium Idolatrorum...sicut noster Papa Romanus est caput omnium Christianorum."—BERLIN, "In hac civitate morat *Abassi* quod sonat papa in illa lingua."—B.N., lat. 2584, "In istâ civitate moratur Lo Abassi, id est Papa in linguâ suâ. Iste est caput omnium ydolatrorum...."]

[4] The title *Lo Abassi*, which Odoric gives to [the chief priest, who of course is not the Dalaï Lama subsequent to the preachings of Tsongkhabá, † 1478 (Odoric was travelling during the Sakýa rule)], is a difficulty: for a wonderful hotchpotch of misplaced erudition on the subject, see *Giorgi's Alphabetum Tibetanum*, p. 688.

Three possible solutions have suggested themselves to me. *First*: in the journey of Evesko Petlin, a Russian, in Tartary (1620), which is given by Bergeron, the Mongol Lamas are called *Lobaes*. This seems to suggest some mode of pronunciation not unlike *Lo abassi*. (*Berg.*, *Traité des Tartares*, p. 107.) *Secondly*: the term *Ubashi* is applied to *some* class of the Lamas among the Mongols. (*Reuilly*, *Desc. du Thibet*, p. 36; *Huc and Gabet* in *Jour. As.* iv, sér. xi, 538.) *Lastly*: among the Persian and Arabic writers the name regularly applied to the members of the Buddhistic religious orders is *Bakshi*, supposed to be a corruption of the Sanskrit *Bhikshu*, "a mendicant," which is one of their orthodox appellations. This term is used by Polo (*Baksi*, see i, 24), and by Ricold of Montecroce, who calls them "*Baxitæ*, sc. quidam pontifices ydolorum," on which his editor can only observe in rather a helpless manner, "*Fortasse hoc vocabulum cohæret cum Russico* Bog, *Deus*" (*Peregrinatores Quatuor*, Lips., 1864, p. 117). This last (*Bakshi*) is probably the word intended by Odoric.

Whatever be the origin of the name it is not improbable that it was brought into the precise form presented, by a lodgment in the head of Odoric or his scribes of the name of the *Abassi* Khaliffs, the Popes of the Saracens. Compare these two passages:

And the fashions of this kingdom are thus. The women have their hair plaited in more than one hundred tresses, and they have a couple of tusks as long as those of wild boars[1]. And another fashion they have in this country is

Odoric.	*Benjamin of Tudela* (p. 95).
"In this city dwelleth LO ABASSI, i.e. in their tongue the *Pope, the Head of all the Idolaters*, and who has the disposal of all their benefices," etc.	"The Khalif Emir Al Mumenin AL ABASSI......who is the chief of the Mohammedan religion, and holds the same dignity over them which *the Pope enjoys over the Christians*.'

[See note in French edition of Odoric: *olog bassi=ulug Bakhshy*, in Eastern turki and means simply *great lama*, the chief of one of the large convents visited by Odoric. *Bakhshy* is the name given by Arabs and Persians to the Chinese Ho-shang, buddhist priest, and to the Tibetan lama.]

[1] [FR. 2810, "Portent plus de dens que en autre pays, et ont deux grans dens comme de saingler."—HAK., "Foeminae in hoc regno portant plusquam centum tricas, & habent duos dentes in ore ita longos sicut apri."—B.N., lat. 2584, "Nam mulieres portant plusquam centum tricas seu dresas, habentes duos dentes ita longos sicut habent apri sive porci silvestres."—FARS., "Sicut habent porci."—VEN., "Mulieres enim plusquam C tricas portant, habentesque duos dentes in hore ut apri habent."—CIV., "Habent duos dentes in ore longos et prominentes."—RAM. A., "Nella bocca hanno duï denti cosi longhi, come Cignali."]

The plaits of hair covered with pieces of turquoise, etc., may be seen in most drawings of Tibetan women. The boar's tusks (if there be no misapprehension) must be a rash generalization; though the disfigurement of the women in other respects by certain fashions that they have adopted is noticed in strong terms by both old and recent travellers. There is a hideous figure of a goddess (*Prasrinmo*), which is represented with boar's tusks, and is very common in Tibet.

But I suspect that the statement is an error of the scribe's. For the women in Tibet do commonly use boar's tusks as ornaments, both attached to the head and hung round the neck. (*Giorgi, Alph. Tibet.*, p. 688; *Voyages de Tavernier* (small edition), iv, 179; *Journ. Asiat.*, Sér. 2, iv, p. 247.)

["All ranks of them are at great pains in adorning their heads; plaiting their hair neatly enough with coral and amber beads, bugles, or pearls; they wear also necklaces of them, where the pieces of amber are sometimes as large as a hen's egg. The quantity of the two first kinds of beads that is on the head, even of a peasant's wife or daughter, is amazing. The two last sorts fall to the share only of the ladies." (Bogle, in Markham's *Tibet*, p. 120.)

Les femmes tibétaines "divisent leurs cheveux en deux tresses, qu'elles laissent pendre sur leurs épaules. Les femmes de classe inférieure sont coiffées d'un petit bonnet jaune, assez semblable au bonnet de la liberté qu'on portait sous la République française. Les grandes dames ont pour tout ornement de tête, une élégante et gracieuse couronne, fabriquée avec des perles fines." (Huc, *Voy.*, ii, pp. 257-8.)

"The women [of Gyantsé, Tibet] generally resemble their sisters

this[1]. Suppose such an one's father to die, then the son will say, "I desire to pay respect to my father's memory";

of Phari, though somewhat less unclean, and wear the same head-dress (see p. 251), except a few perceptibly more addicted to washing, who come from Lhasa, who wear as a head-dress over their smoothly-brushed black locks, parted in the middle, a red cloth fillet like a tiara (*patuk*) studded with coral, turquoise, and amber." (Waddell, *Lhasa*, pp. 213–4.)

Sarat Chandra Das, *Journey to Lhasa*, Lond., 1902, gives, p. 157, the following explanation of the origin of the head-dress; when the famous reformer Tsomoling rose to the rank of a regent "one of the first acts of his administration was to expel all public women from Lhasa, and to compel all women to cover their faces with a coating of catechu, so as to hide their comeliness from the public view. Women were also made to wear a bangle cut out of a conch-shell on their right wrist, by which they could be held when arrested. From this time also dates the use by women of aprons (*pang-den*) and of the present style of head-dress, or *patug*. The old style of *patug* is now only worn by the wives (or Lhacham) of the Shape (ministers)."]

[1] Rubruquis says the people of Tibet used to eat their dead parents, but had left off the practice. "But they still make fine goblets from the heads of their parents, that, as they drink from these, in the midst of their jollity they may keep their kin in mind. This was told me by an eye-witness" (p. 289). Carpini heard of the same custom *pro certo* (p. 658). And Giorgi thus describes the Tibetan funeral rites: "The naked corpse, being doubled up like an unborn infant in the womb, is tied in a sack and carried outside the walls, followed by crowds of monks and neighbours, to an enclosed field in which dogs are kept. There the sextons, or I should rather say the butchers, tear all the flesh from the bones and fling it to the mastiffs to eat. They then either break the bones into small pieces, and give these also to the dogs, or they cast them entire into the river. The *top part of the skull*, or some other entire bones, well cleansed, are given to the family to take home and keep devoutly" (*Alph. Tib.* p. 444). To much the same effect is the account in Father Hyacinth's translation of the Chinese Description of Tibet (*Journ. As.*, u.s., p. 254). These practices appear to be less common now in Tibet, but not extinct.

Klaproth quotes passages showing a knowledge of this mode of disposing of the dead from Strabo, Cicero's Tusculan Disputations, and Justin. Strabo also ascribes to the Caspii the opinion that those whose bodies the birds appropriated were blessed. Herodotus and Mela ascribe such practices to the Issedonians and Scythians, "Corpora ipsa laniata, et cæsis pecorum visceribus immixta, epulando consumunt. Capita, ubi fabre expolivere, auro vincta pro poculis gerunt" (*Pomp. Mela*, ii, 1).

Whatever spice of exaggeration there may be in Odoric's narrative is easily accounted for. Tibetan Buddhists deal much in dead men's bones. A trumpet of human thighbone is a common appendage of their devotees; whilst the representations of some of their divinities show goblets or crowns of human skulls. Giorgi also mentions a symbolical performance, which consisted in dancing round the effigy of a boy. This in the course of the dance was cloven open by a leading performer, who seized the heart and devoured it; the others followed,

and so he calls together all the priests and monks and players in the country round, and likewise all the neighbours and kinsfolk. And they carry the body into the country with great rejoicings. And they have a great table in readiness, upon which the priests cut off the head, and then this is presented to the son. And the son and all the company raise a chant and make many prayers for the

tearing limb from limb and also devouring. This, even if it were not a cannibal tradition, might easily provoke the charge of cannibalism. (*Journ. Asiat.*, u.s.; *Schlagintweit's Buddhism in Tibet*, 269, 216; *Alph. Tib.*, 462). [Cf. Rockhill, *Rubruck*, p. 152.]

[Marco Polo, i, p. 301, speaking of the sorcerers called Tebet and Kesimur, which are the names of two nations of idolaters, says: "This people also have a custom which I must tell you. If a man is condemned to death and executed by the lawful authority, they take his body and cook and eat it. But if anyone die a natural death they will not eat the body." See note in *Marco Polo*, i, pp. 311–314, and note in French edition of Odoric.

Sarat Chandra Das relates, *Journey to Lhasa*, p. 163, that the *ragyabas*, or scavengers of Lhásá who form a guild, "besides begging, cut up the corpses which are brought to the two cemeteries of Lhasa, near which they live, and feed them to vultures and dogs." Later on, p. 169, he says: "Further on we came to a place where the corpses of the townspeople are fed to pigs, whose flesh, by the way, is said to be delicious."

Speaking of the neighbourhood of Gyantsè, Waddell, *Lhasa*, p. 233, narrates: "On a hill-top below the above hermitage was the local Golgotha, the place where the dead bodies are thrown to be devoured by dogs, vultures, crows and other carrion feeders. This revolting mode of disposing of the dead is doubtless owing in part, as Bogle says, to the scarcity of wood for cremation, and to the difficulty of digging the frozen soil for graves. Only the bodies of Lamas and of those dying from small-pox and other infectious disease are burned." Later, Waddell writes, p. 422, that, in his rambles round Lhásá, "near the foot of the hill might occasionally be seen the gruesome way in which the Tibetans dispose of their dead. A man carries the dead body doubled up in a sitting posture and tied in a piece of a tent or blanket, deposits it on the recognised place on a rock, and then he and the attendant Lama proceed to cut off the flesh in pieces, so that the vultures and ravens can devour it. As Manning quaintly puts it, when protesting against their close game laws: 'They eat no birds, but, on the contrary, let the birds eat them.'"

There are other cases of disposing of the dead by giving their flesh to be devoured by the birds of prey. Cf. "*Reference to a model of a tower of Silence (with explanatory Notes relating to the mode of the Disposal of Dead Bodies of the Parsees).*" Bombay, 1885, 8vo.

"The food of the inhabitants consists chiefly of salted butter, tea, mutton, beef, pork, and fowls. Rice is not much eaten, owing to its high price, and because it is considered a fruitful source of disease. Other edibles, such as wheat, barley, and kitchen-produce, &c., are

dead. Then the priests cut the whole of the body to pieces, and when they have done so they go up again to the city with the whole company, praying for him as they go. After this the eagles and vultures come down from the mountains and every one takes his morsel and carries it away. Then all the company shout aloud, saying, "Behold! the man is a saint! For the angels of God come and carry him to Paradise." And in this way the son deems himself to be honoured in no small degree, seeing that his father is borne off in this creditable manner by the angels. And so he takes his father's head, and straightway cooks it and eats it; and of the skull he maketh a goblet[1], from which he and all of the family always drink devoutly to the memory of the deceased father. And they say that by acting in this way they show their great respect for their father[2]. And many other preposterous and abominable customs have they[3].

46. Of a rich man in Manzi, and how he was fed by fifty maidens[4].

When I was still in the province of Manzi, I passed by the foot of the palace wall of a certain burgess[5] whose manner of life is thus. He hath fifty damsels, virgins, who

cheap." (Montgomerie's *Report of a Route Survey from Nepal to Lhasa*, *Journ. Roy. Geog. Soc.*, Lond., xxxviii, 1868, p. 175.)]

[1] [FRENCH TEXT, hanap.—HAK., "De testa eius faciens ciphum." —VEN., "De osse uno capitis fieri facit cyphum."—CIV., "De testa vero vel cerebello facit sibi fieri unum scyphum."]

[2] [HAK., "Bibunt cum solemnitate & laetitia in memoriam patris comesti."—VEN., "Semper cum devocione bibunt in memoriam defuncti patris."]

[3] [HAK., "Et multa vilia & abominabilia facit gens illa quae non scribo, quia non valent, nec homines crederent nisi viderent."—VEN., "Et multa alia inconsueta, & dissoluta fiunt ibi ab istis."—CIV., "Multae sunt aliae consuetudines vanae et inutiles in hac terra."]

[4] [The title of this anecdote varies according to the texts: FRENCH 2810, *De celui qui se fait paistre aux pucelles.*—VENNI, *De provincia Manzi.*—CIV., *De homine delicato.*—PAL., *D' un ricco popolano di Manzi.*]

[5] [HAK., WOLF. 40, VEN., CIV., B.N., lat. 2584, Hominis popularis. —DOM., grande popolano.—RAM. A., huomo popolare.—PAL., uomo popolano.]

wait on him continually[1]; and when he goeth to dinner and taketh his seat at table the dishes are brought to him by fives[2] and fives, those virgins carrying them in with singing of songs and the music of many kinds of instruments. And they also feed him as if he were a pet sparrow[3], putting the food into his mouth, singing before him continually until those dishes be disposed of. Then other five dishes are brought by other five maidens, with other songs and kinds of music, whilst the first maidens retire. And thus he leadeth his life daily until he shall have lived it out[4]. Now this man hath a revenue of XXX *tuman* of *tagars*[5] of rice. And each *tuman* is ten thousand, and each *tagar* is the amount of a heavy ass-load[6]. The court of the palace in which he dwells hath an extent of two miles; and the pavement thereof hath one tile of gold and another of silver

[1] [HAK., "Continuè ministrantes, in omnibus pascentes eum sicut auis auiculas, & habet semper 5. fercula triplicata."—VEN., "Sibi continuo servientes, & dum ad comedendum staret ad mensam omnia fercula quinterna sibi portantur ab ipsis cum diversis cantibus...."—CIV., "Nam habet quinquaginta virgines sibi continue servientes, et cum in mensa sederit ad comedendum, omnia fercula sibi quina et quina ab iis virginibus deferuntur."]

[2] [FRENCH TEXT, IIII doubles ou V.]

[3] [VEN., "Ac si esset avicula quedam."—CIV., "Sicut pullus ab avicula pasceretur."—RAM. A., "A modo d' vccello pascendolo."]

[4] There are some things in this quaint story which Odoric heard in Mangi, resembling what Marco tells of the splendid effeminacy of the dethroned king of that country. The idea of being served only by a company of musical maidens was set forth not long ago in a novel by Mr. Peacock as realized in an English country house. The description of the demesne, and reference to hills of gold, etc., reminds us of the accounts of the island called *Kin-shan* or Golden Hill in the Yang tze Kiang.

[Mandeville has made use of this story, since the episode of a chapter of the *Life and Adventures of Robinsòn Crusoe*, Pt. II, chap. vi.]

[5] [FR. 2810, XXX tuman tosgas.—CIV., "Hic triginta chuma tagaris risi habet in censu."—The passage relating to the income of this wealthy man is not in RAM. A.]

[6] *Taghár* (*Turk.* and *Pers.*), "a large sack, of which horsemen carry a pair slung over the horse, to contain provender" (*Meninski*). The *taghar*, according to Timkowsky, contains about four *poods*, or one hundred and forty pounds, of flour. Revenues continued to be estimated in China in sacks of rice until lately, if they are not so still. In Burma they are always estimated in baskets of rice.

in turn. And in the said court there is a hill made of gold and silver, upon which are erected monasteries and bell-towers, and the like [in miniature] such as men make for their amusement[1]. And 'tis said that there be four men such as he in the realm of Manzi.

Moreover 'tis the mark of gentility[2] in that country to have the nails long; and some let their thumb-nails grow to such an extent that they grow right round the hand. And with the women the great beauty[3] is to have little feet; and for this reason mothers are accustomed, as soon as girls are born to them, to swathe their feet tightly so that they can never grow in the least[4].

[1] [HAK., "Iuxta ambitum istius palatii est vnus monticulus artificialis de auro & argento, super quo stant Monasteria, & campanilia, & alia delectabilia pro solatio illius popularis."—VEN., "In cortivo pallacii huius factus est monticulus unus, de auro & argento, super quo facta sunt monasteria & campanilia ut homines fieri faciunt pro delectationibus suis."—CIV., "In medio huius pallacii factus est unus elevatus monticulus de argento et auro, in quo pulchra ciboria et campanilia facta sunt, sicut in monasteriis fieri solet."—RAM. A., "Il cortile del palazzo di questo tiene di grandezza dui miglia, & il solaro di quello, vn lato d' oro, l' altro d' argento è coperto: Sopra del qual sono li monasterij, & campanili, a modo che molti per lor piacere far sogliono."—FRENCH TEXT, "Le pavement du palais a un carel d'or et l'autre d'argent. Et en ces carreaulx a entaillié chastellez, petiz monstiers et clochiers et autres choses que on fait pour sa délectacion."—WOLF. 40 and FR. 2810 do not contain this passage.]

[2] [HAK., "Nobilitas virorum."—WOLF. 40, "Nobilitas istius est habere longas vngulas."—VEN., "Nobilitas vero ipsius est habere longas ungues."]

[3] [HAK., "Nobilitas autem & pulchritudo mulierum."—CIV., "Pulchritudo autem mulierum est parvos habere pedes. Unde quando foemella nascitur, ligant illi pedes, ab infancia, et eos crescere non permittunt."]

[4] It is remarkable that neither of these well-known Chinese fashions is mentioned by Polo. That of the men letting their nails grow long appears to have been becoming obsolete in Du Halde's time; and I am not aware of any recent notice of it.

[This custom is still in use not only in China but in An-nam; see note in French ed. of Odoric; also on the small feet of the Chinese ladies.—Cf. E. T. Hamy, *Sur les ongles chinois, annamites et siamois*, *Bul. Soc. Anth.*, 2e sér., xi, 1876, pp. 80–5, and *La Nature*, 26 fév. 1876, pp. 199–202.]

47. Of the Old Man of the Mountain, and his end.

After I had left the lands of Prester John and was travelling towards the west[1], I came to a certain country which is called Millestorte[2], a fair and very fertile region. In this country used to dwell a certain one who was called the Old Man of the Mountain[3]. Between two of the

[1] [B.N., lat. 2584, WOLF. 40, versus occidentem.—VEN., versus occidens.—PAL., verso Ponente.—BERLIN, versus Orientem.]

[2] [WOLF. 40, "Millestorte. Hec est multu, pulchra et fertilis."—B.N., lat. 2584, DOM., Millestorte.—VIENNA, CIV., Milestorte.—RAM. A., Melistorte.—VEN., Ministorte.—PAL., Mileser.—HAK., Milestorite.—B.N., lat. 3195, Melensorte, et Melestorte.—B.N., FR. 2810 and FRENCH TEXT, Mellestoire.]

[3] This account of the Old Man of the Mountain (*Shaikh-ul-Jibal*) and his Paradise, is almost exactly the same as that given by Marco Polo. But it would be a mistake to suppose that it is therefore copied. Both related the story in the popular form in which it spread over the East. The Mussulman account in De Guignes is substantially the same; so, according to Zurla, is another Arabic account translated in the *Mines de l'Orient*. And an extract from a Chinese history, given by Klaproth, tells the same story. (*Polo*, ii, 18 and 19; *De Guignes*, i, 341; *Zurla*, *Dissert.*, etc., i, 276; *Klap. Mém. Rel. à l'Asie*, i, 171.)

The sect in its original form was a branch of the Shíyas, which was called Ismaelian, from Ismail the eldest son of the fifth Imám, whom they recognised as his father's successor in opposition to the mass of the Shíyas. Their doctrine took the form of a sort of gnosticism, giving a non-natural sense to all revelation, from which they had the name also of *Bathenians*, from a word signifying "esoteric." Hassan Sabah, son of an Arab at Rai, one of their converts in Persia, put himself at the head of the sect in that country, and about 1090 made himself master of the mountainous part of Irak Ajami immediately south of the Caspian. This region included many strong castles, and at one time the power of his successors extended to the gates of Ispahan. From its character the country was called by the Arabs *Ballád-ul-Jibal*, "the Hill Country," and hence the chief's title. This was also applied to the head of a branch society which had its seat in Syria and became well known to the Crusaders. The name of Assassin is now, I believe, generally allowed to be derived from *hashísh*, the drug under the influence of which the emissaries of the society acted. (*D'Ohsson*, book iv, ch. iv.)

The Old Man of the Mountain seems to have made his way into respectable political society, for it is mentioned that the Emperor Frederic II took occasion on the "Saracen Easter" (*i.e.* the termination of their fast) to give a grand dinner to the ambassadors of the Sultan and of the *Vetulus de Montanis*, at which many bishops and lords were present. Probably this, however, was the Syrian Old Man. (*Hist. Diplom. Frid.* II, iv, 370.)

The Chinese author quoted by Klaproth calls the country of the

mountains of that region he had built a wall, and this he carried right round one of the mountains[1]. And inside this wall were the most delightful fountains of water, and beside them were set the most charming virgins on the face of the earth[2], as well as splendid horses and everything else that could be thought of for the gratification of man's senses. Wine and milk also were made to flow there by certain conduits; and the place had the name of Paradise[3]. And when

Shaikh *Mulahi*; Rubruquis, Polo, Benjamin of Tudela, and the Armenians call it *Mulhet* or *Mulehet*. These terms are from (*Arab.*) *Muláhidah*, "atheists or impious persons," one of the names applied to the sect by the orthodox. The name given by Odoric, *Melistorte*, evidently contains the same element. If the termination does not arise from some error, it may represent some such form as *Malhadistán*, "The Land of the Heretics." Wadding indeed mentions, after Bartholomew of Pisa, that the Franciscans had several houses "in Great Tartary near Millescorte," which might be quoted to show that there was a region so called. But, in fact, Bartholomew is here only building on Odoric's own narrative and misunderstanding it. (*Wadding*, vii, 258.) The occurrence of the name *Malascorti* (for *Malasjird*) in the Catalan Map, suggests that the title given to the Assassins' Country may have been in some way confounded with that name.

[Cf. notes in *Marco Polo*, i, pp. 140–142, and note in French edition of *Odoric*, pp. 476–483. See also Rockhill's *Rubruck*, p. 118. The stronghold of Alamūt, north-east of Qazvin in the Rūdbār mountains, was destroyed by Húlakú in 1256, Dec. 20: Alamut means "Eagle's nest"; it was built in 860 by a prince of Dilem, on an inaccessible rock in the Elburs Mountains; and in 1090 Hassan captured this castle. Cf. Bretschneider, *Mediaeval Res.*, ii, p. 109.—See also *La Forteresse d'Alamūt*, par M. Cl. Huart, *Mém. Soc. Linguist. Paris*, xv, pp. 130–132.]

1 [WOLF. 40, "In hac erat qui vocabatur senex de monte qui inter duos montes fecerat unum murum qui circumdabat montem."—B.N., "Qui inter duos montes contratae hujus unum fecerat murum, qui istum circumdabat montem."]

2 [" Hic intus pulcerimi erant fontes apud quos erant posite pulcerime virgines. Equi pulcerimi omneque illud quod pro humana delectatione poterat inveniri, & hunc locum dicebat paradixium, per quosdam vero conductus illic faciebat vinum & lac." (VEN., p. 79.)]

3 [" Hunc autem locum paradisum nominabat. Ubicunque autem vidit juvenes alicuius pulchritudinis et valoris, eos rapiebat, et in paradisum poni faciebat. Nec fuit in curia qui veritatem huius delusionis intelligeret, exceptis suis secretariis valde paucis. Accipiebat enim homo iste iuvenes fortes corpore, et ipsos in fetidis equorum stabulis reposuit, et ibidem miserrime nutriebat, atque despecto habitu induit, nec eos de istis stabulis exire sinebat, ita quod omnino nesciebant quid essent blandiciae vel solacia huius mundi. Sic autem afflictos tandem eos per quandam pocionem fortissime soporabat, et in amoenitate paradisi sui inter illas puellas transportabat. Illuc

he found any youth of promise he caused him to be admitted to his Paradise[1]. And then when he desired to cause any king or baron to be *assassinated*[2], or poignarded, he called on the officer who was set over that paradise to select some one who was most fitted for the business, and who most delighted in the life led in that paradise of his. To this young man a certain potion was given which immediately set him fast asleep, and so in his sleep he was carried forth from that paradise. And when he awoke again, and found himself no longer in paradise, he went into such a madness of grief that he knew not what he did. And when he importuned that Old One of the Mountain to let him back again into paradise, the reply was: "Thither thou canst not return until thou shalt have slain such a king or baron. And then, whether thou live or die, I will bring thee back into paradise again." And so through the youth's great lust to get back into his paradise, he got murdered by his hand whomsoever he list. And thus the fear of this Old One was upon all the kings of the east, and they paid him heavy tribute. But when the Tartars had conquered nearly the whole of the east, they came also to the land of that Old Man, and at last took his dominion from him[3]. And when they had done

eciam per quosdam conductus vinum et lac descendere faciebat. Et cum volebat interimere aliquem regem vel Baronem, iussit, illum, qui huic paradiso praeerat, caute investigare...." (CIVEZZA, p. 777).]

[1] [FRENCH TEXT, "Quant il trouvoit aucun bel homme et vigoureux, il le mettoit en ce Paradis entre toutes ces choses délectables et lui monstroit tellement que cilz jouvenceaulx cuidoit estre en Paradis, car par soutilz engins et conduis, il y faisoit venir et plovoir vin, et faisoit à ces jounes hommes toutes les délices que corps d'homme pouvoit demander."]

[2] [B.N., lat. 2584, "Volebat facere sicari, id est assaxinari."—VEN., "Volebat aliquem baronem vel regem siccari facere idest assassinari."—WOLF. 40, assassinare.—RAM. A., "Fare arrobar & assassinare."]

[3] ["Cum autem Tartari quasi totum cepissent mundum, venerunt ad istum senem; cui finaliter dominium acceperunt. Quod cum ei sic fuisset acceptum multos de istis hiis sicariis emissit de paradiso per quos sicari et interfici faciebat multos Tartarorum. Hoc videntes ipsi Tartari ad illam civitatem, in quâ senex iste erat, venerunt et eam obsederunt; cum ab eâ non discesserint donec illam et ipsum senem

this, he sent forth many of his assassins from his paradise, and by their hands caused many Tartars to be assassinated and slain. And when the Tartars saw this, they came to the city wherein the Old Man dwelt, and besieged it, and quitted it not until they took it and the Old Man also. Him they bound in chains, and caused to suffer a miserable death.

48. How the friars deal with devils in Tartary[1].

In those regions God Almighty[2] hath bestowed such grace[3] upon the Minor Friars that in Great Tartary they think it a mere nothing to expel devils from the possessed, no more indeed than to drive a dog out of the house. For there be many in those parts possessed of the devil, both men and women[4], and these they bind and bring to our

finaliter habuerunt. Et cum eum ceperunt vinculis eum vinxerunt et malam mortem illum sustinere fecerunt." (B.N., lat. 2584.)

"Cum autem Tartari omnes regiones illas occupassent, venerunt ad hunc senem, et eius dominium .invaserunt. Ille. autem multos sicarios de paradiso emisit, per quos de Tartaris plurimos interfecit. Quo comperto, Tartari civitatem in qua senex erat obsederunt, nec ab ea discesserunt, donec eam per omnia subiugarent. Et hunc captum senem vinculis arctissimis constrinxerunt, et ipsum morte turpissima damnaverunt." (CIVEZZA, p. 777.)

"Cum autem tartari quasi iam totum cepissent oriens venerunt ad hunc senem, cui finaliter dominium acceperunt. Quod cum eis sic foret acceptum multum de istis siccariis emissit de huius paradiso per quos siccari & interfici faciebat multos horum tartarorum. Hoc videntes tartari ad civitatem in qua manebat pervenerunt & eam obscederunt, nec ab ea discesserunt donec & ipsam & senem habuerunt, quem vinculis iunxerunt, & malam mortem substinere fecerunt." (VEN., pp. 79–80.)—The A.S. do not give this chapter.]

1 [The title of this chapter varies greatly according to the versions: B.N., 2810 FR. *Comment les freres meneurs par la grace de Dieu guérissent les enragiés.*—FRENCH TEXT, *Des Esragiez.*—B.N., lat. 2584, *De demonibus a fratribus Minoribus expulsis.*—CIV., *De eieccione Demonum.*—VEN., *Miraculum quod fratres minores fecerunt.* WOLF. 40, *De obsessis.*—DOM., *Del Discacciamento dei Demoni.*—PAL., *Della grazia ch'anno i Frati Minori nella Tartaria.*]

2 [B.N., lat. 2584, CIV., VEN., Omnipotens Deus.—DOM., l' onnipotente Dio.—RAM. A., l' omnipotente Iddio.]

3 [A.S., CIV., "Contra immundos spiritus magnam contulit potestatem."]

4 [B.N., lat. 2584, "Unde multi homines et mulieres...."—CIV.,

friars from as far as ten days' journey off. The friars bid the demons depart forth instantly from the bodies of the possessed in the name of Jesus Christ[1], and they do depart immediately in obedience to this command. Then those who have been delivered from the demon straightway cause themselves to be baptised; and the friars take their idols, which are made of felt[2], and carry them to the fire, whilst all the people of the country round assemble to see their neighbour's gods burnt. The friars, accordingly, cast the idols into the fire, but they leap out again[3]. And so the friars take holy water and sprinkle it upon the fire, and that straightway drives away the demon from the fire; and so the friars again casting the idols into the fire, they are consumed. And then the devil in the air raises a shout, saying:—"See then, see then, how I am expelled from my

"Ideo multi."—VEN., "Tam homines tam mulieres."—DOM., "Molti huomini e femine."—RAM. A., "Molti huomini, e donne."]

1 [B.N., lat. 2584, "Ipsi ex parte et nomine Jhesu Christi."—VEN., "In Christi Yhesu nomine."—PAL., Dalla parte di Jesu.—DOM., Signore Iesu Cristo.—RAM. A., Iesu Christo.—FRENCH TEXT, "Ilz leur ostent les deables du corps ou nom du Père et du Filz et du Saint-Esperit."]

2 [CIV., Idola de filtro facto.—B.N., lat. 2584, ydola de feltro.—VEN., ydola illa sua de filtro.—PAL., idoli di feltro.—DOM., idole, le quali sono di feltro.—RAM. A., di feltro fatti.

Carpini writes, *Rockhill's* ed., p. 59: "They have certain idols made of felt in the image of a man, and these they place on either side of the door of their dwelling; and above these they place things made of felt in the shape of tits, and these they believe to be the guardians of their flocks, and that they insure them increase of milk and colts."

Rubruquis has, *l.c.*, p. 58: "And over the head of the master is always an image of felt, like a doll or statuette, which they call the brother of the master; another similar one is above the head of the mistress, which they call the brother of the mistress, and they are attached to the wall; and higher up between the two of them is a little lank one (*macilenta*), who is, as it were, the guardian of the whole dwelling."

Marco Polo, speaking of the god of the Tartars, i, p. 257, says: "They have a certain god of theirs called *Natigay*, and they say he is the god of the Earth, who watches over their children, cattle, and crops. They show him great worship and honour, and every man hath a figure of him in his house, made of felt and cloth." See notes, *Marco Polo*, i, pp. 257–9, and *Rubruck*, pp. 59–60.]

3 [A.S., CIV., "Frequenter, agente diabolo, prosiliunt extra ignem."]

dwelling-place[1]." And in this way our friars baptise great numbers in that country[2].

49. The Friar telleth of a certain valley wherein he saw terrible things[3].

Another great and terrible thing I saw[4]. For, as I went through a certain valley[5] which lieth by the River of

[1] [CIV., and A.S. (with slight changes): "Indignatus ergo Satanas cum suis, quod vasa diu possessa amiserit, in aere vociferat dicens: 'Videte qualiter de meo habitaculo cum iniuria sum expulsus.'"]

[2] Wadding, in his account of Odoric, ascribes these performances to our traveller himself, which must have been from careless reading.

[3] [VEN., *De valle quadam in qua terribillia vidi.*—CIV., *De Valle infernali.*—PAL., *Della Valle terribile.*—DOM., *Della Valle infernale.*—FRENCH TEXT, *Une grande merveille.*—FR. 2810, *Une grande merveille de la Valée d'enfer et perilleuse.*]

[4] [B.N., lat. 2584, "Aliud terribile magnum ego vidi."—VEN., "Aliud terribille magnum vidi."—A.S., CIV., "Aliud quoque stupendum et terribile ego vidi."—DOM., "Un' altra terribile et gran cosa vidi."—RAM. A., "Vn' altra cosa mirabile, & di terror piena ho uista."—PAL., "Un' altra terribil cosa viddi andando per una valle posta sopra il fiume delle delizie."—FRENCH TEXT, "moult hydeuse."]

[5] The account of the terrible valley is one of the most striking bits of narrative in Odoric's story. Whether its exaggeration be wilful, or the unconscious work of an excited imagination, it seems based on some real experience or combination of experiences.

The account of the sandy hill, on which he heard the sound of invisible *nakkaras* or drums, strikingly recalls the phenomenon of the *Khwája Regruwán*, forty miles north of Kabul, near the foot of the Indian Caucasus. Burnes describes the sounds heard there as loud and hollow, *very like those of a large drum*, whilst Sultan Baber speaks of *the sounds of drums and nagarets*, the very instruments specified by Odoric. A still more apt comparison is afforded by Captain Newbold's fuller account of the like phenomenon in the Sinai desert, at the sand hill known as *Jibal Nákús*, "the Hill of the Bell." Dr. Wallin also was told, in crossing a Wadi of the Sinai desert called Hamade, near Wadi Araba, that sometimes very strange sounds, like those of kettle drums (*nakkaras* again) were heard to rise from the earth, without any discoverable cause.

To the examples of this noted here I may add at least two more, making six in all. One is communicated by my friend Mr. C. R. Markham, who says:—"The musical sounds caused by moving sand, which astonished Odoric, are heard also in the deserts of the west coast of Peru. Mrs. Markham and I heard them when we halted amidst the *medanos* or hills of light sand in the Arequipa Desert." Another case was discovered by the late Hugh Miller in the Island of Eigg (see *Cruise of the Betsy*, quoted in *Petermann's Mittheilungen*, 1858, p. 405). See also Mr. Bollaert's notice of the *Bramador* or Rumbling Mountain of Tarapaca, which appears to be an instance distinct from Mr. Markham's (*J.R.G.S.*, xxi, 104).

The awful and gigantic face in the cliff by the valley side might perhaps have been suggested by the great figures at Bamian in the same region as the Regruwan, or some like image. Burnes gives a formidable description of the valley north of Bamian; the precipitous sides of the defile rising to two thousand and three thousand feet, and so closely as in some places to exclude the midday sun. It is not unlikely that Odoric crossed Hindu Kush on his journey from Tibet, of which we have no particulars. It was through Badakshan that the Persian merchants used to go into Tibet (*D'Ohsson*, i, 272), and Badakshan would probably be entered and left by one of the passes of the Hindu Kush. It is just about this quarter that Fra Mauro's map places the "*Valle dita* Fausta, *ne la quale se vede e aldesse spiriti e altre cose monstruose*," etc. If we could trace what Odoric means by the *Flumen Deliciarum*, it might enable us to fix the locality better. The name may be either a translation, or (more probably) a misapprehension of the amanuensis. Suppose that Odoric in dictating called it (as Ramusio does in his Italian version) *Fiume di Piaceri*, we might perhaps recognize in this the river PANCHSHIR, which the Reg Rawán immediately adjoins. And Wood tells us that the valley of Koh-Daman, into which the Panchshir debouches, is full of places to which superstitious legends attach. Moreover Baber tells us that the Pass of Panchshir was that by which were constantly made the inroads of the robbers of Kafiristan, *who used to slay great numbers of the people* in the neighbourhood.

The belief that wildernesses are haunted places is a very old and general one. Our blessed Lord himself in a very solemn passage adopts the Jewish phraseology as to this matter (Luke xi, 24). Pliny says that in the deserts of Africa phantoms in human shape appear to travellers and immediately vanish again (vii, 2). But the belief is especially prevalent among the nations of Central Asia. By them "deserts...and the like, where nature shows herself in vast forms, and in all the terrors of her influences, are held to be the especial headquarters and rendezvous of malignant spirits...hence the wildernesses of Turan, and particularly the great sand-waste of Gobi, have from hoar antiquity had an evil fame" (*Schmidt*, p. 352). The Turks have a saying that evil spirits play at ball in desert places; both Fa hian and Marco Polo allude to the evil genii of the deserts of Central Asia, and Rubruquis tells of a frightful defile, where the demons were said to snatch travellers off their horses. The Afghans believe each of the numerous solitudes in the mountains and deserts of their country to be inhabited by a lonely demon, whom they call the *Ghodlee Beaban*, or Spirit of the Waste; a gigantic and frightful spectre which devours passengers.

In an interesting little book, *The Romance of Travel*, which has a chapter upon Odoric, the story of the dreadful valley is alleged to be still part of the staple of the professed story-teller in Turkey. The author also refers to gigantic rock-sculptures as one of the elements at the base of the story, and describes the awe which certain such images in the defiles of Asia Minor were calculated to impress.

One would almost think that John Bunyan had been reading this bit of Odoric in Hakluyt's version when he wrote his account of Christian's passage through the Valley of the Shadow of Death. E.g., "This frightful sight was seen, and those dreadful noises were heard by him for several days together; and coming to a place where he thought he heard a company of fiends coming to meet him, he stopt

Delights[1], I saw therein many dead corpses lying. And I heard also therein sundry kinds of music, but chiefly nakers[2], which were marvellously played upon. And so great was the noise thereof that very great fear came upon me. Now, this valley is seven or eight miles long[3]; and if any unbeliever[4] enter therein he quitteth it never again, but perisheth incontinently. Yet I hesitated not to go in that I might see once for all what the matter was. And when I had gone in I saw there, as I have said, such numbers of corpses as no one without seeing it could deem credible. And at one side of the valley, in the very rock, I beheld as it were the face of a man very great and terrible[5],

and began to muse what he had best do...but when they were come even almost at him he cried out with a most vehement voice, '*I will walk in the strength of the Lord God*'; so they gave back and came no further," etc. (*Journ. R. A. S.*, vii, pp. 78–83; *Burnes*, ii, 174; *Wood's Journey to the Oxus*, pp. 180–182; *Foe Koue Ki*, p. 2; *Rubruquis*, p. 295; *Polo*, ii, 34; *Macfarlane's Rom. of Travel*, 1846, ii, 22 and 70; *Elphinstone's Caubul*, 1839, i, 291; *Erskine's Baber*, p. 145, 146.)

[Speaking of the great Desert of Lop, Polo says, ii, p. 197: "And sometimes you shall hear the sound of a variety of musical instruments, and still more commonly the sound of drums." See long note, i, pp. 201–3.—On *Nakkáras*, see *l.c.*, i, pp. 339–341.]

1 [B.N., lat. 2584, A.S., CIV., "Super flumen deliciarum."—VEN., "Supra flumen deliciarum."—MUN., "Juxta unum flumen q. egredit de loco deliciarum i. de Paradyso."—RAM. A., "Sopra del fiume, qual si domanda fiume di piaceri, vscendo quello dal paradiso Terrestre."—J. DE ST DENYS, "selon les fleuves de Paradis."]

2 [B.N., lat. 2584, Maxime autem Achara.—VEN., maxime autem Nachara.—CIV., maxime autem cytharam.—A.S., maximè autem citharae.—HAK., maximè de cytharis, undè multum timui.—FARS., Nachara.—RAM. A., Nachari.—DOM., Specialmente Nacheri.—FRENCH TEXT, "instrumens de musique et espéciaument harpes."]

3 [CIV., fere octo milliaribus.—A.S., scilicet octo milliarium terrae.—PAL., lunga da otto miglia.—RAM. A., 708 miglia!!—FRENCH TEXT, VII ou VIII miles de long.]

4 [B.N., lat. 2584, VEN., Si aliquis infidelium.—DOM., alcuno infedele.—FRENCH TEXT, se aucuns.]

5 [B.N., lat. 2584, unam faciem hominis valde terribilem [the word *mirabilem* has been erased from the MS.] ego vidi.—VEN., faciem hominis maximam & terribillem.—A.S., CIV., faciem hominis, quae sic aspectu erat terribilis.—RAM. A., vna faccia di huomo, talmente terribile.—J. DE V., une forme d' ome moult espouventable.—FRENCH TEXT, "un visage humain très horrible et très hydeux."]

so very terrible indeed that for my exceeding great fear my spirit seemed to die in me. Wherefore I made the sign of the cross[1], and began continually to repeat **Verbum caro factum**[2], but I dared not at all to come nigh that face, but kept at seven or eight[3] paces from it. And so I came at length to the other end of the valley, and there I ascended a hill of sand and looked around me. But nothing could I descry[4], only I still heard those nakers to play which were played so marvellously. And when I got to the top of that hill I found there a great quantity of silver heaped up as it had been fishes' scales, and some of this I put into my bosom. But as I cared nought for it, and was at the same time in fear lest it should be a snare to hinder my escape, I cast it all down again to the ground[5]. And so by God's grace I came forth scathless. Then all the Ṣaracens, when they heard of this, showed me great worship, saying that I was a baptised

[1] [VEN., cum signo crucis.—RAM. A., continuamente meco dicendo orationi.—J. DE V., et auoie en ma bouche.—FRENCH TEXT, "Il estoit si horrible que je cuiday bien morir de paour et disoie ces moz."]

[2] [PAL., *Verbo caro factum est.*—John, i, 14, *Et verbum caro factum est.*—Rubruquis relates, Rockhill's ed., p. 161 : "On the second Sunday in Advent (13th December) in the evening, while we were passing through a certain place amidst most terrible rocks, our guide sent me word begging me to say some prayers (*bona verba*), by which the devils could be put to flight, for in this gorge devils were wont suddenly to bear men off, and no one could tell what they might do. Sometimes they seized the horse, and left the rider ; sometimes they tore out the man's bowels and left the body on the horse, and many such things happened there frequently. So we chanted in a loud voice '*Credo in unum Deum*,' when by the mercy of God the whole of our company passed through." See Rockhill's note, pp. 161–2.]

[3] [RAM. A., piu di sei, o vero otto passi.—B.N., lat. 2584, CIV., VII vel VIII passibus.—FRENCH TEXT, VIII andains.]

[4] [B.N., lat. 2584, "Nichil videbam, preter illa àchara quae pulsari mirabiliter audiebam."—VEN., "Nichil videbam nisi quod audiebam Nachara illa pulsare."—HAK., "Nihil vidi nisi cytharas illas...."—FRENCH TEXT, "mais je n'y vi ne oy nullui."]

[5] [HAK., "Pro mirabili ostendendo, sed ductus conscientiâ, in terram proieci, nihil mecum reseruans...." B.N., lat. 2584, "Et quia de ipso non curabam illud totaliter in terram projeci. Et sic dante Deo inde illaesus exivi."—VEN., "Et timens etiam ne tali illuxione forte michi denegare exitus illud totaliter in terra proieci. Et sic Deo dante inde illexus exivi."—FRENCH TEXT, "J'en pris en mon giron mais riens n'en portay et ainsi m'en alay."]

and holy man. But those who had perished in that valley they said belonged to the devil[1].

50. Friar Odoric attesteth the truth of his story.

I, Friar Odoric the Bohemian of Friuli[2], from a certain town called Pordenone, of the Order of Minorites and the Province of St. Anthony, do solemnly declare and attest to my reverend father the Friar Guidotto, the Minister of the Province aforesaid of St. Anthony in the March of Treviso, in accordance with my vow of obedience and the injunction which he hath laid upon me, that all these things hereinbefore written I either beheld with mine own eyes or heard from men worthy of credit. And as for such things as I saw not myself, the common talk of those countries beareth

[1] [B.N., lat. 2584, qui erant mortui in illa valle, dicebant esse homines demonis infernales.—VEN., qui in illa valle mortui erant.—PAL., erano morti in questa valle.—FRENCH TEXT, "Les Sarrazins...dirent que j'estoye baptiziez et sains homs mais cilz qui la estoient demourez estoient tous deables d'enfer."—CIV., "Illos autem mortuos nescio qua delusione vel fantastica imaginacione decepti, dicebant esse homines demonum infernalium."—WOLF. 40, demones infernales.—PAL., nomini del diavolo de lo 'nferne.—DOM., demonio d' inferno.—RAM. A., spiriti infernali.—HAK., "Daemonum infernalium qui pulsant cytharas vt homines alliciant intrare, & interficiant. Haec de visis certitudinalitèr ego Frater Odoricus hîc inscripsi; & multa mirabilia omisi ponere, quia homines non credidissent nisi vidissent."

Here ends French Text 1380 fr. with *Explicit* after the words "tous deables d'enfer"; this text does not give the last lines concerning Jehan le Long to be found in French 2810 (fol. 115 recto and verso): "*Explicet le yteneraire Odric de Foro Julij de lordre des freres meneurs qui fist cest liure en lan de grace mil trois cens et trente. Et puis la mort dieux a fait par lui maint miracle. Et fu cilz liures translatez par frere iehan le lonc ne dyppre et moisne de saint bertin en saint aumer. En l'an de grace mil. iij^{c} lj. acomplis.*"—This translation of John of Ypres does not contain some important additions included in the Latin MSS. and even in the French translation of J. de Vignay.—The printed edition of J. de Saint Denys ends f. lxvi recto with the "vallée périlleuse," *diables d'enfer*.

Here also ends the story of the PALATINE MS.: "*Finita la diceria di frate Oderigo. Deo grazias!*" But to it is added the *Attestazione del Fr. Odorico*.]

[2] I have here placed this attestation as it is in the FARSETTI and BOLLANDIST versions. No one MS. has the whole of the matter from this to the end arranged exactly as here, but it is, I believe, the original arrangement, and the only one admitting of the introduction of the postscripts of *both* William of Solagna and Marchesino of Bassano.

witness to their truth. And many things I have left out and have not caused to be written lest they should be deemed too hard for belief by such as have not seen them with their own eyes. But, as for me, from day to day I prepare myself to return to those countries in which I am content to die, if so it pleaseth Him from whom all good things do come.

Now, all the things hereinbefore contained were faithfully taken down in writing by Friar William of Solagna[1], just as the aforenamed Friar Odoric the Bohemian uttered them, in the year of the Lord M.CCC.XXX, in the month of May, and at the house of St. Anthony in Padua. Nor did he trouble himself to adorn the matter with difficult Latin and conceits of style, but just as the other told his story so Friar William wrote it, so that all may understand the more easily what is told herein[2].

[1] The position of the name-place of this friar appears to have caused some considerable amount of writing to the Italian critics. It seems to be settled that Solagna is a village on the Brenta, near Bassano. (*Nuova Raccolta d'Opuscoli*, etc., Venezia, 1794, vol. xxv, art. 9.)

[2] [The Latin text of the attestation which I give from M. da Civezza is with some variants which I note really the end of the version of Odoric:

"Ego frater Odericus de Foro Julii testificor coram Deo et Christo Jesu[a], quod quae hic scripsi[b], aut propriis oculis vidi, aut a maiori parte a fide dignis hominibus[c] haec audivi. Multa alia vidi quae non scripsi, quia hominibus terrarum nostrarum impossibilia viderentur, nisi qui ea[d] in terris infidelium sicut ego personaliter inspexissent[e]."

This attestation differs of course according to the versions, especially of the version of Henry of Glatz. Generally it includes the addition relating to William of Solagna. However, here are the chief variants of the texts:

A. *Venni.*

"Ego frater odoricus de foro julii" de portu naonis "de ordine minorum testifficor & testimonium perhibeo Reverendo patri fratri guidoto[f] ministro provincie sancti antoni" in "marchia tarvissina"

[a] A.S., Iesu Christo. [b] A.S., quòd omnia haec, quae hîc scripsi.

[c] A.S., dignorum hominum. [d] A.S., eas.

[e] A.S., sicut ego pectator, adspexissent.

[f] WOLF., 40, "Perhibeo reuerendo fratri et domino meo fratri Guidoto prouinciali Sancti Anthonii in marcha treuisina."

cum ab eo fuerim per obedienciam requisitus. quod hec omnia suprascripta, aut propriis occulis vidi. aut audivi ab hominibus fide dignis. que etiam omnes illarum parcium communiter testabantur. multa tamen dimissi que scribi non feci. quia quasi incredibillia apud plurimos viderentur nisi ea propriis occulis conspexissent. predicta autem fideliter...frater gullielmus de solagna in scriptis redegit sicut ipse frater odoricus ore proprio exprimebat. anno. domini. 1330°. mense maij padue. in loco sancti antonii. supradictus vero frater odoricus postea ex hoc seculo transsivit ad dominum. in conventu Utini. anno domini. 1331°. die 14. Januariy qui post modicum multis, & magnis corruscat miraculis.

B. *Bibliothèque Nationale*, lat. 2584.

"Ego frater Odoricus *Boemus* de Foro Julii provinciae Sancti Antonii de quâdam terrâ quae dicitur Portus Naonis[a], de ordine fratrum minorum, testificor et testimonium perhibeo Reverendo Patri fratri Guidoto ministro antedictae provinciae Sancti Antonii in Marchia Trevissina, cum ab eo fuerim per obedientiam requisitus quod haec omnia quae superius scripta sunt, aut propriis oculis vidi aut ab hominibus fide dignis audivi ; communis etiam locutio illarum contratarum illa quae non vidi testatur esse vera. Multa etiam alia ego dimisi quae scribi non feci, cum ipsa quasi incredibilia apud aliquos viderentur nisi illa propriis oculis conspexissent. Ego autem de die in diem me preparo ad illas contratas accedere, in quibus dispono me mori ut illi placebit a quo cuncta bona procedunt. Praedicta autem fideliter frater Guillelmus de Solagna in scriptis redegit sicut praedictus frater Odoricus *Boemus* ore proprio exprimebat, anno Domini M.CCC.XXX mense Maii Paduae in loco Sancti Antonii. Nec curavit de latino difficili et curioso ac ornato, sed sicut ille narrabat sic iste scribebat, ad hoc ut omnes facilius intelligerent quae dicuntur, et cetera[b]."

C. *Ramusio A.*

"Io fra Odorico di Friuoli dell' ordine de' frati minori : Al Reuerendo Padre fra Guidotto, Ministro della Prouincia di Santo Antonio, Confesso, che essendo io da quello per obedientia richiesto, che le sopradette cose, si quelle, che con li proprij occhi ho viste, come quelle, che da huomini degni di fede ho intese gli volesse dire, & far scriuere : quelle ho dette. E ben vero, che molte cose ho fatte scriuere, quali non ho viste, ma quelli, che sono di quella contrada, fanno testimonio essere vere : Et molte altre cose ho lasciate, quale se prima con li proprij occhi non fossero viste, non sono credibile."

"Le predette cose io fra Guglielmo di Solona, nell' Anno 133 nel mese di Maggio, a Padoua nel loco di S. Antonio, ho scritte, in quel modo, che il predetto fra Odorico con la propria bocca gli riferiua : non curandomi d' vn alto, & ornato modo di parlare scriuerli : ma con vn domestico, & mezo modo di dire : accioche da dotti, & ignoranti siano

[a] The Latin MS. 2584, f. 126 verso has *Naonis*, not *Maonis* as Yule printed it.

[b] After the Anecdote of the Great Khan, related further on, the Lat. MS. 2584, continues in red ink in the margin : *Explicit descripcio Orientalium partium Fratris Odorici Boemi Foro-Julii provinciae Sancti Antonij* ; then comes this attestation also in red ink which ends the narrative.

quelle intese. Il predetto fra Odorico passò dalla presente vita del Signor Nell' Anno 1331. alli 4. [*sic*] di Gennaio, & dopò la sua morte di molti miracoli risplendette."

D. *Domenichelli*[a].

"Et io Frate Odorico di Friuli (d' una terra ch' è chiamata Porto di Naone), dello Ordine de' Frati Minori, rendo testimonianza al venerevole Frate Guidotto, Ministro della Provincia di Santo Antonio della Marca (Trivisana); concio sia cosa che per obedientia io fosse domandato da lui di tutte queste cose che sono scritte di sopra, overo ch' io le viddi con gli miei occhi, o io le udi da huomini degni di fe. Et il comunale ragionamento di quelle contrade testimonia ch' egli è vero quello ch' io non viddi. Molte altre cose io ho lasciate, le quali io nòn feci scrivere, perch' elle parebbono incredibile appresso alcuna persona che no le vedesse con gli suoi occhi. Et io de dì in dì m' apparecchio d' andare in quelle contrade, ne le quale io oe diliberato di vivere et dimorare si come piacerà a Colui dal quale tutti e beni procedono."

E. *Palatine*.

"Io frate Oderigo da Frigolli, d' una terra che si chiama porto maoni, dell' ordine de frati minori testifico, e rispondo al mio monistero per vera ubidizione che tutte queste cose iscritte in questo memoriale o io le vidi o io l' udi dire a uomini degni di fede e dal cummune parlare delle contrade. Onde quelle che non vidi sapiate che vere sono. Altre molte cose lascio, e no le iscrivo che chi non le vedese non le crederebbe. E di dì in dì m' apparecchio di tornare in quelle contrade, e mi dispongo di finire mia vita. Deo grazias, Amen, amen, amen[b]."

F. *Hakluyt*.

"Haec predicta frater Guilelmus de Solangna in scriptis redegit, sicut praedictus frater Odoricus ore tenus exprimebat. Anno Domini 1330. mense Maij in loco Sancti Antonij de Padua; Nec curavit de latino difficili, & stilo ornato; Sed sicut ipse narrabat ad hoc ut homines facilius intelligerent quae dicuntur. Ego frater Odoricus de Foro Iulij de quadam terra quae dicitur Portus Vahonis de ordine minorum testificor, & testimonium perhibeo reuerendo frati Guidoto ministro prouinciae Sancti Antonij in Marchia Triuisana, cum ab eo fuerim per obedientiam requisitus, quòd haec omnia quae superiùs scripta sunt, aut proprijs oculis ego vidi, aut a fide dignis audivi: Communis etiam loquutio illarum terrarum illa quae nec vidi testatur esse; Multa etiam alia ego dimisissem, nisi illa proprijs oculis conspexissem. Ego autem de die in diem me propono contratas seu terras accedere, in quibus mori, & viuere me dispono, si placuerit Deo meo[c]."]

[a] DOM. gives the Infernal Valley, the Anecdote of the Great Khan, and then the Attestation.

[b] See full text of the Palatine MS. in Appendix II.

[c] Hakluyt gives this passage (followed by *De Morte fratris Odorici* printed further on) after the chapters of the Old Man of the Mountain, the perilous Valley, and the Anecdote of the Great Khan (which ends with the word *munus*).

51. Friar Marchesino of Bassano addeth his say; and telleth a pretty passage that he heard of Odoric.

I, Friar Marchesino of Bassano[1], of the Order of Minorites, desire to say that I heard the preceding relations from the aforesaid Friar Odoric when he was still living; and I heard a good deal more which he has not set down. Among other stories which he told, this was one:—He related that once upon a time, when the Great Khan was on his journey from Sandu to Cambalech, he (Friar Odoric), with four other Minor Friars, was sitting under the shade of a tree by the side of the road along which the Khan was about to pass. And one of the brethren was a bishop[2]. So when the Khan began to draw near, the bishop put on his episcopal robes and took a cross and fastened it to the end of a staff, so as to raise it aloft; and then those four began to chaunt with loud voices the hymn, **Veni Creator Spiritus!** And then the Great Khan hearing the sound thereof, asked what it meant? And those four barons who go beside him replied that it was four of the Frank Rabbans (*i.e.*, of the Christian monks). So the Khan called them to him, and the bishop thereupon taking the cross from the staff presented it to the Khan to kiss. Now at the time he was lying down, but as soon as he saw the cross he sat up, and doffing the cap that he wore, kissed the cross in the most reverent and humble manner. Now, the rule and custom of that court is that no one shall venture to come into the Khan's presence empty-handed. So Friar Odoric, having with him a small dish full of apples, presented that as their offering to the Great Khan. And he took two of the apples, and ate a piece of

[1] I take this from FAR. and BOLL. The story as told by Marchesino in their versions is more simple and genuine than as related in the other manuscripts.

[2] This may have been the venerable John of Monte Corvino, or one of his suffragans appointed in 1312. The Khan was almost certainly Yisun Timur, called by the Chinese Tai-Ting, a great-grandson of Kúblái, who reigned from 1323 to 1328.

one of them whilst he kept the other in his hand, and so he went his way.

Now, it is clear enough from this that the Khan himself had some savour of our Catholic faith, as he well might through the Minor Friars who dwell at his court continually. And as for that cap which he doffed so reverently before the cross, I have heard Friar Odoric say that it was a mass of pearls and gems, and was worth more than the whole March of Treviso[1].

[1] FAR. here has the following nonsense, which is so great a falling off from the preceding pretty anecdote that I will not introduce it into the text : "Also I heard another thing from him. For he said that once every year the Great Khan sends one of his Tartars to the Soldan of Babylon, who receives him with great fear. And on an appointed day, the Soldan takes his place on one bank of a small stream, whilst the Tartar takes his on the other bank, with a bow bent in his hand, and a strongly poisoned arrow fixed therein. The Soldan takes his place with his knees bent and his hands clasped ; he hath nought on his head, and nought on his back but a shirt. And the Tartar after giving him a great deal of harsh language calleth on him three times, saying : 'Confess then that thou hast thy life at the hand of the Great Khan, and that thou art his slave !' And the Soldan in great fear answereth that it is even so. And if he did not the other would incontinently slay him. Now this the Khan causeth to be done in token of his power ; and I think it ought not to be let pass into oblivion."

[The *Acta Sanctorum* have made an Appendix following the Attestation of what is due to William of Solagna and to Henry of Glatz and in this they are right I believe. See French edition, pages 501 et seq. Here we give the various texts of the anecdote of the Great Khan :

A. *Jean de Vignay.*

Et encore raconterai-je une chose du grant Caan [chien] laquele je vi. Quer il ont de coustume en cele partie que se le devant dit seigneur trespasse par aucune contrée de sa terre. les homes alumeront le feu devant leur maisons et mettent dedens des espices très odorans et une maniere de confection qui est apelée aromate et font grant fumée pour donner bonne oudeur à leur seigneur quant il passe par là. et moult d'omes li vont alencontre. Et si comme il venoit une fois à Cambalec et l'en oi certainment de sa venue. Nostre evesque et aucuns de nos freres meneurs et moi alames alencontre de li par II journees et quant nous aprochames de li, je mis la crois sus un faist signe été pover estre veue comunement de tous et si tenoie en ma main un encensier ; et donc nous commençâmes à chanter a haute vois : *Veni Creator*, etc.[a], et si comme nous chantions ainsi celi grant Caan[b] oi et entendi nos vois et nous fist appeler et aler a li. Et come

[a] Veni, Creator Spiritus, Mentes tuorum visita. Imple supernâ gratiâ Quae ut creasti pectora. [b] Chien.

je vous ai dit devant, nul n'ose aprochier a son char d'un jeit d'une pierre se il nest appelé. fore ceulz qui le gardent. et si come nous alames ali la crois levée. il osta tantost son chapel de son chief, qui estoit de si grant value que nul ne le peust estimer la value du chapel et fist reverence a la crois, et je mis tantost encens en l'encensier et nostre evesque le prist et encensa ce seigneur. Et coustume est quant ceulz que ceulz qui vont a ce seigneur portent tousjours aucune chose ali offrir et gardent l'auctorité de l'ancienne loi qui dit: *Tu ne vendras pas vuide devant moi*, et pour ce nous portames pommes et l'en offrimes moult honorablement sus un trechouer et il prist de ces pommes et en menja comme un petit, et après ce nostre evesque li donne sa beneiçon, et quant ce fut fait il nous monstra que nous nous depçisson. si que les chevaus et la multitude des gens qui venoient apres li ne nous grevassent en aucune chose, et tantost nous nous departimes de li et alames a aucuns de ces barons qui estoient convertis a la foi Jhu Crist par nos frères et estoient en cele compaignie et leur offrimes des pommes et ils les reçurent a grant joie et en furent aussi lies comme se ce fust un grant don.

B. *Civezza.*

Adjunctio fratris Marchisini de Baxido.

"Ego frater Marchisinus de Baxido[a] fratrum Ordinis Minorum, protestor quod a fratre Oderico praedicto, dum adhuc viveret, audivi plurima quae non scripsit. Dum enim quadam vice semel Can magnus Imperator Tartarorum iret de Cambalech Sandu, ipse frater Odericus erat cum fratribus Minoribus sub umbra unius arboris iuxta viam, ubi ipse Can erat transiturus. Et cum appropinquare caepisset unus fratrum illorum, qui erat Episcopus indutus pontificali ornatu, accepit crucem, et impositam baculo in altum erexit. Tunc ii quatuor caeperunt altis vocibus hymnum: *Veni, Creator Spiritus*, decantare. Quo audito, ipse Can quaesivit a vicinioribus sibi, quid hoc esset. Cui responderunt: Illos esse quatuor rabant franci, idest religiosi christiani. Et eos ad se *vocavit*, et visa cruce, erexit se in curru, et deposito galerio capitis sui, crucem humiliter deosculabatur. Et quia statutum est, quod nullus audeat appropinquare currui suo manibus vacuis, idcirco frater Odericus parvum calathum plenum pomis pulchris obtulit ei pro xenio. At ille duo poma sustulit et de uno comedit, alterum vero gestans in manibus inde recessit. Ex quo luculenter apparet, quod ipse Cam aliquid sapit de fide catholica, et hoc per inductionem fratrum nostrorum, qui in curia sua continue commorantur. Istud autem galerium quod ob reverenciam crucis deposuit, prout audivi a fratre Oderico ex gemmis et perlis praeciosis factum est, et plus valet quam tota Marchia Tervisana. Insuper audivi a fratre Oderico, quod iste magnus Can semel in anno mittit unum de Tartaris suis, honorifice cum comitatu, ad Soldanum babiloniae, quem Soldanus recipit cum honore.

De potencia imperatoris.

Et die pro hoc constituta iste Tartarus super unam ripam parvi rivuli stat, ponendo in manu arcum tensum cum sagittis venenatis. Soldanus vero in alia ripa manet genibus flexis et manibus complexis, indutus veste communi, in capite nihil habens. Tartarus autem eum grandi voce alloquitur, et ter interrogans dicit: Confiteris quod vitam

[a] A.S., Baiadon.

habeas per magnum Can, et es servus eius? Soldanus autem dicit cum reverencia, quod sic: Et nisi sic humiliter responderet, Tartarus eum interficeret cum sagittis. Hoc autem facit ipse Can, ut signum suae magnificenciae et potenciae manifestet."

C. *Bib. Nat.*, lat. 2584.

"Unum referam de magno Cane quod vidi. Consuetudo est in illis partibus quod quando praedictus dominus per aliquam contratam transit, homines omnes ante hospicia suorum domorum igne accedunt et aromata apponunt ac faciunt fumum, ut domino suo transeunti odorem emittant. Et multi homines obviam sibi vadunt. Dum autem semel veniret in Cambalec et de adventu suo certitudinaliter diceretur, unus noster episcopus et aliqui nostri fratres minores et ego ivimus sibi obviam bene per duas dietas. Et dum appropinquavimus ad eum posui crucem super lignum, ita quod publice videri poterat. Ego vero habebam in manu thuribulum quod mecum detuleram. Et incepimus cantare alta voce, dicentes VENI CREATOR SPIRITUS, etc. Et dum sic cantaremus audivit voces nostras nosque vocari fecit et ad eum accedere nos jussit. Cum superius alias dictum sit, nullus audet currui suo appropinquare ad jactum lapidis nisi vocatus exceptis custodientibus eum. Et dum ivissemus ad eum cruce elevatâ, deposuit statim galerium suum sive capellum inestimabilis quasi valoris, et fecit reverentiam ipsi cruci. Statimque in thuribulum quod habebam incensum reposui, et episcopus noster de manu meâ accepit, eumque thurificavit. Accedentes ad predictum dominum semper aliquid ad offerendum secum deferunt, observantes illam legem antiquam, NON APPAREBIS IN CONSPECTU MEO VACUUS. Idcirco portavimus nobiscum aliqua poma [et ea] sibi super unum incisorium reverenter obtulimus. Et ipse duo accepit de ipsis pomis, et de uno aliquantulum comedit. Et deinde predictus episcopus noster ei benedictionem suam impendit. Et hoc facto nobis innuit ut recederemus ne equi post ipsum venientes et multitudo in aliquo nos offenderent. Statim vero ab eo discessimus et divertimus, et ad aliquos barones suos per fratres nostri ordinis ad fidem conversos ivimus, qui in exercitu ejus erant. Et obtulimus eis de predictis pomis. Qui cum maximo gaudio ipsa recipientes, ita videbantur laetari, ac si illis prebuissemus familiariter magnum munus."

D. *Venni.*

Quomodo presentavit Chaam.

"Unum reffere volo de magno Chaam, quod vidi consuetudo est illis, quod quando predictus dominus per aliquam contractam transsit. homines ante hostia suarum domorum ignem accendunt. & imponunt aromata. & faciunt fumum odoris domino transseunti & multi homines ei oviam vadunt. dum autem quadam vice veniret in cambalec & de adventu suo certitudinaliter diceretur quidam noster episcopus & aliqui nostri fratres & ego ivimus sibi oviam bene per duas dietas. & cum appropinquaremus ad eum possuimus crucem super lignum ita quod publice videri poterat. ego vero habebam in manu turibulum. & incepimus cantare alta voce dicentes. veni creator spiritus, etc. & dum audisset voces nostras nos clamari fecit. & ad eum accedere iussit. nam ut supra dictum est. nullus audet currui suo appropinquare ad iactum lapidis nisi vocatur exceptis custodibus. & dum ivissemus ad ipsum cum cruce ellevata. repossuit statim galerium suum inextimabilis quasi valoris. & fecit reverentiam ipsi cruci, statimque in turibulum quod habebam incenssum repossui & episcopus noster de manu mea accepit eumque turrificavit. accedentes vero ad ipsum dominum. semper aliquid offerendum secum ferrunt, observantes legem illam antiquam. non apparebis in conspectu meo vacuus. idcirco nobiscum tullimus aliqua poma. & ea sibi supra unum incissorium reverenter obtulimus. accepit autem duo. & de uno aliquantulum comedit. deinde episcopus noster ei benedicionem suam impendit. hoc facto inuit nobis, ut recederemus ne equi post ipsum venientes & multitudo in aliquo nos offenderet. statimque discessimus. & ad aliquos barones suos per fratres nostri ordinis ad fidem conversos ivimus qui in exercitu eius erant. & obtulimus eis de predictis pomis. qui cum maximo gaudio receperunt. & ita laetari videbantur. ac si eis maximum portavissemus munus."

E. *Ram. A.*

"Vna cosa hò a dire del gran Cane, qual ho vista ; che passando il predetto per quella contrada, tutti gli huomini auanti l' vscio di sua casa, fanna fuoco : & in quello pongono profumi, accioche quello passando gli inspirino odore, & venendo molti huomini, lo vanno ad incontrare : il qual hauendo vna volta a venir in Cabalec, & sapendosi certo della sua venuta : vn nostro Vescouo & alcuni nostri frati & io con essi in compagnia andassimo per due giornate ad incontrarlo : & essendoci a quello appropinquati, ponessimo la Croce sopra vn legno tal che si potea manifestamente da ciascuno vedere. Io haueua in mani l' incensero, qual meco haueua portato, & incominciassimo ad alta voce cantare, dicendo, Veni creator Spiritus. Qual canti hauendo il detto vdito, ne fece chiamare : & comandò, che ce gli accostassimo : che altramente non si haueressimo appropinquati : (essendo che habbiamo detto,) che nissuno, per meza archata possa, se non chiamato, appropinquarseli. Cosi a quello, auicinati, deponendo il suo capello, qual era di inestimabil valore, fe reuerentia alla nostra Croce, & subito il Vescouo, pigliando l' incensero da mano, qual io haueua, quello con il fumo dell' incenso suffumigo : & perche tutti quelli, che al detto Signore vanno seco, portano alcuna cosa ad offerirgli, seruando quella legge antica, qual dice : Non apparebis in conspectu meo vacuus : per questo noi certi frutti portassimo, quali in vn piatto gli offerissimo : de li quali ne prendette due : dell' vno delli quali ne mangiò vn poco, & a quello il predetto Vescouo dopo questo gli diede la sua benedittione. Il che fatto, comandò, che di li partissimo, acciò dalla moltitudine de' Caualli non fossimo offesi. Per il che, di la partiti, andassimo ad alcuni suoi baroni, quali certi frati del nostro medesimo ordine alla fede conuertirono, quali erano nell' essercito di costui : alli quali offerimmo del resto di quelli pomi, quali non con minor allegrezza, furno da quelli accettati, come se gli hauessimo donati grandissimi presenti."

F. *Domenichelli.*

Feste all' Imperatore.

"Una cosa io voglio contare del Gran Cane. Usanza è in quella parte che quando el ditto Signore passa per alcuna contrada, gli huomini dinanti alle lor case appigliano e fuochi et mettono in questi fuochi molte specie, et fanno fumo per mandare l' odore al suo Signore,

52. The blessed end of Friar Odoric.

Now, the blessed man Odoric[1], after he had come back from foreign parts to his own province, to wit, the March of Treviso, became desirous of visiting the Supreme Pontiff, in order to obtain leave from him to take away with him again a body of fifty friars, no matter from what province, provided they had the will to go. So he departed from Friuli, the district of his birth. But when he got to Pisa he was seized with a sore illness which forced him to return to his own province. And so it was that in Udine, a city of Friuli, in the year of the Lord's Incarnation M.CCC.XXXI, and the day before the Ides of January, he passed triumphantly from this world to the glories of the blessed. And his virtues and miraculous powers have been there most brilliantly displayed. For through his means the blind, the

et molta gente il vanno (retro). Una fiata venendo egli in (Cambalec), et sapiendosi certamente la sua venuta, uno nostro Vescovo con alquanti Frati Minori, et io con loro insieme, gli andammo incontro (ben più giornate); et appressandoci a lui, ponemmo la croce in su l' asta pubblicamente, sì che ogni huomo la potea vedere; et io avea in mano uno teribolo, ch' io m' avea portato, et cominciamo a cantare ad alta boce: *Veni, creator Spiritus*, etc.: et cantando noi così, egli udì le nostre boci, et fece chiamare et fare el comandamento, che noi andassimo a lui; et così come io ho ditto di sopra, neuno s' osava appressarii a lui al carro suo a una gittata di mano, se non era chiamato, altri che quegli che guardavano lui; et quando noi andamo da lui con la croce levata, incontenente egli si levò el capello di valore inestimabile, et fece riverentia a la croce, et incontenente io misi de l' incenso nel teribolo, et diedilo in mano al Vescovo, et egli gli diede de l' incenso. Et tutti quanti che vanno a lui, sempre portano seco alcuna cosa da donargli, osservando quella legge antica che dice: *Non appropinquabis in conspectu meo vacuus.* Imperò portamo con noi alquante pome, et quelle in su uno taglieri gli presentamo con grande riverentia. Et egli ne tolse due et mangione un poco dell' una. Et poscia il Vescovo nostro gli diè la sua beneditione; et fatto questo, egli ci fece segno che ci partissomo, acciochè e cavalli et la moltitudine della giente che venia di dietro a lui, non ci offendesse. Et incontenente da lui ci partimo et venimo ad alquanti de' suoi baroni, e quali sono convertiti a la fe nostra per quegli nostri Frati, e quali erano nello stato del Gran Cane, et presentamogli di quelle pome, et eglino con grande alegrezza ricevendole, così si pareano alegrare come se noi gli avessimo fatto un grande dono."]

[1] This is from FAR., comparing BOLL.

lame, the dumb, the deaf, are, by the Lord's permission, made perfectly whole. Glory to God, Amen[1]!

[1] [We give the various versions of the text of the death of Odoric:

"Beatus autem vir Odericus[a] frater, cum anno Domini MCCCXXX de partibus infidelium ad suam provinciam remeasset, scilicet Marchiam Tervisinam, Provinciam Summi Pontificis, vedelicet domini Ioannis Vigesimi secundi, adire disposuit, ut ab eo licentiam peteret, quòd quinquaginta Fratres de quibusdam provinciis collecti, qui voluntarii essent ad eundum, secum duceret ad seminandam fidem in partibus transmarinis, Cum autem recederet de Foro Iulii unde natus erat, et venisset Pisas[b], gravi infirmitate correptus est. Eapropter ad locum suum redire compulsus est. Et veniens in Utinum, quae est civitas de Foro Iuli[c], Anno Dominicae Incarnacionis MCCCXXXI pridie Idus Ianuarii, de huius mundi naufragio transiit ad gloriam Beatorum. Sed in terris, [d]virtutibus et multis miraculis modo coruscat. Nam ad tumulum eius cœci, claudi, surdi et muti, et alii diversis morbis praegravati, per merita ipsius accipiunt graciam sanitatis[e], a Domino Iesu Christo. Hoc testificatus[f] est litteris suis in Curia Papae Patriarcha Aquilejensis, in cuius dioecesi haec fiunt. Et protestatur Styria et Karintia et multi de Italia, et regiones plurimae circumquaque."

Hakluyt.

De Morte fratris Odorici.

"Anno igitur Domini 1331. disponente se praedicto fratre Odorico ad perficiendum iter suae peregrinationis, prout mente conceperat, & etiam vt via & labor esset sibi magis ad meritum, decreuit primò praesentiam adire Domini & patris omnium summi Pontificis Domini Ioannis Papae 22. cuius benedictione obedientiàque recepta cum societate fratrum secum ire volentium ad partes infidelium se transferret: Cùmque sic eundo versus summum Pontificem, non multum distaret à ciuitate Pisana, in quadam via occurit sibi quidam senex in habitu peregrini eum salutans ex nomine, Aue (inquiens) frater Odorice: Et cùm frater quaereret quo modo ipsius haberet noticiam? Respondit, Dum eras in India noui te, tuùmque noui sanctum propositum; sed et tu modò ad conuentum vndè venisti reuertere, quia die sequenti decimo ex hoc mundo migrabis. Verbis igitur senis attonitus & stupefactus, praesertim cùm Senex ille statim post dictum ab eius aspectu disparuit; reuerti decreuit; Et reuersus est in bona prosperitate nullam sentiens grauedinem corporis, seu aliquam infirmitatem: Cúmque esset in conuentu suo Vtinensi. N. in prouincia Paduana decimo die, prout facta sibi reuelatio, accepta communione, ipsoque ad Deum disponente, etiam corpore existens incolumis in Domino feliciter requieuit: Cuius sacer obitus Domino summo Pontifici praefato sub manu Notarij publici transmittitur; qui sic scribit.

"Anno Domini 1331. decima quarta die mensis Ianuarij obijt in Christo Beatus Odoricus ordinis fratrum Minorum, cuius precibus omnipotens Deus multa, & varia miracula demònstrauit; quae ego

[a] A.S., Odoricus. [b] A.S., Pisis. [c] A.S., postridie.

[d] A.S., "Sed innumeris virtutibus & multis miraculis nunc corruscat."

[e] A.S., sanitatum. [f] A.S., testatus.

Guetelus notarius communis Vtini, filius domini Damiani de portu Gruario, de mandato & voluntate nobilis viri Domini Conradi de Buardigio Castaldionis, & consilij Vtini, scripsi, sicut potui, bona fide, & fratribus Minoribus exemplum dedi ; sed non de omnibus, quià sunt innumerabilia, & mihi difficilia ad scribendum."

We now add the

Declaration of Henry of Glatz.

"Et ego Frater Henricus, dictus de Glatz[g], qui praedicta omnia transcripsi, existens Avinioni[h] in Curia Domini Papae Anno Domini supradicto, si ibidem intellexissem[i] de felice fratre Oderico[k] a[l] sociis suis qui secum fuerant, tot perfectiones et sanctitatis[m] opera ; vix aliquibus hic per eum descriptis credere potuissem. Sed cogit[n] me vitae suae veritas, dictis eius fidem credulam adhibere. Scripsi autem haec Anno Domini MCCCXL in Pragâ, circa festum omnium Sanctorum, et copiosius ea audieram in Avinione[o p]."]

[g] Civ., Glars. [h] A.S., Avenione.

[i] A.S., "Si non intellexissem ibidem." [k] A.S., Odorico.

[l] A.S., et. [m] A.S., ejus. [n] A.S., coëgit. [o] A.S., Avenione.

[p] The Text of Father da Civezza revised with the A.S.

APPENDIX I.

LATIN TEXT OF ODORIC, FROM A MS. IN THE BIBLIOTHÈQUE NATIONALE.

DESCRIPTIO ORIENTALIUM PARTIUM FRATRIS ODORICI BOEMI DE FORO JULII PROVINCIÆ SANCTI ANTONII.

1. *De Trapesondâ et Armeniâ Majori*[1].

LICET alia multa et varia de ritibus et conditionibus hujus mundi a multis enarrentur, tamen est sciendum quod ego frater Odoricus de Foro Julio[2], volens transfretare et ad partes infidelium volens ire ut fructus aliquos lucri facerem animarum[3], multa magna et mirabilia audivi[4] atque vidi quæ possum veraciter enarrare[5]. Nam primo[6] transiens Mare Majus, me[7] transtuli Trapesondam, quæ Pontus antiquitus vocabatur. Hæc terra valde est bene situata; ipsa enim est scala[8] quædam, videlicet Persarum, Medorum et omnium eorum que sunt ultra mare. In hac enim terra vidi quoddam quod michi placuit valde[9]. Nam vidi hominem quemdam secum ducentem plures quam quatuor milia perdicum. Iste homo per terram veniebat, perdices non[10] per aerem volabant; has perdices ipse ducebat ad quoddam castrum quod vocatur Canega[11], distans a Trapesonda tribus dietis. Hæc perdices hujus erant conditionis et proprietatis. Nam cum ille homo vellet quiescere vel dormire, omnes se aptabant circa eum, more pullorum gallinarum; et sic isto modo eas ducebat Trapesondam, usque

[1] These headings have been interpolated by the editor as before stated. (See Biogr. and Introd. Notices.)

[2] *Hak.* de portu Vahonis; *Mus.* de portu Nahomonis.

[3] *Bol.* Et hoc de licentiâ prælatorum meorum qui hoc concedere possunt secundum regulæ nostræ instituta.

ad palatium imperatoris. Quæ cum sic essent ante eum de eis tot accipiebat quot ipse volebat. Alias autem predictus homo ad locum de quo prius illas acceperat perducebat. In hac civitate positum est corpus Athanasii super ipsius portam civitatis[12]. Hinc recedens ivi in Armeniam Majorem, ad quamdam civitatem que vocatur Aritiron[13]; hæc civitas multum erat bona et opulenta multo tempore jam transacto, et adhuc esset nisi fuissent Tartari et Sarraceni, qui eam multum[14] destruxerunt. Nam ipsa multum inundat pane carne et aliis victualibus multis præterquam[15] vino et fructibus. Ista civitas[16] multum est frigida. De ipsa enim dicunt gentes quod altior est terra, quæ hodie habitetur in mundo[17]. Hæc autem multum habet bonas aquas, cujus ratio est hæc ut videtur. Nam venæ harum aquarum oriri videntur et scaturire a flumine Eufrate quod per unam dietam distans ab ista civitate labitur inde. Hæc autem civitas est via media, eundi Thauris. De hac recedens ivi ad quemdam montem qui vocatur Sovisacalo[18].

4 *Bol.* a fide dignis.

5 *Far. then has:* Præsens itaque opusculum in capitula dividens de multis gestis quæ vidi et audivi in oriente septentrione et meridie, intendo aliqua sub brevi compendio enarrare, nec intendo de singulis reddere rationem, multa nihilominus primitus mittens quæ apud multos incredibilia viderentur. Neque enim ego illa crederem nisi propriis auribus audivissem aut hæc talia respexissem. Quatuordecim annis cum dimidio in habitu almi confessoris Christi Francisci in hujusmodi partibus sum moratus. Ad petitionem reverendi fratris Gnidoti tunc præsens provincialis ministri provinciæ sancti Antonii hoc breve opusculum in Paduâ compilavi. Siquid igitur studioso lectori in hoc opusculo visum fuerit divinæ bonitati et non meæ imperitiæ imputetur. Siquid autem nimis incredibile vel a veritate devium fuerit visum diligentis lectoris caritas, non mordax insultus aut latrans dente canino, corrigat et emendet.

6 *Far.* Primo itaque de Venetiis cum galeis recedens.

7 *Hak.* et *Mus.* de Pera juxta Constantinopolim.

8 *Bol.* schola (!).

9 *Ven.* *Ut.* quoddam valde pulchrum.

10 Miscopied probably for *vero* as in most others. *Ven. has* hominem... perdices...sequebantur.

11 *Ven.* Zanega; *Ut.* Zanga; *Far.* Tanegar; *Hak.* Zauena; *Bol.* Tegana; *Ram.* Zanga. *The true reading doubtless* Zegana.

12 *Ven.* Is enim est qui fecit symbolum quod incipit Quicunque vult salvus esse ante omnia opus est ut teneat catholicam fidem, etc.

13 *Ven.* Arziron; *Ut.* Aceron; *Far.* Arzirai; *Hak.* Azaron; *Mus.* Arciron; *Bol.* Caricon; *Ram.* Acron.

14 *Hak.* pro magnâ parte. *Far. omits* multum.

15 *Far.* primitus *instead of* præterquam.

16 *Ven.* regio.

17 Sit altior civitas totius universi.

18 *Ven.* Sobissacelo; *Ut.* Sollisaculo; *Far.* Bobis (?Sobis) Sachalo; *Hak.* as in Ven ; *Mus.* ditto; *Bol.* Sarbi-Sarbolo; *Ram.* Sollisaculo; *Marc.* Sobissacallo.

In hac contrata est mons ille[1] in quo est archa Noæ. In quem libenter ascendissem si mea societas me præstolari voluisset; et quem quum ascendere voluerim tamen gens illius contratæ dicebat quod nullus unquam poterat ascendere illum montem. Nam hoc videtur et dicitur Deo altissimo non placere.

2. *De civitatibus Thauris et Soldoniâ.*

De ista contrata recedens me transtuli Thauris, civitatem magnam et regalem que Susis[2] antiquitus dicebatur. In ista ut dicitur est Arbor Sicca, in una moscheta et[3] in una ecclesia Sarracenorum: hæc civitas nobilior est et melior pro mercimoniis quam alia aliqua civitas que hodie sit in mundo. Nam non reperitur hodie aliquid in mundo quod sit comestibile[4] vel quod sit alicujus mercimonii, cujus illic magna copia non habeatur. In tantum autem est nobilis civitas illa, quod est quasi incredibile de hiis quæ illic habentur, hæc enim multum bene est posita atque sita. Nam quasi totus mundus pro mercimoniis illi correspondet civitati[5]. De hac volunt dicere Christiani quod ex ista civitate plura recipit imperator ille quam rex Franciæ habeat de toto suo regno. Penes hanc civitatem est unus mons salinus magnam copiam salis toti exhibens civitati. De hoc sale unusquisque accipit tantum quantum vult et petit et nichil alicui solvendo. In hac civitate multi Christiani cujuslibet generationis[6] commorantur, quibus ipsi Sarraceni in omnibus dominantur, multa autem alia sunt in ista civitate quæ nimis longum foret aliis enarrare. Ab hac civitate Thauris recedens ivi per decem[7] dietas ad quamdam civitatem que vocatur Soldonia[8]. In hac civitate tempore estivo moratur imperator Persarum. In yeme autem vadit ad quamdam contratam[9] que est super mare quod vocatur mare Bachuc[10]. Hæc civitas magna terra est et frigida, in

[1] *Ram.* il monte Gordico.

[2] *Bol.* Suors. *Ram.* Suci,..qual fu sotto il dominio di Assuero Re. So *Ven.*

[3] Et in *should be* id est, *as in Ven.*, *Mus.* and *Far.*, *Hak.* and *Bol. omit about the* Arbor secco *altogether.*

[4] *Bol. here inserts* nihil alicujus utilitatis, necessitatis, aut mercimonii.

[5] *Hak.* and *Mus. instead of the last three words* confluere potest.

[6] *Mus. has* de omni natione. [7] *Far.* has 14.

[8] *Ut.*, *Hak.* Soldania; *Far.* Solonia; *Bol.* Soldolina; *Marc.* Soldonia.

[9] *Bol. alone has* quæ vocatur Axam.

[10] *Ven.* Bachac; *Ut.* and *Ram.* Bacud; *Far.* Abachuc; *Hak.* and *Mus.* Bakuc; *Bol.* Abacut, *and applies the next sentence to the city on that sea;* hæc magna est et *calida*; *Marc.* Bacuch.

se habens bonas aquas, ad quam civitatem portantur multa et magna mercimonia, quæ illic venduntur.

3. *De Civitate Magorum; De Mari Arenoso, et Terrâ Huz.*

De hac civitate recedens cum caravanis et[1] cum quadam societate ivi versus Indiam Superiorem, ad quam dum sic irem per multas dietas applicui ad unam civitatem trium magorum que vocatur Cassan[2], civitatem regalem et magni honoris; verumptamen Tartari eam multum destruxerunt, hec civitas multum habundat pane et vino et multis aliis bonis. Ab hac civitate usque Iherusalem quo magi iverunt non virtute humana sed virtute divina et miraculose cum sic cito iverint, sunt bene quinquaginta dietæ. Multa autem alia sunt in hac civitate quæ non multum expedit enarrare[3]. Inde recedens ivi ad quamdam civitatem nomine Gest[4] a qua distat mare arenosum per unam dietam, quod mare est valde periculosum et mirabile. In hac civitate Gest est copia maxima victualium et omnium aliorum bonorum quæ jam dici possent: potissime autem ficuum illic copia maxima reperitur; uvæ autem siccæ et virides ut herba, et multum minutæ illic reperiuntur uberius et abundantius quam in aliqua parte mundi. Hæc est tertia melior[5] civitas quam Persarum imperator possideat in toto suo regno. De hac dicunt Sarraceni quod in ea nullus Christianus ultra annum vivere umquam valet[6]. Multa autem alia illic habentur. Ab hac recedens et transiens per multas civitates et terras ivi ad quamdam civitatem nomine Conium[7], quæ antiquitus civitas magna fuit; hæc maximum dampnum intulit Romæ tempore jam transacto: ejus autem muri bene quinquaginta miliarum sunt capaces. In ea sunt palacia integra adhuc inhabitabilia[8], tamen multis victualibus ipsa habundat. Ex hac recedens et veniens per multas terras et civitates

[1] *Should be* id est *as in Ven., who has* haravanis. *Hak.* cum quadam societate caravanorum; *Bol.* quadam soc. Tartarorum.

[2] *Ven.* Cassam; *Far.* Casim; *Hak., Mus.* Cassan; *Bol.* Casan.

[3] *Bol.* quæ scribere non curavi. *Hak.* multa mirabilia quæ pertranseo.

[4] *Far.* Iese, *perhaps* Iesd; *Ven., Hak., Mus.* and *Bol.* Gest.

[5] *Bol.* de melioribus *simply.*

[6] *Far. omits* ultra annum.

[7] Sic in *Ven.*; in *Hak.* and *Ut.* Comum; in *Mus.* Comam; in *Far.* Comerum; in *Bol.* Coprum. *Marc.* Conio; *Ram.* Como; *Wadding's Annals,* Karum. Mandeville has *Cornaa.*

[8] This is also the sense in *Far. Hak. has* non habitata; *Mus.* minime tamen inhabitata; *Ven.* inhabitata tamen.

perrexi ad terram Job[1] quæ est cunctorum victualium multum pulcher situs[2]. Penes hanc terram sunt montes in quibus sunt pulcherrima pascua pro animalibus habundanter. Illic etiam melius manna et in majori copia reperitur, quam in terra aliqua quæ hodie sit in mundo. In ipsa etiam habentur quatuor bonæ perdices minores[3] quam uno grosso veneto. In ea sunt pulcherrimi senes, ubi homines nent et filant, mulieres vero non. Hæc terra correspondet a capite Caldeæ versus tramontanam[4].

4. *De Moribus Caldeorum; de Indiâ infra terram et Ormes.*

Exinde exiens ivi in Caldeam que est regnum magnum, ad quam dum sic irem ivi per juxta turrim Babel quæ per quatuor dietas forte distat ab ea[5]. In hac Caldea est sua lingua propria[6]; in qua sunt pulchri homines, mulieres vero turpes. Illi homines compti vadunt et ornati, ut hic nostræ incedunt mulieres. Qui homines super capita sua sunt portantes fasciola aurea et de perlis, mulieres autem sunt ferentes solum unam vilem interulam[7] attingentem usque ad genua, habentemque manicas largas et longas quod usque ad terram ipsæ attingunt: hæc autem mulieres ambulant discalciatæ portantes sarabulas[8] usque ad terram. Hæc tricas et diezas (?) non portant sed earum capilli undique disparguntur. Hic autem sicut homines post ipsas vadunt mulieres, ita illic prius homines mulieres incedunt[9]. Alia autem multa in hac civitate sunt que non multum expedit enarrare. Hinc ego recedens veni in Indiam quæ est infra terram quam ipsi Tartari multum destruxerunt. In ea sunt homines ut plurimum[10] tantum datulos comedentes, quorum xlii libræ[11] minori uno grosso illic habentur.

[1] *Ven.* nomine Hus, sic in *Far.*, *Hak.*, *Mus.* *Bol. has* Ur; *Marc. has only* città la quale ha nome Hus. *The introduction of Job's name is probably interpolated.*

[2] *Hak.* and *Mus.* omnium victualium plenissima est, et pulcherrime situata. *Bol.* has nearly the same.

[3] *Should be* minoris *or* pro minori *as in the other manuscripts.*

[4] *Hak.* correspondet Chaldeæ versus transmontana.

[5] *Hak.* omits the distance.

[6] *Ram.* Nella ditta Caldea è il vero idioma Caldeo qual noi chiamamo lingua Caldea.

[7] *Hak.* and *Mus.* camisiam; *Bol.* tunicellam.

[8] *Sic Ven.* et *Mus.*; *Ut.* cerabulas; *Hak.* Serablans; *Bol.* scrobullas.

[9] *Par.* 2 *has* hæc etiam mulieres vadunt post viros sicut apud nos viri post mulieres. Et alia multa.

[10] *Bol. instead of* ut plurimum *has* pulchri.

[11] *Mus. has* quatuor libræ, et pro minori quarteria uno grosso. *Ram.* 40 ibre.

Sic etiam de aliis multis. Ex hac India recedens et transiens per multas contratas ad mare occeanum ego veni: prima autem terra quam inveni vocatur Ormes, que est terra multum et bene murata, terra multorum ac magnorum mercimoniorum. In ea tantus et ita immensus calor est quod pilia[1] et testiculi homini exeunt coram et descendunt usque ad dimidium tibiarum. Ideo que gens illius contratæ si vivere volunt sibi faciunt unam unctionem qua illa ungunt. Nam aliter homines penitus morerentur, et dum sic sunt uncta in quibusdam sacculis illa ponunt circumcirca se cingentes.

5. *De Navigio ferrum nullum habente, in quo se transtulit Fr. Odoricus Tanam Indiæ.*

In hac contrata homines utuntur navigio quod vocatur Iasse siccum solem spago[2]. In unum istorum navigiorum ego ascendi in quo nullum ferrum potui in aliquo[3] reperire. In quod dum sic ascendissem in xxviii[4] dietis me transtuli usque ad Tanam[5] in qua pro fide Christi gloriosum martirium passi fuerunt quatuor nostri fratres minores: hæc terra multum bene est situata. In ea magna copia panis et vini et arborum reperitur. Hæc terra antiquitus fuit valde magna. Nam ipsa fuit terra regis Pori[6], qui cum rege Alexandro prælium maximum commisit[7]: hujus terræ populus ydolatrat. Nam adorant ignem, serpentem et arbores. Hanc terram regunt Sarraceni qui eam ceperunt violenter, nunc subjacentes Daldili[8]. In hac reperiuntur diversa genera bestiarum. In qua potissime sunt leones nigri in maxima quantitate. Sunt autem symiæ et gattimaymones[9], et noctuæ[10] ita magnæ sicut habentur hic columbæ. Hi etiam mures sunt ita magni sicut hic

[1] *Ven.* and *Far.* parilia *for* virilia *as in Hak.* and *Mus.*

[2] *Should be* sutum solo spago *as in Mus. Hak. has* sutum sparto; *Ven.* sutum solum spegio; *Bol. has* navigio quod vocatur Iassefutum, *an obvious misreading. Marc. has* vase *for the name of the shipping.*

[3] *Should be* aliqua parte *as in Mus. Bol. has* in quo nullum Fratrum potui reperire, *an absurd misreading.*

[4] *Ram.* vinti giorni.

[5] *This is* Cavam *in the transcript made for me; probably a misreading. Ven. has* Tanam, *the others* Thanam *or* Thana, *except Bol. which has* Chanaam; *Marc.* Tana, *Ram.* Thana.

[6] *Bol. has* Ponti vel Parti.

[7] *Mus.* sicut in vitâ ejusdem Alexandri plenius invenitur.

[8] *Hak. has* regis Daldilo: *all have this name nearly the same.*

[9] *The Italian Marc. has* cocoveggie, 'screech owls,' *but bats are meant.*

[10] *Bol.* cathi magni.

sunt canes scherpi[1]. Ideoque illic canes capiunt mures (quia) muriligæ seu katti ad hoc nihil valent[2]. In hac contrata quilibet homo ante domum suam habet unum pedem faxiolorum[3] ita magnum sicut hic una esset columpna; hic pes faxiolorum minime desiccatur dum modo sibi exhibeatur aqua, et multæ aliæ novitates sunt illic quas multum pulchrum esset audire. In hac contrata quæ Tana nuncupatur, ut jam dictum est, passi sunt gloriosum martirium quatuor fratres minores pro fide Christi quod per hunc modum habetur.

6. *Martyrium iv. Fratrum in civitate Tanæ.*

Dum predicti fratres essent in Ormes, passi[4] fuerunt cum una navi ut irent Polumbum[5]; in qua dum essent portati fuerunt malo suo velle[6], usque ad Tanam ubi sunt xv domus Christianorum, scilicet Nestorinorum, qui sunt scismatici et heretici. Et dum sic essent istic sibi invenerunt hospicium, et hospitati sunt in domo cujusdam illorum. Dum autem sic manerent illic, orta fuit quædam lis inter virum illius domus et ejus uxorem quam ille sero ipse fortiter verberavit. Dum vero sic esset verberata et quæsta fuit coram lo cadi[7] uno episcopo in lingua sua. Quam mulierem ipse cadi interrogavit si probare posset quæ dicebat. Tunc autem ipsa respondit dicens se bene probare posse. Nam quatuor Raban Franchi scilicet quatuor viri religiosi in lingua nostra, illic erant in domo cum michi hoc fecit: hos interrogate, qui vobis dicent veritatem. Ipsa autem muliere sic loquente, unus de Alexandria ibi præsens rogavit Cadi ut mitteret pro eis quos dicebat homines maxime scientiæ et scripturas bene scire. Ideoque dicebat bonum esse de fide disputare cum eis. Quod audiens sic ipse Cadi misit pro eis, qui dum sic ante eum adducti fuissent isti quatuor fratres, scilicet frater Thomas de Tolentino de Marchia Anchonitana, frater Jacobus de Padua, frater

[1] *Far. only has* porci parvi; *Ven. has* sarpi sive canes; *Hak.* sicut sunt hinc scepi; *Mus.* scoipi id est canes tales; *Bol.* sicut in terris nostris canes qui dicuntur Depi. *Marc. also has* scherpi.

[2] *Far. omits* quia...valent.

[3] *Ven.* plantam unam fasiolorum; *Hak.* fasciculorum; *Mus.* fasciolorum; *Far.* omits the sentence entirely.

[4] For *pacti* as in *Ven.*, etc.

[5] *Mus.* Polumbrum.

[6] *Hak. has* violenter deportati sunt; *Mus.* vellent nollent.

[7] *Ut. also has* Locadi; *the others* Cadi *or* Kadi, id est episcopo. *Ven.* mane conquesta est cadi, etc.

Demetrius[1] qui erat frater laycus sciens linguas, et frater Petrus de Senis domi ut res custodiret[2], ad ipsum Cadi perrexerunt. Dum sic essent coram lo Cadi[3], ipse cum ipsis disputare cœpit de fide nostra. Cum autem illi infideles sic disputarent cum istis, dicebant Christum solum purum hominem et non Deum. Quod cum sic dixissent, ille frater Thomas Christum esse unum Deum et hominem probavit rationibus, et exemplis in tantum eos confudit Sarracenos quod penitus ipsi contrarium dicere non volebant[4].

7. *Idem.*

Tunc videns ille Cadi se sic esse confusum ab eis, coram toto populo clamare cœpit voce magna dicens: Et tu quid dicis de Machometo? Quid dicis de Machometo? Nunc autem istam consuetudinem habent Sarraceni, qui si se verbis defendere non possunt se ensibus tuentur et pugnis. Dum autem eum interrogasset sic Cadi[5], responderunt fratres dicentes, si tibi probavimus rationibus et exemplis Christum verum Deum et hominem esse qui legem dedit in terra, et Machometus exinde venit qui legem contrariam isti fuit; si sapiens es, quid sit de Deo tu optime scire potes. Tunc ille cadi et alii Sarraceni alta voce dicentes clamabant: Tu quid in tantum[6] dicis de Machometo? Tunc frater Thomas respondit: Vos tantum dicere poteritis de eo quid dico, quod tacere hoc nimium verecundabor unum ex quo me vultis respondere vobis[7]. Respondeo vobis et dico quod Machometus filius perditionis est, et est cum dyabulo patre ejus positus in inferno; non solum ipse sed et omnes qui hanc legem tenent et observant. Cum ipsa sit pestifera nequam et falsa totaque contra domini[8] et animarum salutem. Hoc audientes Sarraceni omnes alta voce unanimiter clamare cœperunt[9]; Malum dixerunt de propheta! et tunc ceperunt fratres et eos in sole vinxerunt ut

[1] *Bol.* Zorzanus.

[2] *This should be as is noted in the margin,* dimisso fratre Petro domi, etc. It is thus in *Far.*, *Hak.* and *Mus.* *Ven. has* ut rex custodiret, *a slip.*

[3] Better with these last words omitted from *ad ipsum* as in *Ven.*

[4] *Hak. omits from* nunc autem. [5] *Should be* de eo, *as in the other MSS.*

[6] *Ven.* and *the others have* iterum.

[7] *Mus. has* Tu inscius quid dico de eo videre potes? tamen ex quo vultis quod plane vobis respondeo, dico, etc. *Hak.* Vos omnes videre potestis quod dico de eo, etc. The others have nearly the same as above.

[8] Dominum. *Ven.* Deum.

[9] *Ven.* Moriatur! Moriatur! quod malum, etc.

virtute caloris intensi duram[1] paterentur mortem. Cum illic tantus sit calor ut si quis per spatium unius missæ perseveraret in sole, ipse penitus moreretur. Et tum illic in sole fuerunt laudantes et glorificantes Deum, a tertia usque ad nonam semper, ylares et sani. Sic hoc videntes Sarraceni inter se consilium habuerunt et ad fratres venerunt dicentes: Volumus accendere magnum et copiosum ignem in quem vos projiciemus; et si ut dicitis[2] ita sit vera, ignis vos non comburet; si autem falsa sit et mala, penitus vos combureminі ab igne[3]. Tunc fratres responderunt eis dicentes: Parati sumus intrare ignem et carcerem, et quidquid nos, cadi, poteris facere pro fide nostra, semper invenies nos paratos, verum tamen unum facere debes[4], quod si ignis nos comburet, non hoc credas ex fide nostra procedere, sed solum ex peccatis nostris, cum propter peccata nostra nos bene comburi permitteret ipse Deus, hoc semper salvo, quod fides nostra ita perfecta est et bona sicut in mundo umquam esse posset. Nam ab hac non est in mundo alia fides, nec esse potest quæ salvum faciat aliquem nisi ista.

8. *Idem.*

Dum autem sic ordinatum esset quod isti fratres conburi deberent vox evolavit et fama corruit per totam illam terram[5]. Itaque tunc omnes de dicta terra tam parvi[6] quam magni tam homines quam mulieres ad hoc finaliter intuendum penitus occurrerunt. Ipsi autem fratres ducti fuerunt super medanum[7], scilicet super plateam civitatis, ubi accensus erat ignis valde copiosus. Qui dum sic accensus esset, frater Thomas ibat ad projiciendum se in ignem. Et dum vellet se in ignem se projicere quidam Sarracenus eum per capucium cepit dicens: Non vadas tu illuc cum sis senex. Nam super te aliquod experimentum[8] habere possis, propter quod ignis te comburere non posset. Sed alium ire permittas. Tunc statim quatuor Sarraceni fratrem Jacobum de Padua violenter ceperunt, eum in ignem projicere

[1] *Ven.* diram; *Mus.* durissimam. [2] *Ven.* ut ducitis.

[3] *Hak.* si autem vos combusserit patebit quod fides vestra nulla sit; *and Mus.* nearly the same. *The others nearly as here.*

[4] *Ven.* sciatis.

[5] *Ven.* Vox et fama per totam civitatem intonuit. *Far.* Vox evolavit et fama insonuit.

[6] *Ven.* pueri. [7] *Hak. omits* medanum.

[8] *Hak.* carmen aliquid vel experimentum.

satagentes, quibus ipse dixit: Me permittatis quia libens in hunc ignem projiciam memet ipsum[1]. Ipsi autem ad sua verba non attendentes statim in ignem[2] projecerunt. Dum autem sic eum in ignem projecissent, et ipse sic in igne permaneret, ignis tam altus et tam magnus ipse erat quod nullus eum unquam poterat intueri; ejus tamen vocem audiebant invocantis semper nomen Virginis gloriosæ. Tunc igne totaliter consumpto ipse frater Jacobus stabat super prunas lætus et gaudens, cum manibus in modum crucis in cœlum levatis, mente integra et puro corde dominum semper laudando. Et quamquam ignis fulcit ita magnus et copiosus, nichil tamen de eo[3] læsum vel combustum breviter fuit inventum. Hoc videns populus cœpit unanimiter exclamare, dicens: Isti sunt sancti, isti sunt sancti! Nephas est offendere eos. Nam merito videmus quod fides sua sancta est et bona! Hoc dicto frater ille Jacobus vocatus fuit de igne, et sic sanus exivit et illæsus. Tunc hoc videns, lo cadi[4] voce magna cœpit clamare dicens: Sanctus non est, sanctus non est! sed ideo non comburitur quod tunica quam habet in dorso est tela terræ Abrahæ. Ideo nudus expolietur et in ignem sic mittatur. Ut autem finaliter hoc compleretur venerunt pessimi Sarraceni et in duplo plus quam prius ignem accenderunt. Et tunc fratrem Jacobum exuerunt, cujus corpus insuper abluerunt, et ipsum optime oleo perunxerunt, et ut ignis major esset et fortius ageret et arderet, et ad hoc ut ipse frater citius comburi posset, oleum in struem lignorum in copiam maximam dejecerunt, et ipsum fratrem Jacobum in ignem cum impetu impulerunt. Frater autem Thomas et frater Demetrius de foris stabant genibus flexis in orationibus magnis et devotionibus persistentes, et sic frater Jacobus ignem iterum exivit illæsus sicut et prius fecit.

9. *Idem.*

Hoc videns populus unanimiter clamabat dicens; Peccatum est, peccatum est offendere eos quoniam sancti sunt! Et sic in populo rumor maximus habebatur. Hoc secundum miraculum videns Lomelic, scilicet Potestas, ad se fratrem Jacobum vocavit et eum se suis fecit indui vestimentis. Et dixit: Vadete fratres,

[1] *Mus.* pro fide meâ libenter ignem intrabo. So in *Hak.* also.

[2] *Mus.* turpiter. *Hak.* violenter.

[3] *Hak.* nec pannus nec capillus læsus per ignem inventus.

[4] *The others have not the* lo.

ite cum gratia Dei, quia nullum malum patiemini vos a nobis. Nam bene videmus vos esse bonos et sanctos, et fidem vestram esse veram et sanctam et bonam finaliter nos videmus. Sed ut vobis securius consulamus vos hanc terram exite quam citius potestis, quia ipse Cadi pro posse nititur et laborat vobis auferre vitam. Dum hoc sic diceret, completorium quasi erat, et tunc totus populus ydolatræ omnesque alii, stupefacti et exterriti, dicentes permanebant: Tot et tanta magna mirabilia vidimus nos ab istis, quod nescimus quid nos tenere debeamus et observare! Dum sic dixissent tunc Lomelic[1] accipi fecit illos tres fratres quos ipse portari fecit ultra quoddam brachium maris per aliquantulum spacium ab illa terra, ubi burgum unum erat, ad quod ille in cujus jam domo fuerant hospitati illos sociavit[2], et sic in domo unius ydolatræ sibi hospicium invenerunt. Dum sic autem illic manerent perrexit cadi ad Lomelic dicens ei; Quid facimus? lex Machometi destructa est, nec[3] aliud fiat, nam isti Raban Franchi (scilicet viri religiosi), nunc ibunt predicando per totam contratam istam, et cum tot et tanta fecerunt ipsi in hac contrata, quæ totus populus jam vidit, omnes convertentur ad eos, et sic lex Machometi aliquid ulterius non valebit. Verumptamen ut ipsa totaliter non sit destructa, tu unum scire debes, quod Machometus precepit in Alchoran (scilicet in lege sua) quod si aliquis unum interficeret Christianum tantum meritum ipse haberet ut si iret ad Mecham. (Unum scire vos debetis quod Alchoran lex Sarracenorum est sicut Christianorum est lex evangelium. Mecha est locus ubi jacet Machometus, ad quam Mecham vel locum sic vadunt Sarraceni sicut Christiani pergunt ad Sepulchrum[4].) Tum Lomelic respondit Cadi dicens; Vade et facias sicut tu vis.

10. *Idem.*

Hoc dicto, statim ille Cadi accepit quatuor homines armatos ut irent ad interficiendum istos fratres, qui dum sic transissent quamdam aquam facta est nox. Et sic illo sero illos non potuerunt invenire. Statimque Lomelic capi fecit omnes illos

[1] *Hak.* Melich. *Mus.* Melik.

[2] The immediately preceding words are wanting in *Mus.*

[3] *Ven.* nisi; *Far.* ni, *one of which is required.*

[4] The whole of this is expressed in *Mus.* in quite different and more diffused language; but, as the meaning is the same, the variations are not worth specifying.

Christianos qui erant in terra, et eos carceri mancipavit. Cum autem perventum esset ad dimidium noctis, tunc fratres ut dicerent matutinum surrexerunt, et tunc homines illi qui missi fuerant ad eos illos invenerunt, et illos extra terram sub arbore quadam adduxerunt. Dum autem sic illi adduxissent ipsos eis dicebant, Vos scire debetis quod mandatum habemus ab ipso Cadi et Lomelic, ut vos interficere debeamus, quod tamen adinplemus nos invite, cum sitis vita bona homines et sancti. Sed tamen nos aliter facere non valemus. Nam si suæ non obediremus jussioni, nos cum liberis nostris et uxoribus penitus moreremur. Hiis isti fratres responderunt sic dicentes: Vos qui huc venistis ut per mortem temporalem vitam æternam valeamus adipisci, quod vobis est preceptum facite. Nam pro fide nostra et amore Domini nostri Jhesu Christi[1], quæ nobis adhibetis nos tormenta parati sumus viriliter sustinere. Unde sic istis audacter respondentibus et constantius, Christianus ille qui eos associaverat, et illi quatuor homines mali, multum ad invicem altercabant[2]. Nam eis respondebat Christianus et dicebat: Si gladium aliquem ego haberem aut quod vultis non fieret aut me cum ipsis neci finaliter daretis. Tunc illi fecerunt fratres expoliari. Statimque frater Thomas junctis manibus simul in modum crucis capitis abscisionem suscepit. Sed fratrem Jacobum unus percussit in capite et eum usque ad oculos scidit, statimque caput abscidit. Frater autem Demetrius uno gladio in mamilla fortissime fuit percussus. Exinde sibi caput fuit abscisum. Dum autem sic ex martirio suo animas Deo dedissent, statim aer ita lucidus et ita clarus est effectus, quod cuncti fortissime mirabantur; similiter, et luna maximam ostendit claritatem et splendorem. Statim autem post hoc tot et tanta tonitrua et fulmina atque choruscationes evenerunt, quod pene omnes mori finaliter se credebant. Navis etiam illa quæ debebat eos portare Polumbum et portati fuerunt usque ad Canam[3] contra velle suum, taliter fuit submersa, quod de ea et omnibus qui erant in illa nichil unquam breviter scitum fuit.

[1] *Hak.* et *Mus.* qui pro nobis crucifigi et mori dignatus est.

[2] *Mus.* multum audacter et constanter cum illis quatuor armatis altercatus est.

[3] *For* Tanam.

11. *Idem.*

Manę autem facto misit Cadi acceptum res illorum fratrum et tunc inventus fuit frater Petrus de Senis, trium aliorum fratrum socius. Quum eum sic reperissent ipsum ceperunt et eum duxerunt ad Cadi; quem ipse Cadi et alii Sarraceni alloquentes sibi maxima promittebant, si fidem suam vellet abnegare et illam Machometi integraliter confiteri. Ipsi autem dum sic sibi loquerentur, ipse de eis trufabatur et eos mirabiliter deridebat. Eo autem sic ipsos deridente, ipsum tormentare cœperunt a mane usque ad meridiem, diversis generibus tormentorum. Quod quamquam sic ei inferrent semper tamen in fide immobilis permanebat et constanter, illorum falsam ostendendo et eam viriliter destruendo. Cum autem videntes Sarraceni a sua non velle discedere voluntate, illum super quemdam arborem suspenderunt, in quam a nona usque ad noctem ipse permansit. Cum autem ad noctem fuit perventum, de arbore ipsum acceperunt sine aliqua læsione de mundo. Hoc illi videntes[1] ipsum per medium diviserunt, et mane facto nichil de eo breviter fuit inventum. Verumtamen uni personæ fide dignæ fuit revelatum quod Deus occultaverat ejus corpus usque ad certum tempus, in quo tamen sibi placuerit ipse illud manifestabit. Ut autem Deus opem ostenderet quod eorum animæ jam regna celestia obtinebant[2], illa die qua beatissimi fratres gloriosi martires sunt effecti, ille Lomelic dormitioni se dedit; qui dum sic in lecto dormiret ecce sibi apparuerunt isti martires gloriosi lucidi, ut sol ac splendidi, singulos enses in suis manibus retinentes, et super Lomelic taliter eos vibrantes ac si dividere voluerunt ipsum totum. Quod videns ipse Lomelic voce sic alta cepit clamare. Quid ad ejus clamorem tota ipsius familia occurrit festinanter petens ab eo quid ipse haberet atque vellet. Ipsum autem dum sic interrogassent ipse respondit dicens: Illi Raban Franchi quos interfici feci huc ad me venerunt suis ensibus, quos habebant, occidere me volentes. Ideoque ipse Lomelic misit pro Cadi cui totum, quod sibi acciderat enarravit, consulens ipsum quid de hoc esset finaliter peragendum, cum se crederet ab eis penitus interire. Tunc Cadi sibi consuluit ut pro eis magnam elemosinam exhiberet, si vellet

[1] *Hak.* videntes illum lætum vivum et illæsum.

[2] *Hak.* ostenderet animas suorum martyrum jam in cœlis consistere et congaudere cum Deo et angelis et aliis sanctis ejus. *Mus. nearly the same. Ven. omits.*

evadere de istorum manibus interfectorum. Tunc statim misit pro illis Christianis quos ipse in carcere detinebat, qui cum venissent ad eum, ipse indulgentiam ab eis de eo quod sibi fieri fecerat humiliter postulavit, faciens se socium eorum et fratrem. Hoc autem facto tunc precepit ut si quis unquam offenderet aliquem Christianum ipse penitus moreretur; et sic omnes illæsos abire permisit. Post hoc autem ipse Lomelic eis quatuor moschetas, scilicet iiii eclesias fecit edificari, in quarum qualibet quosdam sacerdotes Sarracenos fecit morari.

12. *Idem.*

Audiens ipse imperator Doldali[1] istos fratres talem subiisse sententiam, misit et ordinavit ut ipse Lomelic penitus caperetur, et ipse ad eum vinctis manibus duceretur. Qui cum ante eum sic fuisset adductus, eum interrogabat quare mori fecerat tam crudeliter istos fratres. Cum autem interrogatus sic fuisset, respondit ei: Istos fratres sic mori permisi quia ipsi subvertere volebant legem nostram, et malum etiam dixerunt de propheta. Tunc sibi dixit imperator: Tu, crudelissime canis, cum vidisti quod Deus bis liberavit eos ab igne, quo modo fuisti sic ausus ut eis talem mortem inferres. Hæc cum dixisset, eum cum tota familia sua per medium scindi fecit. Et quia talem mortem istos fratres[2] in suum meritum fecit sustinere, hoc ipse passus fuit tantum in detrimentum[3]. In hac autem contrata consuetudo quædam observatur. Nam nunquam corpus aliquod sepelitur, sed ipsa corpora solum in campaneis dimittuntur, et ex nimio calore cito destruuntur et consumuntur. Verum corpora horum fratrum bene quatuordecim diebus illic fuerunt in sole, et ita recentia et integra sunt inventa sicut erant illa die qua passi fuerunt suum martirium gloriosum. Sic autem videntes qui in illa terra aderant Christiani, sua corpora acceperunt, quæ postea sepulturæ tradiderunt[4].

[1] *Ven.* Dodoli; *Far.* Dodili; *Mus.* Dodili; *Hak.* Dodsi; *Marc.* dol Dali.

[2] *Mus.* Petro de Senis. *Hak.* fratri......inflixerat.

[3] *Far.* Cadi autem hoc audiens de terra illa atque de imperatoris dominio clam fugit. *Hak. also ending* et sic evasit. *Mus.* et evasit.

[4] *Here Far. alone has* "Passi autem fuerunt hi beati martyres pro fide Christi martyrium gloriosum anno ab incarnatione Domini nostri Jhesu Christi MIII......"

13. *Fr. Odoricus colligit ossa fratrum; miracula per illa operata.*

Tunc ego frater Odoricus de suo sciens martirio glorioso illuc ivi,—et sua corpora ego accepi quæ jam fuerunt tradita sepulturæ[1]. Quia per sanctos suos Deus ipse multa et magna mirabilia operatur, per istos voluit potissime operari. Nam ego frater Odoricus cum ossa istorum fratrum sic accepissem et pulchris toaleis[2] alligassem, ipsa in Indiam Superiorem ad unum locum nostrorum fratrum cum uno socio et famulo deferebam[3]. Dum autem ea sic portarem, ibi domo cujusdam habui hospitari[4], et ipsa ossa, imo potius reliquiæ sanctæ dici debent, supposui capiti meo et me dedi dormitioni. Et dum sic dormirem ipsa domus a Sarracenis subito fuit accensa, ut me facerent mori[5]. Alta voce populi universi [sic]. Nam hoc est imperatoris preceptum ut cujus domus accenditur[6] ipse penitus moriatur. Ipsa domo sic accensa socius meus cum famulo exivit domum, me in ea cum ossibus remanente, qui dum sic essem in domo jam ardente, ossa horum fratrum ego accepi et[7] in uno angulo ipsius me aptavi[8]. Sic autem igne domum comburente, tres anguli ipsius domus fuerunt combusti, illo solo in quo eram remanente: me autem sic in illo angulo residente, ignis desuper me aderat non me lædens nec ipsius domus angulum comburens; quamdiu autem in domo cum istis ossibus permanebam, ignis nunquam descendebat sed ad modum æris[9] ipse desuper residebat. Cum autem domum egressus fuissem, tunc ipsa totaliter fuit combusta, non solum ipsa sed et multæ aliæ quæ illi contiguæ videbantur, et sic inde illæsus exivi.

1 *Bol.* et apertis sepulchris suscepi ossa eorum humiliter et devote.

2 Toaleis, *towels*. *Ven. has* manutergiis; *Mus.* tuallis.

3 *Here Bol. has* omnipotens quoque Deus qui per prophetam mirabilis in sanctis suis dicitur, etiam per istos sanctos sua voluit mirabilia demonstrare.

4 *Bol.* et cum cum socio pergerem ad quiescendum.

5 *Mus.* tanquam reus (reum) illius ignis accensi.

6 *Mus.* ut si quis reus incendii domus esset. *These two last variations seem to be glosses.*

7 *Bol.* et invocato Dei auxilio.

8 *Bol.* Mira Dei clementia qui se pie clamantibus non elongat!

9 *Ut. has* ad modum crucis extensus, *which seems an arbitrary embellishment of the copyist.*

14. *Idem.*

Aliud quoque insuper evenit quod michi accidit in eundo Nam dum sic per mare cum istis ossibus ego irem ad unam civitatem quæ vocatur Polumpum[1], ubi piper nascitur habundanter, nobis defecit totaliter ipse[2] ventus. Quapropter venerunt ydolatræ suos deos adorantes ut eis ventum prosperum exhiberent, quem illis tamen dare minime potuerunt. Deinde venerunt Sarraceni, et ut etiam ventum haberent multum laboraverunt, et tum illum suis supplicacionibus nunquam habere potuerunt. Deinde michi et socio meo preceptum fuit ut orationes ad Deum nostrum fundere deberemus[3]; quatenus nobis finaliter exhiberet. Qui si haberi posset nobis honorem maximum exhiberent, et ut alii hoc intelligere non possent, ille rector navis Armorice[4] [*sic*] fuit locutus dicens: Si ventus haberi non posset hæc ossa nos projiciemus in mare. Tunc ego hæc et socius audientes orationes, fecimus ipsi Deo; qui videntes ventum haberi non posse, ad honorem Virginis gloriosæ multas missas promisimus celebrare si ventum possemus nos in aliquo tunc habere. Cum autem ventum nos habere minime poteramus[5], tunc accipiens ex ossibus istis unum, ipsum dedi famulo nostro ut iens ad caput[6] navis ipsum in mare projiceret festinanter. Tunc ipso osse in mari sic projecto, statim ventus ita nobis effectus est prosper, quod nunquam nobis defecit donec accessimus nos ad portum, ad quem meritis istorum fratrum devenimus cum salute.

15. *Idem.*

Cum autem illic in Polumbo fuimus nos ad portum, aliam navim nomine Lonclum[7] nos ascendimus ut jam dictum est. In

[1] *Should be* Polumbum, *as in Ven.*, *Far.*, *Mus.*; *Hak. has* Polumbrum; *Marc.* Polumbo et Polombo.

[2] *Bol.* necessarius nobis.

[3] *Boll.* Posthæc mihi et socio meo mandarunt cuncti qui erant in navi dicentes: Vos surgentes adorate Dominum Deum vestrum; si vestris orationibus salutem consequamur honorem vobis maxime impendemus; sin autem, vos cum ossibus istis in pelago submergemus.

[4] *For* Armenice *as in Ven.* and all the others.

[5] *Boll.* ego clamavi ad Dominum Jesum Christum ut per merita istorum Fratrum dignaretur nostrum desiderium exaudire.

[6] *Far. has* apodium navis.

[7] *Ven.* Zuncum; *Ut.* Zocum; *Far.* Cocum; *Mus.* Conchum; *Hak.* has omitted the term; as also *Boll.*, *Marc.* Zochi.

Indiam Superiorem nos venimus ad quamdam civitatem Zaiton[1], in qua sunt duo loca nostrorum fratrum, ut ibi istas reliquias sanctas poneremus. Nunc autem in ista navi erant bene septingenti[2], inter alios homines et mercatores[3]. Nunc ydolatræ isti hanc consuetudinem in se habent. Nam antequam ipsi applicent ad portum, per totam inquirunt navim ut videant quid esset in ea, maxime si sibi essent ossa mortuorum, quæ si reperirent[4], illa in mare projicerent ipsi statim, et habentibus illa mortis periculum maximum immineret[5]. Cum autem sic requirerent, sed[6] in magna fuerint quantitate, nunquam tum illa invenire in aliquo potuerunt[7]. Sic autem dante Deo illa ad locum nostrorum fratrum tulimus diligenter, ubi cum honore et reverentia maxima fuerunt posita condecenter[8]. Et sic multa alia operatur omnipotens Deus per istos sanctos fratres, cum adhuc hoc habeatur apud ydolatras et Sarracenos. Nam cum ipsi morbo aliquo detinentur, vadunt et accipiunt de terra illa in qua fuerunt imperfecti[9], illam abluentes. Quæ cum sit ipsa lota, eam bibunt, statimque ab infirmitatibus suis totaliter liberantur[10].

16. *Quomodo habeatur Piper; De regno Minibar.*

Ut autem sciamus quomodo habeatur piper, sciendum est quod in imperio[11] quodam ad quod applicui nomine Mimbar[12] nascitur ipsum piper; et non in aliqua parte mundi nascitur nisi ibi[13]. Nemus enim in quo nascitur ipsum piper continet bene in

[1] *Ven.* Caytam; *Ut.* Zaytum; *Far.* Caitam; *Mus.* Caychan; *Hak.* Carchan; *Boll.* Sandon; *Ram.* Zailo.

[2] *Mus. absurdly has* in illa autem navicula erant bene LXX Christiani.

[3] *Ven.* inter nautas et mercatores.

[4] *Ven.* quod si mortuorum ossa reperta essent, statim, etc.

[5] *Ven. has* dicentes habentibus...imminere. *Hak.* Et per hoc bonum portum attingere et mortis periculum evadere crederent.

[6] *Ven. has* licet.

[7] *Mus. embellishes,* licet...illa frequenter tangerent, semper tamen eorum oculi sic miraculose delusi fuerunt, quod illa minime perpenderunt; *Hak. has nearly the same; Boll.* Domino Deo qui absconderat animas eorum in abscondito faciei suæ, ossa eorum ab infidelibus occultante.

[8] *Hak.* Ubi in pace requiescunt.

[9] *For* interfecti.

[10] *Boll.* præstante Domino nostro Jesu Christo.

[11] *Far. has absurdly* in pipere.

[12] *Ven.* Minibar; *Hak.* Do; *Far.* Minibarum; *Mus.* Mimbar; *Boll.* Ezaminibar; *Ram.* Muubar.

[13] *Ven.* Nusquam alibi; *Hak.* in nulla parte mundi tantum quantum ibi; *Far.* non...nisi ibi.

se xviii dietas. Et in ipso nemore sunt duæ civitates, una nomine Flandrina[1], altera vero Zinglin[2]. In ista Flandrina habitancium aliqui sunt Judæi, aliqui vero Christiani. Inter has duas civitates[3] bellum intestinum semper habetur, ita tamen quod Christiani semper superant et vincunt Judæos. In hac contrata habetur piper per hunc modum. Nam primo nascitur in foliis quasi heleræe[4], quæ folia juxta magnas arbores plantantur sicut hic nostræ ponuntur vites; hæc folia producunt fructum ut uvarum racemi producuntur. In tanta autem producunt quantitate quod quasi videntur frangi. Cum autem ipsum erit maturum viridis est coloris. Et sic vindemiatur ut hic vindemiantur uvæ, ponendo[5] illud in solem ut desiccetur, quod cum desiccatum est ipsum in vasis collocatur[6]. In hoc etiam nemore sunt flumina in quibus sunt multæ malæ cocoldrigæ[7] (scilicet multi mali serpentes)[8]. A capite nemoris istius versus meridiem civitas quædam habetur nomine Polumbum[9] in qua nascitur melius zinziber quod nascatur in mundo. Tot et tanta sunt mercimonia in ista civitate quod multis incredible videtur.

17. *De moribus Indorum de Polumbo.*

Omnes in hac contrata adorant bovem pro deo suo, ipsum dicentes esse quasi sanctum, quem sex annis faciunt laborare et in septimo positus est in communi[10]. Hunc autem ritum in se continent et observant, qui est abhominabile[11]. Nam quolibet mane accipiunt duo bacilia de auro vel argento, quæ, quum dimittunt bovem ipsum de stabulo, ponunt sub illo. In uno quorum accipiunt urinam in altero vero immundiciam aliam[12].

[1] *Ram.* Alandrina.

[2] *Hak.* Cyncilim; *Far.* Flandriam...Canglin; *Mus.* Zingelyn; *Marc.* Gingilin; *Ram.* Ziniglin.

[3] *Better Hak.* inter quos.

[4] *Ven.* ederæ; *Far.* oleri.

[5] *Mus.* et grana ponuntur ad.

[6] Et sic piper nascitur et custoditur.

[7] *Ven.* flumina habentia...cochodrillos; *Hak. and Far.* crocodili; *Mus.* cocodrilli.

[8] *Mus.* Et sunt etiam in isto nemore multi alii serpentes quos homines per stupam et paleas comburunt, et sic ad colligendum piper secure accedunt. *Hak.* has the like.

[9] *Hak.* et *Mus.* Polumbrum, *and the former says nothing of the ginger.*

[10] *Mus.* ab omni opere ipsum faciunt quiescere in loco solempni et communi ipsum ponentes et dicentes hunc ipsum animal esse sanctum. So *Hak.*

[11] *Ven. simply* talem autem consuetudinem et modum observant.

[12] *Ven.* stercus.

De urina lavant facies suas, de altera vero immunditia ponunt primo in medio visus in uno loco; deinde super ambabus summitatibus genarum, et postea in medio pectore; ita quod in quatuor locis ipsi ponunt; quæ cum sic fecerunt dicunt se fore sanctificatos[1]. Et sicut facit populus sic et rex et regina. Hii similiter aliud ydolum adorant quod est per dimidium homo et per dimidium bos: hoc ydolum per os respondet quod multotiens sanguinem xl[2] virginum petit et requirit huic ydolo; ita homines et mulieres vovent suos filios[3] et suas [filias] ante ydolum istud, ut sibi eorum sanguis ymmolatur[4]. Unde multi moriuntur isto modo. Sic autem multa alia facit populus iste[5] quæ scribere et audire abhominatio esset quædam. In hac etiam insula multa alia habentur et nascuntur quæ non expedit scribere multum. Aliam autem consuetudinem pessimam habent ydolatræ hujus regni. Nam quando homo aliquis moritur, ipsum comburunt mortuum, et si uxorem habet ipsam comburunt vivam, cum dicant eam ire ad manendum[6] cum marito suo in alio mundo. Si autem mulier filios habet ex marito suo, cum eis manere potest[7] si vult. Si autem mulier moriatur, lex aliqua non inponitur viro, cum possit si vult aliam accipere in uxorem. Alia autem consuetudo illic habetur, nam mulieres vinum bibunt, homines vero non; mulieres etiam faciunt sibi radi visum et barbam, homines vero non[8]; et sic de multis aliis mirabilibus et bestialibus que illic fiunt quæ etiam scribere non expedit multum.

[1] *Hak.* pro tota die illa.

[2] *Far.* has iiiior virgines; *Hak.* aliquotiens pro stipendio petit sanguinem xl, etc.

[3] *Par.* 2. Et filias dare sicut hic alicui religioni, et sic per istum modum homines interficiunt filios suos et filias; *Ven.* to the same effect; also *Far.*, *Hak.*, et *Mus.* sicut Christiani aliqui alicui religioni vel sancto in cœlo. So also *Ram.*

[4] *Ram.* secondo che il profeta dice.

[5] *Hak.* bestialis. Immo, etc.

[6] *Hak.* in aratura et cultura cum viro suo in alio mundo.

[7] *Ven.* nec ei ad verecundiam imputatur; *Mus.* sine verecundia et improprio; *Hak.* improperio. Communiter tamen omnes præeligunt comburi cum marito.

[8] *Mus.* faciunt sibi radi cilia supercilia et barbam, et homines non, et sic est de aliis multis vilitatibus utriusque sexus. In *Hak.* *it is* cilia et supercilia et barbam *also*...et sic de multis aliis vilibus contra naturam sexus eorum.

18. *De regno Mobar ubi est corpus B. Thomæ Apostoli, et de conditionibus ydololatrarum.*

Ab hoc regno sunt decem dietæ usque ad unum aliud regnum, nomine Mobar[1], quod est multum magnum regnum, habens sub se multas civitates et terras. In hoc autem regno positum est corpus beati Thomæ apostoli, ecclesia cujus plena est ydolis multis. Penes etiam quam sunt forte xv domus Nestorinorum et Christianorum qui nequissimi et pessimi sunt heretici[2]. Similiter in regno isto est ydolum mirabile valde quod omnes contratæ Indiæ multum reverentur. Nam ipsum est magnum quantus sanctus Christoforus communiter depingitur a pictoribus, et est totum de auro[3], positum super unam magnam cathedram, quæ etiam est de auro. Et habent ad collum unam cordam de lapidibus[4] preciosis. Quæ autem corda precium multum et maximum valet[5]. Ejus ecclesia tota est de auro puro. Nam tectum totum est de auro; similiter et pavimentum[6]. Ad hoc ydolum orandum occurrunt gentes de longinquo sic christiani de longe vadunt[7] ad Sanctum Petrum. Ipsorum autem ad ydolum venientium alii cum corda ad collum pergunt[8]; alii cum manibus super unam tabulam ad collum ligatam; alii cum cultello in brachio[9] fixo et non removent usque quo pervenerunt ad ydolum, ita quod totum brachium postea habent marcidum[10]. Alii etiam sunt aliter facientes. Nam exeuntes domum suam faciunt tres passus; in quarto autem faciunt unam[11] veniam ita longam super terram sicut unus illorum esset. Accipiunt insuper unum thuribulum cum incenso etiam

[1] *Far. has* Bobarum; *Ram.* Mebor.

[2] *Hak.* et in circuitu ecclesiæ simul Canonici vivunt in 15 domibus Nestoriani, i.e., mali Christiani et Schismatici. *From Mus.* simul *should be* sicut; also...Christiani pessimi cismatici et nequissimi heretici. *Far. has* xvi domus.

[3] *Hak.* et *Mus.* purissimo et splendidissimo.

[4] *Hak.* et *Mus.* Chordulam sericam cum lapidibus.

[5] *Hak.* cum lapidibus pretiosissimis quorum aliquis valet plusquam unum regnum.

[6] *Hak.* et *Mus.* et superficies parietum interius et exterius.

[7] *Ven.* peregre: *Far. has* vadunt Romam; *Mus.* sicut ad Stum. Jacobum aut Stum. Petrum.

[8] Alii cum manibus retro ligatis.

[9] Vel tibia.

[10] *Ven. has* corruptum; *Hak.* et *Mus. add* Illum reputant sanctum et bene cum deo suo.

[11] *Ven.* unam unciam veniam, *which I do not understand*; *Mus. has* unam venam sive lineam, *a mistaken gloss; Marc.* una invenia; *Ram.* una cava.

igne adolentes desuper illam longitudinem veniæ[1] ipsius. Sic enim faciendo usque ad ydolum ipsi vadunt unde bene magno tempore aliquando differunt ire ad ydolum ipsum cum sic ut dictum est semper faciendo vadunt. Cum autem sic vadunt, volentes aliquid facere signum unum[2] faciunt illic ubi faciunt hoc, ut sciant quantum processerunt. Hoc autem sic ipsi continuant donec ad ipsum ydolum devenerunt[3].

19. *De aliis consuetudinibus ydololatrarum.*

Apud autem ecclesiam ydoli hujus est unus lacus manu factus[4] ad quem accedentes peregrini[5] projiciunt in ipsum aurum vel argentum vel aliquos lapides preciosos. Et hoc faciunt ipsi in honorem ydoli hujus et ecclesie edificationem, unde multum aurum et argentum lapidesque preciosi habentur in isto lacu. Ideoque cum in ecclesia ejus aliquid facere fieri volunt[6], inquirunt per lacum istum et inveniunt omnia hæc que in ipso sunt projecta. Die autem[7] illo quo hoc ydolum sanctum[8] fuit, accedunt[9] illi de contrata accipientes ipsum de ecclesia, et illud ponentes super uno pulchro[10] curru. Deinde rex et regina omnesque peregrini ad hoc cum populo toto, hii omnes similiter congregati ipsum educunt de ecclesia cum cantibus magnis et omni genere musicorum. Hoc autem ydolum cum sit eductus de ecclesia ejus, multæ virgines binæ et [binæ] ipsum[11] antecedunt euntes canendo mirabiliter ante ipsum[12]. Deinde accedunt etiam peregrini qui evenerunt ad hoc festum, et ponunt se sub isto curru, facientes eum super se transire cum dicunt se velle mori pro Deo suo. Et sic currus

[1] *Ut. has* unciæ (?); *Far. instead of* veniæ ipsius *has* nomine albius *which seems nonsense*—perhaps misread by my copyist; *Mus.* lineæ sive venæ ipsius.

[2] *Far. has* signum unum abbie, *probably a misreading for* illic.

[3] *The whole of this passage about the* veniæ *is omitted in Hak. though retained in Mus., and this is, I think, the first material difference between these MSS.*

[4] *Hak.* et manifestus.

[5] *Mus.* in honorem ydoli et ad edificationem templi.

[6] *Hak.* quando aliquid debet ornari vel reparari.

[7] *Ven.* Annuatim autem die illo, etc.

[8] *Ven.* factum; *Hak.* et *Mus.* die autem annuo constructionis.

[9] *Mus.* Rex et regina illius terræ cum toto populo et omnibus peregrinis accedunt.

[10] *Hak.* pretiosissimo.

[11] *Ven. instead of* binæ et *has* hinc et hinc; *Far.* binæ et binæ; also *Hak.* et *Mus.*

[12] *Hak.* processionaliter combinate modulantes; *Mus.* nearly the same.

transiens super illos qui sunt sub eo, cunctos illos frangit per medium et scindit, unde statim moriuntur[1]. Sic autem façiendo ydolum ipsum ducunt usque ad unum locum deputatum, ad quem locum cum ipsum adduxerunt illum ad locum pristinum reducunt cum cantibus magnis et instrumentis sicut prius. Et sic non est annus in mundo in quo plures quingentis hominibus non moriantur isto modo. Horum autem corpora ipsi accipiunt et comburunt[2], dicentes ea esse sancta cum se mori promiserint pro deo suo[3]. Aliud quoque fit ab istis, nam venit aliquis dicens, Volo me interficere pro deo meo, unde veniunt amici parentes et omnes hystriones de contrata ad faciendum illi festum, qui voluit pro deo suo mori. Unde appendunt ad collum ejus quinque cultellos acutissimos et ipsum[4] ducunt ante ydolum, tunc ille accipit unum ex cultellis illis acutissimis, et alta voce clamat dicens, Pro deo meo michi incido de carne mea. Cum autem inciderit de carne sua, de loco illo in quo voluit, eam projicit in faciem ydoli dicens; Me mori permitto[5] pro deo meo; et sic ibi tandem se interficit pro deo suo. Statimque ipso mortuo corpus ejus comburitur cum illud credatur ab illis esse sanctum quia pro deo suo se ipsum peremit. Sic autem multa alia magna et mirabilia fiunt ab istis quæ minime sunt scribenda. Rex autem insulæ vel provinciæ[6] hujus multum est dives, videlicet auri argenti lapidum preciosorum. In hac autem insula tot bonæ perlæ inveniuntur sicut in aliqua parte mundi, et sic de multis aliis quæ in ista insula reperiuntur. Quæ etiam nimis longum esset scribere.

20. *De Contrata Lamori quæ non videt tramontanam, et de Sumoltra.*

De hac contrata recedens et iens versus meridiem veni per mare oceanum quinquaginta dietis[7] ad unam contratam que vocatur Lamori[8], in qua incepi amittere tramontanam cum terra michi acceperit eam. In ea autem ita inmensus est calor quod omnes illi [tam] homines quam mulieres vadunt nudi[9], nullo se

[1] *Hak.* et per hoc reputant se mori pro deo suo sancte et secure.

[2] *Hak.* et cineres sicut reliquiæ custodiuntur.

[3] *This about the burning, etc., omitted in Mus.*

[4] *Ven.* cum magnis cantibus.

[5] *Ven.* dicens mori promitto.

[6] *Mus.* illius regionis.

[7] *Far.* has xv dietis.

[8] *Hak.* Lammori; *Mus. has* vocatam Sustabor (?) sive Lamory.

[9] *Far. has only* mulieres...nudæ.

cooperientes. Hii de me multum truffabantur[1], qui dicebant Deum Adam fecisse nudum, et ego me malo suo velle vestire volebam[2]. Nam in ista contrata omnes mulieres sunt positæ in communi. Itaque nemo est qui dicere posset veraciter hæc est uxor mea, hic est maritus meus. Cum autem mulier filium vel filiam parit, ipsum vel ipsam dat uni illorum cui vult, cum quibus ipsa jam jacuit eumque vocat patrem suum. Tota terra posita est in communi, itaque nullus cum veritate dicere potest hæc vel illa pars terræ mea est. Domos tamen habent in speciali[3]. Ista gens pestifera est et nequam; ista gens comedit homines sicut nos boves, nam carnem humanam ita comedunt illic sicut hic carnes manzinæ[4] comeduntur, hæc tamen de se bona terra est. Nam magnam copiam carnium bladi et risi [habent], magnaque copia habetur illic de auro[5], de lignis aloe, [de] ganfara[6], de multisque aliis quæ ibi nascuntur[7]. Ad hanc insulam accedunt mercatores de longinquo portantes secum homines[8] vendentesque illos[9] infidelibus ipsis, quos cum emerent eos interficiunt[10] et comedunt, et sic de multis aliis et bonis et malis quæ non scribuntur. In hac eadem insula versus meridiem habetur aliud regnum nomine Sumolchra[11] in quo est una generatio gentis singularis signantis se ferro calido parvo bene in duodecim locis in facie. Et hoc faciunt tam homines quam mulieres. Hii semper gerunt bellum cum hiis qui vadunt nudi. In hac contrata est magna copia rerum. Penes quam est unum aliud regnum nomine Rotemgo[12] versus meridiem. Multa quæ non scribo nascuntur in illo regno.

1 *Ven.* et tu vis ultra ejus velle vestiri.

2 *Hak.* and *Mus.* qui videntes me vestitum deridebant me, dicentes Deum Adam et Evam fecisse nudos; *Boll.* Deus Adam nudum fecit, cur tu vestitus ambulas contra naturam? *Malo suo velle*=Malgré lui.

3 *Ven.* Domos tamen proprias habent; *Hak.* and *Mus.* speciales.

4 *Far.* Porcinæ.

5 *Boll.* amaraco *instead of the preceding words.*

6 *Mus.* Ganfar.

7 Here *Mus. inserts* Tamen gens pestifera est, etc., omitted before.

8 *Ven.* infantes; *Hak.* homines pingues.

9 *Ven.* more bestiarum; *Hak.* and *Mus.* sicut nos vendimus porcos.

10 *Ven.* in macello; *Boll.* has this much shorter.

11 *Ven.* and *Ram.* Sumoltra; *Far.* Simultam *or* Simultra; *Hak.* Sumolcra; *Mus.* Simoltra sive Sumolara; *Boll.* Zumptloc (probably misread); *Marc.* Sumoltra.

12 *Ven.* Bothonigo; *Far.* Betonigo; *Mus.* Boteingo et juxta illud aliud regnum de quo nihil scribo nec de hiis quæ ibi nascuntur; *Boll.* Resengo; *Ram.* Botterigo; *Hak.* omits this kingdom of Rotemgo, etc., altogether; *Marc.* Botemgo.

21. *De optima insula Jauâ.*

Penes[1] hoc regnum est una magna insula nomine Jaua[2], quæ bene tribus millibus miliarium[3] circumdatur. Rex hujus Jauæ habet bene sub se septem reges coronæ. Hæc insula multum bene habitatur. Et est melior insula que habeatur[4]. In ipsa enim nascuntur[5] cubebæ, melegetæ[6], nucesque muscatæ, multæque aliæ species pretiosæ. In eâ est copia magna victualium preterquam vini. Rex istius insulæ unum habet palatium valde mirabile[7]. Nam ipsum est valde magnum[8], cujus scalæ multum sunt magnæ altæ latæque: horum graduum unus est aureus alter vero argenteus. Pavimentum autem ejus unum laterem habet de auro, alterum vero de argento. Murus vero istius palatii totus est lamatus interius lamis aureis[9], in quibus lamis sculpti sunt equites solum de auro habentes circa caput unum magnum circulum aureum sicut hic habent nostri sancti; hic autem circulus totus est plenus lapidibus preciosis. Insuper tectum ejus totum est de auro puro; ut autem breviter et finaliter nos loquamur, hoc palatium ditius et pulchrius est quod hodie sit in mundo. Canis[10] tamen grandis Cathaii multociens fuit in bello in campo cum isto, quem iste semper vicit et superavit. Sic etiam multa alia sunt quæ non scribo.

22. *De contratâ Talamasin et arboribus ejus farinam dantibus, etc.*

Penes hanc contratam est una alia contrata quæ vocatur Patem[11] quam alii vocant Talamasim[12]. Rex hujus contratæ

[1] *Ven.* Juxta.

[2] *Ven.* Java; *Hak.* and *Boll.* Jaua; *Far.* and *Mus.* have Jana; *Marc.* Java.

[3] *Ven.* Secunda melior insularum; *Far.* tertia melior; *Hak.* melior secunda; *Mus.* secunda melior...ut dicitur; *Bol.* est de melioribus Indiæ una.

[4] *Far.* tribus milliariis; *Hak.* cujus ambitus per mare bene trium millium, etc.

[5] *Ven. has* also camphora; *Far.* ganfora; *Hak. has* garyophylli, cubibæ et nuces muscatæ.

[6] *Mus.* et breviter omnes fere preciosæ species ibi sunt.

[7] *Boll.* quod multis impossibile videretur.

[8] *Hak.* and *Mus.* et altissime stat.

[9] *Hak.* parietes...laminati laminis aureis; *Boll.* muri quoque ejus intrinsecus laminis aureis sunt vestiti.

[10] *Ven.* Chaam; *Hak.* Canis de Katay.

[11] *Ven.* and *Hak.* Panten; *Far.* Panthen; *Ut.* Paten; *Boll.* Pacen; *Marc.* Paten; *Ram.* Paten.

[12] *Ven.* Malamasin; *Far.* Thamalsi; *Ut.* Malamasmi; *Hak.* Tathala masim; *Boll.* Thalamasym; *Mus.* Thalamasin; *Marc.* Talamaxim; *Ram.* Malamasmi.

multas insulas habet sub se. In hac contrata inveniuntur arbores farinam producentes; aliquæ etiam quæ mel producunt[1] aliquodque venenum, quod est periculosius venenum quod sit in mundo. Nam circa ipsum non invenitur aliquod remedium nisi unum. Nam si aliquis de illo veneno sumpsisset accipiat de stercore hominis et ipsum distemperet aqua, quem et[2] bibat, propter quod ab illo veneno totaliter liberabitur[3]. Arbores autem isto modo farinam producunt. Nam ipsæ sunt magnæ, non tamen multum altæ[4], etiam eas una securi incidunt circa pedem[5], propter quod quidam liquor ab ipsis exhauritur ad modum collæ[6] quem liquorem ipsi ponunt in saccis factis ex foliis, quos dimittunt per xv dies in sole et in fine xv dierum ex ipso liquore farina facta est, quam postea ponunt per duos in aqua maris; deinde lavant eam aqua dulci et sic faciunt pastam bonam[7] de mundo. Et tunc de ipsa faciunt quid volunt, seu cibos seu panem multum bonum, de quo ego frater Odoricus[8] jam comedi; hæc autem omnia propriis oculis ego vidi. Hujus modi autem panis exterius pulcher est, interius autem[9] niger est. In ripa[10] hujus contratæ versus meridiem est mare mortuum, aqua cujus semper currit versus meridiem. Et si aliquis per juxta ipsius ripam vadit, et cadit in aquam, nunquam ille qui talis invenitur. In hac etiam contrata sunt canaveriæ[11] seu arundines longæ bene pluribus lx passibus, magnæ ut arbores. Aliæ etiam cannæ reperiuntur que vocantur Casan[12]. Hæc per terram semper diriguntur ut quædam herba quæ apud nos appellatur gramegna. Et in quolibet nodo ipsarum radices producunt quæ[13] bene efficiuntur longæ uno miliari. In

[1] *Ven.* Sunt etiam producentes mel, et aliquæ producentes vinum, etc.

[2] *Hak.* in bona quantitate.

[3] *Hak.* statim fugat venenum faciens exire per inferiores partes; *Mus. to same effect, adding* et sic erit salvatus et a veneno totaliter liberatus.

[4] *Far. has a large hiatus from* quem et bibat *to this.*

[5] *Hak.* magnæ et bassæ: *Mus.* magnæ et multum altæ.

[6] *Hak.* sicut gummæ; *Mus.* sicut gumma collæ.

[7] *Hak.* et *Mus.* et odorifera(m).

[8] *Boll.* non solum pro necessitate sed etiam pro delectatione pluries manducavi.

[9] *Ven., Far., Hak., Mus., Boll.* aliquantulum niger.

[10] *Far.* riveriâ.

[11] *Ven.* Cannæ variæ (*no* seu arundines). *Far. has* Canaveriæ.

[12] *Far.* Cassam; *Mus.* Cassati, *with the absurd addition* ex quibus in apotecariis inveniuntur cassia fistulæ. *Ram. has* casar.

[13] *Ven. has* et *instead of* quæ, *which is better. Far.* ramos producunt qui bene, etc. *Hak.* et *Mus. nearly to the same effect*—per unum miliare fere.

hiis autem cannis inveniuntur lapides de quibus aliquis super se hiis nunquam potest incidi a ferro aliquo nec offendi. Et ut plurimum homines istius contratæ de istis lapidibus sunt super se portantes. Ideoque propter virtutem horum lapidum veniunt homines et accipiunt puerulos suos quos in brachio per quod modicum ipsi incidunt, ubi unum de istis lapidibus isti ponunt ne ipse ferro aliquo cadat. Et ut illum parvum vulnus factum in brachio alicujus pueri cito solidetur, de quodam pulvere unius piscis ipsi[1] ponunt, propter quod vulnus illud parvum statim solidatur. Et quia hujus lapidis magnæ sunt virtutes et de istis illi homines sunt portantes[2], ex hoc in bello efficiuntur fortes[3] et magni cursores[4] in mari. Verum quia navigantes permare ab istis talibus offenduntur unum remedium invenerunt. Nam ipsi portant propugnacula seu palos acutissimos de uno fortissimo ligno, portant[que] sagittas cum[5] ferro[6]. Et quia homines illi male sunt armati, per mare navigantes eos vulnerant et penetrant istis pilis acutissimis et sagittis. Sic isto modo[7] isti tales ab illis se viriliter defendunt. De cannis istis Casan faciunt vela suis navibus, sestoria[8], domunculas[9], multaque alia quæ sibi sunt utilitatis magnæ. Multa etiam alia sunt in contrata ista quæ scribere et audire quasi stupor esset. Quapropter ea scribere ad presens non multum curo[10].

23. *De rege Campa, habente multos elephantes et multos filios filiasque.*

Ab isto regno per multas dietas est distans aliud regnum nomine Campa[11], cujus contrata multum pulchra est. Nam in ipsa est copia magna omnium victualium, et bonorum. Rex

[1] *Hak.* et *Mus.* cujus nomen ignoro.

[2] *Ven.* omits this superfluous sentence.

[3] *Ven.* feroces. *Hak.* et *Mus.* communiter triumphant in bellis et in mari, nec possunt isti homines lædi per aliqua arma ferrea.

[4] *Ven.* maximi pirati.

[5] *Ven.* absque, *which is required.*

[6] *Far.* sine ferro.

[7] *Hak. has* Quod adversarii illius gentis scientes virtutem lapidum provident sibi propugnacula ferrea contra spicula illorum, et arma venenata de veneno, et in manu portant palos ligneos, etc...et sic confundunt aliquos et perforant inermes ex lapidum securitate. *Mus. is to the same effect and more diffusely expressed.*

[8] *Far. omits* sestoria.

[9] *Ven.* tali ergo ingenio.

[10] *Mar.* Case di stuoie.

[11] *This was probably written* Çampa; *Ven.* Zampa; *Far.* Canpa or Carpa; *Hak.* Campa; *Marc.* Campa.

contratæ illius ut dicebatur quando ibi fui inter filios et filias ducentos[1] bene habebat; cum multas habeat uxores aliasque mulieres quas ipse tenet[2]. Hic rex xiiii milia[3] elephantum domesticorum habet. Quos ita teneri facit et observari, ab illis hominibus de villis suis[4] qui sibi sunt subjecti sicut hic boves. Aliaque multa animalia tenentur ad socedam. In ista eadem contrata unum mirabile quid reperitur. Nam unaquæque generatio piscium qui sunt in mari, ad hanc contratam in tanta venit quantitate quod dum sic veniunt nichil aliud videtur in mari nisi pisces[5]. Hii autem cum prope ripam sint se projiciunt super illam[6]. Cum sic autem sunt in ripa veniunt homines et tot de ipsis habent et accipiunt et quod ipsi volunt. Hii autem pisces duobus vel tribus diebus manent super ripam. Deinde venit alia generatio piscis faciens hoc idem sicut prima. Sic etiam de aliis singulisque usque ad ultimam ordinate procedunt, quod tantum semel faciunt in anno. Cum de isto quæritur ab illis de ista contrata quare sic fiat, ipsi respondent et dicunt: Quod hoc faciunt isti pisces qui isto modo veniunt suum imperatorem revereri. In eadem etiam contrata vidi unam testitudinem majorem quam esset revolutio trulli ecclesiæ sancti Antonii de Padua[7]. Sic etiam de multis aliis quæ forte aliquibus incredibilia viderentur nisi illa viderent, quare ea scribere non curo. Cum etiam in contrata aliquis moritur habens uxorem, ipse mortuus comburitur, uxor ejus [vero] viva[8]. Nam dicunt quod ipsa cum suo marito vadit ad alium mundum ut illic moretur cum eo[9].

24. *De Insula ubi Cynocephali.*

De ista contrata recedens et navigans per mare Occeanum versus meridiem reperi multas insulas et contratas. Quarum una

[1] *Hak.* 300.

[2] *Bol. has in this place* nec mirabar de hoc cum plures habuerit uxores.

[3] *Hak.* decies millesies et quatuor; *Mus.* xiii millia.

[4] *Bol.* qui nutriuntur a villanis sibi subjectis sicut apud nos boves et alia animalia conservantur.

[5] *Hak.* et *Mus.* per magnum spatium maris nihil videtur nisi dorsa piscium.

[6] *Hak.* et *Mus.* super aridam.

[7] *Hak.* et *Mus.* Ibi etiam sunt testudines ita magni sicut est unus furnus.

[8] *Hak.* et *Mus.* sicut superius de alia contrata dictum est.

[9] *Ven.* ut in alio mundo similiter conversetur cum eo; *Hak.* et *Mus. add* ne ibi aliam uxorem accipiat.

est quæ vocatur Sacimeram[1]. Hæc insula magna est, circuiens bene per duo milia miliarium; in qua homines et mulieres facies caninas habent. Hii unum bovem adorant pro deo suo, propter quod unusquisque unum bovem de auro vel argento semper portat in fronte, in signum quod ille bos est deus eorum. Omnes istius contratæ tam homines quam mulieres nudi vadunt, nihil de mundo portantes nisi unam toaleam[2] qua suam verecundiam ipsi tegunt. Hii sunt magni corpore et valde fortes in bello, ad quod dum sic nudi pergunt solum unum scutum[3] portant quod eos cooperit à capite usque ad pedes. Dum sic autem vadunt ad bellum et eos contingat capere aliquem in bello qui pecunia exigi[4] non possit, statim comedunt ipsum. Si vero pecunia exigi possit eum habita pecunia abire permittunt. Rex istius contratæ bene tres centas[5] perlas portat ad collum multum magnas, propter[6] quod pro diis suis quotidie trecentas orationes ipse facit. Habet etiam unum lapidem preciosum bene[7] longum et magnum unâ spensâ, in manu sua[8] portat, quem lapidem sic portans una flamma ignis ipse videtur esse[9]. Et ut dicitur iste est nobilior et preciosior lapis qui hodie sit in mundo. Verumptamen magnus imperator Tartarorum Cathaii illum lapidem preciosum nec vi, nec pecunia nec etiam ingenio unquam habere potuit. In hac etiam contratâ ipse rex bene justitiam tenet et observat, unde per totum suum regnum quilibet potest ire securus[10]. Multa etiam in hac contrata sunt quæ etiam ego scribere non curo.

25. *De Insula Sillan et ejus mirabilibus.*

Alia est insula Sillan[11], circuiens bene plura quam duo milia miliarium in qua sunt serpentes infiniti, multaque alia animalia

[1] *Ven.* Nicuueran; *Far.* Nichovera; *Hak.* Moumoran; *Mus.* Mochimoran; *Bol.* Insimezan, *probably misread; Marc.* Nicuveran.

[2] *Hak.* et *Mus.* unum pannum lineum.

[3] *Hak. has* unum scutum de ferro; *Mus. to same effect.*

[4] *Ven.* redimi.

[5] *Mus.* cc.

[6] *Ven.* propterea.

[7] *Ven. instead of* bene *has* rubinum; *Far. as in text.*

[8] *Hak.* in digito suo; *Boll.* ita magnam quam sicut unâ manu gestare possem.

[9] *Ven. instead of* quem......esse, *has* qui recte flamma ignis esse videtur; *Hak.* dum habet illum videtur ab aliis quasi una flamma ignis et ideo nullus audet sibi appropinquare; *Mus. nearly the same.*

[10] *Hak. omits this sentence about the king's justice, etc.*

[11] *Ven.* Sillam; *Far.* Silam; *Hak.* Ceilan (the MS. in B. M. has Sylan, almost the only difference from Hakluyt's printed copy); *Mus. has* Salam.

silvestria in magna quantitate[1] ut potissime elephantes. In hac contrata est unus maximus mons de quo dicunt gentes quod super illo Adam planxit filium suum centum[2] annis. In medio montis hujus[3] est quædam pulcherrima planicies in qua est unus lacus non multum magnus[4]. Sed tamen est bene in eo aqua magna quam dicunt gentes esse lacrimas quas Adam et Eva effuderunt, quod tamen non creditur esse verum[5], cum tamen intus nascatur aqua illa. Profunditas[6] hujus aquæ plena est lapidibus preciosis. Quæ aqua multum est yrundinibus[7] et sanguisugis plena. Hos lapides non accipit ille rex, sed pro anima sua semel vel bis in anno sub aquas ipsos pauperes ire permittit, et quotquot ex lapidibus istis capere possunt omnes dimittit eis[8]. Et ut ipsi pauperes ire sub aquam possint accipiunt limonem et quemdam fructum quem bene pistant[9], et illo bene se ungunt et tunc in aquam se mergunt. Et cum sic sint uncti yrundines[10] et sanguisugæ illos offendere non valent. Sic isto modo pauperes subintrant aquam, et exeunt accipientes si possunt de lapidibus istis preciosis. Aqua quæ descendit per montem exit ab isto lacu. Et[11] ibi fodiuntur boni robini et boni dyamantes reperiuntur et multi, sic et multi lapides alii boni; ibi etiam reperiuntur bonæ perlæ, quo aqua ista descendit ad mare. Unde dicitur quod rex iste habet plures lapides preciosos quam aliquis alius rex qui hodie sit in mundo. In hac insulâ sunt diversa genera animalium sicut avium et multorum animalium quæ morantur ibi. Unde dicunt illi de contrata quod hæc animalia multum forensem lædunt non illos qui ibi sunt nati[12].

[1] *Hak.* et *Mus.* et max. multit. leonum ursorum et omnium animalium rapacium.

[2] *Hak.* 500 annis; *Mus. as in text.*

[3] *Ven.* In montis cujus cacumine.

[4] *Far. has omitted the* non; *Hak.* et *Mus. have* parvus.

[5] *Hak.* et *Mus.* sed probavi hoc falsum esse quia vidi aquam in lacu scaturire; *Boll.* gentes errore delusæ......cum tamen videatur ipsa aqua e visceribus terræ scaturire.

[6] *Ven.* Fundus; *Far. as in text.*

[7] Yrundinibus *for* hirundinibus.

[8] *Hak.* et *Mus.* ut orent pro anima sua, *omitting these last three words above.*

[9] *Ven.* limonibus optime frictis optime corpus totum linunt; *Ut.* accipiunt bavoyrem, id est quemdam fructum quem bene pistant; *Far.* acc. limones quos bene pistant.

[10] as above.

[11] *Mus.* et in transitu quando retrahit se fodiuntur, etc.

[12] *Ven. better* nullum forensem lædunt, et solummodo illos qui nati sunt in ipsa; *Far.* to the same effect, also *Hak.*

In hac insula etiam sunt aves multum magnæ sicut sunt anseres, qui duo capita in se habent[1]. Hæc etiam insula maximam copiam habet victualium et multorum aliorum bonorum quæ non scribo.

26. *De Insula Dondin et ejus consuetudinibus turpissimis.*

De ista insula recedens et pergens versus meridiem ad quamdam magnam insulam me applicui quæ vocatur Dondin[2], quæ idem est quod immundum[3]. In insula ista mali homines commorantur. Nam ipsi carnes aridas[4] comedunt omnemque aliam immundiciam quæ jam dici posset[5]. Turpem inter se consuetudinem habent. Nam pater comedit filium et filius comedit patrem, uxor maritum et maritus uxorem; et hoc per istum modum. Ponatur quod pater alicujus illorum infirmetur; filius tunc ipse ibit ad astrologum et ad[6] sacerdotem cui sic dicet: Domine, ite vos ad sciendum a Deo nostro, si pater meus possit ab ista infirmitate liberari vel ex ipsâ mori debet. Tunc ipse sacerdos et alius homo cujus pater infirmatur accedunt ad ipsum ydolum quod est de auro vel de argento eique faciunt orationem et dicunt: Domine, tu es Deus noster, quem pro Deo nos adoramus, nobis respondeas ad ea quæ tibi nos dicemus. Taliter homo multum infirmatur; ideo te petimus si mori debeat ex hoc languore vel liberari. Tunc demon per os ydoli respondet et dicit: Pater tuus non morietur, sed de ista liberabitur infirmitate; verum tale quid sibi facere debes et sic liberabitur ipse. Ita quod ille demon totum ipsum illum modum [dicit] quem circa patrem suum tenere debet[7]. Deinde filius ad patrem accedit, et sibi diligenter servit donec ipse totaliter liberatur[8]. Si autem demon

[1] *Far. absurdly has* mille capita. *Probably* II *taken for* M.

[2] *Ut.* Dandin; *Hak. alone has* Bodin, *but probably a misprint, as it is* Dodin *in the MS., which I take for Hakluyt's original*; *Mus.* Dodyn; *Boll.* Dodyn; *Marc.* Dondin.

[3] *Mus.* idem est quod mundus.

[4] *For* crudas *as in Ven.*

[5] *Hak.* quæ quasi excogitare non poterit, *to which Mus. adds* sive dici.

[6] *Ven. has* id est.

[7] *Boll.* Tunc dæmon quandoque ex Idolo de convalescentia respondit, jubens procuratione illius in fine aliquas fieri ceremonias et oblationes et docens filium quomodo nutriat patrem.

[8] *Mus.* Usque ad plenam convalescentiam juxta documentum diaboli patri ministrat.

ille dicat ipsum debere mori, sacerdos ad eum accedet et unum pannum[1] super os suum ipse ponet, et sic eum statim suffocabit et morietur. Cum autem sic interfecit eum ipsum incidet in frusta et ad ipsum comedendum invitabuntur amici, parentes, omnesque hystriones[2] de contrata, et ipsum comedent cum cantibus et gaudio magno; ejus tamen ossa accipient, illa ponentes sub terra cum magna sollempnitate. Parentes autem illi qui ad has nuptias non fuerunt sibi ad verecundiam maximam reputabant. Hos tales[3] multum reprehendebam, dicens: Quare sic facitis vos cum hoc quod facitis sit contra omnem rationem. Nam si canis aliquis occideretur et ante alium canem poneretur ipse de illo nullatenus manducaret; nedum vos qui homines videmini rationales. Ad hoc mihi respondebant dicentes, hoc facimus ne vermes comedant ejus carnes. Nam si ejus carnes vermes comederent ipsius anima magnas pateretur pœnas; ideoque carnem ejus comedimus, ut ejus anima aliquas non patiatur pœnas. Et sic eis tantum dicere poteram quantum ego volebam quia nunquam aliud credere ipsi volebant nec ab isto ritu discedere quem tenebant.

27. *De Indiâ et* xxiv *millibus Insularum quas habet.*

Multæ aliæ novitates hic habentur quæ non scribo, nam nisi homo eas videret, eas credere non posset, cum in toto non sint mundo tot et tanta mirabilia quæ sunt in isto regno. Hæc autem scribi feci quæ certus sum, et in nullo dubito quia sicut refero ita est[4]. De[5] hac insula[6] diligenter inquisivi multos qui hoc sciunt et omnes uno ore locuntur et dicunt, quod hæc India bene xxiiii[7] milia insularum continet sub se, in qua etiam sunt bene lxiiii reges coronæ. Major pars hujus insulæ[8] bene ab hominibus habitatur. Hic ipsius Indiæ facio finem et nichil de ea dicere volo aliud, sed solum intendo aliquid dicere de India superiori.

1 *Ven.* pannum linum. 2 *Ut.* jaculatores. 3 Ego frater Odoricus.

4 *Hak.* Ego autem coram Deo nihil hic refero nisi illud de quo certus sum sicut homo certificare poterit.

5 *Ven. has* in *instead of* de.

6 *Far.* De hac India Inferiori (*no doubt* Insula *is wrong*) sunt aliæ hæc insulæ quæ nominavi et inquisivi multos qui hoc sciunt, etc.; *Boll.* De magnitudine hujus inferioris Indiæ a multis, etc.

7 *Hak.* 4400; *Boll.* Viginti quatuor millia.

8 *Mus.* istius Indiæ; *so also Boll. Marc. has* queste isole, *which indicates the right reading.*

28. *Venit Fr. Odoricus ad Indiam Superiorem et Provinciam Manzi.*

Ubi sciendum est quod dum navigarem per mare Occeanum versus Orientem per multas dietas ad illam nobilem provinciam Mansi[1] ego veni quam Indiam vocamus superiorem[2]. De ista India quæsivi diligenter Christianos, Sarracenos, ydolatros, omnes officiales magni Canis[3] qui omnes uno ore loquuntur et dicunt quod provincia Manzi[4] habet bene duo millia magnarum civitatum, quæ in tantum sunt magnæ illæ civitates quod Trevisium[5] neque Vincentia in ipsarum numerum ponerentur; unde tanta multitudo est in ista contrata quod apud nos esset incredibile quoddam[6]. In ipsa est maxima copia panis, vini, risi, carnium, piscium, omniumque victualium, quibus homines utuntur in mundo. Omnes homines hujus provinciæ sunt artifices[7] et mercatores qui paupertatem quam habeant[8] dummodo se suis manibus valeant adjuvare nunquam aliquam peterent elemosinam. Hii homines satis sunt corpore pulchri[9], pallidi tamen, habentes barbam ita raram et longam sicut[10] murilegæ, id est cattæ; mulieres vero pulcherrimæ de mundo[11].

29. *De Civitate Cens-Kalan.*

Prima civitas hujus provinciæ quam inveni vocatur Censcolan[12]; hæc civitas bene ita magna est pro tribus Venetiis[13], distans a mari per unam dietam, posita super unum flumen, cujus aqua propter[14] ipsum mare ascendit ultra terram bene xii dietis.

[1] *Mus.* Mansiæ; *Ven.* et *Far.* Manzi; *Hak.* Manci; *Boll.* Manzy.

[2] *Hak.* quæ India vocatur a Latinis.

[3] *Ven.* Chaam. [4] *Mus.* Mancy. [5] *Far.* Tarvisium.

[6] *Boll.* intra muros ipsarum cujuslibet possent stare.

[7] *Ven.* artistæ.

[8] *Mus.* nullam paupertatem habent; *Boll.* qui numquam depauperantur.

[9] *Hak.* Satis formosi.

[10] *Hak* rasas et parvas barbas habentes; *Mus.* raras et parvas sed tamen longas sicut murilegi.

[11] *Mus.* Pulcherrimæ et formosæ; *Boll.* nimium sunt formosæ.

[12] *Ven.* Conscala; *Ut.* Censcula; *Far.* Censcalam; *Hak.* Censkalon, *also Mus. Boll.* Soustalay (*probably misread*); *Marc.* Censscalan.

[13] *Ven.* quæ est in triplo major Vincencia; *Ut. as in text*: so also *Far.*; and *Mus.*, though in another place.

[14] *Far. has* prope; *Hak.* prope mare cui contiguatur (?); *Mus.* cujus aqua propter mare ita contiguum bene per XII dietas super ipsam terram ascendit. *Boll. as in text.*

Totus populus hujus civitatis totiusque provinciæ Manzi Indiæque superioris ydolatrat[1]. Hæc civitas tantum navigium habet et ita magnum quod quasi aliquibus incredibile videretur, unde tota Ytalia non habet navigium ita magnum sicut hæc civitas sola habet[2]. In hâc civitate haberi possunt bene trecentæ[3] libræ zinziberis recentis minori uno grosso. In hac etiam sunt majores et pulchriores anseres ac melius forum[4] quam hoc sit in mundo, unde unus illorum anserum est bene magnus pro duobus de nostris, totus albus ut lac, habens unum os super caput unius ovi quantitate, qui talis coloris est qualis sanguis est. Et hii anseres habent sub gulâ unam pellem per unum semissem[5] pendentem; hii etiam sunt pinguissimi; unus quorum bene coctus et conditus minor uno grosso haberetur. Et sicut est de anseribus sic etiam de anatibus et gallinis, quæ illic sunt ita magnæ quod magnum mirum est. Hic etiam majores sunt serpentes qui sunt in mundo; hii multum capiuntur ab istis a quibus postea dulciter comeduntur. Unde in tam sollempne ferculum habentur ii serpentes, quod faciens fieri convivium unum[6] de istis non habens serpentibus nil facere diceretur. Hæc etiam civitas magnam habet habundantiam omnium victualium quæ sunt in mundo.

30. *De nobili civitate Zayton et de pastu ydolorum.*

De ista contrata recedens et inde transiens per multas terras et civitates, veni ad quamdam nobilem terram nomine Zayton[7]. In qua nos fratres minores habemus duo loca; ad quæ portavi ossa illorum nostrorum fratrum minorum qui passi fuerunt martirium pro fide Jhesu Christi. In hac civitate est copia omnium illorum quæ sunt necessaria humanæ vitæ[8]. Nam tres libræ et octo ucziæ zuchari minori dimidio grosso[9] habentur ibi. Hæc civitas magna est sicut bis esset[10] Bononia. In hac multa sunt monasteria religiosorum qui ydola universaliter adorant. In

[1] *Ven.* Ydola colit.
[2] This last comparison is omitted by *Hak.*
[3] *Boll.* centum libræ......uno minori grosso Veneto.
[4] *Ven.* in meliori foro; *Hak.* maius forum (*probably misread*).
[5] *Hak.* et *Mus.* semipedalem.
[6] *Mus.* has unum ad minus (*au moins*).
[7] *Far.* Caicham: *Mus.* Kaycon; *Hak.* Kaitam; *Boll.* Saiton; *Marc.* Zaitan.
[8] *Hak.* pro lenissimo foro. [9] *Ut.* minori pretio uno grosso.
[10] *Mus.* ut fideliter assero.

uno autem istorum monasteriorum ego fui in quo bene erant tria milia religiosorum habentium[1] xi millia ydola[2]; et unum illorum ydolorum quod minus aliis esse videbatur erat bene ita magnum esset sicut Sanctus Christophorus. Illâ autem horâ quâ istis diis suis dant ad manducandum ivi ad videndum. Et hii isto modo comedere sibi dant. Omnia quæ illis offerunt comedenda eis calidissima[3] porrigunt, ita quod fumus illorum ascendit ad ydola quem ipsi pro comestione istorum ydolorum esse dicunt, aliud autem totum pro se habent et manducant[4]; et sic isto modo dicunt se bene pascere deos suos[5]. Verumptamen hæc terra de melioribus est quæ hodie sint in mundo: et hoc in iis que posset habere corpus humanum[6]. Multa alia de hac terra dici possent quæ non ulterius modo scribo.

31. *De civitate Fuzo et de mirabilibus modis piscandi.*

De hac contrata veni versus orientem ad unam civitatem quæ vocatur Fucho[7], quæ bene circuit per xxx miliaria, in qua sunt majores galli qui sunt in mundo. Gallinæ vero[8] sunt albæ ut nix, non habentes pennas sed solum lanam ut pecus sunt portantes. Hæc civitas multum pulchra et sita super mare de quâ recedens ivi xviii dietis transiens per multas terras et civitates, aliaque diversa multa. Dum autem sic irem veni ad unum magnum montem, in unius cujus latere montis, omnia animalia illic habitancia nigra sunt[9], et homines et mulieres valde estraneum modum vivendi habent. Ab alio autem latere montis omnia animalia alba sunt[10], hominesque et mulieres ab aliis diversum modum vivendi habent. Omnes mulieres innuptæ unum magnum barile de cornu in capite portant ut cognoscantur quia nuptæ sunt. Hinc transiens per xviii alias dietas et per multas terras et civitates,

[1] *Boll.* sub curâ suâ.

[2] *Far.* omits the millia.

[3] *Hak.* et *Mus.* et fumigantia.

[4] *Boll. has* sumunt et pro suis usibus reservant.

[5] *Mus.* Et sic de fumo tantum deos suos pascunt.

[6] *Ven.* Et hoc in necessariis corpori (*sic*) humani.

[7] *Ven.* Fuzo; *Far.* Fuc; *Hak.* Fuko; *Mus.* Fuco; *Boll.* Suctio (*misread probably*); *Marc.* Fuzo.

[8] *Boll.* ita magnæ non sunt, sed.

[9] *Hak.* ut carbo; *Bol. has simply* in cujus latere nigra animalia morabantur, ex alio autem latere ejusdem montis animalia sunt alba.

[10] *Hak.* ut nix.

et veniens ad unum magnum flumen, applicui ad unam civitatem quæ per transversum istud flumen habet unum pontem, in capite cujus in domo cujusdam hospitis fui, qui michi volens complacere dixit: Si tu vis videre bene piscari veni mecum; et sic me duxit super pontem istum. In quo dum sic essem aspexi atque vidi in illis suis barchis[1] mergos[2] super perticas alligatos, quos postea ille homo uno filo ligavit ad gulam ne illi se in aquam submergentes et pisces capientes illos comedere possent[3]. Unde in barcha una posuit tres magnas cistas unam ab uno capite navis, secundam ab alio, tertiam vero posuit in medio. Dum autem sic fecisset illos dissolvit mergos, qui se postea in aquam submergebant, et sic pisces quam plurimos capiebant, quos ipsimet postea in illis cistis ponebant, unde in parvâ horâ omnes illæ cistæ fuerunt plenæ. Ipse autem dum sic plenæ essent a collo eorum filum accipiebat et eos in aqua submergere permittebat, ut inde piscibus pascerentur; cum autem pasti essent ad sua loca revertuntur, et eos ibi ligat sicut prius erant; ego autem de piscibus illis manducavi[4]. Transiens inde per multas dietas alium modum piscandi ego vidi. Nam sunt homines habentes unam tinam calidâ aquâ plenam in unâ barchâ, qui nudi erant habentes singuli post collum unum saccum, et se submergentes in aquam, pisces manibus capiebant ponentes eos in saccis suis, et cum ascendebant eos in barcha sua ponebant; postea in aquam illam calidam se ponentes[5]; tunc alius ibat faciens sicut primus, et sic isto modo multos pisces capiebant[6].

32. *De civitate Cansaiâ quæ maxima est de mundo.*

Hinc ego recedens veni ad aliam civitatem nomine Cansaiæ[7] quod idem est quod civitas cœli. Hæc civitas major aliquâ quæ sit in mundo[8], et bene circuit c miliaria. In ipsa non est spansa[9]

[1] *Hak. has* brachiis (*clearly an error*) *and so translated.*

[2] *Far. has* smergos.

[3] *Ven.* ne cum pisces cepissent ipsos deglutire possent.

[4] *Hak.* et optimi mihi videbantur.

[5] *Ven.* ponebant; *Mus.* balnearunt.

[6] *Hak.* quite omits this second fishing story.

[7] *Ven.* Campsay; *Far.* Chansanæ; *Hak.* et *Mus.* Kanasia; *Bol.* Chamsana; *Marc.* Camsaye.

[8] *Boll.* omni aliâ quam conspexi.

[9] *Ven.* Particula; *Far.* non est terra; *Mus.* nec in ea vidi spatium sive placeam vacuam quin bene inhabitaretur.

terræ que non habitetur bene; et multociens erit domus aliqua quæ bene x vel xii supellectiles[1] habebit[2]. Hæc civitas etiam habet burgia[3] magna habentia majorem gentem quam ipsa civitas tenet. Hæc xii portas [habet] principales, et prope quamlibet illarum portarum ferme ad viii miliaria sunt civitates majores quam essent civitas Venetiarum et Padua, unde bene ibitur sex vel septem dietis per unum illorum burgorum, et tamen videbitur modicum permeasse. Hæc civitas posita est in aquis lacunarum quæ manet et stat, sicut civitas Venetiarum[4]. Ipsa etiam habet plures quam xii millia pontium[5], in quolibet quorum morantur custodiæ custodientes ipsam civitatem pro magno Cane. A latere hujus civitatis labitur unum flumen juxta quod sita est civitas ista, sicut Ferraria ipsa manet[6], unde longior est quam lata[7]. De ipsa autem diligenter scivi et quæsivi a Christianis Sarracenis ydolatris cunctisque aliis, qui omnes loquuntur uno ore quod bene centum miliaria circuit. Per dominum etiam unum mandatum habetur; nam quilibet ignis solvit unum balis[8] annuatim ipsi Cani magno id est quinque cartas ad instar bombicis[9], quæ unum cum dimidio florenum valent. Hunc etiam habent modum; nam bene x vel xii supellectiles[10] faciunt unum ignem, et sic solum pro uno igne solvent; hii autem ignes sunt lxxxv[11] Thuman, cum aliis quatuor Sarracenorum qui constituunt lxxxviii[12]. Unum autem Thuman bene x milia ignium facit. Reliquorum vero alii sunt Christiani, alii mercatores, aliique transeuntes per contratam, unde multum fui miratus quod tot corpora humana poterant habitare simul. In

[1] *Hak. has* imo vidi multos domos habentes x vel xii solaria unum supra aliud, *which is enough to condemn the authority of that version; Mus. has the same.*

[2] *Hak.* et *Mus.* suburbia.

[3] *Bol.* id est familias.

[4] *Hak.* Sita est in aquis quæ semper stant et nec fluunt nec refluunt: vallum tamen habent propter ventum sicut civitas Venetiarum; *Mus. to same effect.*

[5] *Hak.* decem millia et 2... quorum multos numeravi et transivi; *Mus.* xii millia.

[6] *Ven.* et *Far.* Sicut Ferraria juxta Padum; *so Boll. also.*

[7] *Mus.* Hæc sicut Ferraria ipsa manet nam longior est quam lata.

[8] *Mus.* balistorium.

[9] *Far.* unum balis 15 cartas bombicis; *but this should probably be* balis *i.* 5 cartas, etc. (*i. for* id est), *as Hak. has it actually.*

[10] *Mus. adds gratuitously* id est solaria sive domus.

[11] *Far.* lxxv; *Hak. as in text.*

[12] *Far.* lxxviiii; *Hak. as in text; Mus. has* viii^{c}v et ix^{c}ix, but evidently means 85 and 89.

ea est copia magna panis, carnium de porco[1], et vini, ac risi; quod vinum vigim[2] aliter nominatur, quod etiam potacio nobilis reputatur: omnium etiam aliorum victualium illic copia maxima reperitur.

33. *De quodam mirabili quod vidit Fr. Odoricus in quodam monasterio ydololatrarum.*

Hæc est civitas regalis in quâ rex Manzi olim morabatur. Et in ea quatuor nostri fratres minores[3] unum potentem hominem converterunt, in domo cujus[4] hospitabar, unde mihi aliquando dicebat *Atha*[5], id est, Pater, vis venire videre terram? Et sibi semel dixi me velle ire, unde ascendimus unam barcham et sic ivimus ad unum magnum illorum monasteriorum quæ ibi erant, ad quod cum ivissemus unum illorum religiosorum vocavit dicens: Vides hunc Raban[6] Franchi (scilicet istum virum religiosum Franch), iste venit inde ubi occidit sol, et nunc vadit Cambaleth[7], ut roget[8] vitam pro magno Cane. Ideo sibi ostendas aliquid quod ipse videre possit, si hic est mirabile[9], ut si reverteretur ad suas contratas, dicere possit tale quod novum vidi in Cansai[10]. Tunc iste dixit se libenter velle ostendere sibi aliquid novum. Et tunc iste duos magnos mastellos[11] accepit plenos hiis quæ superfuerunt a mensâ[12]. Et ipse tunc statim[13] apperuit cujusdam viridarii portam per quam intravimus in viridarium illud, nunc autem in eo est quidam monticulus[14] plenus arboribus amœnis; et dum in eo sic essemus, ipse Cimbalum[15] unum accepit, et illud incepit

[1] *Hak.* et carnium de porco præcipue. *He omits the* bigini.

[2] *This should run as in Ven.* risi et vini, quod vinum bigini aliter nominatur; *Far. also has it in an unintelligible shape; Mus. has* carnium porcinorum vini et risi quod bignii aliter nominatur, de quo nobilis fit potatio inter eos.

[3] *Boll. has erroneously* prædicti.

[4] *Far.* Continue; *also Mus.*; *Hak.* in cujus hospitio continue habitabam dum fui ibi.

[5] *Ven.* Archa; *Far.* Arra; *Hak.* Ara; *Boll.* Ara.

[6] *Ven.* Franchum; *Boll. has* Rabi.

[7] *Ven.* Cambalech.

[8] *Hak.* deprecetur.

[9] *Ven. omits these four words, as do Ut. and the others.*

[10] *Mus.* Kanasià; *Hak.* Canasiâ.

[11] *Boll.* sportas.

[12] *Hak.* et duxit me ad unam perclusam parvam quam aperuit cum clave, et apparuit viridarium gratiosum, etc.

[13] *Mus.* cum clave.

[14] *Hak.* sicut unum campanile.

[15] *Ven.* Timpanum; *Far.* timbalum; *Boll.* Tintinnabulo.

pulsare[1], ad cujus sonitum multa animalia varia et diversa de illo monticulo descenderunt, sicut nunc essent symiæ, catti, maymones, similiter et multa alia animalia[2] circa ipsum se aptaverunt ad se invicem ordinata. Et cum circa ipsum sic essent posita et ordinata, ipse paropsides[3] posuit ante illa et sicut competebat comedere sibi dabat[4]; hæc autem cum sic comedissent cymbalum pulsare cœpit, et ad sua loca revertebantur cuncta. Dum autem sic viderem ista, multum cœpi ridere[5], dicens: Qualia sunt ista animalia[6]. Qui respondit: Hæc animalia animæ sunt nobilium virorum quæ nos hic pascimus amore dei[7]. Ei autem sic respondenti, dicens[8], Hæc animæ non sunt sed solum bestiæ et animalia ipsa sunt. Michi autem respondebat dicens, Verum non est quod hæc animalia sint, sed solum animæ nobilium sunt istæ, unde unus illorum sicut fuit nobilis homo, sic ejus anima in aliquid istorum animalium nobilium ipsa intrat; animæ vero rusticorum in animalia vilia intrant et habitant. Sic autem isto modo dicere poteram sibi multa quæ tamen aliud nunquam credere volebat[9]. Si quis autem dicere et enarrare hujus civitatis magnitudinem vellet, illiusque magna mirabilia quæ sunt in eâ, unus bonus quaternus stationis hæc talia tenere non posset. Verum ista est nobilior et major civitas pro mercimoniis quam habeat totus mundus[10].

[1] *Hak.* sicut percutitur quando monachi intrant refectorium.

[2] *Ven. has here* quæ faciem habebant humanam quæ erant circa tria millia quæ circa, etc.; *Far.* animalia habentia faciem hominis; *Mus. absurdly has* cciii millia, *probably miscopied for* circa iii milia; *Hak.* 4000.

[3] *Ven.* parassides.

[4] *Boll.* Secundum naturæ suæ......distribuit illis cibum.

[5] *Boll.* illi seni.

[6] *Ven. has instead* Quid hoc indicare vellit; *Mus.* Tunc admiratus quæ essent animalia ista quasi ridendo multum inquisivi; *Boll.* dixi Edissere mihi quid iste significat?

[7] *Hak.* et *Mus.* Dei qui regit orbem.

[8] *For* dixi.

[9] *Hak.* Incepi istam abusionem improbare, sed nihil valuit sibi. Non enim poterat credere quod aliqua anima posset sine corpore manere; *Boll. has* Et licet multa sibi dicerem et prædicarem nunquam tamen ipsum ab hâc perfidia potui revocare.

[10] *Hak. omits this sentence about the city altogether; Mus.* Si quis ergo mirabilia et mercimonia quæ in eâ sunt dicere et enarrare vellet nemo occidentalis partis mundi credere sibi posset.

34. *De civitate Chilenfu, de maximo flumine Talay, et pygmæis.*

De istâ recedens civitate per sex dietas veni ad unam aliam civitatem magnam quæ vocatur Chilenfo[1]; hujus muri civitatis bene per xl miliaria circueunt ipsi. In ista etiam civitate sunt bene tres centi et xl[2] pontes lapidei pulchriores quam totus habeat mundus. In hac civitate fuit prima sedes Regis Manzi in qua ipse morari solebat. Hæc bene habitatur a gente et in ea est ita magnum navigium quod est mirabile valde. Ipsa bene sita est omniumque bonorum copiam habet magnam. Ab hac civitate recedens veni ad quoddam flumen magnum quod vocatur Talay[3], et est majus flumen quod sit in mundo, nam ubi strictius est bene est latum septem miliaribus. Hoc flumen per mediam terram pigmeorum scilicet vidinnorum[4] transit, quorum civitas vocatur Chathan[5], quæ de melioribus et pulchrioribus civitas est quæ sint in mundo; hii pigmei sunt magni tribus spansis, qui faciunt magna opera Goton, id est bombicis[6], quam aliqui homines qui sunt in mundo. Homines autem magni qui ibi sint filios generant qui plus quam pro dimidietate similes illis pigmeis sunt qui sunt ita parvi. Ideoque tot istorum parvorum ibi generantur et nascuntur quod sine numero quasi sunt[7].

[1] *So also in Ven.*; *Ut. has* Chilemphe; *Far.* Chilopho *or* Chilepho; *Hak.* Chilenzo, *but the greater museum MS. has* Chilemfo; *Mus.* Chilefu *or* Chilenfu; *Boll.* Chyleso, bene muratam; *Marc.* Chilenfo.

[2] *Ven.* trecenti et sexaginta; *Far.* iii^c^lx: *Boll. only* quadraginta.

[3] *Ven. also has* Talay; *Mus.* et *Hak.* Thalay; *Marc.* Talay; *Ut.* Dotalay; *Far.* Thanai; *with the following interpolation to justify the blunder*, de quo scripsit Isidorus 12° libro etymologiarum, a Thano primo rege Sitharum denominatus qui ex nivosis (?) fluviis descendens determinavit Europam ab Asia et est inter ii partes mundi medias currens, atque in Pontum fluens; *Boll. has* Thannay.

[4] *Ven. omits these two words*; *Ut. has* id est biduinorum; *Far.* per medium terram biduinorum; *Mus.* pigmeorum, i.e., vidimiorum; *Marc.* Bidoyni *and* Biduini.

[5] *Ven.* Cacham; *Ut.* Tachara; *Far.* Cathan; *Hak.* Kakam; *Mus.* Kaycon.

[6] *Hak.* Goton et Bombycinam. *Omits all that follows about pigmies.*

[7] *Ven. adds* hi pigmæi formosi sunt tam mares quam feminæ per magnitudinem suam, et feminæ nubunt in quinto anno; habent autem animam rationalem sicut nos; *Ut. has the same, with* famosi *instead of* formosi.

35. *De civitatibus Iamzai et Menzu.*

Dum per istud flumen del Talai sic irem transivi per multas civitates et veni ad unam que vocatur Jamzai[1], in qua est unus locus nostrorum fratrum minorum. In hac etiam sunt tres ecclesiæ Nestorinorum, scilicet virorum religiosorum[2]: hæc civitas nobilis est et magna, habens bene xlviii[3] vel lviii tuman ignium, quorum unumquisque tuman bene est x milia. In hac civitate sunt omnia illa quibus vivunt Christiani et sunt in copiâ magnâ[4]. Unde Dominus istius civitatis solum de sale bene habet de redditu quinquaginta milia[5] Tuman balisi. Balisus autem valet unum florenum et dimidium, et ita unum tuman balisi bene constituit quindecim milia florenorum. Verumptamen unam gratiam huic populo fecit Dominus iste. Nam sibi dimittebat cc tuman ne[6] caritudinem[7] haberent. Hanc autem consuetudinem habet civitas ista; nam quando unus homo vult facere unum magnum pastum vel convivium suis amicis, ad hoc sunt hospicia deputata; nam illis hominibus qui hoc hospicium tenent dicet ille homo: Tu hospes facias mihi convivium istud pro quibusdam[8] amicis meis, et pro illo volo expendere tantum; sic autem convivium mihi fiet bene et ordinate, et michi melius servietur ibi quam in domo mea propria[9]. Hæc etiam civitas maximum navigium habet, per x miliaria ab ista civitate. In capite istius fluminis magni del Talai una alia civitas est quæ vocatur Menzu[10]: hæc civitas majus navigium et pulchrius habet quam alia civitas quæ forte sit in mundo. Omnes illæ naves albæ sunt ut nix,

1 *Ven.* Iamzay; *Ut.* Jamzai; *Far.* Iantu; *Hak.* Ianzu; *Mus.* Jancus; *Boll.* Ianzi; *Marc.* Jamzai.

2 *Far.* omits this explanation, which appears to be officious and inaccurate.

3 *Hak.* 48 Thuman *simply*; *Mus.* xlviii vel l thumam.

4 *Hak.* omnia victualia et animalia in magna copia, etc.

5 Both *Ven.* and *Far.* *have* manus, *which seems a mistake*; *Hak.* *has* 50 Thuman, *but* 200 *below*; *Marc.* mani di Thuman balis.

6 *Ven.* Balissius; *Far.* *has* balis autem 4 valet, etc.

7 *Ven.* carestiam.

8 *Ven.* *has* pro tot amicis meis.

9 *This is wrong. It should be as in Ven.*; et melius servitur eis quam in domo propriâ factum esset. *Far. has to this effect also. Hak. has it stupidly:* Et per illum modum melius convivant amici in pluribus hospitiis quam facerent in unâ. *Mus. to effect of Ven.*

10 *Far.* Menchu; *Hak.* Montu; *Mus.* Mencu; *Boll.* Mensy; *Marc.* Menzu.

zesso[1] depictæ. In ipsis etiam sale[2] hospicia multa quæ alia ita pulchra habent et ordinata, sicut unquam in mundo possent, unde est quasi quoddam incredibile audire et videre hujus navigii magnitudinem.

36. *De Flumine Caramoran, et de quibusdam civitatibus.*

Ab ista civitate recedens et transiens per iiii[3] dietas per multas terras et civitates per aquam dulcem, veni ad quamdam civitatem quæ vocatur Lenzin[4]: hæc civitas super posita est unum flumen quod vocatur Caramoram[5]; hoc flumen per medium Cathaii transit, cui magnum dampnum infert quando rumpit, sicut est Padus transiens per Ferrariam[6]. Dum sic irem per flumen istud versus orientem, multis dietis transiens per terras multas et civitates veni ad civitatem unam quæ vocatur Suzumato[7]. Hæc civitas habet majorem habundantiam serici quam forte aliqua terra de mundo, nam quando ibi major caritudo serici possit esse, bene tamen xl libræ habentur minori viii solidorum grossorum[8]. In ea etiam est magna copia omnium mercimoniorum, similiter etiam panis[9], omniumque aliorum bonorum.

37. *De civitatibus magnis Cambalec atque Taydo, et de Palatio Canis.*

Tunc de ista civitate recedens, transiens per multas civitates et terras versus orientem, veni ad illam[10] nobilem civitatem Cambalec: hæc civitas multum est vetus et antiqua, quæ est [in] illa provincia Cathaii. Hanc ceperunt Tartari, juxta quam ad dimidium miliare unam aliam civitatem fecerunt nomine Caydo[11]; hæc xii portas

[1] *Ven.* gippso.

[2] *Both Ven.* et *Far. have this* sale, *which I do not understand. If* salæ *for Halls, it should apparently have been* salas. *Marc. has* in quelle vi sono le sale, alberghi e molte altre cose, etc.

[3] *Ven.* viii; *Far.* octo, *and so the others.*

[4] *Far.* Lencim; *Hak.* et *Mus.* Lencyn; *Boll.* Lensium; *Marc.* Lenzin.

[5] *Ven., Hak.* Caramoran; *Far.* Tharamoram; *Boll.* Tharamorim; *Marc.* Caramoram.

[6] *Ven.* Dum rumpitur sicut facit Padus Ferrariæ.

[7] *Far.* et *Boll.* Sucumat; *Hak.* Sumacoto; *Mus.* Sumakoto; *Marc.* Suzumato.

[8] *Ven.* viii grossorum *simply. So Far. Boll.* octo solidis grossorum minorum.

[9] *Far.* vini; *Hak.* panis vini carnium piscium et omnium specierum electarum. *Nearly so also in Mus.*

[10] *Mus.* nominatam et nobilem.

[11] *Ven.* Taydo; *Far.* et *Hak.* Caido; *Mus.* Taydo; *Boll.* Thayde; *Marc.* Taydo.

habet, intra quamlibet quarum sunt duo miliaria magna, unde in[1] utramque civitatem bene habitatur[2,3] et circuitus istarum duarum civitatum plura ambit quam xl miliaria. In hâc civitate, Canis[4] ille magnus suam sedem habet, ubi etiam unum palatium suum magnum habet, cujus muri[5] bene per quatuor miliaria circueunt. Intra quod spatium multa alia pulchra palatia[6] sunt. In curtivo hujus palatii magni factus est mons unus, in quo edificatum est unum palatium aliud quod est pulcherrimum de mundo. Hic etiam mons arboribus est plantatus, propter quod Mons Viridis nominatur. A latere montis hujus factus est unus magnus lacus, per transversum cujus unus pons pulcherrimus factus est. In isto lacu tot sunt anseres silvestres, anathes, et Cesenæ[7] quod valde mirabile est, unde quando vult venari non oportet eum domum exire pro venatione, cum illa sit in domo. In hoc etiam palatio sunt viridaria plena diversis generibus bestiarum, quas quantumque vult ipse venari potest absque hoc quod extra domum vadat. Palatium autem ipsum in quo sedes sua est multum magnum et pulchrum est, cujus terra duobus passibus elevata est. Ipsum interius habet xxiiii[8] columpnas de auro. Omnes muri ejus cooperti sunt pellibus rubeis, de quibus dicitur quod nobiliores pelles sunt quæ sint in mundo. In medio autem palatio est una magna pingua[9] alta passibus pluribus quam duobus, quæ tota est de uno lapide precioso, nomine merdatas[10]. Ipsa etiam tota est auro ligata et in quolibet angulo ipsius est unus serpens qui verberat os fortissime, hæc etiam pinona retia habet de perlis magnis quæ pendent ab eâ, que retia forte sunt lata una spansa. Per pignam hanc defertur potus per conductus qui in curiâ regis habetur[11]. Juxta hanc etiam pignam manent multa vasa aurea, cum quibus omnes volentes bibere bibunt. In ipso autem palatio sunt multi pavones de auro. Cum aliquis Tartarus aliquod festum vult facere domino suo, tunc sic sunt percutientes ad invicem

1 *Ven.* et inter, *instead of* unde in, *and Mus.*

2 *Hak.* ita quod faciunt quasi unam civitatem.

3 *Boll. incorrectly* et numquam civitas bene per homines habitatur.

4 *Ven.* Chaam.

5 *Boll.* cujus muri per quadrum se extendunt.

6 *Hak.* et *Mus.* dominorum de familiâ suâ.

7 *Ven.* Cesani; *Far.* Cesenæ; *Hak. has only* anserum silvestrium; *Mus.* anserum, anatum et omnium aliarum avium aquaticarum; *Marc. has* Cesani.

8 *Hak.* 14.

9 *Ven.* pigna.

10 *Ven.* Merdacas; *Far.* Merdatas; *Hak.* Merdochas; *Marc.* Merdacas.

11 *Ven.*, *Far.* habentur.

manus suas; tunc hii pavones suas alas emittunt et ipsi tripudiare videntur. Hoc autem fit vel arte dyabolica vel ingenio quodam sub terra fit[1].

38. *De curiâ Domini Canis.*

Quum ipse dominus super suam sedem sedet imperialem a sinistro latere manet regina, et uno gradu inferius duæ aliæ morantur mulieres quas ipse tenet[2]; in infimo autem cunctæ dominæ parentelæ. Omnes illæ quæ nuptæ sunt unum pedem hominis super caput habent, longum bene brachium cum dimidio; subter illo pede sunt pennæ gruis in summitate, et totus ille pes est ornatus perlis magnis, unde si perlæ magnæ in mundo sunt et pulchræ hæc ita sunt in ornamentum istarum dominarum[3]. A latere autem dextro ipsius regis moratur ejus filius primogenitus, qui post ipsum regnare debet; inferius autem ab istis morantur omnes illi qui sunt de sanguine regio. Illic etiam quatuor sunt scriptores scribentes omnia verba quæ dicit ipse rex. Ante cujus conspectum stant barones sui multique alii innumerabiles, nullus quorum loqui auderet ullo modo nisi a magno domino peteretur, istis etiam hystrionibus exceptis[4], qui suum dominum vellent lætificare. Hii tamen hystriones nil aliud facere audent nisi secundum quod rex ipse legem imposuit eis. Ante portas ipsius palatii stant barones custodientes et videntes ne aliquid limen[5] hostii tangat, quod si aliquis faciens reperiretur ipsi eum acriter verberarent[6]. Cum autem dominus iste magnus aliquid convivium facere fieri vult, secum habet xiiii milia barones[7] cum coronis in capite sibi in convivio servientes, et quilibet vestem talem[8] habet in dorso, quod solum perlæ quæ ibi sunt super qualibet veste valent plus quam xv milia florenorum. Curia ipsius optime ordinata est videlicet per denarium[9] centenarium[10] et millenarium, unde omnes inter se taliter sunt ordinati et sibi invicem respondentes, quod de officiis suis, nec de aliquo alio nunquam defectus

[1] *Hak.* arte magicâ vel aliquâ cautelâ subterraneâ; *Mus. nearly so.*

[2] *Hak.* et *Mus.* pro se quando non potest ad reginam accedere.

[3] *Hak. omits this sentence.*

[4] *Ven. better* tamen; *Hak.* et *Mus.* exceptis fatuis et histrionibus.

[5] *Far.* limitem.

[6] *Hak. omits* quod......verberarent.

[7] *Hak.* portantes circulos et coronulas.

[8] *Mus.* talari veste.

[9] *Ven.* decenarium.

[10] *Far. has only* videlicet per C. *This MS.* (*or the transcript furnished*) *would be unintelligible in many places without collation.*

aliquis invenitur. Ego frater Odoricus ibi fui bene tribus annis in hac sua civitate et multotiens in istis suis festis presens fui, nam nos fratres minores in hâc curiâ suâ habemus locum deputatum, et nos semper sic oportet ire[1] et dare sibi benedictionem nostram, unde diligenter petii et inquisivi a Christianis, Sarracenis cunctisque ydolatris a nostris etiam conversis ad fidem[2], qui in illa curia magni sunt barones aspicientes solum ad personam regis, et hii omnes uno ore loquuntur dicentes quod solum hystriones sui sunt bene tredecim tuman[3], unum quorum bene x milia constituit hystrionum; alii autem custodientes canes, bestias silvestres, et aves bene sunt [......] tuman[4]. Medici vero qui custodiunt personam regis sunt ydolatræ numero quadringenti[5], Christiani autem viii, et unus Sarracenus: hii omnes totum illud habent quod est sibi necessarium a curiâ regis. Ejus autem reliqua sua familia ibi sine numero possidetur.

39. *De itinere Domini Canis.*

Dominus vero ille in estate moratur in quadam terra quæ vocatur Zandu[6], posita sub tramontana et frigidior habitabilis que hodie sit in mundo, in hyeme vero in Cambalec ipse manet[7]. Et cum vult ab unâ terrâ ad aliam equitare, hunc modum ipse tenet. Nam quatuor exercitus equitum ipse habet, quorum unus dietâ unâ ipsum antecedit, secundus aliâ dietâ, tertius similiter, et quartus; ita quod semper in medio vadit in modum crucis[8]. Cum autem sic vadunt omnes habent suas dietas ordinatas, unde omnia illa ibi inveniunt quæ sibi sunt necessaria ad comedendum. Gens vero quæ vadit cum eo ambulat isto modo; nam rex ille super uno curru a duabus rotis vadit, in quo facta est una pulcherrima sala[9], tota de lignis aloe et auro ornata, insuper perlis[10] magnis et pulchris et multis lapidibus preciosis; quatuorque elephantes bene ordinati et parati ducunt istum currum, quem

1 *Boll.* primos procedere.

2 *Boll. has* idololatris non modo ab illis qui *per me* ad fidem Christi conversi sunt, etc., *which looks as if it had been tampered with.*

3 *Far.* 12 tuman; *Hak.* 18 thuman; *Mus.* xiii; *Marc.* xiv.

4 *Ven.*, *Far.* xv tuman; *Marc.* xv.

5 *Mus.* ccc[ti].

6 *Ven.* Sanday; *Ut.* Sanay; *Far.* Sandu; *Mus.* Sandu; *Marc.* Sandu.

7 *From* Dominus vero *is omitted by Hak.*

8 *Far.* in modum gradus (in *échelon*).

9 *Hak.* Sella.

10 *Ut.* pellibus.

etiam et quatuor equi pulcherrimi[1] bene cooperti insuper sunt ducentes. Et juxta quem et quatuor barones qui vocantur Zuche[2] vadunt custodientes et tenentes currum ne aliquis offenderet currum ne aliquid offenderet istum regem. Insuper et secum super currum portat xii[3] zirifalcos, quos dum sic sedet in curru super cathedra sua vel sede et videt aliquas volantes aves post eas abire permittit. Et ad unius lapidis jactum nullus currui audet appropinquare nisi illi qui ad hoc sunt specialiter deputati. Unde sicut iste rex magnus vadit, sic et in gradu suo suæ vadunt mulieres isto modo; quod et suus primogenitus tenet et observat, unde quasi incredibile esset illam gentem ymaginari quam dominus iste habet. Exercitus autem illi qui ipsum dominum attendunt[4] quingenti[5] thuman habentes illa a domino quæ sibi sunt necessaria integraliter et complete. Et si aliquem istorum mori contingerit qui de numero computatur alius statim ponitur loco sui unde numerus semper manet.

40. *De imperio Magni Canis et de hospitiis in eo, et de modo expediendi nova ad Dominum.*

Hoc imperium ipse in xii partes condivisit (?)[6] quælibet quarum Syno[7] xii nominatæ. Una autem istarum partium est illud Manzi, quod sub se habet duo millia magnarum civitatum. Unde tam magnum est illud suum imperium quod [si] unus pedes per quamcumque partem ipsius vellet ire in sex[8] mensibus haberet satis, sine tamen insulis quæ sunt bene v milia quæ etiam in numerum non ponuntur[9]. Et ut transeuntes suis possint necessitatibus subvenire per totum regnum suum facit hospicia preparari sicut domos et curtiva quæ domus *Yam*[10] vocantur. In istis autem domibus sic paratis sunt omnia illa quæ sunt necessaria humanæ vitæ. Cum autem novitas aliqua in suo habetur imperio statim ambaxiatores sui ad ipsum super equos velociter currunt. Si autem negotium arduum nimis esset et periculosum, super dromedarios ipsi ascendunt. Et cum ad ista Yam, scilicet

1 *Hak. has* altissimi (albissimi ?).
2 *Far.* Cuthe.
3 *Hak.* duo et albissimi. *The latter also in Mus.*
4 *Ven.* antecedunt.
5 *Ut.* l; *Far.* v^c; *Hak.* xv Thuman.
6 *Ven.* Dominus divisit.
7 *Ven.* Singo; *not in the other copies collated, except Ut., which has* Signo.
8 *Mus.* v.
9 *All this is much abridged in Hak.*
10 *Ven.* Iam.

hospicia sive domos, incipiunt appropinquare, pulsant unum cornu, ad cujus sonitum hospes illius hospitii unum hominem facit velociter preparari, cui ille qui ita velociter venit ad domum illam illam litteram representat quam portavit; et sic iste qui nuper venit ut reficiatur in illa domo manet. Tunc ille qui litteram jam recepit usque ad aliam Yam, scilicet usque ad aliam domum, properat festinanter. Et iste secundus eodem modo facit quo fecit ille primus. Sic per istum modum in una naturali die unum novum xxx dietarum ille recipit imperator[1]. Illic etiam alius modus mittendi pedites observatur. Nam aliqui ordinati cursores in domibus quæ Chidebo[2] nominantur assidue commorantur, habentes cingulum unum circum circa nolarum seu sonaglorum[3]. Harum domorum una distat ab alia miliaribus forte tribus. Cum autem ad illam domum appropinquat istas duas[4] nolas seu sonaglos incipit pulsare fortiter ac valenter; tunc autem ille alius qui est in domo se velociter parat et ad domum vadit quam citius ipse potest. Sic et isto modo, hoc idem et alii cursores tenent et observant donec deventum est ad ipsum Magnum Canem unde in imperio suo [nihil] breviter fieri potest, quin statim vel cito multa penitus ipse sciat[5].

41. *De Venatione Magni Canis.*

Cum ille Canis Magnus ad venandum vadit hunc modum in se habet. Nam extra Cambalec ad xx dietas est unum pulcherrimum nemus[6], viii[7] dietarum per circuitum, in quo tot animalium genera sunt diversa quod valde mirabile est. Circa ipsum nemus positi sunt aliqui pro Magno Cane, qui ipsum custodiunt diligenter. In fine autem trium vel quatuor annorum ad nemus cum gente sua vadit. Cum autem pervenit illic ipse circumdat totum sua gente et in ipsum permittunt canes intrare et aves assuetas post illos emittunt. Et ipsi ad invicem pressi vadunt reducendo illa silvestria ad unam pulcherrimam quæ in medio nemoris habetur planiciem, et sic in ea congregatur bestiarum silvestrium maxima multitudo, sicut sunt[8] leones, cervi,

[1] *Ven. has* nova dietarum trium *only*; *Far. has* xxx; and *Hak. Mus.* xx; *Marc.* xxx.

[2] *Ut.* Chidebeo.

[3] *Ven.* nolis, i.e., sonalis plenum; *Mus.* cum multis pendentibus sonaliis sive nolis.

[4] *Should be* suas.

[5] *Hak. greatly abridges all this again.*

[6] *Hak.* una foresta.

[7] *Far.* vi, *also Hak. and Mus.*

[8] *Far.* boves silvestres; *Ven.* ursi.

multaque alia tam varia quam diversa, quod ibi videtur maximus esse stupor. Unde tantus est rumor atque clamor avium et canum quos in illud nemus emiserunt quod unus non intelligit alterum; et cuncta illa silvestria tremunt clamore illo magno. Dum autem hæc silvestria sic sunt in illa planicie congregata, tunc Magnus Canis ascendit[1] super tres elephantes, et in illa silvestria quinque sagittas jacit, quas cum ejecerit tota societas sua hoc idem similiter facit. Et cum omnes suas jecerunt sagittas, quarum quælibet suum signum habet per quod una ab alia cognoscatur, tunc ille imperator magnus vocari facit *Syo*, id est immani (?) bestiis illis[2] quas de nemore pepulerunt[3]. Et statim bestiæ illæ silvestres quæ ibi vivæ sunt demissæ intrant nemus. Ad alias autem interfectas cuncti barones accedunt accipientes sagittas, quas post illas emiserunt, nam eas bene cognoscunt cum illi inposuerunt sibi signum, unde unusquisque aliud silvestre habet quod sua percussit sagitta. Sic isto modo fit venacio sua[4].

42. *De quatuor festis quæ tenet Canis Magnus.*

Quatuor magna festa in anno iste facit imperator; scilicet, festum Circumcisionis, ejusque Nativitatis diem[5], et sic de reliquis. Ad hæc festa convocat omnes barones hystriones omnesque de suâ parentelâ qui omnes ordinate ponuntur in festo. Maxime autem convocat omnes istos ad duo festa de istis, scilicet, ad festum Circumcisionis et ad festum diei Nativitatis suæ. Cum ad aliquod festum istorum sunt isti convocati, tunc accedunt barones cum coronis in capite ipso, imperatore in sua sede residente, sicut superius dictum est; et omnes barones in locis suis deputatis ordinate morantur. Diversimode autem isti sunt barones vestiti. Nam aliqui sunt vestiti de viridi[6], scilicet primi; secundi de sanguineo sunt induti; tercii vero de glauco seu zamno[7] sunt vestiti. Omnes isti sunt in capite coronati, habentes in manu unam tabulam de dentibus elephantum albam, et singulos circulos aureos, bene uno semisse altos[8], stantesque in pedibus et silencium

1 *Ven. has better* accedit.

2 *Ven. Scio*, id est misericordiam bestiis illis, &c. *So in Far. Marc.* Syon.

3 *Far.* repulerunt.

4 *All much more concise in Hak. and Mus.*

5 *Hak.* et *Mus.* coronationis et desponsationis.

6 *Ven.* de serico; *Ut.* de serico viridi.

7 *Ven.* zauno; *Far. has* tertii de croco; *Hak.* et *Mus.* de croceo.

8 *Ven.* latos.

observantes. Circa istos morantur hystriones cum suis insignis et banderiis. In uno autem angulo cujusdam palacii magni manent philosophi omnes aspicientes et accedentes ad certas horas et puncta. Et cum occurrerit punctum vel hora quam ipsi philosophi petunt, unus clamat valenter et dicit, Debeatis inclinare nostro imperatori domino magno. Tunc omnes barones ter de capite dant in terra. Deinde ille idem exclamabit dicens, Vos surgite cuncti. Et statim ipsi surgunt. Ad alia etiam puncta iterum ipsi attendunt. Cum venit punctum, iterum ille clamabit dicens, Ponite vobis in auriculam digitum. Et faciunt. Et tunc statim dicet, Extrahite. Et obediunt iterum. Sicque modicum stabunt et dicent, *Buratate farinam*[1]: sic et multa alia signa faciunt isti quæ magnam significationem dicunt importare[2]. Deinde sunt officiales multi inquirentes et videntes cunctos barones et hystriones, ne aliquis illorum deficiat. Nam si aliquis ibi deficeret, magnam incurreret pœnam cum autem occurrit punctum et hora istorum hystrionum. Tunc philosophi dicunt facite festum domino. Tunc statim omnes incipiunt pulsare omnia instrumenta sua, et tantus est ille cantus et clamor quod est quasi stupor unus. Deinde vox una clamat dicens, Taceant omnes et sileant! Sic statim omnes tacebunt[3]. Post hæc statim illi de parentela sunt parati cum equis albis. Exinde vox una clamabit dicens, talis de tali parentela, tot centenaria paret equorum domino suo! Ibique statim aliqui sunt parati, ducentes illos equos per ante domum suum[4], ita quod quoddam incredibile est de tot equis albis qui illi domino exenniantur. Deinde sunt barones exennia[5] portantes ex parte aliorum baronum, omnes etiam de monasteriis principales ad ipsum accedunt cum exenniis et suam benedictionem sibi tenentur dare; hoc idem facere nos omnes[6]. Hoc facto et ordinato, tunc aliqui hystriones ad ipsum accedunt, et etiam aliquæ hystrionatrices ante ipsum tam dulciter cantant quod quædam magna jocunditas est audire. Deinde hystriones faciunt venire leones qui

[1] *Far.* omits this.

[2] *Hak.* et *Mus.* quæ scribere nolui quia vana sunt et risu digna.

[3] *Ven. omits this last sentence; and Hak. alone adds:* Tunc accedunt histrionices ante dominum dulciter modulantes quod mihi plus placuit.

[4] *So in Ven. with* dicentes *for* ducentes; *Ut. has* dicentes illos equos parasse domino suo.

[5] Exennia = Xenia.

[6] *Ven., Mus.* nos fratres minores facere oportet. *The* omnes *in the text is probably miscopied for* oportet.

reverentiam faciunt ipsi imperatori. Deinde hystriones vehi faciunt ciphos aureos per aerem plenos bono vino et ad ora omnium volentium bibere de isto vino porrigunt istos cyphos. Sic hæc et multa alia coram isto domino fiunt. Dicere autem et referre magnitudinem istius domini et illa quæ in curia sua fiunt esset incredibile quoddam nisi ista oculis viderentur. De hoc tamen quod multas expensas facit nemo mirari debet, cum nichil aliud pro moneta expendatur in toto suo regno quam quædam cartæ[1] quæ pro monetâ reputantur ibi, et infinitus thezaurus ad suas recurrit manus[2].

43. *De pepone in quo invenitur bestiola ad modum agni.*

Aliud insuper mirabile valde dici potest, quod tamen non vidi sed illud a personis fide dignis audivi. Nam dicitur quod Caoli[3] est unum regnum magnum in quo sunt montes qui montes Caspei vocantur[4, 5]. Unde in eis ut dicitur nascuntur pepones[6] valde magni qui quando sunt maturi ipsi aperiuntur et invenitur una bestiola ad modum unius agni parvi unde ipsi illos pepones habent et illas carniculas quæ sunt ibi[7]. Et quamquam illud forte aliquibus incredibile videatur tamen ita potest esse verum, sicut dicitur quod in hiberniâ sunt arbores aves facientes[8].

44. *De regionibus diversis.*

De isto Cataio recedens[9] et veniens versus occidentem, L.[10] dietis transeundo per multas civitates et terras, veni versus terram

[1] *Far.* cartæ confectæ corticibus morariorum, quæ, etc.

[2] *Far.* unde sicut dixi v^c (for v) cartæ quæ constituunt unum balis, ballis unum florenum cum dimidio.

[3] *Far. adds*: Cum autem moritur iste Canis omnes Tartari adorant ipsum pro deo.

[4] *Ven.* Cadeli; *Ut.* Cadellis; *Far.* et *Marc.* Caoli; *Mus.* Kaloy.

[5] *Hak.* in uno regno istius Canis in quo sunt montes Kapsei et dicitur illud regnum Kalor.

[6] *Ven.* melones.

[7] *Far. has* et illac carunculæ pro nobilissimo ferculo reputantur.

[8] *Far. adds* Nam in Imberniâ sunt arbores super aquam quarum folia statim ut cadunt in ipsam aquam mutantur in aves. *Hak.* Sicut audivi quod in mari Hibernico stant arbores supra ripam maris et portant fructum sicut essent cucurbitæ, quæ certo tempore cadunt in aquam et fiunt aves vocatæ Bernakles et illud est verum. *To which adds Mus.*: Hoc cuilibet Hibernicam legenti historiam satis patet.

[9] *Hak.* post tres annos.

[10] *Mus.* dietis pluribus.

Pretozoan[1], de quo non est centesima pars ejus quod quasi pro certo de ipso dicitur. Ejus civitas principalis Chosan[2] vocatur [......] sua civitas principalis[3] multas tamen alias civitates sub se habet. Sed semper pro pacto accipit in uxorem filiam magni Canis. Deinde veni per multas dietas et deveni in unam provinciam quæ vocatur Casan[4]. Ista est secunda melior provincia et melius habitata quam aliqua quæ sit in mundo[5], ubi autem est minus stricta[6], bene tamen est lata l. dietis, et longa pluribus lx, unde ista provincia taliter habitatur quod quando ab una porta alicujus civitatis exitur portæ alterius civitatis videntur[7]. In hâc est magna copia victualium, maxime autem castaneorum. In hâc autem contratâ vel provinciâ nascitur malus barbarus[8], cujus tanta copia habetur illic quod unus asinus minori sex grossis ponderaretur. Hæc autem provincia est una de xii partibus imperii magni Canis.

45. *De regno Tybot, ubi est Papa ydololatrorum.*

De hâc provinciâ recedens veni ad unum magnum regnum nomine Tybot[9] quod ipsi Indiæ est confine[10]. Totum hoc regnum est subjectum magno Cani[11], et in ipso est major copia panis et vini quam sit in mundo. Gens istius contratæ moratur in tentoriis quæ ex[12] feltris sunt facta nigris. Tota civitas sua regalis et principalis est facta ex muris[13] albis et nigris, omnesque suæ viæ sunt optime scelatæ[14]. In hâc civitate non audet aliquis

[1] *Ven.*, *Far.* Pretezoan; *Mus.* et *Hak.* Pretegoani; *Marc.* Pretegianni.

[2] *Boll.* Tozan, quæ sola de melioribus est in terrâ; *Far.* Cosan; *Hak.* et *Mus.* Kosan; *Marc.* Chosan.

[3] *Read as in Ven.* quâ tamen Vicencia melior diceretur licet ipsa sit sua civitas principalis.

[4] *Ven.* Chasan; *Ut.* Cassan; *Far.* Consan; *Mus.* Chosan; *Hak.* Kasan; *Boll.* Kansan; *Marc.* Casan.

[5] *Mus.* et spissius ut dicitur civitatibus ornata.

[6] *So most MSS. But Marc. which has* dov' ella è più stretta *seems best.* So also *Ram. It should be* magis stricta.

[7] *Hak.* Sicut egomet vidi de multis.

[8] *Ven.* reubarbarum; *Far.* as in text; also *Mus. Marc.* reobarbaro.

[9] *Ven.* Tibot; *Mus.* Tybek; *Hak.* Tibek; *Boll.* Tibet; *Marc.* Tibot.

[10] *Boll.* contiguum est.

[11] *Ven.* Cahaam.

[12] *Mus.* et *Boll.* magnis, *the latter has not* nigris.

[13] *Mus.* ex lapidibus albis et nigris ut scaccarium dispositis et curiose compositis pulcherrime est murata. *Hak.* to like effect.

[14] *Ven.* Sillexatæ; *Far.* Salizate; *Mus.* et *Hak.* pavati; *Marc. has* mattonate *in Italian.*

effundere sanguinem alicujus hominis vel animalis; Et hoc ob reverentiam unius ydoli quod ibi colitur et adoratur. In istâ civitate moratur Lo Abassi[1], id est Papa in linguâ suâ. Iste est caput omnium ydolatrorum[2], quibus dat et distribuit secundum morem suum omnia illa beneficia quæ ipsi habent. Hoc regnum hanc consuetudinem habet. Nam mulieres portant plus quam centum tricas seu dresas, habentes duos dentes ita longos[3] sicut habent apri sive porci silvestres. Hæc etiam alia consuetudo habetur in hâc contratâ. Nam ponatur quod pater alicujus moriatur, et tunc filius ipse sic dicet, Volo honorare patrem meum. Unde faciet convocari omnes sacerdotes, religiosos, omnesque hystriones de contratâ vicinos, similiter et parentes, qui ad campaneam[4] ipsum portant cum gaudio magno, ubi habent paratum unum discum magnum super quo ipsi sacerdotes sibi caput amputabunt, quod postea filio suo ipsi dabunt. Deinde ejus filius cum sua tota societate cantat et pro eo multas orationes facit. Exinde sacerdotes totum corpus ejus incidunt in frusta quod cum sic fecerunt tunc sursum se reducunt cum societate pro eo orationes facientes. Post hæc veniunt aquilæ et vultures de montibus et sic unusquisque suum frustum accipit et asportat. Deinde omnes altâ voce clamant dicentes: Audias[5] qualis homo iste fuit quia ipse sanctus est; nam veniunt angeli Dei et ipsum portant ad paradisum! Sic isto modo faciendo filius ejus multum reputat se honoratum. Cum pater ejus ab angelis Dei, scilicet, ab avibus illis ita honorifice sit portatus, tunc statim filius caput patris accipit, quod coquit et comedit. De testâ autem[6] seu osse capitis sibi fieri facit unum ciphum cum quo ipse et omnes de domo sua semper cum devotione bibunt, et in memoriam patris sui defuncti[7]. Nam sic faciendo, ut dicunt, reverentiam magnam exhibent patri suo; unde multa alia inconsueta et dissoluta fiunt ab istis[8].

[1] *Ven. the same*; *Ut.* lo albafi; *Far.*, *Mus.* et *Hak.* abassi; *Boll.* abbassi; *Marc.* lo abiss.

[2] *Mus.* et *Hak.* sicut noster papa est caput omnium Christianorum.

[3] *Ven. Far.*, et *Mus.* in ore; *Far.* sicut habent porci.

[4] *Mus.* et *Hak.* campum.

[5] Videatis.

[6] *Mus.* id est de crepâ (?).

[7] *Hak. with a touch of humour has* comesti.

[8] *Hak.* Et multa vilia et abhominabilia facit gens illa quæ non scribo, quia non valent, nec homines crederent nisi viderent.

46. *De Divite qui pascitur a* L *Virginibus.*

Dum autem essem in provincia Manzi veni per juxta pedem palacii cujusdam hominis popularis cujus vita per hunc habetur modum. Ipse enim habet L[1] domicellas virgines sibi continue servientes. Et cum vadit ad comedendum et in mensa jam sedet omnia fercula quaterna et quinterna[2] sibi portantur ab ipsis cum diversis cantibus et multis generibus musicorum, et sibi cibum in os ponunt sicut si esset unus passerinus[3] et insuper ante ejus conspectum continue cantatur, donec omnia fercula sunt comesta. Deinde alia quinque fercula ab aliis portantur et recedentibus istis primis cum aliis multis cantibus et diversis generibus musicorum. Sic isto modo ducit vitam suam dum est in mundo[4], hic XXX *tuman tagaris* risi de redditu habet, quorum quodlibet tuman X milia facit; unum autem *tagar* pondus est unius asini magni. Curtivum palatii sui per duo miliaria tenet; palatium autem illud in quo ipse moratur est factum per istum modum; nam pavimentum[5] ipsius unum laterem habet de auro alterum de argento. In curtivo istius palatii factus est unus monticulus de auro et argento, super quo facta sunt etiam monasteria et campanilia, ut homines fieri faciunt pro delectacionibus suis. Unde dicitur quod quatuor tales homines qualis iste est sunt in regno ipsius[6] Manzi. Nobilitas vero ipsius est habere ungues longas, et in tantum aliqui crescere permittunt ungues pollicis, quod cum ipsis circumdant sibi manus. Pulchritudo autem mulierum est parvos habere pedes. Unde hanc consuetudinem habent matres illarum mulierum, nam quando eis nascuntur aliquæ puellæ sibi ligant pedes quos nunquam crescere vel modicum dimittunt illis.

47. *De morte Senis de Monte.*

Dum autem recederem de terris Pretezoan[7], veniens versus occidentem applicui ad quamdam contratam quæ Millestorte[8]

[1] *Far.* 40. [2] *Far.* quinterna et quinterna.

[3] *Ven.* avicula quædam; *Hak.* pascentes cum sicut avis aviculas, et habet semper 5 fercula triplicata, etc.

[4] *Ven.* donec vixerit vitam suam; *Mus.* et sic hoc modo ducit in hoc seculo vitam suam.

[5] *Mus.* aulæ in qua ipse infra illud palatium moratur.

[6] *Ven.* ipso. [7] *Ven.* Preteian.

[8] *Ven.* Ministorte; *Ut.* Millistorte; *Mus.* Melescorte; *Hak.* Milestorite; *Marc.* Milestorte.

nominatur. Hæc contrata pulchra est et multum fertilis[1]. In hac contrata unus erat qui vocabatur Senex a Monte, qui inter duos montes contratæ hujus unum fecerat murum, qui istum circumdabat montem. Infra istum murum pulchriores erant fontes qui unquam possent reperiri. Apud istos fontes positæ erant pulchriores domicellæ virgines quæ unquam possent reperiri, equi pulcherrimi, omneque illud quod pro aliâ delectatione alicui humano corpori poterat inveniri; unde hunc locum vocabant paradisum. Cum autem juvenem valoris aliquem ipse videbat in istâ suâ paradiso ipsum poni faciebat[2] per quosdam autem conductus vinum et lac illuc descendere faciebat[3]. Et cum volebat facere sicari, id est assaxinari, aliquem regem vel baronem, illum qui preerat illi paradiso petere faciebat, ut aliquem inveniret qui magis esset aptus delectari in ista sua paradiso, et morari. Iste autem talis dum sic esset inventus et ibi positus esset, ei potacionem unam dari faciebat quæ ipsum statim sopiebat. Tunc ipsum taliter dormientem de paradiso extrahi faciebat. Qui cum excitabatur et extra paradisum se videbat in tantâ erat positus agonia quod quid ageret penitus nesciebat. Quare illum Senem a monte rogabat constanter ut eum in illam reduceret paradisum in qua prius positus erat. Tunc senex ille dicebat, Tu illic ire non potes ni talem regem interficias vel baronem. Unde seu moriaris sive non, te in ista ponam paradiso. Et quia iste sic delectabatur morari paradiso, per eum sicari id est assaxinare faciebat omnes illos quos volebat. Ideoque omnes reges orientis timebant istum senem sibique tributum magnum exhibebant. Cum autem Tartari quasi totum cepissent mundum[4], venerunt ad istum senem; cui finaliter dominium acceperunt. Quod cum

[1] *Mus.* atque fortis.

[2] *This should come before* cum autem juvenem, *as in Ven.*

[3] *Far. here has a considerable diversity from the rest:*—Per hunc modum; nam nullus erat in curiâ suâ præter paucos secretarios suos qui veritatem delusionis sciret de hoc suo paradiso. Unde accipi faciebat juvenes fortes corpore et ipsos poni faciebat in stallis ubi morantur eques (equi) et ibidem vivere miserrime faciebat. Et faciebat eos de spreto habitu indui et nunquam de illis stallis exibant. Itaque quasi nesciebant quod essent mundi blanditiæ, et quasi desperabantur. Cum autem sic erant afflicti faciebat eis unam potationem dari quæ eos fortissime soporabat (*sic*), et tunc ponebat illos in hoc paradiso inter illas puellas; per quosdam autem conductas, etc. *Hak. has* Iste senex cum voluerit sibi vindicare vel interfecere regem aliquem vel Baronem, dicit illi qui præerat illi Paradiso ut aliquam de notis illius regis vel Baronis introduceret in Paradisum illum, et illum deliciis frui permitteret, et tunc daret sibi potionem, etc. *Mus. has the same a little more diffusely.*

[4] *Ven.* Oriens.

ei sic fuisset acceptum multos de istis hiis sicariis emissit de paradiso per quos sicari et interfici faciebat multos Tartarorum. Hoc videntes ipsi Tartari ad illam civitatem in quâ senex iste erat, venerunt et eam obsederunt; cum ab eâ non discesserint donec illam et ipsum senem finaliter habuerunt. Et cum eum ceperunt vinculis eum vinxerunt et malam mortem illum sustinere fecerunt.

48. *De demonibus a fratribus Minoribus expulsis.*

In hâc autem contratâ Omnipotens Deus fratribus minoribus hanc dedit gratiam magnam[1]. Nam in magnâ Tartariâ ita pro nichilo habent expellere demones ab obsessis, sicut de domo expellerent unum canem. Unde multi homines et mulieres a demone sunt obsessi, quos ligatos bene de x dietis ipsi ad fratres nostros conducunt. Isti autem demoniaci cum adducti sunt ad fratres, ipsi ex parte et nomine Jhesu Christi precipiunt demonibus illis ut exire debeant de illis corporibus obsessorum quam citius ipsi possunt. Tunc statim mandato facto exeunt ab illis. Deinde qui sunt à demone liberati se statim faciunt baptizari[2]. Tunc fratres illa sua ydola de feltro accipientes quæ ipsi habent cum cruce et aquâ benedictâ illa portant ad ignem. Deinde omnes de contrata veniunt videre comburi deos suorum vicinorum. Tunc fratres ista ydola accipientes illa ponunt in ignem et tunc illa de igne exeunt[3]; propter quod fratres postea de aqua accipiunt benedicta quam in ignem projiciunt et statim demon fugit ab igne[4], et sic fratres in ignem ydolum projiciunt ibique conburitur, et tunc demon clamat in aere, dicens[5]; Videas! videas! quod de meâ habitatione sum expulsus! Et sic statim per istum modum nostri fratres multos in illâ contratâ baptizant[6].

[1] *Boll.* contra immundos spiritus magnam contulit potestatem.

[2] *Hak.* et idola sua et pecorum suorum statim dant fratribus, quæ sunt communiter de feltro et de crinibus mulierum.

[3] *Boll.* frequenter agente diabolo prosiliunt extra ignem.

[4] *Hak.* demones in effigie fumi nigerrimi fugerunt et idola remanserunt et combusta sunt.

[5] *Boll.* Indignatus ergo Sathanas cum suis, quia vasa diu possessa amisit, in aere vociferat dicens, Videre qualiter de meo habitaculo cum injuria sum expulsus, etc.

[6] *Instead of this, Hak. has an unintelligible sentence meant for the following as found in Mus.* ...baptizant, qui cito ad ydola et errores suos multotiens recederent nisi fratres semper cum illis stent ad illos in fide Christi continue confirmandos.

49. *De valle quâdam in quâ terribilia vidit Fr. Odoricus.*

Aliud terribile magnum ego vidi. Nam cum irem per unam vallem quæ [est] posita super flumen deliciarum, in ea multa et innumerabilia corpora mortuorum ego vidi, in quâ etiam audivi diversa genera musicorum, maxime autem Achara[1], quæ ibi mirabiliter pulsabantur. Unde tantus erat ibi clamor, quod timor michi maximus incumbebat. Hæc autem vallis forte longa est vii vel viii miliaribus terræ, in quâ, si aliquis infidelium intrat nunquam de illa exit, sed statim moritur sine mora[2]. Et quamquam in illa sic omnes moriantur, tamen volui intrare ut viderem finaliter quid hoc esset. Dum sic autem vallem ego intrassem, ut jam dixi, tot corpora mortua ibi vidi quod nisi aliquis illa vidisset quasi sibi incredibile videretur. In hac etiam valle ab uno latere ejus in ipso saxo unam faciem hominis valde[3] terribilem ego vidi, quæ in tantum terribilis erat quod præ nimio timore spiritum me perdere penitus credebam[4]. Qua propter[5] VERBUM CARO FACTUM EST continue meo ore proferebam. Ad ipsam faciem nunquam fui ausus totaliter appropinquare sed ab ipsa vii vel viii passibus distans ego fui. Cum autem illic accedere non auderem, ad aliud caput vallis ego ivi[6] et tunc ascendi super unum montem arenosum, in quo undique circumspiciens nichil videbam preter illa achara[7] quæ pulsari mirabiliter audiebam. Cum autem in capite montis ego fui illic, argentum reperi in maxima quantitate, ibi, quasi squamæ piscium, congregatum de quo posui in gremio meo[8]. Et quia de ipso non curabam[9] illud totaliter in terram projeci. Et sic dante Deo inde illæsus exivi. Deinde omnes Sarraceni cum hoc sciverunt reverebantur me multum, dicentes

[1] *Ven. Far.*, Nachara; *Hak. has* Maxime de cytharis unde multum timui; *Mus. the like.*

[2] *Hak.* Et ideo omnes de contrata declinant a latere. Et tentatus eram intrare et videre quid hoc esset, *and so on, telling the same story, but in words generally quite different; Mus.* agrees as usual with *Hak.*, but expresses things a little more wordily.

[3] *Ven.* Maximum et terribilem.

[4] Videbam.

[5] *Ven.* Cum signo crucis.

[6] *Ven. simply* Ivi tandem ad aliud caput vallis.

[7] *Ven.* nihil videbam nisi quod audiebam Nachera illa pulsare; *Hak.* nihil vidi nisi cytharas illas, etc.; *Mus. has the like.*

[8] *Hak. adds* pro mirabili ostendendo, sed ductus conscientiâ in terram projeci nihil mecum reservans, etc.

[9] *Ven.* et timens etiam ne tali illusione forte mihi denegare exitus.

me esse baptizatum et sanctum; illos autem qui erant mortui in illa valle dicebant esse homines demonis infernalis[1].

50. *Unum refert de magno Cane Fr. Odoricus*[2].

Unum referam de magno Cane quod vidi. Consuetudo est in illis partibus quod quando prædictus dominus per aliquam contratam transit, omnes homines ante hospicia[3] suorum domorum igne accendunt et aromata apponunt ac faciunt fumum, ut domino

[1] *Hak.* demonum infernalium qui pulsant cytharas ut homines alliciant intrare et interficiant. Hæc de visis certitudinaliter ego Fr. Odoricus hic inscripsi; et multa mirabilia omisi ponere quia homines non crediderint nisi vidissent.

[2] *Here occurs one of the marked differences in the copies. For at this place the copies* Far. *and* Boll. *conclude Odoric's narrative and introduce his attestation of veracity,* Ego Frater Odoricus, etc., *as below. After this they add an appendix, as it were:* Notandum quod ego frater Marchesinus de Bassano de ordine Minorum ista audivi a fratre Odorico predicto, ipso adhuc vivente, nam plura audivi quæ ipse non scripsit. Inter alia quæ ipse locutus est hoc quoque dixit. Nam dixit quod semel dum Canis Magnus iret in Cambalec [de] Sandu ipse frater Odoricus erat cum iiii^or fratribus minoribus sub una arbore quæ plantata erat juxta viam per quam ipsum Canem transitum facere oportebat. Unus autem istorum fratrum erat episcopus. Cum autem iste Canis cœpit appropinquare iste episcopus induit se habitu episcopali, et accepit crucem et posuit eam in fusto, et tunc isti iiii^or fratres inceperunt altâ voce cantare ymnum VENI CREATOR SPIRITUS. Et tunc Canis Magnus hoc audito rumore interrogavit quid hoc esset. Tum illi iiii^or barones qui erant juxta eum dixerunt quod erant iiii^or Rabani Franchi. Tunc ipse Canis fecit eos ad se accedere. Ille autem episcopus acceptâ cruce de fusto tradidit eam osculandam ipso Magno Cani. Ipse vero jacebat, et statim visâ cruce erexit se in sedendo, et deposito galerio de capite crucem fuit devote et humillime osculatus. Iste autem Dominus unam consuetudinem habet. Nam nullus audet in conspectu suo vacuus apparere, unde ipse Fr. Odoricus habens unum parvum calathum plenum pomis ipsi magno Cani fecit exenium. Ipse autem Canis accepit duo poma unum quorum medietatem comedit, aliud vero in manibus ipse gestabat et sic inde recessit. Ex quo satis aparet quod ipse Canis aliquid habuit in fide nostrâ, propter Fratres Minores qui continue in sua curiâ commorantur, cum deposuerit galerium et fecerit tam devote hanc reverentiam ipsi cruci; quod galerium secundum quod audivi a fratre Odorico plus valet quam tota Marchia Trevisana, propter perlas quæ sunt ibi et lapides preciosas. *The preceding is given by the Bollandists after H. de Glatz in the same manner with slightly different language. The following is omitted by* BOLL., *but is added to the above in the Farsetti MS., and as far as I have seen, appears in no other:* Præterea unum aliud audivi ab eo. Nam dixit quod semel in anno Magnus Canis mittit unum de Tartaris suis ad Soldanum Babilloniæ, quem recepit cum magno timore. Et die constitutâ Soldanus stat super unius parvi rivuli ripam et Tartarus stat in alia ripâ cum arcu in manu tenso et cum sagittâ fortissime venenatâ. Stat Soldanus genibus flexis et manibus cancellatis, nihil breviter habens in capite nec in dorso præter interulam. Quem iste Tartarus crudeliter multum alloquens, ter interrogat, dicens: Confiteris tu quod habeas vitam pro Magno Cane, et quod sis servus ejus. Soldanus autem respondet cum magno timore quod sic. Alioquin statim illum interficeret. Hoc autem Canis in signum suæ potentiæ fieri facit: præterea nec arbitror oblivioni mandandum.

[3] *Ven.* hostia (i.e., ostia).

suo transeunti odorem emittant. Et multi homines obviam sibi vadunt. Dum autem semel[1] veniret in Cambalec et de adventu suo certitudinaliter diceretur, unus noster episcopus et aliqui nostri fratres minores et ego ivimus sibi obviam bene per duas dietas. Et dum appropinquavimus ad eum posui[2] crucem super lignum, ita quod publice videri poterat. Ego vero habebam in manu thuribulum quod mecum detuleram. Et incepimus cantare alta voce, dicentes Veni Creator Spiritus, etc. Et dum sic cantaremus audivit voces nostras nosque vocari fecit et ad eum accedere nos jussit. Cum superius alias dictum sit, nullus audet currui suo appropinquare ad jactum lapidis nisi vocatus exceptis custodientibus eum. Et dum ivissemus ad eum cruce elevatâ, deposuit statim galerium suum sive capellum inestimabilis quasi valoris, et fecit reverentiam ipsi cruci. Statimque in thuribulum quod habebam incensum reposui, et episcopus noster de manu meâ accepit, eumque thurificavit. Accedentes ad predictum dominum semper aliquid ad offerendum secum deferunt, observantes illam legem antiquam, Non apparebis in conspectu meo vacuus. Idcirco portavimus nobiscum aliqua poma [et ea] sibi super unum incisorium reverenter obtulimus. Et ipse duo accepit de ipsis pomis, et de uno aliquantulum comedit. Et deinde predictus episcopus noster ei benedictionem suam impendit. Et hoc facto nobis innuit ut recederemus ne equi post ipsum venientes et multitudo in aliquo nos offenderent. Statim vero ab eo discessimus et divertimus, et ad aliquos barones suos per fratres nostri ordinis ad fidem conversos ivimus, qui in exercitu ejus erant. Et obtulimus eis de predictis pomis. Qui cum maximo gaudio ipsa recipientes, ita videbantur lætari, ac si illis prebuissemus familiariter magnum munus.

51. *Testimonium perhibet Fr. Odoricus.*

Ego frater Odoricus Boemus[3] de foro Julii provinciæ sancti Antonii de quâdam terrâ quæ dicitur Portus Maonis[4], de ordine fratrum minorum, testificor et testimonium perhibeo Reverendo

[1] *Ven.* quâdam vice. [2] *Ven.* posuimus.

[3] This addition to Odoric's description of himself occurs in no other copy that I have seen, Latin or Italian.

[4] *Ven. correctly* Naonis; *Hak.* Vahonis; *Mus.* Nahomonis.

Patri fratri Guidotto ministro antedictæ provinciæ sancti Antonii in Marchia Trevissina, cum ab eo fuerim per obedientiam requisitus quod hæc omnia quæ superius scripta sunt, aut propriis oculis vidi aut ab hominibus fide dignis audivi; communis etiam locutio illarum contratarum illa quæ non vidi testatur esse vera[1]. Multa etiam alia ego dimisi quæ scribi non feci, cum ipsa quasi incredibilia apud aliquos viderentur nisi illa propriis oculis conspexissent[2]. Ego autem de die in diem me preparo ad illas contratas accedere, in quibus dispono me mori ut illi placebit a quo cuncta bona procedunt[3]. Prædicta autem fideliter frater Guillelmus de Solagna in scriptis redegit sicut prædictus frater Odoricus Boemus ore proprio exprimebat, anno Domini M.CCC.XXX[4] mense Maii Paduæ in loco Sancti Antonii. Nec curavit de latino difficili et curioso ac ornato, sed sicut ille narrabat sic iste scribebat, ad hoc ut omnes facilius intelligerent quæ dicuntur, etc[5].

[*This is the end of the Parisian MS., No.* 2584. *The following conclusion is from* MS. FAR.]

52. *De morte fratris Odorici.*

Ipse Beatus Frater Odoricus cum de ultramarinis partibus ad suam provinciam remeasset, marchiam scilicet Trevisanam, presentiam summi Pontificis adire volebat, ut ab eo licentiam peteret

[1] *Ven.* Quæ etiam omnes illarum partium communiter testabantur.

[2] *Hak. incorrectly* Multa etiam alia ego dimisissem nisi illa propriis oculis conspexissem.

[3] These last words are not in *Venni*, nor in *Ut.*

[4] *In* UT. *this runs as written by William in the first person*—Ego Fr. Gulielmus...redegi...nec curavi de Latino difficili et ornato stilo, sed sicut ille narrabat ego scribebam cum domestico eloquio et communi ad hoc ut omnes facilius intelligerent quæ hic scribuntur, vel in isto libro dicuntur.

[5] HAK. *and* MUS. *relate the same at greater length, with addition of visions etc., and end by quoting the attestation of the notary Guetellus to the detail of Odoric's miracles, which has been mentioned in the biographical notice prefixed to his Itinerary.* BOLL. *has substantially the conclusion that is in the text, adding to the mention of the miracles:* Hoc testatus est litteris suis in curiâ Papæ Patriarcha Aquileiensis in cujus diœcesi hæc fiunt. Et protestatur Styria et Carinthia et multi de Italia et regiones quam plurimæ circumquaque. *And then:* Ego Fr. Henricus dictus de Glatz, qui prædicta omnia transcripsi existens Avenione in curiâ D'ni. Papæ anno D'ni. supradicto, si non intellexissem ibidem de felice Fr. Odorico et sociis qui secum fuerant, tot perfectiones et sanctitatis ejus opera, vix aliquibus hic per eum descriptis credere potuissem: Sed coegit me vitæ suæ veritas dictis ejus fidem credulam adhibere. Scripsi autem hæc anno D'ni. trecentisimo quadragesimo in Pragâ circa festum omnium Sanctorum, et copiosius ea audieram in Avenione.

per [ut] L fratres, de quâcumque provinciâ essent dummodo ire vellent, secum ducere posset, recessit de Foro Julii unde ipse natus est. Dum esset Pisis gravi infirmitate correptus, quamobrem compulsus est ad propriam [provinciam] remeare. Quapropter in utino de Foro Julii civitate, anno ab incarnatione Domini MCCCXXXI, pridie idus Januarii de hoc mundo triumphans pervenit ad gloriam beatorum. Ubi virtutibus et miraculis quam plurimis coruscat. Nam per eum cæci, claudi, muti, surdi sunt saluti, permittente Domino, restituti. Deo gratias. Amen.

APPENDIX II.

OLD ITALIAN TEXT OF ODORIC, FROM A MS. IN THE BIBLIOTECA PALATINA AT FLORENCE.

INCOMINCIA LA STORIA DI FRATE ODORIGO.

I. *Viaggio di Trebisonda e dell Erminia Maggiore.*

[*In questo anno corrente del* MCCCXVIII *divotamente prego il mio Signore Iddio che porga tal lume al mio intelletto, ch' io possa o in tutto, o in parte rammemorare le maravigliose cose da me viste con questi occhi: alle quali perche maravigliose siano, non perciò se gli deve haver minor fede: Poscia che appresso Iddio niuna cosa è impossibile. Voglio dunque a coloro, che queste cose, che io dirò, vedute non hanno, quanto meglio potrò, brevemente scrivendo, dimostrarle. E giuro per quell' Iddio, che in mio aiuto ho chiamato, in questa narratione non dovere io dire, ne meno, ne più di quel che in varie parti del mondo camminando ho visto*[1].]

Anno Domini MCCCXVIII io frate Odorigo[2] da Friolli de l'ordine de' frati minori della provincia di Padova [*nel mese d'Aprile, con buona licenza del mio superiore*], partimi de la detta provincia e [*navigando con l'ajuto di Dio, e buon vento*] veni in Gostantinopoli con altri miei compagni, e di quindi passai il mare Maggiore e veni in Trebisonda nella contrada detta metropolli di Ponto nella qual terra giace il corpo del beato Atanasio[3] che fece il simbolo. E [in] questa terra vidi una mirabil cosa[4] ch' uno[5] che menava più di dumilia pernici[6] le quali il seguitavano per

[1] *From* MIN. RAM.

[2] MIN. RAM. di Porto Maggiore.

[3] MIN. RAM. quale tanto più oserò di dirla, quanto che moltí, con quali ho parlato in Venetia, m' hanno riferito d' haver visto simil cosa.

[4] MIN. RAM. un' huomo barbuto e di feroce aspetto.

[5] MIN. RAM. a quella guisa che menano i Pastori loro armenti.

[6] MIN. RAM. Quali perdici volando, & andando via le menò a donare all' imperatore di Costantinopoli.

mirabile modo; perchè sempre andavano e volavano e stavan con lui per più di, e ubidielo, e parean quasi che parlassono con lui nella lingua sua. E quando andavano lo 'mperadore prendea delle pernici quante volea, e l' altre se ne venieno co lui infino al castello che si chiama Zavengha[1].

[*Delche maravigliandomi fortemente, udì da coloro, che sarebbe egli per far altre prove più maravigliose di queste: fra le quali fu questa, che un giorno essendo stato ammazzato un caro, & fidelissimo fameglio dello imperatore*[2], *e non trovandosi il mal fattore, ne fu questo barbuto dallo imperatore con istanza pregato, che non qualche via lo scoprisse. Il quale, fatto portare il giovane morto nel mezzo della piazza tutto insanguinato, in presenza di molta gente, scongiurando con li suoi incantesmi, gli messe in bocca una crescia piccola di fior di farina. Il quale non si presto hebbe in bocca la crescia, che si rizzò in piedi, e disse.chi l' haveva ammazzato, e perche cagione: E ciò detto ricadde subito morto*[3].]

Di Trebisonda andai a Zangha, ch' è castello de lo 'mperadore, e quivi si cava l' argento[4] e 'l cristallo, secondo che si dice. Quindi andai in Erminia Maggiore, e pervenni ad Arzelone, ch' è presso d' una giornata al fiume del Paradiso detto d'Eufrates. In questa terra una gran donna lasciò in testamento che de' beni suoi si facessoro un munistero di meretrici al servigio degli uomini in ogni carnalità, per l' anima sua maladeta[5]. Di quindi veni al monte ov' è l' Arca Noè, e volentieri sarei salito alla cima del monte avegnache mai non si trovava chi vi potesse salire, ma perchè non volle aspettare la carovanna non volli provarmene. Il monte è altissimo e bellissimo, e quasi va la neve insino a la terza parte del monte[6].

2. *Delle cittade di Taurisio e di Soldania.*

Poi veni[7] in Persia nella citade ch' è detta Taurisio, e 'n quella via passai il fiume Rosso, ove Alessandro isconfisse il Re d'Asia Dario, e in quella cittade noi abbiamo due luoghi: è nella

[1] MIN. RAM. Zanicco.

[2] *The* MIN. RAM. *has* di Costantinopoli, which is probably an interpolation.

[3] From MIN. RAM.

[4] MIN. RAM. l' oricalco.

[5] This extraordinary story is given more diffusely in MIN. RAM. It is in no Latin MS. that I know of.

[6] MIN. RAM. *has*—perche il monte è santissimo, & oltre ciò inaccessibile per l' altissima, neve che vi sta tutto l' anno, e piglia almeno le due parti del monte.

[7] MIN. RAM. *has absurdly* navigammo e venimmo.

cittade (?) mirabile moltitudine, e di mercatanti molti, ove è uno monte di sale, del quale può prendere chi ve ne vuole[1]. Di quindi veni in Soldania ov' è la sedia dello Re di Persia, nella quale è un luogo de' Frati Predicatori, e uno de' Frati Minori.

3. *Della cittade de' tre Magi, e del Mare Sabuloso.*

Di quindi venni in Saba cittade e terra della quale furono i tre Magi. E tutti i Saracini che dimorano ivi dicono che i Magi furono di quella terra ch' è cittade grande e ben sicura; ma ora è molta diserta. Ed è di lunge da Gerusaleme ben sessanta giornate. Di quindi pervenimo al mare Sabuloso[2], cioè il mare della rena, ov' io isteti quatro dì nel porto[3]. E la carrovana non fu ardita d' entrare nel Sabulo, ch' è una rena secca, che si muove al modo del mare della tempesta del vento; che se alcuno allora v' entrasse incontinente sarebbe ricoperto e affogato. Ov' io vidi monti altissimi di rena i quali in poco tempo si disfanno e altri in poco tempo si rifanno[4]. Di quindi pervenni a una cittade grande ch' è chiamata Geste, la quale è ultima terra di Persia verso l' India; nella quale terra è grande abondanza di grano e di fichi, e uve paserine[5] molto buone, e sono verdi come erba e saporitissime. E di quindi entrai in Caldea, nella quale contrada vanno gli uomini ornati al modo delle donne della nostra contrada, e portano in capo cufie ornate di pietre e d' oro e di preziose cose; ma le femine per contrario vanno mal vestite con camice corte insino a ginocchio, e scalze, e le maniche si larghe che toccano infino in terra[6], e portano eziandio le brache lunghe

[1] MIN. RAM. *has another ignorant interpolation*, e già se n' erano carche navi, e mandato dove ne era carestia.

[2] MIN. RAM. Sabbionoso. *It is* Sabuoso in the *Palatine*; *I have inserted the* l, *as it occurs below.*

[3] ID. E ci convenne star colla caravana in porto ben quatro giorni. E non fu niuno di noi, che ardisse d' intrar in questo loco.

[4] MIN. RAM. E si muta, a quella guisa che fa il mare, quando è in tempesta, hor qui, hor li, e fa nel muoversi l' istesso ondegiar che fa il mare, in guisa tale, che un infinità di persone s' è trovata, caminando per viaggio, oppressa, & sommersa, e coverta da queste arene, le quali dal vento dibattute, & trasportate, hor fanno come monte in un loco, & hor in un, altro, secondo la forza del vento, da cuì sono elle agitate.

[5] *For* passoline. MIN. RAM. *has* d' uva passa grossissima, *which last word is another interpolation, as the Persian raisins are very small, a fact noted in the best Latin MSS.*

[6] MIN. RAM. *after* ginocchio *has* con braghesse, e legazze, che pendono insino al collo del piede.

insino in terra, e 'n capo un poco di panno corto quasi un mezo braccio; e capelli non sono legati. Quivi vidi uno giovane che dovea prender moglie. Quando venne il tempo de lo sposare, tutte le fanciulle vergini della contrada istavan con lei e piangeano, ma lo isposo istava ornato con vestimenti preziosi[1], il quale cavalcoe sopra un asino, e la moglie gli andò dietro a piede, mal vestita e scalza[2]. Il padre della fanciulla gli diede la benedizione, e in quel modo si maritano quivi le fanciulle[3]. Di quindi dopo molte terre veni a la terra di Giobo. E ottimamente sicura e fertile, e gli uomini de la contrada mi narraro la storia di Giobo. Quivi gli uomini filano e non le femmine.

4. *Della Torre di Babel; et della cittade Ormes.*

Di quindi veni a la tore di Babel presso a quattro giornate per selve di datteri ove non avemo che mangiare niente altro che datteri; e l'aque di quindi son salse e poche ven' avea. E per questa selva andai ben quatordici giornate e volentieri sarei ito a la torre, ma nonne avea compagnia e però lasciai di non irvi. Poi venimmo a Ormes ch' è cominciamento de l' India ed è in capo del mare la quale terra è in un isola ed è dilunge a terra ferma ben cinque miglia: in su la quale non nasce albore e non v'ha aqua dolce ed è citta molto bella, e ben murata. Quivi ae si grande abondanza di datteri che per tre soldi n' arebe altri quantunque e ne potesse portare. Ed eziandio v' è grande abondanza di pane e di pesce e di carne ma non è terra sana. [E] pericolosa, e incredibile di calura. E gli uomini e le femmine son tutti grandi. E passando io quivi fu morto uno, e venirvi tutti i giulari della contrada, e puosollo nel mezzo della casa nel' letto; e due femmine saltavano intorno al morto, e giulari sonavano cemboli ed altri istormenti. Poi due femmine abbracciavano il morto, e lodavallo, e l' altre femmine si levavano ritte, e ciascuna tenea un canello in boca e zufolavo; e quando avea zufolato, ed ella si ponea a sedere, e cosi fecero per tutta la notte. E la matina il portaro al sepolcro.

[1] Min. Ram. stando il giovane sposo con la testa bassa, e leggiadrissimamente vestito.

[2] Id. toccando l' asino.

[3] *Here the* Min. Ram. *and the* Palat. *cease to run parallel. The former passes at once to the traveller's arrival at Tana.*

5. *Passa il Fr. Odorico alla Tana d' India.*

Di quindi navicammo per lo mare oceano venti otto dì; poi pervenimmo in Tana, la quale fu cittade del Re Porro; la quale terra è posta in buon luogo, ed a grande abondanza di vittuaglia, e spezialmente di burro, di *susuan* [sisamo ?], e riso. Quivi sono molti diversi animali, leoni neri, e pipistrelli grandi come anitre, topi grandi come cani communi, nè non sono presi da gatti ma da cani per la loro grandeza[1]. In questa terra sono idolatrici, ma 'l signore adorano i saracini il bue[2] e dicono ch' egli è il grande Idio, e non mangiano carne di bue, e lavorano col bue sei anni, il settimo anno i lasciano libero. Prendono anche dello sterco del bue, e pongolosi a la faccia, e dicono da indi inanzi che sono santificati. Alcuno altri adorano gli albori ed alcuno altri adorano il fuoco ed altri i pesci ed altri il sole ed altri la luna. In questa terra non prendono moglie altro che del mese di febraio, e questo è appo loro il primo mese de l' anno. Gli uomini e le femmine vanno tutti ignudi, e 'n cotal modo menano le mogli. Il marito e la moglie salgono insu uno cavallo insieme; è 'l marito di dietro, e tiene la moglie in braccio, e non hanno indosso altro ch' una camicia e 'n capo una mitera grande piena di fiori[3]. E 'l marito tiene un coltello[4] grande ingnudo sopra le spalle della moglie, e tutte le vergini vanno innanzi cantando ordinatamente, e ora restano un poco e poi vanno oltre[5]. In questa terra sono albori che fanno vino che 'l chiamano *loahc*[6] e inebria molto gli uomini. Quivi eziandio non si sopeliscono i morti ma portansi con gran festa a campi alle bestie e gli ucelli che gli divorano. E sono qui i buoi bellissimi, che hanno le corna bene uno mezzo passo, e sono iscrignuti a modo d'un camello. In questa terra vidi il

[1] MIN. RAM. Qui viddi uno Leon grande, e negrissimo, alla guisa di un bufalo: e viddi le nottole, o vogliam dire vespertiglioni, come sono le anatre di qui da noi. E topi, chiamati Sorici di Faraone, che sono grandi come volpi, etc.

[2] *The scribe has made a hash of this. It is intended to be the equivalent of* MIN. RAM.—Il paese è di Saracini; la gente è idololatra e adora il bue. *It probably ran,* In questa terra sono Signori i Saracini, ma la gente, etc.

[3] MIN. RAM. una cuffia alta alla guisa d' una mitra, e lavorata di fioretti bianchi.

[4] MIN. RAM. appontato alla gola.

[5] ID. fino a casa, dove lo sposo, e la sposa si restano soli, e la mattina levati, vanno pur nudi come prima.

[6] See note on translation *in loco*.

luogo e gli uomini qua sono i quatro frati minori[1] come si narra nella storia loro. Da questa terra insino a Panche[2] sono xiiii giornate, e qui è la sedia del Re Poro che fu isconfito dal grande Alessandro.

16[3]. *Del Pepe e come si lo vendemiano; e del regno di Minabar.*

Poi veni per lo mare Oceano quaranta giornate, e pervenni a lo 'mperio di Pirabar[4] dove nasce il pepe. E nasce in cotal modo. L' albore che fa il pepe è fatto come l' elera che nasce su per gli muri. Questo pepe sale su per gli albori che gli uomini piantano a modo de l'elera, e sale sopra tutti li albori più alti[5]. Questo pepe fa i rami a modo dell' uve; e in peruno inproducono tanta quantità di frutto ch' è incredibile; e maturo si lo vendemiano a modo de l'uve e poi pongono il pepe al sole a seccare come uve passe, e nulla altra cosa si fa del pepe. E del pepe ricente fanno composto e io ne mangiai, ed ebbine assai. E ivi cosi grande abondanza di pepe come qui in nostra terra di grano. E la selva dura per diciotto giornate, en tutto il mondo non nasce pepe altro che qui. Quivi sono due citadi, una che si chiama Filandria e l'altra Sigli. Quivi sono molte calcatrici o vero cocolgrilli, e leoni in grande moltitudine, e diverse bestie che non sono in Franchia. Qui si arde il verzino per legne, e tutti i boschi son pieni di paoni salvatichi. Poi venni a Colonbio, ch' è la migliore terra d'India per mercatanti. Quivi è il gengiovo in grande copia e del buono del mondo. Quivi vanno tutti ignudi, salvo che portano un panno innanzi a la vergogna istremo (?) e legalosi di dietro.

17. *Delle consuetudini strane della gente di Minabar.*

Quivi adorano il bue e l' idolo loro è mezzo buoe e mezzo uomo, e favella alcun' ora e vuole sangue di xxx uomini e più, e sangue di femmina, e vuole che sieno uccisi dinanzi da lui. E

[1] *Sic. Probably should be to this effect:* Vidi il luogo, e gli uomini che uccisero i quattro frati, etc.

[2] *Sic. Perhaps it should be* Paroche (Broach) *mentioned by Jordanus in a letter in this collection.*

[3] The Nos. 6–15 are omitted in order to maintain correspondence with the Latin text.

[4] *Or Pinibar* (for Minibar).

[5] *The original here is a tangle, which I have tried to reduce to sense.*

come noi faciamo voti di dare a Dio nostri figliuoli o figliuole, cosi costoro a loro idolo e 'ncontinente che egli il vuole e egli il recano e soenalo dinanzi a lui per reverenza. E spesse volte lo 'mperadore per maggior reverenza o 'l re fa torre a damigelli una vacca, e tolgono un bacino d' oro, e ricevono entrovi l' orina di questa vacca, e lo re se ne lava le mani e 'l volto: poi toglie de lo sterco di questa vacca, e ponselo a la faccia e unguesene le mascelle e'l petto, e poi dice ch' è santificato. E facendo egli questo, tutti fanno il semigliante. In questa terra sono albori che conducono [producono ?] mele, ed è del buono del mondo. Sonvi altri albori che producono vino ed albori che producono lana di che si fa tutto corde e funi, e sonvi albori che producono frutti che di due sarebbe carico un forte uomo, e quando si vengono a manicare conviene che altri s' unga le mani e la boca, e sono odorifili e molto saporiti e chiamansi frutto *chabassi*. Quivi udi dire che sono albori che producono uomini e femmine a modo di frutti, e sono di grandezza un gomito, e sono fitti nell' albore insino al bellico, e cosi istanno; e quando trae vento e sono freschi, e quando non, pare che si seccano. Questo non vidi io, ma udilo dire a persone che l' aveano veduto. Sono anche qui più diverse cose che sarebbe lungo a dire e 'ncredibile e però lascio.

18. *Del reame de Mobar dove giace il corpo di San Tomaso Apostolo.*

Poi pervenni a uno imperio che si dice Mabare, ove fu morto San Tomaso apostolo. Quivi è il massimo imperio. Questa Mabor è provincia. Qui si truova le perle, le maggiori e le migliori del mondo. Qui è uno idolo d'oro puro e massiccio della grandezza che si dipingue Santo Cristofano, ed a intorno al collo una corda piena di priete preziose, e di perle grandi. Tutta la chiesa di questo idolo è d'oro puro. Tutti gl' idolatri del paese vanno in peligrinnaggio a questo idolo come i cristiani a Roma, e adorano in questo modo: che prima fanno tre passi, poi si stende in terra boccone; e qui gli fa incenso col turibolo, e poi fa altri tre passi e fa il simigliante, e questo fanno da certo luogo insino a l' idolo, andando e reggendo (?). In cotale peligrinagio molti portano una tavola in collo, ovvero mensa forata, e mettono il capo per lo foro, e cosi la tiene infino che perviene a l' idolo, e quivi la gettano dinanzi da lui. Altri sono che si forano il braccio con uno coltello, nè non se nel' tragono da la casa insino a l' idolo. E io vidi questo e tuto il braccio era gia fracido. E molte altre diverse penitenzie quivi fanno.

19. *Delle feste che fanno del loro Idolo.*

E quando è la festa di questo idolo, una volta l' anno, pongono l' idolo in su un carro e menalo in certo luogo. Allora in prima [viene] lo 'mperadore, e poi il papa e altri sacerdoti che si chiamano *tuin*, e altri che si sono botati[1] si vanno sotto il carro, alcuno col capo, alcuno col corpo, secondo il voto che fa, si che le ruote pasando sopra loro muoiono e ogni anno impromettono cosi d' esserne uccisi da cc infino cccc, e cosi è cosa oribilissima a vedere. Altri si offeriscono ispontaneamente a l' idolo, e fannosi un fornimento di fiori e gittano a l' idolo della carne sua, la quale tagliano col coltello d' ogni membro. Poi si percuotono col coltello insino al cuore, dicendo ecco che io muoio per lo Iddio mio. E cosi molti uccidono lor medesimi; e cosi si santificano tra loro, come i martiri tra noi. Molti altri fanno voto de' figliuoli loro e menagli dinanzi da questo idolo e scannagli. Et al lato di questo idolo è un luogo nel quale per la divozione gettano oro e argento, e in questo modo quella chiesa è mirabilmente richissima e chiamasi questo luogo *celai* in lor lingua.

20. *De' reami di Java e di Lamori.*

Di Mabara ci partimmo ed entrai nel mare Oceano, e navicai per più dì; e pervenni a una nobile isola appellata de Iava; la quale è molto grande ed è qui abondanza quasi di tutti i beni. Nella quale isola sono dodici reami ed in ciascuno reame a uno imperadore. Quivi nascono le noci moscade e gherofani, e 'l cubebe, e molte altre ispezie in grande quantità. E qui massimamenta abonda i legno aloe e oro ottissimo. Poi navicai per xl. giornate e arivai ad uno regno che si chiama Lamori, e 'n questa contrada cominciai a perdere la tramontana però che la terra me la togliea. Nella quale terra gli uomini e le femmine senza nulla distinzione vanno ignudi, non abendo niente in alcuna parte, se non che alcuna femmina certo tempo quando partoriscono portano dinanzi a la vergogna una foglia d' arbore e legansela con una

[1] Botati *for* votati.

coreggia d' albore. E faceansi beffe di me, dicendo Iddio fece Adamo ignudo, ed io mi vesti a mal suo grado. E tutte le femmine sono in commune in tal modo che nulla n' è appropiata a niuno omo, ma ciascuno si può pigliare qual più gli piace, pur che non facia impedimento a l' altro. E quando ingravida puote la femmina appropiare il figliuolo a cui ella vuole. Eziandio tutta la terra è a commune, si che or nullo può dire questa casa è mia ma ci seno hanno in ispeziale[1]. Quivi eziandio mangiano le carni umani, e Saracini vi recano de l' altre provincìe gli uomini e vendogli loro in mercatanzia; e sono mangiati da coloro e sono uomini bianchi, che de' neri come sono eglino non mangiano. E sono uomini fieri in battaglia e vanno a la battaglia ignùdi, salvo che portano in braccio uno iscudo che gli quoprono insino a piedi. E se prendono alcuno nella battaglia si lo mangiano.

21. *Del Reame ch' e chiamata Sumetra.*

Di quindi ci partimmo e venimmo ad un altro regno di questa Isola ch' è chiamata Sumetra, e qui portano alcun cosa per vestimento, cio è un panno istretto sopra la vergogna. E sono eziandio fieri uomini e pigliano bataglia co' sopra detti. E tutti questi uomini e femine sono segnati in della fronte, cioè nella faccia, d' un ferro di cavallo a nostro modo. In questa contrada è grande mercato di porci e di galline e di burro e di riso, e qui è frutto ottimo cioè *Mussi.* E trovasi quivi oro e stagno a grande quantità. Quivi si pigliano le tartugi, cioè testugini, mirabili, e sono di molti colori e paiono quasi dipinte. Poi veni a l' altro regno di questa Isola ch' è chiamata Bucifali e 'l mare di turci (?), questo regno si chiama il mar morto. Ed egli è tutto il contrario, che 'l mare pende e corre si forte ch' è incredibile, e se marinai si partono punto dallito vanno discendendo, e non tornano mai. E non è alcuno che sapiano dove si vadono, e molti sono cosi iti e non seppono mai che se ne fossono. E la nave nostra fuè in grande pericolo, andando quindi, se non se che Idio ci aiutoe miracolosamente.

[1] *Not intelligible. It runs in the MS.*—Ma ciseno (*or*) cifeno ano in ispeziale. *It is probably meant for*, "except that they have houses to themselves," *as in the Latin MSS. If that be so, perhaps* casa *should read* cosa.

22. *Dell' albori che danno farina; e de' aghi velenatì che soffiano i corsali da certe canne.*

In questa isola sono albori che producono farina e 'l pane che se ne fa è asai bianco di fuori, ma dentro è alquanto nero ma in cucina questa farina è molto buono. E non ti maravigliare che gli albori facciano farina, imperciò che 'l modo è questo. Prendono una iscure, e perquotono l' albore in quella l' albore fa schimma e fa gromma molto grossa. Poi prendo[no] vasi ovvero ceste, e tolgono quella gromma e mettolavi dentro poi per xxx dì per se medesimo sanza tocarla. Divien farina in quello modo. Poi per tre dì prendono aqua marina e colano quella farina in quella aqua, poi gettano quella aqua marina, poi per tre dì prendono aqua dolce e 'ntridola con quella; poi ne fanno la bella massa, e pare il più bello pane che sia al mondo nel sapore. Onde nel regno ove noi savamo (?) ci vene meno tutti gli altri alimenti fuori che questa farina en grande quantità e a buono mercato. E questa contrada tiene insieme bene quatordici migliaia d' isole e altri dicono di meno. Alcuno chiama questa contrada da Talamosa e alcuni altri Panthe. En queste isole sono molte cose maravigliose e strane. Onde alcuni albori ci sono che fanno farina come detto, e alcuni fanno mele, alcuni seta, alcuni lana e alcuni che fanno veleno pessimo. Contro al quale nullo v' è rimedio se non se lo sterco de l' uomo. E quelli uomini sono quasi tutti corsali, e quando vanno a battaglia portano ciascuno una canna in mano, di lunghezza d' un braccio e pongono in capo de la canna una ago di ferro atossiato in quel veleno, e sofiano nella canna e l' ago vola e percuotolo dove vogliono, e 'ncontinente quelli ch' è percosso muore. M' a egli hanno le tina piene di sterco d' uomo e una iscodella di sterco guarisce l' uomo da queste cotali ponture. In questa contrada a canne alte più di lx passi, si grosse che sarebbe impossibile a credere. Anche v' ae un' altra generazione di canne che si istendono per terra e chiamassi *cansalle*. E 'n ogni nodo di quelle canne fanno barbe a modo di gramigna, e queste cane crescono e prolungansi per diritto tramito per tera più d' un miglio ma non sono molto grosse, ma a modo delle canne di Franchia. In queste canne vi nascono entro priete[1] che chiunque tiene di queste priete sopra se, dicono che nullo ferro lo può tagliare. Or quando vogliono

[1] *As once before for* pietre.

trovare la prieta, si percuotono la canna col ferro e se 'l ferro nola taglia ede cercano per la prietra, e tolgono legni agutisimi, e taglienti e cepi e tagliono e 'ncidono tanto che pervengono a la pietra, el padre ch' à figliuoli tolgono questa pietra e fanno una fenditura nel dosso al figliuolo e mettonvi entro questa pietra; poi la fa saldare il del corpo del fanciullo poi nullo ferro può mai tagliare della carne di questo uomo. Quegli che vogliono combattere con questi cotali ch' ano questa pietra portano pali di legno apuntatissimi, e con quelli gli fierono e uccidono. Li uomini di questa contrada sono tutti grandisimi ladroni. Quivi nasce un pesce ch' à cotale natura che quando altri pigliase questo pesce e ricideselo in più parti e una di queste parti si racożi e tochi l' altra incontinente si rapica insieme e saldasi come se mai non v' avesse; avuto niente. Di questo pesce fanno seccare e fannone polvere, e portala con loro duunche vanno in battaglia, e pongosela i loro ferite e 'ncontinente salda. En questa contrada a due vie, l' una va in Zapa, e l' altra in Silania[1].

23. *Dell' Isola di Silan.*

(Silan) è una grande isola nel la quale sono diverse bestie e massimamente serpenti i magiori del mondo. Ed è incredibile ed è ancora mirabile cosa, che nè bestia nè serpenti noe impediscono nessuno uomo forestiere, e [offendono ?] massimamente que' dell' isola. E sono quivi molti leofanti salvatichi. Ed avi una generazione di serpenti ch' anno collo di cavallo e capo di serpente e corpo di cane e coda di serpente ed anno quatro piedi e sono grandi come buoi e piccoli com' asini. Il rè di questa isola è molto ricco in oro e 'n pietre preziose. Quivi si truovano i buoni diamanti e rubini e perle in grande copia. Quivi è 'l monte grande come dicono quelli della contrada ch' Adamo e Adeba piansono Abello per Caino. In sulla cima del monte à alcuna pianura bella ed avi un lago, e dicono che l' aqua di quello lago sono le lagrime d' Adamo ed *Adeba*. Nel fondo di questo lago sono pietre preziose. Il Re di quindi no vi lascia pescare se no se gente povera è bisongnosa. Quando alcuno a licenza di pescare si va ed ugnesi tutto quanto del sugo *lunbors*[2] e poi vae al

[1] *Here is a very manifest interpolation by way of accounting for the double narrative, noticed in the introduction.*

[2] *Sic. Probably for* limbone.

fondo e quante può prendere di queste pietre vae e recale suso. E sonvi tante di queste mignatte che se non fosse il sugo di questo albore uciderebbe gli uomini. E ciascuno vi puote entrare una volta e quello che prende è suo. Questo fa il Re per cagione umile.

Di questo lago esce un rivo e 'n questo rivo si truovano i buoni cherubini[1] in grande quantita, e quando questo rivo entra in mare quivi si truovano le buone perle. E questa isola è delle maggiori ch' abbia l' India ed a grande abondanza di formento e d' olio e d' ogni bene. Molti mercatanti vanno a questa isola per la grande abondanza delle pietre che vi sono. Avi assai altre cose delle quali narrare non curo.

24. *Dell' Imperadore di Zapa, che a gran copia de' leofanti.*

Poi andai per molte giornate navicando e pervenni a lo 'mperio di Zapa[2]; ch' è bella terra ed è molto abondante, quasi in ogni cosa. Quello imperadore al ne torno di xiiii^{m} di leofanti, e gli altri uomini anno i leofanti come noi abbiamo nella nostra contrada i buoi. E quello imperadore secondo che si dice ae da dugento figliuoli e figliuole, tutte propie e propii.

Un' altra maravigliosa cosa a 'n questa contrada che ciascune generazioni di pesci che sono in mare vengono in questa contrada in si grande quantità che nulla altra cosa si vede in mare se non se pesci; e medesimamente si gettano sopra la riva e catuna persona ne prende quanti ne vole; e stanno cosi in sulla riva per due dì o tre e poi viene un' altra generazione de pesci, e fanno il simile, e cosi tutte l' altre generazioni di pesci, una volta l' anno. Ed essendo domandati gli uomini della contrada perchè cosi facciano, rispondono che vengono a fare reverenza a lo 'mperadore. In questa contrada vidi una testugine maggiore per tre volte che non è la chiesa di santo Antonio di Padova, ed altre maraviglie v' à assai. Quando alcuno muore in questa contrada, il marito morto ardollo e con esso lui la moglie, e dicono che la moglie va a stare col marito nell' altro mondo, e cotali modi tengono.

[1] *Sic.* [2] *Doubtless for* Zāpa, *i.e.*, Zampa.

25. *Dell' Isola di Nichoverra dove anno gli uomini la testa a modo d' un cane.*

Partendomi di questa contrada navicai per lo mare Oceano per lo merizzo[1], e trovai molte isole e contrada, tra le quali n' a una che si chiama Nichovera[2]. E gira bene dumila miglia; nella quale tutti gli uomini anno il capo a modo d' un cane, e adorano il bue. E ciascuno porta in della fronte un bue d' oro o d' argento, e tutti vanno ignudi, le femmine e gli uomini, salvo che la vergogna si cuoprono con una tovagliuola. Sono queste genti grandi del corpo, e forti in battaglia, e vanno ignudi nella battaglia, salvo che portano uno iscudo che 'l cuopre tutto, e se pigliano alcuno in battaglia che no si possa ricomperare pecunia, si lo mangiano[3]. E lo Re loro[4] porta ccc. gran pietre a collo, e conviene che faccia ogni dì ccc. orazioni agli Iddi suoi. E porta in della mano ritta un grande cherubino, e[5] lungo bene una ispana, pare una fiamma di fuoco[6]: la quale il Gran Cane s' è molto ingegnato d' averla, e no l' à potuta avere. Questo Re[7] tiene giustizia, si che ogni uomo può ire liberamente per lo suo reame.

Evvi un' altra isola che si chiama Sillia[8] che gira anche bene *m m* miglia, ne la quale son serpenti e molti altri animali salvatichi e leofanti e diversi uccelli.

Sonci uccelli grandi come oche ed anno due capi, e grande quantità di vettuaglia.

26. *Della gente dell' Isola domandata Dodin, e delle sue consuetudini orribili.*

Partendomi quinci verso oriente perveni a una grande isola chiamata Dodin[9], nella quale sono pessimi uomini e mangiano la carne cruda [ed] immondizia. Questi anno sozza consuetudine:

[1] MIN. RAM. *has* verso il Nirisi, whatever that may mean.

[2] MIN. RAM. Nicoverra.

[3] MIN. RAM. Se gli mangiano arrostiti. E 'l simile vien fatto a loro da inemici.

[4] MIN. RAM. di queste bestie.

[5] MIN. RAM. che per lo vero Iddio, *the occasional introduction of which oath is peculiar to that copy.*

[6] ID. che parea d' haver in mano un carbone infocato.

[7] ID. benche sia idololatra, e col viso rassembri un cane, tien ragione e giustitia, & ha gran quantità di figliuoli, & e di gran possanza: e per tutto, etc.

[8] Here we have Ceylon again, showing that the work has been tampered with.

[9] MIN. RAM. Diddi.

il padre mangia il figliuolo, e 'l figliuolo il padre, il marito la moglie, e la moglie il marito; in questo modo, che vanno al sacerdoto e dicono cosi (quand' anno alcuna malatia), domanda lo Dio s' io debbo guarire di questa malatia. Se lo idolo risponde (ch' è 'l diavolo che favella) e dice che debbia guarire, si dice loro andate e fate cosi, e guarà, e cosi fanno. E se lo idolo risponde che debbia morire; e 'l sacerdote viene con uno panna in mano e pogliele in sulla bocca e afogallo. Poi il tagliano per pezzi, e invitano tutto il parentado, e mangiollo con canti e con festa. Poi mettono l' ossa di per se, tutte quante, e prendole e metonle soterra con solennitade. E quelli parenti che non vi fossono invitati se 'l riputano a disonore[1]. Io ripresi costoro[2]; rispuosonmi che 'l mangiavano, perchè se gli inverminasse l' anima patirebbe pena[3].

27. *Delle* xxiv *mila isole d' India.*

Molte novità sono in questa India le quali se l' uomo no le vedese no le crederebbe, però no le iscrivo qui ma in altro luogo ne farò memoria; che in tutto il mondo no ae tante novità quanto sono in questa. E dimandando diligentemente del tenore di questa India tutti mi dissono che questa India tiene xxiiii^{mo} d' isole in se, e sono più di sessantaquatro Re, e la maggiore parte è bene abitata.

28. *Come pervene Frate Odorico all' India Superiore ed alla nobile provincia di Manzi.*

Navicando per più giornate verso l' oriente perveni a l' India superiore, e pervenimmo a la nobile provincia di Manzi, la quale è chiamata l' India di Sopra. Nella quale provincia ae duemila grandi città di tra le quali città Trevigi nè Vicenza no sarebono nominate per cittadi[4]. Ed è si grande moltitudine di genti in

[1] MIN. RAM. E quali sono lieti quando alcuno s' interma, per posserlo mangiare, e farne festa.

[2] MIN. RAM. e dettogli che farebbono meglio a lasciarli morire naturalmente, e sotterrarli.

[3] MIN. RAM. di modo che Iddio offeso dalla puzza non gli riceverebbe nella gloria sua.

[4] MIN. RAM. Più di due mila grosse cittadi, & altre tante tenute, e grosse castella, che sono come Vicenza o Trivigi, che non han nome di città. In questo paese è tanta moltitudine di gente, che è una cosa incredibile, di tal sorte, che in molte parti di detta provincia viddi più stretta la gente, che non è a Vinetia al tempo dell' Ascensione.

quella India che tra noi non sarebbe (in)credibile. Nella quale a grande quantità di pane, di vino, di carne, di pesci e d' ogni vettuaglia, come in nulla terra di mondo. E gli uomini [sono] artifici e mercatanti, nè per nulla povertà ch' abbia nullo di loro no adomandano limosina, insino che possono atarsi con le loro mani. Gli uomini di questo paese sono assai belli di corpo, ma nel viso sono alquanto pallidi, avendo barba a modo di gatto[1]. Le femmine sono le più belle del mondo.

29. *Della gran cittade di Tescalan.*

In questa provincia la prima citade che io trovai si chiama Teschalan[2], la quale è maggiore che tre volte Vinegia, di lunge dal mare una giornata, posta in su un fiume. Questa cittade a tanto naviglio ched è incredibile, che tra tutta Italia non a tanto. In questa terra ae le maggiori oche del mondo che sono ben per due delle nostre[3] e sono bianche come latte. Ed ano sopra del capo un osso grande come un novo vermiglio come una grana, e sotto la gola pende una pelle bene per uno semisso ed assi l' uno di questi cotali per un grosso, e cosi l' oche come l' anitre, e cosi le galline sono si grandi ch' è maravigliosa cosa a vedere. In questa cittade s' à per meno d' un Viniziano[4] ben trecento lib. di gengiovo fresco. In questa contrada sono maggiori serpenti ch' abbia il mondo, e pigliogni e mangialli in ogni convito da bene, e no è tenuto bello convito se di questo nu a[5]. Qui è abondanza d'ogni vittuaglia.

30. *Della nobile città di Zaiton; e de' munasteri degli idolatri.*

Di quindi mi parti di questa contrada e veni per xxxvi[6] giornate e trovai dimolte cittadi e castella, poi veni a una nobile cittade che si chiama *Zataiton*[7]; nella quale nostri frati minori anno due [luoghi]. E 'n questa terra portammo l' ossa de' frati che furo martirizati per Gesò Cristo. In questa terra ae abondanza di tutte le cose necessarie al corpo de l' uomo, più che 'n tera che

[1] MIN. RAM. con i peli della barba irti, e male composti alla guisa delle capre.

[2] MIN. RAM. Tescol.

[3] MIN. RAM. maggiori tre volte delle nostre.

[4] ID. per un ducato viddi dar 700 libre, etc.

[5] ID. Anzi quando vogliono far convito più famosó, tànto più serpenti apparecchiano, e danno in tavola a convitati.

[6] ID. 27.

[7] ID. Zanton.

sia al mondo. Averebbonsi bon tre libre de zuchero per un grosso. Ed è citade grande per due volte Bologna[1]. Sonci molti munasteri di religiosi di l' idolatri, ne' quali sono ben dumilia riligiosi, ed anno bene xi^{m} d' idoli. E 'l minore[2] è a modo d' un grande san Christofano, ed anno loro dimolte vivande calde che vanno insino al naso. Gli altri vivande si mangiano eglino[3].

31. *Della città di Fozzo; e del modo che pescano i pescatori.*

Partendomi di questa terra e venendo verso oriente ad una citade che si chiama Fozzo[4] che gira ben trenta miglia. Qui sono i maggiori galli del mondo; e le galline bianche come latte, e non anno penne ma lana a modo di pecore. Quindi partendoci andai per xviii giornate passando per molte cittadi e castella, veni a un grande monte. E da un lato di questo monte tutti gli animali son neri e gli uomini e le femmine a nostro modo di vivere; da quali de l' altro lato del monte verso oriente per contrario tutti gli animali vi sono bianchi[5]. Inte (?) quelle che sono maritate in questo luogo per segno di matrimonio portano un grande barile di corno[6].

Partendomi per altre xviii giornate passando cittadi e castella arrivai a[7] un grande fiume ch' ae un grande ponte a traverso sopra il fiume; e albergai in capo del ponte. E l' oste, volendomi fare a piacere, mi disse, "Vo tu venire a vedere pescare, vieni qui." E menomi in sul ponte; quivi di sotto erano barche. E vidi maragoni[8] in su pertiche; e l' uomo gli legò la bocca, ovvero la gola con filo, che non potessono mangiare de pesci. Poi puose tre gran ceste nella barca; poi isciolse i maragoni in quali si gitavano nell' aqua, e prendeano de' pesci, e metevagni nella barca, e tosto l' ebbero piene. Poi isciolsono i maragoni il filo ch' aveano legato a collo, e mandavano nel fiume a pascergli. E

[1] ID. Huomini e donne sono piacevoli, e belli, e cortesi, massime a forastieri.

[2] ID. è due volte più grande d' un huomo.

[3] ID. e loro si mangiano le bevande refreddate che sono. [4] ID. Foggia.

[5] ID. Ma l' una parte, e l' altra mi pareva che vivessino, e vestisseno come bestie.

[6] ID. portano in testa un corno di legno coverto di pelle, lungo più di due spanne, a mezzo la fronte.

[7] ID. ad una città chiamata Belsa, che ha un fiume, etc.

[8] Marangone *is a diver (sea bird so called). In this story the* MIN. RAM. *has the extraordinary variation which has been noticed in a note on the translation.* Marigione, *apparently intended for the same word, is there applied to a seal.*

pasciuti tornavano a loro luoghi, e passando per molte giornate vidi pescare in altro modo. Gli uomini della barca erano ignudi, e aveano sacco a collo e gittandosi nell' aqua pigliavano i pesci con mano e metteano nel sacco[1]. Tornando gelati nella barca si entravano in uno tinello d' aqua calda, e poi faceano il semigliante.

32. *Della maravigliosa citta de Chansai.*

Di questo luogo e cittade partendomi perveni ad una grande e maravigliosa citade chiamata Chansai, ch' è a dire in nostra lingua "Cittade del Cielo." Questa è la magiore cittade del mondo[2]. Nella quale non ae ispana di terreno che non s' abiti. E sonvi case di dieci e dodici famiglie e masserizie[3]. La detta cittade a borghi grandissimi, ne' quali abitano assai più gente che nella cittade. La cittade ae dodici porte principali e a ciascuna porta preso a otto miglia sono cittadi, ciascuna maggiore che Padova o Vinegia; nelle quali andammo sei e sette dì per uno di que' borghi[4]. Questa cittade è in aqua di lagune a modo di Vinegia, nella quale à più di xii^{m}[5] ponti e 'n ciascuna istanno guardie che guardano la cittade per lo gran Cane. A lato a questa cittade corre un fiume cheposcha[6], lo quale è più largo che lungo. Della quale diligentemente domandai i Cristiani e Saracini e idolatri, e tutti mi rispuosono per una lingua, Catuno papa per lo signore una bastise[7], ciò cinque carte bambagine, che sono bene uno fiorino e mezzo. E per questa cagione sono ben dodici famiglie ad un fuoco. Questi focolari sono lxxxv tumani ed anche iv tumani di Saracini, si che in tutto sono lxxxix tumani. Ed è il tumano x^{m} fuochi[8]. Gli altri sono mercatanti e gente che va e viene. Maravigliomi molto come tanta gente possono insieme abitare, ed avi si grande dovizia di pane e di vino e di porci, e

1 MIN. RAM. per un ottavo d' hora.

2 MIN. RAM. E si grande che a pena ardisco di dirlo: Ma ho ben trovate in Vinetia assai persone che vi sono state.

3 MIN. RAM. Casa vi ne sono assaissime di otto e di dieci solari, che in ogni solaro habita una fameglia con le sue massarie per la gran carestia di terreno (*the interpolation of some self-sufficient scribe*).

4 ID. Noi eravamo 7 che andassimo per quei borghi.

5 ID. *again has* per Dio vero e sono di certo di più di dieci miglia.

6 *Sic*.

7 *For* Balisi; *still further corrupted in* MIN. RAM. *to* Bastagne.

8 The MIN. RAM. has got all wrong here, but it is scarcely worth quoting.

di riso, e bigini, ch' è un nobile beveraggio, e di tutte altre vittuaglie, ch' è maraviglia a vedere. Questa è cittade reale nella quale dimora il Rè di Manzi.

33. *Della maraviglia che vede il Fr. Odorico in un munistero degli idolatri.*

In questa cittade nostri frati minori[1] convertirono a la fede un potentissimo ne la cui casa io albergai, e diceami, "Atta," (cioè a dire Padre) "vieni e mostreroti la terra." E saliti in una barca, e menoci al munistero[2] di Rabani, cioè religiosi, e dissemi [*should be* disse ad] uno di questi religiosi[3]; vedi un Rabani che viene di quelle parti dove si pone il sole, e vae a Chanbalu[4], a ciò che qui prieghi per lo gran signore, e però mostragli alcuna cosa che possa racontare nel suo paese. E quegli prese due grandi mascelle di quelle ch' erano soperchiate alla mensa, e menoci in uno giardino a un monticello ch' era pieno d' albori. E sonando un cembalo venero molti animali salvatichi socio sal[5] gattimaimoni, iscimie e molte altre bestie salvatiche, tra quali venoro ben tre milia ch' aveano forma d' uomo, i quali s' acconciaro l' uno alato a l' altro, ed a catuno puose una iscodella in mano, e dava loro mangiare. Poi sonando un tamburo, tutti questi animali si tornavano a luogo loro ed io veggendo questo dimandai, che ciò voleva dire. Ed e mi rispuosono ch' erano anime di certi nobili uomini che si veniano a pascere quivi per l' amore di Dio. Ed io istogliendogli di questo, e dicendo loro che non erano anime ma bestiuoli, nulla ne volono credere, e dicono che come l' uomo è nobile in questo mondo, cosi quando muoiono entrano in nobili animali. E del vilano dicono ch' entra in brutti animali. Questa è la maggiore città del mondo e la migliore per mercatanti, ed è molto doviziosa d' ogni bene come detto è.

1 LIR. RAM. *says*, dove è un luogo di Frati minori.

2 MIN. RAM. In un monastero chiamato Thebe.

3 MIN. RAM. *has* Et uno di quei religiosi mi disse, O Rabin...va con questo che è del tuo ordine: che vi mostrera qual cosa di nuovo, etc. *It is very much corrupted and interpolated by one who misunderstood things.*

4 *It is in the MS.* Ghabatau; *but as it is right elsewhere I have corrected it here.*

5 *Not intelligible in MS.*

34. *Della cittade Chilensi; e del gran fiume Talay.*

Partendomi quindi andai per sei giornate e perveni a una grande cittade che si chiamo Chilensi[1]. I muri di questa cittade girano bene xl miglia, ne' quale sono ccclx ponti[2] di pietra de' belli ch' abbia nel mondo. Questa cittade fue la prima sedia del Re de Manzi ed è cittade molto bene abitata, e di grande naviglio maravigliosa, e [di] copia di tutti i beni del mondo. Di quindi partendomi per tre giornate veni a uno grande fiume de maggiori del mondo che là dove gli è più istretto è largo ben vii miglia[3]. Questo fiume passa per mezzo la città Piomario[4] la cui contrada si chiama Chaicho, ch' è delle più belle cittadi del mondo, e delle maggiori. I quali uomini ch' abitano in questa terra son grandi tre spanne, e fanno il maggiore lavoro di bambagia (cioè di cotone) che si vedesse mai. E grandi uomini che sono tra loro ingenerano figliuoli e figliuole che sono più che la metà di que' piccoli e 'ngenerano sanza novero.

35. *Delle città di Jamsai e di Menzu.*

Andando per questo fiume del Talaigi[5], passando per più cittadi venni ad una cittade che si chiama......[6] nella quale a un luogo di frati minori. In questa cittade sono chiese di cristiani Nestorii. Questa cittade e nobile e grande ch' ane lviii tomani di focolari ch' evve il tomano x^{m} focolari[7]. In questa cittade sono tute quelle cose di che debbiono vivere gli christiani.

Il senore a solamente di rendita di questa di sale L tomani di balissi che vale il balisso un fiorino e mezzo, che monta il tumano xv^{m} fiorini d' oro. Questa terra a questa usanza, che quando alcuno vol fare alcuno convito a suoi grandi amici, sonvi alberghi diputati cione, e dice a l' oste Fami un convito di cotanti danari. E nullo è che faccia nullo convito in casa. Questa terra a grandissimo navigli in gran copia. Presso a questa cittade, a dieci miglia ane un' altra cittade, la quale si chiama Menzu, la

[1] MIN. RAM. Chilense.

[2] ID. Porte.

[3] MIN. RAM. Ma perche no vi erano cose degne di meraviglia, poco vi dimorammo, e navigando trovammo un fiume largo più di 20 miglia, di cui un ramo passo per la terra chiamata Piemaronni, etc.

[4] *Or* Piomazio.

[5] *Should be* del Talay e.

[6] MIN. RAM. Sai.

[7] MIN. RAM. 18 Tomani *of* focolari, *each of which is* 10,000 fochi, *and each* foco 10 *or* 12 *families!*

quale ane il maggiore naviglio che città del mondo ched è incredibile la quantità, e sono tutte bianche dipinte di gesso, avendo in loro quelle belle sale e difici.

36. *Del gran fiume Caramoran.*

Partendomi di questa cittade per otto giornate passando per molte cittadi e castella e d' aque dolci, veni ad una cittade la quale è chiamata Launcj[1], la quale è fondata sopra un fiume che si chiama Chiaramoran, il quale passa per mezzo del Cataio e fa grande danno quando si corrompe a modo del Pò. E andando per questo fiume passando molte cittadi e castella verso l' oriente per molte giornate, perveni a una grande cittade chiamata Sogomerca[2], la quale cittade a maggiore abondanza di seta ch' altra cittade che sia al mondo, che quando vene la maggiore carestia se n' arebbe ben xl lib. per[3] meno di viii di grossi, ed ane grande copia d' ogni mercatanzia di pane e d' ogni bene.

37. *Delle grandi città di Chambalu e di Taido, e del palagio del Gran Cane.*

Partendomi della cittade di Sozomacho passai per molte cittadi e terre verso oriente, e perveni[4] à la nobile cittade di Chanbalu[5]. Questa cittade è molto antica ed è nella provincia del Catai. Questa cittade presoro i Tartari, e presso a questa città à un mezzo miglio ne fecero un' altra, che la chiamano Taido. Ed ane xii porti e da l' una a l' altra sono due grandi miglia, e tra l' una cittade a l' altra ben s' abita. E 'l circuvito di queste due cittadi che sono insieme gira bene lx miglia. In questa cittade il gran Cane ane la sua sedia, e dentro ene il suo palagio che gira quatro miglia, e contiene in se molti palagi e belli. Egli è quadro, ed a tre cerchi di mura, e in catuno canto d' ogni muro è un grande palagio, si che pur questi son dodici, e catuno è diputato

[1] MIN. RAM. Laurenza.

[2] MIN. RAM. Sunzomaco, *and below* Sozomacho.

[3] MIN. RAM. per un soldo......E perche vi era in questo loco più gente che in niun altro che havessi visto domandando donde ciò avenisse mi fu risposto per conto che l' aria e il luogo sono alla generazione molto salutiferi, di modo tale che poco sono che muoiono se non di vecchiezza.

[4] ID. Navigando da quattro giornate. *It is* Chanbanau *in the MS. But, as it is right elsewhere, I have corrected it.*

[5] MIN. RAM. *has* Cambalù.

a diverse cose. E nel miluogo è quello dove ista il Signore[1]. E 'l primo cercuito delle mura ane tre porti in ogni faccia, e dentro a questo circuito ene il Monte Verde nel qual' è edificato un molto bello palagio de' più belli del mondo. Questo monte gira bene un miglio, nel quale son piantati albori che d' ogni tempo tengono la verzura. A lato a questo monte è fatto un molto bello lago sopra il quale ane un gran ponte de' più belli del mondo, nel quale lago son oche salvatiche ed anitre e ceceri[e][2] anitrocoli, ch' è maraviglia a vedere. Onde quando lo segnore vole cacciare non gli bisogna d' uscire di casa, però che 'n questo circuito son molti giardini di molte bestiuole e di tutte maniere. Il palagio principale nel quale ista la sedia del Gran Cane è quivi. (Ane) levata la terra più ch' altrove due passi; nel qual palagio a dentro xxiv colonne d' oro, e tutti i muri del palazzo son coperti di pelli rosse le più nobili pelle che sieno in India. E nel mezzo del palagio ane una grande pigna tutta d' una pietra preziosa che si chiama Medachas[3], ed è tutta legata d' oro; e nel canto di questa pigna a un serpente d' oro, e che la batte continuamente; ed una rete d' oro, e di perle grandi, dipende da questa pigna, ed è larga forse una ispana. E questa pigna porta per condotto il beveragio della corte del segnore. A lato a questa pigna istanno molti vaselli d' oro da bere. In questo palagio sono molti paoni d' oro, e quando alcuno Tartero vol far festa allora battono le mani e paoni allora battono l' alie, e pare che giuochino[4]. Questo si fa per arte diavolica, e per altro ingegno che sotterra nascono.

[1] MIN. RAM. Il cui Palazzo gira più di quattro miglia, ed ad ogni cantone è un palazzo dove dimora uno de' quatro sui baroni principali. E dentro al palazzo grande è un altro circuito di muro, che da un muro all' altro e forse mezza tirata d' arco, e tra questi muri vi stanno i suoi provisionati con tutte le sue famiglie. E nell' altro circuito abita il Gran Cane con tutte i suoi congionti, che sono assaissimi, con tanti figliuoli, figliuole, generi, de nepoti: con tante moglie, consiglieri, secretarii, e famegli, che tutto il palazzo che gira 4 miglia, viene ad esser habitato.

[2] *This is probably meant for the* cesanæ *of the Latin MSS.*, whether that be a genuine word or a mistake for *cycne*. MIN. RAM. *has* Eran nell' acqua le centinaia dell' anatre, e de assaissimi uccelli, che vivono di pesce, d' ogni sorte, che quel lago producè.

[3] MIN. RAM. Medecas.

[4] ID. A torno la mensa sua son molti pavoni smaltati, che paiono che sian vivi; e tal volta si mettono a cantare fino che 'l Signore mangia.

38. *Della corte e della gloria del Gran Signore Cane.*

Quando il Gran Cane siede in sulla sedia imperiale da lato sinistro ista la reina, e un grado più giù istanno due altre sue mogli; e poi di sotto tutte le donne del parentado ordinatamente. E le maritate portano un pie d' uomo in sul capo, lungo un mezzo braccio, e sotto le piante di questo piede portano penne di grù, e 'l dosso del piede tutto ornato di grandi perle del mondo. Da lato destro poi si pone a sedere il suo figliuolo primogenito che del regnare dopo lui, e di sotta a quelli istanno tutti quelli che sono di sangue reale. Poi di sotto a quelli sono iv scrittori, che scrivono tutto ciò che dice il Signore. Dinanzi da lui istanno suoi baroni assai sanza novero, de' quali nullo è ardito di parlare se non è domandato dal Signore maggiore. Poi vi sono i giuccolari che vogliono fare allegrezza al Signore, ma no fano mai se non se le leggi a loro imposte[1]. Dinanzi alla porta del palagio istanno baroni a guardia che non sia nullo che tocchi la porta del palagio; che se per alcuno si tocasse è duramente battuto[2].

Quando il Signore fane alcuno convito allora i suoi anno xiv^{m}[3] di baroni colle corone in capo, che servono nel convito; catuno de' quali ane tale vestimento in dosso che solo le perle di ciascuno vestimento vale xv^{m} fior d' oro. La sua corte è ordinata per decime, e ventine, e centinaia e migliaia, che tra loro ordinatamente si rispondono, e ne loro ufici non è difetto nullo. Ed io frate Oderigo fui ben tre anni in questa sua cittade, e noi frati minori aviamo nella terra un luogo diputato a darli la nostra benedizione[4]. E domandando io diligentemente da cristiani e saracini e idolatri e da nostri convertiti, che sono grandi baroni guardando solo a la persona del Signore, e tutti mi dissono per una bocca che giucolatori sono xiii tumani (il tumane è x^{m}) e quelli che guardano e nudriscono i cani e bestie e uccelli da cacciagioni sono xv^{m} di tumani, si che tra giucolari e costoro sono

[1] MIN. RAM. E di quei buffoni ciascnno ha l' hora sua deputata, quando dee star in guardia, e trattenimento del Signore.

[2] MIN. RAM. Ma nelle porte sono guardie grandissime: e se alcuno vi s' appressasse senza licenza del capitano sarebbe amaramente battuto; *which is a misunderstanding of the matter* (see note on transl. *in loco*).

[3] MIN. RAM. quindeci milia.

[4] ID. ......Frati minori che vi hanno il monastero; dove dalla corte vi veniva tanta robba, che sarebbe stata bastante per mille frati. E per lo Dio vero è tanta differenza da questi Signore a questi d' Italia, come da un huomo richissimo ad un che sia il più povero del mondo.

xxviii^{m} di tumani[1]. Si che montano in tuto cclxxx migliaia d' uomini. I medici che guardono la persona sono cccc idolatri, ed otto cristiani e i saracino[2]. E tutti costoro anno ciò ch' è loro necessario dalla corte del signore. L' altra sua famiglia è sanza novero.

39. *Del modo nel quale cavalca ogni anno il Gran Cane di Cambalu.*

Lo signore Gran Cane dimora nel tempo della istate in una terra che si chiama Sandau, la quale è sotto tramontana, ed è la più fredda terra ad abitare del mondo e di verno dimora in questa città Chanbalu che detta è. Quando il signore cavalca da una terra à un' altra, cavalca in questo modo. Egli a iv eserciti di cavalieri, l' una gli va innanzi un dì; l' altra un altro dì; e 'l terzo dopo un altro dì; e 'l quarto il quarto dì; ed egli sempre vane in mezzo, a modo di croce e gli aserciti detti sempre gli vano d' intorno, e catuno gli va di lunge una giornata e andando sempre ano la loro giornata ordinata nella quale truovano tutte queste cose che sono loro necesarie a mangiare. La gente che va con questo signore va sempre per lo detto modo, ed egli vane sopra un carro sopra due ruote, sopra il quale è fatta una bella sala tutta di legni d' aloe, ch' è tanto odorifero e prezioso, ed anche d' oro è ornata, e di perle e di pietre preziose. E questo carro menano v leofanti...[3] e sopra il carro porta xii girfalchi. In quello sedendosi si vede alcuni uccelli sigli lascia andare. E nullo è oso d' appressarsi al carro a una gittata di pietra, se non se questi diputati a queste cose. E cosi va questo signore, e cosi vanno le mogli nello grado e 'l suo figliuolo primogenito. Onde è cosa incredibile a immaginare la grande gente ch' ane questo signore. Quelli iv eserciti che vanno con lui sono v tumani, e catuno tumane è x^{m}; e tutta questa gente anno dal signore ciò ch' è loro necessario; e se nullo di costoro [sia] presente[4] è rimesso un altro in luogo di costui; si che rimane intero il numero[5].

1 The last two figures, etc., are in the MS. xv^{m} and xxviii^{m}.

2 MIN. RAM. quali non si scemano ne aumentano, ma morto l' uno, in suo loco si mette l' altro.

3 Defective and unintelligible.

4 *Meaning, if* any one *is* not *present?* But *below we have* nulla novità *for* any news.

5 *Here* MIN. RAM. *has a long passage peculiar to it.* Le bestie poi di tante sorti strane sono infinite che lui tiene. Fra quali erano sei cavalli, che haveano

40. *Come è doviso l' imperio del Cane et come son parati ospizii per li trapassanti.*

Questo signore Gran Cane lo suo imperio è doviso in xii parti, e catuna si chiama Siglo[1]. L' una di queste parti è il Manzi, ch' ave sotto di se ii^{m} grandi cittadi. Onde ene a sapere che 'l suo imperio è si grande che ben vi mesi si pena ad andare per lungo e per traverso sanza l' isole che sono v^{m}, che non si pongono nel detto novero[2]. E ave fatto per tutto il suo imperio fare case e cortili per li trapasanti, le quali case si chiamano uman[3]. Nelle quali case sono tutto quelle cose ch' a necessaria alla vita dell' uomo. E quando nulla novità viene nel suo imperio incontinente gli mesaggi corrono in su camelli, e se 'l fatto porta pondo montano in su dromedradi, e 'ncontinente che s' appressano a questa [jam] suonano un corno e 'ncontinente uno s' apparecchia e vane insino a l' altro jam e portale quelli rimane e cosi va l' altro al simigliante modo. E per questo modo in un dì naturale a novelle di x giornate dalla lunga. Anche v' ane un altro modo di quelli che corrono. E le case di questi corrieri si chiamano chidebo, e stanno corrieri per queste case, ed anno una cinghia di campanelle. E l' una casa a l' altra ene dilunge tre miglia, ma quella de corrieri de' gamelli xx miglia. E quando s' appressa a una di queste case incontinente comincia a sonare queste campanelle, e quel altro ch' è nella casa s' apparecchia, e corre insino a l' altra casa, e cosi l' uno a l' altro, insin che giungono

sei piedi e sei gambi per uno: e viddi dui grandissimi struzzi, e dui piccioli dietro di loro con dui colli per ciascuno, e dui teste, dalle quali mangiavano, senza far mentione di altri huomini salvatichi che stanno nello giardino di detto Signore, e donne tutte pelose di un pelo grande e bigio, quali han forma humana, e si pascono di poma, e d' altre bevande, che gli ordina il Signore che se gli dia. Fra quali erano huomini non più grandi di dui spanne, e questi si chiamano *Gomiti*. Nella corte ho visto huomini di un, occhio nella fronte, che si chiamavano Minocchi. Et a quel tempo furono appresentati al Signore dui, un maschio, & una femina, quali havevano una spanna di busto, colla testa grossa, e le gambe lunghe, e senza mani, e s' imboccavano con uno dei piedi. E viddi un gigante grande circa 20 piedi, che menava dui leoni, l' un rosso e l' altro nero, e l' altro haveva in guardia leonesse, e leopardi, e con si fatte bestie andava il Signore a far caccia a prender cervi, caprioli, lupi, cingiali, orsi, & altre bestie salvatiche.

[1] *Probably for* Singlo *or* Sing.

[2] Min. Ram. E vi sono proposti quattro che governano l' imperio di questo gran Signore. E ciascuna persona, che facendo viaggio, passa per quei paesi, di qual condition si sia è ordinato, che per dui pasti che fa, non paghi nulla.

[3] *For* iam *as below;* Min. Ram. Per tutto il paese vi sono torri altissime, dove sono assaissime guardie, etc.

ov' ene il signore. Onde nulla si può fare nel suo imperio che 'ncontinente nol sapia, come detto è.

41. *Della cacciagione del gran Cane.*

Quando il gran Cane vane a cacciare fuori di Chanbalu, a venti giornate ene un gran bosco, che gira ben vii giornate. E tante bestie salvatiche quivi conversono ch' è maraviglia. Intorno al bosco istanno guardie che 'l guardano per lo signore. E 'n capo di tre o di quattro anni il signore vi va colla sua gente, il quale intorniano tutto quanto questo bosco. Poi lasciano andare i cani per terra e gli ucelli in aria. Poi si vengono ristriguendo insieme e conducono tutte queste bestie in un piano ch' è nel mezzo. E leoni e parugiani[1] e cerbi e molte altre bestie ch' ene incredibile. E son tanto le grida di quelli uccelli e cani che l' uno nove intende l' altro, si che tutte le bestie salvatiche che trieman di paura[2]. Allora il Gran Cane viene sopra tre leofanti, e saetta tra queste bestie cinque turcassi di saette e com' egli saetta cosi fa tutta la sua compagnia il simigliante. E catuno signore ave un suo segnale nella sua saetta. Allora lo signore fane chiamare Sio! cioè Misericordia! a quelle bestie, e 'ncontinente quelle bestie che son vive si dipartono. Allora vengono i baroni e truovano le loro saette e catuno prende quella bestia ch' à morta la sua saetta. Per questo modo si fane la sua cacciagione.

42. *Delle quattro Feste che tiene ogn' anno il Gran Cane.*

Ancora questo imperadore gran Cane fane ogni anno iiii gran feste. La prima è il primo dì di Febraio, la seconda il dì de la sua nativitade[3]. E convita e fa venire tutti i suoi baroni e bufoni e giucolari, e tutto suo parentado, e tutti si pongono ordinati. E spezialmente a quella di Febraio e a quella della natività tutti i baroni vanno con corone in capo, e lo 'mperadore siede in della

[1] (?)

[2] MIN. RAM. Quivi è si forte il gridar delle genti, l' abbaiar de' cani, l' ulular delle fiere, e 'l sonar de' corni, e l' altri stromenti, che le povere fiere assalite da tema grande, & horror di morte, che porta seco, e lo presente stato che versa negli occhi delle infelici bestie, e 'l ricordarsi delle altre volte, che vi sono incappate, che fa tremare, come debole canna, e non ben ferma, percossa di crudelissimi, e violentissimi soffiar di Borea, o d' Aquilone! Le quali vengono uccisi quasi per tema.

[3] MIN. RAM. La prima è per il dì della sua natività: la seconda è dell' incoronatione sua: la terza è del matrimonio, quando meno per moglie la regina: la quarta è della natività del suo primogenito figliuolo.

sua sedia come detto è adietro, e tutti i baroni. Ciascuno ista nel suo lato; e sono tre divisata di baroni. I primi sono vestiti di verde; i secondi di sanguigno; i terzi d' azurro, e tutti sono incoronati e anno in mano una tavola di dente di leofante, e le cinture tutte d' oro e larghe bene un somesso, e tengono silenzio e 'ntorno a loro istanno i giucolari con sue insegne e bandiere. E in uno poggicciuolo ov' è un grande palagio dimorano i filosofi guardando certi punti[1]. Quando viene quel punto uno grida altamente saliziati (?) cioè inchinatevi al signore. Allora tutti i baroni danno del capo in terra com' è loro usanza quando inchinano. Allora quel medesimo grida levatevi e allora si levano tutti. Ancora questi filosofi guardono a certi punti, e allora quegli grida, Ponetevi il dito nel' orecchie! e poi dice Cavatene! Allora istanno un poco e dicono, Buratate farina! e molti altri segni stolti, e dicono che tutti sono grandi segni. E poi sono ufficiali che richeggiono i baroni e giucolari e se alcuno vene fallo, cade in grande pena. E filosofi quando viene il punto e l' ora dicono a giucolari, Fate festa al Signore; e quelli incontinente cominciano a sonare gli stormenti; ed è si grande il romore ch' è quasi uno isturbamento. Allora dice una boca, Tutti tacete. Allora tutti taciono. Allora tutti quelli del parentado s' apparecchiano di cavalli bianchi. Allora comincia a gridare una voce, Cotali di cotal parentado s' apparecchia di cotante migliaia o vero centinaia di cavalli! Allora sono certi apparecchiati certi che menano i cavalli apparecchiati al signore, ch' è incredibile di tanti cavalli bianchi quanti gli donono. E allora sono tutti famigliari che portano presenti al signore da parte degli altri baroni. E allora tutti i principi di munistero vengono con doni, e donagli la loro benedizione, e quel medesimo conviene fare a noi altri frati minori. E fatte queste giucolaresche cose vengono alcuno altro giucolare dinanzi al signore e cantano molto maravigliosamente, e alcuno altro menano con seco leoni che fanno reverenza a lo mperadore e questi giucolari fanno venire per aria nappi d' oro pieni di buon vino, e cosi vanno a le bocche d' ogni uomo che vuol bere. E questo modo fanno, e molte altre cose dinanzi al signore. A dire la grandezza, e le gran cose della corte di costui sarebbe cosa incredibile se no le vedese. Niuno si maravigli se fa grandi ispese però che nel suo regno no si ispende altra moneta

[1] ID. Non so che ponti, o di stelle, o di pianeti.

che di carta, che no gli costa nulla, e a le sue mani viene tutto tesoro.

43. *Una maraviglia del popone che contiene una bestiuola.*

Un' altra maraviglia vi dirò sua la quale io non vidi, ma udiela dire a persona degna di fede. Alcuni dicono che Chadli ene un gran regno, e qui sono monti che si chiamano monti Caspeos, ne' quali dicono che nascono poponi grandissimi, ne' quali poponi quando sono maturi s' aprono per loro istessi, e truovavisi entro una bestiuola grande, e fatta a modo d' uno agnello; si che ano quella carne a ano il popone. Questo può essere altresi bene si com' ene ne reame d' Inghilterra o di Scozia che dicono che sono albori che fanno uccelletti[1].

44. *Del reame del Presto Giovanni ed altre contrate.*

Partendomi dal Chataio e venendo verso il ponente cinquanta giornate, passando cittadi e castella venni nelle terre del Presto Giovanni, e non è delle cento parti l' una quello che si dice di lui. La prencipale cittade di lui si chiama Casan, ch' ene Vincienza maggiore cittade di quella, e molte altre cittadi à sotto di se, e sempre per patto piglia per moglie la figliuola del Gran Cane. Poi andando per molte giornate perveni a una provincia che si chiama Chansi. Questa è la seconda migliore provincia e la meglio abitata ch' abbia il mondo. E ov' ella è più stretta è larga ben l giornate, e lunga più di lx giornate. Ed è si bene abitata che quando s' esce della porta de l' una cittade si vede le mura dell' altra cittade. Nella quale a grande copia di vittuaglia e spezialmente di castagne. In questa provincia nasce il mal barbaro, ed avene tanto che per meno di vi grossi se ne caricherebbe un asino. Ed è questa provincia una delle xii ch' ane il gran Cane.

45. *Del regno di Tibet dove si truova il Papa degli Idolatri.*

Passando questa provincia grande perveni a un altro gran regno che si chiama Tibet, ch' ene ne confini d' India ed è tutta al gran Cane. Quivi è maggior copia di pane e di vino che in nulla parte del mondo. E la gente di questa contrada dimora in

[1] MIN. RAM. *says* Un dì fra gli altri *viddi* una bestia grande come un' agnello etc. *And here that version stops.*

tende che sono fatte di feltri neri. La prencipale cittade è fatta tutta di pietre bianche e nere, e tutte le vie lastricate. In questa cittade nullo ardisce a spander sangue d' uomo o di femmina, o d' altra bestia. Questo fanno per reverenza d' un loro idolo. In questa cittade dimora il Atassi[1], che viene a dire in nostro modo il Papa. Ed è capo di tutti idolatrici. Questi distribuisce da tutti i benifici e partegli tra loro secondo la loro legge. Ed ane in questo regno questa usanza che le femmine portano in capo più di c paia di trecce avendo ii denti lunghi[2] a modo di porco salvatico. Ed è ancora cotale usanza in questa contrada che quando il padre d' alcuno more, e 'l figliuolo gli vol fare grande onore, convita e rauna tutti i sacerdoti e religiosi e giucolari e vicini e parenti e portano il corpo a la campagna con gran festereccia; e quivi è apparecchiato un gran desco, e quando v' è posto suso e sacerdoti gli mozzano il capo, e danno al figliuolo. E poi il tagliano tutto a pezzi, e 'l figliuolo con tutta la compagnia cantano e cessandosi quindi un pezzo fanno orazioni. Allora vengono aguglie e avoltoi de' monti e ciascuno piglia il suo pezzo. Allora gridano e dicono Vedete che santo uomo questi fu, che vengono gli angeli per lui, e portanelo in paradiso! Poi il figliuolo se ne porta il capo e mangialo cotto poi del teschio fa fare un vaso e mangiano e beono con esso tutti quelli della casa con grande divozione. Piu altre sozze usanze sono tra quelli pagani d' oriente le quali non dico.

46. *D' un ricco popolano di Manzi.*

Nella provincia de Manzi veni ad uno palagio d' un uomo popolano la cui vita ene in questo modo. E tiene cinquanta donzelle vergini, le quali il servono. Quando viene a mangiare ogni vivanda o 'mbandigioni si portano v delle donzelle predette con molti istormenti di diverse maniere, e cantano e del continuo cantano mentre che la vivanda e nanzi. Poi costoro si partono e altre cinque delle dette donzelle si vengono col' altra vivanda, e 'mbastigione e con altri diversi istormenti e con diversi canti e per questo modo mena la sua vita. Questo signore à di rendita xxx tumani tagiai[3] di riso. Il tumano è numero di x^{m}; e 'l tegiar è soma d' asino. E 'l cortile del suo palagio gira ben ii miglia e 'l palazzo è fatto inquesto modo, che l' uno mattone o

[1] *For* Abassi. [2] *Lunghi*, I think. [3] *For* tagar.

vero pietra è d' oro e l' altro d' ariento. Nel cortil dentro ave un monte d' oro e d' argento, sopra il quale son fatti monasteri e campanili per suo diletto. E dicesi che tra questi Manzi sono iiii° uomini per lo modo di costui. Gli uomini di questo paese tengono per nobiltà ad avere lunghe l' unghia, e la bellezza della femmina d' avere piccioli piedi. Però quando nasce la femmina le madri istringono loro i piedi, a ciò che non crescono loro più che vogliono.

47. *Del Vecchio della Montagna.*

Partendomi delle terre del Presto Giovanni, venendo verso ponente, veni a una contrada che si chiama Mileser[1], bella e abondevole d' ogni bene. Nella quale si dicea che sole istare il Vecchio della montagna. Egli avea fatto tra due monti un cercuito di muro, e dentro le più belle fonti del mondo. E dentro eran poste donze' vergini belle le più del mondo, e cavalli bellissimi, e tutte quelle cose che potessono dilettare corpo umano. E facea dire che questo era paradiso; e quando vedea un giovane valoroso si lo metea in questo luogo; nel quale facea andare vino e latte per condotto: e quando volea fare uccidere alcun re o barone, facea dire al soprastante di quel luogo ch' egli facesse venire il più atto e amoroso a diletti e nel dimoro di questo paradiso, e quelli allora dava beveraggi a quel cotale, che 'l facea fortemente adormentare; e cosi dormendo nel facea trare. E quelli risentendosi e trovandosi fuori di questo luogo era in grande tristizia e dolore, e pregava a quel signore che vel facesse ritornare. E allora gli dicea, Vo' tu ritornare, vane e uccidi il cotale uomo poi ci ritornerai, o campi o muoi. E 'n questo modo facea uccidere chiunque e volea. Per la qual cosa era temuto da tutti i re d' oriente, e mandavagli tributo. E 'n questo modo facea uccidere molti de' Tartari quando venieno pigliando il mondo. Per la qual cosa vi venono a oste e puosonvi l' assedio e mai non se ne partiro infino che non ebbero la cittade e 'l vecchio e feciollo morire di mala morte.

48. *Della grazia ch' anno i Frati Minori nella Tartaria.*

In questa contrada a Iddio data questa grazia a' frati minori che nella Grande Tartaria cosi anno per niente di cacciare un

[1] *Probably* Milehet *originally.*

demonio d' un corpo d' uomo, come di cacciare un can di casa. Molti ve ne sono in demoni. E se sono di lunge ben x giornate si gli menano a' frati e al comandamento loro dalla parte di Jesù incontinente si partono via le demonia. E poi quelli che sono liberati si fanno battezzare, e frati prendono i loro idoli di feltro che quegli anno, e colla croce vanno e portagli al fuoco. E quelli della contrada tutti tragono a vedere. E l' idolo salta del fuoco e frati tolgono aqua benedetta e prizalla nel fuoco e le demonia escono del fuoco, e frati vi rimettono entro l' idolo, e 'ncontinente arde. E 'l demonio grida in aria, Io sono cacciato della mia abitazione! E per questo modo i nostri frati ne battezzano molti.

49. *Della Valle Terribile.*

Un' altra terribil cosa viddi andando per una valle posta sopra il fiume delle delizie. Vidi in questa valle molti corpi morti e vidi di diversi istormenti che quivi pareano che sonasono, onde qui era tanto timore e paura che non si potrebbe dire. Questa valle è lunga da otto miglia, nella quale qui v' entra incontinente muore. Nella quale io volli entrare per vedere quello che questo era, ed entrandovi trovai molti corpi morti, ed è cosa incredibile era ad immaginare quant' egli erano in questa valle. In sul monte trovai una testa d' uomo morto tanta terribile che mi mise si gran paura che parea che lo spirito si volesse partire da me. E [in] questa paura sempre andava dicendo, *Verbo caro factum est etc.* Poi montai sopra un monte renoso e guardando d' ogni parte non vidi niente, se non se che molte nacchere udia; e quando fui in capo del monte trovai tanto argento a modo quasi come uno iscogliame di pesce in grande quantità. Del quale niente presi, e cosi sanza alcun danno mi parti. E per questa cagione tutti i saracini m' aveano in grande reverenza, dicendo ch' io era battezzato e santo, e quelli ch' erano morti in questa valle erano istati uomini del diavolo de lo 'nferno.

Finita la diceria di frate Oderigo. Deo grazias!

50. *Attestazione del Fr. Odorico.*

Io frate Oderigo da Frigolli, d' una terra che si chiama porto maoni, dell' ordine de frati minori testifico, e rispondo al mio monistero[1] per vera ubidizione che tutte queste cose iscritte in questo memoriale o io le vidi o io l' udi dire a uomini degni di fede e dal cummune parlare delle contrade. Onde quelle che non vidi sapiate che vere sono. Altre molte cose lascio, e no le iscrivo che chi non le vedese non le crederebbe. E di dì in dì m' apparecchio di tornare in quelle contrade, e mi dispongo di finire mia vita. Deo grazias, Amen, amen, amen.

[1] *For* Ministro.

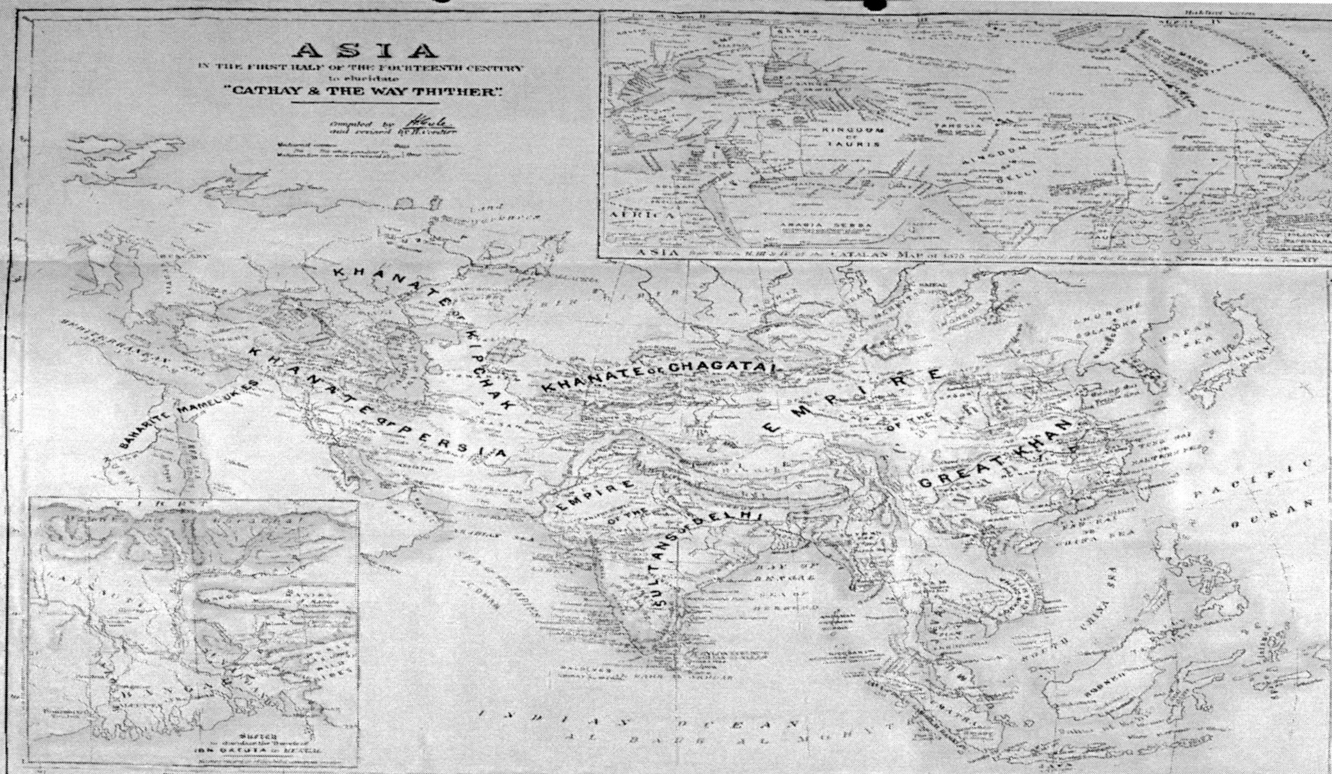
ASIA
IN THE FIRST HALF OF THE FOURTEENTH CENTURY
to elucidate
"CATHAY & THE WAY THITHER".
KINGDOM OF TAURIS
KINGDOM OF DELLI
AFRICA
ARABIA SERRA
KHANATE OF KIPCHAK
KHANATE OF PERSIA
KHANATE OF CHAGATAI
EMPIRE OF THE GREAT KHAN
EMPIRE OF THE SULTANS OF DELHI
BAHARITE MAMELUKES
PACIFIC OCEAN
INDIAN OCEAN
SOUTH CHINA SEA
JAPAN SEA